Essentials of Health Justice

Law, Policy, and Structural Change

SECOND EDITION

Elizabeth Tobin-Tyler, JD, MA
Department of Health Services, Policy, and Practice
School of Public Health
Department of Family Medicine
The Warren Alpert Medical School
Brown University
Providence, Rhode Island

Joel B. Teitelbaum, JD, LLM
Department of Health Policy and Management
Milken Institute School of Public Health
George Washington University
Washington, DC

JONES & BARTLETT
LEARNING

World Headquarters
Jones & Bartlett Learning
25 Mall Road
Burlington, MA 01803
978-443-5000
info@jblearning.com
www.jblearning.com

Jones & Bartlett Learning books and products are available through most bookstores and online booksellers. To contact Jones & Bartlett Learning directly, call 800-832-0034, fax 978-443-8000, or visit our website, www.jblearning.com.

Substantial discounts on bulk quantities of Jones & Bartlett Learning publications are available to corporations, professional associations, and other qualified organizations. For details and specific discount information, contact the special sales department at Jones & Bartlett Learning via the above contact information or send an email to specialsales@jblearning.com.

24819-7

Production Credits
Vice President, Product Management: Marisa R. Urbano
Vice President, Content Strategy and Implementation: Christine Emerton
Director, Product Management: Matthew Kane
Product Manager: Sophie Fleck Teague
Director, Content Management: Donna Gridley
Manager, Content Strategy: Carolyn Pershouse
Content Strategist: Sara Bempkins
Content Strategist: Tess Sackmann
Director, Project Management and Content Services: Karen Scott
Manager, Project Management: Jackie Reynen
Project Manager: John Coakley
Senior Digital Project Specialist: Angela Dooley
Senior Marketing Manager: Susanne Walker

Content Services Manager: Colleen Lamy
Vice President, Manufacturing and Inventory Control: Therese Connell
Composition: Straive
Project Management: Straive
Cover Design: Michael O'Donnell
Text Design: Michael O'Donnell
Media Development Editor: Faith Brosnan
Rights & Permissions Manager: John Rusk
Rights Specialist: Maria Leon Maimone
Cover Image (Title Page, Part Opener, Chapter Opener):
　© Johnny Miller/Unequal Scenes
Printing and Binding: McNaughton & Gunn

Library of Congress Cataloging-in-Publication Data
Names: Tobin Tyler, Elizabeth, author. | Teitelbaum, Joel Bern, author.
Title: Essentials of health justice : law, policy, and structural change /
　Elizabeth Tobin-Tyler, Joel B. Teitelbaum.
Description: Second Edition. | Burlington, MA : Jones & Bartlett Learning,
　[2023] | Includes bibliographical references and index. | Summary:
　"Given the national reckoning around structural inequality, racism, and
　intractable health disparities, there is an unrequited demand among
　faculty and scholars who teach and write about health equity and social
　justice for texts that go beyond a discussion of the social determinants
　of health and access to care to provide analysis that offers a
　structural and legal lens for understanding entrenched health inequity
　in the U.S. The COVID-19 pandemic has only made the need for this
　approach more compelling and urgent. With the assistance and expertise of
　new co-author Ruqaiijah Yearby, authors Elizabeth Tobin-Tyler and Joel
　Teitelbaum build and expand upon their first edition, Essentials of
　Health Justice: A Primer, to meet that need with their significantly
　expanded text, Essentials of Health Justice, Second Edition. This new
　edition explores the historical, structural, and legal underpinnings of
　racial, ethnic, gender-based, and ableist inequities in health, and
　provides a framework for students to consider how and why health
　inequity is tied to the ways that laws are structured and enforced.
　Additionally, it offers analysis of potential solutions and posit how
　law may be used as a tool to remedy health injustice. Written for a wide,
　interdisciplinary audience of students and scholars in public health,
　medicine, and law, as well as other health professions, this accessible
　text discusses both the systems and policies that influence health and
　explores opportunities to advocate for legal and policy change by public
　health practitioners and policymakers, physicians, health care
　professionals, lawyers, and lay people. Key Features:- Significantly
　expanded and divided into 5 Parts that conclude with discussion
　questions or case studies- New chapter 2 looks at social movements from
　the history of the U.S. such as the Civil Rights Movement, Poor People's
　Campaign, Women's Movement, and the Gay Rights Movement- New Part 4 on
　Historically Excluded Populations and Health Injustice includes new
　chapters focusing on specific populations BIPOC, immigrants, women,
　LBGQ, and people with disabilities"- Provided by publisher.
Identifiers: LCCN 2022011866 | ISBN 9781284248142 (paperback)
Subjects: LCSH: Discrimination in medical care–Law and legislation–United
　States. | Social medicine–United States.
Classification: LCC KF3821 .T635 2023 | DDC 344.73/041–dc23/eng/20220420
LC record available at https://lccn.loc.gov/2022011866

6048

Printed in the United States of America
26 25 24 23 22　10 9 8 7 6 5 4 3 2 1

Brief Contents

Contents

PART 1 Context and Background   1

CHAPTER 1 Introductory Frameworks, Definitions, and Theories for Health Justice...... 3

CHAPTER 2 Lessons from U.S. Social Movements for Health Justice 29

PART 2 Aspects of the Legal System that Undermine Health Justice   49

CHAPTER 3 The Roles of the Three Branches of Government in Health Law and Policy....... 51

PART 4 Historically Marginalized Populations and Health Injustice   197

Foreword

by Angela P. Harris and Georges C. Benjamin

In this foreword, we (Harris, a legal scholar, and Benjamin, a public health scholar) offer some reflections on the "health justice" framework. The World Health Organization describes health as "a state of complete physical, mental, and social well-being and not merely the absence of disease and infirmity."[1] This definition of health is a holistic one, reminding us that 80% of what makes people healthy occurs outside the doctor's office and that social drivers may either hinder the quest for health or help improve it. Health is a fundamental human right under the United Nations' Universal Declaration of Human Rights, but not under U.S. law. Nevertheless, in order for the people of this nation to benefit at the highest level from the human right to health, we must have just and equitable social systems and a framework of accountability through law, policy, and social norms.

In the past few decades, the United States has seen an explosion of organizing and policy frameworks that incorporate the word *justice*: environmental justice, reproductive justice, water justice, land justice, food justice, data justice, and more. These "[x] justice" frameworks share at least three central commitments.[2] First, they analyze social inequalities as the outcome of structural oppression. For example, as the authors of this book explain in the Introduction, "laws, policies, and deeply rooted norms and practices have far more to say about the health and well-being of individuals and the communities they form than do human biology, individual behavioral choices, and access to medical care services." Without conscious and persistent policy intervention across institutions, structural inequalities reproduce themselves across space and time. Moreover, structural inequalities appear in the lives of individuals, families, and groups along preexisting power differentials that interlock and overlap in complex ways, a phenomenon that legal scholar Kimberlé Crenshaw calls "intersectionality."[3]

Second, the health justice framework, like other [x] justice frameworks, adopts a social change perspective in recognition of how structural inequalities affect existing institutions and professional discourses. For instance, as this book explains, as a result of historical racism and sexism, discourses of law and public health tend to emphasize universalist and individualist policy interventions, even though such interventions fail to address the structural root causes of unjust disparities.[4] Social movements are essential to structural change. They can shift the policy landscape quickly, moving the needle of public opinion. They can also effectively challenge oppressive norms and analytical blind spots within elite discourses. Indeed, several justice frameworks, including those used in environmental justice and reproductive justice, emerged in reaction to blind spots in established legal, scientific, and policy frameworks.[5] Health justice, like these other frameworks, seeks to remedy historic oppression and work toward a future in which, as the authors of this book put it, "all people have the opportunity to reach their full health potential."

Third, the health justice framework, like other [x] justice frameworks, provides a holistic language for addressing human flourishing. As this book emphasizes, the drivers of health and disease exist at multiple scales, from the planetary (as we have witnessed during the COVID-19 pandemic) to the individual. Linked to the global concept of "health," the aspirational language of "justice" calls our attention to these multiple scales and challenges us to imagine what it might look like to put human health at the center of each one. For example, "health law" conventionally focuses on the laws and regulations that shape individual access to health care services, such as the law relating to insurance reimbursement for clinical care.[6] "Health justice" asks us to imagine—as this book does—how purportedly non-health-related legal arenas, such as the carceral system, affect human health. What might it mean to orient all political, economic, and social institutions around the promotion of human flourishing?

Imagine a future where society focuses its efforts on achieving equitable access to health care and public health services, equity in the quality of care received within the health care setting, and the absence of discrimination based on race, ethnicity, sexual orientation, age, or disability across all human interactions and where the non-health societal factors that influence health are viewed through the lens of promoting human flourishing. This text tries to create a better understanding of how such a vision might be achieved through the use of law, policy, and structural change. We hope its readers adopt this vision in their daily work to achieve health justice for all.

—Angela P. Harris, JD
Distinguished Professor of Law, University of California, Davis, School of Law
—Georges C. Benjamin, MD
Executive Director,
American Public Health Association

References

1. World Health Organization. Constitution. Accessed December 8, 2021. https://www.who.int/about/governance/constitution.
2. Harris AP. Anti-colonial pedagogies: "[X] justice" movements in the United States. *Canadian Journal of Women and the Law.* 2018;30(3):567–594.
3. Crenshaw K. Mapping the margins: Intersectionality, identity politics, and violence against Women of Color. *Stanford Law Review.* 1991;43(6):1241–1300.
4. Harris AP, Pamukcu A. The civil rights of health: A new approach to challenging structural inequality. *UCLA Law Review.* 2020;67(4),758–833.
5. Harris AP. Anti-colonial pedagogies: "[X] justice" movements in the United States. *Canadian Journal of Women and the Law.* 2018;30(3):567–594.
6. Wiley LF. Health law as social justice. *Cornell Journal of Law and Public Policy.* 2014;24(1).

Acknowledgments

We are grateful to several people who generously contributed their guidance and assistance to us during the writing of this text. At the top of the list is the entire team at Jones & Bartlett Learning—particularly Sophie Teague, Sara Bempkins, and Susanne Walker—to whom we are grateful for their support, patience, and expertise. For both editions of this book, we have been blessed by the help of multiple research assistants. The first edition could not have been completed without Joanna Theiss, JD, LLM while Emma Giustozzi, Monica Zhang and Joanna Griffin provided invaluable assistance for this edition. To all of them, we send our deep appreciation for their help and steady supply of good cheer. Finally, we wish to thank those closest to us. Liz sends special thanks to John, Graham, Tobin, and Clare for their perpetual sustenance and encouragement and to her students and clinical, legal, and community partners who work so hard to achieve health justice. Joel sends special thanks to Laura, Jared, and Layna for their unique brand of alchemy and to all the legal-aid lawyers, clinicians, and community workers who leverage the power of law to help lift up those in society whose life circumstances have other ideas.

About the Authors

Elizabeth Tobin-Tyler, JD, MA, is associate professor of health services, policy and practice at the Brown University School of Public Health and Associate Professor of Family Medicine at the Alpert Medical School of Brown University. She is the director of the Master's in Public Health and Master's in Public Policy joint degree program at Brown University. Her research and writing focus on socioeconomic, racial, gender-based, and legal drivers of health and health inequity; public health law and policy; poverty law and the social and health care safety nets; and health system and community-based interventions that promote health equity. She teaches, writes, and consults in the areas of health justice, health care law and policy, public health law, and medical and public health ethics.

Professor Tobin-Tyler is an international expert in the development of medical–legal partnerships, which integrate health care, public health, and legal services to identify, address, and prevent health-harming social and legal needs of underserved patients and populations. She is senior editor and a contributor to the first textbook on the topic, *Poverty, Health and Law: Readings and Cases for Medical-Legal Partnership*, published in 2011. She has published numerous articles and blogs, including in *Academic Medicine, Public Health Reports, The Lancet, Health Affairs, Health and Human Rights, Journal of Legal Medicine, Journal of Law, Medicine and Ethics, Journal of Health and Biomedical Law, Journal of Health Care Law and Policy, Georgetown Journal of Legal Ethics, American Journal of Preventive Medicine,* and *American Journal of Public Health.*

Professor Tobin-Tyler has served on numerous advisory boards and committees related to health justice, including the State of Rhode Island Pregnancy and Postpartum Death Review Committee, the Advisory Board for the Center for Prisoner Health and Human Rights, and the Advisory Council for the Child and Family Policy Center's Learning Collaborative on Health Equity and Young Children. She is also the recipient of several awards including the pro bono service award from the Legal Services Corporation, the Distinguished Advocate award from the National Center for Medical-Legal Partnership, and, for multiple years, the Dean's Excellence in Teaching award at the Alpert Medical School. She has also been selected for several fellowships, including as a Postgraduate Fellow in Public Policy by the A. Alfred Taubman Center at Brown, as a Bray Visiting Scholar at the Cogut Center for Humanities at Brown, and as a Public Health Law Education Faculty Fellow by the Robert Wood Johnson Foundation. In 2018–2019, she served a visiting fellow at the Law, Health, Justice Centre at the University of Technology in Sydney, Australia.

Joel Teitelbaum, JD, LLM, is professor of public health and law, director of the Hirsh Health Law and Policy Program, and co-director of the National Center for Medical-Legal Partnership at the George Washington University in Washington, D.C. For 11 years, Professor Teitelbaum served as vice-chair for academic affairs for the Department of Health Policy and Management.

Professor Teitelbaum has taught law, graduate, or undergraduate courses on health care law, health care civil rights, public health law, minority health policy, and long-term care law and policy. He was the first member of the School of Public Health faculty to receive the University-wide Bender Teaching Award, he has received the School's Excellence in Teaching Award, and he is a member of the University's Academy of Distinguished Teachers and the School's Academy of Master Teachers. He has authored or coauthored dozens of peer-reviewed articles and reports in addition to many book chapters, policy briefs, and blogs on law and social drivers of health, health equity, civil rights issues in health care, health reform and its implementation, medical–legal partnership, and insurance law and policy, and he has delivered more than 100 invited lectures/presentations at leading universities and national conferences. In addition to *Essentials of Health Justice,* he is coauthor of *Essentials of Health Policy and Law* (5th ed.). In 2000, Professor Teitelbaum was corecipient of the Robert Wood Johnson Foundation Investigator Award in Health Policy Research, which he used to explore the creation of a new framework for applying Title VI of the 1964 Civil Rights Act to the modern health care system.

Among other organizations, Professor Teitelbaum is a member of Delta Omega, the national honor society recognizing excellence in the field of public health, and the ASPH/Pfizer Public Health Academy of Distinguished Teachers. In 2016, during President Obama's second term, Professor Teitelbaum became the first lawyer named to the U.S. Department of Health and Human Services Secretary's Advisory Committee on National Health Promotion and Disease Prevention Objectives (a.k.a. "Healthy People"), the national agenda aimed at improving the health of all Americans over a 10-year span. He serves as a member of the board of advisors of PREPARE, a national advanced care planning organization, and on multiple committees of the American Bar Association: as a liaison to the Task Force on Eviction, Housing Stability, and Equity, as an advisor to the Coordinating Committee on Veterans Benefits and Services, and as a member of the Advisory Board of the Public Health Legal Services Research Project in the Center for Human Rights.

Contributors

Chapter 10: Asian, Black, Indigenous, and Latinx People
Ruqaiijah Yearby, JD, MPH
Professor of Law
St. Louis University School of Law
Co-Founder and Executive Director,
Institute for Healing Justice
and Equity
St. Louis University

Chapter 13: LGBTQ+ People
Heather Walter-McCabe, JD, MSW
Associate Professor
Wayne State University School of Law &
School of Social Work

Chapter 14: People with Disabilities
Elizabeth Pendo, JD
Joseph J. Simeone Professor of Law
St. Louis University School of Law

Introduction

The photograph on the front cover of this textbook is of San Francisco's first "safe sleeping village," located in the shadow of City Hall and opened during the early months of the COVID-19 pandemic. The city had long resisted authorizing homeless-tent encampments, but the pandemic ultimately forced San Francisco—along with several other cities in the United States—to embrace the idea, at least temporarily, in the name of safeguarding unhoused people against the pandemic.

Putting aside the fact that no reasonable person should be euphemistically referring to that encampment as a "village" and despite the fact that its occupants have access to food, water, toilets, showers, and health care, readers of this textbook should, in our view, be clear-eyed about what the photo represents: structural inequity, systemic disadvantage, concentrated deprivation, flawed social safety nets, and major wealth inequities. Put differently, the photo represents the opposite of *health justice*, which we define to mean that all people have the opportunity to reach their full health potential through the recognition of two things: (1) that individual and population health and well-being are primarily driven by upstream structural factors (laws, policies, practices, and systems) rather than by genetics and individual behaviors or choices and (2) that health justice is impossible unless the human rights, civil rights, value, and dignity of all people are acknowledged and actively fostered. The meaning of health justice is discussed more fully in Chapter 1.

This textbook aims to acknowledge, describe, analyze, and spur change to the root causes of the many types of health injustices exemplified by the image on the front cover, which in turn translate into the nation's relatively poor health and well-being. These root causes—oftentimes referred to as "structural drivers" for reasons explained later—include laws, policies, systems of governance, and societal norms and practices that are, in many cases, deeply grounded in history. Just a few of the questions explored in this book include: Are current laws designed to ensure that people can optimize their health over their life span? What can we observe about how laws actually operate as opposed to how they were intended to operate? By what methods should stakeholders evaluate the effects of laws and policies? In an intensely polarized environment, when cultural factors seemingly play an outsized role in political participation and social solidarity, how can policymakers be convinced to act in ways that benefit all people rather than narrow constituencies? These are not mere theoretical questions; as you will discover, laws, policies, and deeply rooted norms and practices have far more to say about the health and well-being of individuals and the communities they form than do human biology, individual behavioral choices, and access to medical care services. This is a key assertion of this textbook, and it bears restating in various ways:

- Structural drivers—laws, policies, systems, practices—are leveraged by those in power to determine whether resources, opportunities, and ultimately well-being are equally distributed or unjustly distributed based on characteristics such as race, ethnicity, gender, social class, and so on.

- Health inequities (defined in Chapter 1)—whether based on race, ethnicity, socioeconomic status, age, geography, language, gender, disability status, citizenship status, sexual identity and/or sexual orientation, or other categories—stem primarily from structural drivers, not from biological differences or solely from individual decisions around health behaviors such as tobacco/alcohol/drug use, sexual practices, diet, or exercise.

- Of the various factors that drive health injustice, most operate on a level outside the control of individuals and communities, and most exact a toll on individuals and populations long before people actually become unwell. This effectively means that at the individual and community level, there may be no amount of knowledge, health-promoting behavior, or political engagement that will actually make people physically, mentally, or emotionally healthy or even healthier.

- Of the various factors that drive health injustice, most are mutable. Existing laws and policies that have created inequitable systems and enabled unfair practices need not be permanent; they can be changed. These laws and policies represent choices we make as a society.

- If structural drivers are utilized by those in power to shape society and distribute resources, opportunities, and wellness, then the conditions and material circumstances that result from the design and operation of those structures can be thought of as social drivers (or "social determinants") of health (more fully defined later and in Chapter 1). Studies have shown that over the course of one's life span, social drivers—education, housing, access to health insurance, environmental factors, access to healthy foods, and the like—may account for fully 80% to 90% of the modifiable contributors to healthy outcomes.[1]

One crucial and undeniable aspect of structural drivers of health is that some of the nation's laws, policies, norms, and practices date back to the founding of the country—which is to say, they are rooted in a time marked by overt, legally sanctioned racism and discrimination. Indeed, America's earliest social mores, economic systems, and laws were conceived during an era of genocide, enslavement, and legalized racial oppression, as North America colonizers tortured Native Americans and Black Americans alike. As barbaric as this treatment was, its long-term consequences have been equally damaging: centuries of race-based prejudice, discrimination, and injustice that flow from laws, policies, and societal practices that perpetuate the myth that People of Color are inferior to White people. This is called *systemic racism* (which, as you will read about in Chapter 1, includes *discrimination*), and it remains a devastating driver of health even today, as the legacy of racialized laws, policies, and practices are carried through generations, generally relegating People of Color—Black and Indigenous people, in particular—to a lower social, financial, educational, and health status relative to White people. Systemic racism refers, quite literally, to discrimination that is woven into the fabric of society, and it has left an indelible mark on the health of People of Color (and, it should be noted, frequently on impoverished people of all races and ethnicities), who have been systematically excluded from the health-promoting resources and opportunities necessary for maximal health outcomes.[2] The U.S. Centers for Disease Control and Prevention, the American Medical Association, and the American Public Health Association all agree, as each one has declared systemic racism to be a public health crisis.

One of the many ways that systemic racism affects health is through the fostering of racial wealth gaps. As you will read below and in others parts of this textbook, wealth and health are closely correlated: The wealthier are generally healthier, and the better one's health, the easier it is to amass wealth. Alongside that axiom sit more than 400 years of federal and state housing and education law and policy that have largely benefited White households and in some cases completely excluded Black, Latinx, and Asian people. For example, today, the typical White household holds 10 times more wealth than the typical Black household.

The health effects of systemic racism are also evident in the COVID-19 pandemic, which set in motion the worst economic, social, and health crisis since World War II. The loss of lives, homes, jobs, opportunities, and connections has been felt across the globe and the country. But the pandemic's burden has fallen disproportionately on historically marginalized populations, including Communities of Color and women, LGBTQ+ individuals, and people with disabilities of all races and ethnicities. For example, across every facet of the pandemic—susceptibility, exposure, infection/hospitalization/death rates, job loss, ability to pay rent/mortgage, and more—Communities of Color have been far more ravaged than those of White people. Data released during the writing of this book indicate that between 2018 and 2020, White Americans lost 1.36 years of life expectancy, while Black Americans and Hispanic Americans lost 3.25 years and 3.88 years, respectively.[3]

Similarly, women have disproportionately experienced economic harm and stress from the pandemic due to their traditional caretaking roles; they were more likely than men to become unemployed during the pandemic. Women in low-wage jobs—particularly Black and Latina women—are also more likely to be deemed "essential workers" (e.g., those who work in health care, the service industry, and agriculture), which both amplified their job loss (in industries that shut down) and heightened their exposure to COVID-19 when they could not work from home. Furthermore, LGBTQ+ people, who have long endured stigma and social alienation,

experienced higher rates of mental health and substance use problems during the pandemic; systemic barriers to health care and reinforced social stigma likely played a part. People with disabilities also experienced greater isolation during government shutdowns than nondisabled individuals. In a nutshell, the pandemic illuminated in stark terms the long-standing linkages between one's social status and the opportunity to maintain health. Indeed, while COVID-19 may be the technical "cause" of much of the national destruction that began in early 2020, that's only true to a point; for People of Color and other historically marginalized populations, the real cause is properly located in centuries of systemic racism that permitted COVID-19 a foothold that simply was not available to it in other communities. This point will be elucidated at various places throughout this text.

Before giving way to a description of the specific topics covered in the textbook, this introduction contextualizes the concept of health justice by touching briefly on four overarching topics, all of which are more fully discussed at later points:

1. Wealth equals health—and the United States currently faces historically high levels of economic inequality.
2. Social factors play a critical role in individual and population health.
3. U.S. society is too willing to medicalize social needs and criminalize social deficiencies.
4. There is no across-the-board right to health, health care services, or health insurance in the United States.

Wealth Equals Health

The United States is, unfortunately, a prolific purveyor of both wealth and health inequities. As to the former, it is widely understood that income inequality in the United States is greater than in any other high-income nation, has been growing for decades, and currently rests at historically high levels, with the top 1% of earners taking home nearly a quarter of the nation's income. As to the latter, while health inequities are a global concern, it is well known that they are more acute in the United States than in all other wealthy nations. These two facts are linked: In the United States, a person's or community's wealth effectively determines that person's or community's overall level of health; in turn, one's level of health affects one's ability to improve upon his/her/their economic status, since it is exceedingly difficult to overcome the forces associated with low economic status without good health. Consider the following:

- The risk of dying before the age of 65 is more than three times greater for those with low socioeconomic status (SES) than for those with high SES.[4]
- Almost every chronic condition, including stroke, heart disease, and arthritis, follows a predictable pattern: Prevalence increases as income decreases.[5]
- People living in poverty are disproportionately burdened by higher crime rates (which can lead to injury and poor mental/emotional health), decreased residential home values (which further contributes to the wealth–health cycle), and higher health care costs.[6]
- Poor and middle-class individuals pay a larger share of their incomes for health care than do the affluent, thereby deepening inequities in disposable income.[7]
- Because health care indebtedness is the single largest cause of personal bankruptcy, many low-income individuals forego needed health care rather than risk indebtedness.

Taken together, the literature on the connection between wealth and health provides "overwhelming evidence that economically disadvantaged groups have poorer survival chances and a higher mortality rate, die at a younger age, experience a blighted quality of life, and have overall diminished health and well-being when compared to other members of society."[8] This wealth–health connection ties in with the other overarching topics you will next read about: The nation's treatment of health care as a commodity makes it more difficult for people stuck on the lower rungs of the SES ladder to achieve good health, and economic deprivation is a type of social driver that would require purposeful correction if health justice is to be achieved.

The Role of Social Drivers in Individual and Population Health

According to the U.S. Department of Health and Human Services, social drivers of health are those "[c]onditions in the environments in which people are born, live, learn, work, play, worship, and age that affect a wide range of health, functioning, and quality-of-life outcomes and risks."[9] There are many examples of these types of social factors—neighborhood conditions (including the amount of crime and violence), housing quality, early childhood education and development, economic stability, access to transportation, employment status, access to sufficient amounts of healthy food, access to health care services, a community's level of social cohesion—and they are key drivers of health and health care inequalities (defined in Chapter 1). Sadly, the overall level of these inequalities has been on the rise in the United States over the past several decades and is now among the highest in high-income countries as measured by differences, for example, in life expectancy, the number of people who are uninsured, and the amount of money that individuals spend on health care needs relative to their overall income.

One immediate takeaway for readers is that the conditions in which people live, work, and play have an enormous impact on individual (and thus community) health irrespective of whether a person ever sees the inside of a physician's office. To better understand this, consider for a moment differences in life expectancy, one of the metrics frequently used to comparatively measure health inequality. At time of birth, life expectancy in the United States can vary by 20 years or more, depending on the location in which a person is born. For example, the next baby born in Summit County, Colorado—which is nearly 95% White—has a life expectancy of approximately 87 years. The next baby born in Ogala Lakota County, South Dakota—which is nearly 95% Native American—has a life expectancy of approximately 66 years. One can drive from one county to the other in about 7 hours. Even starker, perhaps, is an example from Philadelphia, Pennsylvania. A child born today in the area covered by the 19106 zip code—near the Delaware River and the famed Liberty Bell—has a life expectancy of 88 years. Less than four miles away in the area covered by the 19132 zip code, a child's life expectancy at birth is just 68 years. That 20-year difference represents approximately 1 year for each minute it takes to drive between the two locations. In these examples you get a sense of why social and environmental factors are more significant drivers of health than either genes or access to health care services: No number of "good genes" or doctor visits could ever correct these differences in life expectancy, but realigning social factors that influence health could dramatically level the playing field. In fact, the concept of "luck egalitarianism"—the idea that justice requires correcting disadvantages resulting from brute luck—has gained ground in recent years, including in the context of health and health care.[10] If the nation did more correcting of this type, it could reduce the differential burdens of

key drivers of health, in turn reducing health inequalities and moving closer to achieving health justice.

Society Medicalizes Social Needs and Criminalizes Social Deficiencies

Next, we contextualize the concept of health justice by focusing briefly on the ways in which the nation underappreciates and misconstrues the role played by social supports in the overall health of the population. To begin, review **Figure 1**.

Note how, as a percentage of gross domestic product (GDP), combined U.S. spending on health and social care sits right in the middle of the pack when compared to some other high-income nations. But the real story resides in how the country spends that money: Unlike every other nation represented, the United States spends more money on health care than on social care (services targeting education, housing, nutrition, poverty, and the like), and it spends less money on social care (as a percentage of GDP) than every other nation. Given these spending patterns, readers might think that while the United States spends less than perhaps it should on social care, its runaway spending on health care services would nonetheless keep the population relatively healthy. Unfortunately, this is far from the case. Compared to most other high-income countries, the United States actually has similar or worse outcomes on several key measures of health, including maternal health, infant mortality, and chronic disease prevention. What may be occurring is that instead of spending money on supports and programs that could keep people healthy (or healthier) in the first instance, the nation is overspending on relatively expensive medical treatments and procedures once individuals become ill[11] and

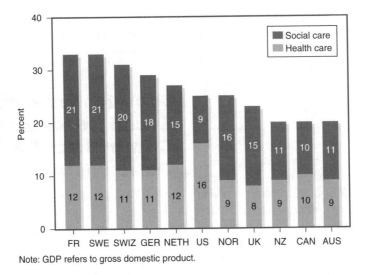

Figure 1 Health and social care spending as a percentage of gross domestic product (GDP)

then sending people back into communities that lack sufficient social supports, thus starting the cycle over again. This is what we mean when we say that the United States "medicalizes" social needs: Essentially, health care services are compensating for a lack of social services spending.

In addition to medicalizing social needs, our society too often criminalizes social deficiencies. Let's use the lack of affordable housing as the first example of a social deficiency. No state in the United States has an adequate supply of rental housing affordable and available for low-income households, and the same can be said for every major metropolitan area.[12] Making matters worse, the poorer the household, the worse the situation, as families with incomes in the bottom 15% of all earners face the prospect of just 17 affordable units available per 100 households. Two root causes of these deficiencies include a lack of investment in affordable housing development and generally relentless rent inflation, which usually hits the lowest-income earners the hardest.

The lack of affordable housing—coupled with the lack of available shelter space, which represents another social deficiency—subjugates hundreds of thousands of people to a life on the streets, as illuminated by the picture on the front cover. Being unhoused often prompts responses from law enforcement, particularly as states and localities pass laws and ordinances making it a crime to perform life-sustaining activities (e.g., eating, sleeping, begging, etc.) in public spaces. Interactions with police, in turn, can have terrible consequences for people already struggling to survive, as some people without adequate shelter have their personal property destroyed, some are pushed out of the urban centers that tend to have more reliable social supports, some accumulate fines they can't afford to pay, and many develop criminal records, which makes it more difficult to secure employment or housing. Additionally, many unhoused persons who come into contact with the police are temporarily incarcerated, which in itself can be devastating: Research indicates that being incarcerated for even just a few days can adversely impact future chances of employment and the well-being of dependent children. (It is worth noting that incarcerating unhoused persons costs two to three-times as much as providing long-term supportive housing.[13])

A second example—this one related to the nation's mental health and substance use crises—drives home the point about how society too easily criminalizes social deficiencies. To start, it is important to understand that compared to every other nation in the world, the United States has the highest incarceration rate: Approximately 640 people for every 100,000 residents are in U.S. jails and prisons, while only two other countries (El Salvador and Rwanda) top 500 people per 100,000 residents, and virtually all other nations are below 350 people per 100,000 residents.[14] The median rate is approximately 150 prisoners per 100,000 residents. Another way to understand the nation's incarceration rate is to grasp that while the United States has only 5% of the world's population, it has nearly 25% of its prisoners—which equates to approximately 2.2 million people on any given day. It must also be noted that U.S. prisons and jails are disproportionately populated with members of racial and ethnic minority groups. For example, while People of Color make up just over 30% of the general population, they comprise more than half of the jail/prison population.[15] While Blacks make up approximately 13% of the nation's population, they account for 28% of all arrests, 40% of the incarcerated population, and 48% of people serving life, life without parole, or "virtual life" sentences.[16] And Native Americans are incarcerated at more than twice the rate of Whites, while Latinxs are held under state jurisdiction at 1.7 times the rate for Whites.[17] Emerging research indicates that this level of mass incarceration may be harming entire communities and contributing to health inequities in the United States.[18]

A few of the factors driving the U.S. incarceration rate have more to do with criminal justice policy than social care deficiencies. For example, the move to mandatory minimum sentences and the implementation of tough-on-crime policies—including "three-strikes" laws and requirements that prisoners serve at least 85% of their sentences—help keep prisons well stocked. But another significant driver of the incarceration rate is society's unwillingness to grapple with its mental health and substance use crises. A majority of jail and prison inmates report mental health concerns, and studies have shown that some two-thirds of jail inmates meet standards for a diagnosable substance abuse disorder.[19] Overall, most of prisoners suffer from either drug addiction or mental illness, and many suffer from both.[20] Indeed, the number of individuals with serious mental illness in prisons and jails now exceeds by 10 times the number in state psychiatric hospitals, and there are more people behind bars for a drug offense than the number of people who were in prison or jail for *any* crime in 1980.[21] Essentially, prisons and jails have become a stand-in for treatment clinics and rehabilitation facilities. Rather than provide prevention, treatment, and other supports in the first instance to individuals who suffer from treatable mental health and substance use disorders, society defaults to the more dangerous, less effective, and more expensive option—criminalizing behavior that often results from illness. (The U.S. carceral state and its effect on health and well-being are discussed in detail in Chapter 9.)

No Generalized Right to Health, Health Care, or Health Insurance

The final topic worth touching on at this early stage is that there is no universal right to health, to health care services, or even to insurance coverage of health care expenses in the United States. This sets the country apart from every other high-income nation and from some middle- and low-income countries as well. The key distinction is that the United States generally treats access to health services like it treats access to food, shelter, and vacuum cleaners—which is to say, one is welcome to them if one can afford them—while other high-income countries generally accept that basic human rights standards include a distinct right to health care services. In the former instance, health care services are viewed as a commodity, whereas in the latter case, health care is seen as a public good worthy of promoting through wealth redistribution.

The choice to commodify health care services—and therefore exclude tens of millions of people from being able to afford them—comes with significant costs to society, and many of the more obvious costs are discussed at points throughout this text. At the same time, there are less obvious ways in which our for-profit health care system harms people. For example, one consequence of the nation's failure to grant equal access to health care services is to actually make people *feel* excluded. Indeed, access to health insurance and health care services functions as a type of social institution, in that having access to these goods shapes behaviors, offers the potential for upward mobility, and fosters feelings of belonging and dignity. The reverse is also true: "In addition to the stress, powerlessness and social disrespect that have been shown to be associated with poorer health status, [uninsured individuals'] awareness of their disadvantaged social status has the potential to undermine self-respect and their sense of themselves as the moral equals of the more fortunate members of society."[22] Furthermore, "where state and local governments have made a concerted effort to integrate marginalized populations into the health care system, researchers find greater connectedness, collaboration, and feelings of a shared fate."[23]

The topics previously summarized have common threads: They are "structural" in nature, they deeply affect health and well-being, and they are changeable. Economic inequality, affordable housing shortages, and a commodified health care system are societal policy choices, not laws of nature. They are, without debate, hugely significant drivers of health that fall outside the control of individuals and have nothing to do with how individuals choose to live their lives. And they all could be modified and improved, and rather quite easily, provided that population-wide welfare—the chief object of social justice—was the goal. In the end, this becomes the primary aim of those committed to health justice: To understand that health *in*justice results from a range of unmet human needs that are not experienced evenly across populations; to accept that the United States has the means to both ameliorate and prevent this type of disuniform deprivation; and to strive for a framework of laws, policies, systems, and practices that effectively rewrite the nation's existing social contract in favor of one that actually secures the opportunity for optimal health and wellness for everyone.[24]

Rationale for and Structure of *Essentials of Health Justice*

This textbook was originally conceived as a primer that would serve as a companion to another textbook in a course on law, medicine, public health, nursing, or health care administration in which health justice was just one of many covered topics. That was in the spring of 2017, and while stand-alone courses on health justice existed, they were not widespread and rarely more than one credit in scope. The social, political, and health events of the intervening years have reshaped what it means to study, teach, and work in the health justice space. Criminal justice reform is now regularly viewed—at least among most academicians and some policymakers—as a health justice concern. So, too, are voting rights and rights to a quality education. Efforts to promote opportunity and prosperity for all while reducing persistent wealth inequities now comfortably fall under the health justice umbrella, as do many other topics not historically linked to the study of "health justice." As a result, professors and students across a range of disciplines are seeking textbooks that holistically analyze entrenched health injustice in the United States and that can serve as the primary text for an extensive variety of courses that fall along a health and social justice spectrum.

This edition of *Essentials of Health Justice* reflects the events of the past 5 years. It has a new subordinate title—the "Primer" designation has been replaced with "Law, Policy, and Structural Change"—is double the length of its predecessor, and covers a far wider range of topics than did the previous book. *Essentials of Health Justice: Law, Policy, and Structural Change* is divided into five parts. Part I provides context and background. Chapter 1 covers definitions, theories, and frameworks that influence conceptions of health justice, while Chapter 2 describes lessons learned from a diverse range of past social justice movements. In Part II, the legal underpinnings of health injustice are discussed from four different vantage points. First, Chapter 3 considers how each of the three branches of government operates in ways that can hamper widespread health justice. Chapter 4 then covers an array of health-harming legal doctrines, including the no duty to treat principle and the "negative Constitution." Chapter 5 describes health justice through the lens of human rights, a perspective that is too often missing in U.S. policy making and jurisprudence. Chapter 6 completes Part II by focusing on legal theories related to proving discrimination.

Across three chapters, Part III describes the role of structural inequity in health injustice. Chapter 7 covers socioeconomic inequality, Chapter 8 gives attention to place-based health inequities, and Chapter 9 details the role of the American carceral state in shaping population health and wellness. Part IV tackles health justice for historically excluded populations, including Asian, Black, Indigenous, Latinx, and other People of Color (Chapter 10); immigrants (Chapter 11); women (Chapter 12), LGBTQ+ people (Chapter 13), and people with disabilities (Chapter 14). Finally, Part V lays out a more vibrant health justice agenda. Chapter 15 summarizes existing efforts to achieve health justice, including medical care system innovations and public health initiatives that target structural change. Lastly, Chapter 16 offers new directions for addressing the root causes of health injustice through community empowerment, policy change, multisector policy advocacy, and a reframing of health justice that leverages human rights perspectives. The text concludes with a call to action to recognize and affirm that the lives of medically and socially vulnerable populations can be immeasurably improved by respecting those populations' right to health justice.

It is our hope that this textbook provides a useful frame for instructing students from different disciplines about the structural role of law in health and well-being, illuminates for students the particular pathways between social policies and the injustices they can create, and offers students concrete ideas about how to practice health justice advocacy skills. By delving into the historical, structural, and legal underpinnings of racial, ethnic, gender-based, and ableist inequities in health, readers will explore (1) how health and justice intersect; (2) how law and policy structure medical, public health, and other social service systems in the United States; (3) how extant social structures lead to inequities that disproportionately harm particular populations; and (4) how health and other social systems could be reshaped to be more responsive to health injustice.

References

1. Epstein WN. A legal paradigm for the health inequity crisis. February 17, 2021. https://ssrn.com/abstract=3787539.

2. Ford CL, Airhihenbuwa CO. The public health critical race methodology: Praxis for antiracism research. *Social Science & Medicine.* 2010;71:1390–1398.

3. Woolf SH, Masters RK, and Aron LY. Effect of the covid-19 pandemic in 2020 on life expectancy across populations in the USA and other high-income countries: Simulations of provisional mortality data. *BMJ.* 2021. Available at: http://dx.doi.org/10.1136/bmj.n1343.

4. Benfer EA. Health justice: A framework (and call to action) for the elimination of health inequity and social justice. *American University Law Review.* 2015;65(2):281.

5. Dickman SL, Himmelstein DU, Woolhandler S. Inequality and the health-care system in the USA. *Lancet.* 2017;389:1431–1444.

6. Benfer EA. Health justice: A framework (and call to action) for the elimination of health inequity and social justice. *American University Law Review.* 2015;65(2):277.

7. Dickman SL, Himmelstein DU, Woolhandler S. Inequality and the health-care system in the USA. *Lancet.* 2017;389:1431–1444.

8. Benfer EA. Health justice: A framework (and call to action) for the elimination of health inequity and social justice. *American University Law Review.* 2015;65(2):279.

9. U.S. Department of Health and Human Services. The Secretary's Advisory Committee on National Health Promotion and Disease Prevention Objectives. 2020 topics and objectives: Social determinants of health. 2021. https://www.healthypeople.gov/2020/topics-objectives/topic/social-determinants-of-health.

10. Segall S. *Health, Luck, and Justice* . Princeton, NJ: Princeton University Press; 2009.

11. Butler SM. Social spending, not medical spending, is key to health. Brookings Institution; 2016. https://www.brookings.edu/opinions/social-spending-not-medical-spending-is-key-to-health/; Bradley EH, Taylor LA. How social spending affects health outcomes. Robert Wood Johnson Foundation; 2016. http://www.rwjf.org/en/culture-of-health/2016/08/how_social_spending.html.

12. Aurand A, Emmanuel D, Threet D, Rafi I, Yentel D. The gap: A shortage of affordable homes. The National Low-Income Housing Coalition. March 2021. https://reports.nlihc.org/sites/default/files/gap/Gap-Report_2021.pdf.

13. Hodge Jr. J, DiPietro B, Horton-Newell AE. Homelessness and the public's health: Legal responses. *Journal of Law, Medicine & Ethics.* 2017;45(1):28–32.

14. Trends in U.S. corrections. The Sentencing Project; May 2021. https://www.sentencingproject.org/wp-content/uploads/2021/07/Trends-in-US-Corrections.pdf.

15. National Association for the Advancement of Colored People (NAACP). Criminal justice fact sheet. 2022. http://www.naacp.org/criminal-justice-fact-sheet/.

16. Prison Policy Initiative. 2021. https://www.prisonpolicy.org/research/race_and_ethnicity/.

17. Prison Policy Initiative. 2021. https://www.prisonpolicy.org/research/race_and_ethnicity/.

18. Wildeman C, Wang E. Mass incarceration, public health, and widening inequality in the USA. *Lancet.* 2017;389:1464–1474.

19. American Psychological Association (APA). Incarceration nation. 2014. https://www.apa.org/monitor/2014/10/incarceration.

20. Austin J, Eisen LB, Cullen J, Frank J. *How many Americans are unnecessarily incarcerated?* Brennan Center for Justice, NYU School of Law; 2016. https://www.brennancenter.org/sites/default/files/publications/Unnecessarily_Incarcerated_0.pdf.

21. The Sentencing Project. Criminal justice facts. 2020. http://www.sentencingproject.org/criminal-justice-facts/.

22. Faden R, Powers M. Incrementalism: ethical implications of policy choices. *The Kaiser Family Foundation.* 1999. Available at: https://www.kff.org/wp-content/uploads/2013/01/incrementalism-ethical-implications-of-policy-choices-issue-paper.pdf.

23. McKay T. The social costs of repealing the ACA. Health Affairs Blog. March 7, 2017. http://healthaffairs.org/blog/2017/03/07/the-social-costs-of-repealing-the-aca-2/.

24. Harris AP, Pamukcu A. The civil rights of health: A new approach to challenging structural inequality. *UCLA Law Review.* 2020;67:758.

PART 1

Context and Background

CHAPTER 1

Introductory Frameworks, Definitions, and Theories for Health Justice

LEARNING OBJECTIVES

By the end of this chapter you will be able to:

- Discuss the frameworks, definitions, goals, values, and ethics of the fields of medicine, public health, and law and how these relate to health justice
- Explain key terminology used by scholars and advocates associated with race, sex and gender, and disability
- Describe some critical theories (race, feminist, queer, and disability) and how they have been applied to medicine, public health, and law and ultimately to health justice

Introduction

This text is designed for a wide range of disciplines and readers, as noted in the Introduction. One of the challenges of confronting and addressing health injustice is that so many factors, systems, and players converge along the way to produce the inequities that harm health. Indeed, if health justice is to be achieved, disciplinary siloes (between and among medicine, public health, law, and public policy) must be dismantled and intersectoral solutions must be collaboratively identified and implemented. This chapter is designed to build some common ground among disciplines and professions to facilitate better understanding of one another's language, goals, values, and practices.

But health justice also requires deep reflection about how power is unevenly distributed among people in American society and how this leaves groups of people marginalized and silenced based on their socioeconomic status, racial or ethnic identity, sexuality, gender, and/or disability. To explore how systems of power exclude particular groups, this chapter also presents how critical theories—critical race, feminist, queer, and disability theories—interrogate the exclusion and marginalization of people considered to be different from the "norm." Linking these theories to health, this chapter investigates how these theories inform and can be applied to medicine, public health, and law to promote health justice.

We begin the chapter with some foundational definitions to create a common understanding of terms as we use them in the text.

Health, as defined by the World Health Organization, is "a state of complete physical, mental and social wellbeing and not merely the absence of disease or infirmity."[1]

Health care inequalities are "differences in the quality of health care provided that are not due to access-related factors or clinical needs, preferences, and appropriateness of interventions. These differences would include the role of bias, discrimination, and stereotyping at the individual (provider and patient), institutional, and health system levels."[2]

Health inequities are "differences in health status or in the distribution of health resources between different population groups, arising from the social conditions in which people are born, grow, live, work and age. Health inequities are unfair and could be reduced by the right mix of government policies."[3]

Social drivers of health are "the conditions in the environments where people are born, live, learn, work, play, worship, and age that affect a wide range of health, functioning, and quality-of-life outcomes and risks."[4] We intentionally use the word *drivers*, rather than the more common *determinants*, to acknowledge the complex causal pathways between and among social, environmental, and biological factors that influence the health of individuals and populations.

Health justice means that all people have the opportunity to reach their full health potential. It recognizes that individual and population health and well-being are primarily driven by upstream structural factors (i.e., laws, policies, practices, and systems), not by the individual behaviors or choices of those in poor health. Health justice addresses health inequities and health care inequalities by recognizing the human rights, civil rights, value, and dignity of all people. Health justice requires self-determination for those who have experienced exclusion, discrimination, and stigma; demands structural changes (in law, policy, practices, and systems) that promote equitable power-sharing across all groups; and, ultimately, secures equitable, health-promoting conditions and communities in which all people can thrive.

How people define health justice may be influenced by their particular vantage points and experiences. For students, the discipline they are studying and/or profession they are preparing for may affect their perspective and understanding of health justice. To bridge understanding and facilitate inquiry and discussion across disciplines, we offer an overview of the frameworks, definitions, goals, values, and ethics of medicine, public health, and law. We start with how these disciplines traditionally have been defined and framed and then explore how they are changing, including how each is confronting and addressing concepts of health justice.

Medicine, Public Health, and Law: Frameworks for Health Justice

Medicine
Frameworks and Definitions

Typically, people think of medicine as primarily concerned with the diagnosis and treatment of disease. In the United States, it is often said that medicine is both a science and an art, meaning that clinicians apply scientific knowledge when diagnosing and treating disease, but they also draw on their own experience and intuitions to help guide them. Traditionally, medicine has been primarily associated with doctors and patients. But medical care involves a range of professionals and practitioners, including nurses, social workers, physician assistants, medical assistants, direct care workers, community health workers, and many others. Increasingly, medicine is becoming a team-based multidisciplinary affair, drawing on the knowledge and expertise of various players. Therefore, when we discuss medical professionals in this text, we are referring to the various practitioners who make up the medical team, not just doctors. Furthermore, medicine cannot be understood in a vacuum. Patients and health care providers exist within larger systems—not only the health care system, but also the political system, legal and regulatory systems, and the many other systems (e.g., educational, criminal justice, environmental) that influence health and health care. **Figure 1.1**

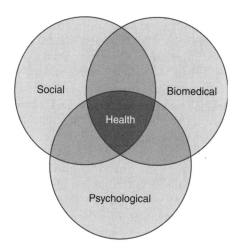

Figure 1.1 The biopsychosocial model of health

demonstrates the biopsychosocial model of health, which incorporates the many factors affecting health.

Goals and Values

How one defines medicine and constructs its frameworks depends first on articulating its goals. The goals of medicine, no doubt, vary based on social context (i.e., where and when medical care is being delivered) and on specialty (the type of medicine being practiced). Nonetheless, scholars have proposed four basic goals of medicine, so we begin with these:

1. Preventing disease and injury and promoting and maintaining health
2. Relieving pain and suffering caused by maladies
3. Caring for and curing those with a malady and caring for those who cannot be cured
4. Avoiding premature death and pursuing a peaceful death[5]

You may detect in these goals a strong focus on the relationship and interaction between the clinician (physician, nurse, or other health care provider) and the patient. But, increasingly, American medicine is embracing broader social goals for clinicians that extend beyond the care of individual patients. For example, in 2001, just after the attacks of September 11, the American Medical Association drafted the *Declaration of Professional Responsibility: Medicine's Social Contract with Humanity*, in which it articulated a more far-reaching vision of clinicians as advocates for "social, economic, educational and political change" in addition to their obligations to care for individual patients and contribute to medical science. Indeed, the declaration states that "humanity is our patient."[6] Though the declaration speaks specifically about physicians, its principles can be applied to all medical professionals.

Nonetheless, the notion that physicians and other health care professionals are obliged to use their skills and knowledge to improve society was certainly not new in 2001. Rudolf Virchow, a German physician, anthropologist, pathologist, writer, and politician, first coined the term *social medicine* in the 1800s to describe how social factors influence and harm health and inequality as a causal factor in disease. Virchow explained that:

> Medicine is a social science, and politics is nothing else but medicine on a large scale. Medicine, as a social science, as the science of human beings, has the obligation to point out problems and to attempt their theoretical solution. . . . The physicians are the natural attorneys of the poor, and the social problems should largely be solved by them.[7]

Social medicine, therefore, extends the medical provider's role well beyond the exam room or lab into the social sphere, including weighing in on public policy, law, and politics. While not all of the medical community embraces social medicine, it has become increasingly adopted in primary care, which centers on holistic and preventive approaches that acknowledge and work to help address social factors related to health. In recent years, some in primary care have embraced a "population medicine" perspective that is concerned with patterns of disease among a population of patients and employs data (including data related to broader social factors) to better understand those patterns.[8] The ethical obligation of physicians and other health care providers to use their knowledge and skills to address their patients' social needs and to promote public policy reform is still debated, but it has gained traction in recent years. Later chapters in this book discuss how medical providers are working both within clinical settings and outside them to address health inequities and injustice.

Ethics

The term *biomedical ethics* emerged in the 1970s as a way to apply philosophical moral principles to ethical dilemmas in medicine. Tom Beauchamp and James Childress's book *Principles of Biomedical Ethics* describes four ethical principles that they argue should be applied to medical practice and biomedical research.[9] See **Table 1.1**. Beauchamp and Childress intend for all four principles to be applied equally to an ethical dilemma; if one or more of the principles must be violated, the violation should be minimal. The principle of autonomy invokes individual rights: the right of patients and research subjects to make their own decisions, without interference from medical professionals, family members, or others. The principles of beneficence and non-maleficence speak to the obligations of medical professionals to ensure that they are acting in the patient's best interest (not their own) and without harm to the patient. Beneficence and nonmaleficence intersect with the principle of autonomy in that medical professionals should not paternalistically make decisions about a patient's health based on what they believe is best when those decisions violate the patient's rights and values. The principle of justice concerns equal treatment of individuals and populations (without regard to race, class, gender, disability, etc.) and with the equitable distribution of health and health care services across populations.

As an ethical principle, justice is not only relevant to individuals; it should also be applied to communities. Community justice "insists on respect for the meanings and values that diverse communities create and hold dear." Therefore, "[c]ommunity justice

Table 1.1 Principlist Biomedical Ethics

Autonomy	Respect for persons. Humans are a means unto themselves and not a means to an end. This encompasses the right to be free to make choices about your body.
Beneficence	Obligation to contribute to person's welfare. Interventions and provisions should provide benefit directly to the patient. This focuses on doing things that are of benefit to another. It requires positive steps to help, and not merely avoiding doing harm.
Nonmaleficence	Obligation not to inflict harm on other persons. Harm is to be avoided or minimized. Underlying tenet of medical professional mission statements (Hippocratic oath).
Justice	For health care, this is the distribution of health (and health care) in a fair and equitable manner. This requires attention to prioritization and rationing. There is no one just way to allocate resources, and most systems utilize several prioritization schemes in concert to attempt to achieve a just distribution.

- The four principles are meant to be used in concert with each other and not in isolation. To use them one aims to uphold ALL of the principles for any issue. If one or more are violated, the violation needs to be minimal. Additionally, there is no hierarchy of principles—which principle is most important (or which two or three) is dependent on the context of the dilemma.
- Principlist moral theory can be problematic in that there is no guidance for proceeding when the four principles cannot be balanced (or upheld). It also considers ONLY the four principles, although there are many other principles, considerations, and values to be considered and weighed into decision-making in most ethical dilemmas.
- In Western nations, such as the United States, autonomy tends to have a higher emphasis than in many other places.

DiNardo M, et al. Principlism and Personalism. Comparing Two Ethical Models Applied Clinically in Neonates Undergoing Extracorporeal Membrane Oxygenation Support. Frontiers in Pediatrics. July 30, 2019.

does not describe in a fine-grained way what just [health and] health care would look like; rather it articulates standards or norms required for reaching agreed-to understandings of health and health care that are needed for the provision of just health care services" and community health.[10] In addition, critics have noted that bioethicists often fail to account for social context: "[B]ioethics tends to view the patient or research subject generically, without attention to race, gender, or insurance status…, and,

thus bioethics has traditionally adopted rules and has applied them with little, if any, concern for how race or other characteristics affect the working of the rules."[11] The notion of justice in bioethics, therefore, necessarily raises important questions about the ways in which medicine has historically and continues to treat marginalized and vulnerable populations. Concepts of justice—as they relate to health care access as well as to the fair and equitable opportunity to be healthy—are analyzed throughout this text.

Public Health

Frameworks and Definitions

Public health focuses on the promotion and protection of the health of populations. "This work is achieved by promoting healthy lifestyles, researching disease and injury prevention, and detecting, preventing and responding to infectious diseases."[12] In promoting the health of populations, a core question for public health is how to define the term *population*. In the case of the COVID-19 pandemic, public health researchers and practitioners may define the population as all of the people in the world. On the other end of the spectrum, a small rural community may identify a population of 100 or fewer people for the purposes of public health research or testing an intervention to prevent or treat disease. Often, public health researchers and practitioners define a population by a specific category, such as people having a particular disease or people from a certain racial, ethnic, or socioeconomic group. Public health's focus on populations has traditionally been what has distinguished it from medicine. But as noted previously, medicine is increasingly concerning itself with the broader social drivers of health through the perspective of "population medicine."

Nonetheless, public health has long been concerned with the social-ecological model of health that describes the individual, social, socioeconomic, cultural, and environmental factors and conditions that affect the health of individuals and populations and that distribute health inequitably. See **Figure 1.2**.

Goals and Values

At its core, public health is focused on the prevention of disease and injury. The impact of public health actions on population health varies based on the degree to which these actions change the social environment and how much effort is required of individuals. See **Figure 1.3**. The term *upstream* is often used

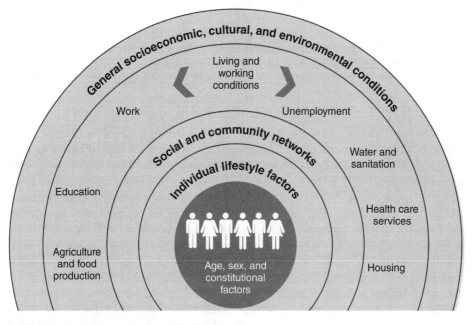

Figure 1.2 The social-ecological model of health

Reproduced from Dahlgren G, Whitehead M. Policies and strategies to promote social equity in health. Stockholm Institute for Future Studies;1991.

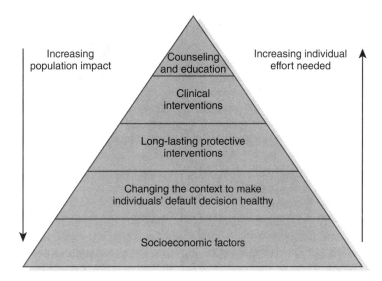

Figure 1.3 The health impact pyramid

Reproduced from Frieden, T.R. A framework for public health action: The health impact pyramid. *American Journal of Public Health.* 2010; 100 (4), 590–595.

to describe interventions that address harmful social and structural drivers that, if avoided, prevent *downstream* disease and injury.

As the field of public health has grappled with the entrenched health disparities evident in America, it has increasingly embraced equity as a core goal. This is clear from the Centers for Disease Control and Prevention's (CDC) recently updated 10 *Essential Public Health Services.* See **Figure 1.4**. As you can see, the 10 services, which include the broader categories of policy development, assurance, and assessment, surround a core value: equity. The original 1994 version of the 10 essential services surrounded the core tool of research.[13]

Public health's attention to the social and structural drivers of health inequity builds on the theory of *social epidemiology,* which "assumes that the distribution of health and disease in a society reflects the distribution of advantages and disadvantages in that society. Based on this premise, social epidemiology examines which sociostructural factors affect the distribution of health and disease, as well as how these factors influence individual and population health."[14]

The theory that public health encompasses a wide range of "conceptual, methodological, scientific, political and moral factors recognizing the interdependency and interrelationship of the health of people, communities, and nations" is articulated in what has been deemed the *new public health,* which promotes "an integrative approach to protecting and promoting the health status of both the individual and the society."[15] The new public health promotes interdisciplinary and intersectoral approaches, including law and policy reform, as important means to addressing the root causes of poor population health and health inequities. The "health in all policies" (HIA) approach is an example of an intersectoral *new* public health strategy. It considers the population health implications of a broad range of policies, such as education, transportation, and housing. Chapter 15 describes HIA in greater detail.

Public Health Ethics

Ethical principles in public health are intended to guide decision-making by public health

THE 10 ESSENTIAL PUBLIC HEALTH SERVICES

To protect and promote the health of all people in all communities

The 10 Essential Public Health Services provide a framework for public health to protect and promote the health of all people in all communities. To achieve optimal health for all, the Essential Public Health Services actively promote policies, systems, and services that enable good health and seek to remove obstacles and systemic and structural barriers, such as poverty, racism, gender discrimination, and other forms of oppression, that have resulted in health inequities. Everyone should have a fair and just opportunity to achieve good health and well-being.

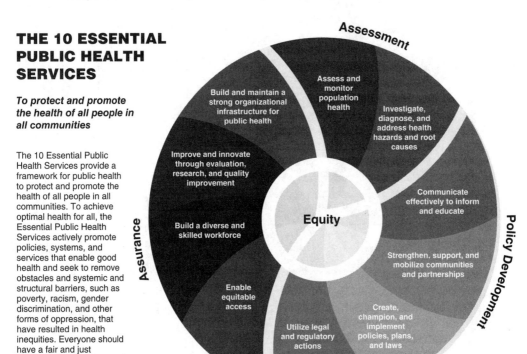

Figure 1.4 The 10 essential public health services

Centers for Disease Control and Prevention. Ten Essential Public Health Services. 2020. https://www.cdc.gov/publichealthgateway/publichealthservices/essentialhealthservices.html.

officials and policymakers to ensure that competing interests are carefully acknowledged and weighed before action is taken. Federal, state, and local public health officials carry significant authority to regulate a wide range of business, community, and individual behaviors in order to promote and protect public health, as you will read in Chapter 3. Ethical principles for public health intervention and policy articulate the values of the public health field. For example, the American Public Health Association's 2019 Code of Ethics demonstrate the field's commitment to transparency and public trust; policies and practices that reflect scientific evidence; equity; inclusivity; respect for individual rights; and promotion of communal interests.

As has been apparent throughout the COVID-19 pandemic, balancing all of these

ethical principles in public health decision-making, especially during a time of crisis, is extremely fraught. Currently in the United States, ethical decision-making in public health is complicated by political polarization, scientific uncertainty, competing messages from traditional and social media, and general distrust by the public of government authority and institutions.

Law
Frameworks and Definitions

Law as a discipline is broad and diverse. Here, we describe the essential role of law in organizing society and governing human relationships and conduct and also how law relates to health. To begin, we offer a definition of law from *Black's Law Dictionary*:

That which is laid down, ordained, or established. A rule or method according to which phenomena or actions co-exist or follow each other. Law, in its generic sense, is a body of rules of action or conduct prescribed by controlling authority, and having binding legal force. That which must be obeyed and followed by citizens subject to sanctions or legal consequences is a law.[16]

But law is more than rules. Law reflects the evolving customs, beliefs, and value systems of a given nation, state, or locality. Indeed, law "takes an understanding, a norm, an attitude, and hardens it into muscle and bone."[17] It reaches into nearly every corner of American life. People encounter laws daily pertaining to the environment, property ownership, the workplace, civil rights, copyright, energy, banking, and much more. Hence, a society as sprawling and complex as ours needs formal, enforceable rules of law to provide a measure of control (for example, the need to regulate entities or actions that are potentially dangerous or invidious—a polluting power plant or acts of discrimination based on race or gender). Law is also expected to achieve "justice" by producing outcomes based on fairness and equality. The legal system in the United States encompasses the complex interactions among the three branches of government (legislative, executive, and judicial) charged with writing, implementing, and interpreting the law, as discussed in detail in Chapter 3.

Law relates to medicine and public health in multiple and distinct ways. Traditionally, the law of medicine or what is typically called *health care law* has been understood as the rules and regulations governing the health care industry, including hospitals and other health care organizations and providers, insurers, and pharmaceutical and device manufacturers, as well as individual medical professionals. Health care laws include, among many others, antitrust laws governing hospital system mergers, medical fraud and abuse by providers and insurers, medical malpractice, and privacy laws such as the Health Insurance Portability and Accountability Act (HIPAA). As discussed later, in recent years, the definition of health care law has been expanded to incorporate a broader range of laws that implicate health equity and justice. Furthermore, the field of public health law utilizes a definition that is distinct from health care law. Consider scholar Lawrence Gostin's definition of public health law:

> Public health law is the study of the legal powers and duties of the state, in collaboration with its partners (e.g., health care, business, the community, the media, and academe), to assure the conditions for people to be healthy (to identify, prevent, and ameliorate risks to health in the population) and the limitations on the power of the state to constrain the autonomy, privacy, liberty, proprietary, or other legally protected interests of individuals for the common good. The prime objective of public health law is to pursue the highest possible level of physical and mental health in the population, consistent with the values of social justice.

In addition to regulating the actions of stakeholders in the medical care system and defining the duties and limits of public health authority, law plays a vital role in structuring the conditions in which people live. In so doing, law is an important social driver of health. It governs physical environments, such as through laws regulating environmental hazards, workplace safety, and rental property standards. It also shapes social environments and norms through laws that, for example, regulate smoking, tax sugar-sweetened beverages, and require restaurants to publish calorie counts on their menus. Perhaps most importantly, it structures the distribution of resources needed for people to be and stay healthy, including through tax laws, health care policies, and regulations structuring and governing safety net programs.[18]

Values and Goals

With greater attention to the many ways in which law shapes health outcomes and inequities, health care law and public health law scholars and practitioners are redefining the goals and values of law and legal practice. They are also finding common ground in recognizing the upstream role that law plays in both individual and population health, thus implicating both medicine and public health. As medical professionals confront the downstream effects of failed social policies in meeting patients' unmet social needs, they are acknowledging the critical role that law plays in shaping not only the medical care and public health systems but also their patients' health potential. Medical-legal partnerships are offering opportunities for lawyers and medical teams to work together to aid patients not only in enforcing legal rights that affect their health but also in jointly advocating for legal and policy changes that promote and support health, as discussed in Chapter 15.

Similarly, public health professionals and practitioners are joining forces with lawyers to identify ways to employ law as a tool to promote and protect health, including through addressing social drivers of health. Public health lawyers are also studying how specific laws—as written and as implemented and enforced—affect the health of the people subject to those laws. This approach is called *legal epidemiology*, defined as "the scientific study and use of law as a factor in the cause, distribution, and prevention of disease and injury in a population." This empirical approach helps public health officials and public health lawyers to better understand "*how* law influences health…and *whether* it does so."[19] As interdisciplinary approaches to health care law and public health law take hold, they share

two values and goals: improving and promoting individual and population health in the United States and eliminating the health inequities that have plagued this country for so long.

Ethics

Legal ethics are generally understood as the professional rules of conduct for lawyers. Lawyers are governed by state ethics rules that address issues such as the lawyer-client relationship, the lawyer's duty to serve as a zealous advocate for the client, client confidentiality, conflicts of interest, and professional independence. The legal profession highly values lawyers' duties to their clients above all else. Strict ethical rules for lawyers can sometimes make interdisciplinary collaboration with other professionals, such as medical and public health professionals, difficult. For example, a lawyer working with medical professionals to assist a patient with a legal barrier to health—such as the risk of an eviction from the patient's home—may only share information with a medical team if the patient/client permits it. Increasingly, medical-legal partnerships and other interdisciplinary collaborations are finding effective ways to protect patients' rights while also engaging in collaborative problem-solving without running afoul of professional ethical rules.[20]

Lawyers in public health agencies or those working collaboratively with public health partners must also be mindful of ethical rules guiding their behavior. They must balance duty to their client and fidelity to existing law and its limits with their partners' broader public health goals. This may mean that they must sometimes advise a more measured approach to public intervention or action than their colleagues are seeking. Nonetheless, working in tandem with public health colleagues, lawyers often find innovative ways to use the law as a tool for prevention and for promoting public health. As medical, public health, and legal professionals apply intersectoral approaches to population health improvement and equity, they are reimagining their professional boundaries and developing innovative approaches and strategies to health justice. We explore these approaches and strategies in later chapters.

Critical Theories: Challenging Norms and Shaping Definitions of Health Justice

With that overview of the fields of medicine, public health, and law, we now turn to discussion of some of the critical theories driving discourse around inequality, marginalization, and power in the United States. We present these theories to challenge you to think about how norms shaped by dominant power structures serve to control not only the distribution of opportunities and resources but also whose voices are heard and valued. Here we focus on critical race, feminist, queer, and disability theories. We begin each topic with some definitions. In presenting these definitions, we acknowledge that readers may disagree with our choices and language. Language, after all, is powerful: It shapes norms, creates mental images that are inclusive or exclusive, and either reinforces or disrupts biases. We challenge you to critique our language and definitions as you think critically about what health justice means or should mean in the future. After presenting definitions and theories, we explore the ways in which these critical theories apply to medicine, public health, and law.

Race and Ethnicity

Definitions of race and ethnicity are far from static. In the areas of medicine and public health, definitions of race and ethnicity have profound implications for the health of People of Color and for approaches to addressing health inequities. Historically (and still in some circles today), race has been defined as a biological category. Biological notions of race have been used to justify health inequities and perpetuate notions of White superiority. The way race is defined in the law shapes legal responses to discrimination and racism and structures the obligations of governmental officials to address injustices. We start with definitions to delineate the different ways in which race and racism have been construed in the past and how they are being redefined. We then explore critical race theory, which confronts how definitions of race and racism have been used by those in power to categorize and subjugate people based on their assigned race and/or ethnicity.

Definitions

Race is a social construct that artificially categorizes people by phenotype—"the societal box into which others put you based on your physical features."[21] The United States has a disturbing history with regard to racial classification, given how much those classifications have been infused with bigoted beliefs about White superiority. Therefore, race is a "harmful way to think about human biological differences."[22] From a scientific perspective, racial taxonomy is inadequate because "(1) the concept of race is based on the idea of fixed, ideal, and unchanging types; (2) human variation is continuous; (3) human variation is nonconcordant; (4) within-group genetic variation is much greater than variation among 'races'; (5) there is no way to consistently classify by race; and (6) there is no clarity as to what race is and what it is not."[23] As legal scholar Dorothy Roberts notes, race is not just a social construct, it is a "political category that is defined by invented rules"[24] that have profound consequences for "people's health, wealth, social status, reputation, and opportunities in life."[25]

Ethnicity is a social construct that sorts people into groups based on common national and/or cultural traditions, language, sense of group membership, or values.[26] At times in American history, ethnicity has been equated with race. For example, until the 1970s, Mexicans were classified in the Census simply as "White." Then, in the 1980s, the Census included the word *Hispanic*, which was later changed in the 2000 Census to *Latino*.[27]

Assigned ethnicity may or may not correspond to how people identify themselves.

Racism is the combination of racial prejudice (a prejudgment about a person or group based on negative stereotypes) and the power to subordinate people based on their assigned "race." Racism "is a system of structuring opportunity and assigning value based on phenotype (race) that: unfairly disadvantages some individuals and communities; unfairly advantages other individuals and communities; [and] undermines realization of the full potential of the whole society through the waste of human resources."[28] Racism can operate at various levels, including (1) interpersonal racism, or experiences of discrimination and prejudice experienced in everyday life; (2) internalized racism, in which victims of racism internalize prejudicial attitudes resulting in stress or loss of self-esteem; and (3) structural and institutionalized racism, which are "the structural elements of racism that are codified in our institutions of customs, practice and law so there need not be an identifiable perpetrator."[29]

Critical Race Theory

Critical race theory (CRT) developed in the 1970s and 1980s post–civil rights era at a time when the "prevailing sense was that the law was not at all involved in creating and sustaining racial hierarchies."[30] Law professor Derrick Bell, one of the founders of CRT, argued that the persistence of racial inequality in the post–civil rights era resulted in part from the failure of civil rights laws to fundamentally address racial injustice. His scholarship focused on interrogating the ways in which law continued to both construct and justify racial inequality. He argued that American institutions, either intentionally or unintentionally, justify or minimize racism.[31] Kimberlé Crenshaw, who coined the term *critical race theory*, has acknowledged that CRT is "fundamentally eclectic" and is "not a fully unified school of thought."[32] Instead, she says, it is a framework for interrogating racial hierarchy and inequality. Indeed, "the scholars who produce CRT

are an interdisciplinary bunch, and they bring a broad range of investigative tools—including anthropology, history, qualitative and quantitative sociology, political theory, and economics, among others—to bear in their inquiries."[33] (As discussed later, CRT has been applied not just to law but also to medicine and public health and has been an important tool for analyzing the connections between racial inequality and health injustice.)

According to legal scholar Khiara Bridges, there are four basic tenets that animate CRT: First is the understanding that race is not biological; it is a social construct (as noted previously). CRT scholars argue that, while race is not a biologic reality, the *social* reality must be analyzed in terms of how racial classification affects the lives of People of Color. Second, racism is a foundational part of American society. Bell argued that racism runs through and is reinforced by all U.S. institutions. Therefore, racist incidents (e.g., recurring events of police brutality in Communities of Color) are not aberrations, but rather are indicative of structural/institutionalized racism. Third, CRT rejects the idea that racism is equated with race consciousness. Scholars argue that "colorblindness" not only papers over structural racism, it makes remediation for past harms impossible. For example, Supreme Court decisions that employ colorblindness and that make racial discrimination only actionable with proof of intentional discrimination have severely hindered racial justice, as touched on in Chapter 6. Fourth, CRT privileges the lived experiences of People of Color as critical to scholarly analysis (i.e., scholarship is only valuable if it contributes to dismantling racial oppression and improves the lives of real people).[34]

Equality Versus Equity. Arguing that racism is deeply embedded in the fabric of American law, systems, and institutions, CRT scholars assert that remedies for racial injustice must be based on the principle of equity. They contend that it is not sufficient to assume that all racial groups have equal opportunities (e.g., educational and economic) when the legacy of legalized racial discrimination and structural racism continue to disproportionately limit the opportunities of certain racial and ethnic groups. They assert that *equity* (as opposed to *equality*) demands that policies allocating the distribution of resources (e.g., taxes, public benefits, health care, housing) acknowledge past discrimination, structural racism, and power differentials. Thus, equitable policies should focus on what historically marginalized people actually need in order to have the opportunity to achieve their full potential.

Interest Convergence. Some CRT scholars have argued that "the interests of blacks in achieving racial equality have been accommodated only when they have converged with the interests of powerful whites."[35] Derrick Bell described this "interest convergence" to help explain why, even after passage of civil rights laws, racial injustice continues. Writing about *Brown v. Board of Education*, the Supreme Court decision holding racially segregated schools unconstitutional, Bell says the Court's decision "cannot be understood without some consideration of the decision's value to whites, not simply those concerned about the immorality of racial inequality, but also those whites in policymaking positions able to see the economic and political advances at home and abroad that would follow abandonment of segregation."[36] Specifically, he pointed out that during the Cold War, the hypocrisy of America's racial segregation made it look bad to the rest of the world. Additionally, policymakers feared that the communist movement was gaining support among some in the Black community because racial minorities were treated better in some communist countries than they were in the United States. However, he noted, the promise of equal educational opportunity did not materialize for most Black children, as schools remain as racially segregated today as they were before the Civil Rights Movement.[37] Thus, Bell suggests that as long as racial equality threatens the interests of privileged White people, change will not occur.[38]

Intersectionality. CRT legal scholar Kimberlé Crenshaw first coined the term *intersectionality* in 1989 to articulate the legal "Catch-22" that Black women experienced when alleging employment discrimination. Under most courts' interpretation of employment discrimination law, Women of Color are forced to choose whether to allege that they are being discriminated against because of their race or their gender but not both. Instead of acknowledging that Women of Color have more than one identity (e.g., racial, ethnic, sex, gender identity) affecting their status in society, they are boxed into selecting one over another. Crenshaw explains that "[i]ntersectionality is a lens through which you can see where power comes and collides, where it interlocks and intersects. It's not simply that there's a race problem here, a gender problem here, and a class or LBGTQ problem there. Many times that framework erases what happens to people who are subject to all of these things."[39] (Later we discuss how Crenshaw's theory of intersectionality has been applied through other critical theories and also its relevance for health justice.)

Application of Critical Race Theory and Intersectionality to Medicine, Public Health, and Law
Medicine

CRT theorists critique the notion that racism is only present in medicine when there is overt individual discrimination that occurs in interactions between health care providers and patients. While they acknowledge that interpersonal racism is a problem in medicine, they focus on the ways in which racism is deeply imbedded and institutionalized in medical science and medical practice through the misuse of race as a biological category.[40] Historically, the medical and scientific communities have employed biological race as a means to reinforce racial hierarchies.[41] Bogus theories of genetic differences based on race fueled the eugenics movement (which had as its goal the elimination of undesirable genetic traits in human beings, often associated with race)[42] and the Bell Curve intelligence theory (the idea that IQ is associated with race),[43] and they continue to influence understandings of race in medicine.[44]

Science has disproven genetic theories of race. Indeed, 99.9% of the genetic makeup of human beings is identical and the 0.1% variation among them is not associated with any racial grouping.[45] However, despite this evidence, the use of biological or genetic race has not disappeared from medical research or guidelines. A 2021 article in the *Journal of the American Medical Association* asserts that:

> [R]ace variables have become part of the norm of accepted medical knowledge and practice. This applies to both therapeutics (incorporation of race to identify clinically meaningful treatment effect modification for various interventions, as in hypertension or heart failure) and other clinical tools (incorporation of race to improve diagnosis or prognosis in, for example, calculation of kidney function or pulmonary function).[46]

Using race when diagnosing and treating patients gives rise to pseudo-biological explanations for health inequities. CRT scholars continue to challenge references to biological race in medicine as the underlying cause of health inequities and instead insist that researchers identify and call out how racism is the root cause of these inequities.

Public Health

Public health scholars have also embraced CRT as a way to identify and investigate how structural racism infects health. Public health scholars Chandra Ford and Collins Airhihenbuwa point out that CRT is useful as a way to critique racial bias in public health research: "Racism was rarely considered an important determinant of health. The introduction of CRT for empirical research helps address these concerns directly. Its tools help researchers illuminate racial biases embedded in a field or in a study's aims, methods, conclusions, etc., and develop strategies to address them."[47] To help public health researchers and practitioners incorporate the tools of CRT inquiry, they developed public health critical race praxis (PHCR). PHCR is a framework for health equity research that "examines the causes of racial/ethnic patterns of health and disease" and interrogates "the racial context in which the research is conducted."[48]

Law

CRT was born out of critical legal studies theory, which challenged the "objectivity and neutrality of the law."[49] Legal scholar Roy L. Brooks articulates the goals of CRT in law as:

> attempt[ing] to analyze law and legal traditions through the history, contemporary experiences and racial sensibilities of racial minorities in this country. The question always lurking in the background of CRT is this: What would the legal landscape look like today if people of color were the decision-makers?[50]

CRT scholars note that, because law is primarily concerned with resolving individual disputes—such as employment discrimination—it leaves in place the structural underpinnings of inequality and disadvantage. However, they also recognize that law can be used as "a tool for emancipation and for securing racial equality."[51] Thus, CRT legal scholars ask these types of questions: How does the law construct race? How has the law protected racism and upheld racial hierarchies? How does the law reproduce racial inequality? How can the law be used to dismantle race, racism, and racial inequality? The law's treatment of racism and racial discrimination has played a major role in perpetuating health injustice, as discussed in Chapter 6.

Sex and Gender

Understandings of sex, gender, and sexuality continue to evolve. Following we offer some initial definitions. (A more extensive glossary of terms is provided in Chapter 13.) We then turn to how definitions of sex, gender, and sexuality have been influenced and transformed by social and political theories that subvert underlying assumptions about what it means to be "male" and "female." Feminist and queer theories both challenge the extant power structures (including the language and definitions that sustain them) that subordinate people based on their sex and/or gender and sexuality.

Definitions[52]

Sex is the sex (male or female) assigned to an infant, most often based on the infant's anatomical and other biological characteristics. In law, the term *sex* may include gender identity and sexual orientation status.

Sexism describes bias and discrimination against a person based on their sex or gender. Like racism, there are interpersonal, internalized, and structural levels of sexism. Sexism most affects women and LGBTQ+ people, but it also can also affect cisgender men, who are expected to conform to societal expectations of masculinity.

Gender is the characteristics and roles of women and men according to social norms. While sex is described as female, male, and intersex, gender can be described as feminine, masculine, androgynous, and many more.

Gender identity is a person's inner sense of being a girl/woman/female, boy/man/male, something else, or having no gender.

Cisgender describes a person whose gender identity is consistent in a traditional sense with their sex assigned at birth—for example, a person assigned female sex at birth whose gender identity is woman/female.

Gay is a sexual orientation describing people who are primarily emotionally and physically attracted to people of the same sex and/or gender as themselves. Commonly used to describe men who are primarily attracted to men but can also describe women attracted to women.

Feminism/Feminist. Definitions of "feminism" and what it means to be a "feminist" have varied over time and across different countries and cultures. Feminism is generally understood as the belief in and commitment to social, economic, and political equality for all people regardless of sex or gender. A feminist is a person who advocates for equal rights for all people regardless of sex or gender.

Heteronormativity is the assumption that everyone is heterosexual or that only heterosexuality is "normal." It also refers to societal pressure for everyone to look and act in a stereotypically heterosexual way. Heteronormativity can manifest as heterosexism, the biased belief that heterosexuality is superior to all other sexualities.

LGBTQ+ stands for lesbian, gay, bisexual, transgender, queer, and other persons whose sexual orientation or gender identity falls outside societal norms.

Nonbinary describes a person whose gender identity falls outside the traditional gender binary structure of girl/woman and boy/man. Sometimes abbreviated as NB or enby.

Queer is an umbrella term describing people who think of their sexual orientation or gender identity as outside societal norms.

Sexual orientation is how a person characterizes their emotional and sexual attraction to others.

Transgender describes a person whose gender identity and sex assigned at birth do not correspond based on traditional expectations—for example, a person assigned female sex at birth who identifies as a man or a person assigned male sex at birth who identifies as a woman.

Woman is a person who identifies as female regardless of the person's sex assigned at birth.

Feminist Theory

Feminist theory continues to evolve over time and has been shaped by historical, political and cultural contexts. The feminist or women's movement in the United States has had many iterations, as we discuss in more detail in Chapter 2. Nonetheless, feminist theory can be described as "the range of committed inquiry and activity dedicated first, to describing women's subordination—exploring its nature and extent; dedicated second, to asking both how—through what mechanisms, and why—for what complex and interwoven reasons—women continue to occupy that position; and dedicated third, to change."[53] "Inquiry and activity" in feminist theory centers on several themes that are relevant to gender inequity in medicine, public health, and law. We describe these in the following sections.

The Private Versus Public Spheres.
Feminist theory challenges traditional social role divisions that assign women to the "private sphere" (e.g., responsibility for housework, child care, and eldercare) and provide men greater access to the public sphere (e.g., paid work, politics, business). Feminist theorists have challenged this dichotomy and critiqued the ways in which it structures and maintains male power and female subordination. They call for the full participation of women in society's social, economic, and political spheres equal to that of men; they also call for men to share equal responsibility for domestic responsibilities, arguing that this is both fair and better for families and society.

Equality Versus Difference.
Feminists' call for full equality between men and women in all aspects of society has been met with resistance based on two claims: Men and women are biologically different and therefore should be treated differently in some contexts (e.g., military service), and women may have different preferences and make different choices than men (e.g., the idea that women are more inclined toward child care than are men). In essence, this argument is that gender inequity is the result of nature (biological difference) and choice (women want different things than men), not unequal power differentials between men and women. Feminist theorists have grappled with the *equality versus difference dilemma*, which asks: Should women try to conform to male standards of behavior in order to obtain full equality with them, or should they embrace notions of women's differences from men (e.g., the idea that women are more interested in relationships and caretaking than are men)? This question requires a deeper interrogation of the role of biology in constructing differences between men and women versus the role of social structures in constructing them.

The Male Norm.
As women have sought power in the workplace, politics, and other seats of power and privilege, the equality versus difference dilemma has required feminist theorists to uncover and expose the ways in which systems (including health care and public health systems), laws, and policies have been constructed around a male norm. Indeed, the notion that women were somehow defective versions of men took root as early as the third century BC when the philosopher Aristotle described the female as a "deformed male."[54] Feminist critiques have extended from biblical references to women's bodies being molded out of the male model (Adam and Eve) to demonstrating how ostensibly neutral rules and practices ignore women's experiences and are formulated with men in mind. Feminist legal scholar Catherine McKinnon explained that societal norms have been largely built around a male model: "Men's physiology defines most sports, their needs define auto and health insurance coverage, their socially designed biographies define workplace expectations and successful career patterns, their

perspectives and concerns define quality in scholarship, their objectification of life defines art…."[55]

In the 1980s, feminist theorists began to redefine the quest for equality, rejecting the idea that women should have to conform to a (traditional) male role in order to be treated equally. Instead, they argued that when women differed from men (e.g., in the ability to become pregnant), society, law, and policy should change to accommodate women, not the other way around. This shift led to feminists asserting the ways in which women's experiences were different from those of men and demonstrating how women's experiences have been devalued and deprioritized by society.

The Female Body. Early philosophers viewed women as lacking the rationality required for public discourse and public life. Instead, they associated women with emotion, nature, the body, and reproduction.[56] This association has often been used to justify women's domestic role, as they were seen as too irrational (based on their deep connection to nature resulting from menstruation and childbirth) to participate in public life. Feminist critics have not only rejected assumptions about women as less rational, they have confronted the ways in which the female body has been presented and objectified through the dominant male perspective. In particular, they have challenged the historical and contemporary images of women's body in art and media such as "the maternal body, the vulnerable body, the victimized body, the hysterical body, the body with no desire of its own, the regulated body, the rebellious body, the thin body."[57] They call for women to reimagine and represent their own images of the female body in order to reclaim power and self-worth.

Anti-Essentialism and Intersectionality. As feminist theory evolved during the 1970s and 1980s, scholars began to critique the ways in which feminism and the feminist movement were primarily associated with the experiences of White, middle-class, cisgender women, ignoring the diverging experiences of women by race, ethnicity, class, sexual orientation, and gender identity. Feminist scholarship in this area has been most robust in legal studies. Legal scholar Angela Harris coined the term *essentialism* to describe "the notion that a unitary, 'essential' women's experience can be isolated and described independently of race, class, sexual orientation, and other realities of experience."[58] Essentialism, for example, has forced Black women into an either/or dichotomy to explain their oppression (i.e., gender discrimination versus racial discrimination but not both). As discussed earlier, legal scholar Kimberlé Crenshaw instead proposed an "intersectional" approach to understanding the discrimination and subordination based on multiple identities. Applying intersectionality to Black women, for example, acknowledges that they "experience double-discrimination—the combined effects of practices that discriminate on the basis of race and the basis of sex. And sometimes, they experience discrimination as Black women—not the sum of race and sex discrimination, but as Black women."[59] Thus, in feminist theory, an intersectional approach rejects the notion that women should have to check only one box. As discussed later, intersectionality has also been critical to queer theory.

Application of Feminist Theory to Medicine, Public Health, and Law
Medicine

Feminist theory has been applied to medicine in several ways. First, it has been used to challenge the primacy of the male body and men's health in everything from medical research and education to health insurance coverage.[60] Second, because much of medicine has historically ignored women's health, feminists have focused on elevating women's knowledge about their own bodies, symptoms, and health.[61] This includes deconstructing medical myths about women as inferior due to menstruation, pregnancy, and menopause and empowering them to see their bodies as not only normal but powerful.[62] Third, challenging myths about women's health has been particularly important in countering the historical notion of "hysteria" in medicine—that women's symptoms were a function of their emotions, not real medical problems. Feminists in the medical community note that these stereotypes are still prevalent in medicine today: Women are often told by medical providers that their physical ailments, especially their pain, are "all in their heads."[63] Fourth, feminists have sought to dismantle what they view as the medicalization of women's health, especially control by male doctors of the natural process of childbirth. Instead, they advocate for traditional models of women supporting one another during pregnancy and childbirth, such as through midwifery and doula care. Finally, feminists have promoted equity in the profession of medicine and scientific research, highlighting how women have been historically excluded from and continue to be marginalized in medicine, especially from positions of power.

Public Health

Feminist scholars in public health have similarly sought to disrupt ways of conceptualizing health that have been largely constructed around men by centering research on women's health experiences and developing theoretical frameworks that challenge assumptions based on gender norms. They have explored public health methods that are sensitive to gender differences and the wide diversity within and across genders. Intersectional feminist theory is applied to public health in its growing attention to the complex social drivers of health that call upon multidisciplinary approaches and perspectives. Finally, feminists have supported collective action approaches to structural change by employing an anti-subordination framework to public health problems.[64]

Law

In law, scholars have applied feminist theory to critique the very structures of the law: how gender assumptions influence the development, interpretation, and effect of the law on women and men. These include identifying how biases and discrimination affect women's opportunities (e.g., in the workplace, politics, leadership); illuminating how assumptions based on a male norm devalue women's experiences, voices, and contributions; challenging power structures that reduce or eliminate women's choices; and promoting an intersectional approach that draws on critical race theory and other frameworks for understanding women's subordination. In practical terms, feminist theory is applied to issues such as reproductive rights and caretaking responsibilities, sexual and domestic violence, and women's economic opportunity and subordination. Women's legal rights are vital to health justice, as we discuss rom more detail in Chapter 12.

Queer Theory

Developing out of gay and lesbian studies and women's and feminist studies, queer theory took hold in the 1990s to theorize and describe gender identities and sexuality that do not conform to the heterosexual "norm." Queer theory disrupts essentialist heterosexual and cisgender notions of identity and sexual desire. Thus, "queer theory and politics necessarily celebrate transgression in the form of visible difference from norms. These 'Norms' are then exposed to be norms, not natures or inevitabilities."[65]

Challenging Gender Binaries and Hierarchies. Like feminist theory, which calls into question assumptions about biological differences between men and women and how those assumptions have been employed to subordinate women to men, queer theory interrogates societal and cultural norms that label people as abnormal based on their sexual orientation and gender identity. Queer theorist Judith Butler challenges traditional feminist theory's static definition of "woman," arguing that in queer theory "the very subject of women is no longer understood in stable or abiding terms."[66] Butler argues that gender—being labeled a man or woman—is essentially a performance based on culturally constructed behaviors (i.e., how people dress, walk, speak, wear their hair) that define maleness or femaleness as though these categories are natural.[67] Indeed, queer theory contests binaries—such as male or female, straight or gay—that simplify and ignore the fluidity of sexuality and gender identities. It also points to the ways in which these binaries are hierarchical, assigning value to some over others (e.g., male over female, straight over gay, cisgender over transgender) to justify disparate treatment.[68]

Questioning Sexual and Gender Norms. Queer theorists also analyze the ways in which science, which is viewed as neutral and objective, has shaped understandings of what is "normal" and "abnormal" in gender identity and behavior, noting that behavioral norms have fluctuated and evolved over time and across cultures. They challenge the ways in which science and medicine have pathologized homosexuality and gender-nonconforming behaviors as diseases, mental illness, and social deviance. (Chapter 13 discusses the history of medical and psychiatric treatment of LGBTQ+ people in detail.) Queer theory also rejects societal expectations that, to avoid the stigma associated with their sexual orientation and gender identity, LGBTQ+ people must hide their true selves (i.e., "staying in the closet"). In this way, queer theory, like feminist theory and CRT, rejects assimilation into the dominant culture and instead calls into question societal (White, male, cisgender) norms themselves.

Intersectionality: The Queer of Color Critique. As with feminist theory, queer theory has expanded to recognize overlapping, multiple identities and how people who are, for example, queer, female-identifying, and Black, confront compounding oppression from homophobia, cisgenderism, sexism, and racism. The queer of color critique decenters the White gay male as the frame of reference for queer theory and embraces an intersectional analysis. In *Unapologetic: A Black Queer and Feminist Mandate for Radical Movements*, Charlene Carruthers describes a queer of color critique as "a political praxis (practice and theory) based in Black feminist and LGBTQ traditions and knowledge, through which people and groups see to bring their full selves into the process of dismantling all systems of oppression."[69]

Application of Queer Theory to Medicine, Public Health, and Law
Medicine

Queer theory critiques medicine and medical treatment in at least three ways. First, queer theorists deconstruct the historical (and often current) treatment of LGBTQ+ people as deviating from the norm in their sexuality and gender identities. Queer theory rejects medicine's categorization of people's sex, sexuality, and gender into hierarchical binaries—male versus female, sexually normal versus sexually abnormal, and healthy gender-conforming versus unhealthy gender-deviant. Queer theorists and activists ask the medical community to recognize and honor gender diversity and fluidity. Second, they challenge how medical and other health professions education reinforces heteronormativity and binary approaches to gender not only by failing to acknowledge the spectrum of gender identities but also by reproducing gender subordination in failing to teach future physicians about LGBTQ+-affirming care. Third, queer theory supports structural changes to health care that support dignified and safe spaces for the care of LGBTQ+ patients. Queer theory demands that the medical community engage in "further analysis into the contradictions between the urgency of ethical biomedical practice and critical healing alongside the various discourses, ideologies, and cultures which shape biomedicine, and by which biomedical knowledge and clinical practices are themselves shaped."[70]

Public Health

Queer theory has been applied to public health by promoting an intersectional and intersectoral understanding of and approach to gender and health. In addition to calling for restructuring health education and health care, queer theorists articulate and critique the multiple social drivers of LGBTQ+ people's health. Recognizing that social drivers, including where people live, work, and go to school, have profound effects on health, theorists demand structural changes that lead to language, education, and spaces that support and affirm LGBTQ+ people in all aspects of their lives. These changes include using inclusive, nonbinary language; promoting sex education that is not heteronormative; and creating nonbinary public spaces, such as bathrooms. These societal changes, they argue, will improve public health by reducing stigma that is health-harming to LGBTQ+ people. Queer theory also critiques public health research that is not inclusive of gender-nonconforming people and promotes research that challenges normative assumptions about gender but also supports better health for LGBTQ+ populations.[71] This would mean, for example, designing research studies that divide people not by male/female but instead by subpopulations based on research subjects' gender identities.

Law

Queer legal theory interrogates the way in which law normalizes and sustains the subordination of LGBTQ+ people based on privileging heteronormative notions of sex, sexuality, and gender. Since America continues to permit legalized discrimination against LGBTQ+ people, many queer legal scholars focus on challenging overtly discriminatory laws, such as those in employment, housing, and education. But like feminist theorists, queer legal theorists have struggled with the ways in which concepts such as "equality" may, on the one hand, lead to expanded legal rights for LGBTQ+ people but, on the other hand, reinforce the requirement that they assimilate to heteronormative expectations and behavior in order to obtain legal rights and status. For example, some queer theorists have critiqued the focus on legalizing marriage equality for gays and lesbians as embracing a patriarchal heterosexual norm in order to pursue state recognition. Thus, queer legal theory involves a "reflexive and ongoing engagement with legal issues around sex, gender and sexuality that sit at the nexus of power and knowledge."[72]

Disability

Disability studies as a unique field of study began in the United States in the late 1960s as part of the disability rights movement. As disability scholars Rabia Belt and Doron Dorfman explain, advocates "challenged ableist assumptions about their existence and catalyzed the still-evolving academic field of disability studies…[which] concerns itself with human difference and the ways people with disabilities have been pushed out of what society conceives as the 'normal.' The critique of normalcy as a socially constructed category has thus been a cornerstone in the field."[73] Defining what is meant by *disability* has profound medical, social, legal, and political implications for people determined to be *disabled*. Critical disability theory developed out of disability studies as a method to "scrutinize[e] not bodily or mental impairments but the social norms that define particular attributes as impairments, as well as the social conditions that concentrate stigmatized attributes in particular popula-tions."[74] We explore the evolution of definitions of disability and the ways in which critical dis-ability theory seeks to empower people with disabilities to define themselves.

Definitions

Ableism is "[the] negative rating of a person's abilities and productivity based on assump-tions about that person's capabilities as assessed by non-disabled people. Ableism encompasses deeply held beliefs about productivity, attrac-tiveness, and the value of human life."[75]

Disability. We begin with the definition of disability used by the World Health Organiza-tion, acknowledging that disability theorists and activists take issue with it. We do so to introduce some of the terminology (*impairment*, *activity limitation*) that is often used to describe disability. Following we will highlight the evo-lution of different definitions of disability. The WHO describes three dimensions of disability:

1. **Impairment** in a person's body structure or function, or mental functioning; examples of impair-ments include loss of a limb, loss of vision, or memory loss
2. **Activity limitation**, such as diffi-culty seeing, hearing, walking, or problem solving
3. **Participation restrictions** in nor-mal daily activities, such as working, engaging in social and recreational activities, and obtaining health care and preventive services[76]

Critical Disability Theory

Critical disability theory shares common ground with critical race theory, feminist the-ory, and queer theory in that it probes "basic assumptions about identity, ideology, poli-tics, meaning, social justice and the body."[77] Like other critical theories, disability theory is employed to resist static definitions of dis-ability in favor of evolving understanding of

what it means to be disabled, driven by dis-abled people themselves. It is also political in that "scrutiny of normative ideologies should occur not for its own sake but with the goal of producing knowledge in support of justice for people with stigmatized bodies and minds."[78] Here we consider the medical and social mod-els of disability and how critical disability theorists have critiqued these models with an eye toward social and health justice for people with disabilities.

The Medical Model of Disability. In some ways, the medical model of disability has been driven by the status and authority that medical professionals have in diagnos-ing illness and defining bodily, cognitive, or psychiatric impairment. The medical model seeks to "fix" disability to the extent pos-sible through a biomedical cure or remedy. From the perspective of critical disability theory, the medical model begins with the assumption that the "problem" begins with the patient, who is somehow faulty. Thus, the medical model is normative in that it com-pares the disabled person to the so-called "normal person." Under the medical model, disabled people are viewed as unable to care for themselves and in need of charity, relying on clinicians to define and categorize their disability and to determine their needs and rights, including access to certain government supports and legal protection from discrimi-nation. Thus, the medical model is viewed as a deficit-based approach to disability in which disabled people are defined by their disability without regard to how they define themselves, their needs, and their wants.[79]

Social Model of Disability. The social mod-el of disability developed as part of the disability studies movement in response to critiques of the medical model of disability. Rather than center-ing the individual's impairment as the site of the problem, the social model focuses on the ways in which disability is socially constructed by societal norms, attitudes, laws, and policies. The social model divorces impairment from disability in order to focus on how society excludes, disadvantages, and erects barriers for disabled people. The isolation and exclusion of disabled people, therefore, are viewed as the result of societal choices and the unwillingness by those holding power to construct and organize the social world with disabled people in mind.[80]

Crip Theory. Building on other critical theories, crip theory contests centers of power to probe how definitions of disability act to subordinate, marginalize, and stigmatize people with disabilities. Just as queer theory inverted the meaning of *queer*, an epithet, to a term embracing gender diversity, disability theorists and activists appropriated the term *crip* (a version of the derogatory word *crippled*) to define disability as an identity and as "life enriching and contributing to human diversity."[81] Crip theory contests the dominant deficit-based view of disability and privileging of ableism, instead centering the perspectives of disabled people in order to conceptualize their own identities and futures. It also critiques the ways in which capitalism and its ableist approach to work, economic, and social value define power in society. Finally, it fully embraces an intersectional understanding of disability, sexuality, and gender identity and probes questions related the connections between racial, ethnic, and disability discrimination.[82]

Application of Critical Disability Theory to Medicine, Public Health, and Law

Medicine

As discussed previously, critical disability theory rejects the medicalization of disability, instead pointing to its social construction. It has sought to give disabled people voice in making their own decisions about how they wish to live and how they construct their identities, apart from medical interference and paternalism. Indeed, "disability is not fundamentally a question of medicine or health, nor is it just an issue of sensitivity and compassion; rather, it is a question of politics and power(lessness), power over, and power to."[83] On the other hand, in recent years some critical disability theorists and activists have criticized the social model in failing to fully recognize and address the very real medical needs of disabled people, including the pain and mental stress associated with impairment, divorced from social stigma and treatment. They point out that only focusing on social discrimination may undermine important efforts to ensure disabled people obtain appropriate, accessible, and respectful health care.[84] Furthermore, like critical race, feminist, and queer theories, critical disability theorists and activists call for better training for clinicians so that medical professionals are forced to confront their own biases about disability and so that disabled patients are empowered through shared decision-making and patient-centered models of care.[85]

Public Health

Public health's focus on prevention has sometimes led to an uncomfortable relationship with disability. How can public health embrace disability theory and at the same time maintain its focus on prevention? Increasingly, public health organizations and practitioners are embracing disability theory by advocating for and employing secondary prevention strategies that support disabled people to define their own health, well-being, and health care needs. Public health researchers are using disability theory to critically analyze how disabled people have been excluded from research studies. Public health practitioners also advocate for the elimination of health inequities between disabled and nondisabled people.[86] Some argue that a human rights framework is where public health and disability theory find synergy. From this perspective, disability theory and public health together focus on health equity—ensuring all people have a right to their highest attainable health—and on the social drivers of health—eliminating oppressive barriers to health and well-being to support "social flourishing."[87]

Law

Disability legal studies and theory deconstruct how disability is defined and shaped in the law in order to preserve an ableist power structure. Disability legal scholar Sagit Mor explains: "The law in this view is an arena of struggle in which the meaning of disability is constantly formed and transformed, contested, negotiated, defied, and interrogated, constrained and liberated."[88] Hence, disability legal theorists and scholars dissect the "values, histories and intentions behind rules and court decisions"[89] in multiple areas of law, including welfare, civil rights, institutionalization, criminal justice, sterilization, euthanasia, and reproductive rights.

Disability legal theory is increasingly intersectional. Theorists point out how historically marginalized people have been devalued and subjugated based on normative categories that have elevated White, middle-class, cisgender, able-bodied men but also the ways in which their unequal treatment under the law was justified based on "the idea of medicalization and embodying social difference as biological."[90] For example, slaves were defined as mentally and physically different and inferior in order to justify their legally sanctioned oppression and bondage; immigrant, LGBTQ+, disabled, Black,

and poor people were sterilized during the twentieth-century eugenics movement (which advanced the theory that human genetics must be tailored to increase superior traits in the U.S. population by excluding people and groups considered inferior and undesirable) with full support of the law; and, as noted earlier, women's bodies were considered anomalous and their health concerns labeled as mental and physical deficiencies and disabilities in order to justify their exclusion from public life.[91]

Conclusion

Historically, medicine, public health, and law have each played a role in sustaining definitions, norms, and practices that subordinate groups of people. Critical race, feminist, queer, and disability theorists continue to interrogate how the legacy of the subjugation of people deemed different and inferior continues to affect how these individuals and populations are treated today. Health justice demands that scholars, practitioners, and others continue to probe and disrupt the underlying assumptions in medicine, public health, law, and public policy that subordinate people based on their status. In Chapter 2, we turn to the role of social movements (often supported by critical theory) in not only driving law and public policy reform but also altering norms and attitudes. These movements have also helped transform medical and public health systems and practice and inspired medical, public health, and legal professionals to fight for social change.

References

1. World Health Organization. Constitution. 2022. https://www.who.int/about/governance/constitution.
2. Smedley B, Stith A, Nelson A, eds. Institute of Medicine. Unequal treatment: Confronting racial and ethnic disparities in health care. Washington, DC. 2003. http://www.nap.edu/openbook.php?isbn=030908265X.
3. World Health Organization. Health inequities and their causes. February 22, 2018. https://www.who.int/news-room/facts-in-pictures/detail/health-inequities-and-their-causes
4. Healthy People 2030. Social determinants of health. 2022. https://health.gov/healthypeople/objectives-and-data/social-determinants-health.

5. The goals of medicine: Setting new priorities. *Hastings Cent Rep.* 1996;26:S9–S14.

6. American Medical Association. AMA Declaration of Professional Responsibility. Preamble. December 4. 2001. https://www.ama-assnorg/delivering-care/public-health/ama-declaration-professional-responsibility

7. Wittern-Sterzel R. "Die Politik ist weiter nichts, als Medicin im Grossen"—Rudolf Virchow und seine Bedeutung for die Entwicklung der Sozialmedizin ["Politics is nothing else than large scale medicine"—Rudolf Virchow and his role in the development of social medicine]. *Verh Dtsch Ges Pathol.* 2003;87:150–157. German.

8. White J, Riese A, Clyne B, Vanvleet M, George P. Integrating population and clinical medicine: A new third-year curriculum to prepare medical students for the care of individuals, panels, and populations. *Rhode Island Medical Journal.* 2015;98(9):32–35.

9. Beauchamp T, Childress J. *Principles of Biomedical Ethics.* New York, NY: Oxford University Press; 1979.

10. Galarneau C. *The Communities of Health Care Justice.* New Brunswick, NJ: Rutgers University Press; 2016.

11. Randall V. Slavery, segregation and discrimination: Trusting the health care system ain't easy! An African American perspective on bioethics. *St. Louis Univ. Public Law Rev.* 1996;15:199.

12. CDC Foundation. What is public health? 2022. https://www.cdcfoundation.org/what-public-health .

13. Centers for Disease Control and Prevention. Original Essential Public Health Services Framework. 2020. https://www.cdc.gov/publichealthgateway/publichealthservices/originalessentialhealthservices.html.

14. Honjo, K. Social epidemiology: Definition, history, and research examples. *Environmental Health and Preventive Medicine.* 2004;9:193–199.

15. Tulchinsky TH, Varavikova EA. What is the "new public health"? *Public Health Reviews.* 2010;32(1):26.

16. Garner B. *Black's Law Dictionary.* 10th ed. Eagan, MN: Thomson West; 2014.

17. Friedman LM. *Law in America: A Short History.* New York, NY: The Modern Library; 2002.

18. Burris S, Berman M, et al. *The New Public Health: A Transdisciplinary Approach to Practice and Advocacy.* New York, NY: Oxford University Press; 2018.

19. Burris S, Berman M, et al. *The New Public Health: A Transdisciplinary Approach to Practice and Advocacy.* New York, NY: Oxford University Press; 2018: 42–44.

20. Campbell AT, Sicklick J, Galowitz P, Retkin R, Fleishman SB. How bioethics can enrich medical-legal collaborations. *J Law Med Ethics.* 2010 Winter;38(4):847–862.

21. Jones CP. Confronting institutionalized racism. *Phylon* 2002;50:7–22.

22. Goodman, AL. Why genes don't count (for differences in health). In: LaVeist TA, Isaac LA, eds. *Race, Ethnicity, and Health: A Public Health Reader.* 2nd ed. San Francisco, CA: Jossey-Bass; 2013:50–53.

23. Goodman, AL. Why genes don't count (for differences in health). In: LaVeist TA, Isaac LA, eds. *Race, Ethnicity, and Health: A Public Health Reader.* 2nd ed. San Francisco, CA: Jossey-Bass; 2013:50–53.

24. Roberts D. *Fatal Invention: How Science, Politics, and Big Business Re-Create Race in the Twenty-First Century.* New York, NY: The New Press; 2011:23.

25. Roberts D. *Fatal Invention: How Science, Politics, and Big Business Re-Create Race in the Twenty-First Century.* New York, NY: The New Press; 2011:5.

26. MP Associates, Center for Assessment and Policy Development, and World Trust Educational Services. Racial Equity Tools. Glossary. October 2021. https://www.racialequitytools.org/glossary.

27. Parker K, Horowitz JM, Morin R, et al. Race and multiracial Americans in the U.S. Census. Pew Research Center. June 11, 2015. https://www.pewresearch.org/social-trends/2015/06/11/chapter-1-race-and-multiracial-americans-in-the-u-s-census/#fn-20724-28.

28. Jones CP. Confronting institutionalized racism. *Phylon* 2002;50:7–22.

29. Grumbach K, Braveman P, Adler N, Bindman AB. Vulnerable populations and health disparities: an overview. In: King TE, Wheeler MB, Bindman AB, et al., eds. *Medical Management of Vulnerable and Underserved Populations: Principles, Practice and Populations.* New York, NY: McGraw Hill; 2007.

30. Bridges, K. *Critical Race Theory: A Primer.* St Paul: Foundation Press; 2019.

31. Brown BA. *Critical Race Theory: Cases, Materials and Problems.* St. Paul, MN: Thompson West; 2003:3–4.

32. Crenshaw KW. The first decade: Critical reflections, or a foot in the closing door. *UCLA Law Review.* 2002;49:1361.

33. Bridges, K. *Critical Race Theory: A Primer.* St Paul, MN: Foundation Press; 2019:11.

34. Bridges, K. *Critical Race Theory: A Primer.* St Paul, MN: Foundation Press; 2019:10–14.

35. Lawrence CR. The id, the ego, and equal protection: reckoning with unconscious racism. *Stanford Law Review.* 1987;39:317 (discussing the work of Derrick Bell).

36. Bell D. *Brown v. Board of Education* and the interest-convergence dilemma. *Harvard Law Review.* 1980;93(3):518–533.

37. García E. Schools are still segregated, and black children are paying a price. Economic Policy Institute. February 12, 2020. https://www.epi.org/publication/schools-are-still-segregated-and-black-children-are-paying-a-price/ .

38. Bell D. *Brown v. Board of Education* and the interest-convergence dilemma. *Harvard Law Review.* 1980;93(3):518–533.

39. Columbia Law School. Kimberlé Crenshaw on intersectionality, more than two decades later. June 8, 2017. https://www.law.columbia.edu/news/archive/kimberle-crenshaw-intersectionality-more-two-decades-later .

40. Roberts D. *Fatal Invention: How Science, Politics, and Big Business Re-Create Race in The Twenty-First Century.* New York, NY: The New Press; 2012; Yearby R. Race-based medicine, colorblind disease: how racism in medicine harms us all. *American Journal of Bioethics.* 2021;21(2):19–27; Roberts D. Abolish race correction. *Lancet* 2021;397(10268):17–18; Gampa V, Bernard K, Oldani M. Racialization as a barrier to achieving health equity for Native Americans. *AMA Journal of Ethics.* 2020;22(10):E874–E881.

41. Washington H. *Medical Apartheid.* New York, NY: Anchor Books; 2006; Chowkwanyun M. Race is not biology. *The Atlantic.* 2013. https://www.theatlantic.com/health/archive/2013/05/race-is-not-biology/276174/.

42. Black E. *War Against the Weak: Eugenics and America's Campaign to Create a Master Race.* Washington, DC: Dialog Press; 2003.

43. Herrnstein RJ, Murray C. *The Bell Curve: Intelligence and Class Structure in American Life.* New York NY: The Free Press; 1996.

44. Roberts D. *Fatal Invention: How Science, Politics, and Big Business Re-Create Race in The Twenty-First Century.* New York, NY: The New Press; 2012;

45. Roberts D. *Fatal Invention: How Science, Politics, and Big Business Re-Create Race in The Twenty-First Century.* New York, NY: The New Press; 2012.

46. Ioannidis JPA., Powe NR, Yancy C. Recalibrating the use of race in medical research. *JAMA.* 2021;325(7):623.

47. Ford C, Airhihenbuwa C. Commentary: Just what is critical race theory and what's it doing in a progressive field like public health? *Ethnicity & Disease.* 2018;28(1):223.

48. Ford C, Airhihenbuwa C. Commentary: Just what is critical race theory and what's it doing in a progressive field like public health? *Ethnicity & Disease.* 2018;28(1):223.

49. Brown BA. *Critical Race Theory: Cases, Materials and Problems.* St. Paul, MN: Thompson West; 2003:1.

50. Brooks RL. Critical race theory: A proposed structure and application to federal pleading. *Harvard Blackletter Law Journal.* 1994;11:85.

51. George J. A lesson on critical race theory. *American Bar Association Human Rights Magazine.* January 11, 2021;46(2). https://www.americanbar.org/groups/crsj/publications/human_rights_magazine_home/civil-rights-reimagining-policing/a-lesson-on-critical-race-theory/.

52. Many of these definitions come from the Fenway Institute, National LGBTQIA+ Health Education Center. LGBTQIA+ Glossary of Terms for Health Care Teams. https://www.lgbtqiahealtheducation.org/publication/lgbtqia-glossary-of-terms-for-health-care-teams/.

53. Dalton C. Where we stand: Observations on the situation of feminist legal thought. *Berkeley Women's Law Journal.* 1988–89;3:1,2.

54. Witt C. Feminist history of philosophy. In: Alanen L, Witt C, eds. *Feminist Reflections on the History of Philosophy. The New Syntheses Historical Library (Texts and Studies in the History of Philosophy), vol. 55.* Dordrecht: Springer; 2004.

55. MacKinnon CA. Difference and dominance: On sex discrimination. In: *Feminism Unmodified: Discourses on Life and Law.* Cambridge, MA: Harvard University Press; 1987.

56. Lloyd G. Reason, gender, and morality in the history of philosophy. *Social Research.* 1983;50(3):490–513.

57. Chrisler JC, Johnston-Robledo I. Woman's embodied self: Feminist perspectives on identity and image. *American Psychological Association.* 2018:8.

58. Harris AP. Race and essentialism in feminist legal theory. *Stanford Law Review.* 1990;42:581, 585.

59. Crenshaw K. Demarginalizing the intersection of race and sex: A black feminist critique of antidiscrimination doctrine, feminist theory and antiracist politics. *University of Chicago Legal Forum.* 1989;1:139–167,149.

60. Sharma M. Applying feminist theory to medical education. *Lancet.* 2019;393:570–578.

61. Cleghorn E. *Unwell Women: Misdiagnosis and Myth in a Man-Made World.* New York, NY: Dutton; 2021.

62. Reverby S. Feminism and health. *Health and History.* 2002;4(1):5–19.

63. Lines L. The myth of female hysteria and health disparities among women. RTI International. May 9, 2018. https://www.rti.org/insights/myth-female-hysteria-and-health-disparities-among-women.

64. Hammarström A. Why feminism in public health? *Scand J Public Health.* 1999 Dec;27(4):241–244.

65. Richards C, Bouman WP, Barker MJ. Genderqueer and non-binary genders in critical and applied approaches in sexuality, gender and identity. In: *Behavioral Science and Psychology.* London, UK: Palgrave Macmillan; 2017.

66. Butler, J. *Gender Trouble: Feminism and the Subversion of Identity.* 2nd ed. New York, NY: Routledge; 1999.

67. Butler, J. *Gender Trouble: Feminism and the Subversion of Identity.* 2nd ed. New York, NY: Routledge; 1999.

68. Phelan S. *Playing with Fire: Queer Politics, Queer Theories.* New York, NY: Routledge; 1997.

69. Carruthers C. *Unapologetic: A Black, Queer, and Feminist Mandate for Radical Movements.* Boston, MA: Beacon Press; 2018.

70. Spurlin WJ. Queer theory and biomedical practice: the biomedicalization of sexuality/the cultural politics of biomedicine. *Journal of Medical Humanities.* 2019;40:7–20.

71. American Public Health Association. Promoting transgender and gender minority health through inclusive policies and practices. November 1, 2016. https://www.apha.org/policies-and-advocacy/public-health-policy-statements/policy-database/2017/01/26/promoting-transgender-and-gender-minority-health-through-inclusive-policies-and-practices.

72. Thomas K. Practicing queer legal theory critically. *Critical Analysis of Law.* 2019; 6(1):8–22.

73. Belt R, Dorfman D. Disability, law, and the humanities: The rise of disability legal studies. In: *The Oxford Handbook of Law and Humanities.* New York, NY: Oxford Press; 2019:146.

74. Minich JA. Enabling whom? Critical disability studies now. *Lateral.* 2016;5. http://csalateral.org/wp/issue/5-1/forum-alt-humanities-critical-disability-studies-now-minich/.

75. Belt R, Dorfman D. Disability, law, and the humanities: The rise of disability legal studies. In: *The Oxford Handbook of Law and Humanities.* New York, NY: Oxford Press; 2019:149.

76. Centers for Disease Control and Prevention. Disability and health overview. 2020. https://www.cdc.gov/ncbddd/disabilityandhealth/disability.html.

77. Siebers T. *Disability Theory.* University of Michigan Press; 2008:1.

78. Minich JA. Enabling whom? Critical disability studies now. *Lateral.* 2016;5. http://csalateral.org/wp/issue/5-1/forum-alt-humanities-critical-disability-studies-now-minich/.

79. Haegele JA, Hodge S. Disability discourse: Overview and critiques of the medical and social models. *Quest.* 2016;68:2,193–206.

80. Haegele JA, Hodge S. Disability discourse: Overview and critiques of the medical and social models. *Quest.* 2016;68:2,193–206.

81. Belt R, Dorfman D. Disability, law, and the humanities: The rise of disability legal studies. In: *The Oxford Handbook of Law and Humanities.* Oxford Press; 2019: 150.

82. Hall MC. Critical Disability Theory. The Stanford Encyclopedia of Philosophy. Winter 2019 Edition. Edward N. Zalta (ed.). https://plato.stanford.edu/archives/win2019/entries/disability-critical/

83. Pothier D, Devlin R. *Critical Disability Theory: Essays in Philosophy, Politics, Policy, and Law.* Vancouver: UBC Press; 2006.

84. Shakespeare S. Still a health issue. *Disability & Health Journal.* 2012;5:129–131.

85. Cuff S, McGoldrick K, Patterson S, Peterson E. The intersection of disability studies and health science. *Transformations: The Journal of Inclusive Scholarship and Pedagogy.* 2016;25(2):37–50.

86. Hayward K. A slowly evolving paradigm of disability in public health education. *Disability Studies Quarterly.* 2004;24(4). https://dsq-sds.org/article/view/890/1065.

87. Berghs M, et al. Rights to social determinants of flourishing? A paradigm for disability and public health research and policy. *BMC Public Health.* 2019;19:997.

88. Mor S. Between charity, welfare, and warfare: A disability legal studies analysis of privilege and neglect in Israeli disability policy. *Yale Journal of Law & the Humanities.* 2006;18:63–136, 78.

89. Belt R, Dorfman D. Disability, law, and the humanities: The rise of disability legal studies. In: *The Oxford Handbook of Law and Humanities.* New York, NY Oxford Press; 2019:157.

90. Belt R, Dorfman D. Disability, law, and the humanities: The rise of disability legal studies. In: *The Oxford Handbook of Law and Humanities.* New York, NY: Oxford Press; 2019:153.

91. Belt R, Dorfman D. Disability, law, and the humanities: The rise of disability legal studies. In: The *Oxford Handbook of Law and Humanities.* New York, NY: Oxford Press; 2019.

CHAPTER 2

Lessons from U.S. Social Movements for Health Justice

LEARNING OBJECTIVES

By the end of this chapter you will be able to:

- Define what is meant by a "social movement"
- Describe the major U.S. social movements
- Discuss what lessons may be learned from prior social movements for those seeking health justice

Introduction

Much of the social change that has occurred in the United States is due to social movements. Although definitions of the term *social movement* vary, in this chapter we use this one: "collective forms of protest or activism that aim to affect some kind of transformation in existing structures of power that have created inequality, injustice, disadvantage and so on."[1] Generally, social movements bring together ordinary people (those on the outside of institutionalized power) who apply a variety of tactics (protests, marches, sit-ins, petition-drives, media events) to achieve specific aims for social change.[2] Studies of these movements by sociologists have pointed to a few key drivers of success. These include clearly defined goals

directed at institutions that have the capacity to make change; engaging "rank and file of the constituencies they are representing" in decision-making; building sympathetic allies who can support the movement with funding, access to media, and so on; allowing members to determine the level of risk they are willing to take (e.g., violence by the police, arrest, etc.); and developing agreed-upon responses to repression.[3] But perhaps most importantly, social movements are long-term projects that often require enormous patience, learning from failure, and regeneration:

> Persistence—sustaining commitment, perhaps over the course of a lifetime; expanding networks while forming and reforming coalitions; assessing

failures and devising new strategies; exploiting new political opportunities with fresh tactical repertoires; and integrating new generations into the life of the movement—is key to assuring further moments of success.[4]

This chapter highlights the history, goals, tactics, successes, and failures of several social movements in U.S. history. Not only do many of these movements inform how marginalized groups of people have achieved social change, including making America more just and equal, but they also demonstrate the challenges of confronting institutionalized power structures. As you read about these movements, apply the elements of successful social movements described previously to concepts of health justice. How has each of these movements worked to disrupt institutionalized power, and how have they tried to work with those in power to bring about change? What lessons can we learn from these movements for a health justice movement?

The Civil Rights Movement

The Civil Rights Movement is the best-known social movement in U.S. history. When most people think of the Civil Rights Movement, they think about historic events, such as Rosa Parks's refusal to give up her seat during the Montgomery bus boycott in 1954 or Martin Luther King's famous "I Have a Dream" speech at the March on Washington in 1963. But the movement in the 1950s and 1960s was built upon earlier movements demanding civil rights for African Americans. These included the anti-lynching campaign led by Ida B. Wells at the turn of the twentieth century and the efforts in the 1930s led by the National Association for the Advancement of Colored People (NAACP). In the 1930s, Charles Hamilton Houston, the first Black man to attend Harvard Law School, engineered a legal strategy

to challenge the fallacy of "separate but equal" educational opportunities for Black students. These cases laid the legal groundwork for the U.S. Supreme Court's 1954 decision in *Brown v. Board of Education* (which was argued by Thurgood Marshall, Houston's protegee), in which the court held that unequal racially segregated schools were unconstitutional.[5]

The Civil Rights Movement encompassed many different organizations and stakeholders that shared the goals of racial equality and the dismantling of Jim Crow laws; but did not always agree on tactics and strategy. Younger African Americans, in particular, became frustrated in the late 1950s with the slow pace of change through the courts, including the failure of schools in the South to desegregate with "all deliberate speed," as ordered by the Supreme Court in *Brown*. Economic exploitation, disenfranchisement, the government's failure to hold White perpetrators of unspeakable racial violence accountable, and the daily indignities and material deprivation that resulted from America's racial apartheid made the lives of Black people in the United States intolerable for decades. The young Baptist minister Martin Luther King and others argued that mobilizing Black people and their allies across the country to carry out protests and acts of civil disobedience was the most effective way to accelerate the dismantling of Jim Crow laws in the South. (It's important to note here that racial discrimination and violence were prevalent in the North as well). Working with national organizations—the Southern Christian Leadership Conference (SCLC), the NAACP, the Congress of Racial Equality (CORE), and the Student Nonviolent Coordinating Committee (SNCC)—King preached nonviolent civil disobedience as the most effective means to capture the minds and hearts of White lawmakers and White Americans. King led boycotts (like the Montgomery Bus Boycott of 1955–56), sit-ins (in which Black people and their allies sat at lunch counters in violation of segregation laws in the South, for example), and marches demonstrating against racist laws (such as the Selma to Montgomery march to fight for voting rights), and he lobbied the president and members of Congress to enact legislation to desegregate American institutions and make racial discrimination illegal. These efforts led to the passage of the Civil Rights Act of 1964, the Voting Rights Act of 1965, and the Fair Housing Act of 1968.

After passage of the Civil Rights and Voting Rights Acts, King increasingly focused on the effects of economic inequality and poverty on African Americans, including the effects on their health. Notably, in a speech at the Convention of the Medical Committee for Human Rights in Chicago in March 1966, King said: "Of all the forms of inequality, injustice in health care is the most shocking and inhumane."[6] As the Civil Rights Movement drew on in the late 1960s and progress slowed despite passage of civil rights laws, King sought ways to build coalitions of poor people of all racial and ethnic groups to press for policy changes to address economic inequality and poverty. (See the discussion of the Poor People's Campaign, initiated by King, later in the chapter.)

While the Civil Rights Movement of the 1950s and 1960s demonstrated the power of widespread mobilization and a coordinated strategy of nonviolent resistance and direct action to pressure lawmakers toward law reform, some civil rights leaders saw King's approach as too conciliatory toward and dependent upon the White power structure. In contrast, the Black nationalist movement promoted Black pride, self-determination, and economic self-sufficiency. The most well-known leader of this movement was Malcolm X, who was a national representative of the Nation of Islam, a Black nationalist Muslim organization that advocated Black separatism, "any means necessary" to achieve Black liberation, and economic self-sufficiency. Malcolm was a vocal and public critic of the mainstream Civil Rights Movement led by King, calling the March on Washington a "farce."[7] However, after parting ways with the Nation of Islam in

1963 and visiting Mecca, the holiest site for Muslims, Malcolm reached out to civil rights leaders, including King, and began to express misgivings about the use of violence as the solution to America's "race problem." From 1964 until he was assassinated allegedly by members of the Nation of Islam, Malcolm continued to advocate for Black self-defense and economic independence but no longer called for racial separation.[8]

The Black nationalist movement continued into the late 1960s and 1970s through the work of the Black Panther Party, started by college students Huey Newton and Bobby Seale in Oakland, California. The party called for revolution against the White power structure, which had oppressed African Americans for more than three centuries. Newton saw the Party as a continuation of the Black Nationalist movement led by Malcolm X, advocating Black self-defense and rejecting King's nonviolent approach:

> Malcolm, implacable to the ultimate degree, held out to the Black masses the historical, stupendous victory of Black collective salvation and liberation from the chains of the oppressor and the treacherous embrace of the endorsed spokesmen [King]. Only with the gun were the black masses denied this victory. But they learned from Malcolm that with the gun, they can recapture their dreams and bring them into reality.[9]

But in addition to its more militant rhetoric, the Panthers developed what they called "survival programs" that provided all kinds of social, educational, and medical services for Black communities. These included the following:

> …breakfast programs for school-children, liberation schools, medical clinics, clothing programs, buses to prison programs, a sickle cell anemia research foundation, housing cooperative programs, pest control

programs, plumbing and maintenance programs, food programs, child development centers, escort services for the elderly, and ambulance programs.[10]

Civil rights leaders and leaders of other movements for Black liberation and equality have long debated strategies and tactics: employing nonviolent civil disobedience versus asserting the right to self-defense and armed resistance; seeking full integration within the dominant White society versus Black self-sufficiency and independence; making demands to policymakers to address economic and social inequities versus providing separate social, educational, and medical services to people within the Black community. As you read about other social movements, consider whether the lessons learned from the Civil Rights Movement have influenced the approaches and tactics used in other movements for social change.

The Poor People's Campaign

As discussed previously, Martin Luther King increasingly focused toward the end of his life on economic justice as a way for Black people and other marginalized groups to achieve true equality. Reportedly at the suggestion of Robert Kennedy (former U.S. attorney general and senator) and Marion Wright Edelman, director of the NAACP Legal Defense and Educational Fund in Jackson, Mississippi, King announced the Poor People's Campaign in 1967. The campaign involved the mobilization of 3,000 poor people of all racial and ethnic backgrounds to travel to Washington, D.C., to lobby government officials for better educational opportunities that promoted children's self-image and "federal funding for full employment, a guaranteed annual income, anti-poverty programs, and housing for the poor."[11] The campaign assembled poor African Americans, Native Americans, Puerto Ricans, Mexican Americans, and Whites from

53 organizations. King viewed economic injustice as inherently linked to racism and wanted to directly confront the hypocrisy of the American Dream: "I think it is absolutely necessary now to deal massively and militantly with the economic problem…to dramatize the gulf between promise and fulfillment, to call attention to the gap between the dream and the realities, to make the invisible visible."[12]

King was assassinated on April 3, 1968, before the campaign was fully underway. King's widow, Coretta Scott King, insisted that the campaign continue. In May 1968, Coretta Scott King and representatives from the National Welfare Rights Organization led a march with 7,000 people in Washington, D.C. "Resurrection City," a series of 3,000 wooden tents, was erected on the National Mall to demonstrate to lawmakers that the activists would not back down until their demands were met. Demonstrators camped on the mall for 42 days until they were evicted by federal authorities.[13]

In 2018 (50 years after the 1968 campaign), Protestant ministers William J. Barber and Liz Theoharis co-founded the Poor People's Campaign: A National Call for Moral Revival. Recognizing that King's vision and goals for the poor people's campaign were never realized and that racism, poverty, and social inequality remain unresolved problems in America, they set out to again raise awareness about economic inequality. The modern-day campaign's demands echo those of the 1968 campaign but extend even further. The campaign seeks "federal and state living-wage laws, equity in education, an end to mass incarceration, a single-payer health-care system, and the protection of the right to vote."[14] The campaign disputes the official government poverty measure, which estimates that roughly 37 million people live in poverty in the United States. Instead, it argues that using the more realistic supplemental poverty measure—which takes into account expenses for basic needs—140 million people currently live in poverty in the United States.[15]

Figure 2.1 Supporters of the Poor People's Campaign demonstrate outside the U.S. Capitol, 2018
© Jose Luis Magana/AP/Shutterstock

In 2018, employing nonviolent civil disobedience, Barber and Theoharis organized direct actions in Washington, D.C., and in 40 states to confront "the interlocking evils of systemic racism, poverty, ecological devastation, militarism and the war economy and the false narrative of religious nationalism."[16] (See **Figure 2.1**). In 2020 the campaign released its "Poor People's Moral Budget," with Barber testifying before the House Budget Committee. On June 20, 2020, the organization held a digital "Mass Poor People Assembly and Moral March on Washington."[17]

The Women's (Feminist) Movement

Although the distinction is sometimes disputed, most scholars divide the women's movement in the United States into three "waves." We describe the movement through the lens of these three waves for simplicity but acknowledge that the movement is more complicated that this structure provides. The first wave spans from the mid-1800s to 1920, when women obtained the right to vote. Early American law was based on English common law, including incorporation of the doctrine of "coverture," which considered "husband and wife one, and that one is the husband."[18] In other words, married women's legal rights and obligations were subsumed by their husbands'. Married women could not own property or contract in their own names. Many of the early feminists were inspired by the abolitionist movement (calling for the abolition of slavery) and sought women's equality by protesting women's subjugation in political, economic, and social life. Their top priority became the right to vote. While White female property owners were allowed to vote in some communities at the time that the Constitution was ratified, all states had excluded women's suffrage within the 20 years after ratification.[19] The National American Woman

Suffrage Association (NAWSA) was formed in 1890 and fought state by state, finally achieving ratification of the Nineteenth Amendment in 1920 giving women the right to vote.[20] But the movement for women's suffrage was "long, difficult and divisive."[21] White leaders of the suffrage movement prioritized women's suffrage over Black suffrage and often demeaned and marginalized Black women, including pacifying racist members by asking Black suffragists to march behind the state delegations.[22]

Despite the suffragists' victory in 1920, many laws in the early to mid-twentieth century continued to treat women as inferior to men and restricted their activities. For example, laws limited how many hours women could work (based on the idea that they were more fragile than men) and obligated men to support their wives (based on the idea that women were solely responsible for domestic duties).[23] By the 1960s, inspired by the Civil Rights Movement, women began advocating for equality across all domains of their lives—from domestic life to work to sexuality and reproductive choice.

The second wave of the women's movement was strongly influenced by feminist books. French writer Simone DeBeauvior's *The Second Sex*, published in 1949, depicted cultural assumptions about femininity as oppressive and called for women's liberation.[24] In the United States, Betty Friedan published the national bestseller *The Feminine Mystique* in 1963, which called attention to the ways in which societal limitations placed on women, relegating them solely the responsibilities of domestic chores and child care, left them unfulfilled and unhappy. She argued that women, trying to live up to the ideal of femininity cast upon them, weren't even able to articulate the reason for their unhappiness.[25]

Friedan's book helped galvanize "consciousness raising" in which groups of women came together to discuss their lives. From these groups, the idea that "the personal is political" served as a catalyst for the new women's movement, which sought full equality for women with men. The National Organization for Women (NOW), formed in 1966 by Betty Friedan and others, advocated "to bring women into full participation in the mainstream of American society now, exercising all the privileges and responsibilities thereof in truly equal partnership with men."[26] NOW advocated for the enforcement of antidiscrimination laws, such as Title VII of the Civil Rights Act of 1964, which banned employment discrimination based on sex. They also sought repeal of laws prohibiting abortion and fought for maternity leave, funding for child care, and equal educational opportunities for girls and women. They exposed the prevalence of violence against women by men through rape and domestic violence.[27] NOW also focused enormous energy between 1967 and 1982 on lobbying for the passage of the Equal Rights Amendment (ERA). A constitutional amendment written by feminist Alice Paul in 1943, the ERA asserts: "Equality of rights under the law shall not be denied or abridged by the United States or by any state on account of sex." Although it was passed by Congress in 1972, it failed to garner enough support among the states after years of lobbying by activists, and thus it has never been ratified.[28]

Nonetheless, major accomplishments of the second wave of the women's movement include, among other things, advancement of women's equality under the law through Supreme Court decisions (including advancement of property, employment, and reproductive rights); promotion of equal rights for girls and women in education through the federal Title IX statute, passed in 1972; passage of state rape shield laws, which prevent cross-examination of rape survivors about their prior sexual history; and enactment of the Pregnancy Discrimination Act in 1978 prohibiting discrimination in the workplace based on pregnancy.[29]

Like the suffrage movement of the late nineteenth and early twentieth centuries, the leaders of the second wave feminist movement were often divided along ideological, racial, ethnic, and class lines. Largely built around the experiences and agenda of White middle- and upper-class women, the early part of the movement neglected and marginalized the voices of Black, Latina, and other Women of Color and/or poor women. Black feminists and other Women of Color criticized the movement for seeking to unify all women around a common agenda while ignoring how racism and classism compound the subordination for Women of Color.[30] They pointed out that Women of Color, for example, were not discouraged from working by societal ideas about domesticity; instead, they were relegated to working demeaning, low-wage jobs that took them away from their own children. Women of Color, too, sought reproductive rights, such as the right to contraception and abortion, but they also wanted an end to forced sterilization, something few White women experienced.[31]

The women's health movement emerged as part of the larger women's movement in the 1960s and 1970s to improve health care for all women. Activists fought to end sexist and paternalistic treatment within the medical community[32] and helped establish health centers and self-help organizations controlled by and for women. This movement, generally speaking, was quite successful: It helped expand abortion and other reproductive services; publicized stories of sterilization abuse, particularly among Women of Color, which led to new regulations; and created more public awareness around a range of policy issues, including the lack of women's health research, insufficient programming for the prevention of breast and ovarian cancer, and the need for enhanced education in the areas of sexually transmitted infections, contraception, infertility, osteoporosis, and adolescent pregnancy.[33] Despite these successes, activists recognized that without universal health care, women would not experience these gains equally because so many lacked access to basic health care.[34]

Although scholars debate whether there was an actual third wave of the women's

movement, they point to a few features of feminist activism and mobilization during the 1990s as contributing to the movement. First, they note the importance of Anita Hill's 1991 testimony before Congress alleging sexual harassment by Clarence Thomas, then a U.S. Supreme Court nominee, as a defining moment in galvanizing women around the issue of workplace sexual harassment. Second, they suggest that third-wave feminism in the 1990s was decidedly "intersectional" in that it more directly engaged with the experiences of women who differ across gender identity, race, ethnicity, disability, and social class. Third, they argue that feminists began to break with what they viewed as the rigid ideas of the second wave. For example, feminists in the 1990s and early 2000s rejected the idea that women should not be called "girls," instead embracing the words *girl* and *grrrl* as terms of empowerment, not weakness.[35]

Some even argue that the Women's March of 2017 and the #MeToo movement are part of a "fourth wave" of feminism. But others reject the labeling of women's rights activism and feminism as part of discrete waves: "...the wave metaphor suggests the idea that gender activism in the history of the United States has been for the most part unified around one set of ideas, and that set of ideas can be called feminism."[36] Indeed, notions of what "feminism" means continue to evolve as diverse perspectives are included in the movement for gender equality.

The Gay Rights/ LGBTQ+ Movement

The gay rights movement is thought to have taken root in the 1950s with the establishment of the Mattachine Society, a gay rights organization, in Los Angeles. The group's mission was to eliminate discrimination and distain toward gay people. The first lesbian organization, Daughters of Bilitis, was formed in 1955 in San Francisco. Employing a tactic from the Civil Rights Movement, members of the Mattachine Society staged a "sip in" in New York City in 1966 to protest a bar's unwillingness to serve gay people. The protest resulted in the New York City Commission on Human Rights declaring that gay people have a right to be served.[37]

However, the beginning of the modern LGBTQ+ movement is usually associated with the Stonewall riots in June 1969, when gay people and straight allies resisted a routine police raid of the Stonewall Inn, a gay bar in New York City. Rioting and protests continued for six days. Two gay rights organizations were formed following the Stonewall riots: the Gay Liberation Front, which advocated for sexual liberation, and Gay Activist Alliance, which sought to "work within the political system, seeking to abolish discriminatory sex laws, promoting gay and lesbian civil rights, and challenging politicians and candidates to state their views on gay rights issues."[38] To commemorate the Stonewall riots, the first gay pride parade was held in New York City in June 1970. In the early 1970s, gay rights organizations began to form in major cities across the United States, and soon thereafter openly gay people began to successfully run for political office. In 1974 in Ann Harbor, Michigan, Kathy Kozachenko, an out lesbian, was elected to the city council. In California, Harvey Milk, who campaigned on a gay rights platform, was elected San Francisco city supervisor in 1978. Milk was assassinated in 1978, but attention to his successful election was vital to the growing gay rights movement. Before his death, Milk had asked artist and gay rights activist Gilbert Baker to design a flag to represent the movement; Baker created the rainbow flag, which he unveiled at the gay pride march in 1978.[39]

In the late 1970s, backlash to gay rights began to build in conservative parts of the country. Anita Bryant, a singer and conservative southern Baptist, successfully advocated to repeal a gay rights ordinance in Dade County, Florida.[40] Nevertheless, the momentum of the movement continued to grow, and in 1979,

75,000 people participated in a march on Washington demanding equal rights for LGBT people. The movement's focus, however, took a turn in the early 1980s when gay men began becoming ill and dying from HIV/AIDS. The failure by the government and the medical and public health communities to take seriously the devastation of the health crisis for the gay community became a pivotal moment for the movement. It starkly illustrated the country's indifference to the rights and dignity of gay people. (See the discussion that follows on the HIV/AIDS movement.)

In the 1990s, the movement confronted both state and federal laws that excluded LGBT people from protection under the law. Colorado amended its state constitution to preclude government officials in all three branches of government from passing or interpreting laws to protect people from discrimination based on their "homosexual, lesbian, or bisexual orientation, conduct, practices or relationships." Gay rights advocates challenged the amendment as a violation of the Equal Protection Clause of the federal Constitution's Fourteenth Amendment. The U.S. Supreme Court rejected the state's outright ban on protecting LGBT people's rights: "If the constitutional conception of 'equal protection of the laws' means anything, it must at the very least mean that a bare desire to harm a politically unpopular group cannot constitute a legitimate governmental interest."[41] That same year, Congress passed the Defense of Marriage Act, defining marriage as between a man and a woman and declaring that no state need recognize a marriage between same-sex partners granted in another state.[42] The law was not ruled unconstitutional by the Supreme Court until 2013.

In 1993, advocates also fought President Bill Clinton's policy of "Don't Ask, Don't Tell," which barred military officials from asking recruits about their sexual orientation. At the same time, the policy continued to forbid gay relationships among military personnel and required gay servicemen and women to remain silent about their sexual orientation or face discharge.[43] For years, gay rights organizations, including the Human Rights Campaign, mobilized a multistate effort to have the policy repealed. Finally, in 2011, President Barack Obama repealed the policy, and service members who had been discharged for their status were allowed to re-enroll.[44]

Legal advocacy organizations, such as Gay and Lesbian Advocates and Defenders (GLAD), also played a momentous role in expanding equality for LGBTQ+ people in the 2000s. Initially achieving victories in state courts and legislatures, GLAD and other legal advocacy organizations sought national recognition of marriage equality for LGBT people. In 2015, in *Obergefell v. Hodges*, the U.S. Supreme Court declared that marriage is a fundamental right and that denying same-sex couples that right would violate both the due process clause and the equal protection clause of the Fourteenth Amendment.[45]

Despite these important triumphs, LGBTQ+ people and their advocates continue to face enormous barriers to full equality in the United States, including discriminatory laws in housing, employment, and health care. As the movement has expanded in recent years to include fighting for the rights of transgender and other gender-nonconforming people, states and the federal government have adopted discriminatory laws and policies targeted at these populations. Many of these policies directly implicate and harm LGBTQ+ health, as described in Chapter 13.

The HIV/AIDS Movement

Acquired Immune Deficiency Syndrome (AIDS) was recognized as a new disease in 1981, as young gay men increasingly succumbed to opportunistic infections their immune systems should have successfully fought off.[46] In short order, the disease would come to be known as a disease of gay men and intravenous drug users, sectors of the population usually ignored; as a result, the U.S. government and medical system did little to address it.[47] The budget for AIDS research was minimal, only one pharmaceutical company was seriously pursuing treatments, and President Ronald Reagan refused to publicly address the growing crisis.[48]

From the onset of the epidemic, gay and lesbian communities mobilized to create networks of care providers focused on providing comfort to the sick and dying.[49] However, many activists believed that simply treating the sick was insufficient and demanded action and accountability, particularly in light of the U.S. government's inaction. Six years and 20,000 deaths later, the AIDS Coalition to Unleash Power—known as ACT UP—was born. Designed to be a confrontational movement, ACT UP was motivated by its members' fury over inaction and the bureaucratic processes impeding access to treatment.[50] Gay men and their allies took to the streets of New York City, protesting at City Hall, demonstrating on Wall Street, and practicing civil disobedience to command the nation's attention.[51] Members found success with these tactics and put them to use to demand access to an experimental drug the Food and Drug Administration (FDA) refused to release. Days after activists marched on FDA headquarters holding tombstones inscribed with "dead from FDA red tape"; (see **Figure 2.2**), the FDA revised its position on public access to experimental drugs.[52]

ACT UP came to call its approach the "inside-outside strategy."[53] Aggressive protests were followed by well-researched, viable policy proposals that addressed the major roadblocks standing in the way of developing an AIDS treatment. The group's advocacy was evidence-based and demanded greater transparency in every aspect of the response to the AIDS crisis. Through this method, ACT UP was instrumental in writing and pushing through legislation, redirecting federal funding, addressing the exclusion of persons with AIDS from insurance policies, and eventually succeeding in securing an effective antiretroviral drug in 1996.[54]

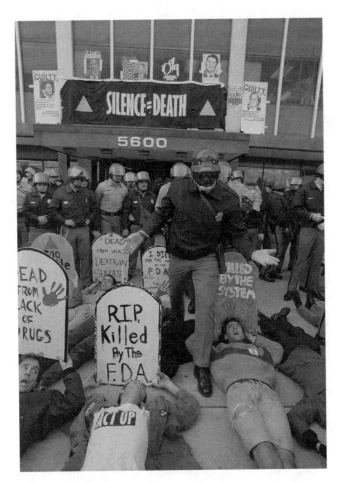

Figure 2.2 ACT UP demonstrators protest in front of the headquarters of the Food and Drug Administration
© J Scott Applewhite/AP/Shutterstock

While ACT UP's strategy for grassroots mobilization and creating policy change was fairly unique, it owes much of its success to its ability to build upon the more established gay rights movement and to leveraging the support of the women's health movement of the 1970s.[55] The intersectional nature of the AIDS epidemic also allowed ACT UP to mobilize support across racial and socioeconomic lines and to engage with other marginalized communities suffering from AIDS.[56] The organization formed committees to address specific issue areas ignored by the government response, including the need-for-needle exchange programs and housing policies that recognized the many people who lost their homes following lengthy AIDS-related hospitalizations.[57]

ACT UP and the AIDS movement more generally were successful not only in achieving the distribution of an effective antiretroviral therapy but also in revolutionizing practices within the field of pharmaceutical science and the provision of health care.[58] The AIDS movement was instrumental in the switch from the testing of experimental drugs on small population samples over long periods of time to the testing of larger samples over shorter periods, thereby speeding up the time it took to conduct drug trials.[59] The movement was also involved in jump-starting research into treatments for the opportunistic infections killing AIDS patients waiting for a cure.[60] And the movement pioneered new models for patient advocacy within the research and health care systems by empowering disease sufferers to have a voice in the research process.

The Disability Rights Movement

Some scholars view the beginning of the disability rights movement as coinciding with other social justice movements (e.g., the Civil Rights and women's movements) in the 1960s and 1970s. But others point out that disability rights activism actually started in the mid-nineteenth century with the rise of industrial capitalism, which placed a "premium on self-sufficiency and the work ethic, tethering citizenship rights to economic participation."[61] The Social Security Disability system initiated in the 1930s reinforced the long-held belief that people with disabilities could not work and needed charity from the government. Disability rights activists fought against exclusion from employment and developed new organizations focused on advocacy for people with specific disabilities, such as the National Federation of the Blind.[62] After World War II, disabled veterans organized to demand better government programs such as medical care, rehabilitation services, and pensions.[63] World War II veteran Charles Caniff called attention to the plight of people with disabilities, comparing the structural barriers that excluded them from society to the exclusion of Black people in the Jim Crow South.[64]

Nonetheless, there is no doubt that the disability rights movement was ignited in the 1960s along with other movements seeking equality for marginalized groups. Like many of the other movements for social justice, the disability rights activism of the late 1960s took root on college campuses. Ed Roberts, who had contracted polio as a teenager and who used a wheelchair and required an iron lung to help him breathe, moved into the Cowell infirmary at the University of California, Berkeley, and began taking classes. By the time Roberts graduated in 1967, other students had done the same, living in the infirmary and pursuing their degrees. They called themselves the "Rolling Quads" while fighting to make the campus accessible, and by 1972, they had successfully created the Center for Independent Living, entirely run by disabled people. The model quickly spread to other universities.[65]

At the same time, parents of children with disabilities had been fighting for deinstitutionalization (a policy of moving people with disabilities out of large state institutions and closing part or all of those institutions) and for equal educational opportunities for their children. In 1969, the Pennsylvania Association of Retarded Citizens (PARC) sued the state of Pennsylvania, demanding access for disabled children to public education. The case made its way to the Supreme Court, which held that disabled children have a right to free and equal education.[66] Congress codified this right in 1975 in the Education for All Handicapped Children Act, which was renamed the Individuals with Disabilities Education Act (IDEA) in 1988.[67]

Meanwhile, in New York, Judith Heumann, who had been denied a teaching certificate because she used a wheelchair, sued the New York Board of Education. After settling her lawsuit, Heumann moved to Berkeley to work at the Center for Independent Living.[68] She then cofounded the organization Disabled in Action, which focused on ending discrimination against people with disabilities.[69] In 1977, Heumann led a 25-day occupation of the San Francisco offices of the Department of Health, Education and Welfare. The occupation was a protest of the long delay by the department in carrying out its obligation to promulgate regulations to implement and enforce Section 504 of the Rehabilitation Act of 1973, which prohibited discrimination based on disability in government programs.[70] Passage of Section 504 had been a major accomplishment for the movement, but government officials had been excruciatingly slow to move forward with implementation.

In 1990, frustrated by the lack of enforcement of Section 504 and other antidiscrimination laws, 1,000 disability rights activists converged in Washington, D.C., for the "Wheels of Justice" campaign. While Section 504's antidiscrimination provisions were a major step forward, the law only covered places (employers, schools) that were federally financed. There were still many public accommodations (e.g., restaurants, doctor offices, retail stores, and other privately owned establishments open to the public) that were not required to provide access to people with disabilities. The "Wheels of Justice" protestors blocked traffic, making their way to the U.S. Capitol to demand that Congress pass the Americans with Disabilities Act (ADA). The proposed ADA was a comprehensive antidiscrimination law that would require that accommodations be made for people with disabilities in public accommodations in addition to government-funded entities. Some activists left their wheelchairs and other assistive devices and crawled up the 83 marble steps to the Capitol.[71] The media attention to the demonstration helped to pressure lawmakers to pass the ADA, and on July 26, 1990, President George H. W. Bush signed it into law as the first comprehensive disability rights law in the world.[72] However, the work of disability activists was not finished. In cases interpreting the ADA, courts consistently narrowed its reach. Activists again turned to Congress, which passed the ADA Amendments Act in 2008, expanding the definition of disability and changing the way courts must interpret discrimination under the act.[73] Chapter 14 describes in detail the current advocacy by disability rights activists.

The Immigrants' Rights Movement

The United States has long been conflicted about immigration. On the one hand, America sees itself as the country that welcomes immigrants from across the globe. Indeed, the Statue of Liberty contains these words from the poem "The New Colossus": "Give me your tired, your poor, Your huddled masses yearning to breathe free, The wretched refuse of your teeming shore. Send these, the homeless, tempest-tossed to me, I lift my lamp beside the golden door!" On the other hand, the U.S. history of immigration is rife with ambivalence, hostility, and hatred toward immigrants. America's notion of itself as a melting pot has long been at odds with the actual embrace of diversity. Should immigrants fully assimilate (e.g., be required to speak English and adapt to American culture), or is it beneficial for America to encompass multiple cultures and languages? As scholar Ronald Bayor remarks, "The United States has had a love-hate relationship with its immigrants."[74] Bayor notes that historically and in present times, the tension between America's view of itself as a country of immigrants and its disdain for and fear of immigrants originates from its racist and nationalistic sense of itself as a White Protestant nation. Concerns about the loss of this identity, fears about how increasing immigration would threaten the country's culture and institutions, and growing economic insecurity fuel anti-immigrant sentiment:

> Nativism and anti-immigrant attitudes ha[ve] many sources, mainly based on concerns about job competition, crime, disease, increasing poverty, radicalism or terrorism, religious and cultural differences, and a sense of invasion by racially inferior peoples who would outbreed the real Americans of Anglo-Saxon backgrounds, or by those who would not understand American democratic principles.[75]

After the large-scale immigration from Europe in the early twentieth century, immigration slowed between 1920 and 1960. Immigration policy during this period was based on setting quotas by country for how many people could enter the United States.[76] But in 1965, Congress revamped immigration law with the Immigration and Nationality Act, which discontinued the consideration of nationality, ancestry, race, and gender and instead prioritized family members, certain types of professionals, low-skilled workers in short supply, and refugees.[77] As more undocumented immigrants began entering the country, Congress passed legislation (the Immigration Reform and Control Act) in 1986 criminalizing the hiring of undocumented immigrants while offering amnesty to some others. Then the Immigration Act of 1990 again capped the number of immigrants who could enter, this time based on family and employment status but also allowing for a smaller number of "diversity" immigrants.

In response to the growing number and diversity of immigrants entering the United States, "ethnonationalism bubbled up from the four corners of America in the 1990s."[78] Hostility to "illegal immigrants" led to angry rhetoric, repressive policies, discrimination, and marginalization, but at the same time it helped shape political identity for undocumented immigrants and build solidarity with some documented immigrants and other allies.[79] Immigrants with legal status found themselves racially profiled and stigmatized; some American citizens who knew undocumented immigrants through employment arrangements or personal relationships disliked their harsh treatment.[80] Coalitions began to form focused on immigrants' rights. Early activists for immigrants' rights used different, and sometimes inconsistent, arguments. Some used a "postnationalist" frame, arguing that undocumented immigrants should be protected based on their fundamental human rights, regardless of citizenship. Others employed a "liberal nationalist" frame, suggesting that undocumented immigrants were entitled to rights based on their "cultural assimilation, rootedness and contributions to the national community."[81]

The immigrants' right movement was initiated in the late 1990s through local grassroots efforts widely dispersed across the United States. Some groups focused on specific immigrant populations (e.g., Latinx immigrants, Southeast Asian immigrants). While the movement has been primarily driven by local and regional associations focused on protecting immigrants' legal rights and supporting immigrant communities, some national umbrella organizations drive priorities around immigration law reform. For example, the Immigrant Solidarity Network serves as a clearinghouse for information;[82] the National Network for Immigrant and Refugee Rights brings together local coalitions and immigrant, refugee, community, religious, civil rights, and labor organizations and activists to support just immigration policies;[83] and the Immigration Advocates Network provides resources to nonprofits, community organizers, service providers, and lawyers serving immigrant communities.[84] National organizations have supported public health practitioners and health care providers by educating them about the impact of immigration and other laws on immigrants' access to health care and to other health-promoting services. For example, they inform health care providers and institutions what to do in the event that Immigration and Customs Enforcement (ICE), the federal agency charged with arresting and detaining undocumented immigrants, approaches a patient at a health clinic or hospital. They also educate medical and public health practitioners about which government programs are available to immigrants depending on individuals' immigration status.

Immigrants' rights activists organized "A Day without Immigrants" on February 16, 2017, in response to the anti-immigrant rhetoric and policies of President Donald Trump. The day consisted of a boycott and protest. Immigrants were encouraged not to go to work or spend money. The goal was to demonstrate the importance of immigrants to the U.S. economy and resist racial profiling by ICE.[85] Also in 2017, #AbolishICE began trending on Twitter, leading to the Abolish ICE movement, which called for the agency to be disbanded after years of aggressive detention and deportation of immigrants. U.S. Representative Mark Pocan, a Wisconsin congressman, proposed legislation to abolish ICE, diverting some of its responsibilities (such as investigating human trafficking) to other agencies and limiting deportations to immigrants who have committed serious crimes.[86] Without comprehensive immigration law reform on the horizon, the immigrants' rights movement continues to primarily organize at the grassroots level around reacting to the harms of anti-immigrant policies.

The Environmental Justice Movement

The Environmental Protection Agency (EPA) defines environmental justice as "the fair treatment and meaningful involvement of all people regardless of race, color, national origin, or income, with respect to the development, implementation, and enforcement of environmental laws, regulations, and policies."[87] The goal, according to the EPA, is for everyone to have "the same degree of protection from environmental and health hazards and equal access to the decision-making process to have a healthy environment in which to live, learn, and work."[88]

Although government agencies like the EPA have embraced the idea of environmental justice, the movement itself is defined by grassroots efforts that have pressured the government to step in when industry locates environmental hazards disproportionately in low-income and/or Communities of Color.

Robert Bullard, an academic and former marine, is regarded as the "father of the environmental justice movement."[89] In 1979, Bullard's wife, Linda McKeever Bullard, an attorney, brought the first environmental

justice lawsuit using civil rights laws to challenge the placement of a landfill in a middle-class Houston neighborhood in which 82% of the people were Black.[90] Serving as an expert witness in the case, Robert Bullard collected data and talked to Black residents; he found that the siting of hazardous waste dumps in Houston was far from random.[91] All of the city-owned landfills in Houston were in Black neighborhoods.[92]

Bullard observed that the environmental movement had been predominantly made up of middle-class Whites and had paid little attention to issues of racial and socioeconomic equity. He identified the need to marry the Civil Rights Movement's focus on eliminating institutionalized racism and discrimination with environmentalism through a new movement for environmental justice.[93] The core question of the early environmental justice movement was one of distributive justice. In his book *Dumping in Dixie*, Bullard poses these questions: "How are the benefits and burdens of environmental reform distributed? Who gets what, where, and why? Are environmental inequities a result of racism or class barriers or a combination of both?"[94] One scholar notes that the early environmental justice movement's focus on using civil rights laws to challenge racial injustice did not provide much opportunity to address class-based inequities: "The EJ [environmental justice] lens in its first generation was not developed for application to poverty-related threats" as poor communities have no remedy under the law for disparate treatment.[95] Hence, the movement expanded to a broader procedural justice approach: listening to and mobilizing the people living in affected communities. More specifically, this is intended to give people a seat at the table when decisions are being made that affect the environment in which they live.

A prime example of a community coming together to fight environmental racism and injustice is the 1982 protests and demonstrations in Warren County, a predominantly

Black county in North Carolina. The state sited a hazardous waste landfill there to hold 6,000 truckloads of PCB-laced soil. Concerned about the potential for the PCB to leach into the water supply as well as other health-related effects of the landfill, community members blocked the road to prevent the trucks from reaching the landfill and held nonviolent protests for six weeks. See **Figure 2.3**. Five hundred people were arrested. The effort was ultimately unsuccessful in blocking the landfill, but it received significant national media attention and raised awareness about the environmental justice movement. It also led Walter Fauntroy—who had participated in the protests as Washington, D.C.'s congressional delegate in the U.S. House of Representatives—to request a study by the Government Accountability Office to investigate whether Communities of Color experienced a disproportionate burden of environmental hazards. The study found that "three-quarters of the hazardous waste landfill sites in eight southeastern states were located in primarily poor, African-American and Latino communities."[96]

In 1990, environmental justice activists sent a letter to major environmental organizations calling for them to address racial bias in their policies and hiring and demanding that they address environmental racism. As a result, many of these mainstream groups developed environmental justice platforms. Environmental justice leaders held the First National People of Color Environmental Leadership Summit in Washington, D.C., in 1991, bringing together environmental and

Figure 2.3 Protestors block the delivery of toxic PCB waste to a landfill in Afton, North Carolina, 1982
© Steve Helber/AP/Shutterstock

civil rights leaders from across the country.[97] Pressure by activists also facilitated incorporation of environmental justice into federal government policy. For example, in 1994, President Bill Clinton signed Executive Order 12898 directing federal government agencies to "identify and address the disproportionately high and adverse human health or environmental effects of their actions on minority and low-income populations."[98]

The environmental justice movement has played an essential role in raising awareness among policymakers and the public about how racism and socioeconomic inequity influence environmental decision-making and how the disproportionate burden of environmental hazards and toxins affects the health of low-income people and Communities of Color. Nonetheless, environmental concerns remain a core feature of health injustice in the United States. See Chapter 8 for further discussion of current issues related to environmental justice.

The Health Care Reform Movement

The twentieth century witnessed two distinct forces advocating for reform in the U.S. health care system. On the one hand, grassroots activism was rooted in and motivated by individuals' experiences with the health care system and led by patients and others who, inevitably, would need to access health care services. This activism was dispersed and often inspired by a single issue or need but premised on mobilizing a broader base of support.[99] On the other hand, a national health care reform movement—this one led by professional advocates—was created to push comprehensive reform through lobbying, op-ed pieces, and scholarly articles.[100] There was a lack of cooperation between the two movements in part because of their different goals: The grassroots movement was focused on a variety of relatively immediate needs,

while the national movement was focused on longer-term reform. While neither movement achieved comprehensive reform, their dual efforts spurred important conversations and improvements.

Furthermore, many grassroots leaders came to realize that their demands could only be fully realized through more comprehensive reform (e.g., universal access to health care services).[101] As a result, the labor, Civil Rights, women's health, HIV/AIDS, and disability rights movements all broadened their single-issue demands to include fundamental, systemic change. For example, the organized labor movement realized as early as 1913 that while health care clinics created and staffed by union workers could help fulfill some workers' unmet health care needs, universal health care was needed to provide a more stable solution.[102] The Western Miners' Federation established similar worker-run hospitals and through those experiences came to endorse universal health insurance.[103] Similarly, civil rights leaders in the 1960s came to understand through their fight to desegregate hospitals that their demands could not be fully met without universal access to quality health care. As a result, they endorsed Medicare as part of President Lyndon B. Johnson's anti-poverty programming and worked to ensure that hospitals would accept Medicaid and provide inner-city patients with quality health care.[104] As described previously, the women's health movement also called for universal health coverage. As a result, the health care reform movement issued broader demands for a health care system that provided medical care equal in quality irrespective of race, gender, and socioeconomic status.[105]

Today, the national health care reform movement continues to expand, as changes in the system (e.g., the Affordable Care Act) break down forces that once divided popular support, employer cutbacks and layoffs illustrate the instability of the job-based health insurance model, and Medicare and Medicaid resources are stretched thin in the face of growing patient populations.[106] Indeed, many people who previously felt secure—protected by job benefits and large public health insurance programs—now have more in common with the underinsured and uninsured.[107] Chapter 7 describes in more detail the challenges to health care reform since passage of the Affordable Care Act in 2010.

Conclusion

This chapter has highlighted many of the social movements—particularly those that were most active in the 1960s and 1970s—that have brought about change to the social fabric of American society. But the chapter also demonstrates the slow pace of change when it comes to addressing inequality and injustice for people who have been historically excluded from economic and political spheres of power. Many of these movements have influenced or directly addressed health injustice as a result of deeply rooted social inequality in the United States. Chapter 3 now turns to America's centers of political power—the three branches of government—a discussion of how they affect the health of the U.S. population as a whole, and the specific health inequities suffered by historically marginalized groups.

References

1. Martin G. *Understanding Social Movements*. New York, NY: Routledge; 2015:1.
2. Almeida P. *Social Movements: The Structure of Collective Mobilization*. Berkeley: University of California Press; 2019:6.
3. Zwerman G, Schwartz M. How "good" social movements can triumph over "bad" ones. *Scientific American*. March 16, 2021. https://www.scientificamerican.com/article/how-lsquo-good-rsquo-social-movements-can-triumph-over-lsquo-bad-rsquo-ones/.
4. Zwerman G, Schwartz M. How "good" social movements can triumph over "bad" ones. *Scientific American*. March 16, 2021. https://www.scientificamerican.com/article/how-lsquo-good-rsquo-social-movements-can-triumph-over-lsquo-bad-rsquo-ones/.
5. National Association for the Advancement of Colored People (NAACP). Charles Hamilton Houston. 2022. https://naacp.org/find-resources/history-explained/civil-rights-leaders/charles-hamilton-houston.
6. Luther King M. Presentation at the Second National Convention of the Medical Committee for Human Rights, Chicago, IL. March 25, 1966.
7. PBS. American experience: Timeline of Malcolm X's life. 2022. https://www.pbs.org/wgbh/americanexperience/features/malcolmx-timeline-malcolm-xs-life/.
8. Haley A, X Malcolm. *The Autobiography of Malcolm X*. New York: Random House; 1964.
9. Newton H. In defense of self defense. Essays from the Minister of Defense. July 3, 1967:9. https://archive.lib.msu.edu/DMC/AmRad/essaysministerdefense.pdf .
10. Delli Carpini MX. Black Panther Party: 1966–1982. In Ness I, Ciment J. *The Encyclopedia of Third Parties in America*. Armonke, NY: Sharpe Reference; 2000: 192. http://repository.upenn.edu/asc_papers/1.
11. Diamond A. Remembering Resurrection City and the Poor People's Campaign of 1968. *Smithsonian Magazine*. May 2018. https://www.smithsonianmag.com/history/remembering-poor-peoples-campaign-180968742/.
12. Dellinger D. The last march of Martin Luther King Jr. *The Atlantic*. April 4, 2018. https://www.theatlantic.com/politics/archive/2018/04/mlk-last-march/555953/.
13. Diamond A. Remembering Resurrection City and the Poor People's Campaign of 1968. *Smithsonian Magazine*. May 2018. https://www.smithsonianmag.com/history/remembering-poor-peoples-campaign-180968742/.
14. Cobb J. William Barber takes on poverty and race in the age of Trump. *The New Yorker*. May 7, 2018. https://www.newyorker.com/magazine/2018/05/14/william-barber-takes-on-poverty-and-race-in-the-age-of-trump.
15. Poor People's Campaign. Our demands.2020. https://www.poorpeoplescampaign.org/about/our-demands/.
16. Poor People's Campaign. About. 2022. https://www.poorpeoplescampaign.org/about/.
17. Poor People's Campaign. About. 2022. https://www.poorpeoplescampaign.org/about/.
18. Goldstein L, Baier J, et al. *The Constitutional and Legal Rights of Women*. 4th ed. St. Paul: West Academic Publishing; 2019:7.
19. Goldstein L, Baier J, et al. *The Constitutional and Legal Rights of Women*. 4th ed. St. Paul: West Academic Publishing; 2019:7.
20. Kraditor A. *The Ideas of the Woman's Suffrage Movement, 1890–1920*. New York, NY: W.W. Norton; 1981:4.

21. Goldstein L, Baier J, et al. *The Constitutional and Legal Rights of Women.* 4th ed. St. Paul: West Academic Publishing. 2019;8.

22. Bleiweis R, Phadke S, Frye J. 100 years after the 19th Amendment, the fight for women's suffrage continues. Center for American Progress. August 18, 2020. https://www.americanprogress.org/issues/women/news/2020/08/18/489651/100-years-19th-amendment-fight-womens-suffrage-continues/.

23. Goldstein L, Baier J, et al. *The Constitutional and Legal Rights of Women.* 4th ed. St. Paul: West Academic Publishing. 2019;8

24. De Beauvoir S. *The Second Sex.* Paris, France: Editions Gallimard; 1949.

25. Friedan B. *The Feminine Mystique.* New York, NY: W.W. Norton; 1963.

26. The National Organization for Women. The National Organization for Women's 1966 statement of purpose. 1966. https://now.org/about/history/statement-of-purpose/.

27. The National Organization for Women. Highlights. https://now.org/about/history/highlights/.

28. Francis R. Equal Rights Amendment. January 2022. FAQ. https://www.equalrightsamendment.org/faq.

29. The National Organization for Women. Highlights. 2022. https://now.org/about/history/highlights/.

30. hooks b. *Ain't I a Woman? Black Women and Feminism.* Boston, MA: South End Press; 1981.

31. Grady C. The waves of feminism, and why people keep fighting over them, explained. *Vox.* July 20, 2018. https://www.vox.com/2018/3/20/16955588/feminism-waves-explained-first-second-third-fourth.

32. Munch S. The women's health movement. *Social Work in Health Care.* 2008;43:1, 17–32. https://doi.org/10.1300/J010v43n01_02.

33. Norsigian J. Our bodies ourselves and the women's health movement in the United States: Some reflections. *American Journal of Public Health.* May 8, 2019. https://ajph.aphapublications.org/doi/full/10.2105/AJPH.2019.305059.

34. Norsigian J. Our bodies ourselves and the women's health movement in the United States: Some reflections. *American Journal of Public Health.* May 8, 2019. https://ajph.aphapublications.org/doi/full/10.2105/AJPH.2019.305059.

35. Grady C. The waves of feminism, and why people keep fighting over them, explained. *Vox.* July 20, 2018. https://www.vox.com/2018/3/20/16955588/feminism-waves-explained-first-second-third-fourth.

36. Grady C. The waves of feminism, and why people keep fighting over them, explained. *Vox.* July 20, 2018. https://www.vox.com/2018/3/20/16955588/feminism-waves-explained-first-second-third-fourth.

37. PBS. American experience. Milestones in the American gay rights movement: Stonewall uprising. 2022. https://www.pbs.org/wgbh/americanexperience/features/stonewall-milestones-american-gay-rights-movement/.

38. Rapp L. Gay Activists Alliance. GLBTQ. 2004. http://www.glbtqarchive.com/ssh/gay_activists_alliance_S.pdf.

39. 150 years of LGBT+ history: Paying tribute to the past, present, and future. *Bloomberg.* June 28, 2019. https://www.bloomberg.com/company/stories/150-years-lgbt-history-paying-tribute-past-present-future/.

40. Johnson E. The myth that has shaped the Christian Right and the LGBTQ rights movement for four decades. *Washington Post.* June 21, 2019. https://www.washingtonpost.com/outlook/2019/06/21/myth-that-has-shaped-christian-right-lgbtq-rights-movement-four-decades/.

41. Romer v. Evans, 517 US 620 (1996).

42. The Defense of Marriage Act. 1 U.S.C. § 7 and 28 U.S.C. § 1738C (1996).

43. Pruitt S. Once banned, then silenced: How Clinton's "Don't Ask, Don't Tell" policy affected LGBT military. *History Stories.* July 3, 2019. https://www.history.com/news/dont-ask-dont-tell-repeal-compromise.

44. Human Rights Campaign. Repeal of "Don't Ask, Don't Tell." 2022. https://www.hrc.org/our-work/stories/repeal-of-dont-ask-dont-tell.

45. Obergefell v. Hodges. 576 US 644 (2015).

46. Greene, W. A history of AIDS: Looking back to see ahead. *European Journal of Immunology.* 2008;Suppl 1:S94–102. 10.1002/eji.200737441.

47. Shilts R. *And the Band Played On: Politics, People, and the AIDS Epidemic.* New York, NY: St. Martin's Press; 1987.

48. Aizenman, N. How to demand a medical breakthrough: Lessons from the AIDS fight. NPR. February 9. 2019. https://www.npr.org/sections/health-shots/2019/02/09/689924838/how-to-demand-a-medical-breakthrough-lessons-from-the-aids-fight.

49. Aizenman, N. How to demand a medical breakthrough: Lessons from the AIDS fight. NPR. February 9. 2019. https://www.npr.org/sections/health-shots/2019/02/09/689924838/how-to-demand-a-medical-breakthrough-lessons-from-the-aids-fight.

50. Elbaz, G. Beyond anger: The activist construction of the AIDS crisis. *Social Justice* 1995;22:4(62). https://www.jstor.org/stable/29766907.

51. Aizenman, N. How to demand a medical breakthrough: Lessons from the AIDS fight. NPR. February 9. 2019. https://www.npr.org/sections/health-shots/2019/02/09/689924838/how-to-demand-a-medical-breakthrough-lessons-from-the-aids-fight.

52. Aizenman, N. How to demand a medical breakthrough: Lessons from the AIDS fight. NPR. February 9. 2019. https://www.npr.org/sections/health-shots/2019/02/09/689924838/how-to-demand-a-medical-breakthrough-lessons-from-the-aids-fight.

53. Aizenman, N. How to demand a medical breakthrough: Lessons from the AIDS fight. NPR. February 9, 2019. https://www.npr.org/sections/health-shots/2019/02/09/689924838/how-to-demand-a-medical-breakthrough-lessons-from-the-aids-fight.

54. France, D. How ACT UP remade political organizing in America. *The New York Times*. April 13, 2020. https://www.nytimes.com/interactive/2020/04/13/t-magazine/act-up-aids.html.

55. Pai, M. AIDS activism: A playbook for global health advocacy. *Forbes*. November 30, 2019. https://www.forbes.com/sites/madhukarpai/2019/11/30/aids-activism-a-playbook-for-global-health-advocacy/?sh=6a2246e640a1.

56. Pai, M. AIDS activism: A playbook for global health advocacy. *Forbes*. November 30, 2019. https://www.forbes.com/sites/madhukarpai/2019/11/30/aids-activism-a-playbook-for-global-health-advocacy/?sh=6a2246e640a1.

57. France, D. How ACT UP remade political organizing in America. *The New York Times*. April 13, 2020. https://www.nytimes.com/interactive/2020/04/13/t-magazine/act-up-aids.html.

58. Aizenman, N. How to demand a medical breakthrough: Lessons from the AIDS fight. NPR. February 9. 2019. https://www.npr.org/sections/health-shots/2019/02/09/689924838/how-to-demand-a-medical-breakthrough-lessons-from-the-aids-fight.

59. Aizenman, N. How to demand a medical breakthrough: Lessons from the AIDS fight. NPR. February 9. 2019. https://www.npr.org/sections/health-shots/2019/02/09/689924838/how-to-demand-a-medical-breakthrough-lessons-from-the-aids-fight.

60. Aizenman, N. How to demand a medical breakthrough: Lessons from the AIDS fight. NPR. February 9. 2019. https://www.npr.org/sections/health-shots/2019/02/09/689924838/how-to-demand-a-medical-breakthrough-lessons-from-the-aids-fight.

61. Patterson L. The disability rights movement in the United States. In Rembis M, Kudlick C, Nielsen KE, eds., *The Oxford Handbook of Disability History*. Oxford: Oxford University Press; 2018:440.

62. Patterson L. The disability rights movement in the United States. In Rembis M, Kudlick C, Nielsen KE, eds., *The Oxford Handbook of Disability History*. Oxford: Oxford University Press; 2018:440.

63. Patterson L. The disability rights movement in the United States. In Rembis M, Kudlick C, Nielsen KE, eds., *The Oxford Handbook of Disability History*. Oxford: Oxford University Press; 2018:440.

64. Patterson L. The disability rights movement in the United States. In Rembis M, Kudlick C, Nielsen KE, eds., *The Oxford Handbook of Disability History*. Oxford: Oxford University Press; 2018:440.

65. Belt R, Dorfman D. Disability, law, and the humanities: The rise of disability legal studies. In Stern S, Del Mar M, Meyler B, eds., *The Oxford Handbook of Law and Humanities*. Oxford: Oxford University Press; 2019.

66. Patterson L. The disability rights movement in the United States. In Rembis M, Kudlick C, Nielsen KE, eds., *The Oxford Handbook of Disability History*. Oxford: Oxford University Press; 2018:440.

67. The Individuals with Disabilities Education Act. 20 U.S.C. 1412 (1988).

68. Belt R, Dorfman D. Disability, law, and the humanities: The rise of disability legal studies. In Stern S, Del Mar M, Meyler B, eds., *The Oxford Handbook of Law and Humanities*. Oxford: Oxford University Press; 2019.

69. Patterson L. The disability rights movement in the United States. In Rembis M, Kudlick C, Nielsen KE, eds., *The Oxford Handbook of Disability History*. Oxford: Oxford University Press; 2018:440.

70. Belt R, Dorfman D. Disability, Law, and the Humanities: The Rise of Disability Legal Studies. Stern S, Del Mar M, Meyler B, eds., *The Oxford Handbook of Law and Humanities*. Oxford: Oxford University Press; 2019.

71. Patterson L. The disability rights movement in the United States. In Rembis M, Kudlick C, Nielsen KE, eds., *The Oxford Handbook of Disability History*. Oxford: Oxford University Press; 2018:440.

72. The Americans with Disabilities Act, 42 U.S.C. § 12101 (1990).

73. The Americans with Disabilities Act Amendments Act. Pub L 110-325 (2008).

74. Bayor R. Introduction: The making of America. In Bayor R, ed., *The Oxford Handbook of American Immigration and Ethnicity*. Oxford: Oxford University Press; 2016:6.

75. The making of America. In Bayor R, ed., *The Oxford Handbook of American Immigration and Ethnicity*. Oxford: Oxford University Press; 2016:65.

76. Georgetown Law Library. A brief history of civil rights in the United States. Immigrant and refugee civil rights. 2021. https://guides.ll.georgetown.edu/c.php?g=592919&p=4171684.

77. Georgetown Law Library. A brief history of civil rights in the United States. Immigrant and refugee civil rights. 2021. https://guides.ll.georgetown.edu/c.php?g=592919&p=4171684.

78. Nicholls WJ. *The Immigrant Rights Movement: The Battle over National Citizenship*. Palo Alto, CA: Stanford University Press; 2019:4.

79. Nicholls WJ. *The Immigrant Rights Movement: The Battle over National Citizenship*. Palo Alto, CA: Stanford University Press; 2019.

80. Nicholls WJ. *The Immigrant Rights Movement: The Battle over National Citizenship*. Palo Alto, CA: Stanford University Press; 2019.

81. Nicholls WJ. *The Immigrant Rights Movement: The Battle over National Citizenship*. Palo Alto, CA: Stanford University Press; 2019:8.

82. Immigrant Solidarity Network. 2022. http://www.immigrantsolidarity.org/.

83. National Network for Immigrant and Refugee Rights. 2020. https://nnirr.org/.

84. Immigration Advocates Network. 2022. https://www.immigrationadvocates.org/.

85. Chappell B. "A Day Without Immigrants" promises a national strike Thursday. NPR. February 16, 2017. https://www.npr.org/sections/thetwo-way/2017/02/16/515555428/a-day-without-immigrants-promises-a-national-strike-thursday.

86. Levinson-Waldman R. The Abolish ICE movement explained. Brennan Center for Justice. July 30, 2018. https://www.brennancenter.org/our-work/analysis-opinion/abolish-ice-movement-explained.

87. Environmental Protection Agency. Environmental justice. 2020. https://www.epa.gov/environmental justice.

88. Environmental Protection Agency. Environmental justice. 2022. https://www.epa.gov/environmental justice.

89. Dr. Robert Bullard Biography. 2018. https://drrobertbullard.com/biography/.

90. Bean v. Southwestern Waste Management, Inc. 482 F. Supp. 673 (S.D. Tex. 1979).

91. Bullard RD. *Dumping in Dixie: Race, Class, and Environmental Quality*. New York: Taylor and Francis; 1990.

92. Meet Robert Bullard, the father of environmental justice. *Grist*. March 15, 2006. https://grist.org/article/dicum/.

93. Bullard RD. *Dumping in Dixie: Race, Class, and Environmental Quality*. New York, NY: Taylor and Francis; 1990.

94. Bullard RD. *Dumping in Dixie: Race, Class, and Environmental Quality*. New York, NY: Taylor and Francis; 1990: 2.

95. Vanderheiden S. Environmental and climate justice. In Gabrielson T, Hall C, Meyer JM, Schlosberg D, eds., *The Oxford Handbook of Environmental Political Theory*. Oxford: Oxford University Press; 2016: 323.

96. NRDC. The environmental justice movement. March 17, 2016. https://www.nrdc.org/stories/environmental-justice-movement.

97. NRDC. The environmental justice movement. March 17, 2016. https://www.nrdc.org/stories/environmental-justice-movement.

98. Environmental Protection Agency. Summary of Executive Order 12898—Federal Actions to Address Environmental Justice in Minority Populations and Low-Income Populations. 59 FR 7629. February 16, 1994. https://www.epa.gov/laws-regulations/summary-executive-order-12898-federal-actions-address-environmental-justice.

99. Hoffman B. Health care reform and social movements in the United States. *American Journal of Public Health*. September 2008. https://www.ncbi.nlm.nih.gov/pmc/articles/PMC2518596/.

100. Hoffman B. Health care reform and social movements in the United States. *American Journal of Public Health*. September 2008. https://www.ncbi.nlm.nih.gov/pmc/articles/PMC2518596/.

101. Hoffman B. Health care reform and social movements in the United States. *American Journal of Public Health*. September 2008. https://www.ncbi.nlm.nih.gov/pmc/articles/PMC2518596/.

102. Hoffman B. Health care reform and social movements in the United States. *American Journal of Public Health*. September 2008. https://www.ncbi.nlm.nih.gov/pmc/articles/PMC2518596/.

103. Hoffman B. Health care reform and social movements in the United States. *American Journal of Public Health*. September 2008. https://www.ncbi.nlm.nih.gov/pmc/articles/PMC2518596/.

104. Hoffman B. Health care reform and social movements in the United States. *American Journal of Public Health*. September 2008. https://www.ncbi.nlm.nih.gov/pmc/articles/PMC2518596/.

105. Hoffman B. Health care reform and social movements in the United States. *American Journal of Public Health*. September 2008. https://www.ncbi.nlm.nih.gov/pmc/articles/PMC2518596/.

106. Hoffman B. Health care reform and social movements in the United States. *American Journal of Public Health*. September 2008. https://www.ncbi.nlm.nih.gov/pmc/articles/PMC2518596/.

107. Hoffman B. Health care reform and social movements in the United States. *American Journal of Public Health*. September 2008. https://www.ncbi.nlm.nih.gov/pmc/articles/PMC2518596/.

PART 2

Aspects of the Legal System that Undermine Health Justice

CHAPTER 3

The Roles of the Three Branches of Government in Health Law and Policy

LEARNING OBJECTIVES

By the end of this chapter you will be able to:

- Explain key roles of the legislative branch of government in health law and policy
- Explain key roles of the executive branch of government in health law and policy
- Explain key roles of the judicial branch of government in health law and policy

Introduction

This chapter provides an overview of the ways in which the three branches of government—legislative, executive, and judicial—influence individual and population health and well-being through law and policy. It describes how the unique role of each branch plays out in the context of making and/or interpreting health law and policy, notes how these roles may be different at the federal and state levels, and provides examples of the range of laws, committees, and agencies that influence individual, community, and population health.

Health law and policy encompass a vast range of issues in health care, public health, bioethics and biotechnology, the social safety net, and civil and human rights, thus

providing the government ample opportunity to shape the many drivers that ultimately lead to health (in)justice. While a full exploration of these opportunities is beyond the scope of this chapter, our hope is that by grasping the general roles of each of the three branches of government in designing and interpreting health law and policy, readers will be better able to advocate for needed structural and policy change. We note that this chapter and the next one could be studied in concert: This chapter focuses on each branch's ability to control the levers of government in the context of health, while Chapter 4 describes the types of legal doctrines that can take hold and negatively influence the health of tens of millions of people when lawmakers and policymakers display a lack of attention to health justice. These legal doctrines—the "no duty to treat" principle, the exclusion of impoverishment from protection under federal antidiscrimination law, the "negative Constitution," and the general lack of right to legal counsel in civil legal matters—help explain how laws seemingly unrelated to health equity regulate population health in deeply disproportionate ways.

The Legislative Branch of Government and Health

Overview

Article I of the U.S. Constitution makes Congress the lawmaking body of the federal government by granting it "all legislative powers" and the right to enact "necessary and proper laws" to effect its prerogatives.[1] Congressional responsibilities are fulfilled by the two chambers of Congress, the Senate and the House of Representatives. As part of its overall legislative powers, the Constitution grants to Congress the specific powers to levy taxes, collect revenue, pay debts, provide for the general welfare, regulate interstate and foreign commerce, establish federal courts inferior to the Supreme Court, and declare war.[2] The Senate alone has the power to ratify treaties and confirm nominations of public officials.

Of course, the federal government does not have a monopoly on lawmaking; many important laws are dispatched by state and local legislatures. This is particularly true in areas related to health (e.g., think health care provider licensing, health care organization accreditation, some aspects of health insurance regulation, and many paramount public health issues), and we discuss in more detail later the importance of state and local police powers in the context of public health. For purposes of this chapter, the legislative branches of various governments can be thought of as a collection of elected representatives who make policy decisions—which they then transform into statutory law—and who oversee the activities of executive branch agencies through the authorization of programs and the appropriation of funds.

Legislative Powers and Health Policy

The powers granted to the legislative branch of government include the ability to create health laws directly and also to deeply affect population health and well-being through laws that would not, on their face, be described as "health laws" (think, for example, of housing policy). At the federal level, for instance, the ability to shape population health is represented by a range of committees and subcommittees, some of which are depicted in **Table 3.1**.

Depending on one's view, legislators either are uniquely able to protect population health and promote health justice or are in reality too partisan and/or self-serving to make "the nation's health"—as complex as it is—a meaningful policy priority. On the one hand, the legislative branch of government is publicly accountable through the electoral process. It has the capacity to collect information from a wide range of objective sources. It can gather and analyze vast amounts of scientific data necessary for sound policy development. And it can deliberate and debate important policy topics. On the other hand—as witnessed most recently throughout the COVID-19 pandemic—the glaring polarization and lack of shared values around population health infect all levels (local, state, federal) of the legislative branches of government.

To an extent, some polarization is to be expected; the legislative branch is one of two political branches in government (the executive branch being the other), legislators belong to political parties, and legislators are frequently indebted to individuals, advocacy organizations, interest groups, and industries that were key to their election success. But

Table 3.1 Key Health Committees and Subcommittees and Their Health-Related Jurisdictions

Committee/Subcommittee	Health-Related Jurisdiction
Senate Finance Committee	

• Subcommittee on Health Care	• Department of Health and Human Services
	  • Centers for Medicare and Medicaid Services (includes Children's Health Insurance Program [CHIP])
	  • Administration for Children and Families
	• Department of the Treasury
	  • Group health plans under the Employee Retirement Income Security Act (ERISA)

Senate Appropriations Committee	
• Subcommittee on Labor, Health and Human Services, Education, and Related Agencies	• Department of Health and Human Services • All areas except Food and Drug Administration, Indian Health, and construction activities
• Subcommittee on Agriculture, Rural Development, Food and Drug Administration, and Related Agencies	• U.S. Department of Agriculture (except Forest Service) • Includes child nutrition programs; food safety and inspections; nutrition program administration; special supplemental nutrition program for Women, Infants, Children (WIC); Supplemental Nutrition Assistance Program (SNAP) • Food and Drug Administration
Committee/Subcommittee	**Health-Related Jurisdiction**

• Subcommittee on Interior, Environment, and Related Agencies	• Department of Health and Human Services
	  • Indian Health Services
	  • Agency for Toxic Substances and Disease Registry

Senate Health, Education, Labor, and Pensions Committee	
• Subcommittee on Children and Families • Subcommittee on Primary Health and Retirement Security	• Occupational safety and health, public health, Health Resources and Services Act, substance abuse and mental health, oral health, health care disparities, ERISA
Senate Committee on Agriculture, Nutrition, and Forestry	
• Subcommittee on Food and Nutrition, Specialty Crops, Organics and Research	• Food from fresh waters; SNAP; human nutrition; inspection of livestock, meat, and agricultural products; pests and pesticides; school nutrition programs; other matters related to food, nutrition, and hunger
Senate Committee on Environment and Public Works	
• Subcommittee on Clean Air, Climate, and Nuclear Safety • Chemical Safety, Waste Management, Environmental Justice, and Regulatory Oversight • Fisheries, Water, and Wildlife	• Air pollution, environmental policy, research and development, water pollution, nonmilitary control of nuclear energy, solid waste disposal and recycling

(continues)

Table 3.1 Key Health Committees and Subcommittees and Their Health-Related Jurisdictions   *(continued)*

Committee/Subcommittee	Health-Related Jurisdiction
House Committee on Ways and Means	
• Subcommittee on Health	• Programs providing payments for health care, health delivery systems, and health research • Social Security Act • Maternal and Child Health Block Grant • Medicare • Medicaid • Peer review of utilization and quality control of health care organizations • Tax credit and deduction provisions of the Internal Revenue Service relating to health insurance premiums and health care costs

• Subcommittee on Worker and Family Support	• Social Security Act
	  • Public assistance provisions
	  • Supplemental Security Income provisions
	  • Mental health grants to states

House Committee on Appropriations	

• Subcommittee on Labor, Health and Human Services, Education, and Related Agencies	• Department of Health and Human Services
	  • Administration for Children and Families
	  • Administration for Community Living
	  • Agency for Healthcare Research and Quality
	  • Centers for Disease Control and Prevention
	  • Centers for Medicare and Medicaid Services
	  • Health Resources Services Administration
	  • National Institutes of Health
	  • Substance Abuse and Mental Health Services
	  • Federal Mine Safety and Health Review Commission
	  • Medicaid and CHIP Payment and Access Commission
	  • Medicare Payment Advisory Committee
	  • National Council on Disability
	  • Occupational Safety and Health Review Commission
	  • Social Security Administration

• Subcommittee on Agriculture, Rural Development, Food and Drug Administration, and Related Agencies	• Food and Drug Administration • Department of Agriculture (except Forestry)
• Subcommittee on Energy and Water Development, and Related Agencies	• Department of Energy • National Nuclear Strategy Administration • Federal Energy Regulatory Commission • Department of Interior • Bureau of Reclamation • Defense Nuclear Facilities Safety Board • Nuclear Regulatory Commission

Committee/Subcommittee	Health-Related Jurisdiction
• Subcommittee on Interior, Environment, and Related Agencies	• Department of Interior (except Bureau of Reclamation and Central Utah Project) • Environmental Protection Agency • Indian Health Service • National Institute of Environmental Health Sciences • Chemical Safety and Hazard Investigation Board
House Committee on Agriculture	
• Subcommittee on Nutrition, Oversight, and Department Operations	• Nutrition programs, including SNAP
• Subcommittee on Biotechnology, Horticulture, and Research	• Policies and statutes relating to horticulture, bees, organic agriculture, pest and disease management, bioterrorism, biotechnology
• Subcommittee on Livestock and Foreign Agriculture	• Policies and statutes relating to inspections of livestock, dairy, poultry, and seafood; aquaculture; animal welfare

Wilensky, SE, & Teitelbaum, JB. (2020). Essentials of Health Policy and Law (Fourth Edition), Ch. 2. Burlington, MA: Jones & Bartlett Learning.

partisanship leads legislators to view policy through a relatively narrow lens, and its divisiveness oftentimes leads to noncooperation. Furthermore, legislators often operate on a time horizon that is more in tune with their own reelection cycles than with the longer-term outlook necessary for many key health justice issues.[3]

Examples of Federal Statutes that Shape Health Policy

There is no concise way to describe the dozens of federal, state, and local statutes that impact health, and it is fair to say that the examples that follow do not do justice to the broad topic of health policy. Nonetheless, the examples are useful in helping to portray the legislative branch's role (in this case, the federal legislative branch) in creating laws that affect individual and population health, both directly and indirectly. Some of the examples (listed chronologically) receive no additional treatment in this textbook, while others are described in more detail.

1. *Social Security Act (1935).*[4] The Social Security Act was a cornerstone of President Franklin D. Roosevelt's New Deal domestic policy program and a response to the fact that by the 1930s, the United States was the only industrialized nation without any national social security system. The law included retirement benefits (which, over time, have contributed to a decline in poverty among the elderly), survivors' benefits, unemployment insurance, and aid to families headed by single mothers.

2. *Medicaid and Medicare (1965).*[5] Thirty years after the original social security legislation was signed into law, it was amended to include Medicaid and Medicare, two behemoths of U.S. health law and policy. Medicaid provides health insurance coverage to low-income families and individuals, including children, parents, pregnant women, seniors, and people with disabilities. It is funded jointly (though not equally) by the federal government and each individual state.

Medicare provides health insurance coverage to people ages 65 and over and to some individuals under age 65 who have a long-term disability. Together, the two programs provide health insurance to some 136 million Americans.

3. *Employee Retirement Income Security Act (ERISA; 1974).*[6] One of the most complex areas of federal civil law, ERISA was established in 1974 mainly to protect the employee pension system from employer fraud. However, the law was drafted in such a way as to extend to all benefits offered by ERISA-covered employers, including health benefits. The nearly 150 million people in this country who receive health and other benefits through a private employer can be said to work for an "ERISA-covered" employer. ERISA employs two main devices to protect employee benefits. First, it imposes "fiduciary"—or good faith—responsibilities on those individuals or entities that administer various types of employer-sponsored benefit plans. (In the case of health benefits, this is oftentimes a managed care organization.) The second tool used by Congress in ERISA to regulate employee benefits is a set of uniform, nationwide rules for the administration of employee benefits. However, while ERISA closely regulates the structure and operation of pension plans, the law includes few substantive standards governing the design or administration of health (or other) employee benefits. As a result of the dearth of substantive standards pertaining to employee health benefits, employers enjoy discretion under ERISA to decide whether to offer health benefits at all and, if they do, to offer a benefit package of their choosing. ERISA's lack of substantive health benefit regulations is compounded by the fact that the law contains few avenues for employees to remedy negligent benefit plan administration, including

substandard conduct in the administration of health plan benefits.

4. *Emergency Medical Treatment and Active Labor Act (EMTALA; 1986).*[7] Because EMTALA represents the only truly universal legal right to health care in this country—the right to access emergency hospital services—it is often described as one of the building blocks of health rights. EMTALA was enacted to blunt the practice of "patient dumping": the turning away of poor or uninsured persons in need of hospital care. By refusing to treat these individuals and instead "dumping" them on public hospitals, private institutions were effectively limiting their patients to those whose treatment costs would likely be covered out-of-pocket or by insurers. EMTALA was thus a conscious effort on the part of Congress to create legally enforceable rights to emergency hospital care for all individuals regardless of their income or health insurance status. At its core, EMTALA includes two related duties (which technically attach only to hospitals that participate in the Medicare program, but nearly every hospital in the country participates in that federal program). The first duty requires covered hospitals to provide an examination to all individuals who present at a hospital's emergency department seeking care for an emergency medical condition. The second duty requires hospitals to either stabilize any condition that meets EMTALA's definition of emergency medical condition or, in the case of a hospital without the capability to treat the emergency condition, undertake to transfer the patient to another facility in a medically appropriate fashion. The legal rights established under EMTALA are accompanied by heavy penalties for their violation.

5. *Americans with Disabilities Act (ADA; 1990).*[8] The ADA is a broad civil rights law prohibiting discrimination against individuals with disabilities in many

facets of everyday life, including employment, public services, public accommodations (i.e., privately owned entities open to the general public), transportation, and more. Not a "health law" per se, the ADA's impact on health care for disabled individuals is nonetheless notable. Like discrimination in health care based on race or ethnicity, health care discrimination premised on disability has a sordid history in the United States. (This is discussed more fully in Chapter 14.) Historical discriminatory practices and perspectives resonate even in today's health care system, as treatment opportunities for those with disabilities are skewed toward institutional, rather than community, settings and disease-specific limitations in health insurance are commonplace. The ADA helps remedy some of these deficiencies. For example, the law defines "places of public accommodation" to include private hospitals and other private health care providers. So, for example, a dentist in private practice who does not receive any federal funds for his services is nonetheless prohibited from discriminating against a person who has a health condition that meets the definition of "disability" under the ADA.[9]

6. *Health Insurance Portability and Accountability Act (HIPAA; 1996).*[10] HIPAA is a federal law that aims to protect patient health information from being disclosed without the patient's consent or knowledge. The idea behind the law was to permit the flow of health information in order to improve the delivery of health care services and promote public health while ensuring that individual patient health information is secured and protected. The statute led to the development of what is known as the "HIPAA Privacy Rule," a federal regulation that governs the use and disclosure of individually identifiable health information.[11]

7. *Patient Protection and Affordable Care Act (ACA; 2010).*[12] The ACA represents the most monumental piece of U.S. federal health policymaking since passage of Medicaid and Medicare in 1965. It reordered many aspects of the health insurance and health care delivery systems, lowered the number of uninsured individuals and thus increased access to care for millions of people, helped reduce racial and ethnic health and health care disparities, and resulted in economic benefits for states that implemented the Medicaid expansion that was made available under the ACA.[13] That said, even its staunchest supporters recommend changes to improve health insurance affordability, increase access to care, strengthen the insurance "marketplaces" that are a hallmark of the law, and contain health care costs.[14] Even more than a decade after the ACA's passage, implementation of the law remains an ongoing, dynamic process involving the federal government, states, employers, insurers, providers, patients, and others. The ACA's benefits and limitations are discussed in greater detail in Chapter 7.

State and Local Police Powers

One focal point of public health law and policy is locating the appropriate balance between the regulation of private individuals and corporations and the ability of those same parties to exercise rights that allow them to function free of overly intrusive government intervention. Achieving this balance is not easy for lawmakers and policymakers, as stakeholders disagree on issues like the extent to which carmakers should alter their operations to reduce environmentally harmful vehicle emissions, the degree to which companies should be limited in advertising cigarettes, or whether gun manufacturers should be held liable in cases where injuries or killings result from the negligent use of their products.

These competing interests are mainly addressed through two types of laws: those that define the functions and powers of public health agencies and those that aim to directly protect and promote health. State legislatures create these types of laws through what are known as their *police powers*. These powers represent the inherent authority of state and local governments to regulate individuals and private business in the name of public health promotion and protection. The importance of police powers cannot be overstated; it is fair to say that they are the most critical aspect of the sovereignty that states retained at the founding of the country, when the colonies agreed to a governmental structure consisting of a strong national government.

Nor should the reach of police powers be underestimated, as they grant lawmakers the authority to coerce private parties to act (or refrain from acting) in certain ways. This is so because, in a country founded upon the twin ideals of individualism and a limited government, many individuals and businesses will not voluntarily conform with principles that promote the public good but that limit their own preferred behaviors or their bottom line. The COVID-19 pandemic serves as an obvious example (and, in fact, all of the major communicable disease outbreaks in the United States have been thwarted by some combination of compulsory screening, examination, treatment, isolation, and quarantine programs). Over the course of the pandemic, state and local legislative bodies have used their police powers to pass laws relating to stay-at-home orders, business closures, occupancy limits, face coverings, vaccine mandates, workforce issues, and more. While in some places these laws were met with hostility and derision, laws curbing personal and corporate interests in the name of public health have long been accepted tools of legislatures. Examples abound: mandatory licensing for health care professionals, food safety laws for restaurants, occupational health and safety laws, pollution control measures, building codes, seatbelt and helmet

laws, and many more. As described in Chapter 1, as part of the "new public health," state and local lawmakers have experimented with a range of public health laws geared toward curbing the growth of chronic diseases such as obesity, diabetes, cardiovascular disease, and asthma. Taxes on sugary drinks, mandates to publish calorie counts on restaurant menus, regulation of the sale of tobacco to minors, and requirements for physical education in public schools are all examples of the ways in which state legislators use their police powers to promote public health.[15]

The Executive Branch of Government and Health

Overview

Article II of the U.S. Constitution establishes the federal executive branch and vests executive power in the most well-known member of the branch, the president.[16] Of course, the president does not act alone in running the executive branch, instead relying on a range of agencies (e.g., the Office of Management and Budget), staff (e.g., the Domestic Policy Council), and departments (e.g., the Department of Health and Human Services) that are responsible for implementing the laws passed by Congress and setting policy through executive orders, administrative rule making, and interpretive guidance.[17]

As is true with legislative matters, many important health policy decisions are made by state and local—rather than federal—executive branch officials. While states reserve the right to organize in any way they wish, for purposes of this chapter, it is enough to say that state and local executive branches of government are structured enough like their federal counterpart to speak about them as a whole. For example, in all cases there is a president-like chief executive who is directly elected by the people: All 50 states have a governor, each of the five U.S. territories with permanent residents has a governor, and the District of Columbia has a mayor. Then—at least in most states—there are lieutenant governors, attorneys general, secretaries of state, and so on. Finally, all state and local executive branches employ administrative agencies to implement laws passed by their state's legislature and set policy in furtherance of a governor's agenda.

Executive Powers and Health Policy

The head of an executive branch of government, whether a president, governor, or mayor, sets the administration's policy agenda and promotes key priorities. The chief executive is also an elected official who is a member of a political party, thus infusing politics and partisanship into many important health justice issues and frequently leading to substantial swings in policy as administrations flip from one party to the other. One example, among many, will suffice to make the latter point. In 1985, the second Ronald Reagan administration implemented what's known as the "Mexico City policy." It requires foreign nongovernmental organizations that receive funding from the U.S. government to certify that they will not perform or actively promote abortion as a method of family planning—even if they do so using *non*-U.S. funds. (This is why the policy's detractors refer to it as a "global gag rule.") The policy was rescinded by Democratic President Bill Clinton in 1993, reinstated in 2001 by Republican President George W. Bush, rescinded in 2009 by Democratic President Barack Obama, reinstated in 2017 by Republican President Donald Trump, and then rescinded again by Democratic President Joe Biden in 2021.

The president is able to shape public policy in three key ways. The first is through the use of the veto power. This power can take two forms. First, presidents are free to veto legislation passed by Congress that they dislike, although this has happened with only 3% of all federal legislation since George Washington was president[18] and vetoes can be overridden by a two-thirds vote in both the Senate and the House of Representatives. The second form of veto power is that of a veto threat, wherein presidents try to persuade Congress to alter a piece of legislation to their liking simply by threatening to veto it.

The second way a president can shape health and other policy is through the use of executive orders (EO). These are legally binding decisions that can influence the internal operations of the executive branch, the degree to which laws are enforced, the response to natural disasters and other emergencies, the waging of wars, and more. For example, one week into office President Biden issued an executive order titled "Strengthening Medicaid and the Affordable Care Act."[19] Among other things, the EO created a new, additional enrollment period to be used by people shopping for health insurance coverage under the Affordable Care Act and called on the Secretaries of the Departments of Health and Human Services, Labor, and Treasury to (1) suspend, revise, or rescind any regulations that limited Americans' access to health care and (2) consider actions that protect and strengthen health care access. Like the statutes written by the legislative branch and the regulations (described next) promulgated by executive branch agencies, EOs can be overturned by the judicial branch of government (in the case of EOs, if they are contrary to existing statutory or constitutional law). Finally, given their potential breadth, EOs are sometimes viewed as controversial because, as described previously, the legislative branch of government is alone tasked with "enacting" laws.

The third way the executive branch can shape health policy is through the implementation of statutes passed by Congress and signed into law by the president. By necessity, statutes are usually written broadly: Legislators simply do not have the expertise to include every detail about how a new program should operate or how a new department will be structured. As a result, executive branch agencies are left to fill in the details, which they do by promulgating regulations, developing rules, and issuing policy statements. Because executive branch agencies are created to deal with specific policy subject matters (think the Department of Education, the Department of Defense, the Department of Labor, and so on), they are best able to carry out statutory prerogatives that fall under their respective policy umbrellas.

Administrative law—as the rules and regulations of executive branch agencies are called—is crucial in the area of health law and policy. For example, consider the Medicaid program, which functions primarily as a health insurance program for low-income individuals. The Medicaid statute embodies Congress's intentions in passing the law, including standards pertaining to program eligibility, benefits, and payments to participating health care providers. Yet there are literally thousands of Medicaid administrative regulations and rules, which over the past 55 years have become the real battleground over the stability and scope of the program.

It is important to note that assuming the process for creating the regulations was itself legal and provided that the regulations do not stray beyond the intent of the enacted statute, regulations have the full force of law. In order to be lawful, regulations must be proposed and established in a way that conforms to the requirements of the federal Administrative Procedure Act of 1946, which provides procedural restrictions for agency rule making and adjudication.

Examples of Federal Executive Agencies That Influence Population Health and Well-Being

There are two main types of federal agencies: executive department and independent. Executive department agencies fall under direct control of the president. There are 15 of these

cabinet-level departments, and their directors (i.e., secretaries) serve at the pleasure of the president. By contrast, independent agencies are those that are established by Congress as functioning outside the Executive Office of the President. While still a part of the executive branch, these agencies are considered independent because they are not required to report to a higher official (e.g., a department secretary) and because the president has limited power to remove the agency's leader or staff. Instead, independent agency heads serve a fixed term unless they are removed "for cause" (i.e., for violating existing law or policy). There are dozens of federal independent agencies, including the Consumer Product Safety Commission, the Corporation for Public Broadcasting, the Equal Employment Opportunity Commission, the Securities and Exchange Commission, the National Transportation Safety Board, and the National Labor Relations Board.

Several federal administrative agencies—both executive department and independent—are concerned with health, health care, and/or public health. The most obvious of these is the U.S. Department of Health and Human Services (HHS), a sprawling entity that houses hundreds of medical, public health, and social services programs that provide care, information, research, and more to tens of millions of U.S. residents. The department includes 11 operating divisions; the main purpose of each one is described in **Table 3.2**.

Several other federal departments and agencies, in addition to HHS, play important roles in the health of the nation. For example, the Department of Agriculture is the federal government's leader on food, agriculture, natural resource, and nutrition policy. The Department of Defense (DoD) provides health insurance coverage to current and retired military personnel and their families through its TRICARE program, and it maintains a public health division that aims to prevent disease and disability across the armed services. The DoD also plays an important role in U.S. health security—an identified national

Table 3.2 U.S. Department of Health and Human Services Operating Divisions

Division	Main Purpose
Administration for Children and Families (ACF)	To "promote economic and social well-being of families, children, individuals, and communities" through educational and supportive programs
Administration for Community Living (ACL)	To increase "access to community support and resources" for older adults and people with disabilities
Agency for Healthcare Research and Quality (AHRQ)	To "produce evidence to make health care safer, high quality, more accessible, and affordable, and to work with HHS and other partners to make sure the evidence is understood and used"
Agency for Toxic Substances and Disease Registry (ATSDR)	To prevent "exposure to toxic substances and reduce the adverse health effects" associated with such exposure
Centers for Disease Control and Prevention (CDC)	To protect "the public health of the nation by providing leadership in the prevention and control of diseases and other preventable conditions" and to respond the public health emergencies
Center for Medicare and Medicaid Services (CMS)	To provide "oversight of Medicare, the federal portions of the Medicaid and State Children's Health Insurance Program, the Health Insurance Marketplace, and related quality assurance activities"
Food and Drug Administration (FDA)	To ensure that "food is safe, pure, and wholesome," drugs and medical devices are "safe and effective," and that "electronic products that emit radiation are safe"
Health Resources and Services Administration (HRSA)	To provide "health care to people who are geographically isolated, or economically or medically vulnerable"
Indian Health Services (IHS)	To provide "American Indians and Alaska Natives with comprehensive health services"
National Institutes of Health (NIH)	To support and conduct "biomedical and behavioral research," to train "promising young researchers," and to promote "collecting and sharing knowledge"
Substance Abuse and Mental Health Services Administration (SAMHSA)	To improve access to and "reduce barriers to high-quality, effective programs and services for individuals who suffer from or are at risk for addictive or mental disorders, as well as for their families and communities"

Wilensky, SE, & Teitelbaum, JB. (2020). Essentials of Health Policy and Law (Fourth Edition), Ch. 2. Burlington, MA: Jones & Bartlett Learning.

security issue—by countering biological threats through public health activities in conjunction with civilian agencies domestically and internationally. The Department of Education assesses national levels of health literacy (the degree to which individuals have the capacity to obtain, process, and understand basic health information and services) and recommends policy designed to promote the health and well-being of students (e.g., policy related to violence and drug prevention, homelessness, and exploited youth). The Environmental Protection Agency implements law across a range of areas, including air and water quality, climate change, hazardous waste cleanup, and sustainable energy, and it conducts research to better understand how health disparities can arise from unequal environmental conditions. The Department of Transportation collaborates with the HHS Centers for Disease Control and Prevention to examine the health impacts of transportation systems. And the Department of Veterans Affairs oversees the largest integrated health care system in the country, consisting of thousands of medical centers, nursing homes, and outpatient clinics. While the preceding list is not exhaustive, it gives a sense of the range of federal agencies that dedicate their expertise to the nation's health.

State and Local Executive Branch Health Policymaking

As noted earlier, the U.S. Constitution places primary responsibility for protecting the public's health with the states. In carrying out this responsibility, states utilize various health-related agencies not unlike those at the federal level. It is common for states to employ agencies concerned with health care financing and delivery, aging, behavioral health, environmental health, children and family services, student health, facility licensing and inspection, provider credentialing, and more, although their structure, powers, and lines of authority vary across the country. Furthermore, because population health is impacted by many social, economic, and environmental factors, state health agencies also conduct policy-relevant research, disseminate information aimed at helping people engage in healthy behaviors, provide prevention services like counseling and education, and establish collaborative relationships with health care providers and with other government policymaking agencies. Indeed, state health agencies are increasingly collaborating with government agencies with expertise in transportation, housing, and education to address the social drivers of health.

In addition, states empower local health departments (LHDs) to assist with public health responsibilities. Most commonly, LHDs report to a local government—such as a

county commission or local board of health—although in some states, state and local governments jointly oversee the LHD. The services provided by LHDs vary considerably, though there is an emphasis on addressing communicable diseases (through immunizations and disease surveillance systems), environmental health, mental health and substance use disorders, and children's health issues.

The Judicial Branch of Government and Health

Overview

Article III of the U.S. Constitution establishes the federal judicial branch of government,[20] and the constitution and laws of each state establish state courts.[21] Although the federal and state court systems have distinct authority, they do not look very different structurally; typically, there is a collection of justices, judges, magistrates, and other "adjudicators" spread across a collection of trial courts, a group of intermediate appellate courts, and a "court of last resort" (i.e., the single highest court in the federal or state system).

The main responsibility of courts is to interpret and apply the nation's laws. This entails deciding the meaning of constitutions, statutes, and regulations; protecting and enforcing individual legal rights; overseeing criminal and civil trials and appeals; and maintaining stability in the law through the application of legal precedent. One additional job of the judicial branch is to determine whether the legislative and executive branches of government have acted in a way that violates the law. This responsibility is carried out through the doctrine of "judicial review."[22] The theory behind judicial review is that, as the branch of government originally designed to be most independent of the political process (a topic further discussed later), courts can pass judgment on the actions of the political branches free of partisanship, financial pressure, and interest group influence.

Judicial Powers and Health Policy

The judiciary influences population health and health justice in myriad ways, and in so doing it frequently addresses some of the most emotionally charged social questions in the United States. When courts decide whether public health laws are constitutional (e.g., COVID-19-related mandates), determine the scope of individual legal rights (e.g., state abortion regulations), rule on whether executive branch agencies are acting according to their legislative authority (e.g., the termination of an individual's Medicaid benefits), or decide legal issues impacting the human rights of individuals or groups (e.g., the mental health care of border and immigrant youth), they are not just answering legal questions that affect individual litigants—they are setting legal precedents that potentially affect millions of people. What follows is just a fractional list of some of the more potent health justice topics commonly addressed by the judicial branch.

1. *Right to privacy*. The scope of the due process clause of the federal Constitution's Fourteenth Amendment is one of the most incandescent topics in health care and health justice because the clause rests at the heart of the U.S. Supreme Court's "right to privacy" jurisprudence, including the right to obtain an abortion. The provision prohibits states from depriving "any person of life, liberty, or property, without due process of law."[23] Although the Constitution makes no mention of "privacy," the Supreme Court, as early as the 1890s, has interpreted the word *liberty* to include some level of individual autonomy from governmental interference when making personal decisions. The right to privacy achieved real promi-

nence in 1965, when the Supreme Court ruled that the due process clause protects the liberty of married couples to buy and use contraceptives without government restriction.[24] After that decision, advocates of an expanded right to privacy flooded the federal courts with personal privacy cases. Two years later, the Supreme Court struck down laws banning interracial marriage.[25] In 1972, laws prohibiting unmarried individuals from using contraception were invalidated.[26] At that point, the stage was set for the Supreme Court's 1973 decision in *Roe v. Wade*, wherein the court ruled that the liberty guaranteed by the due process clause protects a pregnant woman's right to choose to have an abortion—up until the time of viability of the fetus—without excessive government interference.[27] Chapter 12 details the current state of the law with regard to reproductive rights.

2. *Police powers*. Earlier, we described police powers as the ability of states and localities to require conformance with standards of conduct designed to promote and protect the public's health, safety, and welfare. But the fact that government coercion *can* be justified by important public health goals does not answer the question of *when* it is justified or to what extent. These questions were addressed in the well-known case of *Jacobson v. Massachusetts*,[28] wherein the Supreme Court upheld the authority of states to enforce compulsory vaccination laws. Although the court put up some guardrails around states' coercive power, the decision is primarily animated by the notion of a social compact: Because each of us is part of a greater whole, there is no absolute individual right to live free from government restraint. If this idea sounds familiar even 115 years after the decision was handed down, chalk it up to the COVID-19 pandemic—the *Jacobson* decision has been described, debated, and cited by

many courts analyzing states' and cities' use of their emergency powers in an attempt to control the pandemic.[29]

3. *The Affordable Care Act.* The ACA has been challenged in state and federal courts nearly 2,000 times since its passage in 2010,[30] and the U.S. Supreme Court has already ruled on three separate occasions that there is nothing unconstitutional about the law (once ruling that the penalty for not carrying health insurance is a valid exercise of the congressional power to tax,[31] once ruling that ACA subsidies to help individuals and small businesses buy insurance were not somehow unlawful,[32] and most recently deciding that states that challenged the constitutionality of the individual mandate did not have the legal standing to bring the lawsuit in the first place[33]). This is a remarkable track record for a statute that is still in adolescence. The law has become enormously important for several reasons, not the least of which is the health insurance coverage it provides to some 31 million people. However, given that the ACA has become a political cudgel, there is little reason to expect the flow of lawsuits to slow. Chapter 7 describes in more detail how the court's assessment of the ACA affects health equity and justice.

4. *Firearm regulations.* One of the most contested issues in public health policy concerns the meaning and scope of the Second Amendment of the U.S. Constitution. One side of the debate argues that the amendment confers an individual right to possess firearms for private use; the other side claims that the language of the provision means that guns can only be tied to the collective right to maintain state militias.[34] The most prominent U.S. Supreme Court decision in this space is *District of Columbia v. Heller*,[35] a 2008 decision in which the court held that the Second Amendment protects an individual right to possess and use a gun for reasons unrelated to militia service, such as for self-defense within one's home. Ever since, federal and state courts have attempted to discern and apply the *Heller* decision to a range of state firearm regulations, resulting in confusion and additional lawsuits. For a country that eclipses the rest of the world in civilian-owned firearms,[36] experiences far higher rates of gun-related deaths than all other high-income countries,[37] and needs to confront the fact that young Black men and teens are killed by guns 20 times more frequently than their White counterparts,[38] the future direction of firearm jurisprudence is of paramount importance to health justice.[39]

5. *Religious liberty.* For many decades, the religious freedoms that Americans enjoy under federal and state law have been successfully balanced, more or less, with public health laws (e.g., the exemption of people with religious objections from public school vaccination mandates).[40] However, the nation may be witnessing an important shift to this delicate balance. In 1993, Congress passed the Religious Freedom Restoration Act,[41] and since that time 23 states have followed suit, greatly expanding the number of people who are able to seek religious-based exemptions from all manner of health and safety laws. Furthermore, in 2014 the U.S. Supreme Court interpreted the federal religious freedom law to mean that certain *corporations* can be exempt from regulations to which their owners religiously object (in this particular case, an ACA regulation requiring employers to cover certain contraceptives for their female employees).[42] If the trend of interpreting religious freedom laws expansively should continue, it has the potential to undermine the ability of government officials to act aggressively in the name

of public health. Later chapters in this book explore how religious freedom laws are affecting the health rights of particular population groups.

The Politicization of the Judicial Branch

The judicial branch is viewed as uniquely able to fulfill its responsibilities because by original design, it is the branch of government most insulated from politics. At the state level, however, this insulation is now more or less a fiction, as most state judges are subject to popular election, either at the time of initial selection or subsequently, when it is determined whether they will be retained as judges.[43] This is a practice carried out almost nowhere else in the world. At the federal level, at least, judges and justices are not elected but rather are nominated by the president and voted on by the Senate. If approved for the bench, they are granted life tenure under the Constitution (which may insulate them from politics, but the flip side of that coin is that it insulates them from public accountability too).

However, whether the federal judicial appointment process results in an impartial, nonpolitical judiciary is an open—and important—question in today's partisan environment given the many health injustices described throughout this text. Indeed, it is now common for individuals to spend decades being "groomed" for federal appellate judgeships; for politicians to portray the federal courts—and especially the U.S. Supreme Court—as little more than a political prize to be "won" or "lost"; for Senate votes on judicial nominees to fall along partisan lines; for federal law clerks to match the ideology of the president that appointed the judge or justice for whom they work; and for lawmakers to call out and sometimes attempt

to rein in judges' rulings with which they disagree.

There are several problems with a politicized judiciary,[44] but they all fall under the umbrella of legitimacy. Courts have no power to enforce their rulings or to allocate funds to bring them to life. Instead, the American public and the policymaking branches of government must be persuaded that court decisions are reasoned, just, and based on law, not on politics or ideology. As people become convinced that politics plays a role in judicial decision-making, the legitimacy of courts—and their decisions—erode.[45] After enough erosion, the public may begin to question the need to abide by judges' decisions, and policymakers may begin to question the need to respect the separation of powers between branches of government. Essentially, as politics eat into courts' perceived authority to make unpopular decisions and reign in legislative and regulatory abuses, individual rights—say, the ability of historically disenfranchised populations to participate in elections devoid of unlawful barriers—stand to suffer.

Conclusion

This chapter explored the ways in which the legislative, executive, and judicial branches of government influence population and individual health and well-being. Hopefully, you got a sense of the enormous range of population health drivers influenced by federal, state, and local governments and thus of the many ways that health justice advocates can strive for structural and policy change. Indeed, bear these governmental roles in mind as you turn to the next two chapters—on health-harming legal doctrines and human rights principles, respectively—and then as you begin to deeply explore structural inequity in Part 3.

References

1. U.S. Const. art. I, § 1; U.S. Const. art. I, § 8.

2. U.S. Const. art. I, § 1.

3. Gostin L. The formulation of health policy by the three branches of government. National Academy of Sciences. 1995. https://www.ncbi.nlm.nih.gov/books/NBK231979/.

4. Pub.L. 74–271, 49 Stat. 620 (1935).

5. 42 U.S.C. §§ 1396 et seq. (1965).

6. Pub.L. 93–406, 88 Stat. 829 (1974). Like the statute itself, even citations to ERISA are complicated, as the law's section numbers in the U.S. Code (where much of ERISA can be found under Title 29) do not always correspond to the section numbering in the original act as written by Congress. For a helpful website effectively decoding where ERISA provisions are located in the U.S. Code, go to http://benefitslink.com/erisa/crossreference.html.

7. 42 U.S.C. §§ 1395dd et seq. (1986).

8. Pub. L. No. 101-336, 104 Stat. 328 (1990).

9. Bragdon v. Abbott, 524 U.S. 624 (1998).

10. Pub. L. 104–191, 110 Stat. 1936 (1996).

11. 45 C.F.R. pt. 164 subpt. E (2000).

12. Pub. L. No. 111–148, 124 Stat. 119 (2010).

13. Lantz P, Rosenbaum S. The potential and realized impact of the Affordable Care Act on health equity. Journal of Health Politics, Policy, and Law. 2020;45(5):831–845.

14. Blumberg J, Holahan J, Buettgens M, Wang R. A path to incremental health reform: Improving affordability, expanding coverage, and containing costs. Robert Wood Johnson Foundation. December 2018. https://www.rwjf.org/en/library/research/2018/12/a-path-to-incremental-health-care-reform.html.

15. Dietz WH, Benken DE, Hunter AS. Public health law and the prevention and control of obesity. The Milbank Quarterly. 2009;87:215–227.

16. U.S. Const. art. II, § 1.

17. Wilensky SE, Teitelbaum JB. Essentials of Health Policy and Law. 4th ed., Ch. 2. Burlington, MA: Jones & Bartlett Learning; 2020.

18. H.R. Doc. No. 106-216, at 43 (2000).

19. Executive Order on Strengthening Medicaid and the Affordable Care Act. 2021. https://www.whitehouse.gov/briefing-room/presidential-actions/2021/01/28/executive-order-on-strengthening-medicaid-and-the-affordable-care-act/.

20. U.S. Const. art. III.

21. United States Courts. Comparing federal & state courts. https://www.uscourts.gov/about-federal-courts/court-role-and-structure/comparing-federal-state-courts.

22. Marbury v. Madison, 5 U.S. 137 (1803).

23. U.S. Const. amend. XIV, § 1.

24. Griswold v. Connecticut, 381 U.S. 479 (1965)

25. Loving v. Virginia, 388 U.S. 1 (1967).

26. Eisenstadt v. Baird, 405 U.S. 438 (1972).

27. Roe v. Wade, 410 U.S. 113 (1973).

28. Jacobson v. Massachusetts, 197 U.S. 11 (1905).

29. Parmet WE. The Covid cases: A preliminary assessment of judicial review of public health powers during a partisan and polarized pandemic. San Diego Law Review. 2020;57:999. https://digital.sandiego.edu/sdlr/vol57/iss4/6.

30. National Conference of State Legislatures. Legal cases and state legislative actions related to the ACA. 2021. https://www.ncsl.org/research/health/state-laws-and-actions-challenging-ppaca.aspx.

31. National Federation of Independent Business v. Sebelius, 567 U.S. 519 (2012).

32. King v. Burwell, 576 U.S. 473 (2015).

33. California v. Texas, 593 U.S. ___ (2020)

34. Teitelbaum J, Spector E. District of Columbia v. Heller: implications for public health policy and practice. Public Health Reports. 2009;124(5). https://journals.sagepub.com/doi/pdf/10.1177/003335490912400519.

35. District of Columbia v. Heller, 554 U.S. 570 (2008).

36. BBC News. America's gun culture in charts. 2021. https://www.bbc.com/news/world-us-canada-41488081.

37. NPR. How the U.S. compares with other countries in deaths from gun violence. 2019. https://www.npr.org/sections/goatsandsoda/2019/08/05/743579605/how-the-u-s-compares-to-other-countries-in-deaths-from-gun-violence.

38. Educational Fund to Stop Gun Violence. A public health crisis decades in the making. 2021. https://efsgv.org/wp-content/uploads/2019CDCdata.pdf.

39. Gostin LO, Parmet WE, Rosenbaum S. Health policy in the Supreme Court and a new conservative majority. JAMA. 2020;324(21):2157–2158.

40. Hodge Jr. JG. Respecting religious freedoms and protecting the public's health. Public Health Reports. 2015;130(5):546–549. https://www.ncbi.nlm.nih.gov/pmc/articles/PMC4529841/.

41. Pub. L.103-141, 107 Stat. 1488 (1993).

42. Burwell v. Hobby Lobby Stores, Inc., 573 U.S. 682 (2014).

43. Brennan Center for Justice. Judicial selection: Significant figures. 2015. https://www.brennancenter.org/rethinking-judicial-selection/significant-figures.

44. Brennan Center for Justice. Promote fair courts. 2021. https://www.brennancenter.org/issues/strengthen-our-courts/promote-fair-courts.

45. Brennan Center for Justice. New poll: Vast majority of voters fear campaign cash skews judges' decisions. 2013. https://www.brennancenter.org/our-work/analysis-opinion/new-pollvast-majority-voters-fear-campaign-cash-skews-judges-decisions.

CHAPTER 4

Health-Harming Legal Doctrines

LEARNING OBJECTIVES

By the end of this chapter you will be able to:

- Explain the meaning of the "no duty to treat" principle
- Describe how poverty is excluded from protection under federal antidiscrimination law
- Discuss what is meant by the term "the negative Constitution"
- Explain the difference between the right to legal counsel in criminal and in civil legal matters

Introduction

This chapter provides readers with an overview of the types of broad legal doctrines that can influence the health of tens of millions of people—even in cases in which the doctrines themselves have nothing specific to do with health care or public health practice. It thus considers the topic of health justice through a wide lens, so that from the outset readers understand that even arcane legal doctrines seemingly unrelated to health equity are at work to influence the nation's health in disproportionate ways. As the text progresses, the lens zooms in more and more, providing a series of images that portray health injustices in sharper relief.

Four legal doctrines were selected to serve as examples, a couple of which receive additional treatment in subsequent chapters. The selected doctrines were not chosen for their interrelatedness; indeed, in some cases, they have little to do with one another, aside from the fact that they all work in their own way to make it more difficult for many people to get and/or stay healthy. The first doctrine discussed is the only one of the four that is specific to health care services: the "no duty to treat" principle. This long-standing principle helps explain why there is no overarching right to health care in the United States. The second doctrine has to do with the fact that federal civil rights protections have never been extended to poverty in the same way they have been extended to race, ethnicity, gender, disability, age, and other traits or distinguishing qualities. We next discuss the notion of a "negative Constitution," which refers to the fact that the federal Constitution has been interpreted by the U.S. Supreme Court as not requiring the government to affirmatively act to protect the public's health and welfare. Lastly, we explain the difference between the right to legal counsel in criminal matters and in civil legal matters. The lack of such a right in the latter context can have enormous health consequences for low-income individuals and families.

The "No Duty to Treat" Principle

One of the most basic tenets in U.S. health law is that, generally speaking, individuals have no legal right to health care services (or to health insurance). As a result, there is no legal responsibility on the part of clinicians to provide health care upon request. This doctrine is referred to as the "no duty" or "no duty to treat" principle, which is perhaps most famously described in the case of *Hurley v. Eddingfield*. In that case, the Indiana Supreme Court was asked to pass judgment on the actions of one Dr. Eddingfield, whose lack of medical attention led to the death of a pregnant woman named Charlotte Burk. In the course of discussing whether the doctor had a legal relationship to Mrs. Burk sufficient to trigger a duty to treat, the court wrote that Indiana's medical licensing statute

> provides for . . . standards of qualification . . . and penalties for practicing without a license. The [state licensing] act is preventive, not a compulsive, measure. In obtaining the state's license (permission) to practice medicine, the state does not require, and the licensee does not engage, that he will practice at all or on other terms than he may choose to accept.[1]

In other words, according to the court, Dr. Eddingfield's medical license did not confer upon him an *obligation* to provide health care

services; rather, Indiana's licensure requirement existed in order to make sure that should a person actually decide to provide health care services, that person would have the necessary knowledge and skills to do so in an appropriate fashion. Viewed in this way, medical licenses are a form of quality control, not a mechanism for gaining access to services. The same can be said for the driver's licenses many of you have in your book bag or purse: In no way does a driver's license require that you take a vehicle out for a spin, today or ever; rather, as with a medical license, the point of your driver's license is to guarantee that should you choose to operate a motor vehicle, you are qualified to do so. Note, too, that just as Dr. Eddingfield's medical license did not grant Mrs. Burk access to his services, your driver's license does not grant you access to a car or truck.

In order to understand the power of the "no duty" principle, you should know one other thing about Dr. Eddingfield: Prior to Charlotte Burk's death, he served as her family physician. Put in more formal terms, the doctor had a preexisting relationship with the now-deceased patient. Clearly, the Indiana Supreme Court was aware of this fact from the record that was produced during the doctor's trial, and surely, you must be thinking, this fact would establish enough of a fiduciary relationship to hold Dr. Eddingfield accountable for the death of Mrs. Burk. However, under the law, physician–patient relationships must be established (and reestablished) for each specific "spell of illness," and thus past treatment alone is not enough to form a legally binding relationship in the present. Put differently, a physician–patient relationship does not exist as a general, continuous legal matter—even with one's primary care doctor—but rather it exists for a specific period of time and must be (re)established accordingly.

The United States generally treats health care as a commodity subject to market forces and to one's own economic status. Indeed, during the public debate in 1993 over President Bill Clinton's failed attempt at national health reform—one of several times the nation has debated whether to move away from the "no duty" principle and establish a right to health care—then—U.S. Representative Dick Armey (R-TX) stated that "health care is just a commodity, just like bread, and just like housing and everything else."[2] What is instructive about Representative Armey's quote is that, far from being a legal anomaly, the lack of a right to health care services is in line with the nation's overall approach to access to basic necessities. During the 1960s and early 1970s, with the tailwinds of the Civil Rights Movement filling their sails, a determined group of public interest lawyers and social reform activists pressed the federal courts for an interpretation of the Constitution that would have created an individual right to welfare. Under this view, the government would be required to provide individuals who suffered from "brutal need" with minimally adequate levels of health care, food, housing, and so on—the types of things referred to by Representative Armey. But in a series of cases, the Supreme Court rejected this notion of a constitutional right to welfare. Underpinning these decisions were views about the nature and design of the Constitution, the nation's free market philosophies, and more.

At the same time, the scope of the "no duty to treat" principle is not all-encompassing, as there are a few laws that chip away at it and thus carve out a right to health care services where otherwise it would not exist. For example, a federal law called the Examination and Treatment for Emergency Medical Conditions and Women in Labor Act grants all individuals, irrespective of one's ability to pay or a hospital's willingness to provide services, the right to an "appropriate screening examination" and, if an emergency condition is uncovered, to clinical services necessary to stabilize the patient. Basically, the law prevents hospitals from turning away people with medical emergencies—at least until those emergencies have been addressed to the point that the individual's condition will not materially worsen upon leaving the facility, at which time the "no

duty" principle kicks back in and the hospital is free to refuse further treatment. Additionally, both Medicaid and Medicare create legal rights to health care benefits and services for individuals who meet the programs' eligibility criteria, but then again, these services are only carried out by health care providers who choose in the first instance to participate in the programs themselves. (Recall the analogy between a medical license and a driver's license; in the case of providers who choose not to participate in Medicaid and Medicare, they are effectively choosing the types of cars they don't want to drive.) Finally, some private health insurance products obligate physicians participating in the delivery of those products to provide care to individuals who purchase those products; essentially, for purposes of this discussion, delivery of care under these private health insurance policies operates like the delivery of Medicaid and Medicare services, in the sense that physicians decide whether to become "participating providers" in private health insurance plans.

The basic upshot of the "no duty" principle is that individuals can access health care services if (1) they have the means to pay for health care services outright; (2) they have the means to pay for private health insurance premiums, deductibles, and copayments; (3) they have been singled out for public insurance coverage on the basis of medical condition, age, or income; or (4) they are lucky enough to stumble into free services through the magnanimity of ethics-conscious health care providers. It almost goes without saying that this approach to health care results in enormous gaps: The nation suffers from disparities in health care access, diagnosis, treatment, and outcomes, based on a range of factors including race, ethnicity, socioeconomic status, physical and mental disability, age, gender, sexual orientation, and immigration status, as discussed in various chapters throughout this textbook. Furthermore, it is not uncommon for people to delay or forgo care altogether on the basis of cost.[3]

The Exclusion of Poverty from Protection Under the Constitution

In the chapter on socioeconomic status and health, you will learn about the close connection between poverty and poor health. As a backdrop to that discussion, we describe here the way in which poverty has been treated under the federal Constitution—namely, as undeserving of rigorous antidiscrimination protection. Certain characteristics such as race, national origin, religion, and sex have been declared "suspect" or "quasi-suspect" classes by the U.S. Supreme Court, a designation that indicates that people have suffered governmental discrimination on the basis of these characteristics in the past. As a result, the Court has interpreted the federal Constitution's Equal Protection Clause in a way that grants special protection against discrimination to these classes. However, the Court has never ruled that the impoverished are a protected class. Furthermore, the Court has protected over time certain fundamental rights—including rights not explicitly set out in the Constitution—under the Constitution's Due Process Clause. Notwithstanding a series of cases the Court heard during the civil rights era, the Court has yet to find that individuals have a fundamental right to even the most basic necessities.

Overview of Equal Protection Jurisprudence

Under the Equal Protection Clause of the Fourteenth Amendment to the federal Constitution, states are generally prohibited from governing in ways that single out particular groups for unequal treatment.[4] Nonetheless, a state will often pass laws that treat certain groups differently than others, such as a law that prohibits men—but not women—under a certain age from purchasing alcohol.[5] As described later, whether this law (and many others that similarly differentiate among groups of people, regardless of the context) is constitutional depends in large part upon how deeply a court scrutinizes a legislature's goals in passing the law. The important idea that there should be different levels of judicial scrutiny when undertaking equal protection analyses was born in a surprising place: a footnote in a 1938 Supreme Court decision considering a state law concerning milk. In discussing the Court's practice to normally defer to states about their reasons for passing laws, Justice Harlan Stone recognized that, in contrast to economic laws like the one before the Court, "prejudice against discrete and insular minorities may be a special condition, which tends seriously to curtail the operation of those political processes ordinarily to be relied upon to protect minorities, and which may call for a correspondingly more searching judicial inquiry."[6] In other words, when legislatures pass laws that disadvantage "discrete and insular minorities," the lawmakers may have been motivated not by neutral governmental goals like safety but rather by prejudice or animus. As a result, courts should be in the habit of carefully scrutinizing those laws that may have been corrupted by hostility toward certain minority groups.

One question the Court has had to answer several times since 1938 is: Which groups are "discrete and insular minorities"? Although the Court has not ruled that any particular set of criteria must be satisfied in order to qualify a group as a "suspect class," it has generally asked at least three questions when considering this question:

1. Has the group in question historically been discriminated against or been subject to prejudice, hostility, or stigma?
2. Does the group possess an immutable or highly visible trait?
3. Is the group generally powerless to protect itself through the political process?

Only a few years after writing its famous footnote, the Supreme Court determined that laws "which curtail the civil rights of a single racial group are immediately suspect," and as a result, the Court will apply "the most rigid scrutiny" when deciding their constitutionality.[7] Under this "strict scrutiny" test, as it has come to be known, race-based classifications will be upheld only if the law has a compelling government interest and is narrowly tailored to achieving it. Strict scrutiny has proven to be a difficult standard to overcome because it is very hard for a state legislature to show that a law favoring one race over another has a compelling governmental objective behind it. The Court now also applies strict scrutiny to laws treating U.S. citizens differently than noncitizens, laws singling out individuals based on their national origin, and laws infringing fundamental rights.

Through the process of deciding which groups are worthy of enhanced protection from discrimination, the Supreme Court determined that laws that treat men and women differently are not as plainly troubling as classifications based on race, national origin, or citizenship status. As a result, the Court deemed sex-based laws "quasi-suspect," subjecting them not to strict but to "intermediate" scrutiny. Under this standard, states must show that a law that classifies people on the basis of sex serves important governmental objectives and is substantially related to the achievement of those objectives.[8]

Applying a variety of factors, with varying degrees of consistency, the Court has found that not all groups singled out for disparate treatment should be subjected to strict or even intermediate scrutiny.[9] If the Court determines that the classification is neither suspect nor quasi-suspect, it applies the lowest standard of review, termed "rational basis" review. Laws nearly always survive this type of review. For example, the Supreme Court upheld a Massachusetts law that required police officers to retire at age 50, refusing to find that age was a suspect or quasi-suspect classification, citing no history of discrimination and the fact that older people cannot be a discrete, insular minority because everyone ages. The Court scrutinized the law only to the extent of asking whether the law was rationally related to a legitimate state interest and was satisfied with testimony that, because people tend to decline physically at age 50, the law serves the state's interest in public safety.[10] However, even when applying rational basis review, the Court will refuse to uphold a law if it is based upon "a bare ... desire to harm a politically unpopular group."[11]

Overview of Substantive Due Process Jurisprudence

Just as the Fourteenth Amendment limits the ability of governments to single out particular groups for unequal treatment, it also protects individuals from laws that infringe too severely upon fundamental rights guaranteed by the Constitution. This is known as the guarantee to "substantive due process" because the protections stem from the Fourteenth Amendment's due process clause. Some fundamental rights, like the right to vote, are explicitly included in the text of the Constitution. Others, however, are not explicitly mentioned but are so "deeply rooted in the nation's history and tradition" and "implicit in the concept of ordered liberty" that the Supreme Court has deemed them to be fundamental (for example, rights related to marriage, contraception, procreation, and child-rearing).

As with determining which suspect or quasi-suspect groups fall under the equal protection umbrella, the Court has grappled with determining which implicit rights are worthy of being classified as fundamental. In what is clearly the most famous example, the Court found in *Roe v. Wade* that the fundamental (but implicit) right to privacy was expansive enough to encompass a woman's right to choose to terminate a pregnancy under certain circumstances.[12]

Efforts to Apply Equal Protection and Substantive Due Process to Laws Affecting the Poor

Concurrent with other social movements of the time, the 1960s and early 1970s brought about a fight for equality for poor people, as advocates sought to publicize the harms associated with persistent poverty, poor nutrition, dangerous housing, and substandard education. And while the federal Aid to Families with Dependent Children (AFDC) program (which started in 1935 as a relatively minor expenditure but became a nearly $30 billion program by the mid-1970s) provided assistance for struggling families, the often humiliating and burdensome legal requirements imposed by states in administering it solidified the general view that recipients were second-class citizens.[13] Poverty lawyers launched challenges to these state laws on various grounds, including the argument that they infringed upon an implicit fundamental right: the right to live at a basic level of subsistence.

The first state welfare law challenge that made its way to the U.S. Supreme Court, in a case called *King v. Smith,* was successful—just not on constitutional grounds. In the *King* case, the state of Alabama terminated welfare benefits to a single mother because she occasionally cohabitated with a man who was not her husband, on the grounds that this man acted as a "substitute father" and could support the woman's children. The Supreme Court rejected this argument, finding it to be a violation of the federal AFDC statute, which only denied benefits where legal parents—but not men who cohabitate with single mothers—were able to provide support.[14] *King v. Smith* marked a victory for the welfare rights movement, but it did nothing to improve efforts to gain special status for the poor under the Constitution.

The second welfare benefits case to be heard by the Court, *Shapiro v. Thompson,* challenged a Connecticut rule that denied welfare benefits to families that had lived in the state for less than a year. This time, the Court decided the case on constitutional grounds, holding that the rule infringed on the plaintiff's implicit fundamental right to travel and could not survive strict scrutiny.[15] Even though the Court held that the law infringed upon the right to travel and not on a right to live, the decision resulted in a "euphoric reception from welfare lawyers," who hoped "that strict scrutiny would soon be extended to state welfare law classifications, heralding the end of geographic differences in welfare grants and moving inexorably toward a constitutional right to live."[16]

Soon after, in 1970, poverty lawyers recorded another victory in *Goldberg v. Kelly*, when the Court held that welfare benefits could not be terminated without an evidentiary hearing. Importantly, the Court considered the welfare benefits to be "statutory entitlements" rather than charity, but it did not go so far as to find that the poor have a constitutional right to receive welfare benefits.[17] Nevertheless, the Court noted that

…important governmental interests are promoted by affording recipients a pre-termination evidentiary hearing. From its founding, the Nation's basic commitment has been to foster the dignity and wellbeing of all persons within its borders. We have come to recognize that forces not within the control of the poor contribute to their poverty…Welfare, by meeting the basic demands of subsistence, can help bring within the reach of the poor the same opportunities that are available to others to participate meaningfully in the life of the community… Public assistance, then, is not mere charity, but a means to "promote the general Welfare, and secure the Blessings of Liberty to ourselves and our Posterity." The same governmental interests that counsel the provision of welfare, counsel as well its uninterrupted provision to those eligible to receive it; pre-termination evidentiary hearings are indispensable to that end.[18]

The Court's strong language—and its quotation of the Preamble to the Constitution—suggested to some that the Court was sloping toward a future ruling that those mired in poverty had a right to public assistance, thus taking another step closer to recognizing a right to live.

However, the Court abruptly halted this trajectory in *Dandridge v. Williams*, decided just a few weeks after *Goldberg*. The issue in *Dandridge* was whether a Maryland regulation setting a family maximum limit for welfare benefits violated the Equal Protection Clause because it unfairly disadvantaged families with more children by providing less money per child. The Court was blunt in its assessment, characterizing state welfare rules as the type of "intractable economic, social and even philosophical problems" that are "not the business of this Court." Applying the lowest level of scrutiny, the Court upheld the law as rationally related to the state's legitimate interests, including encouraging employment.[19]

In another case arguing for special legal status for poor people, called *San Antonio Independent School District v. Rodriguez*, students in a poor area of San Antonio challenged Texas' method of funding public education. The method, wherein school districts in relatively wealthy areas provided more funding per student than did districts with poorer residents, was challenged under the Equal Protection Clause for providing lower-quality education to poor children. In response, the Supreme Court refused to find that children living in poorer school districts were entitled to a public education equal to that of children from wealthier families, noting that it had never found that wealth is a suspect class entitled to strict scrutiny.[20] The Court wrote that "at least where wealth is involved, the Equal Protection Clause does not require absolute equality or precisely equal advantages." The Court contrasted this case to earlier decisions, in which wealth-based classifications completely deprived individuals of important services and were struck down as a result. As a result, the Court applied rational basis review and affirmed Texas's funding scheme.

Future Prospects for Granting Poverty Special Status

The line of welfare rights cases culminating in *Dandridge* seems to foreclose a finding that there is a fundamental right to live, a right for which many poverty lawyers had fought.[21] But the Court's language in *Goldberg* at least suggests a way forward for future arguments that a person mired in poverty has a right to a basic level of subsistence. Since public assistance, in the form of welfare, subsidized housing, subsidized nutrition, a quality education, and more, is needed to sustain even a meager existence for millions of adults and kids, perhaps society should consider whether a legally recognized, even if implicit, fundamental right to live should be "found" in the nation's Constitution.[22]

Furthermore, although the Supreme Court in *Rodriguez* was stating the obvious when it said it has never held that poverty is a suspect class, this is primarily a product of the Court's unwillingness to address the question directly.[23] Were the Court to consider the standards under which other classifications have been deemed suspect, it could certainly find that laws singling out the poor should be more closely scrutinized. As the state welfare laws noted previously demonstrate, there is a long history of discrimination against the poor. Further, there can be no doubt that low-income individuals lack political power, given that ordinary political processes are often dominated by corporate interests and wealthy individuals.[24] At the very least, laws that discriminate against the poor and are rooted in "a bare ... desire to harm a politically unpopular group" should be subjected to more searching review.[25]

The "Negative Constitution"

We turn now to a third health-harming legal doctrine, this one termed "the negative Constitution." This discussion certainly dovetails with the preceding one, since the negative Constitution helps explain why certain positive rights (like rights to tangible things, including food or health care services) are not often found to exist as a federal constitutional matter.

By way of background, we start with a description of what are known as "police powers." These powers represent state and local government authority to require conformance with certain standards of conduct meant to protect the public's health, safety, and welfare. Put less formally, a state's police powers allow it to control—to some extent—personal and corporate activities that may harm the public's health if left unbridled. There are many examples of police powers: Health care providers must obtain licenses from state agencies before practicing medicine; health care facilities must meet and maintain certain accreditation standards; restaurants are heavily regulated by states and localities; employers must follow many occupational health and safety rules; buildings have "codes" that must be followed when they are designed, built, and maintained; certain industries are constrained by pollution control measures; the marketing and sale of tobacco products are regulated by law; motorcyclists must wear helmets; and passengers in cars must wear seat belts. If you stopped to think about it for a couple minutes, you would likely generate many more examples of the ways in which your daily activities are shaped by governmental police powers.

As the preceding list indicates, police powers can be rather coercive, if not downright invasive. However, these powers are not absolute, and at some point they give way to the individual freedoms and liberties we have come to cherish as Americans. Furthermore, police powers can never be used to purely punish individuals—since their purpose is the promotion of public health—they cannot be administered arbitrarily, and they cannot be used for purposes unrelated to public welfare.

After reading about police powers, many students reasonably believe that states must protect the public health and welfare through affirmative use of these powers. The U.S. Supreme Court has never interpreted the Constitution in this way, however. Rather, the Court has viewed the Constitution as empowering the government to act in the name of public health, in the event a state chooses to do so. (This is reminiscent of the act of licensing—for both doctors and drivers—discussed in the previous section on the "no duty to treat" principle.) This, you may have guessed, is what is meant by "the negative Constitution." This doctrine holds that the Constitution does not require government to provide any goods or services whatsoever, public health or otherwise, and derives from the fact that the Constitution is phrased mainly in negative terms—for example, the Constitution's First Amendment doesn't affirmatively state that citizens have a right to free speech, it says that Congress "shall make no law" abridging the freedom of speech. This view of the Constitution, to paraphrase Judge Richard Posner, maintains that the drafters of the document were more concerned with what government would do to people rather than what government should do for them. In this way, the Constitution exerts a negative force that limits governmental power to restrain us as individuals rather than compelling government to promote public health through tangible goods and services.

The application of the negative Constitution doctrine is starkly witnessed in two Supreme Court decisions—*DeShaney v. Winnebago County Department of Social Services* and *Town of Castle Rock, Colorado v. Gonzales*[26]—which both have terribly distressing facts at their core. In the *DeShaney* case, a one-year-old named Joshua DeShaney was placed in his father's custody after his parents divorced.

Over the span of the next three years, multiple people—including the father's second wife and various emergency room personnel—complained to social services workers in Wisconsin that the father had been abusing Joshua physically. While county officials opened a case file and interviewed Joshua's father on multiple occasions, each time they decided that they didn't have sufficient evidence of child abuse to remove Joshua from the house and place him in court custody. When Joshua was four years old, he suffered a horrific beating at the hands of his father. He eventually survived a life-threatening coma but was left with permanent brain damage, and he was expected to live the remainder of his life in an institution for the mentally disabled. Subsequently, Joshua's father was convicted of child abuse.

Joshua's mother filed a civil rights lawsuit against the Wisconsin social services workers who failed to remove him from his abusive father's home. A 6–3 majority of the U.S. Supreme Court turned away the lawsuit in 1989, finding that under the Due Process Clause state officials had no affirmative constitutional duty to protect Joshua:

> [N]othing in the language of the Due Process Clause itself requires the State to protect the life, liberty, and property of its citizens against invasion by private actors. The Clause is phrased as a limitation on the State's power to act, not as a guarantee of certain minimal levels of safety and security. It forbids the State itself to deprive individuals of life, liberty, or property without "due process of law," but its language cannot fairly be extended to impose an affirmative obligation on the State to ensure that those interests do not come to harm through other means.[27]

The Court majority then went even further, ruling that while the state knew that Joshua was in danger and expressed a willingness to protect him against that danger, those facts were not enough to establish the type of affirmative duty to rescue reserved for parties who have (for purposes of the Constitution) a "special relationship."

Three Justices dissented. They argued that the State of Wisconsin, through its establishment of a child protection program, undertook a duty to intervene in Joshua's life and that its failure to meet this duty violated the Constitution. The dissenters complained that, in effect, Wisconsin's program displaced private sources of child protection but then ignored the very harm it was meant to prevent.

Sixteen years after *DeShaney*, the Supreme Court again took up the question of whether the government has a duty to affirmatively protect its citizens. Sadly, the facts in *Castle Rock v. Gonzales* are as tragic as those in *DeShaney*. Jessica Gonzales received a restraining order protecting her and her three young daughters from her husband, who was also the girls' father. One June afternoon, all three girls disappeared from in front of her home. She suspected that her husband had taken the girls in violation of the court order, a suspicion she was able to confirm through a phone call to her husband. In two initial phone conversations with the Castle Rock (Colorado) Police Department, Mrs. Gonzalez was told there was nothing the police could do and to wait until 10:00 p.m. to see if anything changed.

Nothing had changed by 10:00 p.m., so Jessica again called the police, at which time she was again told to wait, this time until midnight. After this process played out yet another time, she went to her husband's apartment. Finding it empty, she went to the police station in person. Rather than attempt to locate the missing girls, the police officer who wrote up Jessica's report went to dinner. A couple hours later, Jessica's husband pulled his truck up to and began shooting at the Castle Rock Police Department. The police returned fire, killing him. Jessica's three daughters were found dead in the back of her husband's truck, having been murdered by their father some hours earlier.

Jessica sued the police department, claiming that its inaction violated the Constitution. Specifically, she argued that the restraining order she received was "property" and that the police effectively "took" this property in violation of the Due Process Clause's requirement that no state "deprive any person of life, liberty, or property, without due process of law." By a 7–2 margin, however, the Supreme Court ruled in favor of the town of Castle Rock, ruling that Jessica did not have an individual entitlement to enforcement of a Colorado law that requires police officers to use all reasonable means to execute restraining orders. The Court then said that even if it had found such an entitlement, there was uncertainty as to whether the entitlement would rise to the level of a protected "property" interest that triggers constitutional protections. According to the Court, the Due Process Clause does not protect all government "benefits," including things that government officials have discretion to grant or deny. (For example, because police departments have finite resources, officers have discretion to consider whether a violation of a restraining order is too minor to justify enforcement.)

Taken as a whole, the negative Constitution doctrine and the cases that apply it raise a couple important questions in the broad context of health, welfare, and safety. First, given our deep reliance on government to organize social and economic life in a way that creates conditions for us to be healthy, what do you think about a legal doctrine that holds that government has no affirmative obligation to provide services or to shield even the most vulnerable among us from another person's violence? Second, if we can't rely on the courts to check even the worst instances of government workers' failure to act, what's to prevent those same workers from "using" their inaction to harm certain people or groups (e.g., withholding important benefits from certain groups or withholding necessary services from certain neighborhoods)?

No Right to Counsel in Civil Legal Matters

The fourth and final legal doctrine discussed as a background matter concerns the ability of individuals to afford and access help when trying to enforce complex civil legal rights. This ability is, in many ways, as important as the right itself, for what good are rights to, say, food stamps, a mold-free apartment, and Medicaid benefits if the holder of the rights can't actually get those things? Because the enforcement of legal rights is so important—particularly for low-income and other vulnerable populations whose reliance on social programs and services is often a quality-of-life or life-and-death matter—it makes sense to ask what rules and systems are in place to help people enforce their legal rights. To answer this somewhat complicated question in a succinct way, it is instructive to consider the difference between rights that attach in the area of criminal legal representation and those that exist in the realm of civil legal assistance. It is worth noting at the outset that the United States is one of the only countries that completely separates access to criminal and civil legal services.

Criminal Legal Representation

Per the Sixth Amendment to the U.S. Constitution, the government is required to provide legal counsel to all federal defendants who are unable to afford their own attorneys. The right to counsel in state criminal prosecutions was established (though only for serious offenses) by the U.S. Supreme Court in the well-known case of *Gideon v. Wainwright*.[28] The case started after Clarence Gideon was arrested for burglary. Indigent and unable to secure the services of private legal counsel, he asked the trial court to assign him a lawyer. Denied by the court, Gideon represented himself. He was found guilty and sentenced to five years in state prison.

Gideon appealed his conviction to the U.S. Supreme Court, claiming that the state court's refusal to grant him legal assistance violated his constitutional rights. The Supreme Court agreed to hear Gideon's case (and assigned him a highly respected lawyer). The Court eventually ruled in Gideon's favor, holding that the assistance of counsel, if desired by an indigent defendant, was a guaranteed right under the U.S. Constitution when states prosecuted people for serious crimes. Along with a new trial, Gideon received government-financed legal services, and he was cleared of all charges just a few months after the Supreme Court's landmark ruling.

Gideon v. Wainwright led to many changes in how the indigent are represented in criminal cases. For example, the decision effectively created the need for criminal lawyers employed at public expense—what are known today as public defenders—and its importance extends not only to subsequent cases concerning legal representation at trial and on appeal but also to cases dealing with police interrogation and the well-known right to remain silent.

Civil Legal Assistance

Unlike the case for serious or high-risk criminal cases, there is no generalized right to the assistance of a lawyer in civil matters—even for the indigent and even when the most basic human needs are at stake. While states have created rights to counsel in situations dealing with the termination of parental rights, paternity, juvenile abuse, and involuntary commitment to mental health facilities, it is rare for individuals to have rights to legal assistance in very common and critical areas of civil law, including health care, immigration status, domestic violence, veterans benefits, disability needs, child custody, housing, public benefits, employment disputes, special education needs, and more. In all of these types of disputes—which can be incredibly complex and which can have life-altering consequences—individuals and families can harbor no

expectation that an attorney will be on hand to help them. Instead, because they cannot afford legal fees, it is commonplace for the indigent, a growing portion of the middle class, and many small businesses to simply give up or go it alone when it comes to important civil legal needs. (Contrast this with the approach of the countries in the European Union, all of which have had a right to civil legal assistance for decades.)

Importantly, there is a legal safety net for the poorest segment of our population, who can at least try to access what are known as civil legal aid services. These services are provided by a network of publicly funded legal aid agencies, private lawyers and law firms offering free or near-free legal assistance, and law school clinics run by faculty and staffed by students. Unfortunately, however, there is far more need than there is capacity to handle that need. In the end, usually only those individuals with the lowest incomes receive assistance: some 80% of low-income individuals and 40% to 60% of middle-class individuals suffer from legal needs that go unmet. This equates to tens of millions of people who cannot access the legal assistance they need to save their homes, their jobs, their rightful public benefits, and the like.[29]

As a matter of pure funding, the U.S. Congress is most to blame for the enormous gap that exists between civil legal needs and resources. Congress holds the purse strings of the Legal Services Corporation (LSC), a not-for-profit corporation established by federal law in 1974 as the single largest funder of civil legal aid for low-income Americans. In today's dollars, LSC's congressional appropriation in 1976 was about $479,000,000; in 2019, that number was $440,000,000. But this $39,000,000 reduction does not tell the whole story, for over the 43-year-period just referred to, need has soared—meaning that LSC's budget should be much higher than even its inflation-adjusted 1976 budget just to keep pace with increased need over time.

The link between civil legal problems and health is underlined by the Community Needs and Services Study, an examination of the civil justice experiences of the American public.[30] According to the study, two-thirds of adults in a middle-sized American city experienced at least 1 of 12 different categories of civil justice situations in the previous 18 months. Notably, the average number of situations reported rested at 3.3, and poor people, Blacks, and Hispanics were more likely to report civil justice situations than were middle- or high-income earners and Whites. The most commonly reported situations concerned employment issues, government benefits, health insurance, and housing. The study uncovered significant connections between civil justice situations and health: Respondents indicated that nearly half of the situations resulted in feelings of fear, a loss of confidence, damage to physical or mental health, or verbal or physical violence or threats of violence. In fact, adverse impacts on health were the most common negative consequence, reported for 27% of situations. Also important is the fact many of those who responded indicated that they didn't even know that the problems they were experiencing were rightly considered "legal" in nature. The link between civil legal needs and health will be more fully explored in subsequent chapters.

Conclusion

As evidenced by the legal doctrines described in this chapter, the nation's health has much more than just social support deficiencies and luck working against it; it has long-standing, deeply rooted legal doctrines to account for as well. Creating universal health insurance coverage? That could easily be done by way of a federal statute, assuming the political will was present. A shift in national spending priorities away from downstream medical procedures in favor of more upstream social care? In other nations similar to our own, this is the norm, so it can't be that difficult. And universal health insurance and social drivers of health are, at least, relatively common discussion topics among policymakers. But realigning bedrock legal principles that in some cases don't even conjure up the notion of "health consequences" for most people? That is a true challenge. One of the aims of this text is simply to help laypeople understand that things like "suspect classifications" and "the negative Constitution" are important legal principles that pertain to the nation's health. After you've read the text in its entirety, it is our hope that it will become one of your aims as well.

References

1. *Hurley v. Eddingfield*, 59 N.E. 1058 (Ind. 1901).
2. Reinhardt U. The debate that wasn't: the public and the Clinton health care plan. In Aaron H., ed. *The Problem That Won't Go Away: Reforming U.S. Health Care Financing.* Washington, DC: Brookings Institution; 1996:70–109, 102.
3. Amin K, Claxton G, Ramirez G, Cox C. How does cost affect access to care? Peterson-KFF Health System Tracker. January 5, 2021. https://www.healthsystemtracker.org/chart-collection/cost-affect-access-care/#item-start.
4. Nice JA. No scrutiny whatsoever: Deconstitutionalization of poverty law, dual rules of law and dialogic default. *Fordham Urban Law Journal.* 2008;35:630–631.
5. See *Craig v. Boren*, 429 U.S. 190 (1976).
6. *United States v. Carolene Products Co.*, 304 U.S. 144, 152–153 n. 4 (1938).
7. *Korematsu v. United States*, 323 U.S. 214, 216 (1944).
8. *Craig v. Boren*, 429 U.S. 190, 197 (1976).
9. For a summary of the Court's analyses in determining suspect and quasi-suspect classes, see Rose H. The poor as a suspect class under the Equal Protection Clause: An open constitutional question. *Nova Law Review.* 2010;48:419–420.
10. *Massachusetts Board of Retirement v. Murgia*, 427 U.S. 307 (1976).
11. *Romer v. Evans*, 517 U.S. 620, 635 (1996).
12. *Roe v. Wade*, 410 U.S. 113, 152–153 (1973).

13. Davis MF. *Brutal Need: Lawyers and the Welfare Rights Movement, 1960–1973.* New Haven, CT: Yale University Press; 1993:Chapters 1–2.

14. *King v. Smith*, 392 U.S. 309, 332–333 (1968).

15. *Shapiro v. Thompson*, 394 U.S. 618, 633 (1969).

16. Davis MF. *Brutal Need: Lawyers and the Welfare Rights Movement, 1960–1973.* New Haven, CT: Yale University Press; 1993:80.

17. *Goldberg v. Kelly*, 397 U.S. 254, 262 (1970).

18. *Goldberg v. Kelly*, 397 U.S. 254, 262 (1970).

19. *Dandridge v. Williams*, 397 U.S. 471, 486–487 (1970).

20. *San Antonio Independent School Dist. v. Rodriguez*, 411 U.S. 1, 29 (1973). The Court also held that education is not a fundamental right but went on to say that the children were receiving an education, even if it was substandard.

21. Davis MF. *Brutal Need: Lawyers and the Welfare Rights Movement, 1960–1973.* New Haven, CT: Yale University Press; 1993:Chapter 9.

22. See Nice JA. No scrutiny whatsoever: Deconstitutionalization of poverty law, dual rules of law and dialogic default. *Fordham Urban Law Journal.* 2008;35:633.

23. Rose H. The poor as a suspect class under the Equal Protection Clause: An open constitutional question. *Nova Law Review.* 2010;34(2):408.

24. Nice JA. No scrutiny whatsoever: Deconstitutionalization of poverty law, dual rules of law and dialogic default. *Fordham Urban Law Journal.* 2008;35:648.

25. *Romer v. Evans*, 517 U.S. 620, 635 (1996). See Dyson MR. Rethinking Rodriguez after Citizens United: The poor as a suspect class in high-poverty schools. *Georgetown Journal on Poverty Law & Policy.* 2016;24(1),1–58.

26. 489 U.S. 189 (1989) and 545 U.S. 748 (2005), respectively.

27. 489 U.S. at 195 (1989).

28. 372 U.S. 335 (1963).

29. Legal Services Corporation. The Justice Gap: Measuring the Unmet Civil Legal Needs of Low-Income Americans. Prepared by NORC at the University of Chicago for Legal Services Corporation. Washington, DC; 2017. https://www.lsc.gov/sites/default/files/images/TheJusticeGap-FullReport.pdf.

30. Sandefur RL. *Accessing justice in the contemporary USA: Findings from the Community Needs and Services Study.* Chicago, IL: American Bar Foundation; 2014. http://www.americanbarfoundation.org/uploads/cms/documents/sandefur_accessing_justice_in_the_contemporary_usa._aug._2014.pdf.

CHAPTER 5

International Human Rights, Health, and the Failure of United States Leadership

LEARNING OBJECTIVES

By the end of this chapter you will be able to:

- Describe the international human rights regime
- Explain the right to health under international human rights standards
- Discuss predominant U.S. government attitudes concerning international human rights standards, including the human right to health

Introduction

Conceptually, human rights are universally recognized principles and opportunities that apply to everyone, independent of location, status in society, culture, religion, race, nationality, and so on. In other words, they are rights afforded to all human beings simply as a function of being human. Human rights represent a key component of a truly just society.

Notwithstanding the universal nature of human rights, countries vary widely in their approach to them—some countries weave human rights principles throughout their organizing documents and public systems and strive to enforce them (e.g., Iceland, Norway), others flaunt human rights protections on the global stage (e.g., Egypt, Syria), and the others fall somewhere on a spectrum between these two poles. Furthermore, some nations contend that cultural and/or religious idiosyncrasies represent acceptable limitations to the concept of human rights universality, but outside these nations, this view is widely shunned.

As you will read in more detail in the text that follows, the United States, generally speaking, is more talk than action when it comes to human rights enforcement. While the U.S. government champions human rights around the world—insisting that other countries protect human rights, even imposing sanctions for a failure to do so—it is not nearly as robust in championing and protecting these rights on U.S. soil. In fact, given its general unwillingness to join other countries in "advancing and adhering to the international framework of human rights laws," some experts have characterized the United States as a human rights "rogue state."[1] At the very least, the United States' focus on civil and political rights at the expense of economic and social ones disappoints human rights advocates in and outside the United States.

The U.S. approach notwithstanding, applying a human rights framework to notions of health justice is not a novel concept. For example, the 1948 Universal Declaration of Human Rights (UDHR)—which for the first time laid out fundamental human rights to be universally protected and which inspired dozens of human rights treaties—includes a reference to health as part of the right to an adequate standard of living. More than a decade ago, the World Health Organization Commission on the Social Determinants of Health wrote that "[t]he international human rights framework is the appropriate conceptual and legal structure within which to advance towards health equity...."[2] And even a cursory search for literature that links human rights and health results in hundreds of documents.

These links between human rights and health are explored later. This chapter begins by describing generally the international human rights regime. It then turns to a discussion of the ways in which this regime promotes and protects health as a human right and concludes by exploring U.S. attitudes toward widely accepted international human rights standards.

The International Human Rights Regime

Overview

An international regime is a "set of principles, norms, rules and decision-making procedures" established by nations to guide their behavior in a specific subject area.[3] In the case of human rights, the regime came to life near the close of World War II in 1945, when representatives of 50 countries gathered in San Francisco, California, to discuss matters of world peace. After two months, a new international organization— the United Nations (U.N.)—was born, and to this day it remains the essential organization working to protect global human rights, maintain international peace, provide humanitarian assistance, and uphold international law.

The original U.N. charter included the promotion of human rights as one of the organization's main purposes, and in 1946 the U.N. Commission on Human Rights was established to spearhead the development of international human rights law. (The commission was replaced in 2006 with the U.N. Human Rights Council.) Two years later, in 1948, the U.N. General Assembly adopted the UDHR, which in turn led to a cascade of international, regional, and country-specific treaties, declarations, guidelines, and customary law meant to protect basic human rights.

Declarations and Treaties

A declaration is a statement recognizing a universally valid principle; it is not an agreement by which countries bind themselves under international law. As a result, declarations are not subject to ratification by countries, and there is no international effort associated with their compliance. A treaty, by contrast, is an internationally binding agreement. Also referred to as conventions or covenants, treaties enter into force as countries undergo the process of first signing and then ratifying them.

Treaty signature is an act by which a nation provides a preliminary endorsement of the treaty and obligates itself to refrain from acts that would defeat or undermine the treaty's objective and purpose; however, signature does not commit the nation to the instrument's ratification. Ratification, in turn, is an act by which a country agrees to be legally bound by the terms of a particular treaty by fulfilling its own particular national legislative requirements.

Countries can also "accede" or "adhere" to treaties rather than ratify them. The former is an act in which a country accepts the opportunity to become a party to a treaty that is already negotiated and signed by other states; the latter refers to acceptance by a non-signatory nation of some, though not all, of a treaty's provisions. Partial acceptance of an international convention is permitted through what are called "reservations"—provided that the treaty itself does not prohibit them. Where the treaty is silent on the topic of reservations (not uncommon in human rights treaties), they may be taken—but they may then be examined to determine whether they are compatible with the treaty's object and purpose. If incompatible, a reservation is deemed invalid. In this situation, one of two possibilities results: Either the treaty applies in full to the country without the benefit of the reservation, or the invalidity vitiates the country's consent and prevents it from being a party to the treaty. Depending on the treaty, certain international courts or other monitoring bodies make decisions on the validity of reservations.

The most important human rights declaration is the UDHR,[4] which for the first time spelled out the basic civil, political, economic, social, and cultural rights that should be enjoyed by all people. While aspirational and not legally binding, it remains a groundbreaking document for the way it promoted a comprehensive and universal set of principles meant to apply regardless of culture, religion, ideology, political system, or legal system. Among all of the treaties and other legal instruments influenced by the UDHR, the 1966 International Covenant on Civil and Political Rights[5] and the 1966 International Covenant on Economic, Social and Cultural Rights[6] are two of the most crucial. (These are discussed further later.) Together, these three instruments are referred to as the "international bill of human rights."

It should be noted that existing treaties do not cover all human rights that, arguably, should be guaranteed. For example, the U.N. General Assembly has adopted human rights declarations on matters for which there are no U.N. treaties, including religious and ethnic tolerance,[7] international development,[8] and Indigenous Peoples.[9]

Customary International Law

Like declarations and treaties, customary law is a component of international law. But customary international law refers to international obligations that arise from established practices "accepted as law" rather than from written documents. For example, customary law is key to the regulation of armed conflict that arises between two or more nations.

Compared to treaties, however, customary international law is a less important source of law for protecting human rights. This results for a few reasons. First, not many human rights standards—particularly as they relate to social and economic rights—are a part of long-standing custom. Second, the right holders in customary international law are nations themselves rather than individuals, and when there are breaches, the harmed nation may be hesitant to act against the delinquent one. Third, there are few remedies available in international law tribunals for breaches of custom. But customary law does have one advantage over treaty law: It is binding upon *all* states (unless it is a regional or local custom, though this is rare), as opposed to applying only to countries that elect to be bound.

Protected Rights: Civil, Political, Economic, Social, Cultural, and More

Human rights are often divided into three categories, called generations. First-generation rights encompass individual civil and political rights. These rights are most obviously represented by the International Covenant on Civil and Political Rights (ICCPR) and can be subdivided into physical and civil security on the one hand and civil-political liberties on the other.[10] Physical and civil security rights include the right to be free of torture, enslavement, and other inhumane treatment; civil-political liberties include the rights to freely practice a religion and to participate in political processes.[11] First-generation rights are considered "negative" rights, in that rather than providing a right to something tangible, they protect rights to liberty and to being free from excessive government intervention. The U.S. Bill of Rights—the first 10 amendments to the federal Constitution—is one example of the way in which first-generation rights are manifested in national law.

Social, economic, and cultural rights animate the second generation of human rights. This generation of rights aims to promote the fulfillment of basic needs (e.g., adequate housing and health care), economic needs (e.g., fair wages), and cultural needs (e.g., access to research).[12] The International Covenant on Economic, Social and Cultural Rights (ICESCR) is the primary international instrument promoting and protecting these rights. Second-generation rights are considered "positive" rights in that they do provide rights to tangible things, such as health care, wages, and information.

Third-generation human rights refer to collective group rights, such as the right to self-determination, the right to a healthy environment, and the right to peace. Self-determination includes the right to community development, which can be defined as "promoting participative democracy, sustainable development, rights, economic opportunity, equality, and social justice, through the organisation, education, and empowerment of people within their communities."[13] Generally speaking, third-generation rights have not made much progress as human rights, but they are being increasingly acknowledged. For example, the African Charter on Human and Peoples' Rights is unique in guaranteeing a full set of third-generation human rights.[14]

Civil and political rights differ from economic, social, and cultural rights in important ways, owing mainly to history. In the aftermath of World War II, political divisions among nations resulted in two separate treaties: the ICCPR and the ICESCR. This division allowed for a hierarchy of sorts to take hold, with economic, social, and cultural rights playing second fiddle to civil and political rights, due mainly to the West's downplaying of the former as "socialist."[15]

The distinctions between the two types of rights take several forms. First, the language in the ICCPR is relatively rights-affirming (e.g., "everyone has the right to…"), whereas the ICESCR is more aspirational (e.g., "undertake to guarantee"). Relatedly, the ICESCR states that the included rights are subject to nations' "available resources," language that has destabilized economic and social rights as compared to its civil and political cousins, permitting scholars and policymakers to argue that the former are conditional while the latter are fully justiciable.

A second difference between the two types of rights concerns their enforcement mechanisms. While both the ICCPR and ICESCR include methods by which countries report on implementation, only the ICCPR included an individual enforcement mechanism. This distinction further fed the idea that economic, social, and cultural rights were somehow not as justiciable as civil and political rights. (While the ICESCR finally adopted an optional individual complaint mechanism in 2013, the damage had been done.) Furthermore, although both covenants include monitoring and implementation schemes, the nature of economic, social, and cultural rights—given their connection to "available resources"—makes many monitoring and implementing tactics less effective than is the case with civil and political rights.

Nearly 30 years after the two treaties were drafted, the World Conference on Human Rights aimed to curb the disparate ways in which the two bodies of rights were viewed by many. Conference attendees drafted what is known as the Vienna Declaration, which stated that "[a]ll human rights are universal, indivisible, and interdependent and interrelated. The international community must treat human rights globally in a fair and equal manner, on the same footing, and with the same emphasis."[16] While the concepts of universality, indivisibility, and interdependence were not new to human rights in the 1990s, the Vienna Declaration was a direct effort to dispel the gap that had been created between civil and political rights on the one hand and economic, social, and cultural rights on the other.

U.N. Monitoring and Enforcement

While a full discussion of international human rights monitoring and enforcement is beyond the scope of this chapter, a brief discussion of the role of the United Nations is warranted. By becoming parties to international treaties, countries assume legal obligations to respect, protect, and fulfill human rights.[17] The obligation to respect—for example, the duty not to torture—means that countries must refrain from interfering with or curtailing the enjoyment of a human right; this is a negative obligation because it only requires a country to *not* do something. The obligation to protect requires nations to protect individuals and groups against human rights abuses; this represents a positive obligation to protect people from violations of their rights by other private individuals or by someone acting on behalf of the government. Finally, the obligation to fulfill means that countries must take positive action to facilitate the enjoyment of basic human rights; this could range from adopting legislation to implement international treaties to providing schools and hospitals.

Various components of the United Nations play a role in monitoring and enforcing international treaties and other instruments. For example, the General Assembly can adopt resolutions that declare human rights standards or condemn particular breaches of human rights; the Security Council can take enforcement action against human rights violations that amount to a threat to peace; the High Commissioner for Human Rights coordinates human rights activities throughout the U.N. system; and many human rights treaties—including the ICCPR and ICESCR—have treaty monitoring bodies, which are committees of independent experts who monitor compliance.

Yet above all, it is the U.N. Human Rights Council that has the responsibility to promote and protect human rights around the globe. The Council is composed of 47 countries elected from the General Assembly, with a specified number of seats going to each major geographic region. The Council has multiple roles: drafting treaties and declarations, which require adoption by the General Assembly; investigating allegations of treaty breaches; and monitoring compliance with human rights standards and instruments, through three primary mechanisms—"special procedures," a practice called universal periodic review, and the hearing of individual complaints.

Special procedures refer to a process by which the Council appoints independent experts/working groups to monitor and report annually on the human rights situation in countries that have been identified by the Council as problematic or to brief the Council on a particular worldwide human rights problem. Under the process of universal periodic review, the Council considers the human rights record of all U.N. member countries every four and a half years. For each review, countries submit a report on the steps they've taken to address Council recommendations from the previous review cycle, and civil society organizations (nongovernmental organizations

[NGOs], faith-based organizations, etc.) weigh in on nations' performance as well. Finally, the Council hears complaints from individuals or NGOs via a confidential procedure in which it examines allegations of patterns of human rights violations in particular countries.

The Right to Health Under International Standards

Overview

Historically, "health" was described as the absence of disease or illness. However, evolving concepts of public health in the nineteenth century changed this perception, and today the right to health is broad enough to be linked with several other human rights, including rights to food, water, sanitation, and housing; the right to safe and adequate working conditions; the right to life; the right to education; the right to freedom from torture; the right to privacy; and the right to access vital information.

The positive right to health was first articulated, for purposes of modern international human rights standards, by the World Health Organization (WHO) Constitution in 1946. It defines health as "a state of complete physical, mental and social well-being and not merely the absence of disease or infirmity" and the right to health as "the enjoyment of the highest attainable standard of health."[18] Two years later, the UDHR stated that "[e]veryone has the right to a standard of living adequate for the health and well-being of himself and of his family, including food, clothing, housing and medical care and necessary social services, and the right to security in the event of unemployment, sickness, disability, widowhood, old age or other lack of livelihood in circumstances beyond his control."[19] Importantly, this provision recognizes that, more than anything else, the *context* of people's lives—social conditions, opportunities, community

resources—determines their health and well-being.[20] Then, in 1966, Article 12 of the ICESCR declared that "States Parties to the present Covenant recognize the right of everyone to the enjoyment of the highest attainable standard of physical and mental health."[21] (The interpretation and implementation of Article 12 are discussed further later.) Finally, health has been addressed in various additional conventions in the context of specific issues and populations. For example, the International Convention on the Elimination of All Forms of Racial Discrimination, the Convention on the Elimination of All Forms of Discrimination Against Women, the Convention on the Rights of the Child, and the Convention on the Rights of Persons with Disabilities all include language pertaining to the right to health.

Resource Limitations and the Principle of Progressive Realization

As just noted, Article 12 of the ICESCR states that everyone has the right to "the enjoyment of the highest attainable standard of physical and mental health." But what does this mean? It is very broad and quite vague. Ask yourself: How would you enforce this provision?

Whatever Article 12 of ICESCR means, there is agreement on what it *doesn't* mean: The right to health has not been understood to mean a right to be *healthy*. This interpretation results for two main reasons. First, no country can fully account for all of the individual genetic predispositions and behavioral choices that impact the ability to get and remain fully healthy. Second, countries vary widely in their access to wealth and resources, a reality recognized by the ICESCR. Article 2(1) of the ICESCR states that "[e]ach State Party to the present Covenant undertakes to take steps, individually and through international assistance and cooperation, especially economic and technical, to the maximum of its available resources, with a view to achieving progressively the full realisation of the rights recognised in the present Covenant by all appropriate means, including particularly the adoption of legislative measures."[22] This language refers to what is known as the principle of "progressive realization"—the idea that nations must, in carrying out their human rights duties, strive to fulfill economic and social rights obligations to the greatest extent possible given contextual resource constraints. Like the language used to describe the right to health itself, the progressive realization language is open-ended and ambiguous. (For example, what exactly does "to the maximum of its available resources" mean?) But this ambiguity is no accident: Because many of the rights contained in the ICESCR require complex and expensive social systems and because nations' relative wealth and available resources vary widely, many countries demanded the progressive realization language in order to agree to enshrined economic, social, and cultural rights. Yet some nations exploit the open-ended "available resources" language to sidestep their responsibilities.[23]

In an attempt to thwart such proclivities, the UN Committee on Economic, Social and Cultural Rights—the group of experts that reviews reports submitted by UN member countries on their compliance with the ICESCR—explicated the progressive realization principle to make clear to nations that the committee would determine whether countries were, in fact, using "all appropriate means" to realize economic, social, and cultural rights.[24] Furthermore, the committee introduced the "minimum core" concept, which aims to ensure that countries satisfy, at the very least, minimum essential levels of each ICESCR right.[25] Essentially, the concept represents a floor that countries must meet and maintain regardless of the ways in which their available resources are affected.

Given the way that ICESCR rights are structured, economic policies and downturns at the local, national, and international levels have major implications for the enjoyment of economic, social, and cultural rights. As noted previously, the systems needed to implement and deliver these rights are expensive; thus, when under pressure to reduce budget deficits, countries too often turn instinctively to social program austerity measures (cuts to social spending, regressive tax hikes, pension reforms, etc.) that create or exacerbate economic and social problems for their populations. Since the global economic downturn in 2008, the overall impact of austerity measures on economic and social rights, poverty, and inequality has been enormous.[26] In fact, nations' knee-jerk efforts to implement austerity measures post-2008 have created widespread crises in the areas of labor, food, health, housing, social security, and more, resulting in an "ascendant belief in a new normal of resource scarcity."[27] The COVID-19 pandemic, unfortunately, is likely to only accelerate these concerns.

The Scope of the Right to Health

Notwithstanding resource constraints and the notion of progressive realization, Article 12 of the ICESCR has been interpreted to require something more than mere access to health care services. As noted previously, the right to health was drafted with the intent to encompass a wide range of socioeconomic factors that promote conditions in which people can attain their maximum well-being, and thus the right extends to the underlying drivers of health. Understood in this way, the right to health encompasses a range of entitlements and freedoms, including rights to food and nutrition, adequate shelter, safe and potable water, adequate sanitation, adequate education, health information, safe and healthy working conditions, effective and equitable health facilities and services, and bodily integrity.[28]

The U.N. Committee on Economic, Social and Cultural Rights has distilled these entitlements and freedoms down to four elements:

availability, accessibility, acceptability, and quality.[29] Availability refers to having functional programs and services (e.g., potable water, sanitation facilities, hospitals, clinics, trained health care providers) in sufficient quantity. The accessibility element demands physical access without discrimination to the noted services, goods, and facilities but also economic accessibility with a particular emphasis on marginalized populations for whom affordability is key. This element also requires information accessibility. Acceptability means that health services, goods, and facilities must be provided in accordance with medical ethics (think confidentiality, privacy, and informed consent) and in culturally appropriate ways, with particular sensitivities to age groups and gender orientations. The final element—quality—refers to the fact that health services, goods, and facilities must be scientifically and medically appropriate.[30] Notwithstanding the committee's efforts to further define the scope of the right to health, the right remains one of the more controversial and nebulous human rights.[31]

U.S. Government Attitudes Concerning International Human Rights Law

Overview

As a starting point for analyzing U.S. attitudes toward international human rights law, review **Table 5.1**.

Table 5.1 Where the United States Stands on 10 Key International Treaties

Treaty	Signed	Ratified	Notables
International Covenant on Civil and Political Rights	1977	1992	U.S. took a reservation to Article 7 and considers itself bound to the extent that "cruel, inhuman or degrading treatment or punishment" is prohibited by the Fifth, Eighth, and Fourteenth Amendments to the U.S. Constitution. The United States took a reservation to Article 20 so as to not require any action that would restrict the right to free speech and association protected by the U.S. Constitution. The United States also reserved the right to impose capital punishment on any person duly convicted under laws permitting the imposition of capital punishment. The United States also reserved the right to treat juveniles as adults in the criminal justice system, under exceptional circumstances. The United States declared that the convention is not self-executing. (A self-executing treaty is one that may be directly applied by courts; a non-self-executing treaty cannot be applied by courts until it has first been implemented through national legislation.)

Treaty	Signed	Ratified	Notables
International Convention on the Elimination of All Forms of Racial Discrimination	1966	1994	The United States took a reservation to Articles 4 and 7 and declared that it would not accept any obligation to limit freedom of speech, expression, and association—essentially stating that the United States will not take steps to restrict or limit hate speech. The United States declared that it would not take stricter measures to regulate private conduct than what already exists under U.S. law, and thus it took reservation to paragraph 1 of Articles 2, 3, and 5. The United States took a reservation to Article 22, which sends any dispute between state parties to the International Court of Justice. The United States declared that the convention is not self-executing.
Convention Against Torture and Other Cruel, Inhuman or Degrading Treatment or Punishment	1988	1994	The United States took a reservation to Article 16, the definition of torture, and instead looks to the Eighth Amendment of the U.S. Constitution for legal guidance. The United States took a reservation to Article 30, which submits a dispute between state parties concerning the interpretation or application of the Convention to the International Court of Justice. The United States declared that the convention is not self-executing.
Convention on the Prevention and Punishment of the Crime of Genocide	1948	1988	The United States took a reservation to Article 9, which submits a dispute between State Parties to the International Court of Justice; specific consent of the United States is required in each case. The United States reserved that nothing in the convention will require legislation or action by the United States that is prohibited by the Constitution.
Convention on the Rights of Persons with Disabilities	2009	N/A	The United States failed to ratify by five votes in December 2012. The George W. Bush Administration stated that ratification of the convention was unnecessary because of the federal Americans with Disabilities Act, which the administration believed to be more effective than the ratification of an international disability treaty.

(continues)

Table 5.1 Where the United States Stands on 10 Key International Treaties   *(continued)*

Treaty	Signed	Ratified	Notables
Convention on the Elimination of All Forms of Discrimination Against Women	1980	N/A	The United States is one of only six countries in the world—the others being Iran, Sudan, Somalia, Palau, and Tonga—yet to ratify the treaty.
International Covenant on Economic, Social, and Cultural Rights	1977	N/A	The United States is among just 23 countries yet to ratify the treaty.
Convention on the Rights of the Child	1995	N/A	This is the most widely accepted human rights treaty. Of all the United Nations member countries, only the United States has not ratified.
International Convention on the Protection of the Rights of Migrant Workers and Members of Their Families	N/A	N/A	Forty-nine countries have ratified this treaty; another 17 have signed.
International Convention for the Protection of All Persons from Enforced Disappearance	N/A	N/A	Sixty-two countries have ratified; another 36 have signed.

Table 5.1 paints an unflattering picture for a country that views human rights promotion as an important foreign policy goal[32] and once played a leadership role in promoting and protecting global human rights. (For example, Eleanor Roosevelt, former first lady of the United States, was appointed by President Harry S. Truman in 1946 as a delegate to the U.N. General Assembly. In this capacity, she served as the first chairperson of the U.N. Human Rights Commission and is recognized as the driving force behind the UDHR's adoption.[33]) Unfortunately, this leadership has waned over time. Today, the United States holds the distinction of having ratified or acceded to fewer key human rights treaties than any other country in the G20, an international economic and development forum composed of 19 countries and the European Union, which together account for 60% of the world's population.[34] Indeed, it is not unfair to say that the United States partially and selectively embraces international human rights law, exempts itself from certain treaties altogether and from many treaty provisions, generally denies the applicability of international human rights law to domestic affairs, and takes the position that domestic law prevails over international treaty law even when treaties provide broader protections against human rights abuses.

Further, the United States sometimes resists full implementation of the treaties it *has* ratified, including the International Convention on the Elimination of All Forms of Racial Discrimination (ICERD). As a party to ICERD, the United States has committed to "undertake to pursue by all appropriate means and without delay a policy of eliminating racial discrimination in all its forms and promoting understanding among all races...."[35] As shown in Table 5.1, however, the United States took several reservations that effectively nullify important aspects of

ICERD, and the United States has neither passed federal implementing legislation for this particular treaty nor allowed citizens to bring lawsuits seeking the convention's enforcement.[36] The United Nations has taken note; according to a *New York Times* article from July 2021, the U.N. set up a panel of experts in law enforcement and human rights to "investigate the root causes and effects of systemic racism in policing [in the United States], including the legacies of slavery and colonialism, and to make recommendations for change. It will look at issues ranging from excessive use of force, racial profiling and police handling of peaceful protests to links between racial supremacy movements and the police and the criminal justice system."[37]

As the ICERD example illuminates, the U.S. approach to human rights policy and enforcement is not a mere abstraction; it is broadly reflected in the daily reality of tens of millions of people who live in the United States.[38] Indeed, compared to the other 38 countries that are members of the Organisation for Economic Co-operation and Development (an intergovernmental organization of mainly democratic, market-based, high-income nations that aims to stimulate economic progress), the United States has one of the highest rates of income inequality;[39] one of the highest youth poverty rates;[40] one of the highest infant mortality rates;[41] below-average life expectancy rates at time of birth;[42] below-average enrollment rates in secondary and tertiary education;[43] relatively high rates of youth not in employment, education, or training;[44] and so on.

What accounts for the United States' apathetic approach to human rights leadership? The answer is multifactorial. First, there's the notion of "American exceptionalism"—the idea that the United States is somehow unique due to its historical development and values and as a result is inherently supportive of human rights regardless of its behavior.[45] While an attractive worldview for some, there is a robust body of literature deeply critical of this concept.[46] Second, during the 1940s and 1950s, there was a concerted effort by some powerful (mainly Southern) federal legislators to avoid international scrutiny of the nation's racial caste system represented by Jim Crow laws and policies.[47] This effort was successful in preventing U.S. ratification of certain human rights treaties. Third, as noted previously, the East–West political divide that persisted in the aftermath of World War II led to unfortunate separations of political and civil rights on the one hand and economic and social rights on the other—and the United States took a decidedly political/civil approach to its human rights policy.[48] In fact, the U.S. retreat from the promotion of economic and social rights went beyond mere opposition to socialism; it also resulted from U.S. concerns that ratification of the ICESCR could obligate it to ensure economic stability in low-income nations and could force a redistribution of wealth in the United States.[49]

U.S. Government Attitudes Concerning Health as a Human Right

Unsurprisingly, the United States' general view of international human rights law influences its view of the internationally recognized right to health. As described throughout this text, there is in the United States no universal right to health, health care services, or health insurance nor to the many things that make good health possible and sustainable (e.g., adequate shelter, adequate nutrition, a solid education, and so forth).

The closest the United States has come to a universal "health program" is a handful of attempts to enact a national health insurance scheme.[50] The early 1900s witnessed the first attempts to make a right to health insurance coverage more recognizable, but these efforts fizzled without much fanfare, and the national health insurance movement was dormant until the mid-1930s. During and in the immediate aftermath of the Great Depression, there was a significant increase in government aid programs, including old-age assistance, unemployment compensation, and other forms of public aid. Yet a national health insurance program remained elusive due in part to strong opposition from the American Medical Association and its belief that "socialized medicine" would limit physician freedom and interfere with the doctor–patient relationship.

Once World War II neared an end, President Franklin D. Roosevelt called for an "economic bill of rights" that included insurance for medical care. After Roosevelt's death in 1945, President Harry Truman strongly advocated for the same. While there was some public support for national health insurance at the time, a greater number of people preferred modest voluntary plans over a national, compulsory health insurance program. National health insurance proposals returned to the scene in the early 1970s as part of a broader effort to expand patient rights, including the areas of informed consent, involuntary commitment, and equal access to health care services. Richard Nixon was president at the time, and at various points in his time in office he supported both comprehensive health insurance coverage and more limited coverage schemes. Yet again, there was no majority support for any of the proposals.

Fast-forward to 1993, when President Bill Clinton promoted what was called the Health Security Act, a national health insurance proposal that combined elements of managed care and market competition. Like the national health insurance plans before it, Clinton's plan was too divisive to draw majority support, and the proposal never came to a vote in Congress. The most recent effort to create universal health insurance came in the lead-up to passage of the Patient Protection and Affordable Care Act (ACA), which is discussed at various other points in this textbook. For purposes of this discussion on the human right to health, it is enough to say that the ACA has received mixed reviews: On one hand, the law

is praised as more firmly pointing the United States in the direction of international human rights norms; on the other hand, it is criticized as being only a statutory right that is subject to modification or revocation as the political winds shift and also for avoiding the specific language of international human rights law.[51]

In addition to the factors described previously that have led the United States to abstain from international human rights leadership, additional factors have made it difficult to achieve universal health care and/or health insurance programs in the United States. These include the country's vast cultural differences and focus on individualism, which together have made health reform consensus hard to come by for more than a century; the country's system of government, which traditionally leaves social welfare programming to states (with exceptions for certain populations, such as the elderly); and the power of the many interest groups that represent each aspect of the incredibly complex U.S. health care and public health systems.

Yet another factor in the quest to achieve universal health care and/or health insurance programs is the fact that the U.S. Constitution guarantees neither economic nor social rights (another way in which the United States stands apart from most other nations[52]). There are four leading theories as to why this is the case. The first is simply the age of the Constitution itself, which is the oldest in force in the world and which was written long before the modern human rights movement took hold.[53] While this fact could be neutralized by simply amending the Constitution to account for these types of rights, it is anything but simple to amend the Constitution, even in the face of widespread support for an amendment. A second theory as to why the U.S. Constitution lacks economic and social rights has to do with their enforceability: Even if these types of rights had a constitutional foothold, their enforcement would strain judicial capacities.[54] While it is true that no court could guarantee adequate food, shelter, and medical care for everyone, it is equally true that some U.S. states and many other countries have strategies for enforcing economic and social rights. (For example, in 2010 Vermont became the first state to use a human rights framework to design a new health care system;[55] many countries perform well at using their resources to make sure rights to health, education, food, housing, and work are fulfilled.[56]) A third rationale has to do with the fact that no political group deeply associated with social and economic rights has achieved enough power in the United States to bring them to fruition.[57] Finally, there is the view that if not for President Nixon's election in 1968—which resulted in the seating of four new conservative justices to the Supreme Court—the progressive judicial movement of the 1960s would eventually have led to an interpretation of the Constitution that recognized basic economic and social rights.[58]

Whether viewed through the frame of human rights leadership, national culture and politics, or the scope of the Constitution, it is not difficult to understand why economic and social rights—and, specifically, the human right to health—have not found a home in the United States. The results are not pretty: massive wealth and income inequality; extreme poverty; the population health status of a low-income country; the commodification of health insurance and health care services, which prices millions of people out of needed health care; a wispy social safety net; and seemingly intractable health and health care disparities across a wide range of metrics. All of these topics and more are discussed in more detail in the next two parts of this textbook.

Conclusion

Given the gap between the scope and flexibility of the human right to health and the United States' lamentable track record of invoking and fulfilling this right domestically, it is clear that there is much that could be done to redeem past failures.[59] Although these failures create a strong drag on potential future reform, recent developments offer small glimmers of hope. For example, nearly one-third of state constitutions now at least mention health or health care and even more address broader economic and social rights (though their mentions says little about their implementation/enforcement);[60] since its passage in 2010, the ACA has provided health insurance coverage to some 31 million people; and some state and federal courts (including the U.S. Supreme Court) are at least acknowledging, with a bit more frequency, international human rights norms in their decisions interpreting and applying domestic law.[61] These reforms, however, are far short of what is needed in light of the complex and deeply rooted health injustices described throughout the remainder of this book. Whether, for example, the United States will *ever* ratify—and then comply with—the ICESCR is a matter of an entirely different magnitude and, sadly, very much an open question.

References

1. Blau JR, Brunsma DL, Moncada A, et al. *The Leading Rogue State: The United States and Human Rights.* Routledge (London, England and New York, NY); 2008.
2. World Health Organization. A conceptual framework for action on the social determinants of health. 2010. https://www.who.int/sdhconference/resources/ConceptualframeworkforactiononSDH_eng.pdf.
3. Muñoz AA. International human rights regimes. *SUR: International Journal on Human Rights.* 2017;25. https://sur.conectas.org/en/international-human-rights-regimes-matrix-analysis-classification/.
4. United Nations. Universal declaration of human rights. 1948. https://www.un.org/en/about-us/universal-declaration-of-human-rights.

5. United Nations Human Rights Office of the High Commissioner. International covenant on civil and political rights. 1966. https://www.ohchr.org/en/professionalinterest/pages/ccpr.aspx.

6. United Nations Human Rights Office of the High Commissioner. International covenant on economic, social and cultural rights. 1966. https://www.ohchr.org/en/professionalinterest/pages/cescr.aspx.

7. Office of the United Nations High Commissioner for Human Rights. Declaration on the elimination of all forms of intolerance and of discrimination based on religion or belief. 1981. https://www.ohchr.org/en/professionalinterest/pages/religionorbelief.aspx.

8. Office of the United Nations High Commissioner for Human Rights. Declaration on the right to development. 1986. https://www.ohchr.org/en/professionalinterest/pages/righttodevelopment.aspx.

9. United Nations. Declaration on the rights of Indigenous Peoples. 2007. https://www.un.org/development/desa/indigenouspeoples/wp-content/uploads/sites/19/2018/11/UNDRIP_E_web.pdf.

10. Reid L. The generations of human rights. UAB Institute for Human Rights Blog. 2019. https://sites.uab.edu/humanrights/2019/01/14/the-generations-of-human-rights/.

11. Reid L. The generations of human rights. UAB Institute for Human Rights Blog. 2019. https://sites.uab.edu/humanrights/2019/01/14/the-generations-of-human-rights/.

12. Reid L. The generations of human rights. UAB Institute for Human Rights Blog. 2019. https://sites.uab.edu/humanrights/2019/01/14/the-generations-of-human-rights/.

13. The International Association for Community Development. 2017. https://www.iacdglobal.org/about/.

14. African Commission on Human and Peoples' Rights. African Charter on Human and Peoples' Rights. 1981. https://www.achpr.org/legalinstruments/detail?id=49.

15. Betts, P. Socialism, social rights, and human rights: the case of East Germany. *Humanity.* 2012. http://www.humanityjournal.org/wp-content/uploads/2014/06/3.3-Socialism-Social-Rights-and-Human-Rights.pdf.

16. United Nations Human Rights Office of the High Commissioner. Vienna Declaration and Programme of Action. 1993. https://www.ohchr.org/en/professionalinterest/pages/vienna.aspx.

17. United Nations. Universal Declaration of Human Rights: The foundation of international human rights law. https://www.un.org/en/about-us/udhr/foundation-of-international-human-rights-law.

18. World Health Organization. Constitution of the World Health Organization. 2006. https://www.who.int/governance/eb/who_constitution_en.pdf.

19. United Nations. Universal Declaration of Human Rights. 1948; Art. 25(1). https://www.un.org/en/about-us/universal-declaration-of-human-rights.

20. Tobin Tyler, E. "Small places close to home": Toward a health and human rights strategy for the US. *Health and Human Rights.* 2013;15(2):80–96.

21. Office of the United Nations High Commissioner for Human Rights. International Covenant on Economic, Social and Cultural Rights. 1966; Art. 12. https://www.ohchr.org/en/professionalinterest/pages/cescr.aspx.

22. Office of the United Nations High Commissioner for Human Rights. International Covenant on Economic, Social and Cultural Rights. 1966; Art. 2(1). https://www.ohchr.org/en/professionalinterest/pages/cescr.aspx.

23. See, e.g., Inter-American Commission on Human Rights. Corruption and human rights in the Americas: Inter-American standards. 2019. https://www.oas.org/en/iachr/reports/pdfs/CorruptionHR.pdf.

24. Office of the United Nations High Commissioner for Human Rights. CESCR general comment no. 3: The nature of states parties' obligations (Art. 2, Para. 1, of the Covenant). 1990. https://www.refworld.org/pdfid/4538838e10.pdf.

25. Office of the United Nations High Commissioner for Human Rights. CESCR general comment no. 3: The nature of states parties' obligations (Art. 2, Para. 10, of the Covenant). 1990. https://www.refworld.org/pdfid/4538838e10.pdf.

26. Office of the United Nations High Commissioner for Human Rights. Report on austerity measures and economic and social rights. 2013. https://www.ohchr.org/documents/issues/development/rightscrisis/e-2013-82_en.pdf.

27. Center for Economic and Social Rights. Austerity and its alternatives. 2015. https://www.cesr.org/austerity-and-its-alternatives.

28. Office of the United Nations High Commissioner for Human Rights and the World Health Organization. The right to health, fact sheet No. 31. 2008. https://www.ohchr.org/documents/publications/factsheet31.pdf.

29. Office of the United Nations High Commissioner for Human Rights. CESCR General Comment No. 14: The right to the highest attainable standard of health (Art. 12). 2000. https://www.refworld.org/pdfid/4538838d0.pdf.

30. World Health Organization. Human rights and health. 2017. https://www.who.int/news-room/fact-sheets/detail/human-rights-and-health.

31. Tobin-Tyler E. "Small places close to home": Toward a health and human rights strategy for the US. *Health and Human Rights.* 2013;15(2):80–96.

32. Council on Foreign Relations, International Institutions and Global Governance Program. The global human rights regime. 2012. https://www.cfr.org/report/global-human-rights-regime.

33. United Nations. History of the declaration. https://www.un.org/en/about-us/udhr/history-of-the-declaration.

34. American Civil Liberties Union. What you should know about the U.S. and human rights. https://

www.aclu.org/sites/default/files/assets/121013-humanrightsfacts.pdf.

35. Office of the United Nations High Commissioner for Human Rights. International Convention on the Elimination of All Forms of Racial Discrimination (Article 2(1)). 1965. https://www.ohchr.org/en/professionalinterest/pages/cerd.aspx.

36. Watson MK. American Bar Association. The United States' hollow commitment to eradicating global racial discrimination. 2020. https://www.americanbar.org/groups/crsj/publications/human_rights_magazine_home/black-to-the-future-part-ii/the-united-states--hollow-commitment-to-eradicating-global-racia/.

37. Cumming-Bruce N. U.N. to form panel to investigate systemic racism in policing. *New York Times* (July 13, 2021). https://www.nytimes.com/2021/07/13/world/united-nations-panel-human-rights-council-racism.html.

38. See, e.g., United Nations General Assembly, Human Rights Council. Report of the special rapporteur on extreme poverty and human rights on his mission to the United States of America. 2018. https://digitallibrary.un.org/record/1629536?ln=en.

39. Organisation for Economic Co-operation and Development. OECD data: Income inequality. 2020. https://data.oecd.org/inequality/income-inequality.htm#indicator-chart.

40. Organisation for Economic Co-operation and Development. OECD data: Poverty rate. 2020. https://data.oecd.org/inequality/poverty-rate.htm#indicator-chart.

41. Organisation for Economic Co-operation and Development. OECD data: Infant mortality rates. 2020. https://data.oecd.org/healthstat/infant-mortality-rates.htm.

42. Organisation for Economic Co-operation and Development. OECD data: Life expectancy at birth. 2020. https://data.oecd.org/healthstat/life-expectancy-at-birth.htm#indicator-chart.

43. Organisation for Economic Co-operation and Development. OECD data: Enrolment rate in secondary and tertiary education. 2019. https://data.oecd.org/students/enrolment-rate-in-secondary-and-tertiary-education.htm.

44. Organisation for Economic Co-operation and Development. OECD data: Youth not in employment, education or training (NEET). 2020. https://data.oecd.org/youthinac/youth-not-in-employment-education-or-training-neet.htm.

45. Tobin-Tyler E. "Small places close to home": Toward a health and human rights strategy for the US. *Health and Human Rights*. 2013;15(2):80–96.

46. See, e.g., Ignatieff M. *American Exceptionalism and Human Rights*. Princeton University Press (Princeton, NJ); 2005; Pease DE. *The New American Exceptionalism*. University of Minnesota Press (Minneapolis, MN); 2009.

47. Soohoo C, Albisa C, Davis MF, eds. *Bringing Human Rights Home: A History of Human Rights in the United States*. University of Pennsylvania Press (Philadelphia, PA); 2009.

48. Tobin-Tyler E. "Small places close to home": Toward a health and human rights strategy for the US. *Health and Human Rights*. 2013;15(2):80–96.

49. Tobin-Tyler E. "Small places close to home": Toward a health and human rights strategy for the US. *Health and Human Rights*. 2013;15(2):80–96.

50. The summary that follows of national health insurance efforts is heavily influenced by Wilensky SE, Teitelbaum JB. *Essentials of Health Policy and Law* (4th ed.). Ch. 10. Jones & Bartlett Learning (Burlington, MA); 2020.

51. Willen SS. Invoking health and human rights in the United States: museums, classrooms, and community-based participatory research. (2019). *Health and Human Rights*. 21(1):157–162.

52. Jung C, Hirschl R, Rosevear E. Economic and social rights in national constitutions. *The American Journal of Comparative Law*. 2014;62(4):1043–1093.

53. Sunstein CR. Why does the American constitution lack social and economic guarantees? *Syracuse Law Review*. 2005;56:1.

54. Sunstein CR. Why does the American constitution lack social and economic guarantees? *Syracuse Law Review*. 2005;56:1.

55. MacNaughton G, McGill M. Economic and social rights in the United States: Implementation without ratification. *Northeastern University Law Journal*. 2012;4(2):365.

56. Human Rights Measurement Initiative. Right to Health. 2021. https://rightstracker.org/en/metric/health.

57. Sunstein CR. Why does the American constitution lack social and economic guarantees? *Syracuse Law Review*. 2005;56:1.

58. Sunstein CR. Why does the American constitution lack social and economic guarantees? *Syracuse Law Review*. 2005;56:1.

59. Roth K. Biden's challenge: Redeeming a US role for human rights. Human Rights Watch. 2021. https://www.hrw.org/world-report/2021/bidens-challenge.

60. Matsuura H. State constitutional commitment to health and health care and population health outcomes: Evidence from historical US data. *American Journal of Public Health*. 2015;105(Suppl 3): e48–e54. https://www.ncbi.nlm.nih.gov/pmc/articles/PMC4455512/; Soohoo C, Goldberg J. The full realization of our rights: The right to health in state constitutions. 2010. https://scholarlycommons.law.case.edu/caselrev/vol60/iss4/5.

61. Tobin-Tyler E. "Small places close to home": Toward a health and human rights strategy for the US. *Health and Human Rights*. 2013;15(2):80–96.

CHAPTER 6

Discrimination, Implicit Bias, and the Limits of the Law

LEARNING OBJECTIVES

By the end of this chapter you will be able to:

- Provide an overview of federal antidiscrimination law
- Describe a range of laws that have been enacted to shield "protected classes" from discrimination and to prevent discrimination from leeching into key areas of social life
- Discuss key limitations of antidiscrimination law, including the difficulty of remediating implicit bias through law

Introduction

This chapter closes Part II, which focuses on various aspects of the legal system that can blunt full-throttled efforts to achieve health justice. The other chapters in Part II covered the roles of the three branches of government in health law and policy, including some ways in which each branch operates to create barriers to health justice; certain health-harming legal doctrines, such as the "no duty to treat" principle and the exclusion of poverty from protection under the Constitution; and the ways in which the United States excuses itself from serious application of international human rights standards.

In closing Part II—and in preparation for Parts III and IV, which discuss structural inequity and historically disadvantaged populations, respectively—this chapter provides an overview of federal antidiscrimination law.[1] Unfortunately, the roots of persistent discrimination in this country were buried deeply and exhaustively hundreds of years ago, and the nation has never truly done the hard work of digging them out. At the hands of those who colonized North America, Indigenous People and African Americans suffered unconscionable genocide, enslavement, and legalized racial oppression. This treatment in and of itself, however—as barbaric as it was—is not what locked in subsequent centuries of discrimination and maltreatment. Rather, it set in motion in the United States an evolving and durable belief system that perpetuated the myth that People of Color—Black people, in particular—are inferior to White people.[2] This had the long-term effects of legitimizing slavery and relegating People of Color to a lower social, financial, and educational status relative to Whites. This belief system has been resistant enough to survive the Civil War, passage and implementation of the Constitution's Thirteenth and Fourteenth Amendments, the Civil Rights Movement of the 1960s, and the election of the first Black president. The nation's history of discrimination against People of Color—and other marginalized populations, including women, people with disabilities, LGBTQ+ people, and immigrants—has also prevented tens of millions of people from obtaining equal access to critical resources and opportunities. In fact, Eduardo Porter, author of *American Poison*, contends that the American majority concluded that if public goods had to be shared with minoritized populations, it would rather not have them at all:

> That's why the United States failed to build the safeguards erected in other advanced countries to protect those on the wrong side of wrenching economic and social change. Americans may hope to rationalize the omission as some sort of historical inevitability, the only natural choice for a self-reliant people bred on a rugged, ungoverned frontier. But their choice to leave those sinking to sink further has a darker parentage.[3]

Indeed, the enduring belief system about White supremacy and the miserly approach to social solidarity that emerged from this nation's discriminatory past are so profound in the area of health care that the most authoritative treatise on the subject of health care discrimination—Michael Byrd and Linda Clayton's *An American Health Dilemma*[4]—is nearly 1,500 pages in

length. Over two volumes, the authors cover the historical relationship in the United States between race, biology, and health care; Black health from the precolonial period through 1900; a discussion of the dual (and unequal) health systems that were created for Black and White people and the ways in which these systems persisted through the civil rights era; the role of civil rights law in Black health; and much more.

This chapter begins with an overview of federal antidiscrimination law. It then describes a range of laws that have been enacted to specifically shield certain "protected classes" from discrimination and thus prevent discrimination from leeching into key areas of social life, such as employment, housing, education, and public accommodations. (Recall that Chapter 4 discussed protected classes and the criteria the U.S. Supreme Court uses to determine which groups gain heightened protection from discrimination under the federal Constitution; refer back to that chapter's discussion of equal protection jurisprudence if you would like a refresher.) Following that description, the chapter turns to two key limitations of antidiscrimination law: the fact that it is better designed to prevent and punish intentional discrimination (i.e., "disparate treatment") but not unintentional discrimination that nonetheless results in harm (i.e., "disparate impact") and the fact that it is exceedingly difficult to remediate the consequences of implicit biases through law.

Overview of Federal Antidiscrimination Law

Discrimination refers to the act of treating someone less favorably based on a group, class, or category to which they belong. Antidiscrimination law, then, refers to laws that are designed to prevent discrimination against particular groups or classes of people. (Federal antidiscrimination law can take the form of constitutional provisions, statutes, and regulations; in this chapter, we focus on statutory law.) Importantly, and as discussed further later, antidiscrimination laws are generally designed to prevent *intentional* discrimination, although some laws go further to reach unintentional discrimination that nonetheless disproportionately and adversely impacts a protected group. Laws can be designed to protect against discrimination committed by individuals and/or discrimination that arises from policies or practices that operate on a societal level.

While the country's earliest civil rights laws addressed some forms of discrimination (e.g., the Civil Rights Act of 1866 declared all persons born in the United States to be citizens; the Civil Rights Act of 1875 provided for equal treatment of Black people in public accommodations and public transportation), the most important development in U.S. antidiscrimination law was the Civil Rights Act of 1964.[5] This federal law was far broader than anything that came before it, prohibiting discrimination on the basis of race, color, religion, sex, and national origin in areas of society as varied as voting, education, employment, and public accommodations (i.e., a place that offers goods and services to the general public, whether owned and operated privately or by the government). The 1964 Civil Rights Act also paved the way for other federal antidiscrimination laws.

Some commentators go even further, contending that passage of the 1964 law was responsible for important shifts in the views of the American public with regard to discrimination and antidiscrimination law.[6] Under this view, at the time that *Brown v. Board of Education*[7] was decided by the U.S. Supreme Court in 1954, there was strong majority resistance to broad antidiscrimination legislation; many Whites still believed in White supremacy, and many others simply held strong prejudices against People of Color and other disadvantaged groups.[8]

Over the next 10 years, as the Civil Rights Movement (1954–1968) picked up speed and the Supreme Court released additional decisions recognizing discrimination as a serious societal problem, support grew little by little for federal antidiscrimination law. Support for disparate impact discrimination protection was germinated during this time, and support (in some circles) for affirmative action policies increased.[9] With the country primed in this way, passage of the Civil Rights Act in 1964 was apparently transformative. By the late 1970s, most White Americans agreed (at least publicly) with the need for powerful antidiscrimination laws, public expressions of racism and other prejudices were generally not tolerated, and implicit (i.e., subconscious) bias became the next battlefield in terms of creating equality in areas such as education, employment, housing, and more.[10] With that brief overview in place, we turn now to a description of several key federal antidiscrimination laws.

Antidiscrimination Law: Protecting Specific Classes and Promoting Equality

Under the federal Constitution, certain characteristics such as race, national origin, religion, and sex have been declared "suspect" or "quasi-suspect" classes by the U.S. Supreme Court, a designation that indicates that people have suffered governmental discrimination on the basis of these characteristics in the past (see Chapter 4). As a result, the Supreme Court interprets the Constitution's equal protection clause in a way that grants special protection against governmental discrimination to these classes, and Congress has passed laws to protect these populations from nongovernmental discrimination as well. Furthermore, Congress has determined that various populations and characteristics not singled out under equal protection jurisprudence also deserve antidiscrimination protections (e.g., the Vietnam Era Veterans' Readjustment Assistance Act[11] prohibits federal contractors from discriminating in employment against veterans and requires employers to take affirmative action to recruit, hire, promote, and retain them).

Due to space constraints, we focus here on those antidiscrimination laws most relevant to the populations and themes highlighted in this text. In Part IV of this book—which describes in detail the health justice struggles of Asian, Black, Indigenous, and Latinx people; immigrants; women; LGBTQ+ people; and people with disabilities—several of the laws noted receive additional treatment. The laws are listed in chronological order.

- The Civil Rights Act of 1866[12] declared that all people born in the United States were U.S. citizens and had the rights to make contracts, own property, sue in court, and enjoy the full protection of federal law. Although the law's original purpose was to protect the rights of the newly freed slaves, courts have interpreted it to protect people of all races from discrimination and harassment.

- The Equal Pay Act (1963)[13] was aimed at abolishing wage disparities based on sex and requires employers to provide equal pay for equal work (though employers are permitted under the law to pay different salaries for equal work if the difference is based on seniority, merit, an incentive system, etc.).

- Title VI of the Civil Rights Act of 1964[14] prohibits discrimination on the basis of race, color, or national origin by programs and activities that receive federal funding. The statute passed by Congress bans intentional discrimination, while the statute's implementing regulations go further to reach conduct and practices that, even if unintentional, nonetheless have a disproportionate adverse impact

on minority groups.[15] Although Congress has never passed a comprehensive health care antidiscrimination law comparable to, say, laws in the areas of employment, voting, or housing, health care discrimination was very much in the minds of those who designed and passed Title VI.[16] However, while Title VI remains deeply important to efforts to stamp out discrimination in health care, the ability of individuals to enforce their rights under the law was deeply undercut by a controversial U.S. Supreme Court decision in 2001 (discussed later).

- Title VII of the Civil Rights Act of 1964[17] prohibits employers from discriminating against job applicants and employees on the basis of race, color, religion, sex, and national origin and further bans employers from retaliating against a job applicant or employee who asserts their rights under the law. Title VII reaches working conditions, hiring and firing processes, compensation, benefits, job assignments, promotions, and disciplinary matters. Like Title VI, Title VII prohibits both intentional discrimination and also seemingly neutral decisions and practices that nonetheless adversely impact groups covered by the law. Furthermore, in the 2020 case of *Bostock v. Clayton County*,[18] the U.S. Supreme Court held that employment discrimination on the basis of sexual orientation or gender identity also violates Title VII.

- The Voting Rights Act of 1965[19] is one of the most important civil rights laws in the nation's history. Enacted to make the promise of the right to vote under the Constitution's Fifteenth Amendment a reality, it brought about several changes: It outlawed the use of literacy tests in the voting process; required jurisdictions with a history of voting discrimination to obtain "preclearance" for any new voting practices (although in the 2013 decision

Shelby County v. Holder,[20] a deeply divided U.S. Supreme Court eviscerated this requirement); it prohibited the denial or abridgment of the right to vote on account of race or color; and it directed the attorney general to challenge the use of poll taxes in state and local elections, after which the Supreme Court held these taxes to be unconstitutional.[21] (The use of poll taxes in national elections had already been abolished by the Constitution's Twenty-Fourth Amendment.)[22]

- The Fair Housing Act (1968)[23] protects people from discrimination on the basis of race, color, national origin, religion, sex, familial status, and disability when they are renting or buying a home, applying for a mortgage, and more. For example, it is illegal under the act to do any of the following on the basis of any of the noted protected characteristics: refuse to rent or sell housing; refuse to negotiate for housing; set different terms, conditions, or privileges for the sale or rental of a dwelling; provide different housing services or facilities; refuse to make a mortgage loan or provide other financial assistance for a dwelling; impose different terms or conditions on a mortgage; discriminate in appraising a dwelling; and more.

- Title IX of the Education Amendments (1972)[24] prevents any education program or activity receiving federal funding from excluding from participation, denying benefits, or discriminating on the basis of sex (which the law defines to include pregnancy, sexual orientation, and gender identity). Because "programs and activities" are defined as including "all of the operations of . . . a college, university, or other postsecondary institution, or a public system of higher education,"[25] Title IX's reach is long: Its nondiscrimination protections apply to student recruitment, admissions, educational programs and courses, research, housing, counseling,

financial and employment assistance, health and insurance benefits, health services, and more.

- Section 504 of the Rehabilitation Act (1973)[26] prohibits discrimination on the basis of disability in programs conducted by federal agencies, in programs receiving federal funding, in federal employment, and in the employment practices of federal contractors. Additionally, the law requires covered entities to provide "reasonable accommodations" to people with disabilities, meaning, for example, that an employer is required to take reasonable steps to accommodate an employee's disability (unless doing so would cause the employer "undue hardship").

- The Pregnancy Discrimination Act (1978)[27] amended Title VII of the 1964 Civil Rights Act to make it illegal for employers to discriminate on the basis of pregnancy, childbirth, or a related medical condition (including those related to miscarriage or termination of a pregnancy). The act forbids pregnancy-related discrimination in all aspects of employment, including hiring, firing, pay, job assignments, promotions, layoff, training, fringe benefits, and any other term or condition of employment. (This includes prohibitions against forcing employees to take leave when they are still able to perform their jobs and making assumptions about their ability or willingness to work after childbirth.)

- The Immigration Reform and Control Act (1986)[28] prohibits employers from discriminating against job applicants and employees on the basis of their citizenship or national origin in the areas of hiring, firing, compensation, benefits, job assignments, promotions, and discipline.

- Although the Emergency Medical Treatment and Active Labor Act (1986)[29] is technically a health care access law, it is an antidiscrimination law at its core.

The law was enacted to prevent hospitals from "dumping patients"—denying care to poor or uninsured persons in need of emergency health care. (Patient dumping was a common strategy among private hospitals aiming to shield themselves from the potentially uncompensated costs associated with treating poor and/or uninsured patients. By "dumping" these individuals onto public hospitals, private institutions effectively limited their patients to those who were insured or able to pay for their care out-of-pocket.) The law requires that everyone—regardless of race, health insurance status, or ability to pay—presenting at a hospital emergency room be screened and treated for an emergency medical condition.

- The Americans with Disabilities Act (1990)[30] is a landmark civil rights law that prohibits discrimination on the basis of physical and mental disability and guarantees that people with disabilities have equal employment opportunities, equal access to the goods and services offered by public accommodations, and equal participation in government programs. Importantly, the law expands on the antidiscrimination protections offered by Section 504 of the Rehabilitation Act—which applies only to entities receiving federal funds—by covering "places of public accommodation," including private hospitals and other private health care providers.

- Section 1557 of the Affordable Care Act (2010)[31] expands the reach of several existing federal civil rights laws by applying them to programs and activities covered by the ACA. The provision prohibits discrimination on the basis of race, color, national origin, sex, age, or disability, and it represents the first time that federal law has broadly prohibited sex discrimination in health care. Specifically, Section 1557 extends its antidiscrimination protections to (1) individuals participating in any

health program or activity, any part of which receives funding from the federal government (an important declaration because it effectively bars private entities that participate in public programs from limiting their compliance only to certain areas or services); (2) individuals participating in any program or activity that is administered by the U.S. Department of Health and Human Services under Title I of the ACA, including the ACA's federally facilitated insurance marketplace; and (3) individuals who purchase health insurance products through state-level ACA marketplaces. Importantly, Section 1557 also makes clear that federal funding includes health insurance policies purchased with federal subsidies, meaning that Section 1557 applies, for example, to insurers that participate in Medicaid, Medicare, and the Children's Health Insurance Program.

As noted, readers will encounter deeper analyses of many of these laws in Part IV of this book. For now, with these summaries in place, we turn to a discussion of two key limitations of federal antidiscrimination law: the narrowing of "disparate impact" protections and the challenge of remediating implicit bias.

The Limits of Federal Antidiscrimination Law

The Narrowing of "Disparate Impact" Protections

As alluded to earlier in this chapter, several federal laws protect against two different types of discrimination: disparate treatment (intentional discrimination) and disparate impact (unintentional discrimination that nonetheless produces disproportionate adverse results for a protected group). In the case of disparate impact, the aim of antidiscrimination law is to remedy the impact of the prohibited conduct rather than focus on an offender's motive. In today's society, intentional discrimination against protected classes is less common than it used to be, and when it is alleged, it is rarely proven because offenders are careful not to leave behind "smoking gun" evidence of their discriminatory intent. As a result, disparate impact protections take on heightened importance in federal antidiscrimination law. Unfortunately, over the past 20 years—as the membership of the U.S. Supreme Court has become more conservative in its approach to civil rights law—disparate impact protections have been constricted, a trend that is likely to continue. We describe this change through the lens of three cases: *Alexander v. Sandoval*,[32] decided by the U.S. Supreme Court in 2001; *Texas Department of Housing & Community Affairs v. The Inclusive Communities Project, Inc.*,[33] decided by the same court in 2015; and *CVS Pharmacy, Inc. v. Doe*,[34] a case the U.S. Supreme Court agreed to hear in 2021 but that was ultimately settled by the litigants.

The Decision in Alexander v. Sandoval

Alexander v. Sandoval is a case that revolves around Title VI of the 1964 Civil Rights Act. Recall two things about Title VI: It prohibits discrimination on the basis of race, color, or national origin by programs and activities that receive federal funding, and it bans disparate treatment (by statute) and disparate impact (by the regulations passed to enforce the statutory prohibition). The lawsuit in *Sandoval* began in 1996 when non-English-speaking residents of Alabama alleged that the state's Department of Public Safety discriminated against them on the basis of national origin by refusing to offer drivers' licensing exams in any language other than English. The plaintiffs did not contend that Alabama intentionally discriminated against them, as they weren't prohibited from applying for their drivers' licenses; rather, they

argued that the *impact* of Alabama's neutral policy was to discriminate against individuals who hailed from countries where English was not spoken. Because the claim was one of discriminatory impact, it arose under the Title VI regulations, not the statute.

Title VI does not include what's called a private right of action (i.e., an explicit statement that individuals who allege discrimination under the law could themselves file lawsuits in court to enforce their rights). This was not uncommon for legislation written during this era, as federal courts commonly inferred this private right of action when litigants preferred private enforcement over that provided by federal agencies. (For example, the Office for Civil Rights in the U.S. Department of Health and Human Services has the authority to enforce Title VI claims that arise in a health care setting.) And, in fact, prior to the Supreme Court's *Sandoval* decision, every federal Court of Appeals to address the enforcement question concluded that a private right of action existed to enforce Title VI's statutory and regulatory protections. Put differently, for the 35 years between passage of Title VI and the *Sandoval* decision, there was no disagreement in the federal courts concerning the ability of individuals harmed by discriminatory conduct at the hands of federally funded entities to enforce their own rights.

In a single, deeply divisive opinion, a 5–4 majority of the Supreme Court overturned decades of settled civil rights law. In a technical opinion that should make a contortionist proud, the majority ruled that while statutory claims of disparate *treatment* may be enforced by the individuals suffering the discrimination, claims of regulatory disparate *impact* may not; rather, only the federal government has enforcement authority over the most common type of discrimination in today's society. This interpretation of Title VI is neither obvious (a point made clear by the court's four dissenters) nor practical, given that it "leaves persons who allege *de facto* discrimination in the position of having legal protections but no effective legal remedy other than the discretionary and grossly under-staffed federal enforcement machinery" (i.e., enforcement provided by government agencies).[35]

The fallout from *Alexander v. Sandoval* has been far-reaching because of the nature of Title VI: The law reaches discrimination on the basis of race, color, or national origin by *any* entity, program, or activity that receives federal funding. Stop to consider just how vast that universe of recipients must be— including people and entities in the nation's massive health care system—and how many individuals might possibly allege disparate impact discrimination by those recipients. As a result, a discussion of the *Sandoval* fallout is beyond the scope of this section; however, in the endnote to follow, we point readers interested in further discussion of this topic to just a few relevant articles.[36]

The Decision in Texas Department of Housing & Community Affairs v. The Inclusive Communities Project, Inc.

The 2015 case of *Texas Department of Housing & Community Affairs v. The Inclusive Communities Project, Inc.* revolves around the Fair Housing Act (FHA). Recall from earlier in this chapter that the FHA protects people from discrimination on the basis of race, color, national origin, religion, sex, familial status, and disability when they are renting or buying a home, applying for a mortgage, and much more. While the facts, law, and outcome that pertain to this case are different from those just described in *Alexander v. Sandoval*, it is hard when looking ahead to the application of the *Inclusive Communities Project* opinion to not read it as imposing significant limitations on disparate impact law under the FHA.

The facts of the case centered on the distribution of federal low-income housing tax credits to developers that construct low-income housing. In 2009, the Inclusive Communities Project—a Dallas-area not-for-profit community organization committed to racial and economic integration—sued the Texas Department of Housing and Community Affairs (TDHCA), the state housing authority in charge of administering the low-income tax credits in Texas. The community organization claimed that the housing authority disproportionately granted tax credits to developments in predominantly minority neighborhoods over developments in White neighborhoods, resulting in a concentration of low-income housing in minority neighborhoods in violation of the FHA.

The specific legal question in the case was whether the federal trial court used the correct standard for evaluating an FHA claim of disparate impact discrimination. The Supreme Court answered in the affirmative, ruling that the FHA's statutory language sufficiently focuses on the consequences of the actions in question rather than on an actor's intent. However—perhaps to lure to the majority Justice Anthony Kennedy, who at the time was the key swing vote on the Supreme Court— the majority spoke of important limitations on the application of disparate impact law going forward. Indeed, a theme that rises to the top of the majority opinion is the need to "protect potential defendants against abusive disparate-impact claims." For example, the court sent a series of signals to lower federal courts hearing future FHA disparate impact claims to "examine with care" the lawsuits' validity; to be certain that plaintiffs establish a "robust" causal connection between the challenged practice and the alleged disparate impact; to grant a defendant's justification for its behavior unless the justification is "artificial, arbitrary, and unnecessary"; and to ensure that "disparate-impact liability is properly limited."[37]

While technically a close "win" for disparate impact claims under the FHA, the language noted may actually serve to narrow FHA disparate impact law going forward. Furthermore, Justice Kennedy is no longer a member of the Supreme Court, and the court's membership is easily more conservative in its interpretation of civil rights law than it was in 2015. In this new environment, it is not hard to read *Inclusive Communities Project* as a long-term win for future defendants in FHA disparate impact cases.

The Case of CVS Pharmacy, Inc. v. Doe

In 2021, the U.S. Supreme Court agreed to hear the case of *CVS Pharmacy, Inc. v. Doe*. Although the case ended up being settled by the litigants just weeks before oral arguments were to take place, the fact that the court agreed to hear the case at all is noteworthy, given what was at stake. (Under Supreme Court rules, if at least four justices want to hear a case, it is added to the court's docket.) The plaintiffs were individuals with HIV/AIDS who relied on their employer-sponsored health plans to obtain necessary medications. Typically, the plaintiffs filled medicine prescriptions at their local pharmacies. However, CVS Pharmacy, Inc. altered its rules so that the only way that health plan enrollees could obtain specialty medications—including HIV/AIDS drugs—as an "in-network" benefit was through a pharmacy program that only dispensed the drugs by mail or by shipments to CVS pharmacy stores (which then require pickup). The plaintiffs sued, claiming that CVS's program violated Section 1557 of the Affordable Care Act by charging out-of-network prices for specialty medications dispensed at non-CVS pharmacies. (Recall that Section 1557 of the ACA incorporates the antidiscrimination provisions of various federal statutes including, for people with disabilities, Section 504 of the Rehabilitation Act.)

CVS responded that the mail-order program reflected the cost and complexity of specialty medications rather than any particular disability status. However, rather than sticking to the specific facts and merits of the plaintiffs' claim, CVS went further, arguing that disability-based disparate impact claims should *never* be permitted under Section 504 of the Rehabilitation Act (and therefore, by extension, under Section 1557 of the ACA). A federal trial court dismissed all of the plaintiffs' claims. On appeal, the U.S. Court of Appeals for the 9th Circuit revived the plaintiffs' Section 504/ACA claim.

Needless to say, *CVS Pharmacy, Inc. v. Doe* had potentially far-reaching implications for disability antidiscrimination law specifically and disparate impact law more generally. Given that at least four Supreme Court justices were willing to entertain the broad legal attack lodged by CVS, it may only be a matter of time before a different litigant tries to place the same claim in front of the court. And given the court's recent disparate impact jurisprudence, the next case could bring about significant changes to long-standing antidiscrimination law.

The Challenge of Remediating Implicit Bias Through Law

Recall that the beginning of this chapter called out the earliest forms of violence and oppression against Indigenous and Black people. While this type of *overt* persecution is no longer the norm, it laid the groundwork for a cascading, multigenerational belief system premised on the idea of White superiority that persists today through mainly *implicit* biases. Similarly, implicit biases about immigrants and ethnic minorities, women, LGBTQ+ people, and people with disabilities are based on long-standing societal stereotypes and stigma, and they permeate individuals' perceptions and behaviors. "Implicit bias" refers to "bias in judgment and/or behavior that results from subtle cognitive processes (e.g., implicit attitudes and implicit stereotypes) that often operate at a level below conscious awareness and without intentional control."[38] Implicit biases are not inherently bad; according to social psychology research, they allow our brains to structure and categorize information to quickly respond to potentially dangerous situations and to process the huge amount of information we encounter in our daily lives.[39] That said, these fast-acting "automatic beliefs" absolutely have the potential to lead to discriminatory and other harmful behaviors:

> [A]utomatic associations become problematic when they are assumed to predict real world behavior and when decision making is based on them. Automatic negative associations with stereotypes or implicit racial attitudes, while existing in the unconscious, become displayed through the individual's behavior. These behaviors are often apparent in microaggressions, which are "brief and commonplace daily verbal, behavioral, and environmental indignities, whether intentional or unintentional, that communicate hostile, derogatory, or negative racial slights and insults to the target person or group."[40]

What makes implicit biases so enduring is that, generally speaking, individuals consciously hold nonprejudiced beliefs and do not realize that they are being motivated by implicit biases.[41]

There are innumerable ways that implicit biases could influence decision-making around many of the topics and populations discussed in this text—everything from cultural norms and practices, to the nation's system of governance, to the manner in which public institutions and systems operate, to the laws and decisions that dictate housing, education, employment, and opportunities, to daily interpersonal interactions. By way of brief examples, consider the following:

- Implicit bias may explain why the amount of cash assistance available to low-income people depends more on the state in which a family lives rather than the family's experience of poverty. (As you will read in Chapter 7, governmental cash assistance is a critical lifeline to health for many low-income individuals and families.) The Urban Institute—an economic and social policy research organization in Washington, D.C.—found that under the Temporary Assistance to Needy Families (TANF) program, states with larger populations of White people provide more cash assistance and have more generous access rules than states that have larger Black populations. Thus, low-income Black families are more likely to live in states with more restrictive policies for obtaining or keeping TANF benefits.[42]

- Systems designed to spark the use of health information technology can introduce bias into provider–patient relationships. In one electronic medical record system, an airplane icon is displayed for so-called "frequent flyers": patients with chronic physical, mental, or substance use conditions who frequently use emergency departments or psychiatric crisis centers. Usually used pejoratively in a health care context, "frequent flyers" are assumed to be problem patients. (A better term for patients who require relatively high levels of health care is "high need, high cost.") Rather than provide care based on the patient's medical problems, a health care provider using this particular electronic medical record system may instead react to the icon—perhaps without ever having even spoken to the patient—and make assumptions based upon the "frequent flyer" designation. If providers begin encounters with patients with a "problem patient" stereotype in their mind, they may fail to diagnose genuine medical issues or fail to provide quality care.[43] (As discussed in Chapter 12, studies suggest that gender bias plays a role in the diagnosis and treatment of illness in women.)

- Medical education may unwittingly reinforce or encourage implicit bias, thus indoctrinating new generations of health care providers into unconscious stereotyping. For example, clinical vignettes that rely upon racial or gender stereotypes may encourage students to draw conclusions based on these stereotypes rather than on the individual characteristics of patients.[44] Negative role modeling may also contribute to systemic bias in health care. During their formative training years, medical students witness physicians acting upon their implicit biases and may replicate this "hidden curriculum" in practice. Indeed, physicians may assume that patients with limited English proficiency are more difficult to treat because of the time required to engage an interpreter and thus may provide less information to those patients in an effort to save time. Medical students, told in class to provide high-quality care to all patients, receive a different message when they see physicians cut corners as a result of their biases.[45]

It is true that implicit biases are universal. But it is also true that in our society, there are tremendous power imbalances that mean that some implicit biases—say, for example, those held by police officers or federal regulators—are potentially far more forceful than others. Given these two facts, what, if anything, should the law do about implicit biases? In an influential 1987 law review article, Professor Charles Lawrence urged the legal system to take seriously the problem of unconscious bias,[46] and a federal court in 2017 was blunt in its assessment that implicit bias is "no less corrosive of the achievement of equality" than explicit and overt discrimination.[47] But it is at best an open question as to whether existing antidiscrimination law prohibits actions driven by implicit bias, and legal scholars point to the obvious problem of proving causation between unconscious behavior and allegedly unlawful outcomes.[48] Indeed, as much as current antidiscrimination law aims to stamp out differential treatment based on

protected traits, "implicit bias presents obvious difficulties. In many cases entirely unaware of their bias and how it shapes their behavior, people will frequently fail to override their [intuitive] inclinations. Ordinary antidiscrimination law will often face grave difficulties in ferreting out implicit bias even when this bias produces unequal treatment."[49]

It would appear that disparate impact law could serve as a starting point for adjudicating claims premised on implicit biases, given that both concepts traverse areas where there may be harmful outcomes but no perceptible evidence of discriminatory intent. However, one commentator delinks the two concepts (in this instance, in the area of employment):

> Whereas disparate impact claims focus on the impact of a broadly applicable employment policy on a group of employees, implicit bias theory explains how an individual decision maker's unconscious bias may influence a discrete employment decision affecting an individual employee. In many cases challenging an employment decision caused by alleged implicit bias, particularly when the adverse employment action is an individual termination, plaintiffs will struggle to identify the neutral employment policy required to pursue a disparate impact claim.[50]

As the nation's understanding of the role that implicit biases play in decisions and behaviors continues to grow, there would seem to be little doubt that individuals harmed by these biases will resort to legislatures and courts for potential solutions. What happens at that point remains to be seen, but two things bear noting. First, when people are treated differently and adversely because of a protected trait, the principle that underpins antidiscrimination law has been violated, and it shouldn't matter whether the origin of the adverse treatment is implicit or not.[51] Second, while the purpose of antidiscrimination law as applied to claims of disparate treatment is to remedy an *individual's* discriminatory conduct toward another person, the purpose of the law as it pertains to disparate impact is to remedy *systemic* unequal treatment. By undermining the law's reach in the latter context, lawmakers and the courts are effectively treating structural discrimination as if—like slavery and de jure oppression—it is a thing of the past.

Conclusion

This chapter surfaced two of the more unsavory drivers of health injustice—discrimination and bias—both of which remain an enduring component of a society that relegates far too many fellow human beings to the fringes of well-being. While many forms of discrimination are now illegal, the legacy of de jure discrimination—and, indeed, the effects of discriminatory conduct simply not actionable through law—still resonates deeply, as you will read about in Parts III and IV. As for implicit biases, there is much to be done on this front as well. All of us can and should make a more concerted effort to become better aware of our biases because the fact that we have them does not dictate that we act on them. Indeed, implicit bases, once identified, can be controlled—assuming that people are sufficiently motivated to control them.[52] Yet while there are efforts afoot to mainstream these ideas, the legal system is not, as it stands, well equipped to address situations in which unconscious biases end up resulting in harm.[53] According to one legal scholar, "[t]he scientific evidence … provides abundant proof that antidiscrimination law must be refined to fit the empirically supported social science record that demonstrates how unconscious racism causes discrimination and harm in health care and in other contexts as well. The scientific basis for legally distinguishing unconscious and implicit bias from intentional bias has eroded."[54]

References

1. States and cities have their own antidiscrimination laws, of course, and some of them go further in protecting people from discrimination than do their federal counterparts. However, space limitations prevent us from discussing this plethora of state and local law in a meaningful way. By way of example, see Hunt J. A state-by-state examination of nondiscrimination laws and policies [discussing gay and transgender nondiscrimination laws and policies]. Center for American Progress. 2012. https://www.americanprogress.org/article/a-state-by-state-examination-of-nondiscrimination-laws-and-policies/.

2. Equal Justice Initiative. Slavery in America: The Montgomery slave trade. 2018. https://eji.org/reports/slavery-in-america.

3. Porter E. *American Poison: How Racial Hostility Destroyed Our Promise*. New York, NY: Knopf Doubleday Publishing Group; 2020:125.

4. Byrd W, Clayton LA. *An American Health Dilemma: A Medical History of African Americans and the Problem of Race*. New York, NY: Routledge; 2000.

5. Pub. L. No. 88-352, 78 Stat. 253 (codified as amended at 42 U.S.C. § 2000a *et seq.* (1994)).

6. Mercat-Bruns M. *Discrimination at Work: Comparing European, French, and American Law* (Chapter 1). Oakland, CA: University of California Press; 2016.

7. *Brown v. Board of Education of Topeka*, 347 U.S. 483 (1954), was the landmark ruling that U.S. state laws establishing racial segregation in public schools were unconstitutional.

8. Mercat-Bruns M. Discrimination at work: Comparing European, French, and American Law (Chapter 1). Oakland, CA: University of California Press; 2016.

9. Mercat-Bruns M. *Discrimination at Work: Comparing European, French, and American Law* (Chapter 1). Oakland, CA: University of California Press; 2016.

10. Mercat-Bruns M. *Discrimination at Work: Comparing European, French, and American Law* (Chapter 1). Oakland, CA: University of California Press; 2016.

11. 38 U.S.C. § 4212 (1974).

12. 14 Stat. 27–30 (1866).

13. 77 Stat. 56 (1963).

14. 42 U.S.C. 2000d et seq. (1964).

15. Civil Rights Div., U.S. Dep't of Justice, Title VI Legal Manual. 2001. https://www.justice.gov/crt/fcs /T6manual; Barton Smith D. *Health care divided: Race and healing a nation.* Ann Arbor, MI: University of Michigan Press; 1999.

16. Rosenbaum S, Teitelbaum J. Civil rights enforcement in the modern healthcare system: Reinvigorating the role of the federal government in the aftermath of *Alexander v. Sandoval. Yale Law Journal of Health Policy, Law, & Ethics.* 2003. https://digitalcommons.lawyale .edu/yjhple/vol3/iss2/1.

17. 42 U.S.C. § 2000e-2 (1964).

18. 140 S. Ct. 1731 (2020).

19. 79 Stat. 437 (1965).

20. 570 U.S. 529 (2013).

21. *Harper v. Virginia State Board of Elections*, 383 U.S. 663 (1966).

22. National Archives. Our Documents Initiative: Voting Rights Act. https://www.ourdocuments.gov/doc.php? flash=false&doc=100.

23. 42 U.S.C. §§ 3601-3619 (1968).

24. 20 U.S.C. §§ 1681 et seq. (1972).

25. 20 U.S.C. § 1687(2)(A) (1972); see also 45 C.F.R. § 86.2(h) (1977).

26. 29 U.S.C. § 794 (1973).

27. 42 U.S.C. § 2000e(k) (1978).

28. 100 Stat. 3359 (1986).

29. 42 U.S.C. § 1395dd (1986).

30. 42 U.S.C. § 12101 (1990).

31. 42 U.S.C. § 18116 (2010).

32. 532 U.S. 275 (2001).

33. 135 S. Ct. 2507 (2015).

34. 982 F.3d 1204 (9th Cir. 2020).

35. Rosenbaum S, Teitelbaum J. Civil rights enforcement in the modern healthcare system: Reinvigorating the role of the federal government in the aftermath of *Alexander v. Sandoval. Yale Law Journal of Health Policy, Law, & Ethics.* 2003. https://digitalcommons.lawyale .edu/yjhple/vol3/iss2/1.

36. Welner KG. *Alexander v. Sandoval*: A setback for civil rights. Education Policy Analysis Archives. 2001. https://www.researchgate.net/publication/49610050 _Alexander_v_SandovalA_Setback_for_Civil_Rights; Black DW. Picking up the pieces after *Alexander v. Sandoval*: Resurrecting a private cause of action for disparate impact. *North Carolina Law Review.* 2002;81(356). https://papers.ssrn.com/sol3/papers.cfm? abstract_id=2519668; and Core LS. *Alexander v. Sandoval*: Why a supreme court case about driver's licenses matters to environmental justice advocates. *Boston College Environmental Affairs Law Review.* 2002;30:191. https://lawdigitalcommons.bc.edu/ealr/vol30 /iss1/9/.

37. Hancock P, Glass AC. Symposium: The supreme court recognizes but limits disparate impact in its Fair Housing Act decision. SCOTUSblog. 2015. https:// www.scotusblog.com/2015/06/paul-hancock-fha/.

38. Casey PM, Warren RK, Cheesman FL, Elek JK. Helping Courts Address Implicit Bias: Resources for Education B-2. National Center for State Courts; 2012. http:// www.ncsc.org/~/media/Files/PDF/Topics/Gender%20 and%20Racial%20Fairness/IB_report_033012.ashx.

39. Tabesh E. Combating implicit bias in the workplace. Fisher Phillips Blog. 2017. https://www.fisherphillips .com/news-insights/combating-implicit-bias-in-the -workplace.html.

40. Benfer EA. Health justice: A framework (and call to action) for the elimination of health inequity and social justice. *American University Law Review.* 2015;65(2):278–279 (internal footnotes omitted). See also Devine PG, Forscher PS, Austin AJ, Cox WTL. Long-term reduction in implicit race bias: A prejudice habit-breaking intervention. *Journal of Experimental Social Psychology.* 2012;48(6):1267–1278.

41. For examples in the fields of medicine, law enforcement, and law, see, respectively, Sabin JA, Nosek BA, Greenwald AG, Rivara FP. Physicians' implicit and explicit attitudes about race by MD race, ethnicity, and gender. *Journal of Health Care for the Poor and Underserved.* 2009;20:896–913; Correll J, Park B, Judd CM, Wittenbrink B, Sadler MS, Keesee T. Across the thin blue line: Police officers and racial bias in the decision to shoot. *Journal of Personality and Social Psychology.* 2007;92:1006–1023; and Rachlinski JJ, Johnson SL, Wistrich AJ, Guthrie C. Does unconscious racial bias affect trial judges? *Notre Dame Law Review.* 2009;84:1195–1246.

42. Hahn H, Aron LY, Lou C, Pratt E, Okoli A. Why does cash assistance depend on where you live? Washington, DC: Urban Institute. 2017. https:// www.urban.org/research/publication/why-does -cash-welfare-depend-where-you-live.

43. Joy M, Clement T, Sisti D. The ethics of behavioral health information technology: Frequent flyer icons and implicit bias. *JAMA.* 2016;316(15):1539–1540.

44. Buchs S, Mulitalo K. Implicit bias: An opportunity for physician assistants to mindfully reduce health care disparities. *The Journal of Physician Assistant Education.* 2016;27(4):193–195.

45. Kenison TC, Madu A, Krupat E, Ticona L, Vargas IM, Green AR. Through the veil of language: Exploring the hidden curriculum for the care of patients with limited English proficiency. *Academic Medicine.* 2017;92:92–100.

46. Lawrence III CR. The id, the ego, and equal protection: Reckoning with unconscious racism. *Stanford Law Review.* 1987;39:317.

47. *Woods v. City of Greensboro*, 2017 WL 174898 (4th Cir. May 5, 2017) (finding the lower court erred in dismissing minority-owned business's claim of discrimination based on implicit bias).

48. See, e.g., Bagenstos SR. The structural turn and the limits of antidiscrimination law. *California Law Review.* 2006;94:1. https://www.jstor.org/stable/20439026.

49. Jolls C, Sunstein CR. The law of implicit bias. *California Law Review.* 2006;94:969, 976.

50. Tabesh E. Combating implicit bias in the workplace. Fisher Phillips Blog. 2017. https://www.fisherphillips.com/news-insights/combating-implicit-bias-in-the-workplace.html.

51. Jolls C, Sunstein CR. The law of implicit bias. *California Law Review.* 2006;94:969.

52. Bagenstos SR. The structural turn and the limits of antidiscrimination law. California Law Review. 2006;94:1. https://www.jstor.org/stable/20439026.

53. Bagenstos SR. The structural turn and the limits of antidiscrimination law. California Law Review. 2006;94:1. https://www.jstor.org/stable/20439026.

54. Matthew DB. Just medicine: A cure for racial inequality in American health care. New York, NY: NYU Press; 2015.

PART 3

Structural Inequity and Health Injustice

CHAPTER 7

Socioeconomic Status, Unmet Social Needs, and Health

LEARNING OBJECTIVES

By the end of this chapter you will be able to:

- Describe how each aspect of socioeconomic status (education, occupation, wealth and income) are social drivers of health and how they intersect with race, ethnicity, gender, and other types of status
- Explain how economic inequality and poverty influence health and drive population health outcomes in the United States
- Discuss different safety net programs and their role in promoting health

Introduction

When thinking about socioeconomic status (SES), people most often focus solely on income differences. But, in fact, SES encompasses one's education, occupation, income, and wealth, all of which connect to social status or standing in relation to others. SES, therefore, is intersectional: multiple factors converge to produce one's status and economic position in American society. As we highlight in this chapter, SES (education, occupation, wealth, and income) and race, ethnicity, and gender are intricately intertwined and impact people's opportunities and access to a range of services.

An abundance of research and scholarship points to the complex pathways between these social factors and health inequity. As you read this chapter, consider the multiple, often intersecting factors (SES, race, ethnicity, and gender) that contribute to a person's SES and how those factors shape the opportunity to be healthy.

SES and Health

SES, as an important determinant of health, was first uncovered in the 1960s by a research team led by Michael Marmot, a British physician and epidemiologist, in longitudinal studies known as the "Whitehall Studies." What Dr. Marmot and his team discovered was that, despite universal access to health care through the National Health Service in the United Kingdom, health outcomes varied significantly by SES. Specifically, Marmot tracked health outcomes by differences in employment grade in the British civil service as a marker for social class, finding that participants with lower status in the work hierarchy had worse health outcomes. For example, for coronary heart disease, the researchers found that men in the lowest civil service grade were 3.6 times more likely to die from the disease than men in the highest grade. The differences persisted even after adjusting for health and lifestyle factors.[1]

What was truly groundbreaking in the Whitehall Studies is that researchers found a social gradient in health, meaning that the differences in health outcomes were not only present when comparing the highest and the lowest classes; they were present at every step of the social hierarchy. Marmot explains: "Socioeconomic differences in health are not confined to poor health for those at the bottom and good health for everyone else. Rather, there is a social gradient in health in individuals who are not poor: the higher the social position, the better the health. I have labeled this 'the status syndrome.'"[2] According to Marmot, the status syndrome is determined not just by social class, but also by people's sense of "[a]utonomy—how much control you have over your life—and the opportunities you have for full social engagement and participation"[3] in society.

While Americans may prefer to view the United States as a classless society without the type of social hierarchy that exists in the United Kingdom, a number of studies show that the United States actually lags behind other countries in social mobility—the ability to move from the lower class to the middle class or from the middle class to upper class. A study by the Economic Mobility Project of the Pew Charitable Trusts found that 66% of Americans who started out in families in the top fifth for income remain in the top two-fifths while 66% of those born in the bottom fifth stay in the bottom two-fifths.[4] Additionally, research on SES and health shows that a social gradient in health holds true in the United States, like that described by Marmot in the United Kingdom. For example, a study of multiple health indicators for children and adults by SES found that "those with the lowest income and who were least educated were consistently least healthy, but for most indicators, even groups with intermediate income and education levels were less healthy than the wealthiest and most educated."[5] SES is associated with a range of diseases, including low birthweight, hypertension, diabetes, cardiovascular disease, arthritis, and cancer. Low SES is also correlated with higher mortality.[6]

Recent studies have related SES to a rise in mortality among working-class Americans. In 2015, researchers Anne Case and Angus Deaton published findings of their study showing that death rates for White people at midlife (ages 45 to 54) were rising from what they termed "deaths of despair"—deaths from suicide, drug and alcohol poisonings, and chronic liver diseases and cirrhosis.[7] Case and Deaton posited that these deaths of despair may be driven by economic insecurity experienced by working-class, non-college-educated White people, particularly men. They noted that "self-reported declines in health, mental health, and ability to conduct activities of daily living and increases in chronic pain and inability to work, as well as clinically measured deteriorations in liver function, all point to growing distress in this population."[8] However, a 2021 study that applied a more granular lens to the data found that those at risk for deaths of despair were not limited to the group identified by Case and Deaton. They found that people with functional disabilities, Native American/Alaska Native people, working-age unemployed people, separated and divorced people, those with net income losses, and those with military service were at highest risk for these types of deaths.[9] Nonetheless, both studies connect social status to health outcomes and certain causes of death.

Drug overdose deaths, particularly from opioids like prescription painkillers, heroin, and fentanyl, have played a major role in premature mortality for more than a decade. While, at least initially, the opioid epidemic has been largely concentrated among lower-SES White people, the crack cocaine epidemic of the 1980s and early 1990s devastated low-income, urban, and predominantly Black communities. The lack of data collected during the crack epidemic makes it difficult to calculate the number of drug overdoses.[10] However, studies show that the impact of the epidemic on Black communities was devastating, including the rise in homicide deaths among young Black men and adverse birth outcomes among Black women.[11] During the COVID-19 pandemic, overdose deaths, which had been rising for years, spiked to nearly 90,000 from January to August 2020, nearly 20,000 more deaths than during the same period in 2019. Experts point to pandemic-related stress but also to the inability of many people suffering from substance use disorders to obtain help during the shutdown.[12] The COVID-19 pandemic also appears to have both initiated and exacerbated mental health and substance use disorders for many people. Forty-one percent of respondents in a survey conducted by the Centers for Disease Control and Prevention (CDC) reported detrimental mental and behavioral health problems related to the stress of the pandemic; 31% reported anxiety or depression; 13% said they started or increased substance use; and 10% considered suicide. More than half of Latinx respondents reported having at least one adverse mental or behavioral health problem, while 66% of those without a high school diploma and 54% of essential workers reported at least one problem.[13]

Clearly socioeconomic status is heavily implicated in population health outcomes. But understanding the pathways between SES and health is extremely complex. **Figure 7.1**

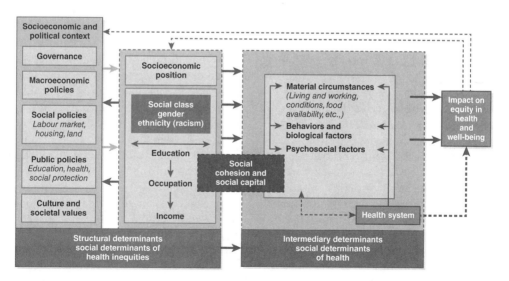

Figure 7.1 Model of the pathways by which SES influences health

Reproduced from Solar, O., & Irwin, A. (2010). A conceptual framework for action on the social determinants of health. WHO Document Production Services. Available at: https://www.who.int/publications/i/item/9789241500852

provides one example of how to map these pathways. But many questions remain. What is the role of education versus occupation versus income in health outcomes? How do these factors influence one another? How do they independently or collectively influence health? What role does SES play in substance use and mental health disorders? How do race and gender intersect with SES to drive health disparities? Does inequality itself shape health outcomes? How does poverty affect health and for how long? We explore each of these factors and their role in health outcomes.

Education

While it is perhaps not as obviously related to health as other basic needs such as access to health care and healthy food, research continues to demonstrate that educational level is closely correlated with health. Compared with college graduates, those who have not completed high school are more than four times as likely to be in fair or poor health. Children's health is also influenced by parental education: Children of parents who have not finished high school are six times as likely to be in fair or poor health as children of college graduates.[14] Health economists have suggested that four additional years of educational attainment can reduce the risk of multiple health outcomes, including mortality, heart disease, and diabetes as well as self-reported poor health status and the number of sick days used.[15] The pathways by which education influences health are multifarious. They are thought to include differences between the more educated and the less educated in health knowledge, literacy, and behavior; the role of educational attainment in employment opportunities and income; and education's effect on sense of control, social standing, and social support.

At the same time, the pathways between education and health are not unidirectional. Health also influences educational attainment. Childhood lead poisoning and asthma can significantly impede educational attainment, as we discuss in Chapter 8. Children who suffer from chronic disease, disability, and mental health disorders are likely to experience disruptions in school functioning, which limits school achievement. Disadvantaged children who are poor or homeless or live in stressful and unstable home environments are also likely to suffer from increased absenteeism and interrupted learning. **Figure 7.2** explains the multiple pathways between education and health.

Health disparities are closely associated with differences in educational opportunity and achievement. For example, health economist Janet Currie reviewed a range of common early childhood physical and mental health conditions known to affect cognitive skills and behavior and for which there are documented racial disparities (lead poisoning, asthma, anemia and iron deficiency, and attention-deficit hyperactivity disorder [ADHD]). She also studied maternal health conditions and behaviors (maternal depression and breastfeeding) believed to influence child cognitive and social functioning. Currie concludes that as much as a quarter of the school readiness gap between Black and White children "might be attributable to health conditions or health behaviors of both mothers and children."[16] She suggests a range of policy responses that may help to reduce these health and educational disparities (including improving access to health care for low-income mothers and children; expansion of early childhood education and development programs that combine multiple services, such as health, child development, and parenting supports; family-based services such as home-visiting programs for high-risk families; and linking nutritional

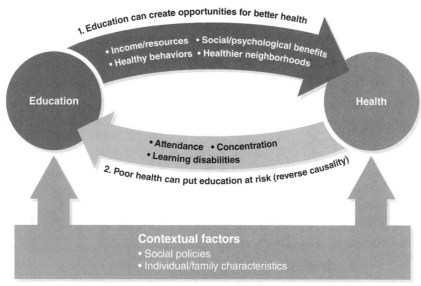

Figure 7.2 How are education and health linked?

supports like the Special Supplemental Nutrition Program for Women, Infants and Children [WIC] to health care).[17] We further explore some of these programs and policies later in this chapter.

Employment

Like education, employment and unemployment are key factors in health. Good jobs provide enough income to allow an individual or family to live in a healthy neighborhood, purchase nutritious food, and have access to quality health care. Additionally, since roughly half of Americans receive their health insurance through employment, a job serves as an important gateway to health care. Just as employment is protective of health, unemployment can harm it. The unemployed are 54% more likely than the employed to be in poor or fair health. They are also at high risk for stress-related

conditions such as heart disease and stroke and to be diagnosed with depression.[18]

But even those who are employed may suffer the health consequences of low-paying, low-quality work. In 2018, 7 million people were classified as "working poor," meaning that they spent at least 27 weeks or more in a year in the labor force (working or looking for work), but their incomes nonetheless fell below the federal poverty level.[19] While the majority of the working poor have full-time jobs, they work in very low-wage jobs. Nearly one-third of American workers are in jobs in which the hourly rate is so low that, even working full time for the full year, their annual earnings would place them below the federal poverty level. Low-wage workers are disproportionately female, young, Black, and/or Latinx.[20]

In addition, many of the working poor cycle in and out of involuntary unemployment, as many low-wage jobs are unstable. Working in a low-wage job has four important consequences for health. First, low-wage workers are more likely to be exposed to dangerous and unhealthy working conditions. Notably, racial and ethnic minorities are more likely to work in jobs with higher risk of injury.[21] Second, many low-wage jobs do not provide workers with affordable health insurance. Third, due to inflexible work schedules and working conditions, access to health care may be impeded. Finally, workers in low-wage jobs are less likely to have access to paid sick and parental leave. Indeed, the United States is the only country among 41 high-income nations that has no nationwide requirement that employers provide some form of paid parental leave.[22] Because many low-wage jobs are part time and/or contingent, low-wage workers are least likely to work for employers that voluntarily provide paid leave. Because women are also more likely to work part time due to caretaking responsibilities, they are less likely than men to have access to health and leave benefits.[23]

The COVID-19 pandemic exposed the vast inequalities that exist across race, gender, and SES in the workplace and presents a stark example of how health and safety are intricately connected to workplace exposures and job status. So-called "essential workers"—those with low-wage frontline jobs such as those working in grocery stores, agriculture, health care, and manufacturing—not only faced greater risk of exposure to COVID-19, but they were also more likely to experience a financial crisis if they were unable to work. Low-wage jobs in these sectors are less likely to provide paid sick leave, further disadvantaging workers if they contracted COVID-19. People of Color and women are more likely to be essential workers, and women are more likely to bear the brunt of the responsibility for child care, leaving them more vulnerable to job loss and economic fragility during a public health emergency (see **Figure 7.3**).[24]

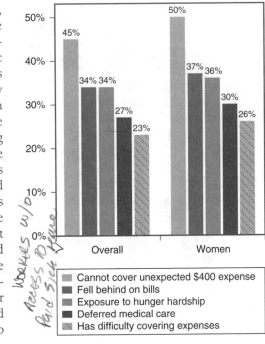

Figure 7.3 Household economic fragility among workers without access to paid sick leave

Reproduced from Schneider D, Harknett K. Essential and vulnerable: service-sector workers and paid sick leave [Internet]. Cambridge [MA]: The Shift Project; 2020 Apr [cited 2021 Apr 29]. Available from: https://shift.hks.harvard.edu/essentialand-vulnerable-service-sector-workers -and-paid-sick-leave/notes: Survey data collected September 2017–November 2019. The exhibit is reproduced with permission of the Shift Project.

Income and Wealth Inequality

Like education level and occupation, income and wealth are highly correlated with health outcomes. Income inequality in America has been growing since the 1980s. While the incomes of the wealthiest 1% of the population grew 226% from 1980 to 2015, incomes of those in the bottom 20% grew only 85% over the same period, and the incomes of those in the middle 60% grew just 47%.[25] Not only has income inequality grown, but wages, when accounting for inflation, have also essentially remained stagnant for the past 40 years (see **Figure 7.4**). There remains a significant wage gap between men and women, which is

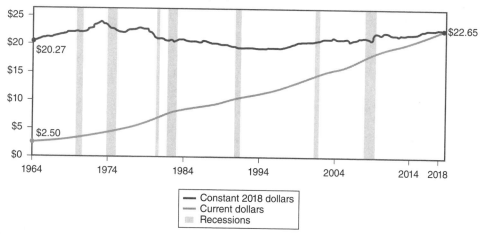

Average hourly wages in the United States, seasonally adjusted

$22.65
$20.27
$2.50

— Constant 2018 dollars
— Current dollars
■ Recessions

Note: Data for wages of production and nonsupervisory employees on private nonfarm payrolls. "Constant 2018 dollars" describes wages adjusted for inflation. "Current dollars" describes wages reported in the value of the currency when received. "Purchasing power" refers to the amount of goods or services that can be bought per unit of currency.

Figure 7.4 Americans' paychecks are bigger than 40 years ago, but their purchasing power has hardly budged

Desilver D. For most U.S. workers, real wages have barely budged in decades. Pew Research Center. August 7, 2018. https://www.pewresearch.org/fact-tank/2018/08/07/for-most-us-workers-real-wages-have-barely-budged-for-decades/

even more pronounced for Women of Color. When taking into consideration all occupations, White women made 78%, Black women made 61%, and Latinx women made 56% of what White men made in 2019 based on annual median earnings.[26]

In addition to rising income inequality and real wage stagnation, there has also been a rising concentration of wealth at the top since the 1980s. Income is the money that a household earns over the course of a year. Wealth is a person's total net worth—assets (property, investments) minus any liabilities (debt). As economists Emmanuel Saez and Gabriel Zucman report, since 1980 the growth in wealth inequality has even outpaced income inequality:

> In 1980, the ratio of aggregate household wealth to national income was 300%. In 2020, this ratio approaches 570%, the highest level ever recorded

in the history of the United States. In other words, during the 1980–2020 period, wealth as a whole has been growing almost twice as fast as income. The result is that relative to what is produced and earned in a given year, the wealth of the rich has skyrocketed.[27]

Furthermore, the wealth gap is not evenly distributed. The Federal Reserve reports that data from the 2019 Survey of Consumer Finances show that White families have eight times the wealth of Black families and five times that of Latinx families.[28]

Inequality and Poverty

As income and wealth inequality have grown, so too have health inequities between the rich and poor.

The gap in life expectancy between the wealthiest and poorest Americans has been widening since the 1970s and is now 10 years for women and nearly 15 years for men.[29] While, as described earlier, health disparities are distributed across a social gradient, here we focus on those at the bottom of the social hierarchy and the large role that poverty plays in poor health. To understand why poverty is such an important predictor of health outcomes, we first explore two key questions about poverty itself: How is poverty defined? and Who is poor in America? We then turn to the causes of poverty, its effects on health, and the role of unmet social needs in health inequities.

What Does It Mean to Be Poor in America?

In his book *Poverty in America*, John Iceland defines poverty simply as "economic, or income, deprivation" and describes two types of poverty measures: an *absolute* measure and a *relative* measure. Absolute poverty measures assume that there is a "measurable subsistence level of income or consumption below which people should be deemed economically disadvantaged or deprived," while relative measures are based on "the notion that poverty is relative to a society's existing level of economic, social and cultural development."[30] In other words, poverty is defined by comparative economic deprivation—people's status relative to others in their country, state, or local community. The United States tends to favor absolute measures of poverty. For example, as discussed later in the chapter, most social safety net programs use a threshold income level—based on family size and regardless of changes to the family's standard of living—for purposes of program eligibility. At the same time, states sometimes use median household income—a relative measure of poverty—to determine eligibility for programs.

Defining who is poor using a relative measure implies that poverty may differ depending on the country in which one lives. In other words, it may be different to be poor in a wealthy nation like the United States than it is to be poor in a very low-income country, such as Bangladesh. It also raises interesting (and controversial) questions about what may be considered the "basic needs" of an individual or family living in the United States. Is having access to a car a basic need in the United States? Can one have a cell phone and be considered poor? Does owning a washing machine, computer, or television or having air-conditioning imply that a family is not poor? What might be considered luxuries in other countries may seem like basic needs in the United States, given the nation's relative overall wealth. Some argue that having items like cell phones and air conditioners means that a family should not be considered poor. As we explore what we call "social needs" and their relation to health, think about those questions.

Who Is Poor in America?

Using official government measures of poverty from the Census, in 2019, 34 million Americans, about 10% of the population, were considered to be living in poverty. The majority of Americans living below the federal poverty level are children. Black people are more than twice as likely to be poor compared to White people, and Latinx people are more than 1.7 times as likely as White people to live in poverty. But as the largest population in the United States, White people make up the majority of the poor—about 22.5 million people. Women are more likely than men to live in poverty, and Women of Color are more likely to be poor than White women (see **Figure 7.5**). The poverty rate is highest among single female–headed households with children under age six.[31]

Although the poverty rate had been declining, it increased from 15% to 16.7% between February and September 2020 largely

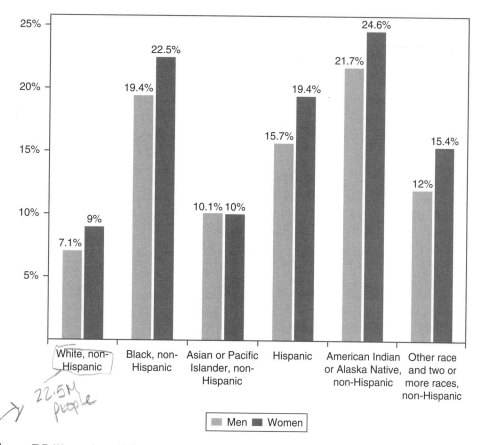

Figure 7.5 Women have higher rates of poverty than men across almost all races and ethnicities

Robin Bleiweis, Diana Boesch, and Alexandra Cawthorne Gaines. The Basic Facts About Women in Poverty. Center for American Progress. August 3, 2020. Available at https://www.americanprogress.org/issues/women/reports/2020/08/03/488536/basic-facts-women-poverty/

due to the COVID-19 pandemic; Black and Latinx Americans saw the largest increases in poverty during this time.[32] As we describe later in the chapter, policies and programs that support people to meet their basic needs are highly effective in reducing the number of families living below the poverty line.

The Effects of Poverty on Health (and Health on Poverty)

While the causal pathways between poverty and health are complex, one thing is clear: Poverty and unmet basic needs are strongly associated with negative health outcomes,[33] and people with limited resources typically present with more "complex clinical needs" than those with more resources.[34] There are a number of theories that attempt to explain these correlations. First, poverty is not just a lack of income; it is associated with a range of other social conditions that may affect health—like access to quality education, health care, housing, nutritious food, and employment opportunities. Second, poverty and health are connected bidirectionally. If one is poor, he or she is more likely to have health problems, but having health problems may also lead one to be poor, as the inability to attend school or work due to illness or disability contributes to poverty. Third, patients with unmet basic needs may not be in a position to direct their attention to long-term goals such as good health because they are focused on surviving day to day. For example, one study found that women with unmet basic needs were less likely to receive diagnostic resolutions after screening positive for cancer. Another study showed that more unmet basic needs are negatively associated with exercise days per week, servings of fruits and vegetables, and being a nonsmoker.[35]

People living in poverty tend to smoke cigarettes more heavily and are less likely to quit smoking cigarettes (34.5%) than those at or above the poverty line (57.5%), even though they try as much as those at or above the poverty line, 66.6% and 69.6%, respectively.[36] Cigarette smoking is associated with the material hardships connected to poverty, such as "lack of social support, unsafe neighborhoods and unmet needs for food and medical care."[37] Furthermore, those with the "lowest educational levels, the least amount of income, the highest levels of poverty, and the lowest occupational status" are the most likely to smoke cigarettes.[38]

Unmet Social Needs and Health

As our understanding of the critical role of social status in producing health continues to expand, researchers are pointing to the fact that the United States stands alone (among its peer nations) in allocating far more resources to medical care than it does to social services and supports. In many respects, the United States has "medicalized" poverty and social problems rather than address them as root causes of poor health. While access to quality health care is imperative, it is but one social driver of health and a relatively small contributor to a person's overall health.

Researchers Elizabeth Bradley and Lauren Taylor first demonstrated how the United States is an outlier among its peer nations in outspending every other one on health care services while significantly underspending on social services such as education, housing, economic development, and food supports. They found that nations in the Organisation for Economic Co-operation and Development (a forum made up of 34 countries with market-based economies who work together to promote economic growth and prosperity) spend two dollars on social services for every one dollar spent on health care—except for the United States, which spends just fifty-five cents on social services for every dollar spent on health care (see **Figure 7.6**). Bradley and Taylor also assessed how this difference in spending might affect health outcomes. Here, they found that countries (and some states) with a higher ratio of social-service-to-health care spending have better health outcomes on many measures. They argue that better integration of medical and social services could improve health outcomes and reduce health disparities.[39] In Chapter 15, we explore initiatives designed to better integrate medical and social services for socially disadvantaged patients and populations.

Next we present some of the ways in which unmet social needs implicate health and present an overview of U.S. safety net programs designed to provide social supports to low-SES individuals and families. We also discuss some of the laws intended to protect health and well-being that, ideally, should protect vulnerable people from injury and harm. As you read about these services and supports, consider these questions: How well do these programs and systems protect the health of low-SES individuals and families? Would greater investment in these upstream services likely help reduce downstream medical costs? What are the benefits and drawbacks of government investment in these services? Is a market-based approach to

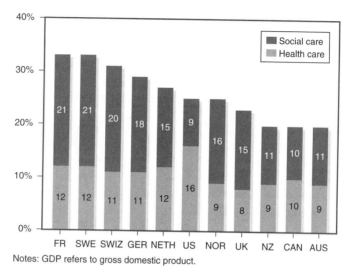

Figure 7.6 Heath and social care spending as a percentage of GDP

Bradley, E., & Taylor, L. (2013). The American health care paradox: Why spending more is getting us less. Public Affairs.

social supports preferred over government intervention? Are there other services and supports that the United States should invest in that would better promote population health and reduce health inequities?

The Structure of the Social Safety Net

We begin with an overview of what is meant by the "social safety net." Who is eligible for safety net programs, and why? Who actually participates in safety net programs? How effective are these programs in reducing poverty (or at least in ameliorating its effects)?

What Is the Safety Net?

The term *safety net* is used to describe the combination of government programs that are designed to prevent individuals and families from falling into poverty. These programs include income supports such as welfare, tax credits, and unemployment insurance as well as subsidies for food and housing and

publicly funded health insurance for eligible individuals.

Who Is Eligible for Safety Net Programs?

Safety net programs may have *categorical eligibility* requirements, *income eligibility* requirements, or both. Categorical eligibility means that a particular category of person is eligible—such as children, people over age 65, or those with disabilities. In the United States, categorical eligibility has historically been determined by making a distinction between the "deserving" and "undeserving" poor. Many safety net programs have been constructed to assist those viewed as particularly vulnerable or deserving of government assistance: single mothers, children, the elderly, and the disabled. Able-bodied adults, regardless of income, have typically been regarded as undeserving of government assistance. Categories of people deemed deserving have evolved over time and still remain controversial. For example, as discussed later in more detail, changes were made to the safety net in 1996 based on the idea that poor single mothers should be considered able-bodied adults and only deserving of government assistance if they demonstrated that they were working or engaged in education and job training.

Generally, income eligibility requirements are based on the *federal poverty guidelines*. Issued each year by the U.S. Department of Health and Human Services (DHHS), these guidelines are based on the *federal poverty threshold*, which is used to calculate the amount of income needed by an individual or family to meet a basic standard of living. **Table 7.1** shows the poverty guidelines for 2021. Safety net program eligibility is often based on a percentage of the federal poverty guideline. For example, eligibility for the Medicaid program (health insurance for low-income and disabled people) may be based on a person's income being 138%

Table 7.1 2021 Poverty Guidelines for the 48 Contiguous States and the District of Columbia

Persons in Family /Household	Poverty Guideline
For families/households with more than 8 persons, add $4,540 for each additional person.	
1	$12,880
2	$17,420
3	$21,960
4	$26,500
5	$31,040
6	$35,580
7	$40,120
8	$44,660

Office of the Assistant Secretary for Planning and Evaluation. 2021 Poverty Guidelines. https://aspe.hhs.gov/topics/poverty-economic-mobility /poverty-guidelines/prior-hhs-poverty-guidelines-federal-register -references/2021-poverty-guidelines

or less of the federal poverty guideline. The federal poverty threshold is criticized as underestimating the number of people who live in poverty because its calculation of the cost of meeting basic needs is too low and does not account for a range of factors affecting actual standard of living, including geographic differences, dramatically different housing costs by region, and other expenses borne by individuals and families in the current economy.[40]

What Is an Entitlement?

The media and policymakers often talk about the rising costs of entitlement programs, but what exactly is an entitlement, and how is it different from other government benefits? Some safety net programs are structured to provide benefits to eligible people on a first-come, first-serve basis. The government appropriates a fixed amount of funding to support the benefit program, and when that funding is spent, there is no additional funding to support more benefits, even if all eligible individuals have not received the benefit. This is true, for example, for housing subsidies, as is described later. Other government benefits, however, are legal entitlements, meaning that by law, the government must supply the benefit to all eligible individuals regardless of cost or funding. There is, therefore, no cap on spending for the program; it is an open appropriation. Medicaid and Medicare are examples of entitlement programs.

Who Participates in Safety Net Programs?

Roughly one in five Americans and one in three children receives assistance from a safety net program. Just over 70% of people eligible for a social safety program participate in at least one. Black people are most likely to participate in safety net programs, but White people make up the largest share of recipients. Whether eligible people receive support varies significantly by where they live. For example, nearly 70% of eligible people in Washington, DC, receive support, while less than 40% of those eligible in Utah do.[41] Immigrants may or may not have access to safety net programs depending on their legal status. Under federal law, undocumented immigrants are not eligible for safety net programs, though some states may extend certain benefits to them. For some safety net programs, such as the Temporary Assistance for Needy Families Program, or TANF (welfare), Medicaid, and SNAP (food stamps), lawful permanent residents may apply only after waiting for five years.

Do Safety Net Programs Reduce Poverty and Improve Health?

Without social safety programs, far more people would live below the federal poverty level. When counting government assistance provided through these programs as additional income, the poverty rate would be twice as high without the safety net.[42] Research also shows that safety net programs focused on economic security render important benefits for health, especially for children. A National Academy of Sciences (NAS) panel on child poverty explains: "The weight of the causal evidence does indeed indicate that income poverty itself causes negative child outcomes."[43] The panel concludes that income supports are connected with a range of improved health outcomes, including lower maternal stress, healthier birth weights, better childhood nutrition, higher reading and math test scores as well as high school graduation rates, and lower rates of drug and alcohol use.[44]

Income Supports

A number of safety net programs are designed to raise household income in order to prevent an individual or family from falling below the poverty line. Income supports are distributed across four main types of government programs: (1) TANF, a welfare program for very poor parents and children; (2) the Unemployment Insurance (UI) program, which provides partial wage replacement during temporary unemployment; (3) the minimum wage, which Congress sets for virtually all workers; (4) the earned income tax credit (EITC), which serves to boost the income of low-wage workers by providing a tax refund for workers earning below a certain annual income. There are additional income support programs for people with disabilities. These are discussed separately in Chapter 14.

The Temporary Assistance for Needy Families Program

The Temporary Assistance for Needy Families Program (TANF) program was created in 1996 as part of the Personal Responsibility and Work Opportunity Reconciliation Act (PRWORA). TANF replaced the Aid to Families with Dependent Children (AFDC) program, which was established in 1935 to provide cash welfare to poor single mothers and their children during the Great Depression. The new program was explicitly designed to "end welfare as we know it" by President Bill Clinton and by the U.S. Congress based on concerns that the AFDC program was creating a "culture of dependency" on the government by its recipients. TANF is a federal program that provides block grants—essentially, a predetermined amount of money—to states to design their own welfare programs; states must contribute "maintenance of effort" dollars to support their programs. TANF shifted the focus of welfare away from cash assistance to needy families toward the use of government funding to support work and personal independence. The goals stated in the TANF statute are to "(1) provide assistance to needy families so that children may be cared for in their own homes or in the homes of relatives; (2) end the dependence of needy parents on government benefits by promoting job preparation, work, and marriage; (3) prevent and reduce the incidence of out of wedlock pregnancies and establish annual numerical goals for preventing and reducing the incidence of these pregnancies; and (4) encourage the formation and maintenance of two parent families."[45]

To meet these goals, the law provides strict work requirements for recipients as well as a five-year lifetime limit on receipt of benefits. Studies of the TANF program show that the number of poor families receiving assistance has dropped dramatically over time as states have continued to reduce benefits. Nationally, in 1996, 68 out of 100 poor families received TANF benefits; in 2019, 23 out of 100 poor families received TANF. But there is vast disparity by state; the number of families receiving TANF for every 100 poor families ranges from four in Louisiana to 70 in California. Federal policymakers have not increased TANF spending since 1996; as a result, the benefit has "lost nearly 40 percent of its value due to inflation."[46]

Some states use federal TANF block grant funds to pay for subsidized child care for low-income working parents. States are permitted under federal law to use TANF funds directly for child care assistance or to transfer up to 30% of their TANF funds to the state's Child Care and Development Block Grant (CCDBG), another federal grant program to states. This assistance is a critically important factor in enabling parents—particularly women—to work, and it helps protect families from falling into poverty by reducing out-of-pocket expenses for child care, which can absorb a large portion of monthly income. Indeed, child care expenses for two children consumes the largest share of family expenses, exceeding housing.[47]

After passage of PRWORA in 1996, many states expanded their child care assistance programs to support low-income parents as they transitioned into work. But funding for child care assistance has declined significantly in the past decade. From 2000 to 2019, TANF funds used by states for child care declined 42%.[48] Without financial assistance, many low-income parents are forced to accept poorer-quality child care in order to work. Studies show that low-income mothers are more likely to rely on informal, lower-quality care arrangements than higher-income mothers. However, when provided financial assistance, they are more likely to select child care centers that provide better opportunities for early learning.[49] Early child development and education programs have been shown to be particularly important to promote school readiness for low-income children, who often present at school as educationally behind their more affluent peers.[50] In addition, according to one study, children who participate in well-designed, responsive preschools have fewer behavioral problems in middle school.[51] As you read earlier, educational success is highly correlated with good health outcomes and vice versa. Not only does access to quality child care enable parents to work and help to alleviate parental stress, it supports critical early development and learning opportunities for their children, affecting kids' health and life course.

Unemployment Insurance

Earlier in the chapter, we outlined the role that employment plays in health and the detrimental effects of unemployment on health. The Unemployment Insurance (UI) program is designed to provide a financial buffer to those who have lost their jobs as they search for employment. It is administered jointly by the U.S. Department of Labor and the states to provide temporary, partial income replacement for workers who have lost their jobs through no fault of their own. States set eligibility and benefit levels. To qualify, workers must certify that they are able to seek and are actively seeking work. UI benefits typically amount to about half of a worker's prior wages, up to a maximum benefit amount, and can be taken for a period up to 26 weeks. During the Great Recession, when the unemployment rate soared, most states extended the period for up to 99 weeks. While some policymakers were concerned that this extension would lead individuals to stop looking for work, some economists suggest that the extension did not affect job growth.[52]

Similar concerns arose during the COVID-19 pandemic when Congress passed the American Rescue Plan in 2021, temporarily allowing states to extend the duration of unemployment insurance, provide additional payments, and cover certain workers (such as "gig" workers) in order to support individuals who lost their jobs when businesses and other employers were forced to shut down.[53]

The Minimum Wage

The federal minimum wage of $7.25 per hour has not changed since 2009, though slightly more than half of the states have a higher rate. Seven states have no minimum wage or their minimum wage is set below the federal one.[53] In recent years, advocates have pushed for a $15 per hour federal minimum wage and have successfully persuaded some state and local lawmakers to increase the minimum wage to $15 per hour. Research demonstrates that a higher minimum wage is associated with a number of health benefits. These include better birth outcomes, reductions in death by suicide, decreases in hypertension, and better health behaviors. Yet some researchers warn that raising the federal minimum wage could bring negative consequences for some workers who are more vulnerable should employers respond to the required wage increase by decreasing hours. These workers include Black and Latinx men and women who are more likely to work in low-wage, less stable jobs. Cecile Joan Avila and Austin Frakt caution that "[w]hile a federal minimum wage increase is overdue, to maximize benefits and minimize harms, it has to be done with a degree of sensitivity to disparate impacts across subpopulations not often present in broad legislative agendas."[55] They argue that policymakers should analyze the research on the impact of raising the minimum wage on these workers and, if there is a detrimental effect, combine the raise with other safety net supports.

The Earned Income Tax Credit

The earned income tax credit (EITC) is a federal tax credit for low- and moderate-income working people—those with children and earning below about $41,000 to $56,000 (depending on marital status and the number of children) and single adults without children earning below about $15,570. The EITC has two core goals: (1) encourage and reward work and (2) reduce poverty. A worker's EITC grows with each additional dollar of wages until it reaches the maximum value. The EITC is refundable, meaning that if it exceeds a low-wage worker's income tax liability, the IRS will refund the balance. The average EITC for a family with children for tax year 2017 was $3,171. The Center for Budget Policy and Priorities—a nonpartisan research and policy institute in Washington, DC—estimates that in 2018, the EITC lifted 5.6 million people out of poverty and reduced the severity of poverty for another 16.5 million people.[56] A 2020 study published in the *Journal of Public Economics* found that children exposed to a 3% increase in the average annual EITC between birth and age 18 are more likely to report good or excellent health and less likely to be obese between the AGES of 22 and 27 than those not exposed to the increase.[57] Given the rise in income inequality in the past 35 years and its role in health inequality, income support programs, like those described here, are critical to reducing health inequities and improving overall population health. However, much of the American public is resistant to expansion of safety net programs.

Employment Protections

It is beyond the scope of this chapter to outline all of the legal protections available to workers; instead, we focus on two that specifically implicate health and safety: workers' compensation and the Family and Medical Leave Act. Employment protections for disabled workers are discussed in Chapter 14.

Workers' Compensation

A state-mandated insurance program, workers' compensation provides compensation to workers for job-related illnesses and injuries. Workers' compensation is a no-fault program, meaning that workers are eligible for compensation regardless of who is at fault for the injury. Workers compensated under the program relinquish their right to sue the employer for damages based on their injuries. Unfortunately, the workers' compensation system appears to be failing most low-wage workers. A study of violations of labor laws

in American cities found that of the workers surveyed who had been seriously injured in their jobs, only 8% had filed a workers' compensation claim, and of all the injured workers in the sample, only 6% ultimately had claims paid through workers' compensation. Fifty percent of individuals who told their employer of their injury experienced an illegal response from their employer—"including firing the worker, calling immigration authorities, or instructing the worker not to file for Workers' Compensation."[58]

The Family and Medical Leave Act

The Family and Medical Leave Act (FMLA) provides up to 12 weeks of unpaid, job-protected leave to qualifying employees for specified circumstances, including the following:

- The birth or adoption of a child
- To care for a seriously ill family member (spouse, child, or parent)
- To care for an injured service member in the family or, in some cases, for circumstances arising out of a family member's deployment
- To recover from the employee's own illness

The law covers government employers, schools, and private-sector employers who employ 50 or more workers. To qualify, an employee must have been employed for at least 12 months and have worked at least 1,250 hours during the previous year. Employees do not have to take all 12 weeks of leave at once; it may be used on an intermittent basis as long as it meets the requirements of the law.[59]

The law applies to only about one in six worksites in the United States because smaller employers are exempted and because it excludes roughly half of employees based on its hourly requirements.[60] Furthermore, while the law protects employees from losing their jobs because of the need to take time off for illness or to care for a family member, it does not require that the employer pay the employee during his or her absence. For low-income workers who are not in a position to take unpaid leave, the law may have little value. Most low-income parents do not get paid when they need to care for a sick child. This includes two-thirds of women with income below 200% of the federal poverty level and three-quarters of women living below poverty.[61]

Lack of access to paid sick and family leave has important implications for health. It puts low-income families in an untenable position of choosing between foregoing income for basic needs, potentially losing employment altogether, or taking needed time during illness or to care for a sick family member. Increasingly, states and some counties and cities are passing paid sick and family leave laws. As of November 2021, ten states had passed legislation providing paid family and medical leave.[62] While these laws vary by eligibility requirements, length of leave allowed (i.e., the number of weeks), and amount of benefit, they all allow employees to take leave with some financial cushion. A study in New York City found that the city's paid leave program was associated with a decrease in the probability of emergency care, particularly for conditions treatable in a primary care setting.[63] In 2021 the Biden administration proposed the American Families Plan, which would guarantee paid leave for the birth or adoption of a child, illness, or to care for an ill family member.[64]

Health Care

Because there is no legal right to health care nor a universal government-sponsored health insurance program, the United States has substantially higher rates of uninsured citizens than other comparable nations, many of which provide government-funded insurance (for core health services) to all citizens. For most low- and moderate-income Americans,

the out-of-pocket costs for health care are prohibitively expensive, and thus having adequate insurance coverage for both preventive and catastrophic care is required to access needed health care services. Of course, having health insurance does not ensure access to appropriate quality health care, but it is the first step in making access to services possible for most Americans.

The Patient Protection and Affordable Care Act of 2010 (ACA) expanded access to health insurance in two ways. First, it expanded eligibility for Medicaid, a federal public insurance program for the poor and disabled, which is primarily funded by the federal government and administered by states. The ACA expanded Medicaid coverage to all individuals below 138% of the federal poverty level. Second, the ACA created a mandate that all citizens acquire health insurance or pay a tax, providing subsidies to low- and moderate-income individuals to offset the cost of insurance premiums. In addition to coverage expansions, the law sought to reform and improve several other aspects of the American health care system, including how health care is paid for, implementing quality metrics, and funding programs to improve public health and equity.

The ACA dramatically reduced the number of uninsured individuals, from roughly 44 million people in 2008 to 27 million people in 2017.[65] From 2010 to 2019, there were significant reductions in the percentage of uninsured Black people (from 19.9% to 11.4%), Latinx people (from 32.6% to 20%), and American Indians and Alaska Natives (32% to 21.7%).[66] Despite these gains, a large segment of the population remains uninsured. There are several reasons for this. First, the law, as envisioned by its drafters, has never been fully implemented. As described later, in *National Federation of Independent Business v. Sebelius* (2012), the U.S. Supreme Court determined that expansion of the Medicaid program under the ACA was optional, not required, for states.[67] The result of this decision is that many of the poorest adults in states that did not expand Medicaid remain without coverage or a regular source of health care. Second, Congressional Republicans and former President Donald Trump sought to repeal the ACA and, when that failed, chipped away at core provisions of the law through legislative, regulatory, and legal actions.

Most notably, in 2017, the Republican-controlled Congress passed a law that repealed the tax penalty imposed by the individual mandate. While the individual mandate is still law under the ACA, the IRS no longer enforces the tax penalty.[68] In February 2018, a group of 18 state attorneys general, led by the Texas attorney general, sued in federal district court arguing that without enforcement of the individual mandate as a tax, the entire ACA was unconstitutional. They contended that, because other provisions of the law rely on the individual mandate, the law cannot stand on its own. However, in *California v. Texas*, the Supreme Court dismissed the case, saying that the plaintiffs in the case did not have standing (i.e., they did not allege a sufficient legal interest and potential injury to bring the lawsuit).[69] For now, the ACA remains the major governing structure for the U.S. health care system, with both its benefits and its gaps.

Medicaid

Created in 1965 as part of President Lyndon Johnson's War on Poverty, the Medicaid program was intended to provide a safety net for the very poor and disabled who otherwise could not afford health insurance or who lacked access to health care. Using both categorical and income eligibility criteria, the program covered low-income pregnant women, children, the disabled, and the elderly poor. In 2010, when the ACA

expanded federal eligibility for Medicaid, all individuals with an income below 138% of the federal poverty level—regardless of category (e.g., disability, age)—became eligible and states were required to cover them. But, as noted previously, in a major case in 2012 (*National Federation of Independent Business v. Sebelius*), which challenged Congress's power to require Medicaid expansion in all states, the U.S. Supreme Court held that Congress could not "coerce" states into expanding their Medicaid programs by threatening the loss of other federal Medicaid funding.[70] Given the choice to expand their Medicaid programs to single poor adults with generous support from the federal government, 39 states and the District of Columbia have expanded their programs, while 12 states have not (as of 2021).[71] Six states—Idaho, Maine, Missouri, Nebraska, Oklahoma, and Utah—all expanded their Medicaid program through ballot initiative, meaning that voters decided that they desired expansion when their elected officials did not act.[72]

Low-income adults living in states that did not expand Medicaid fall into what is known as "the coverage gap," those who are not eligible for Medicaid but are also not eligible for subsidies to buy insurance in the ACA's health insurance exchanges. It is estimated that roughly 2.2 million people fall into this gap, although this number fluctuates over time. Roughly a third of those who fall into the coverage gap are parents, one in six has a disability, and a disproportionate share are People of Color (see **Figure 7.7**).[73]

Research shows that Medicaid improves health care utilization, increases self-reported health, and saves lives. A 2017 study found that people living in states that expanded Medicaid experienced reduced out-of-pocket spending, a 41 percentage point increase in having a regular source of care and preventive visits, and a

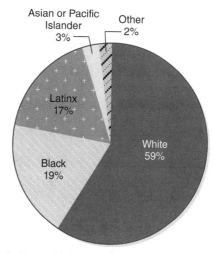

Coverage Gap

American Indian or Alaska Native 1%

Asian or Pacific Islander 1%

Other 2%

Latinx 28%

White 40%

Black 28%

All Nonelderly Adults

Asian or Pacific Islander 3%

Other 2%

Latinx 17%

White 59%

Black 19%

Note: Limited to nonelderly, noninstitutionalized (e.g., not in long-term care or prison) adults aged 19–64 in nonexpansion states. Excludes estimated population lacking legal documentation. Latinx category may include any race; all other categories are non-Latinx.

Figure 7.7 Black and Latinx adults represent more than half the coverage gap despite representing just over a third of all adults in nonexpansion states

Gideon Lukens and Breanna Sharer. Closing Medicaid Coverage Gap Would Help Diverse Group and Narrow Racial Disparities. Center for Budget and Policy Priorities. June 14, 2021. https://www.cbpp.org/research/health/closing-medicaid-coverage-gap-would-help-diverse-group-and-narrow-racial

23 percentage point increase in reports of "excellent" health.[74] In a 2021 study using a novel data set that linked administrative Medicaid enrollment and mortality data to large-scale individual survey records, researchers estimated that from 2014 to 2017, Medicaid expansion prevented the deaths of at least 19,200 adults between the ages of 55 and 64 while 15,600 people in nonexpansion states experienced premature death during the same period.[75]

Medicaid has always been structured as a joint federal–state program in which the federal government matches state funds on an open-ended basis. Apart from core federal standards for coverage and eligibility, states have great flexibility in designing and administering their Medicaid programs. Because Medicaid is an entitlement program, all individuals who are deemed eligible under federal and state requirements

are guaranteed coverage. Medicaid now covers more than 80 million people, or nearly one in five Americans.[76] It is also the major source of coverage for long-term care for older Americans. In addition to providing insurance coverage to individuals, Medicaid finances a large segment of the health care system, including hospitals, nursing homes, community health centers, and physicians and other health care providers.[77]

As the Medicaid program's costs to the federal government and to state budgets have increased over time, some states have limited eligibility and coverage to the minimum federal requirements. Republicans have proposed changing Medicaid from a federal entitlement to a block grant program, similar to TANF, as a way to reduce costs; however, so far, they have been unsuccessful in doing so. Additionally, under the Trump administration, states were encouraged by the Centers for Medicare and Medicaid Services (CMS) to submit applications for waivers from federal requirements that would allow them to impose work requirements for eligibility for their Medicaid programs. Under Section 1115 of the federal Medicaid law, states may submit proposals to CMS for demonstration projects or experiments that "promote the objectives" of the Medicaid program.[78] After receiving approval from the Trump administration, the waiver submitted by Arkansas was struck down by a federal appeals court, which found that the requirements did not help further goals of the Medicaid program (i.e., to provide health insurance to low-income people). In 2021, the Biden administration withdrew the waiver approval for Arkansas granted by the Trump administration, citing evidence that the work requirements in Arkansas led to dramatic reduction in Medicaid enrollment—some 18,000 people were disenrolled—even though 97 percent of them met the work requirements or exemptions. Cumbersome administrative burdens made maintaining coverage challenging for many enrollees.[79] As of July 2021, Arkansas is awaiting a response to its appeal from CMS.

Medicaid enrollment increased during the COVID-19 pandemic by approximately 5 million people. Growth occurred in both expansion and nonexpansion states, though it was larger in expansion states. Economic hardship, including loss of income, and a stronger focus on access to health care during the pandemic likely explain the growth. Congress also provided additional pandemic-related funding to states if they agreed to maintain coverage for current enrollees. This meant that fewer people were disenrolled while new people became eligible.[80]

As you can see, the question of who is deserving of government assistance, whether through income supports or through health insurance coverage, and how much assistance should be provided are issues that remain hotly debated in the United States.

Medicare

Like Medicaid, Medicare was created in 1965 to prevent a vulnerable group—older Americans—from going without health care. Unlike Medicaid, Medicare has no income eligibility requirements but instead is based solely on whether an individual is categorically eligible. Also unlike Medicaid, Medicare has not been subjected to the frequent calls for reform, which most often involve reducing eligibility and reduced funding. Medicare beneficiaries—older Americans—are substantially stronger politically than Medicaid beneficiaries—the poor and disabled. Most individuals ages 65 and over are eligible if they or their spouse have paid payroll taxes for 10 or more years. People under age 65 who are receiving disability benefits (SSI or SSDI) or who have end-stage renal disease or a diagnosis of ALS (Lou Gehrig's disease) are also eligible.

Medicare has four parts to its coverage:

- *Part A.* Hospital Insurance Program, which covers inpatient hospital services, skilled nursing facility, home health, and hospice care
- *Part B.* Supplementary Medical Insurance Program, which covers physician, outpatient, home health, and preventive services
- *Part C.* Medicare Advantage Program, which allows enrollment in private insurance plans
- *Part D.* Prescription drug benefit

"Dual eligibles"—people over the age of 65 who are also low-income—may qualify for both Medicare and Medicaid. In this case, Medicaid pays all of their Medicare premiums, deductibles, and copays and, importantly, pays for long-term care, such as nursing home care.

Children's Health Insurance Program

The Children's Health Insurance Program (CHIP), like Medicaid, is a health insurance program jointly funded by the federal government and the states. It provides coverage to uninsured children up to age 19 in families whose income is too high for them to qualify for Medicaid. States receive a federal match in funding based on the level at which they set eligibility for coverage. For example, if a state sets eligibility at 300% of the federal poverty level (FPL), its match will be higher than if it sets eligibility at 200% of the FPL.[81] Unlike Medicaid and Medicare, CHIP is not a federal entitlement; funding is capped, and Congress must renew funding every few years. Most recently, the Bipartisan Budget Act of 2018 funded CHIP through 2027. Generally, CHIP has been a popular program, garnering bipartisan support.

Community Health Centers

Much of the discussion up to this point has been focused on how the government funds health insurance coverage for particular populations. But as you know, access to insurance does not always equate with access to health care. As a result, the government also makes direct investments in health care delivery for low-income and medically needy individuals through community health centers (CHCs). CHCs provide primary health care to low-income and vulnerable patient populations across the United States, regardless of ability to pay or insurance status. CHCs exist in all states and serve some 28 million people. Ninety-one percent of CHC patients are low-income, 46% are on Medicaid, and 22% are uninsured. Forty-two percent of CHCs are located in rural areas and provide critical care to residents of underserved areas.[82]

Community health centers are organized as nonprofit clinics and are governed by four primary federal requirements. The health centers must (1) be located in underserved areas and serve medically underserved populations, (2) provide comprehensive primary

health care services, (3) operate on a sliding payment scale, and (4) be governed by a community board from which the majority of members must be health center patients. Because the ACA increased direct funding to community health centers, they have been able to grow their services and the number of patients served, particularly in states that expanded their Medicaid programs. Medicaid payments make up 44% of revenue for CHCs.[83]

Although the ACA has expanded access to health insurance and has promoted important reforms to health care systems, U.S. health care ranks 11th, and last, among peer high-income countries across five domains: access to care, care process, administrative efficiency, health care outcomes, and, not surprisingly, equity.[84] Health care reform remains one of the most pressing issues for the nation, as health care costs consume a large percentage of federal and state budgets, while many Americans go without needed health care.

Food Assistance

Just as access to a regular, quality source of health care improves health outcomes, access to sufficient amounts of nutritious and affordable food is necessary for optimal health, including physiological, cognitive, and emotional functioning. Food insecurity in a household may be described as the following: "At times during the year, these households were uncertain of having, or unable to acquire, enough food to meet the needs of all their members because they had insufficient money or other resources for food."[85] The U.S. Department of Agriculture (USDA), which tracks food insecurity in the United States, distinguishes between low food security and very low food security. *Low food security* is associated with "reports of reduced quality, variety, or desirability of diet but little or no indication of reduced food intake." *Very low food security* is associated with "reports of multiple indications of disrupted eating patterns and reduced food intake."[86]

Because being food insecure is related to income, household resources, and access to healthy foods, it is by definition related to poverty.[87] While one does not have to be poor to experience food insecurity, being food insecure is highly correlated with low income. The USDA reports the results of the U.S. Food Security Scale, which is part of the Census Bureau's Current Population Survey. The survey measures the level of food insecurity experienced by individuals and families, including children. Slightly more than 10% of the population were considered food insecure in 2019; 4% of those (about 5 million households) had very low food security. Food insecurity is highest among households with children headed by single mothers; Black and Latinx households also have a higher prevalence of food insecurity than White households. Furthermore, people living in large cities and rural areas are most likely to be food insecure.[88] While food insecurity had been declining in recent years, it skyrocketed in 2020 with the onset of the COVID-19 pandemic. One study found that food insecurity doubled to 23% of households in 2020, with 36% of Black and 32% of Latinx households not having adequate food.[89]

Food insecurity is related to both inadequate quantity and quality of food. When resources are limited, households may trade quality for quantity to avoid hunger. Nutrient-dense, energy-sparse foods (fruits, vegetables, and dairy) are generally more expensive than low-nutrient, energy-dense foods (refined grains, added sugars, and added saturated/trans fats). Therefore, food insecurity is not always connected to hunger. As pediatricians Debra Frank and John Cook note, "Although a young child subsisting on cheap 'junk food' may not cry from hunger, total intake of both macronutrients (calories and protein) and micronutrients may be insufficient for normal growth, leading to stunted growth (nutritional short stature) and underweight for age or height."[90]

The inability to afford healthy, nutrient-rich foods is also linked to obesity. While obesity rates have risen dramatically in the past 30 years among adults and children from all socioeconomic groups, obesity disproportionately affects people of lower socioeconomic and education levels and those from minority groups. In addition to the trade-offs that low-income households make to reduce food costs (e.g., buying low-cost, high-calorie food rather than more expensive, healthier, lower-calorie foods to stretch food budgets), these households are also more likely than higher-income ones to live in *food deserts*, where healthier foods simply are not available. The USDA defines a food desert as "a part of the country vapid of fresh fruit, vegetables, and other healthful whole foods, usually found in impoverished areas. This is largely due to a lack of grocery stores, farmers' markets, and healthy food providers."[91] To qualify as a "low-access community," at least 500 people and/or at least 33% of the Census tract's population must reside more than 1 mile from a supermarket or large grocery store. (For rural Census tracts, the distance is more than 10 miles.)[92]

Particularly for young children, food insecurity can have a significant impact on development.[93] Comparisons of children under the age of 3 living in households with food insecurity with those in food-secure homes show that food-insecure children have worse overall health and more hospitalizations. Children and adolescents living in food-insecure homes are also more likely to be iron-deficient, which can impact kids' energy and attention.[94] The stress associated with food insecurity can also have a significant effect on child health.

In adults, food insecurity is associated with chronic disease, such as diabetes and hypertension (high blood pressure). Food-insecure adults often report that they cannot afford balanced meals and often cut or skip meals. Replacement of fruits and vegetables with inexpensive carbohydrates raises glycemic (blood sugar) levels in adults predisposed to diabetes.[95] Food insecurity among adults also affects health care utilization. One study found that the risk for admission to the hospital for hypoglycemia increased 27% in the last week of the month for a low-income population versus a high-income population. The study authors attribute this difference to food insecurity and the exhaustion by low-income households of food budgets by the end of the month.[96]

There are three main assistance programs designed to alleviate food insecurity and to support nutrition: the Supplemental Nutrition Assistance Program (SNAP); the Special Supplemental Nutrition Program for Women, Infants and Children (WIC); and the School Breakfast and School Lunch Programs.

Supplemental Nutrition Assistance Program

The Supplemental Nutrition Assistance Program (SNAP) (formerly called the Food Stamp Program) was originally created in 1939 as a way to promote the purchase of unmarketable farm surpluses by low-income populations. Over time, it has become the nation's most important anti-hunger program. SNAP is an entitlement program that provides monthly benefits through a set dollar amount for the purchase of qualifying foods. In 2019, an average of 35.7 million people participated in the program per month.[97] Nearly all low-income individuals are eligible for SNAP, though certain immigrants who are lawful permanent residents must undergo a waiting period before becoming eligible for benefits. Undocumented immigrants are not eligible. Childless unemployed adults are limited to receipt of the benefit for three months every three years. Under federal rules, states may

waive the three-month limit during times of economic crisis.

The amount of the SNAP benefit provided to recipients depends on the size of a participating family and the family's income. Benefits are based on an assumption that families will spend 30% of their income on food. A family with no income would qualify for the maximum benefit, while a family with more income would receive the benefit calculated after their expected contribution. Citing evidence that SNAP benefits are insufficient to provide an adequate diet, in 2021, the Biden administration announced the largest increase in SNAP benefits in the history of the program. Recipients will see an average increase of 25% in their benefits.[98]

While the federal government and states jointly fund the costs of administration of SNAP, the federal government is responsible for the full cost of SNAP benefits. At the federal level, SNAP is funded and administered through the USDA's Food and Nutrition Service, which sets program guidelines and supports states in administering the program at the local level. States are responsible for conducting outreach and education, determining who is eligible, and distributing benefits. Hence, there is wide variance in uptake across states, with some states providing benefits to nearly all eligible individuals and families and other states reaching only a percentage of those eligible. Nationwide, it is estimated that about 16% of food-insecure households do not participate in SNAP.[99] Some of the gap in reaching eligible families may have to do with stigma associated with government assistance, but given that some states have much higher participation rates than others, outreach and education likely also play a large role.

Because SNAP serves to reduce food insecurity and also acts as an income support, studies show that it significantly alleviates financial stress on families. Research by Shaefer and Gutierrez suggests that in addition to reducing food insecurity by 13%, SNAP also provides families with more resources for essential needs such as housing, utilities, and medical bills. They estimate that SNAP participation reduces the risk of falling behind on rent by 7%, while it reduces the risk of being unable to pay for utilities by 15%. Another study found that SNAP participation decreased the likelihood of forgoing medical care by 9%.[100]

The Special Supplemental Nutrition Program for Women, Infants, and Children

The Special Supplemental Nutrition Program for Women, Infants, and Children (WIC) is a federal program focused on protecting the nutritional health of pregnant or nursing women, infants, and children under age 5. The eligibility requirements for participation in WIC are that the applicant must be

- A resident in the state in which they are applying
- A pregnant or nursing woman or a child under the age of 5
- Low income
- At risk for poor nutrition

While federal law sets the categorical eligibility requirements for the program (e.g., that the recipient be a qualifying woman, infant, or child), states have leeway in determining income thresholds for eligibility and nutritional requirements for determining if a recipient is "at risk for poor nutrition."[101] Unlike SNAP, WIC does not have immigration status restrictions. Half of all American infants and a quarter of all children ages 1 to 4 are served by the WIC program. Mothers participating in WIC receive nutrition counseling, assistance with locating health care, and support with breastfeeding. Food packages are designed depending on the recipient (adult, infant, or

child) and may include vouchers for cereal, milk, fresh produce, or formula.

A much smaller program than SNAP, WIC reaches roughly 6.7 million women and children, only slightly more than half of those eligible.[102] Given the health consequences of poor nutrition for pregnant women and young children, WIC serves an important purpose in ensuring that nutritional needs are met during this critical period for mothers and young children. The evidence suggests that WIC improves health and well-being. One study assessing whether prenatal participation in WIC improved birth outcomes showed that it was associated with a significant reduction in the infant mortality rate among Black Americans.[103] Another study found that earlier and longer-term participation in WIC by mothers and children reduces food insecurity.[104]

The National School Lunch and Breakfast Programs

The National School Lunch Act was signed in 1946 by President Harry S. Truman to provide nutritious, low-cost or free meals to school-age children. The National School Lunch Program (NSLP) now operates in more than 100,000 public schools, nonprofit private schools, and child care centers. Children in families with incomes below 130% of the federal poverty level are eligible for free lunch, while those from families with incomes between 130% and 185% of the poverty level are eligible for reduced-price lunch.

School meals must meet the nutrition standards set by the latest Dietary Guidelines for Americans. The Healthy Hunger-Free Kids Act of 2010 authorized funding and set policy for core child nutrition programs.[105] Under the Obama administration, with leadership from First Lady Michelle

Obama, federal standards were changed to increase fruits, vegetables, and whole grains in meals; to include calorie limits by age group; and to reduce sodium content. The stricter nutrition regulations met with significant criticism from school districts that complained that the guidelines were difficult to meet and that children were throwing away the healthier meals rather than eating them. This criticism was echoed by Trump administration Agriculture Secretary Sonny Perdue, who announced soon after taking office that the USDA would delay implementation of the sodium requirements and would allow waivers for the regulations regarding whole grains. Yet evidence does not appear to support the claim that offering healthier meals to children is a waste. For example, a 2015 study published in *Childhood Obesity* found that students consumed more fruit and wasted less of their entrees and vegetables after revised nutritional standards went into effect.[106]

The School Breakfast Program (SBP) was established in 1966 to provide grants to schools to offer breakfast to "nutritionally needy" children. Initiated as a pilot program, schools located in poor areas or in areas where children had to travel a great distance to school were targeted for funding. In 1975, when the U.S. Congress made the program permanent, it continued to emphasize participation by schools with severe need. Similar to the NSLP, the program is governed by federal nutritional standards and eligibility requirements. Supporters of the SBP point to research documenting the relationship between hunger and poor academic achievement and the particular role that breakfast plays in improving cognition and attention in school.[107] In response to this argument, some school districts offer universal free breakfast, and some even provide it in the classroom rather than in the cafeteria to encourage all students to eat breakfast.

A 2013 study by Mathematica Policy Research, a research foundation in Washington, DC, estimated the causal effects of universal free breakfast on academic achievement as measured by test scores. Researchers suggested that by reducing the stigma associated with only offering free breakfast to low-income children, students are more likely to participate. They found that improvements in test scores are "at least partly driven by year round benefits [of offering universal free breakfast] rather than only consumption at the time of testing."[108]

The Justice Gap: Access to Legal Assistance for Low-Income People

Federal and state safety net programs provide access to basic resources that promote health and well-being. But, as we have described, many people who are legally entitled to or eligible for safety net programs do not access them, sometimes due to illegal or unaccountable action by government authorities. Access to a legal advocate who is trained to challenge intractable and unresponsive government systems and help low-income people enforce their legal rights is crucial in countering negative social and structural drivers of health. Yet, like the many safety net programs that fall short in meeting the needs of eligible individuals and families, the legal system is inadequate in enforcing the rights of low-income and disadvantaged people, rights that are vital to protecting health and reducing inequities. The United States suffers from a substantial "justice gap"—"the difference between the level of civil legal assistance available and the level that is necessary to meet the legal needs of low-income individuals and families."[109] Just as there is no right to health care in the

United States, there is no right to legal assistance in civil justice matters. Common civil legal problems affecting low-income individuals and families include wrongful denial of government benefits and entitlements, unlawful housing eviction, housing safety code violations, employment discrimination, and inadequate protection in cases of family violence. All of these problems strongly implicate individual and family health and well-being.

In 1974, Congress established the Legal Services Corporation, an independent nonprofit corporation that provides grants to state legal-aid organizations to provide free legal assistance to qualifying low-income individuals, generally those whose incomes are below the federal poverty level. These include 132 nonprofit legal-aid programs with 800 offices around the country.[110] In addition to LSC-funded programs, there are legal-aid organizations that are funded through other means such as state and local governments, Interest on Lawyers' Trust Accounts (IOLTA), the private bar, and philanthropic foundations.

Current funding for legal-aid programs is wholly inadequate to meet the significant legal needs of low-income individuals and families, as described in Chapter 4. Nearly a million individuals who seek out help with a civil legal problem are turned away due to lack of resources among legal-aid programs, and millions of others who could benefit from assistance don't even seek it. A 2017 study by LSC found that "low-income Americans receive inadequate or no professional legal help for 86% of the civil legal problems they face in a given year."[111] The justice gap has enormous ramifications for people's lives as the National Center for Access to Justice notes in its report "Working with Your Hands Tied Behind Your Back":

> Every year, millions of Americans who need help with their legal problems find out that there is no such help on offer. Some are left to go it alone in court, where they may stand little chance against a better-equipped adversary. Some lose their homes, their savings and their children in cases they might have won with the right kind of help. Others avoid the legal system altogether, in situations where it could help vindicate their rights or win reparation for abuse.[112]

Legal Rights, the Safety Net, and Health

As we noted earlier, some safety net programs are legal entitlements—the government is obliged to provide the benefit to all who meet the eligibility requirements—and eligible individuals who are wrongfully denied benefits or whose benefits are erroneously terminated may have legal recourse. An eligible individual may be denied a benefit for a number of reasons: administrative error, communication problems between a government agency and the recipient, or confusion about changing eligibility standards. Often it is difficult for individuals, especially those living in poverty, to have the time, resources, and knowledge to challenge a government bureaucracy's decision on their own. For some government benefits, initial denials and delays are common. Bureaucratic hurdles are sometimes strategies designed to make the process of applying for and sustaining assistance difficult in order to reduce enrollment, thereby saving money for the state or federal government.[113]

Denial of income supports, health insurance, or food assistance can have devastating effects on the health of individuals and families who are living below or close to the poverty line. Notably, the majority of legal problems reported to legal aid lawyers are related to health care. These include debt collection for health care costs and inadequate health insurance coverage (see **Figure 7.8**).

Access to justice advocates are calling for stronger investment in legal services and the right to free legal representation in some civil matters, particularly those affecting health and safety, as we explore in Chapter 15. Health justice advocates are promoting partnerships among legal advocates, health care providers, and public health practitioners to advance the legal rights of low-income and marginalized individuals and families to protect and promote their health.

Conclusion

This chapter described the manifold ways in which SES influences and is influenced by health. It also detailed current U.S. policy and social safety net programs, their effectiveness in reducing poverty and promoting health, and major gaps. In the next chapter, we consider the role of place—where people live, go to school and work, play, socialize, and carry on their daily lives—in health justice. We explore how place has been shaped by history, law, policy, and investment (or lack of investment).

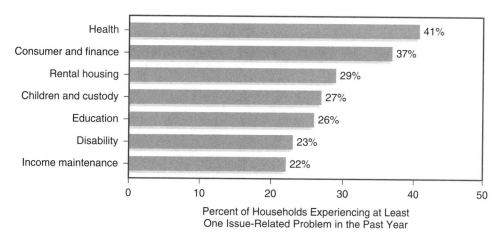

Figure 7.8 Common civil legal problem areas

Legal Services Corporation. 2017. The Justice Gap: Measuring the Unmet Civil Legal Needs of Low-income Americans. Prepared by NORC at the University of Chicago for Legal Services Corporation. Washington, DC.

References

1. Marmot MG, Rose G, Shipley M, Hamilton PJ. Employment grade and coronary heart disease in British civil servants. *Journal of Epidemiology and Community Health*. 1978;32(4):244–249.
2. Marmot, M. Status syndrome: A challenge to medicine. *JAMA*. 2006;295:1304–1307.
3. Marmot, M. Status syndrome: A challenge to medicine. *JAMA*. 2006;295:1304–1307.
4. The Pew Charitable Trusts Economic Mobility Project. Pursuing the American dream: economic mobility across generations. 2012. http://www.pewtrusts.org /~/media/legacy/uploadedfiles/pcs_assets/2012 /pursuingamericandreampdf.pdf.
5. Braveman PA, Cubbin C, Egerter S, Williams DR, Pamuk E. Socioeconomic disparities in health in the United States: What the patterns tell us. *American Journal of Public Health*. 2010 April;100(1):S186–S196.
6. Adler NE, Newman K. Socioeconomic disparities in health: pathways and policies. *Health Affairs*. 2002 March;21(2):60–76.
7. Case A, Deaton A. Rising morbidity and mortality in midlife among white non-Hispanic Americans in the 21st century. *Proceedings of the National Academy of Sciences*. 2015;112(49):15078–15083. http://www .pnas.org/content/112/49/15078.

8. Case A, Deaton A. Rising morbidity and mortality in midlife among white non-Hispanic Americans in the 21st century. *Proceedings of the National Academy of Sciences.* 2015;112(49):15078–15083. http://www.pnas.org/content/112/49/15078.

9. Olfson M, Cosgrove C, et al. Deaths of despair: adults at high risk for death by suicide, poisoning, or chronic liver disease in the US. *Health Affairs.* 2021;40(3):505–512.

10. Wedenoja L. The role of cocaine mortality in a resurgent overdose epidemic. SUNY Rockefeller Institute of Government. December 14, 2020. https://rockinst.org/blog/the-role-of-cocaine-mortality-in-a-resurgent-overdose-epidemic/.

11. Fryer RG, Heaton PS, Levitt SD, Murphy KM. Measuring crack cocaine and its impact. *Economic Inquiry.* 2013;51:1651–1681.

12. Mental health, substance use, and suicidal ideation during the Covid-19 pandemic—United States, June 24–30, 2020. August 13, 2020. Centers for Disease Control and Prevention. https://www.cdc.gov/mmwr/volumes/69/wr/mm6932a1.htm.

13. Mental health, substance use, and suicidal ideation during the Covid-19 Pandemic—United States, June 24–30, 2020. August 13, 2020. Centers for Disease Control and Prevention. https://www.cdc.gov/mmwr/volumes/69/wr/mm6932a1.htm.

14. Robert Wood Johnson Foundation Commission. Education and health. Issue Brief 5; April 2011. https://www.rwjf.org/content/dam/farm/reports/issue_briefs/2011/rwjf70447.

15. Cutler D, Lleras-Muney A. Education and health: Evaluating theories and evidence. *Making Americans Healthier: Social and Economic Policy as Health Policy.* New York, NY: Russell Sage Foundation; 2008.

16. Currie J. Health disparities and gaps in school readiness. *Future of Children. Spring* 2005;15(1):117–138.

17. Currie J. Health disparities and gaps in school readiness. *Future of Children. Spring* 2005;15(1):117–138.

18. Robert Wood Johnson Foundation. How does employment—or unemployment—affect health? Issue Brief. March 2013. https://www.rwjf.org/content/dam/farm/reports/issue_briefs/2013/rwjf403360.

19. U.S. Bureau of Labor Statistics. A profile of the working poor. 2018. https://www.bls.gov/opub/reports/working-poor/2018/home.htm.

20. U.S. Bureau of Labor Statistics. A profile of the working poor. 2018. https://www.bls.gov/opub/reports/working-poor/2018/home.htm.

21. Levy BS, Wegman DH, Baron SL, et al. *Occupational and Environmental Health: Recognizing and Preventing Disease and Injury.* 6th ed. Oxford, U.K.: Oxford University Press; 2011: 70.

22. Pew Research Center. Among 41 nations, U.S. is the outlier when it comes to paid parental leave. September 26, 2016. http://www.pewresearch.org/fact-tank/2016/09/26/u-s-lacks-mandated-paid-parental-leave/.

23. The Henry J. Kaiser Family Foundation. Paid family leave and sick days in the U.S.: Findings from the 2016 Kaiser/HRET employer health benefits survey. May 13, 2017. http://www.kff.org/womens-health-policy/issue-brief/paid-family-leave-and-sick-days-in-the-u-s-findings-from-the-2016-kaiser-hret-employer-health-benefits-survey/.

24. Schneider RWKHD. Inequalities at work and the toll of COVID-19. Health Affairs Brief. *Health Affairs.* June 4, 2021. https://www.healthaffairs.org/do/10.1377/hpb20210428.863621/full/.

25. A guide to statistics on historical trends in income inequality. Center on Budget and Policy Priorities. https://www.cbpp.org/research/poverty-and-inequality/a-guide-to-statistics-on-historical-trends-in-income-inequality.

26. Institute for Women's Policy Research. The Gender Wage Gap by Occupation 2019 and by Race and Ethnicity (fact sheet). March 2020. https://iwpr.org/wp-content/uploads/2020/07/2020-Occupational-wage-gap-FINAL.pdf.

27. Saez E, Zucman G. The rise of income and wealth inequality in America: Evidence from distributional macroeconomic accounts. *Journal of Economic Perspectives.* https://www.aeaweb.org/articles?id=10.1257%2Fjep.34.4.3.

28. Neil B, Chang AC, Dettling LJ, Hsu JW. Disparities in Wealth by Race and Ethnicity in the 2019 Survey of Consumer Finances. Washington, DC: Board of Governors of the Federal Reserve System; 2020.

29. Dickman SL, Himmelstein DU, Woolhandler S. Inequality and the health-care system in the USA. *Lancet.* 2017;389:1431–1444.

30. Iceland J. *Poverty in America: A Handbook.* Berkeley, CA: University of California Press; 2012: 20–28.

31. Semega J, Kollar M, Shrider EA, Creamer J. Income and poverty in the United States: 2019. United States Census Bureau. Report number P60-270. September 15, 2020. https://www.census.gov/library/publications/2020/demo/p60-270.html.

32. Parolin Z, Curran M, Matsudaira J, et al. Monthly poverty rates in the United States during the COVID-19 pandemic. Poverty and Social Policy Working Paper. October 15, 2020. Columbia University. https://static1.squarespace.com/static/5743308460b5e922a25a6dc7/t/5f87c59e4cd0011fabd38973/1602733471158/COVID-Projecting-Poverty-Monthly-CPSP-2020.pdf.

33. Barkley L, Svetaz MV, Chulani VL. *Promoting Health Equity Among Racially and Ethnically Diverse Adolescents a Practical Guide.* Switzerland: Springer Nature Publishing; 2019.

34. Davies JM, Sleeman KE, Leniz J, Wilson R, et al. Socioeconomic position and use of healthcare in the

last year of life: A systematic review and meta-analysis. *PLoS Medicine.* 2019;16(4):3.

35. Thompson T, McQueen A, Croston M, et al. Social needs and health related outcomes among Medicaid beneficiaries. *Health Education & Behavior.* 2019;46(3):436–444.

36. Cigarette smoking and tobacco use among people of low socioeconomic status. Centers for Disease Control and Prevention. https://www.cdc.gov/tobacco /disparities/low-ses/index.htm; Brown-Johnson CG, England LJ, Glantz SA, Ling PM. Tobacco industry marketing to low socioeconomic status women in the U.S.A. *Tobacco Control.* 2014 Nov;23(e2):e139–e146; Balbach E, Gasior R, Barbeau E. RJ Reynolds' targeting of African Americans: 1988–2000. *American Journal of Public Health.* 2003;93(5)822–827.

37. Brown-Johnson CG, England LJ, Glantz SA, Ling PM. Tobacco industry marketing to low socioeconomic status women in the U.S.A. *Tobacco Control.* 2014 Nov;23(e2):e139–e146.

38. Winkleby MA, Jatulis DE, Frank E, Fortmann SP. Socioeconomic status and health: How education, income, and occupation contribute to risk factors for cardiovascular disease. *American Journal of Public Health.* 1992;82:816–820; Cornelius ME. Tobacco product use among adults—United States, 2019. *Morbidity and Mortality Weekly Report.* The Centers for Disease Control and Prevention; 2019. https:// www.cdc.gov/mmwr/volumes/69/wr/mm6946a4 .htm?s_cid=mm6946a4_w.

39. Bradley EH, Taylor LA. American health care paradox: why spending more is getting us less. *Health Affairs.* New York, NY: Public Affairs; 2015; Bradley EH, Canavan M, Rogan E, et al. Variation in health outcomes: The role of spending on social services, public health, and health care, 2000–09. *Health Affairs.* 2016;35(5):760–768.

40. Ryan AM, Dacchille C, Wolf DF, Lawton E. Income and health: dynamics of employment and the safety net. In Tobin-Tyler E, Lawton E, Conroy C, Sandel M, et al., eds. *Poverty, Health and Law: Readings and Cases for Medical-Legal Partnership.* Durham, NC: Carolina Academic Press; 2012:192–193.

41. Minton S, Giannarelli L. Five things you may not know about the US social safety net. Urban Institute: Income and Benefits Policy Center; 2019.

42. Trisi D, Saenz M. Economic security programs cut poverty nearly in half over last 50 years. Center on Budget and Policy Priorities; 2019. https://www.cbpp .org/research/poverty-and-inequality/economic-security -programs-cut-poverty-nearly-in-half-over-last-50.

43. National Academies of Sciences, Engineering, and Medicine. A roadmap to reducing child poverty. National Academies Press; 2019. https://www.nap.edu /read/25246.

44. National Academies of Sciences, Engineering, and Medicine. A roadmap to reducing child poverty. National Academies Press; 2019. https://www.nap.edu /read/25246.

45. Personal Responsibility and Work Opportunity Reconciliation Act of 1996. Pub.L. 104-193 (1996).

46. Meyer L, Floyd I. Cash assistance should reach millions more families to lessen hardship. Center on Budget and Policy Priorities. https://www.cbpp.org /research/family-income-support/cash-assistance -should-reach-millions-more-families-to-lessen.

47. The US and the high price of child care: an examination of a broken system. Child Care Aware of *America.* 2019. https://www.childcareaware.org/our-issues/research /the-us-and-the-high-price-of-child-care-2019/

48. Safari A, Schoot L. To lessen hardship states should invest more TANF dollars in basic assistance for families. Center on Budget and Policy Priorities. January 12, 2021. https://www.cbpp.org/research/family -income-support/to-lessen-hardship-states-should -invest-more-tanf-dollars-inbasic#:~:text=In%20 2019%2C%20states%20spent%20%245,000%20 after%20adjusting%20for%20inflation.&text=Ten%20 states%20spent%20more%20than,spent%20less%20 than%205%20percent.

49. Mather A. Childcare costs: Yet another way we're failing the poor. *Forbes.* February 1, 2016. https:// www.forbes.com/sites/aparnamathur/2016/02/01 /childcare-costs-yet-another-way-were-failing-the -poor/2/#21c93a9427bd.

50. Duncan GJ, Magnuson K. Investing in preschool programs. *The Journal of Economic Perspectives: A Journal of the American Economic Association.* Spring 2013;27(2):109–132.

51. Votruba-Drzal E, Coley RL, Maldonado-Carreño C, et al. Child care and the development of behavior problems among economically disadvantaged children in middle childhood. *Child Development.* 2010;81(5):1460–1474.

52. Boone C, Dube A, Goodman L, Kaplan E. Unemployment insurance extension during great recession did not destroy jobs. Institute for New Economic Thinking. October 13, 2016. https://www.ineteconomics.org /perspectives/blog/unemployment-insurance -extension-during-great-recession-did-not-destroy-jobs.

53. Covid-19 unemployment benefits. USAGov. https:// www.usa.gov/covid-unemployment-benefits.

54. Minimum wage tracker. Economic Policy Institute. https://www.epi.org/minimum-wage-tracker/.

55. Avila CJ, Frakt AB. Raising the minimum wage and public health. *JAMA Health Forum. JAMA.* 2021;2(1): e201587–e201587.

56. Policy basics: The earned income tax credit. Center on Budget and Policy Priorities. https://www.cbpp.org /research/federal-tax/the-earned-income-tax-credit.

57. Braga B, Blavin F, Gangopadhyaya A. The long-term effects of childhood exposure to the earned income tax credit on health outcomes. *Journal of Public Economics*. 2020 Oct;190.

58. Bernhardt A, Milkman R, Theodore N, et al. Broken laws, unprotected workers: Violation of employment and labor laws in America's cities. 2009. http://www.nelp.org/content/uploads/2015/03/BrokenLawsReport2009.pdf?nocdn=1.

59. U.S. Department of Labor. Family and Medical Leave Act. https://www.dol.gov/general/topic/benefits-leave/fmla.

60. Family and medical leave in 2012. Report for the U.S. Department of Labor. September 13, 2013. https://www.dol.gov/asp/evaluation/fmla/FMLA-2012-Executive-Summary.pdf.

61. Ben-Ishai L. Wages lost, jobs at risk: the serious consequences of lack of paid leave. Center for Law and Social Policy. February 5, 2015. http://www.clasp.org/resources-and-publications/publication-1/2015-02-03-FMLA-Anniversary-Brief.pdf.

62. State paid family and maternal leave insurance laws. National Partnership for Women and Families. November 2021. https://www.nationalpartnership.org/our-work/resources/economic-justice/paid-leave/state-paid-family-leave-laws.pdf

63. Ko H, Glied SA. Associations between a New York City paid sick leave mandate and health care utilization among Medicaid beneficiaries in New York City and New York State. *JAMA Health Forum*. 2021;2(5):e210342.

64. Findlay S. Biden and democrats propose national paid leave. *Health Affairs*. June 24, 2021. https://www.healthaffairs.org/do/10.1377/hblog20210617.789833/full/?utm_medium=email&utm_source=hasu&utm_campaign=blog&utm_content=findlay&utm_source=Newsletter&utm_medium=email&utm_content=Life+Expectancy+On+The+US-Mexico+Border%2C+Giving+Birth+With+COVID-19+%26+More&utm_campaign=HASU%3A+6-27-21&vgo_ee=PIsaBHiejM66z3IzHBl%2F3D%2BJLi7DAuyw1lBdDJF3D%2Bo%3D.

65. Garfield R, Orgera K, Damico A. The uninsured and the ACA: A primer key facts about health insurance and the uninsured admits changes to the Affordable Care Act. KFF. January 25, 2019. https://www.kff.org/report-section/the-uninsured-and-the-aca-a-primer-key-facts-about-health-insurance-and-the-uninsured-amidst-changes-to-the-affordable-care-act-how-many-people-are-uninsured/.

66. Artiga S, Hill L, Orgera K. Health coverage by race and ethnicity 2010–2019. KFF. July 16, 2021. https://www.kff.org/racial-equity-and-health-policy/issue-brief/health-coverage-by-race-and-ethnicity/.

67. *National Federation of Independent Business v. Sebelius*, 567 U.S. 519 (2012).

68. Jost T. The tax bill and the individual mandate: What happened, and what does it mean? *Health Affairs*. December 20, 2017. https://www.healthaffairs.org/do/10.1377/hblog20171220.323429/full/.

69. *California v. Texas*, 593 U.S. ___ (2021).

70. *National Federation of Independent Business v. Sebelius*, 567 U.S. 519 (2012).

71. Status of State Medicaid Expansion Decisions: Interactive Map. Kaiser Family Foundation. October 8, 2021. https://www.kff.org/medicaid/issue-brief/status-of-state-medicaid-expansion-decisions-interactive-map/.

72. Jost T. The tax bill and the individual mandate: What happened, and what does it mean? *Health Affairs*. December 20, 2017. https://www.healthaffairs.org/do/10.1377/hblog20171220.323429/full/.

73. Lukens G, Sharer B. Closing Medicaid coverage gap would help diverse group and narrow racial disparities. Center for Budget and Policy Priorities. June 14, 2021.

74. Sommers BD, Maylone B, Blendon RJ, John OE, Epstein AM. Three-year impacts of the Affordable Care Act: Improved medical care and health among low-income adults. *Health Affairs*. 36(2017):1119–1128.

75. Miller S, Johnson N, Wherry L. Medicaid and mortality: New evidence from linked survey and administrative data. *Quarterly Journal of Economics*. January 20, 2021. https://doi.org/10.1093/qje/qjab004.

76. April 2021 Medicaid & CHIP enrollment Data Highlights. Medicaid. https://www.medicaid.gov/medicaid/program-information/medicaid-and-chip-enrollment-data/report-highlights/index.html#:~:text=81%2C046%2C488%20individuals%20were%20enrolled%20in,individuals%20were%20enrolled%20in%20Medicaid.

77. The Henry J. Kaiser Family Foundation. Medicaid Pocket Primer. June 9, 2017. https://www.kff.org/medicaid/fact-sheet/medicaid-pocket-primer/.

78. About section 1115 demonstrations. *Medicaid*. 2022. https://www.medicaid.gov/medicaid/section-1115-demonstrations/about-section-1115-demonstrations/index.html.

79. Biden administration begins process of rolling back approval for Medicaid work experiments, but supreme courts hangs on. Commonwealth Fund. April 8, 2021. https://www.commonwealthfund.org/blog/2021/biden-administration-begins-process-rolling-back-approval-medicaid-work-experiments.

80. Khorrami P, Sommers BD. Changes in US Medicaid enrollment during the COVID-19 pandemic. *JAMA*. 2021;4(5):e219463.

81. Children's Health Insurance Program. Medicaid. 2022. https://www.medicaid.gov/chip/index.html.

82. National Association of Community Health Centers. America's health centers 2021 snapshot. August 2021.

https://www.nachc.org/research-and-data/research-fact-sheets-and-infographics/americas-health-centers-2021-snapshot/.

83. National Association of Community Health Centers. Strengthening the safety net: Community health centers on the front lines of American health care. March 2017. http://www.nachc.org/wp-content/uploads/2017/03/Strengthening-the-Safety-Net_NACHC_2017.pdf.

84. Mirror mirror, 2021: Reflecting poorly: Health care in the U.S. compared to other high-income countries. The Commonwealth Fund. August 2021. https://www.commonwealthfund.org/sites/default/files/2021-08/Schneider_Mirror_Mirror_2021.pdf.

85. U.S. Department of Agriculture, Economic Research Service. Definitions of food insecurity. 2021. https://www.ers.usda.gov/topics/food-nutrition-assistance/food-security-in-the-us/definitions-of-food-security/.

86. U.S. Department of Agriculture, Economic Research Service. Definitions of food insecurity. 2021. https://www.ers.usda.gov/topics/food-nutrition-assistance/food-security-in-the-us/definitions-of-food-security/.

87. Cook JT, Frank DA. Food security, poverty, and human development in the United States. *Annals of the New York Academy of Sciences*. 2008;1136:193–209, 195.

88. Ag and Food Statistics: Charting the essentials. USDA ERS. https://www.ers.usda.gov/data-products/ag-and-food-statistics-charting-the-essentials/.

89. Schanzenbach D, Pitts A. How much has food insecurity risen. Northwestern Institute for Policy Research. June 10, 2020. https://www.ipr.northwestern.edu/documents/reports/ipr-rapid-research-reports-pulse-hh-data-10-june-2020.pdf.

90. Cook JT, Frank DA. Food security, poverty, and human development in the United States. *Annals of the New York Academy of Sciences*. 2008;1136:193–209, 195.

91. American Nutrition Association. USDA defines food deserts. *Nutrition Digest*. 2010;38(2). http://americannutritionassociation.org/newsletter/usda-defines-food-deserts.

92. American Nutrition Association. USDA defines food deserts. *Nutrition Digest*. 2010;38(2). http://americannutritionassociation.org/newsletter/usda-defines-food-deserts.

93. Rose-Jacobs R, Black MM, Casey PH, et al. Household food insecurity: Associations with at-risk infant and toddler development. *Pediatrics*. 2008;121(1):65–72.

94. American Academy of Pediatrics, Council on Community Pediatrics, Nutrition Committee. Promoting food security for all children. *Pediatrics*. November 2015;136(5):1431–1438.

95. Seligman HK, Laraia BA, Kushel MB. Food insecurity is associated with chronic disease among low-income NHANES participants. *The Journal of Nutrition*. February 2010;140(2):304–310.

96. Seligman HK, Bolger AF, Guzman D, et al. Exhaustion of food budgets at month's end and hospital admissions for hypoglycemia. *Health Affairs*. January 2014;33(1):116–123.

97. USDA. Characteristics of supplemental nutrition assistance program households: Fiscal year 2019. Supplemental Nutrition Assistance Program Report Series. March 2021. https://fns-prod.azureedge.net/sites/default/files/resource-files/Characteristics2019.pdf.

98. Deparle J. Biden administration prompts largest permanent increase in food stamps. *The New York Times*. August 15, 2021. https://www.nytimes.com/2021/08/15/us/politics/biden-food-stamps.html.

99. Whitmore DS, Bauer L, Nantz G. Twelve facts about food insecurity and SNAP. Brookings Institution. April 21, 2016. https://www.brookings.edu/research/twelve-facts-about-food-insecurity-and-snap/.

100. Shaefer HL, Gutierrez IA. The supplemental nutrition assistance program and material hardships among low-income households with children. *Social Service Review*. December 2013;87(4):753–779.

101. Special supplemental nutrition program for women, infants, and children. USDA. 2022. https://www.fns.usda.gov/wic.

102. National and state-level estimates of WIC eligibility and WIC Program reach in 2018 with updated estimates for 2016 and 2017. USDA. 2021. https://www.fns.usda.gov/wic/national-and-state-level-estimates-wic-eligibility-and-wic-program-reach-2018-updated.

103. Khanani I, Elam J, Hearn R, et al. The impact of prenatal WIC participation on infant mortality and racial disparities. *American Journal of Public Health*. April 2010;100(1):S204–S209.

104. Metallinos-Katsaras E, Gorman KS, Wilde P, Kallio J. A longitudinal study of WIC participation on household food insecurity. *Maternal and Child Health Journal*. July 2011;15(5):627–633.

105. U.S. Department of Agriculture. School Meals: Healthy Hunger-Free Kids Act. https://www.fns.usda.gov/school-meals/healthy-hunger-free-kids-act.

106. Schwartz MB, Henderson KE, et al. New school meal regulations increase fruit consumption and do not increase total plate waste. *Childhood Obesity*. June 2015;11(3):242–247.

107. Food Action and Research Center. Research brief: Breakfast for learning. October 2016. http://frac.org/wp-content/uploads/breakfastforlearning-1.pdf.

108. Dotter DD. Breakfast at the desk: The impact of universal breakfast programs on academic performance. *Mathematica Policy Research*. October 2016. http://www.appam.org/assets/1/7/Breakfast_at_the_Desk_The_Impact_of_Universal_Breakfast_Programs_on_Academic_Performance.pdf.

109. Legal Services Corporation. The unmet need for legal aid. LSC. 2022. https://www.lsc.gov/about-lsc/what-legal-aid/unmet-need-legal-aid.

110. Legal Services Corporation. America's partner for equal justice. LSC. 2022. https://www.lsc.gov/about-lsc/who-we-are.

111. Legal Services Corporation. Justice gap report. LSC. June 2017. https://www.lsc.gov/our-impact/publications/other-publications-and-reports/justice-gap-report.

112. National Center for Access to Justice. Working with your hands tied behind your back: Non-lawyer perspectives on legal empowerment. June 2021. https://ncaj.org/working-your-hands-tied-behind-your-back.

113. Michener J. *Fragmented Democracy: Medicaid, Federalism, and Unequal Politics*. New York, NY:Cambridge University Press; 2018.

CHAPTER 8

Place-Based Inequities

LEARNING OBJECTIVES

By the end of this chapter you will be able to:

- Discuss the role of different aspects of the ecology of place (family, home, neighborhood, region, and environmental exposure) in health outcomes
- Describe some of the laws and policies that perpetuate place-based health inequities
- Analyze how stronger enforcement of existing laws and policies and development of health-promoting laws and policies can support healthier environments and reduce health inequities

Introduction

In recent years, researchers, advocates, and policymakers have begun paying closer attention to the ways in which place influences population health. This chapter uses a wide lens to describe how the place where people are born, grow up, go to school, work, and age affects their health. It starts by zooming in to the first place people experience—their family environment—to examine how family is part of the "ecology" of place influencing child health and how laws and policies influence family stability and safety. It then turns to the role of the home—specifically, housing affordability and conditions and their impact on individual and family health. Next, the lens expands further to highlight how neighborhood exposures and concentrated poverty and segregation produce inequitable health outcomes and to explore how the area or region in which one lives (i.e., urban versus rural) implicates health. Finally, this chapter zooms all the way out to consider environmental injustice and the ways in which toxic exposures and the effects of climate change are distributed across the U.S. population and drive health inequities.

We consider these domains related to place because all of them structure health opportunities for individuals and communities and because social environment shapes socioeconomic status, which is highly correlated with health outcomes and life expectancy (see Chapter 7). We also focus on these aspects of place because each of them is subject to law and policy interventions that either help support and protect health or hinder health and reinforce health inequities. As you read this chapter, think about all of the ways in which health and life opportunities are structured by place-based conditions and the specific ways that past and current legal and policy decisions shape the environments in which people live.

Family: Stability and Safety

From the time children are born, their environment—their relationships with their caretakers and sense of safety and security, including having their basic needs met—is formative for their health and opportunities in life. In fact, "beginning prenatally, continuing through infancy, and extending into childhood and beyond, development is driven by an ongoing, inextricable interaction between biology (as defined by genetic predispositions) and ecology (as defined by the social and physical environment)."[1] Research continues to point to the importance of the family environment, not only in child development but also in long-term health. We explore the family and the "ecology" shaping a child's early experiences and how these experiences are fundamental to lifelong health.

Adverse Childhood Experiences and Toxic Stress

In 1998, Dr. Vincent Felitti and colleagues published a groundbreaking study on the relationship between health risk behavior and disease in adulthood and adverse childhood experiences (ACEs)—namely, exposure to childhood emotional, physical, or sexual abuse; household dysfunction (including exposure to intimate partner violence, parental substance abuse and/or mental illness, and

incarceration of a parent); and lack of basic necessities.[2] This study became known as the "ACEs study" and has been widely cited in recent years as further research has documented that ACEs not only drive poor adult health, they also appear to alter brain development in young children, leading to a host of negative outcomes.

The ACEs study found a "strong graded relationship between the breadth of exposure to abuse or household dysfunction during childhood and multiple risk factors for several of the leading causes of death in adults."[2] These include significantly heightened risk for substance use disorders, depression, suicide, poor self-rated health, sexually transmitted disease, obesity, heart disease, cancer, chronic lung disease, liver disease, and skeletal fracture.[3] Data from the 2016 National Survey of Children's Health show that a third of U.S. children under the age of 18 have had at least one ACE, while more than 14% have had at least two.[4] Research also indicates that children who have had two or more ACES are significantly more likely to have a chronic health condition that requires special health care.[5]

While ACEs may occur at all socioeconomic levels, children living in poverty who are exposed to multiple stressors—community crime and violence, food insecurity, overcrowding, unstable housing, lack of access to resources, environmental hazards, and underperforming schools—are at higher risk for poor adult health outcomes. In a recent study, economic hardship was the most commonly reported type of adversity.[6] Since one in five children in the United States lives in poverty, it is not surprising that many kids experience deprivation and adversity that influence their health. Screenings conducted in pediatric clinics find that unmet social needs are more commonly reported than other types of ACEs; these included issues related to parental employment, housing, and the ability to pay bills.

The top ACEs reported were parental substance use and mental illness.[7] A study by Child Trends found that ACEs are not distributed equally by race and ethnicity: "Nationally, 61 percent of black non-Hispanic children and 51 percent of Hispanic children have experienced at least one ACE, compared with 40 percent of White non-Hispanic children and 23 percent of Asian non-Hispanic children."[8]

Seeking to explain the pathways between ACEs and negative adult health outcomes, researchers suggest that chronic stress in early childhood, referred to as "toxic stress," actually creates "physiologic disruptions or biological memories that undermine the development of the body's stress response systems and affect the developing brain, cardiovascular system, immune system, and metabolic regulatory controls."[9] These "physiologic disruptions" last into adulthood, often leading to lifelong disease and impairment.[10]

It is important to note that not all stress is bad stress. Stress produces the hormone cortisol, which, if properly regulated, helps us focus on the task at hand. Our bodies are built around the idea of "fight or flight," or hyperarousal, to allow us to respond to a perceived threat or stressful situation. During times of acute stress, we go through a process known as allostasis, whereby our bodies make physiological adaptations to regulate and protect our bodies from exposure to stress. With toxic or chronic stress, our bodies are overloaded by the daily wear and tear of stress. This is known as "allostatic load." When this occurs, our physiological reactions to stress become progressively less effective in protecting our bodies from stress. When people feel that they do not have control over the stressors in their life, they are especially prone to allostatic load. Physician and epidemiologist Camara Phyllis Jones likens allostatic load to a car running at high RPMs continuously for weeks and months; eventually the car breaks down.[11]

The daily wear and tear of these multiple stressors, or cumulative stress, can also affect daily functioning. Toxic stress affects what neuroscientists call executive functioning and self-regulation—the ability to plan ahead, focus, manage emotion, adapt to new situations, and resist impulses. These skills are critical for success in school, social relationships, and productivity. It should be noted that adults, like children, can experience toxic stress and struggle with executive functioning as a result. Studies show that living in poverty with the constant worry of being unable to meet basic needs has a profound effect on adult cognitive functioning.[12]

Although families are often thought of as private entities and family dysfunction as resulting from personal failures by parents, clinicians and others who work with vulnerable families argue that prevention of ACEs and consequential toxic stress requires a comprehensive socioecological approach:

> Given the complex interplay between the individual, the family, the community, and the larger sociopolitical structure, the socio-ecological model provides a good conceptual framework to guide prevention. To have the desired multilevel effect, strategies to prevent the occurrence of ACEs and their adverse impacts are needed at every level.[13]

Indeed, law and policy interventions can play a major role in shaping the family environment by investing in and structuring crucial supports for caregivers that enable them to provide a stable, safe, and nurturing environment for their children. In the following text, we explore family violence as an example of not only how living in an unsafe environment harms the health of both child and adult victims but also how legal and policy interventions are fundamental to preventing violence and protecting victims.

Family Violence

Here we discuss two types of family violence: child maltreatment and intimate partner violence (or domestic violence). Child maltreatment can be defined as "behavior towards [a child] . . . which (a) is outside the norms of conduct, and (b) entails a substantial risk of causing physical or emotional harm. Behaviors included will consist of actions and omissions, ones that are intentional and ones that are unintentional."[14] Generally, four types of maltreatment are recognized: physical abuse, sexual abuse, neglect (including educational neglect, medical neglect, and other forms), and emotional maltreatment.[15]

Childhood exposure to physical, sexual, and emotional abuse and neglect can have severe consequences for child development as well as for adult health outcomes. Exposure to physical and sexual abuse puts children at high risk of chronic health problems, posttraumatic stress disorder (PTSD), eating disorders, substance use disorders, and suicidality.[16] Each year roughly 650,000 children are reported to child protection agencies for maltreatment. The majority of these reports are for neglect, 61%, compared to 10.3% for physical abuse and 7.2% for sexual abuse.[17]

Each state has its own laws that define abuse and neglect and determine who is obligated to report child abuse and neglect as well as the designated agency that will receive and investigate reports. Most state laws require certain professionals to report suspected abuse or neglect when acting in their professional capacity. These usually include physicians, nurses, social workers, teachers, and child care providers. Some states require that all persons report suspected cases of child abuse or neglect.

The government agency responsible for investigating child abuse, usually referred to as "Child Protective Services" (CPS), has the authority to determine if there is credible evidence supporting the allegation of abuse and

what further action will be taken. Typically, once a report is made to the agency, it investigates to determine if a case should be opened or if the report does not warrant further action. Once a case is opened, the agency may petition the court to have the child temporarily removed from the home and placed in foster care, or if it determines that the child is not in immediate danger, it may allow the child to remain in the home with agency oversight and services to the family. State laws and policies set timelines for each stage of the process.

Concerned that too many children were lingering for long periods of time in foster care, Congress passed the Adoption and Safe Families Act of 1997 to specify that CPS agencies must make reasonable efforts to keep the child in the home safely. If the child is removed from the home, the agency must create a permanency plan and a review hearing must be held within 12 months of the child being removed from the home, at which time the child may be reunified with his/her/their family or the agency will file for a termination of parental rights in order to place the child in an adoptive home.[18]

Despite federal efforts to improve the child protection system by pressuring CPS agencies to move children out of the system more quickly, significant problems remain. Lawyers working on child welfare cases cite a laundry list of problems: lack of basic services for vulnerable families, inadequacy of mental health services for children and parents, lack of preventive services to reduce involvement with the system in the first place, and issues with the CPS workforce (including lack of training, high caseloads and turnover, and difficulty recruiting foster parents).[19]

Although child abuse and neglect may occur in families from all socioeconomic groups, poor and extremely poor families are more likely to be reported to authorities. Roughly three times as many Black, Latinx, and American Indian/Alaska Native children live in poverty than do

White and Asian American children. Relative to their populations, Black and Native American children are overrepresented in the child welfare system.[20] Researchers attribute this overrepresentation to

- Disproportionate and disparate needs of children and families of color, particularly due to higher rates of poverty
- Racial bias and discrimination exhibited by individuals (e.g., caseworkers, reporters of abuse)
- Child welfare system factors (e.g., lack of resources for Black, Indigenous, and People of Color families, caseworker characteristics)
- Geographic context, such as the region, state, or neighborhood in which a family lives[21]

Researchers who have studied the child welfare system have identified significant racial disparities in treatment, particularly for Black mothers. Black children are the most likely group to be removed from their parents' care (most often from their mothers), while White families reported to authorities for abuse or neglect are more likely to be offered services in the home.[22] Legal scholar Dorothy Roberts explains:

> This state intrusion is typically viewed as necessary to protect maltreated children from parental harm. But the need for this intervention is usually linked to poverty, racial injustice, and the state's approach to caregiving, which addresses family economic deprivation with child removal rather than services and financial resources.[23]

Understanding the role of poverty and lack of access to resources related to child abuse and neglect as well as disparate systemic responses to reports of child maltreatment is important in identifying appropriate policy reforms. Given the potential health consequences for children associated with abuse, neglect, and family separation, more upstream preventive measures—such as access to resources to meet basic needs, supports for parents, and reduction in community-level stressors—are required.

Like child maltreatment, intimate partner violence (IPV)—also often referred to as domestic violence—is an important contributor to poor health in victims and survivors. IPV is defined as a pattern of purposeful coercive behaviors that may include inflicted physical injury, psychological abuse, sexual assault, progressive social isolation, stalking, deprivation, intimidation, and threats. These behaviors are perpetrated by someone who is, was, or wishes to be involved in an intimate or dating relationship with an adult or adolescent victim and aims to establish control over the other partner.[24]

It is estimated that a quarter of all women will experience IPV in their lifetimes. Although men may also be victims, women are far more likely to experience IPV; it is the leading cause of nonfatal injury to women in the United States. In addition to risk of physical injury, victims of IPV are at greater risk for mental health problems such as depression, anxiety, and PTSD as well as for substance use disorder and cigarette smoking. Because IPV is based on exerting power and control over the victim physically, emotionally, and sexually—whether through social and financial isolation, coercion, or threats—escaping the relationship can be extremely challenging. In fact, victims are most at risk for death when they seek to leave the relationship.[25] **Figure 8.1** demonstrates the dynamics of power and control in IPV.

Poverty, homelessness, and undocumented immigrant status are vital risk factors for IPV because they create significant barriers for victims to leave an abusive relationship. Lack of financial resources and/or no alternative housing options (other than living on the streets) create a strong deterrence to leaving. Undocumented immigrants may fear reporting abuse out of concern that it could lead to deportation.

Figure 8.1 Power and control in physical and sexual violence

DOMESTIC ABUSE INTERVENTION PROGRAMS, 202 East Superior Street, Duluth, Minnesota 55802, 218-722-2781, www.theduluthmodel.org.

Children who are exposed to IPV in their homes can also exhibit significant physical and mental health problems. In young children, these include failure to thrive, developmental delay, withdrawal, and sleep disruption. In older children, these include asthma, headaches, gastrointestinal issues, sleep disorders, aggressive behavior, and substance use. Exposure to IPV undermines children's sense of safety and protection, leading them to see the world as dangerous and unpredictable and violence as a legitimate way to resolve conflict.[26] This can have profound effects on their physical, mental, and emotional development and their opportunities for a healthy life.

The legal system's primary tool for protecting victims from future abuse is the civil protection order (often referred to as a restraining order or no-contact order), which legally bars the perpetrator from contacting or coming within a designated distance from the victim. These orders may also include that the perpetrator stay away from the victim's children. *The Violence Against Women Act of 2000* is a federal law that, among other things, provides grants to support legal assistance to victims in obtaining these orders. Civil protection orders are intended to prevent any future abuse and harassment by the perpetrator. While they are an important tool in providing safety for victims and their children, studies suggest that nearly 50% of civil protection orders are violated at least once.[27]

It is important to acknowledge that protective orders and the legal system are only part of what is needed to provide safety from IPV. Because perpetrators of IPV seek power and control over victims, using the legal system to regain control may actually incite more violence and danger for victims. Careful safety planning should include ensuring that victims and their children have a safe location to which to relocate if necessary. Because low-income victims are less likely to have the financial means to relocate, they require comprehensive supports, such as housing assistance and income supports, to be able to fully separate from an abuser. Since these types of safety net supports are often lacking (as described in Chapter 7), many low-income victims and survivors end up homeless when they leave an abusive home.

It is also important to note that when the victim of IPV has children with the abuser, permanent separation is even more difficult. Courts are loath to completely terminate parents' rights to contact children, particularly if a parent has not directly physically harmed the child. It is common for a perpetrator of IPV to use the legal process as an opportunity to continue to harass, threaten, and abuse the victim parent. As research continues to demonstrate the detrimental effects on children of exposure to violence in the home, courts have increasingly taken into account a parent's history of IPV when making custody decisions and visitation arrangements. However, it is rare for a parent who has engaged in IPV to have visitation terminated altogether. In making custody and visitation decisions, courts generally apply the "best interests of the child" standard, weighing a list of factors to determine the frequency of contact between each parent and the child. Legal advocates and health care providers play a key role in informing the court about the effects of past violence on children as well as the risk of future exposure after divorce or separation. With the growing understanding of how ACEs affect a child's development and lifelong health, advocates can inform judges and other decision-makers about the consequences of failing to protect a child from continued exposure to IPV.

Home: Housing Affordability and Conditions

Research continues to demonstrate the many ways in which access to safe, affordable housing is a key driver of health.[28] The unavailability of affordable housing correlates with poor health in three important ways. First, the stress of housing instability in and of itself appears to have profound consequences for child and adult health. Second, when a high percentage of income is devoted to rent, many families cut back on other basic necessities important to health, notably food and medical expenses. Third, low-income tenants are often forced to live in substandard and unhealthy housing conditions when safe, affordable housing is unavailable, thus affecting their own health and safety. The lack of safe, affordable housing in the United States is well documented. Next we explore the intersections among housing affordability, unsafe housing conditions, and health inequities.

Housing Affordability and Health

The National Low-Income Housing Coalition (NLIHC) estimates that the nation has a shortage of 6.8 million affordable rental homes for extremely low-income households (defined as "households with income at or below the poverty guideline or 30% of area median income, whichever is higher") and that there are only 37 affordable units for every 100 of these households. Housing is generally considered affordable if a family spends less than 30% of its income on rent or to purchase a home. Yet 71% of extremely low-income households in the United States spend more than half of their income on rent and utilities.[29] The number of renters increased 26% from 2006 to 2016, while homeownership decreased more than 5%. The hourly wage required to afford a two-bedroom apartment in the United States is $24.90, nearly $18 higher than the federal minimum wage of $7.25 and $6.12 higher than the average hourly wage of $18.78 earned nationwide.[30]

Federal and state housing assistance programs for low-income individuals and families fall into two types of programs: Public housing are units owned by governmental housing authorities (usually administered at the state or local levels), while the Section 8 voucher program allows eligible individuals and families to rent units in the private market using a subsidy provided by the housing authority. Both the public housing and Section 8 programs are overseen by the U.S. Department of Housing and Urban Development (HUD). Neither of these housing assistance programs are entitlements. Many states have lengthy waiting lists for eligible individuals and families, some as long as several years.[31] Due to limited funding, three out of four eligible families do not receive housing assistance, and for "every assisted household in the United States, twice as many low-income households are homeless or pay more than half of their income for rent and do not receive any federal rental assistance."[32] Federal rules for eligibility are based on targeting the most needy: 75% of new households must be "extremely low income," as defined earlier. Generally, a family using a voucher must contribute either 30% of its income toward

rent or a minimum rent of $50, depending on which is higher. Roughly a third of housing vouchers go to adults with children, about a quarter go to the elderly, and a fifth go to disabled adults.[33]

The gap between available affordable housing and the number of individuals and families needing it generates a range of detrimental health outcomes. First, it contributes to homelessness, which is highly correlated with poor health. People experiencing homelessness have increased risk of infectious disease (e.g., hepatitis C and HIV) and chronic disease (e.g., diabetes, high blood pressure, cardiovascular disease) and higher rates of mental health and substance use disorders, and they confront significant barriers to health care.[34] Children experiencing homelessness (an ACE) are at substantial risk for experiencing toxic stress and have higher rates of physical and mental health problems. Mortality for unhoused people is between three and 11 times higher than for housed individuals.[35] Reasons for homelessness include economic instability, eviction, untreated mental health disorders, substance use disorders, and family violence. Of women who experience homelessness, 20% to 50% cite IPV as the reason for their homelessness. When people are homeless, maintaining access to regular preventive care and treatment of chronic physical and mental health problems is exceedingly difficult. Indeed, "health cannot happen without housing."[36]

Families who struggle to pay unaffordable rents are at high risk of eviction. Eviction from housing is extremely common for low-income individuals and families and has important health consequences, particularly for low-income mothers and children. Because many low-income tenants do not have written tenancy agreements or leases, they have few protections from eviction. In most states, tenants must be provided with adequate notice before they may be lawfully evicted. This time period usually conforms to how tenants pay their rent. For example, if tenants pay rent on a monthly basis, they must be given 30 days' notice before they may be evicted without cause. However, if tenants violate the state's tenancy laws by, for example, failing to pay rent on time, they may be evicted lawfully through a court process set by law.

Since most low-income tenants are evicted for nonpayment of rent, they often have no legal recourse. As long as landlords follow the legal process for eviction based on nonpayment of rent, they are generally within their rights to evict their renters. Nonetheless, tenants sometimes have a defense or counterclaim in an eviction proceeding. For example, if landlords fail to meet their statutory responsibilities under housing health and safety laws, tenants may use this as a defense to eviction and make a counterclaim against their landlords for failing to meet their legal duties. Unfortunately, many low-income tenants are unaware of their legal rights or are unable to obtain legal assistance. Roughly 90% of landlords have legal representation in eviction proceedings, while only 10% of tenants do.[37] Because of the lack of access to legal assistance (as discussed in Chapter 7), most low-income tenants are at a serious disadvantage in protecting their legal rights. For example, a study in Baltimore found that in housing court:

> Judges rapidly accepted landlord allegations of unpaid rent that trigger the eviction process, the most serious penalty that tenants can face. Yet they seldom imposed one of the most serious penalties against landlords who violate their legal obligations to provide livable homes: cash damages. Court records show judges awarded damages to tenants in fewer than 20 cases—less than one half of 1 percent of all cases.[38]

During the COVID-19 pandemic, as many people lost their jobs and were unable to meet their rent obligations, they faced eviction. An estimated 30 to 40 million people were at risk of eviction. Because low-income People of Color, especially women, experienced a disproportionate share of job loss and economic hardship, they were disproportionately exposed to housing instability, eviction, and homelessness.[39] Black and Latinx individuals and families with children were more likely to report fear of eviction at the start of the pandemic.[40] In 2020, the Centers for Disease Control and Prevention (CDC) instituted a moratorium on evictions for nonpayment of rent. When the moratorium ended on July 31, 2021, the CDC issued another, more narrowly tailored moratorium, preventing eviction in communities with high infection rates. Yet many tenants were unaware of their rights under the moratorium, and landlords found ways to evict tenants for reasons other than nonpayment to avoid the constraints imposed by the moratorium rules. The $47 billion in rental aid allocated by Congress—intended to avert an eviction crisis—was painfully slow in reaching people who needed it. By June 2021, only $3 billion had been distributed.[41] In August 2021, in *Alabama Association of Realtors, et al. v. Department of Health and Human Services, et al.*, the U.S. Supreme Court held that the federal eviction moratorium was unlawful because it exceeded the CDC's authority under the Public Health Service Act, which the CDC argued provided justification for the moratorium during times of public health crisis.[42]

Housing instability has been shown to have particularly negative health effects for children. It is not difficult to understand how housing instability affects children's social connections and educational opportunities, which in turn both affect children's cognitive and emotional development. Housing instability also has important consequences for the health of low-income mothers. In a study of the effects of eviction on families, researchers Matthew Desmond and Rachel Tolbert Kimbro found that mothers who were evicted suffered higher rates of depression, poorer health for themselves and their children, and more stress than mothers who had not experienced eviction. Furthermore, Desmond and Kimbro found that they continue to experience material hardship and depression two years after eviction.[43]

Eviction also has long-term legal consequences for tenants' ability to find housing:

> [E]viction cases remain on a tenant's public record for seven years and are visible to landlords, rental agencies, and credit agencies during their screening processes. This black mark can push a resident out of their neighborhood and cripple their ability to get back on their feet—they will be ineligible for many forms of loans, unable to secure public housing benefits, and screened out of most applications for quality housing.[44]

Heat or Eat: Making Untenable Choices Between Housing and Other Necessities

Another vital link between housing and health is the phenomenon known as "heat or eat." A family who pays a disproportionate percentage of household income for housing has less available income for other necessities such as food, medicine, and clothing. Low-income households with high housing and utility costs spend less on food, especially in the winter when utility costs are at their highest.[45] Poor nutrition adversely affects health and development, especially

for children, as discussed in Chapter 7. Cost-burdened households also experience an increased burden of utility shutoffs, in which their utilities, heat, water, and/or electricity are discontinued for some portion of the year. Low-income households are more likely to live in older, less energy-efficient homes and spend on average 7.2% of their income on utility bills, while higher-income households spend roughly 2.3% of income on these bills.[41] Exposure to very high or very low indoor temperatures has detrimental effects on health. For example, exposure to cold temperatures is associated with increased risk of cardiovascular disease and asthma exacerbation.[46]

The "heat or eat" phenomenon has also been associated with "failure to thrive" in children. Failure to thrive broadly describes children who weigh less than the fifth percentile for their age or who show a chronic pattern of poor weight gain. Failure to thrive in low-income children whose families are experiencing utility shutoff may occur because prolonged exposure to cold temperatures puts a child at risk for hypothermia, causing weight loss and neurological damage. Hypothermia increases metabolic rate and shivering to restore normal body temperature, which in turn results in more calorie burn-off. In other words, being cold increases calorie expenditure; this is particularly true for children. Thus, malnutrition is the end result of both food insecurity and utility insecurity.[47] Energy insecurity also places low-income families at risk for injury. Families may choose alternative heat sources for warmth, such as cooking stoves, wood-burning stoves, and space heaters, which are associated with greater risk for burns, fires, and respiratory illness.

A federal program called the Low-Income Home Energy Assistance Program (LIHEAP) was designed to offer assistance to low-income families struggling with high utility bills and with weatherizing their homes to make them more energy efficient.[48] But like many non-entitlement safety net programs, LIHEAP has been chronically underfunded, assisting only 20% of the income-eligible population each year.[49] The Coronavirus Aid, Relief, and Economic Security (CARES) Act of 2020 allocated $900 million toward LIHEAP to assist low-income households in paying energy bills, and many states suspended shutoffs during the pandemic. But this investment is too small to address the COVID-19-related accumulating utility bills for many households.[50]

Conditions: Health-Harming Housing Hazards

In addition to a shortage of affordable housing, the United States also suffers from a lack of available housing that has been built and maintained with health in mind, particularly in low-income neighborhoods. In a 2009 report, the U.S. Surgeon General defined a healthy home as "sited, designed, built, renovated, and maintained in ways that support the health of residents."[51] Yet a HUD study showed that 23 million housing units have lead-based paint hazards, 17 million have high exposure to indoor allergens, and 6 million have moderate to severe infrastructure problems. The health burden from these housing problems include injury (especially for children and the elderly); respiratory illness such as asthma, chronic obstructive pulmonary disease, and emphysema from indoor exposure to pollutants; and childhood lead poisoning from exposure to lead in paint, water, and soil.[52]

Unsurprisingly, these health burdens are not distributed equally across the population. Black people are 1.7 times as likely as White people to live in homes with severe physical problems, and low-income people are 2.2 times as likely to live in substandard

housing as higher income people. Low-income households are also more likely to be poorly insulated, leading to the environment being too warm or too cool and to the use of less safe forms of heating (e.g., space heaters).[53] Substandard housing conditions are shaped by social forces as well as local, state, and federal laws and policies. For example, housing safety laws are often less likely to be enforced in low-income neighborhoods, leaving poor tenants with little recourse.[54] Specific health disparities associated with housing hazards have been well documented, particularly in low-income children. We describe two of the most prevalent ones next: lead poisoning and asthma.

Lead Poisoning

While the overall burden of lead poisoning has diminished substantially in the past 20 years, racial- and socioeconomic-based lead poisoning disparities have not. Black children, low-income children, and children enrolled in Medicaid continue to have higher rates of lead poisoning than other children.[55] These disparities are driven by a number of factors. While the United States banned the use of lead in paint in 1978, homes built before 1978 are likely to have been painted with lead paint. If a home is in disrepair, the lead paint is more likely to chip and produce dust, which can then be ingested by children. Low-income children are more likely to live in older housing that is in disrepair.

Childhood lead poisoning is most often caused by exposure to dust and paint chips from interior surfaces of homes with deteriorating lead-based paint. Young children and babies are most at risk for lead poisoning because they crawl on the floor, exposing them to lead dust and paint chips. Because babies and toddlers engage in hand-to-mouth activities—exploring their world through putting things in their mouths—they are likely to ingest lead dust and chips more easily. In addition, because brain development is so rapid in the first six years of life, children's developing brains are more susceptible to the toxic effects of lead.

Overlaps between housing needs and food needs may also exacerbate childhood lead poisoning disparities. Deficiencies in both iron and calcium are thought to result in increased absorption of lead from the gut. Low-income children are more likely to experience food insecurity and thus anemia and calcium deficiencies, which may increase their lead uptake. Lead poisoning has serious, lifelong consequences for health, development, cognition, and behavior. See **Figure 8.2**.

In addition to poisoning from lead paint, exposure to lead in water is also of concern. The water crisis in Flint, Michigan, which began in 2014, helped raise awareness about the dangers of old pipes leaching lead into drinking water. In Flint, residents were exposed to high levels of lead in their drinking water after the town changed its water source—in order to save money—from Detroit's city water to the Flint River. Because the water was not properly treated, lead from pipes leading into homes from the street leached toxic levels of lead into the drinking water. Forty-one percent of residents in Flint live below the federal poverty level, and 56% are Black. After city, state, and federal government officials failed to recognize the problem and address it in a timely manner, many viewed their failure to act as systemic racism. In 2017, the Michigan Civil Rights Commission issued a report, "The Flint Water Crisis: Systemic Racism through the Lens of Flint," suggesting that "deeply embedded institutional, systemic and historical racism" contributed to governmental officials' decision to tap the Flint River as a cost-saving measure without due regard for the health consequences for Flint's population.[56] Researchers investigating racial disparities in lead exposure and poisoning have labeled it "toxic inequality."[57] While the Flint crisis has led

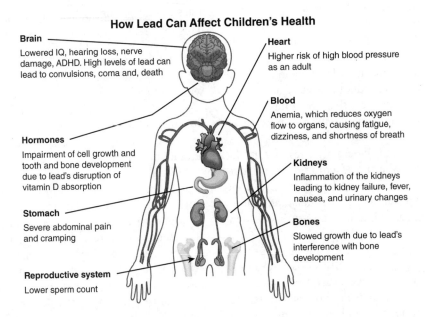

How Lead Can Affect Children's Health

Brain
Lowered IQ, hearing loss, nerve damage, ADHD. High levels of lead can lead to convulsions, coma and, death

Hormones
Impairment of cell growth and tooth and bone development due to lead's disruption of vitamin D absorption

Stomach
Severe abdominal pain and cramping

Reproductive system
Lower sperm count

Heart
Higher risk of high blood pressure as an adult

Blood
Anemia, which reduces oxygen flow to organs, causing fatigue, dizziness, and shortness of breath

Kidneys
Inflammation of the kidneys leading to kidney failure, fever, nausea, and urinary changes

Bones
Slowed growth due to lead's interference with bone development

Figure 8.2 How lead affects children's health

Data from Calderone J, Gould S. Here's how lead is poisoning American children. *Business Insider*. March 7, 2016. http://www.businessinsider.com/lead-health-child-flint-michigan-body-pollution-water-2016-3.

to renewed calls for improving lead safety in homes and water, few municipalities and states have the resources to undergo systematic remediation programs. As a result, children—particularly those in low-income communities—remain at risk.

Housing-Related Asthma Triggers

Another common housing-related health hazard is exposure to indoor pollutants that serve as "triggers" for asthma. Both the development of asthma and the severity of asthma are thought to be related to environmental triggers. Asthma is a chronic respiratory disease causing episodes of wheezing, coughing, and shortness of breath; if severe, it can be fatal. Asthma prevalence has doubled in the past two decades, and asthma accounts for over 10 million office visits, 400,000 hospitalizations, and 10 million missed days of work each year.[58] Asthma triggers include poor ventilation, dust mites, pet dander, cockroach and mice feces, and mold. Housing that has not been well maintained is especially prone to these triggers, and economically disadvantaged families who disproportionately live in substandard housing are at higher risk for asthma.

A study in New York City found that Black and Latinx people were more likely to live in housing units with significant structural and maintenance problems, including water leaks that can lead to mold, chipping paint, broken plaster, holes in surfaces, and pest infestation—in other words, many of the types of substandard housing conditions that cause or exacerbate asthma.[59] Low-income families, particularly those in inner-city neighborhoods, are also at higher risk for exposure to outdoor pollutants such as transportation depots, industrial land use, and transfer stations, all of which can lead to or exacerbate asthma.[60]

Asthma is the most common chronic disease among children, and 40% of asthma diagnosed in children is believed to be attributable to residential exposures.[61] Because these exposures are related to material hardship, there are significant racial and socioeconomic disparities in rates of asthma. "Non-Hispanic Black children have higher rates of asthma diagnosis, asthma morbidity, hospitalizations for asthma, and asthma mortality than non-Hispanic White children."[62]

Asthma is also a leading medical cause of chronic school absenteeism. Asthma flare-ups may cause children to miss school to receive medical attention, including spending time in the emergency department or hospital for particularly severe episodes. Low-income children are more likely to have poorly controlled asthma, leading to flare-ups. Poorly controlled asthma is also associated with problems with attention, cognition, and hyperactivity, which in turn can lead to poor academic performance.[63] Thus, asthma disparities not only contribute to poor health, they perpetuate inequalities in educational opportunity for disadvantaged children. Like childhood lead poisoning, which effects physical, cognitive, and behavioral functioning and thus can disrupt learning, asthma disparities exacerbate racial and socioeconomic inequality by reducing educational and economic opportunity for low-income Children of Color.

Tenants have the legal right to live in a property that does not endanger their health or safety. States and municipalities have housing maintenance and safety laws, usually referred to as the "housing code," that spell out housing conditions that endanger health and safety and that, therefore, violate the code. Most states and localities have agencies that inspect properties for housing health and safety violations. If tenants believe that a property is in violation of the housing code, they may contact this agency and request an inspection. If the inspection determines that a property is in violation of the code, the agency sends the property owner a notice of violation, and the owner is given a specified period of time to correct the violation(s). Failure to remediate the conditions that violate the housing code usually results in fines.

However, low-income tenants face a number of problems enforcing their legal right to safe housing. First, many low-income tenants are unaware of their rights or, if they are, may not know how to exercise those rights. In most jurisdictions, the burden is on a tenant to complain to the appropriate housing code enforcement agency and seek an inspection of the property. For vulnerable tenants who have poor bargaining power and few affordable housing options, the risk of antagonizing a landlord—who, of course, may resort to eviction in retaliation for alerting authorities—is often not in their best interest. While many states have laws protecting tenants from retaliatory eviction, these laws frequently are unenforced. Second, because many housing code agencies are under-resourced and/or poorly administered, the responses to tenant complaints are often discretionary and inadequate. Legal assistance is vital to helping vulnerable tenants enforce their rights, but as discussed in Chapter 7, most low-income tenants have difficulty accessing it. Another option is for cities to implement proactive enforcement in which cities target particular areas for routine inspections based on the likelihood of housing code violations. This approach removes from vulnerable tenants the burden of enforcing their own rights and creates a more systematic way for cities to ensure that housing remains safe.[64]

Community: Racial Segregation and Neighborhood Exposures

Like housing, neighborhoods play a key role in the health of individuals, families, and communities. The neighborhood in which one lives has major ramifications for all aspects of a person's life, opportunities, and health. Political scientist Jamila Michener points out that neighborhoods structure and determine who has what opportunities in America:

> "Place matters" in profound, multitudinous ways and it is acutely consequential for those who inhabit the economic and racial margins of American society. The power of place is neither incidental nor innocuous. Instead, the social, economic, and political significance of where a person lives stems from public policies that create, contour, and reinforce systemic inequity. One way that policy does this is by facilitating the geographic concentration of people who are structurally vulnerable.[65]

Next, we examine how racial segregation and concentrated poverty in neighborhoods not only structure economic opportunity but also have a profound impact on the opportunity for health.

Racial Segregation and Concentrated Poverty

Segregation and neighborhood disadvantage did not happen by accident. Historical legalized discrimination embedded racial and economic segregation into America's place-based disparities, will be discussed in detail in Chapter 10. Current policies and efforts—including the failure to adequately enforce civil rights laws, such as the Fair Housing Act—reinforce and perpetuate neighborhood inequities. Not surprisingly, racial and economic segregation are strongly associated with poor health outcomes. Studies show correlations between neighborhood disadvantage and cardiovascular disease, obesity, depression, cancer, and risk behaviors such as smoking, early sex, and substance use disorders. Life expectancy can vary by as much as 25 years between neighborhoods, even those just a handful of miles apart.[66] This association has led researchers to suggest that your health may be more a function of your zip code than your genetic code. **Figure 8.3** shows the differences in life expectancy in New Orleans, Louisiana, based on neighborhood or region of the city.

Neighborhood Exposures and Health

Neighborhood-related health inequities result from greater exposure in segregated neighborhoods to poverty, lack of access to human capital (i.e., educational and employment opportunities), violence, stress, indoor and outdoor environmental pollutants, and structural problems with the built environment. Legalized racial segregation has left a legacy of multiple structural barriers for people living in low-income neighborhoods, particularly for racial and ethnic minorities, including poor access to quality educational opportunities, employment, and health care. One study found that in metropolitan areas, 76% of Black children and 69% of Latinx children live in worse neighborhood conditions than the worst-off White children.[67]

Researchers have also linked community to social capital, which plays an important role in health. Ichiro Kawachi defines social

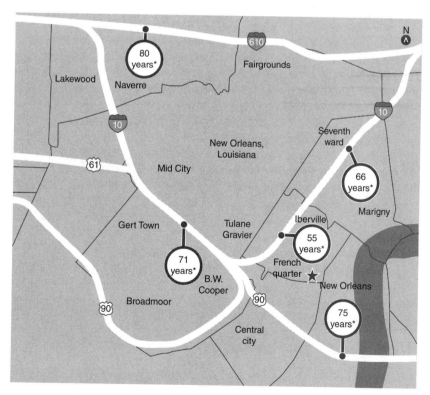

Figure 8.3 Map of New Orleans, Louisiana, showing differences in life expectancy by different regions of the city

"*Social Capital*"

capital as "those features of social relationships—such as levels of interpersonal trust and norms of reciprocity and mutual aid—that facilitate collective action for mutual benefit."[68] In a study of the relationship between social capital and health, Kawachi and his colleagues found that perceptions of trust in other people in one's community were correlated with death rates from heart disease, cancer, and infant mortality.[69] Social capital is closely connected to social inequality in a given community: Living in a community with greater social inequality negatively influences perceptions of that community and the forces at play in the community, such as high levels of violence and social anxiety, as well as increased perceptions of discrimination. "The combination of increasing social status differentials and the deteriorating social relations could hardly be a more potent mix for population health."[70]

It is not difficult to see that the built environment—the physical parts of where we live, work, and play, such as homes, buildings, streets, open spaces, and infrastructure—can significantly affect health. The built environment includes such things as proximity to traffic, walkability, access to parks, availability of healthy food, and mixed-use development. Neighborhoods with sidewalks promote walking; mixed-use development promotes retail markets that are more likely to offer healthy foods; parks improve air quality and provide exercise opportunities. Public health officials suggest that the built environment is crucial to improving population health. Neighborhood planning and design can make individual choices, such as eating healthier food and exercise, the easy choice rather than an uphill battle. Because racially segregated, high-poverty neighborhoods tend to experience more crime and violence and lack many of the healthy attributes described (sidewalks, parks, and access to healthy food), opportunities for good health are severely curtailed.

Research shows that protracted exposure to neighborhood violence is associated with intensified reactivity and heightened cortisol (stress hormone) levels in children. This biological response is thought to indicate a child's heightened vigilance to potential threats.[71] In addition to increased stress and vigilance, exposure to neighborhood violence affects the health of adults and children in a number of ways. First, unsafe neighborhoods appear to reduce physical activity because children and adults may forgo recreational activities in the neighborhood if they are concerned about safety. Second, individuals and families may lack social support, important to health and well-being, and become isolated if they are afraid to leave their homes. Third, people living in neighborhoods with high rates of violence are more likely to have mental health and substance use disorders and to engage in risk-taking behaviors.

It is estimated that two-thirds of children are exposed to different types of community violence by the age of 18. Children living in economically disadvantaged communities are more likely to be exposed to violence.[72] A study of mothers of young children in Baltimore found that over the course of a year, 30% had witnessed a person being shot, more than half saw someone beaten or stabbed, 76% had witnessed someone being arrested, and the majority had been awakened by gunfire or police. The mothers who had witnessed violence had worse health outcomes on five measures than those who had not: self-reported health, smoking, exercise, amount of sleep, and sleep interruption. The study suggested that the mothers' trauma related to exposure to neighborhood violence not only affected their own health but also had detrimental effects on their ability to parent their young children.[73]

Research has shown that moving to a lower-poverty neighborhood appears to improve well-being and life opportunities for low-income children. A 2015 study of a HUD experiment called "Moving to Opportunity" found that children under the age of 13 whose low-income families were offered the opportunity to move to a lower-poverty neighborhood were more likely to go to a higher-quality college and to have higher earnings in adulthood.[74] Because education and income are highly correlated with health outcomes, living in lower-poverty neighborhoods that present opportunities for quality education and higher earnings also provides opportunities for better health. But not all people can or want to move to a different neighborhood. As a result, structural change requires policies that invest in low-income neighborhoods, supporting the infrastructure necessary for health. As discussed at the end of this chapter, there are legal and policy interventions that can remedy these long-standing inequities in neighborhoods.

Area and Region: Rural Health

Health is not only influenced by neighborhood and community but also by the area or region in which one lives. While we often associate poverty-based health inequities with urban communities, the U.S. rural population is more likely to live in poverty than populations living in metropolitan areas. A quarter of the rural population have incomes below the federal poverty level, compared to one-fifth of the population living in metropolitan areas.[75] Furthermore, while rural areas have experienced a loss of manufacturing jobs and subsequent rising rates of unemployment, urban America has experienced population and economic growth as well as expanded health care and public health initiatives focused on addressing chronic disease.[76] Rural communities experience a higher burden of heart disease, stroke, diabetes, tobacco use, substance

abuse, and mental health disorders than metropolitan areas. This is partly explained by the fact that rural areas have a higher percentage of older adults, likely due to younger adults leaving rural communities for metropolitan areas.[77] Rural areas also have a much higher prevalence of injury-related deaths than urban areas: There is a 22% higher risk of injury-related death in rural communities, and more than half of all car accident fatalities occur in rural areas.[78]

Recent research has focused on rural health outcomes and has sought answers as to why they seem to be worsening. The "deaths of despair" study mentioned in Chapter 7, which describes the rising mortality rates among White people ages 45 to 54 with a high school education or less, has been cited as one answer, especially given the high rates of drug overdose in rural communities. But a follow-up study in 2017 that focused on subpopulations found that "in addition to deaths from suicide, accidental poisoning, and liver disease, White people in rural areas saw increases in chronic disease deaths, which contributed to the overall higher increases in death rates in these subpopulations."[79] Furthermore, while the opioid crisis and rising mortality rates from chronic disease have heightened awareness about poor health in predominantly White rural communities, this focus may fail to capture the complexity of rural health inequities. Many rural communities are home to large Native American and Black populations as well as immigrant populations,[80] and these populations in rural areas are more likely to live in poverty than are their White counterparts.[81]

A number of structural drivers of health are particular to rural areas. For example, rural people tend to have less access to quality water, transportation, broadband, and health care; live in food desserts; and be more susceptible to the effects of climate change because of their role in agriculture

Auxillary
Adverse
Economic
Consea

and energy production. They are also more likely to experience social isolation.[82] Lack of access to quality health care undoubtedly contributes to poor health outcomes among rural populations. People living in rural communities have more limited access to health insurance because they are less likely to be covered by employer-sponsored insurance than people living in metropolitan areas. Despite the high rates of poverty in rural areas, rural populations are also less likely to have access to Medicaid, as nearly two-thirds of the rural uninsured live in states that did not expand Medicaid to single adults under the Affordable Care Act. Consequently, rural people are much more likely (15%) than their urban counterparts (9%) to fall into the "coverage gap," meaning that their income is too low for them to qualify for financial assistance to purchase private insurance, which was designed to help more moderate-income people.[83]

Furthermore, rural areas suffer from significant shortages of health care providers. Primary care, behavioral health, dental care, and specialty care are all more limited in rural areas. Studies show that rural patients are also less likely to receive screening and diagnostic testing, including cancer screenings, compared with patients in urban areas.[84] One of the most chronic shortages in rural communities is that of mental health providers. This shortage, combined with heightened stigma around mental health care in rural communities, creates significant barriers for rural populations.[85] Given the prevalence of mental health and substance use disorders in these communities, this remains a major concern for improving health and well-being in rural America.

Another trend that has been devastating to many rural communities is hospital closures. More than 125 rural hospitals have closed since 2010, leaving residents to travel long distances to receive care (see **Figure 8.4**). These hospitals not only provided acute care, but many also provided primary care and specialty services, including maternal and obstetric care. Their closure has further exacerbated provider shortages. Having to travel a greater distance for health care often means that people neglect or delay seeking the care they critically need, whether to address existing chronic or acute conditions or to receive care they need to stay healthy.[86]

Some medical schools are creating training tracks devoted to encouraging future physicians to practice in underserved rural areas.[87] But structural change necessitates federal and state policies that assess the needs of rural communities and invest in sustainable health care infrastructure, particularly in primary care and addiction and mental health treatment. In addition to health care access, further attention by state and federal policymakers to the specific upstream social and economic drivers of poor health and health disparities in rural areas will be vital to improving outcomes. These include investment in job opportunities, access to safety net programs (including Medicaid), community development, and addressing environmental health hazards.

law +
policy

Environment: Toxic Injustice and Climate Change

Just as homes, neighborhoods, areas, and regions create and reinforce disparate exposures that perpetuate health inequalities, pathogens caused by environmental toxins and the effects of climate change are not evenly distributed across populations. Thus, "place matters" to health at multiple levels—from your home to the neighborhood surrounding your home to the air, water, and land that surrounds your home to the area or region where you live. While we all share the environment, People of Color and

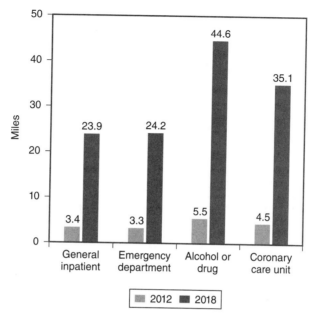

Figure 8.4 Distance in miles from service areas with rural hospital closures to the nearest open hospital that offered certain health care services, 2012 and 2018

GAO Analysis of data from the Department of Health and Human Services and North Carolina Rural Health Research Program. GAO 21-93.

socioeconomically disadvantaged communities (including some rural communities) are more likely to be exposed to hazardous waste and other environmental toxins.[88]

Placement of Environmental Hazards

Spatial planning and zoning play a key role in the location of environmental hazards and the populations who will be exposed to them. As one environmental health researcher notes:

> Vulnerable communities are used (directly or indirectly) to host social and environmental disamenities and externalities through planning, zoning, industrial siting, infrastructure and development inequities.... There is an underdevelopment and/

or destabilization in the growth, health, and quality of life of host communities overburdened by environmental and social externalities and spatially and socially bounded by limited access to environmental amenities.[89]

Studies show that Black people are more likely to live near a Superfund site (locations requiring a long-term response to clean up hazardous material contaminations).[90] Research investigating whether hazardous waste treatment plants are more likely to be placed in existing Communities of Color or whether People of Color move to where existing sites are located found that "[h]azardous waste TSDFs [treatment, storage, and disposal facilities] were sited where white move-out and minority move-in were already occurring, and had been occurring for a decade or two prior to siting for some cohorts of TSDFs."[91]

One of the primary federal legal levers for communities to take action when confronted with environmental injustice is to file a complaint with the Environmental Protection Agency (EPA) under Title VI of the Civil Rights Act. The law prohibits any entity receiving funding from the EPA from discriminating based on race, ethnicity, or national origin. But a series of Supreme Court decisions and lax enforcement by the EPA have made it difficult for communities to succeed in challenging placement of hazardous waste and exposure to environmental toxins.[92] Indeed, in 2016, a commission charged with evaluating the EPA's enforcement of Title VI found that it had failed to take action to protect Communities of Color most burdened by environmental injustice.[93]

There is strong evidence that regulators are more likely to impose stricter enforcement mechanisms against polluters in communities demonstrating greater political power.[94] But neighborhood segregation and poverty concentration often weaken political power. Increasingly, community activists are building political power in marginalized communities through grassroots organizing. Health care and public health professionals are critical allies in these efforts since they can illuminate the negative health impacts and disparities created by environmental injustice.

Climate Change

Economically disadvantaged communities and vulnerable populations are also more burdened by climate change and natural disasters. A 2017 report by National Oceanic and Atmospheric Administration (NOAA) confirmed that 2016 was the warmest year on record and that climate change is contributing to unusual weather patterns, storms, and sea level rise, which can have a disastrous impact on communities.[95] A 2021 report by scientists from the United Nations Intergovernmental Panel on Climate Change stated that human activity is "unequivocally" responsible for global warming, efforts to reduce greenhouse gases are desperately needed, and some damage to the planet is now irreversible. U.N. Secretary-General António Guterres called the report a "code red for humanity."[96] Climate change affects health through heat-related morbidity and mortality due to rising temperatures and prolonged heat waves, air pollution, and increased risk of infectious disease, especially water- or vector-borne diseases, and trauma and mental health impacts of environmental disasters.[97] Refer to **Figure 8.5**.

Relatively vulnerable populations—the elderly, children, people with chronic health conditions, and those living in more marginalized communities—are most at risk for harm from climate change–related events. Hurricane Katrina, an extremely destructive storm that hit the Gulf Coast of the United States in 2005, exemplified the disproportionate toll that natural disasters can take on vulnerable populations. Of the roughly 1,400 Katrina-related deaths in Louisiana, fatalities were largest among the disabled, those living in nursing homes, and those from poor communities without the resources to relocate during the storm. One study reported that 49% of the fatalities were people age 75 or older and that the mortality rate among Black people was 1.7 to 4 times higher than among White people.[98] The economic toll of the storm also disproportionately affected poor and vulnerable people, who were less likely to be able to rebuild their homes or who were dislocated from public housing that was never reopened after the storm. Post-Katrina studies of evacuees have shown that many suffer from resulting mental health problems such as depression and PTSD.[99]

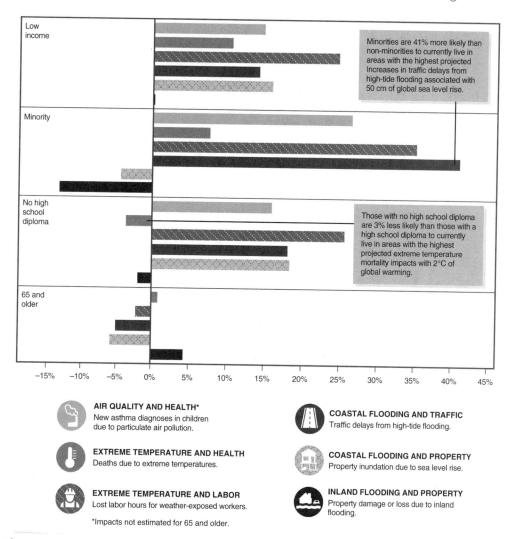

Figure 8.5 Differences in risks to socially vulnerable groups relative to reference populations with 2°C of global warming or 50 cm of global sea level rise

Environmental Protection Agency. Climate Change and Social Vulnerability in the United States: A Focus on Six Impacts. September 2021. https://www.epa.gov/cira/social-vulnerability-report

The increasing number of severe weather events—such as hurricanes, earthquakes, and wildfires—demonstrates that catastrophic storms and natural disasters are likely to continue to wreak havoc on communities for years to come. As discussed earlier, rural populations are affected by climate change in ways that are different from urban populations because of their connection to agriculture and energy production. Droughts and floods are likely to affect the economic stability for farmers as they struggle with rising temperatures and extreme weather events. Power outages are also highlighting the need to improve and update the country's energy infrastructure.

The Biden administration has announced a new target for the United States to "achieve a 50–52 percent reduction from 2005 levels in economy-wide net greenhouse gas pollution in 2030."[100]

The Environmental Justice Movement focuses on both distributive justice (distributing environmental burdens equitably across the population) and procedural justice (ensuring a fair decision-making process that leads to equitable distribution of those burdens), as described in Chapter 2. Using evidence of disproportionate environmental burden on low-income communities, particularly Communities of Color, the Environmental Justice Movement has employed collective action to ensure participation in the decision-making process. (Chapter 16 will further explore the values and tools of collective action in different contexts.) Strengthening the voices of people from marginalized communities to assert what they need and demand the right to live in healthy, safe places is key to structural change. As the effects of climate change threaten all communities, but especially more marginalized communities, political action is vitally important to not just the United States but the planet.

Conclusion

This chapter explored the multiple ways in which place matters to health. From families to homes to neighborhoods to regions to the environment, human beings are shaped by and absorb their surroundings, with important consequences for their health. The conditions in which people live their daily lives may be experienced individually or by subpopulation, but they are all modifiable through policy and targeted interventions focused on health equity and justice.

Law and public policy have, unfortunately, helped structure place-based inequities and environmental harms and injustice, but they can also help remedy them. Policy analysts at the Urban Institute point out that the federal government, in particular, has a large role to play to invest in and drive structural changes needed to protect health and advance fair opportunity:

> Because public policies helped create these equity gaps, they can and should close them. The federal government can play a particularly potent role: it already has a range of civil rights, fair housing, and environmental justice laws creating authority to act but awaiting the will and resources to do so. It can help level the playing field across cities and regions and ensure that fair access to opportunity exists everywhere in the US. And only the federal government manages the public budget and scale of resources necessary to reverse long-standing inequities.[101]

Laws are critical tools in addressing place-based inequities affecting health, but it is not always the case that new laws are needed to bring about change. Political will, targeted advocacy, and investment where laws already exist (e.g., housing codes, civil rights, and environmental protections) are required to ensure that enforcement on behalf of underserved and marginalized communities is taken seriously. Indeed, health justice advocates can and should press federal, state, and local governments to work strategically and collaboratively with marginalized and vulnerable populations in improving the place-based health drivers in their communities.

References

1. Shonkoff JP, Garner AS; Committee on Psychosocial Aspects of Child and Family Health; Committee on Early Childhood, Adoption, and Dependent Care; Section on Developmental and Behavioral Pediatrics. The lifelong effects of early childhood adversity and toxic stress. *Pediatrics*. 2012 Jan;129(1):e232–e246, e234.

2. Felitti VJ, Anda RF, Nordenberg D, et al. Relationship of childhood abuse and household dysfunction to many of the leading causes of death in adults: The Adverse Childhood Experiences (ACE) Study. *American Journal of Preventive Medicine*. 1998;14(4):245–258.

3. Felitti VJ, Anda RF, Nordenberg D, et al. Relationship of childhood abuse and household dysfunction to many of the leading causes of death in adults: The Adverse Childhood Experiences (ACE) Study. *American Journal of Preventive Medicine*. 1998;14(4):245–258.

4. Data Resource Center for Child and Adolescent Health. 2017–2018 National Survey of Children's Health. Indicator 6.13: How many children experienced one or more adverse childhood experiences from the list of 9 ACEs? 2022. http://childhealthdata.org/browse/survey/results?q=4783&r=1.

5. Centers for Disease Control and Prevention. Adverse childhood experiences. April 12, 2021. https://www.cdc.gov/violenceprevention/aces/index.html

6. Novoa C, Morrissey T. Adversity in childhood: The role of policy in creating and addressing adverse childhood experiences. August 27, 2020. https://www.americanprogress.org/issues/early-childhood/reports/2020/08/27/489805/adversity-early-childhood/

7. Selvaraj K, Ruiz MJ, Aschkenasy J, et al. Screening for toxic stress risk factors at well-child visits: The Addressing Social Key Questions for Health Study. *The Journal of Pediatrics*. 2019:205:244–249,246.

8. Sacks V, Murphey D. The prevalence of adverse childhood experiences, nationally, by state, and by race or ethnicity. *Child Trends*. February 12, 2018. https://www.childtrends.org/publications/prevalence-adverse-childhood-experiences-nationally-state-race-ethnicity

9. Shonkoff JP, Garner AS; Committee on Psychosocial Aspects of Child and Family Health; Committee on Early Childhood, Adoption, and Dependent Care; Section on Developmental and Behavioral Pediatrics. The lifelong effects of early childhood adversity and toxic stress. *Pediatrics*. 2012 Jan;129(1):e232–e246, e234.

10. Shonkoff JP, Garner AS; Committee on Psychosocial Aspects of Child and Family Health; Committee on Early Childhood, Adoption, and Dependent Care; Section on Developmental and Behavioral Pediatrics. The lifelong effects of early childhood adversity and toxic stress. *Pediatrics*. 2012 Jan;129(1):e232–e246, e234.

11. Goldberg D, Baxley EG, Fancher TL. Socioecologic determinants of health. In: Skochelak S, et al. ed. *Health Systems Science*. New York, NY: Elsevier; 2017: 134–152,140 (citing Camara Phyllis Jones).

12. Mani A, Mullainathan S, Shafir E, Zhao J. Poverty impedes cognitive function. *Science*. 2013;341:976–980.

13. Oral R, Ramirez M, Coohey C, et al. Adverse childhood experiences and trauma informed care: The future of health care. *Pediatric Research*. 2016;79:227–233,229.

14. *Child Trends*. Databank indicator: Child maltreatment. 2019. https://www.childtrends.org/indicators/child-maltreatment/.

15. *Child Trends*. Databank indicator: Child maltreatment. 2019. https://www.childtrends.org/indicators/child-maltreatment/.

16. U.S. Department of Justice. Children exposed to violence. 2012. https://www.justice.gov/sites/default/files/defendingchildhood/cev-rpt-full.pdf.

17. U.S. Department of Health & Human Services, Administration on Children, Youth and Families, Children's Bureau. *Child Maltreatment*. 2019. https://www.acf.hhs.gov/sites/default/files/documents/cb/cm2019.pdf.

18. The Adoption and Safe Families Act of 1997. PL 105-89.

19. National Association of Counsel for Children. Asking the experts: What are the three most critical issues facing child welfare today? September 12, 2016. https://www.naccchildlaw.org/news/307300/Asking-the-Experts-What-Are-the-Three-Most-Critical-Issues-Facing-Child-Welfare-Today-NACC-Blog.htm.

20. U.S. Department of Health & Human Services, Administration on Children, Youth and Families, Children's Bureau. *Child Maltreatment*. 2019. https://www.acf.hhs.gov/sites/default/files/documents/cb/cm2019.pdf

21. Children's Bureau, Child Welfare Information Gateway. Racial disproportionality and disparity in child welfare. *Issue Brief*; October 2016. https://www.childwelfare.gov/pubPDFs/racial_disproportionality.pdf.

22. Roberts DE. Prison, foster care, and the systemic punishment of Black mothers. *UCLA Law Review*. 2012;59:1474.

23. Roberts DE. Prison, foster care, and the systemic punishment of Black mothers. *UCLA Law Review*. 2012;59:1474.

24. Groves BM, Augustyn M, Lee D, Sawires P. *Identifying and Responding to Domestic Violence: Consensus Recommendations for Child and Adolescent Health*. San Francisco, CA: Family Violence Prevention Fund; 2002.

25. McAlister Groves B, Pilnik L, Tobin Tyler E, et al. Personal safety: Addressing interpersonal and family violence in the health and legal systems. In

Tobin Tyler E, Lawton E, Conroy C, Sandel M, et al., eds. *Poverty, Health and Law: Readings and Cases for Medical-Legal Partnership*. Durham, NC: Carolina Academic Press; 2012.

26. McAlister Groves B, Pilnik L, Tobin Tyler E, et al. Personal safety: Addressing interpersonal and family violence in the health and legal systems. In Tobin Tyler E, Lawton E, Conroy C, Sandel M, et al., eds. *Poverty, Health and Law: Readings and Cases for Medical-Legal Partnership*. Durham, NC: Carolina Academic Press; 2012.

27. McAlister Groves B, Pilnik L, Tobin Tyler E, et al. Personal safety: Addressing interpersonal and family violence in the health and legal systems. In Tobin Tyler E, Lawton E, Conroy C, Sandel M, et al., eds. *Poverty, Health and Law: Readings and Cases for Medical-Legal Partnership*. Durham, NC: Carolina Academic Press; 2012: 359.

28. Taylor L. Housing and health: An overview of the literature. *Health Affairs Health Policy Brief*. June 7, 2018. https://www.healthaffairs.org/do/10.1377/hpb2018 0313.396577/full/.

29. National Low Income Housing Coalition (NLIHC). The gap: a shortage of affordable homes. March 2021. https://reports.nlihc.org/sites/default/files/gap/Gap -Report_2021.pdf

30. National Low-Income Housing Coalition (NLIHC). Out of reach 2021: How much do you need to earn to afford a modest apartment in your state? 2021. https://nlihc.org/sites/default/files/oor/2021/Out-of -Reach_2021.pdf

31. Center for Budget and Policy Priorities. Policy basics: Federal rental assistance. May 3, 2017. https://www.cbpp.org/research/housing/policy-basics -federal-rental-assistance.

32. Center for Budget and Policy Priorities. United States: Fact sheet: Federal rental assistance. March 30, 2017. https://www.cbpp.org/sites/default/files/atoms /files/4-13 -11hous-US.pdf.

33. Center for Budget and Policy Priorities. Who is helped by housing choice vouchers? 2016. www.cbpp.org /who-is-helped-by-housing-choice-vouchers-0.

34. U.S. Department of Housing and Urban Development. 2016 annual homeless assessment report to Congress, part 1: Point-in-time estimates of homelessness. November 2016. https://www .hudexchange.infg.ресources/documents/2016 -AHAR-Part-1.pdf.

35. Baxter AJ, Tweed EJ, Katikireddi S, et al. Effects of Housing First approaches on health and well-being of adults who are homeless or at risk of homelessness: Systematic review and meta-analysis of randomised controlled trials. *Journal of Epidemiology and Community Health*. 2019;73(5):379–387.

36. Bechara C. Housing for health: Why health cannot happen without housing. Kaiser Permanente. August 29, 2019. https://about.kaiserpermanente .org/community-health/news/housing-for-health -why-health-cannot-happen-without-housing.

37. Desmond M. Unaffordable America: Poverty, housing, and eviction. *Fast Focus*. 2015;22:1–6. https://www.irp.wisc.edu/publications/fastfocus/pdfs /FF22-2015.pdf.

38. Donavan D, Marbella J. Dismissed: Tenants lose and landlords win in Baltimore's rent court. *The Baltimore Sun*. April 26, 2017.

39. Jaboa L. The pandemic has exacerbated housing instability for renters of color. Center for American Progress. October 30, 2020. https://www .americanprogress.org/issues/poverty/reports /2020/10/30/492606/pandemic-exacerbated-housing -instability-renters-color/.

40. Benfer E, Robinson DB. The COVID-19 eviction crisis: An estimated 30–40 million people in America are at risk. The Aspen Institute. August 20, 2020. https://www.aspeninstitute.org/blog-posts/the-covid -19-eviction-crisis-an-estimated-30-40-million -people-in-america-are-at-risk/.

41. MacFarquhar N. Evicted, despite a federal moratorium: "I do not know what I am going to do." *The New York Times*. August 11, 2021. https://www.nytimes.com/2021/08/11/us/eviction -moratorium-vegas.html.

42. *Alabama Association of Realtors, et al. v. Department of Health and Human Services, et al.* 594 U. S. ____ (2021).

43. Desmond M, Tobert Kimbro R. Eviction's fallout: Housing, hardship, and health. *Social Forces*. September 2015;94(1):295–324,297.

44. Network for Public Health Law. The Public health implications of housing instability, eviction, and homelessness (fact sheet). April 2021, 2. https:// www.networkforphl.org/resources/legal-and -policy-approaches-towards-preventing-housing -instability/the-public-health-implications-of -housing-instability-eviction-and-homelessness /#:~:text=Housing%20instability%20is%20a%20 public,communities%2C%20and%20drives% 20health%20inequities.&text=Those%20who%20 lack%20stable%20housing,%2C%20food% 20insecurity%2C%20and%20violence.

45. Frank DA, Neault NA, Skalicky A, et al. Heat or eat: The low income energy assistance program and nutritional and health risks amongst children less than three years of age. *Pediatrics*. 2006;118(5):1293–1302.

46. Energy Efficiency for All. Lifting the high energy burden in America's largest cities: How energy efficiency can improve low income and underserved

communities. April 2016. http://energyefficiencyforall
.org/sites/default/files/Lifting%20the%20High%
20Energy%20Burden_0.pdf.

47. Frank DA, Neault NA, Skalicky A, et al. Heat or eat: The
low income energy assistance program and nutritional
and health risks amongst children less than three
years of age. *Pediatrics.* 2006;118(5):1293–1302.

48. U.S. Department of Health and Human Services,
Office of Community Services. Low Income
Home Energy Assistance Program (LIHEAP).
January 20, 2022. https://www.acf.hhs.gov/ocs/low
-income-home-energy-assistance-program-liheap

49. Office of the Administration for Children and Families.
LIHEAP FAQs for consumers. January 19, 2016. https://
www.acf.hhs.gov/ocs/faq/liheap-faqs-consumers

50. Graff M, Carley S. COVID-19 assistance needs to target
energy insecurity. *Nature Energy.* 2020;5:352–354.

51. U.S. Department of Health and Human Services. *Call
to action to promote healthy homes.* Washington, DC:
Office of the Surgeon General; June 2009: i.

52. President's Task Force on Environmental Health
Risks and Safety Risks to Children, Healthy Homes
Workgroup. Advancing healthy housing: A strategy
for action; 2013:13–14.

53. Krieger J, Higgins DL. Housing and health: Time
again for public health action. *American Journal of
Public Health.* May 2002;92(5):758–768,760.

54. Tobin Tyler E. When are laws strictly enforced?
Criminal justice, housing quality, and public
health. *Health Affairs Blog.* November 5, 2015.
http://healthaffairs.org/blog/2015/11/05/when
-are-laws-strictly-enforced-criminal-justice-housing
-quality-and -public-health/.

55. American Academy of Pediatrics Policy
Statement. Lead exposure in children: prevention,
detection, and management. *Pediatrics.* October
2005;116(4):1036–1046,1037.

56. The Michigan Civil Rights Commission. The
Flint water crisis: Systemic racism through the
lens of Flint. February 17, 2017. http://www
.michigan.gov/documents/mdcr/VFlintCrisisRep-F
-Edited3-13-17_554317_7.pdf.

57. Sampson RJ, Winter AS. The racial ecology of lead
poisoning: Toxic inequality in Chicago neighborhoods,
1995–2013. *Dubois Review.* 2016;13(2):2–23.

58. Newacheck PW, Halfon N. Prevalence, impact,
and trends in childhood disability due to asthma.
Archives of Pediatric and Adolescent Medicine. 2000;
154:287–293.

59. Rosenbaum E. Racial/ethnic differences in asthma
prevalence: The role of housing and neighborhood
environment. *Journal of Health and Social Behavior.*
June 2008;49(2):131–145,132.

60. Rosenbaum E. Racial/ethnic differences in asthma
prevalence: The role of housing and neighborhood

environment. *Journal of Health and Social Behavior.*
June 2008;49(2):131–145,132.

61. Robert Wood Johnson Foundation. Where we live
matters for our health: The links between housing and
health. *Issue Brief 2: Housing and Health.* September
2008:6.

62. Hughes HK, Matsui EC, Tschudy MM, Pollack CE,
Keet CA. Pediatric asthma health disparities: Race,
hardship, housing, and asthma in a national survey.
Academic Pediatrics. 2017;17:127–134,128.

63. Basch CE. Healthier students are better learners:
a missing link in school reforms to close the
achievement gap. A Research Initiative of the
Campaign for Educational Equity Teachers College,
Columbia University. March 2010.

64. Change Lab Solutions. Healthy housing through
proactive rental inspection. 2014. http://
www.changelabsolutions.org/sites/default
/files/Healthy_Housing_Proactive_Rental_Inspection
_FINAL_20140421.pdf.

65. Michener J. How health policies affect health equity:
People, places, power: Medicaid concentration and
local political participation. *Journal of Health Politics,
Policy and Law.* October 2017;42(5):865–900.

66. Jutte DP, Miller JL, Erickson DJ. Neighborhood
adversity, child health, and the role for
community development. *Pediatrics.* March 2015;
135(2):S48–S57.

67. Williams DR, Jackson PB. Social sources of racial
disparities in health. *Health Affairs. March/April*
2005;24(2):325–334.

68. Kawachi, I. Social capital and community effects on
population and individual death. *Annals of the New
York Academy of Sciences.* 1999;896:120–130,121.

69. Kawachi, I. Social capital and community effects on
population and individual death. *Annals of the New
York Academy of Sciences.* 1999;896:120–130,121.

70. Wilkinson, RG. Health, hierarchy, and social
anxiety. *Annals of the New York Academy of Sciences.*
1999;896:48–63,50.

71. Theall KP, Shirtcliff EA, Dismukes AR, Wallace M,
Drury SS. Association between neighborhood violence
and biological stress in children. *JAMA Pediatrics.*
2017;171(1):53–60.

72. Aizer A. Neighborhood violence and urban youth.
National Bureau of Economic Research. February
2008.

73. Johnson SL, Solomon BS, Shields WC, et al.
Neighborhood violence and its association with
mothers' health: Assessing the relative importance of
perceived safety and exposure to violence. *Journal of
Urban Health.* July 2009;86(4):538–550.

74. Chetty R, Hendren N, Katz LF. The effects of exposure
to better neighborhoods on children: New evidence
from the moving to opportunity experiment. Harvard

University and National Bureau of Economic Research. May 2015.

75. The Henry J. Kaiser Foundation. The Affordable Care Act and insurance coverage in rural areas. May 29, 2014. https://www.kff.org/uninsured/issue-brief/the-affordable-care-act-and-insurance-coverage-in-rural-areas/.

76. Stein EM, Gennuso KP, Ugboaja DC, et al. The epidemic of despair among white Americans: Trends in the leading causes of premature death, 1999–2015. *American Journal of Public Health.* October 2017; 107(10):1541–1547.

77. Inungu JN, Minelli MJ. *Foundations of Rural Public Health in America.* Burlington, MA: Jones and Bartlett Learning; 2021.

78. National Rural Health Association. About rural health care. 2022. https://www.ruralhealthweb.org/about-nrha/about-rural-health-care.

79. Stein EM, Gennuso KP, Ugboaja DC, et al. The epidemic of despair among white Americans: Trends in the leading causes of premature death, 1999–2015. *American Journal of Public Health.* October 2017; 107(10):1541–1547.

80. Inungu JN, Minelli MJ. *Foundations of Rural Public Health in America.* Burlington, MA: Jones and Bartlett Learning; 2021.

81. Inungu JN, Minelli MJ. *Foundations of Rural Public Health in America.* Burlington, MA: Jones and Bartlett Learning; 2021.

82. Inungu JN, Minelli MJ. *Foundations of Rural Public Health in America.* Burlington, MA: Jones and Bartlett Learning; 2021.

83. MACPAC. Medicaid and Rural Health (Issue Brief). April 2021. https://www.macpac.gov/wp-content/uploads/2021/04/Medicaid-and-Rural-Health.pdf.

84. Spoont M, Greer N, Su J, et al. Rural vs. urban ambulatory health care: A systematic review [Internet]. Washington, DC: U.S. Department of Veterans Affairs. May 2011. Summary and discussion. https://www.ncbi.nlm.nih.gov/books/NBK56140/.

85. Spoont M, Greer N, Su J, et al. Rural vs. urban ambulatory health care: A systematic review [Internet]. Washington, DC: U.S. Department of Veterans Affairs. May 2011.

86. Bailie M, Barton T, et al., Confronting rural America's health care crisis. Bipartisan Policy Center. April 21, 2020. https://bipartisanpolicy.org/report/confronting-rural-americas-health-care-crisis/

87. Association of American Medical College. Attracting the next generation of physicians to rural medicine. February 3, 2020. https://www.aamc.org/news-insights/attracting-next-generation-physicians-rural-medicine

88. Wilson SM. An ecologic framework to study and address environmental justice and community health issues. *Environmental Justice.* 2009;2(1):15–23,15–16.

89. Maantay J. Zoning, equity, and public health. *American Journal of Public Health.* July 2001;91:1033–1041.

90. Kramar DE, et al. A spatially informed analysis of environmental justice: Analyzing the effects of gerrymandering and the proximity of minority populations to U.S. superfund sites. *Environmental Justice.* 2018.

91. Mohai P, Saha R. Which came first, people or pollution? Assessing the disparate siting and post-siting demographic change hypotheses of environmental injustice. *Environmental Research Letters.* 2015.

92. EarthJustice. Federal court still requires EPA to enforce civil rights. October 2, 2020. https://earthjustice.org/news/press/2020/federal-court-requires-epa-to-enforce-civil-rights.

93. U.S. Commission on Civil Rights. Environmental justice: Examining the environmental protection agency's compliance and enforcement of Title VI and Executive Order 12,898. September 2016. https://www.usccr.gov/pubs/2016/Statutory_Enforcement_Report2016.pdf.

94. Banzhaf S, Young A, et al., Environmental justice: The economics of race, place, and pollution. *Journal of Economic Perspectives.* Winter 2019; 33(1):185–208.

95. National Oceanic and Atmospheric Administration (NOAA). International report confirms 2016 was warmest year on record for the globe. August 10, 2017. http://www.noaa.gov/news/international-report-confirms-2016-was-warmest-year-on-record-for-globe.

96. Chestney N, Andrea JA. U.N. climate change report sounds "code red for humanity." Reuters. August 9, 2021. https://www.reuters.com/business/environment/un-sounds-clarion-call-over-irreversible-climate-impacts-by-humans-2021-08-09/.

97. Levy BS, Patz JA. *Climate Change and Health.* Oxford, U.K.: Oxford University Press; 2015.

98. Brunkard JN, Amulanda G, Ratard R. Hurricane Katrina deaths, Louisiana, 2005. *Disaster Medicine and Public Health Preparedness.* December 2008; 2(4):215–223.

99. King RV, Polatin PB, Hogan D, et al. Needs assessment of Hurricane Katrina evacuees residing temporarily in Dallas. *Community Mental Health Journal.* 2016;52:18.

100. The White House. President Biden sets 2030 greenhouse gas pollution reduction target aimed at creating good-paying union jobs and securing U.S. leadership on clean energy technologies. April 22, 2021. https://www.whitehouse.gov/briefing-room/statements-releases/2021/04/22

/fact-sheet-president-biden-sets-2030
-greenhouse-gas-pollution-reduction-target
-aimed-at-creating-good-paying-union-jobs
-and-securing-u-s-leadership-on-clean-energy
-technologies/.

101. Green S, Turner MA, et al., Creating places of opportunity for all. The Urban Institute. September 2020. https://www.urban.org/sites/default/files/publication/102821/creating-places-of-opportunity-for-all_3.pdf.

CHAPTER 9

The Carceral State

20 pages

LEARNING OBJECTIVES

By the end of this chapter you will be able to:

- Explain some customary law enforcement practices and how they affect the health and well-being of low-income Communities of Color
- Discuss the growth of incarceration in the United States, some of the laws and policies that have perpetuated this growth, and how mass incarceration affects individual, community, and public health
- Describe existing and proposed law, policy, and practice changes focused on reducing mass incarceration and its negative health effects

Introduction

Chapter 7 explored the role of socioeconomic status in health inequities, and Chapter 8 described how place—one's family, home, neighborhood, region and exposure to environmental hazards—influences the opportunity to be healthy. This chapter continues the discussion of structural health inequities by focusing on America's unique, unjust, and health-harming approach to criminal justice. It begins by investigating the historical and social roots of law enforcement in the United States and how the construction and inequitable enforcement of criminal laws have a disparate impact on certain populations, especially Communities of Color. It then explores the ways in which American's system of mass incarceration—which we define as jails and prisons, the probation and parole systems, and the post-incarceration consequences of a criminal record—has been driven primarily by policy decisions divorced from evidence about effective ways to reduce crime and promote public safety. These policies—including prioritization of punishment over rehabilitation, strict and harsh sentencing rules, the imposition of large court fines and fees, and the excessive use of probation—help propagate a system that entangles 19.6 million Americans and their families. The chapter then investigates how incarceration and the collateral consequences of a criminal record compound racial, ethnic, socioeconomic, and health-related inequities, harming individual, community, and population health.

1980 -94
$8M → $95M

It ends by describing current and potential models for reducing incarceration and ameliorating its effects on health. This chapter takes a distinctly structural approach to the carceral state in the United States, meaning that it illuminates the upstream decisions that have shaped laws, policies, practices, and systems that render downstream health harms and inequities.

Law Enforcement and the Health of Low-Income Communities of Color

The relationship between law enforcement and low-income Communities of Color, particularly Black communities, is deeply rooted in American history. Policing as a means of social control of poor (and most often) Black people follows a long path—from slavery to Reconstruction-era Black Codes (laws that limited the freedom and economic opportunity of Black people, often enforced by police) to Jim Crow laws to "stop and frisk" policies in urban, predominantly Black neighborhoods. While it is beyond the scope of this chapter to present a thorough history of law enforcement's role in racial injustice, it is important to acknowledge this history as you read about current considerations and controversies in law enforcement in low-income Communities of Color.

This chapter begins with the rise of mass incarceration in the 1970s. In an ostensible effort to crack down on a growing crime rate in the 1970s (which included concerns about a rising drug trade), the federal government initiated the "War on Drugs"—a highly punitive approach to the sale and possession of illegal drugs—as well as other "tough on crime" laws and policies. The War on Drugs was initiated by the Nixon administration in 1971 but was amplified in the 1980s by the Reagan administration. From 1980 to 1984, the federal budget for drug enforcement increased from $8 million to $95 million, penalties for possession of marijuana were raised, and federal mandatory minimum sentences were established.[1] As historian Elizabeth Hinton points out, Reagan's policies not only criminalized addiction, they also produced disparate consequences for low-income Communities of Color:

> [Reagan] led Congress in criminalizing drug users, especially African American drug users, by concentrating and stiffening penalties for the possession of the crystalline rock form of cocaine, known as "crack," rather than the crystallized methamphetamine that White House officials recognized was as much of a problem among low-income white Americans.[2]

Five grams of crack cocaine (used predominantly in low-income Black communities because it was cheaper) carried similar penalties to 500 grams of powder cocaine, which was more typically used by White people. Yet the U.S. Sentencing Commission found on at least three occasions that the chemical compositions of the two drugs and their physical effects were not appreciably different. More than 80% of defendants sentenced for crack offenses were Black despite evidence that more than 66% of crack users were White or Latinx.[3] While championed by the Reagan administration, these policies had bipartisan support.[4]

In the early 1980s, on the heels of these regressive drug policies, police departments initiated another new approach to "criminal justice" termed *proactive policing*. Proactive policing refers to "strategies that have as one of their goals the prevention or reduction of crime and disorder and that are not reactive in terms of focusing primarily on uncovering ongoing crime or on investigating or responding to crimes once they have occurred"[5] The practice of proactive policing as a deterrent to crime manifested in approaches such as "stop and frisk"—stopping, frisking, and sometimes searching individuals based solely on "reasonable suspicion" of criminal activity in neighborhoods labeled high crime areas. At the height of its stop-and-frisk approach to "controlling" crime, New York City police made nearly 700,000 stops in 2011. Lawsuits brought by the Center for Constitutional Rights in 1999 and again in 2008, claiming that the policy violated the federal Constitution's Fourth and Fourteenth Amendments (pertaining to search and seizure and equal protection of the laws, respectively), led to court-ordered quarterly audits. The audits had two purposes: to monitor why the police were making stops and to track the stops by race and ethnicity.[6] Although the number of "stop and frisks" has decreased significantly in New York City since 2011 (down to about 10,000 per year), the majority of people stopped in this manner are Black and Latinx, even though they are less likely than White people to be found with a weapon.[7]

A second type of proactive policing is what is known as the "broken windows" theory," in which "the police seek to prevent crime by addressing disorder and less serious crime problems. Such police interventions are expected to reinforce and enhance informal social controls within communities."[8] The premise of this type of policing, popularized by New York City Police Commissioner William Bratton in the 1990s, is that once a neighborhood begins to tolerate low-level crime, more serious crimes will follow; hence, the theory goes, when people see broken windows in the buildings in their neighborhoods, more deterioration and disorder will follow. Broken windows policies have been hotly debated. While evidence of the effectiveness in reducing crime is mixed, most researchers agree that "aggressive order maintenance strategies that target individual disorderly behaviors do not generate significant crime reductions."[9] In fact, the approach is more likely to undermine law

enforcement: "A sole commitment to increasing misdemeanor arrests stands a good chance to undermine relationships in low-income urban communities of color, where coproduction is most needed and distrust between the police and citizens is most profound."[10]

Combined with stop-and-frisk policies, which have been shown to result in racial profiling, aggressive policing, and other "zero tolerance" policies encouraging police to make arrests for low-level offenses have served to perpetuate police harassment in Communities of Color. Less than 5% of all arrests each year are for violent offenses; most are for low-level felonies and misdemeanors. Black people are more than twice as likely to be arrested than White people.[11] A study in Wisconsin found that White individuals charged with misdemeanors are 75% more likely than Black individuals to have the charges dropped or to serve no time in jail.[12] Despite documented racial disparities in arrests, convictions, and punishments that result from stop-and-frisk policies, many police departments continue to use the tactic alongside other aggressive or "zero tolerance" policies. Some argue that these policies persist—despite the disproportionate harm to Communities of Color and the lack of evidence of their effectiveness—due to entrenched bureaucratic practices, such as basing police productivity on the number of stops and/or arrests made and the ease of intelligence gathering.[13]

Overexposure to Law Enforcement and Health

Persistent police surveillance and the high number of arrests for low-level offenses take an enormous toll on the health of people living in low-income Communities of Color. Perhaps most significantly, overexposure to police can elevate the risk of officer-citizen physical violence that can lead to injury and death.[14] Roughly 1,000 people each year are killed by police. Black people are disproportionately likely to be killed in these interactions; they are more than twice as likely to be killed by police as White Americans."[15]

Although their plight is less publicized, Indigenous people are more likely to be killed by the police than any other group.[16] LGBTQ+ people, people experiencing homelessness, and people with mental illness or substance use disorders disproportionately experience police use of force, and some women, especially Women of Color, experience sexual violence and harassment by police officers.[17]

Recent incidents in which Black people have died while in police custody (e.g., Eric Garner in New York City, Sandra Bland in Houston, Freddie Gray in Baltimore, and George Floyd in Minneapolis) have not only shined a spotlight on police use of force, they have also pointed to the fact that people in police custody do not have a legal right to emergency medical attention. Some advocates are proposing legislation requiring that police immediately request medical services when a detainee requests it or when it is apparent that it is warranted.[18]

A major concern among public health leaders is that data on law enforcement–related fatalities and injuries are not uniformly reported, making surveillance and trend monitoring extremely challenging.[19] Increasingly, however, public health researchers are documenting how overexposure to law enforcement, especially police use of force, has adverse health outcomes for individuals and communities. These include both psychological and physiological responses to stressful experiences with police, whether violent or not. For example, one study of young men in New York City found that those "who reported more police contact also reported more trauma and anxiety symptoms, associations tied to how many stops they reported, the intrusiveness of the encounters, and their perceptions of police fairness."[20] Police stops are also correlated with higher rates of hypertension and diabetes in communities in which these stops are relatively common.[21]

People living in low-income communities that are exposed to high levels of police violence also experience vicarious trauma. A 2021 study in California found that exposure to fatal police violence increased the risk of pre-term birth. The study authors note that acute stress from police violence, combined with higher levels of chronic stress among Black women, likely explained the correlation to adverse birth outcomes.[22] Another study found that there are spillover effects from learning about police killings for the mental health of Black Americans, but not for White Americans.[23] Finally, police presence in Communities of Color may affect access to services, including health care for immigrants. Fear of deportation may induce undocumented immigrants to forego health care and other services to avoid the possibility of encountering law enforcement. (For more discussion of this issue, see Chapter 11).

Scholars who study law enforcement in low-income Communities of Color suggest that policy and practice reforms should include more sophisticated crime analysis to prevent discriminatory crime control approaches, better engagement with residents through community policing strategies, just procedures for police–resident interactions, and problem-solving around crime prevention that does not rely on surveillance and aggressive enforcement.[24] It is worth noting here that in the same communities where police are more likely to make arrests for minor offenses—such as illegally selling cigarettes, loitering, or jaywalking—protective public health laws such as housing safety codes and environmental protection laws often go unenforced (see Chapter 8).[25] Shifting from aggressive policing tactics that harm public health and exacerbate racial and socioeconomic health inequities to more collaborative approaches that engage communities in crime reduction and safety will require state and local investment and policies that prioritize health justice.

LO I

America's Mass Incarceration System: Consequences for Individuals, Communities, and Public Health

The aggressive law enforcement strategies in low-income Communities of Color, undergirded by the War on Drugs, have driven an unprecedented escalation in the number of Americans—disproportionately Black and Latinx men—who are incarcerated, on probation, or on parole. America's mass incarceration system, which as Michelle Alexander explains "refers not only to the criminal justice system but also to the larger web of laws, rules, policies and customs that control those labeled as criminals both in and out of prison," has devastated low-income Communities of Color and has propelled and exacerbated health inequities. We begin by reviewing data on incarceration in the United States, consider some of the explanations for its growth, and analyze some of its implications for socioeconomic and racial inequities. We then turn to the vast number of "collateral consequences" for individuals with a criminal record. Finally, we explore the implications of criminal justice involvement for the health of individuals, families, communities, and the broader public.

The Exponential Growth of Mass Incarceration in the United States

The United States has an incarceration rate that exceeds that of every other nation in the world and that includes significant racial inequities, as noted in the Introduction to this text. **Figure 9.1** highlights international rates of incarceration, demonstrating that the United States is an outlier with regard to the number of people it incarcerates.

Roughly 2.2 million people are incarcerated in federal and state prisons, juvenile detention facilities, and jails each year. More than half a million of those are locked up in jails

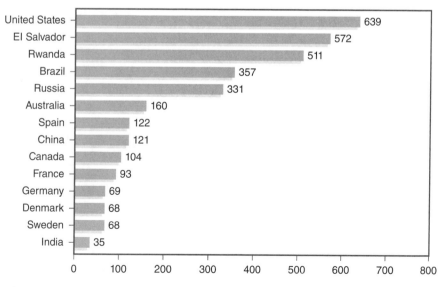

Figure 9.1 International rates of incarceration per 100,000

without having been convicted of a crime.[26] An additional 4 million people are under some sort of criminal justice system control, such as probation or parole.[27] As **Figure 9.2** displays, the growth in the number of people on probation skyrocketed in the mid-1970s but started to decline somewhat in the late 2000s. We discuss the ramifications of the probation system in more detail later in the chapter.

As highlighted previously, a disproportionate number of the people affected by America's mass incarceration are racial and ethnic minorities. A report by the National Academies of Sciences, Engineering and Medicine concluded that "[t]he emergence of high incarceration rates has broad significance for U.S. society. The meaning and consequences of this new reality cannot be separated from issues of social inequality and the quality of citizenship of the nation's racial and ethnic minorities."[28] Overall incarceration rates peaked in 2009 but have been slowly declining in some parts of the country. However, incarceration rates for women, which have grown steadily since the 1980s, have not dropped at the same pace as those for men (see **Figure 9.3**). Growth in the number of women in prison appears to result from the crackdown on drug and minor offenses in low-income neighborhoods discussed earlier in the chapter.[29]

It is also important to note that LGBTQ+ people have long been and continue to be overrepresented in the criminal justice system. Until the U.S. Supreme Court struck them down in *Lawrence v. Texas* in 2003, state sodomy laws were enforced as a way to criminalize sexual activity between same-sex partners, as we discuss in Chapter 13.[30] In 2019, the National Survey on Drug Use and Health

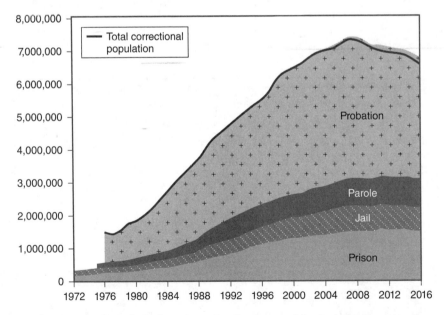

Figure 9.2 The total number of people under correctional supervision includes those in prison, in jail, on parole, or on probation

Note: Figure shows total correction population, including state and federal prison, local jail, and probation and parole populations, from 1972 to 2016. Individuals can have more than one correctional status, so the total correctional population may be less than the sum of those in each status. Data for 1972 to 1979 were compiled from the Sourcebook of Criminal Justice Statistics for The Growth of Incarceration in the United States: Exploring Causes and Consequences, National Research Council Committee on Law and Justice, National Academy of Sciences, April 2014. The 1980 to 2016 data are from the Bureau of Justice Statistics, Annual Probation Survey, Annual Parole Survey, Annual Survey of Jails, Census of Jail Inmates, and National Prisoner Statistics Program.
Reproduced from Institute for Research on Poverty. Connections among Poverty, Incarceration, and Inequality. May 2020. https://www.irp.wisc.edu/resource/connections-among-poverty-incarceration-and-inequality/

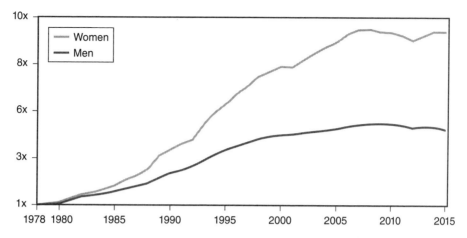

Figure 9.3 Women's state prison populations have grown faster than men's

Reproduced from Sawyer W. The Gender Divide: Tracking Women's State Prison Growth. Prison Policy Initiative. January 9, 2018. https://www.prisonpolicy.org/reports/women_overtime.html

reported that gay, lesbian, and bisexual adults were 2.25 times as likely to be arrested as straight people in the past 12 months.[31] They are also three times as likely as straight people to be incarcerated.[32] Among transgender people, Black transgender people are most likely to report police harassment and assault; they are four times more likely to be incarcerated than White transgender people.[33]

Reasons for the Growth in Incarceration

Criminal justice scholars view the growth in incarceration through several lenses. First, as described earlier, criminal justice policies started to change dramatically beginning in the 1970s. These included the War on Drugs, aggressive policing, and stiffer sentencing laws that increased both arrests and prison sentences. These increases also produced a "chicken and egg" problem: As more people were sentenced to prison, states and the federal government constructed more prisons to hold them. This created what some call the "prison industrial complex," an economy, particularly in small towns, built on incarceration. As funding from the federal government

was funneled to federal agencies and states for the War on Drugs and enhanced law enforcement and as more people were arrested and prosecuted, there was a need for more prison beds. From 1985 to 2019, state expenditures on incarceration grew from $6.7 billion to $56.6 billion (see **Figure 9.4**).

As states built more prisons, the private sector increasingly invested in the prison industry. Beyond the construction of prisons, private businesses now play a role in multiple aspects of the criminal justice

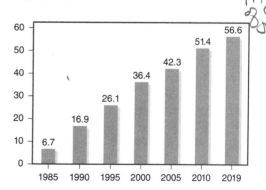

Figure 9.4 State expenditures on corrections in billions, 1985–2019

Reproduced from The Sentencing Project. Criminal Justice Facts. https://www.sentencingproject.org/criminal-justice-facts/

motivation for mass incarceration

system, including contracting inexpensive prison labor, developing surveillance technology used by police, and operating prison food and medical services as well as owning and operating prisons.[34] While some view privatization as beneficial to relieving tight state budgets, others see incarceration as a financial boon to private industry. Privatization, they argue, creates perverse economic incentives to keep prison beds full and runs counter to criminal justice reform. An additional consequence of the growth in the prison industry is that many communities become dependent on prisons for employment. When policymakers attempt to close a prison, they often confront people in local "prison towns" whose livelihood depends on the prison remaining open (e.g., correctional officers and other prison workers, local businesses that serve those workers or produce goods for the prison).[35] To provide some perspective on the sheer number of correctional facilities in operation in the United States, in 2020, there were 110 federal prisons, 1,833 state prisons, 1,772 juvenile correctional facilities, 3,134 local jails, 80 jails on tribal lands, and 218 immigration detention facilities.[36]

# of prisons

One of the primary motives for expanding incarceration and hence building more prisons was to reduce violent crime. Yet a recent study that randomly assigned and then compared criminal defendants to judges who were "more harsh or lenient in their sentencing" found that those who were sentenced to prison were no more or less likely to be convicted of a violent crime within five years and that the benefit of "incapacitating" a person to prevent them from committing crime while in prison was marginal.[37] Furthermore, states that have decreased their prison populations have not seen an increase in crime rates.[38] Indeed, the enormous costs expended on incarceration do not appear to pay off in terms of crime reduction.

A second focus for criminal justice scholars in explaining why the United States leads the world in incarceration is America's penchant for punishment over rehabilitation and for retribution over reintegration. In his recent book, *Inferno: An Anatomy of American Punishment*, law professor Robert Ferguson argues that "America doesn't just punish its criminals. It demonizes them. It turns them from men into monsters so that it then may feel justified in treating them so."[39] Scholars suggest that lengthy prison terms, use of solitary confinement, charging and sentencing juveniles as adults, and executing people with mental illness and development disabilities (which are unique to the United States when compared with other high income nations) all represent a criminal justice system that dehumanizes people who commit crimes—many of them minor—and employs harsh punishment to rid society of those viewed as dispensable.

America's punitive approach to crime cannot be separated from its history of racial discrimination and its policies that treat poverty as more of an individual failure than a structural societal problem. As described earlier, aggressive policing in low-income neighborhoods, criminalizing petty offenses, and racially disparate charging and sentencing for drug crimes all contribute to the number of People of Color, particularly Black men, who are incarcerated. One study estimated that in 2009 the cumulative probability by age 30 to 34 that a Black man would spend time in prison was nearly 70% compared to 15% for a White man.[40]

But the data also make it clear that socioeconomic status is inextricably linked to incarceration. Fifty percent of incarcerated White people and 60% of incarcerated Black people have not completed high school.[41] A study comparing income based on incarceration history found that men who were incarcerated earned less than half (prior to their incarceration) what men who were not incarcerated earned.[42] Unhoused people are 11 times more likely to be incarcerated than housed people.[43] This is likely, at least in part, a function of the increasing number of laws that criminally punish homeless people for activities like camping or sleeping in public.[44] Thus, low socioeconomic status (SES) is a pathway to incarceration that some call the "poverty to prison pipeline."[45] Income and wealth inequality in the United States have grown steadily since the 1980s; so, too, has the criminalization of poverty (see Chapter 7).[46]

Finally, another key policy trend that links low SES and incarceration and may help to explain the dramatic expansion of the criminal justice system is the increase in the number of people who serve extra time for technical violations of the terms of their probation or for failure to pay court fees and fines. As discussed previously, the probation system in the United States has expanded dramatically in the past 40 years. Technical violations of probation, which include missing an appointment with a probation officer, failing a drug test, or not completing court-mandated counseling, account for as many as one in four admissions to state prison.[47]

Court fees and fines have proliferated since the 1980s, likely the result of more punitive criminal justice policies and as a means to pay for the expenses associated with mass incarceration and the prison industrial complex. City, state, and federal policies mandate the payment of these fees, fines, and surcharges associated with court costs; some states assess these fees and fines regardless of whether a person is convicted of a crime.[48] As the American Bar Association reports, these fees and fines are ubiquitous:

> In 44 states and the District of Columbia, defendants can be billed for a public defender [who is supposed to be provided free of charge]. In 41 states, inmates can be charged room and board for jail and prison

stays. In 44 states, offenders can get billed for their own probation and parole supervision.

One study showed that, on average, the families of the formerly incarcerated incurred $13,607 in court fines and fees.[49] Depending on the state, failure to pay court debt can lead to jail time in several ways: It is considered a probation violation, it is a penalty for "willful failure to pay criminal justice debt," and/or it may lead to arrest and pre-detention until a hearing on the ability to pay is held.[50] Since the majority of people who are incarcerated are already poor, accumulating this kind of debt along with the threat of additional jail time can easily lead to a cycle of poverty and reincarceration.

It is important to note that, as with the prison industrial complex, court fees and fines may create perverse financial incentives for cash-strapped governments seeking alternatives to raising revenue through tax increases. An investigation by the U.S. Department of Justice after the 2015 shooting of teenager Michael Brown by a police officer in Ferguson, Missouri, concluded that the city's imposition of a range of fines was for the purpose of building revenue rather than a result of concerns about public safety. The practice of directing police officers to generate city revenue this way "resulted in unconstitutional policing, with an emphasis on exacerbating racial biases, and led to the infliction of unnecessary harm on citizens of the Ferguson community."[51] As a result of persistent advocacy by criminal justice experts and people from affected communities, some states are reforming their court fee and fine systems. But the detrimental consequences of incarceration run much deeper than fees and fines. Indeed, there are a plethora of laws that make any contact with the criminal justice system a lifelong burden long after people have served their time.

Reentry: The Collateral Consequences of Incarceration

Involvement with the justice system serves as a kind of "scarlet letter" in American society. It carries stigma and legal implications that shape the ability of formerly incarcerated people to work, find housing, access resources, and rejoin their community. The stigma of criminal justice involvement also in and of itself harms health and mental health, making a "second chance" exceedingly difficult. Stigma is a process whereby "elements of labeling, stereotyping, separation, status loss, and discrimination co-occur together in a power situation that allows the components of stigma to unfold."[52] Since justice-involved people tend to be undereducated, poor, and often homeless; to suffer from mental illness and/or substance use disorders; and to come from already marginalized groups, the stigma of a criminal record and an incarceration history reinforces and compounds already existing social disadvantage. Stigma affects not only individuals who are or were incarcerated but their family members as well.[53]

The stigma of a criminal record is buttressed by a whole host of local, state, and federal laws that make reentry into society and community even more challenging. The "collateral consequences" of a criminal record refer to the penalties and disabilities that occur automatically as a result of conviction, apart from the sentence itself (i.e., whether a person serves jail/prison time or not). These include a range of disadvantages: disenfranchisement; ineligibility for public benefits, housing, scholarships, and student loans; being barred from obtaining occupational licenses and employment; loss of child custody and the inability to adopt a child; and felon registration requirements.[54] It is estimated that there are 46,000 collateral consequences in local, state, and federal laws and regulations; 60% to 70% of these are related to employment.[55] Even though these collateral consequences have dire effects on most aspects of a person's life, there is generally no requirement that a defendant be warned about these consequences when deciding whether to accept a plea or in the event they are convicted.[56] For immigrants without legal status, deportation may be a collateral consequence of a criminal conviction. Federal law not only bars individuals with certain types of criminal convictions from public housing, it also allows them to be kept from visiting their families upon reentry. Indeed, federal law permits families of individuals who are arrested to be evicted from public housing.[57] A study by the Government Accountability Office found that there are "641 collateral consequences that can be triggered by nonviolent drug convictions," and 497 of these can last a lifetime (see **Figure 9.5**).[58]

There are 19.6 million people in the United States living with felony records, and one-third of these people are Black men.[59] The proliferation of collateral consequences has been calamitous for racial equity and for individual, family, and population health in Communities of Color. Collateral consequences perpetuate poverty, unemployment, homelessness, and food insecurity, all key social drivers of health. Hence, combining the stigma and collateral consequences of criminal justice system involvement with an already heavy burden of disadvantage due to racism, low SES, and untreated health conditions is a recipe for lifelong marginalization and poor health. And, as Reuben Jonathan Miller describes in *Halfway Home: Race, Punishment and the Afterlife of Mass Incarceration*, the consequences of a felony record disrupt the basic fabric of families and communities:

> It whispers in the ears of prospective employers and landlords, urging them to reject applications. And it whispers into the ears of grandmothers and girlfriends as they make life-or-death decisions on behalf of

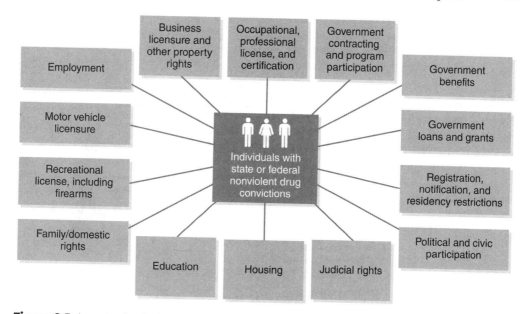

Figure 9.5 Aspects of an individual's life that can be affected by federal collateral consequences for nonviolent drug convictions, as identified by the National Inventory of Collateral Consequences of Conviction

U.S. Government Accountability Office. Nonviolent Drug Convictions: Stakeholders' Views on Potential Actions to Address Collateral Consequences. GAO-17-691. September 7, 2017. https://www.gao.gov/products/gao-17-691

their loved ones, forcing them to withhold a couch to sleep on or risk eviction to help them because the state has labeled the people they care for most criminals.

In recent years, lawyers and policymakers have directed more attention to these laws because, as the American Bar Association notes, "If promulgated and administered indiscriminately, a regime of collateral consequences may frustrate the chance of successful re-entry into the community, and thereby encourage recidivism." For example, in 2018, the American Bar Association published a "judicial bench book" for judges, prosecutors, defense attorneys, defendants, and the general public to guide them through the National Inventory of Collateral Consequences of Conviction (NICCC), which makes transparent all of the potential collateral consequences associated with a conviction.[60] Collateral consequences of a criminal record, whether informal or codified, not only create material hardships—lack of access to housing, benefits, employment—but also serve as key social drivers of health.

Mass Incarceration and Health

As we have highlighted, criminal justice-involved individuals disproportionately experience overlapping and mutually reinforcing disadvantage such as racial injustice, poverty, lack of education, homelessness, and high rates of disability, mental illness, and substance use disorders.[61] American society tends to criminalize mental health conditions, substance use, and various social problems (e.g., criminalizing sleeping in public even when affordable housing and shelters are in short supply), as we discussed in the Introduction. In many ways, prisons have become de facto health and mental health care providers—46.7% of the psychiatric beds in the United States are forensic and are located in or overseen by correctional institutions and agencies. Non-correctional psychiatric inpatient beds decreased 95% between the 1960s and 2016.[62] Similarly, access to treatment in the community for substance use disorders is woefully inadequate, especially for those who lack health insurance. Indeed, there is a strong link between having mental illness or a substance use disorder, lacking health insurance, and being arrested multiple times (see **Figure 9.6**).

In addition to experiencing higher rates of mental illness and substance use disorders, the incarcerated population also has a higher prevalence of disabilities and infectious and chronic diseases than their non-incarcerated counterparts. More than one-third of prison inmates suffer from at least one disability (not including substance use disorders), including 19.5% of prisoners who have developmental

or intellectual disabilities.[63] Incarcerated individuals are four to six times more likely than the general public to report Down syndrome, autism, dementia, learning disorders, and intellectual disabilities.[72] HIV is approximately four times higher in correctional settings than in the general population; hepatitis C virus (HCV) is nine to 10 times higher. Incarcerated individuals also have higher rates of sexually transmitted diseases and tuberculosis when compared with the general public.[64] While some individuals may have already contracted an infectious disease before entering a correctional facility, "prisons have emerged as a risk environment for these infections to be further concentrated, amplified, and then transmitted to the community after prisoners are released."[65]

The COVID-19 pandemic starkly illuminated the spread of infectious disease in

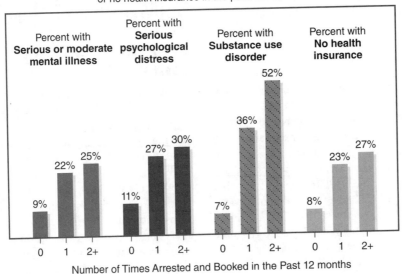

Percentage of individuals who were not arrested and booked in the past 12 months, compared to those arrested and booked once, and those arrested and booked multiple times, that reported having a serious or moderate mental illness (SMMI), serious psychological distress, a substance use disorder, or no health insurance in the past 12 months

Figure 9.6 People with multiple arrests have serious health needs

prisons and the challenges that inmates face in attempting to avoid exposure. As of May 2021, there were an estimated 661,000 cases of COVID-19 in correctional facilities, though experts suggest this is likely an underestimate since cases are not always reported by prison authorities. People living in prisons are at 5.5 times greater risk of contracting COVID-19 and have three times the risk of death as those living in the general population.[66] But the prison-related spread of COVID-19 did not stay within prisons; as people cycled in and out of jail or prison and correctional employees left work, they carried the disease to their communities. A study of Cook County Jail found that in one month alone, 17% of the total COVID-19 cases in predominantly Black and Latinx communities and 21% of COVID-19 racial disparities in Chicago could be attributed to this cycling in and out of prisons.[67]

People also enter prison with untreated chronic diseases. According the U.S. Department of Justice, 40% of state and 33% of federal prisoners report that they currently have a chronic condition, such as high blood pressure (the most common condition), asthma, arthritis, diabetes, or heart or kidney disease. Female inmates are more likely to report chronic conditions (60% in state and 56% in federal prisons).[68] Although there is not extensive research directly linking the experience of incarceration to specific health outcomes, one study found that incarceration is associated with increased C-reactive protein (CRP) and risk for depression, especially for people who spent longer periods in prison.[69] CRP is associated with chronic stress, leading to inflammation and reduced immune response, putting a person at higher risk of heart disease and death. Chronic stress is associated with both poor physical and mental health outcomes, as highlighted in Chapter 8. Incarcerated people are very likely to have had exposure to adverse childhood experiences (ACEs), with women having had greater exposure. This exposure to childhood trauma is strongly associated with criminal system justice involvement (see **Figure 9.7**).[70]

But incarceration itself also produces a number of stressors, including loss of freedom, social isolation, and fear for personal safety, and as described previously, reentry generates substantial stress from the enormous challenges related to securing employment and housing, reconnecting with family and community, and stigma.[71] Thus, the

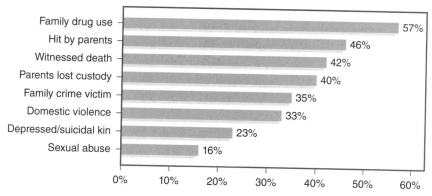

Figure 9.7 Those leaving prison reported high rates of exposure to trauma during early childhood; the most common childhood trauma was growing up with a family member who struggled with serious drug problems

health of incarcerated individuals is affected by exposures and disadvantages they experience before ever setting foot in a prison as well as the experience of incarceration.

Furthermore, access to quality health care is clearly also vital to health during and after a prison sentence is served. Health laws and policies and constitutional law structure access to health care in prisons. Prior to passage of the Affordable Care Act (ACA), access to affordable health insurance was unavailable for most low-income single adults. Thus, most incarcerated individuals were likely to have been uninsured. Without insurance, many in this population had no regular source of primary or mental health care or access to substance use disorder treatment prior to incarceration. A study of jail inmates undertaken prior to ACA passage found that 80% of jail inmates with chronic health problems did not receive regular medical care prior to incarceration, and 90% did not have health insurance.[78]

The ACA's expansion of Medicaid to low-income single adults made it possible for this population to access health insurance, often for the first time. However, because the ACA's Medicaid expansion is optional for states, individuals who live in states that did not adopt the expansion still have no access to affordable health insurance and likely no regular source of health care (see Chapter 7). Furthermore, federal law bars inmates from obtaining Medicaid coverage while in prison. This policy has consequences for health and health care in correctional facilities. First, the costs of medical care are borne by state correctional budgets rather than federal and state governments. This discourages states from investing in prison health care. Second, it further enshrines inequities in health care access by SES, race, and ethnicity. Third, it thwarts successful reentry by fostering "logistical hurdles" to continuity of care.[72]

Ironically, the first time many incarcerated individuals receive primary health care is while in prison. In 1976, the Supreme Court held in *Estelle v. Gamble* that the provision of health care is mandated in correctional facilities, since incarcerated individuals are effectively wards of the state and unable to seek care on their own. The Court said that "deliberate indifference to serious medical needs of prisoners" violates the Eighth Amendment to the U.S. Constitution, which forbids infliction of "cruel and unusual punishment."[73] While the U.S. Department of Justice reports that eight in 10 inmates say that they have seen a health care provider while in prison,[74] the breadth and quality of medical care varies dramatically by state and correctional system. A review of prison health care concludes that "actual medical treatment is consistently provided for only a fraction of those needing it, whether for HIV, chronic conditions, mental health, or substance abuse."[75]

An important legal question related to delivery of medical care in prisons is: What is the standard of care required? This question has arisen in the case of treatment of hepatitis C, a common infectious disease among prisoners. Hepatitis C affects roughly a quarter of the prison population.[76] Direct-acting anti-retroviral agents (DAAs) cure more than 90% of hepatitis C infections and are considered the standard of care for treatment. However, DAAs cost between $20,000 and $84,000 per year. Should correctional facilities be required to treat patients with hepatitis C with DAAs? What if this kind of treatment is not necessarily available to the general public due to cost? Should the fact that hepatitis C is an infectious disease affecting public health factor into this discussion? Federal courts have split on this question. Some states have begun offering DAAs to their incarcerated populations, either as a matter of policy or in order to settle litigation.[77]

A second question regarding health care for incarcerated populations is reproductive health care for female inmates. While nine in 10 pregnant prisoners report having an obstetric exam in prison, only about half say they have received other types of prenatal care, such as testing, diet advice, exercise, or medication.[78] Pregnant people constitute 4,000 admissions to prisons and 55,000 admissions to jails annually.[79] The American College of Obstetrics and Gynecology (ACOG) has developed standards for reproductive care in correctional facilities. These include pregnancy counseling and abortion; treatment for HIV, depression, and substance use disorders; vitamins and diet support; and postpartum contraception.[80] But studies of reproductive health care in prisons and jails show that care falls far short of these standards. A report by the National Women's Law Center that graded states on their provision of reproductive health care in correctional facilities found that 21 states received a D or F. Most states did not have policies on routine exams, treatment of women with high-risk pregnancies, nutrition, or HIV screening.[81]

Third, since roughly 60% of all adults serving time in prison or jails have substance use disorders,[82] what should be the standard of treatment for patients with addiction? Substance use disorder treatment is not routine in carceral settings, and few people access treatment after leaving prison.[83] Formerly incarcerated individuals, particularly those with a history of using opioids such as heroin and fentanyl, are at high risk of overdose upon leaving prison. Most inmates with opioid addiction must withdraw without medication-assisted treatment (MAT) or supportive counseling. Upon leaving prison, formerly incarcerated people often start using drugs again, and if they use at the level they did prior to being in prison, they are likely to overdose as their body can no longer tolerate the higher dose. In 2016, to reduce overdoses among the formerly incarcerated, Rhode Island

began offering MAT to inmates with opioid addiction while in prison and follow-up access to community MAT providers. Post-incarceration overdose deaths were reduced in the state by 61%.[84]

The health and health care inequities experienced by incarcerated and formerly incarcerated populations demonstrate the confluence of social, health, and criminal justice policies and their overlapping effects on health. **Figure 9.8** demonstrates how racial discrimination, economic inequality, and criminal justice policies converge and lead to health inequity.

In addition to the health inequities experienced by incarcerated individuals, mass incarceration has perpetuated health disparities in families of the incarcerated and in communities with high rates of criminal justice involvement. For example, women with incarcerated partners are at increased risk for social isolation and depression,[85] and children who have an incarcerated parent are susceptible to feelings of shame and stigma and are at higher risk for stress-related illness.[86]

A 2021 cross-sectional study found that having any family member incarcerated is associated with a 2.6-year decrease in life expectancy when compared to people who do not have an incarcerated family member. Black people were projected to experience an additional 0.5 year of life expectancy reduction. The study concludes that "[t]hese findings suggest that efforts to decarcerate may improve population-level health and well-being by reducing racial disparities and detrimental outcomes associated with incarceration for nonincarcerated family members."[87] The family and community disruption created by incarceration and the collateral consequences that cause significant barriers to reentry not only undermine the individual's opportunity to start over, they also significantly destabilize social cohesion in the community.

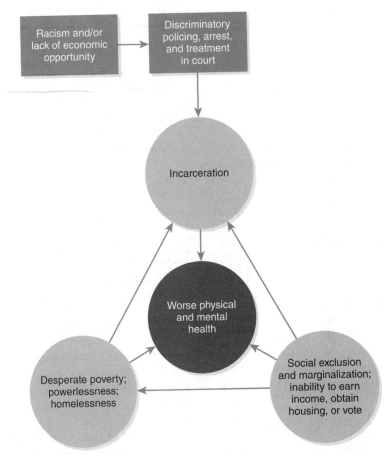

Figure 9.8 Discrimination and incarceration trigger a vicious cycle that threatens health equity

Acker J, Braveman P, Arkin E, Leviton L, Parsons J, Hobor G. *Mass Incarceration Threatens Health Equity in America.* Executive Summary. Princeton, NJ: Robert Wood Johnson Foundation, 2019: 10. https://www.rwjf .org/en/library/research/2019/01/mass-incarceration-threatens-health-equity-in-america.html

Structural Change: Reducing Incarceration and Addressing Its Health Effects

We end the chapter by considering existing efforts to reduce incarceration and to address its effects on the health of individuals, families, communities, and the broader population. We will explore four approaches that move increasingly upstream in their approaches: (1) improving both health care in prisons and the continuity and quality of care post-incarceration; (2) linking legal services and health care for criminal justice–involved individuals and their families through medical-legal partnerships; (3) diversion programs that keep people out of the criminal justice system by connecting them with community-based care and supports; and (4) policy changes, including police reform, reducing collateral consequences, and decarceration (reducing prison populations).

Improving Correctional Facility and Post-Incarceration Health Care

As we have described, people who are incarcerated have higher rates of chronic and infectious diseases and mental health and substance use disorders. Yet the evidence suggests that access to quality health care that could not only support prisoner health but also enable a successful reentry is lacking in most correctional facilities. Indeed, correctional facilities could serve as important providers of high-quality treatment for substance use disorders, including MAT, chronic disease management and screening, and effective treatment of infectious disease. Yet investment in prison health care varies dramatically across states. One study found that per-inmate costs ranged from $2,173 to $19,796.[88] Indeed, providing appropriate, dignified, quality care to people in correctional facilities not only improves health, it also protects society:

> Well-run, forward-thinking prison health care systems are vital to state aims of providing care to incarcerated individuals, protecting communities, strengthening public health, and spending money wisely. Likewise, poorly performing systems threaten to make states less safe, less healthy, and less fiscally prudent. Put simply: The stakes extend far beyond the confines of prison gates.[89]

As a matter of public policy, improving the health of incarcerated people, particularly by addressing addiction, has significant benefits, not just to the individual but also to society. Studies show that investment in addiction treatment has a seven-to-one return on investment by reducing crime and increasing employment earnings of those treated.[90]

But to be effective in improving health and reducing recidivism, there must be seamless continuity between prison health care and community-based care. There are numerous ways for the formerly incarcerated to become disconnected from health care, including homelessness, lack of health insurance, and stigmatizing, unfriendly, or even hostile medical providers. Perceived discrimination by health care providers is associated with worse self-reported health.[91] A relatively recent development to address these gaps in quality post-incarceration care is the growing network of transitions clinics, which are primary care medical homes for people who have been recently released from prison and jail. These clinics have two defining features: They employ a community health worker who is formerly incarcerated, and they are located in neighborhoods most harmed by incarceration. The Transitions Clinic Network (TCN) reports that there are clinics in 14 states and Puerto Rico.[92] One study suggests that patients referred to a transitions clinic by correctional partners were less likely to use the emergency room or to be hospitalized than those referred by other community partners.[93] Investment by correctional systems in continuity of care is critical to successful reentry.

Medical-Legal Partnerships: Preventing Incarceration and Supporting Reentry

An additional opportunity for improving the health of justice-involved people and their families is by joining the efforts of health care providers and legal advocates. Medical-legal partnerships (MLPs) partner health care providers and legal advocates with the goal of addressing social and legal drivers of health for individuals, communities, and populations. MLPs are discussed in greater detail in Chapter 15. Here, we focus on how they may target and support those involved in the criminal justice system at different stages of the process. One MLP model is to partner Transitions Clinic and other medical providers with legal advocates to provide free legal assistance to formerly incarcerated patients and their families to support successful reentry. MLP legal advocates and clinicians work together to identify and address patients' social and legal barriers, such as access to food stamps, cash assistance, disability benefits, child custody, and child support.[94] They also advocate for legal and policy changes that reduce the collateral consequences of incarceration.

A second model of an MLP focused on criminal justice–involved populations is one that seeks to divert people from incarceration in the first place. An MLP in Rhode Island partners a Providence-based Lifespan Transitions Clinic with the Office of the Public Defender. Clinicians identify patients whose medical information may serve as valuable evidence to judges to support diversion to community-based services and treatment rather than incarceration. This medical evidence can be critical in demonstrating that the patient is engaged in appropriate medical, mental health, or SUD treatment and should be diverted from incarceration. The partnership has generated customizable letters that clinicians can use to support their patients, including ones that speak to the effect on the patient's health of court debt and incarceration.[95] MLPs specifically focus on promoting health justice by targeting the laws and policies that perpetuate socioeconomic and racial health inequities and by helping to educate decision-makers—judges and policymakers—about the impact of incarceration on health.

Diversion: Problem-Solving Courts

Given the large percentage of justice-involved people who have untreated mental illness and substance use disorders, it would be far more just, effective, and efficient to address the root causes of criminal behaviors related to these health conditions than to continue our current approach: incarceration. But so long as community-based treatment is underfunded and unavailable, the criminal justice system continues to carry the burden of managing individuals with these health issues. One opportunity to divert people into treatment rather than incarceration is through problem-solving courts. Drug courts target defendants with substance use disorders and employ a multidisciplinary team approach that includes social workers, treatment service professionals, community corrections staff, judges, prosecutors, and defense attorneys. These courts assess defendants' risks and needs, offer treatment and rehabilitation services, implement graduated sanctions and incentives (usually in lieu of incarceration), and monitor and supervise progress (such as drug testing). The evidence on the effectiveness of drug courts is mixed. While some studies suggest that drug courts are effective in diverting people with SUD from the criminal justice system and reducing recidivism, others find the opposite. Consider this statement by the Social Science Research Council, which reviewed the evidence on drug courts:

> We found that drug courts, as implemented in the United States, are a costly, cumbersome intervention that has limited, if any, impact on reducing incarceration. Indeed, for many participants, they may have the opposite effect by increasing criminal justice supervision and subjecting those who fail to graduate to harsher penalties than they might otherwise have received, thus becoming an *adjunct* rather than an *alternative* to incarceration. [They are] disproportionately burdensome to the poor and racial minorities.[96]

Certainly, diverting people from incarceration to treatment is a worthy goal. The effectiveness of a drug court in providing appropriate supports to individual defendants likely depends heavily on the implementation of the program.

Policy Change: Police Reform, Reducing Collateral Consequences, and Decarceration

Since the murder of George Floyd by police in 2020, there has been a nationwide call for police reform. According to the National Conference of State Legislatures, 30 states passed new laws related to police oversight and reform soon after the Floyd murder. These laws included a range of reforms, including mandating body cameras, restricting neck restraints, and limiting officer immunity. Hundreds of additional bills were proposed in 2020, and some were passed into law.[97] Other reform proposals include reducing (or eliminating) aggressive policing tactics in Communities of Color by providing a stricter definition of "reasonable suspicion" for police stops and restructuring protocols for police-community contact that are informed by the community served.[98] But these reforms may still leave in place police practices that harm the health of individuals and populations in low-income Communities of Color and do little to address upstream inequities that lead to overpolicing.

Cities across the country are debating ways to reform (or eliminate altogether) police departments. There are two types of proposals. First, some propose *defunding the police* by substantially reducing police department budgets and then redirecting that funding toward the social safety net and community investment (e.g., affordable housing, mental health care, drug treatment).[99] Second, those calling for *abolition* argue that police departments are an "inherently racist tool of social control" and cannot legitimately be reformed.[100] They propose replacing policing with a model in which empowered communities work to solve their own problems. Abolitionists often support alternatives to policing such as restorative justice—a response to crime that focuses on repairing the harm and restoring the well-being of those involved through a process of reconciliation. Any type of reform, community by community, is slow, and there is plenty of skepticism among substantial parts of the public that smaller reforms will make any real difference. To convince policymakers to undertake structural changes, advocates must demonstrate the benefits to public safety and the return on investment of preventive, upstream supports and services. Furthermore, deeply imbedded racially discriminatory police practices will change only with sustained monitoring, data collection, and advocacy by affected communities and their allies.

In recent years, there have also been a range of policy approaches taken to reducing incarceration. These include implementing alternatives to incarceration (such as diversion programs), reforming sentencing laws (particularly for lower level drug offenses), legalizing marijuana, eliminating or reducing cash bail and court fees and fines, passing state legislation to restore voting rights to people with criminal records, and repealing collateral consequence laws. There have also been some federal bipartisan efforts at criminal justice reform, including the First Step Act, which made important strides by among other provisions:

- Shortening mandatory minimum sentences for nonviolent federal drug offenses
- Expanding the "drug safety-valve," which allows judges more discretion in sentencing for drug offenses
- Applying retroactively the Fair Sentencing Act of 2010, which reduced the sentencing disparity between crack and powder cocaine to address racial inequities

- Improving the conditions in federal prisons by prohibiting the shackling of pregnant women, increasing credit for good behavior, and requiring prisons to offer programming to reduce recidivism[101]

While the act made important reforms, there are two important caveats. First, it was a compromise bill that watered down or eliminated many other policy reforms that were originally proposed. Second, the law only applies to federal prisons. Decarceration became even more urgent in 2020 during the height of the pandemic, when, as described earlier, the spread of COVID-19 was rampant in prisons and jails. Between January and August 2020, populations in state jails decreased by 22%, in state prisons by 4%, and in federal correctional facilities by 10%.[102] Criminal justice experts, the legal community, health care providers, and public health professionals are increasingly calling for systemic multipronged reforms. Proposed reforms include reducing excessive sentences; eliminating incarceration based on inability to pay cash bail, fees or fines; investing in diversion programs and prison-based rehabilitation services; and most importantly, addressing upstream issues like poverty and providing community-based treatment for mental health and substance use disorders.[103]

Conclusion

There are some positive signs that criminal justice reform is taking shape in the United States. The confluence of events—the Black Lives Matter Movement, the worldwide response to the murder of George Floyd, the growing evidence of the costs (both human and monetary) of mass incarceration, and the attention garnered by prisons from the COVID-19 pandemic—is creating momentum for change. It remains to be seen whether this momentum will lead to real legal, policy, and cultural transformation in America's approach to criminal justice. The carceral state was not built overnight; it will take time to dismantle it.

References

1. Beckett K. *Making Crime Pay: Law and Order in Contemporary American Politics*. London: Oxford University Press; 1999: 52–53, 167.
2. Hinton EK. *From the War on Poverty to the War on Crime: The Making of Mass Incarceration in America*. Cambridge, MA: Harvard University Press; 2017: 307–332.
3. Vagins DJ, McCurdy J. Cracks in the system: Twenty years of the unjust federal crack cocaine law. The American Civil Liberties Union. October 2006. https://www.aclu.org/files/assets/cracksinsystem_20061025.pdf?.
4. Hinton EK. In: *From the War on Poverty to the War on Crime: The Making of Mass Incarceration in America*. Cambridge, MA: Harvard University Press; 2017: 307–332.
5. The National Academies of Sciences. Proactive Policing: Effects on Crime and Communities. Effects on Crime and Communities | The National Academies Press. November 9, 2017. https://www.nap.edu/catalog/24928/proactive-policing-effects-on-crime-and-communities.
6. James B. Stop and Frisk in 4 cities: The importance of open police data. Sunlight Foundation. March 2, 2015. https://sunlightfoundation.com/2015/03/02/stop-and-frisk-in-4-cities-the-importance-of-open-police-data-2/.
7. Stop-and-Frisk in the De Blasio Era. ACLU of New York. 2019. https://www.nyclu.org/en/publications/stop-and-frisk-de-blasio-era-2019.
8. National Academies of Sciences. Proactive Policing: Effects on Crime and Communities. Effects on Crime and Communities | The National Academies Press. November 9, 2017. https://www.nap.edu/catalog/24928/proactive-policing-effects-on-crime-and-communities.

9. Braga AA, Welsh BC, Schnell C. Can Policing Disorder Reduce Crime? A systematic review and meta-analysis. *Journal of Research in Crime and Delinquency.* 2015;52(4):567–588. doi:10.1177/0022427815576576.

10. Skogan WG, Frydl K. *Fairness and Effectiveness in Policing the Evidence.* Washington, DC: National Academies Press; 2004.

11. Vera. Arrest Trends. Arrests | Arrests Trends. Accessed October 25, 2021. https://arresttrends.vera.org/arrests.

12. Berdejó C. Criminalizing race: Racial disparities in plea bargaining. *Boston College Law Review.* 2018;59.

13. Fagan J, Geller A, Davies G, West V. Street stops and broken windows revisited: The demography and logic of proactive policing in a safe and changing city. In: Rice SK, White MD (eds.), *Race, Ethnicity, and Policing: New and Essential Readings.* New York, NY:New York University Press; 2009.

14. Esposito M, Larimore S, Lee H. Aggressive policing, health, and health equity. *Health Affairs Blog.* April 2021. https://www.healthaffairs.org/do/10.1377/hpb2021 0412.997570/full/.

15. Tate J, Jenkins J, Rich S. Fatal Force. 931 people have been shot and killed by police in the past year. The Washington Post. January 31, 2022. https://www .washingtonpost.com/graphics/investigations/police -shootings-database/

16. Koerth M. Police violence against Native Americans goes far beyond Standing Rock: and everyone is probably understating the extent of the problem. FiveThirtyEight. December 2, 2016. https://fivethirtyeight.com/features /police-violence-against-native-americans-goes-far -beyond-standing-rock/.

17. Addressing Law Enforcement Violence as a Public Health Issue. American Public Health Association. November 13, 2018. https://www.apha.org/policies -and-advocacy/public-health-policy-statements /policy-database/2019/01/29/law-enforcement-violence.

18. Dluhy LA, Abel B, Dluhy RG. Establishing Medical Civil Rights. *New England Journal of Medicine.* August 2021:490–491.

19. Bylander J. Civil unrest, police use of force, and the public's health. *Health Affairs.* 2015;34(8):1264–1268.

20. Geller A, Fagan J, Tyler T, Link BG. Aggressive Policing and the mental health of young urban men. *American Journal of Public Health.* 2014;104(12):2321–2327.

21. Sewell AA. Collateral damage: The health effects of invasive police encounters in New York City. *Journal of Urban Health.* April 2016:42–67.

22. Goin DE, Gomez AM, Farkas K, et al. Occurrence of fatal police violence during pregnancy and hazard of preterm birth in California. *Paediatric and Perinatal Epidemiology.* 2021;35(4):469–478.

23. Bor J, Venkataramani AS, Williams DR, Tsai AC. Police killings and their spillover effects on the mental health of Black Americans: A population-based, quasi-experimental study. *Lancet.* 2018;392(10144): 302–310.

24. Braga AA, Brunson RK, Drakulich KM. Race, place, and effective policing. *Annual Review of Sociology.* 2019;45(1):535–555.

25. Tobin-Tyler E. When are laws strictly enforced? Criminal justice, housing quality, and public health: *Health Affairs Blog.* November 5, 2015. https:// www.healthaffairs.org/do/10.1377/hblog20151105 .051649/full/.

26. Sawyer W, Wagner P. Mass incarceration: The whole pie 2020. Prison Policy Initiative. March 24, 2020. https:// www.prisonpolicy.org/reports/pie2020.html.

27. Nellis A. Report of The Sentencing Project to the United Nations Special Rapporteur on Contemporary Forms of Racism, Racial Discrimination, Xenophobia, and Related Intolerance: Regarding racial disparities in the United States criminal justice system. The Sentencing Project. May 1, 2018. https://www.sentencingproject .org/publications/un-report-on-racial-disparities/.

28. National Research Council. The growth of incarceration in the United States: Exploring causes and consequences. *The National Academics of Sciences, Engineering, Medicine.* 2014.

29. Prison Policy Initiative. The gender divide: Tracking women's state prison growth. Prison Policy Initiative. January 9, 2018. https://www.prisonpolicy .org/reports/women_overtime.html.

30. *Lawrence v. Texas.* 539 U.S. 558 (2003).

31. Visualizing the unequal treatment of LGBTQ people in the criminal justice system. Prison Policy Initiative. March 2, 2021. https://www.prisonpolicy .org/blog/2021/03/02/lgbtq/.

32. Visualizing the unequal treatment of LGBTQ people in the criminal justice system. Prison Policy Initiative. March 2, 2021. https://www.prisonpolicy .org/blog/2021/03/02/lgbtq/.

33. Grant JM, Mottet LA, Tanis J. Injustice at every turn: A report of the National Transgender Discrimination Survey. National Center for Transgender Equality. 2011. https://transequality.org/sites/default/files/docs /resources/NTDS_Report.pdf. Published 2011.

34. Prashar A. American businesses are raking in billions from the prison-industrial complex: It's time to get serious about dismantling this disgusting system. *Business Insider.* September 14, 2020. https://www .businessinsider.com/prison-industrial-complex -end-business-help-mass-incarceration-2020-9.

35. Branson-Potts H. California's prison boom saved this town. Now, plans to close a lockup are sparking anger and fear. *Los Angeles Times.* June 21, 2021. https://www.latimes.com/california/story/2021-06-21 /newsom-plan-will-shut-rural-california-prison-lose -jobs-susanville.

36. Sawyer W, Wagner P. Mass incarceration: The whole pie 2020. Prison Policy Initiative. March 24, 2020. https://www.prisonpolicy.org/reports/pie2020.html.

37. Harding DJ. Do Prisons Make us safer? New research shows that prisons prevent far less violent crime than you might think. *Scientific American*. June 21, 2019. https://www.scientificamerican.com/article/do -prisons-make-us-safer/.

38. Mauer Nazgol Ghandnoosh M, Ghandnoosh N. Fewer Prisoners, Less Crime: A tale of three states. The Sentencing Project. April 26, 2016. https://www.sentencingproject.org/publications /fewer-prisoners-less-crime-a-tale-of-three-states/.

39. Ferguson RA. *Inferno: An Anatomy of American Punishment*. Cambridge, MA: Harvard University Press; 2014.

40. Pettit B, Sykes B, Western B. Technical report on revised population estimates and NLSY79 analysis tables for the Pew Public Safety and Mobility Project. 2009. https://scholar.harvard.edu/files/brucewestern /files/westernpettit10.pdf.

41. Pettit B. *Invisible Men: Mass Incarceration and the Myth of Black Progress*. New York City, NY: Russell Sage Foundation; 2012.

42. Prisons of Poverty: Uncovering the pre-incarceration incomes of the imprisoned. Prison Policy Initiative. July 9, 2015. https://www.prisonpolicy.org/reports /income.html.

43. Gray B, Smith D. Criminal justice reentry and homelessness. Texas Criminal Justice Coalition. February 1, 2019. http://www.evidenceonhomelessness .com/wp-content/uploads/2020/04/Reentry-and -Homelessness_Synthesis-of-the-Evidence.pdf.

44. National Homelessness Law Center. No safe place. February 2019. https://nlchp.org/wp-content/uploads /2019/02/No_Safe_Place.pdf.

45. FPWA ending the poverty to prison pipeline report 2019. The Federation of Protestant Welfare Agencies. April 2019. https://www.fpwa.org/wp-content/uploads /2019/04/FPWAs-Ending-the-Poverty-to-Prison-Pipeline -Report-2019-FINAL.pdf.

46. Edelman P. *Not a Crime to Be Poor: The Criminalization of Poverty in America*. New York: The New Press; 2017.

47. Confined and costly: How supervision violations are filling prisons and burdening budgets. Council of State Governments Justice Center. September 1, 2021. https://csgjusticecenter.org/publications/confined -costly/.

48. Martin KD, Smith SS, Still W. Shackled to debt: Criminal justice financial obligations and the barriers to re-entry they create. National Institute of Justice. January 2017. https://www.ojp.gov/pdffiles1 /nij/249976.pdf.

49. De Vuono-Powell S, Schweidler C, Walters A, Zohrabi A. Who Pays? The true cost of incarceration on families. National Institute of Corrections. March 31, 2021. https://nicic.gov/who-pays-true-cost-incarceration -families.

50. Jahangeer K. Fees and fines: The criminalization of poverty. Americanbar.org. December 16, 2019. https://www.americanbar.org/groups/government _public/publications/public_lawyer_articles /fees-fines/.

51. Jahangeer K. Fees and fines: The criminalization of poverty. Americanbar.org. December 16, 2019. https:// www.americanbar.org/groups/government_public /publications/public_lawyer_articles/fees-fines/.

52. Link BG, Phelan JC, Conceptualizing stigma. *Annual Review of Sociology*. 2001;27:363–385,367.

53. Tobin-Tyler E, Brockmann B. Returning home: Incarceration, reentry, stigma and the perpetuation of racial and socioeconomic health inequity. *Journal of Law, Medicine & Ethics*. 2018;45(4):545–557.

54. Garretson H. Legislating forgiveness: A study of post-conviction certificates as policy to address the employment consequences of a conviction. National Institute of Corrections. 2016. October 16, 2017. https://nicic.gov/legislating-forgiveness-study-post -conviction-certificates-policy-address-employment -consequences.

55. U.S. Government Accountability Office. Nonviolent drug convictions: stakeholders' views on potential actions to address collateral consequences. September 7, 2017. https://www.gao.gov/products/gao-17-691.

56. American Bar Association. Collateral consequences of criminal convictions: Judicial bench book. American Bar Association, Criminal Justice Section. March 2018. https://www.ojp.gov/pdffiles1/nij/grants/251583.pdf.

57. American Bar Association. Collateral consequences of criminal convictions: Judicial bench book. American Bar Association, Criminal Justice Section. March 2018. https://www.ojp.gov/pdffiles1/nij/grants/251583.pdf.

58. U.S. Government Accountability Office. Nonviolent drug convictions: stakeholders' views on potential actions to address collateral consequences. September 7, 2017. https://www.gao.gov/products/gao-17-691.

59. Miller RJ. *Halfway Home: Race, Punishment and the Afterlife of Mass Incarceration*. New York: Little, Brown and Company; 2021.

60. American Bar Association. Collateral consequences of criminal convictions: Judicial bench book. American Bar Association, Criminal Justice Section. March 2018. https://www.ojp.gov/pdffiles1/nij/grants /251583.pdf.

61. Pettit B, Sykes B, Western B. Technical report on revised population estimates and NLSY79 analysis tables for the Pew Public Safety and Mobility Project. 2009.

https://scholar.harvard.edu/files/brucewestern/files/westernpettit10.pdf.

62. Fuller DA. Going, going, gone: Trends and consequences of eliminating state psychiatric beds, 2016. *Psychiatric Services.* 2017;68(3):306–307.

63. Mizrahi J, Jeffers J, Ellis EB, Pauli P. Disability and criminal justice reform: Keys to success. Respectability. May 2017. https://www.respectability.org/wp-content/uploads/2017/05/Disability-and-Criminal-Justice-Reform-White-Paper.pdf.

64. Rich JD, Wohl DA, Beckwith CG, et al. HIV-related research in correctional populations: Now is the time. *Current HIV/AIDS Reports.* 2011;8(4):288–296.

65. Kamarulzaman A, Altice FL, Verster A, et al. Prevention of transmission of HIV, hepatitis B virus, hepatitis C virus, and tuberculosis in prisoners. *Lancet.* September 10, 2016. https://www.thelancet.com/pdfs/journals/lancet/PIIS0140-6736(16)30769-3.pdf.

66. Reinhart E. How mass incarceration makes us all sick. Health Affairs Blog. May 28, 2021. https://www.healthaffairs.org/do/10.1377/hblog20210526.678786/full/?utm_medium=email&utm_source=Newsletter&utm_campaign=HASU%3A%2B5-30-21&utm_content=Care%2BDelays%2BAs%2BA%2BResult%2BOf%2BCOVID-19%2C%2BHospice%2B%2B%2BMore&vgo_ee=PIsaBHiejM66z3IzHBl%2F3D%2BJLi7DAuyw1lBdDJF3D%2Bo%3D.

67. Reinhart E, Chen DL. Carceral-community epidemiology, structural racism, and COVID-19 disparities. *Proceedings of the National Academy of Sciences.* 2021;118(21).

68. Maruschak L, Berzofsky M, Unangst J. Medical problems reported by prisoners (survey of prison inmates, 2016). Office of Justice Programs. February 2015. https://www.ojp.gov/ncjrs/virtual-library/abstracts/medical-problems-state-and-federal-prisoners-and-jail-inmates-2011.

69. Boen CE. Criminal justice contacts and psychophysiological functioning in early adulthood: Health inequality in the carceral state. *Journal of Health and Social Behavior.* 2020;61(3):290–306.

70. Messina N, Grella C, Burdon W, Prendergast M. Childhood adverse events and current traumatic distress: A comparison of men and women drug-dependent prisoners. *Criminal Justice and Behavior.* 2007;34(11):1385–1401.

71. Boen CE. Criminal justice contacts and psychophysiological functioning in early adulthood: Health inequality in the carceral state. *Journal of Health and Social Behavior.* 2020;61(3):290–306.

72. Edmonds M. The reincorporation of prisoners into the body politic: Eliminating the Medicaid Inmate Exclusion Policy. SSRN. June 8, 2021. https://papers.ssrn.com/sol3/papers.cfm?abstract_id=3861849.

73. *Estelle v. Gamble*, 429 U.S. 97 (1976).

74. Maruschak L, Berzofsky M, Unangst J. Medical problems reported by prisoners (survey of prison inmates, 2016). Office of Justice Programs. February 2015. https://www.ojp.gov/ncjrs/virtual-library/abstracts/medical-problems-state-and-federal-prisoners-and-jail-inmates-2011.

75. Dumont DM, Allen SA, Brockmann BW, Alexander NE, Rich JD. Incarceration, community health, and racial disparities. *Journal of Health Care for the Poor and Underserved.* 2013;24(1):78–88.

76. Katz R. Hepatitis C litigation: Healing inmates as a public health strategy. SSRN. April 29, 2020. https://papers.ssrn.com/sol3/papers.cfm?abstract_id=3568737.

77. Katz R. Hepatitis C litigation: Healing inmates as a public health strategy. SSRN. April 29, 2020. https://papers.ssrn.com/sol3/papers.cfm?abstract_id=3568737.

78. Maruschak L, Berzofsky M, Unangst J. Medical problems reported by prisoners (survey of prison inmates, 2016). Office of Justice Programs. February 2015. https://www.ojp.gov/ncjrs/virtual-library/abstracts/medical-problems-state-and-federal-prisoners-and-jail-inmates-2011.

79. Sufrin C, Jones RK, Mosher WD, Beal L. Pregnancy prevalence and outcomes in U.S. jails. *Obstetrics and Gynecology.* 2020;135(5):1177–1183.

80. Committee on Health Care for Underserved Women of American College of Obstetricians and Gynecologists. Committee opinion no. 511. *Obstetrics & Gynecology.* 2011;118(5):1198–1202.

81. The Rebecca Project for Human Rights/National Women's Law Center. Mothers behind bars: A state-by-state report card and analysis of Federal Policies. Gateless Gate. October 17, 2011. https://gatelessgatezen.wordpress.com/2011/10/17/mothers-behind-bars-a-state-by-state-report-card-and-analysis-of-federal-policies/.

82. Tsai J, Gu X. Utilization of addiction treatment among U.S. adults with history of incarceration and substance use disorders. Addiction Science & Clinical *Practice.* 2019;14(1).

83. Tsai J, Gu X. Utilization of addiction treatment among U.S. adults with history of incarceration and substance use disorders. Addiction Science & Clinical *Practice.* 2019;14(1).

84. Green TC, Clarke J, Brinkley-Rubinstein L, et al. Postincarceration fatal overdoses after implementing medications for addiction treatment in a statewide correctional system. *JAMA Psychiatry.* 2018;75(4):405.

85. Schnittker J, Massoglia M, Uggen C. Incarceration and the health of the African American community. *Du Bois Review.* April 15, 2011. http://users.soc.umn.edu/~uggen/Schnittker_Massoglia_Uggen_DR_11.pdf.

86. Wildeman C. Incarceration and population health in wealthy democracies. *Criminology.* 2016;54(2):360–382.

87. Sundaresh R, Yi Y, Harvey TD, et al. Exposure to family member incarceration and adult well-being in the United States. *JAMA Network Open.* 2021;4(5).

88. Urahn SK, Thompson MD. Prison health care: Costs and quality. The Pew Charitable Trusts. October 27, 2017. https://www.pewtrusts.org/~/media/assets/2017/10/sfh_prison_health_care_costs_and_quality_final.pdf.

89. Urahn SK, Thompson MD. Prison health care: Costs and quality. The Pew Charitable Trusts. October 27, 2017:2. https://www.pewtrusts.org/~/media/assets/2017/10/sfh_prison_health_care_costs_and_quality_final.pdf.

90. Ettner SL, Huang D, Evans E, et al. Benefit-cost in the California Treatment Outcome Project: Does substance abuse treatment "pay for itself"? Health services research. February 2006. https://pubmed.ncbi.nlm.nih.gov/16430607/.

91. Redmond N, Aminawung JA, Morse DS, Zaller N, Shavit S, Wang EA. Perceived discrimination based on criminal record in healthcare settings and self-reported health status among formerly incarcerated individuals. *Journal of Urban Health.* 2020;97(1):105–111.

92. Transitions Clinic Network. Transitions Clinic. 2014. https://transitionsclinic.org/transitions-clinic-network/.

93. Shavit S, Aminawung JA, Birnbaum N, et al. Transitions Clinic Network: Challenges and lessons in primary care for people released from prison. *Health Affairs.* 2017;36(6):1006–1015.

94. Benfer EA, Gluck AR, Kraschel KL. Medical-legal partnership: Lessons from five diverse MLPs in New Haven, Connecticut. *Journal of Law, Medicine & Ethics.* 2018;46(3):602–609.

95. Vanjani R, Martino S, Reiger SF, et al. Physician–public defender collaboration—A new medical–legal partnership. *New England Journal of Medicine.* 2020; 383(21):2083–2086.

96. Social Science Research Council. Drug courts in the Americas. October 2018. https://www.ssrc.org/publications/drug-courts-in-the-americas/.

97. Widgery A. Legislative responses for policing-state bill tracking database. October 8, 2021. https://www.ncsl.org/research/civil-and-criminal-justice/legislative-responses-for-policing.aspx.

98. Lee MESLH. Aggressive policing, health, and health equity: Health Affairs brief. Health Affairs. April 30, 2021. https://www.healthaffairs.org/do/10.1377/hpb20210412.997570/full/?utm_medium=email&utm_source=Newsletter&utm_campaign=HASU%3A%2B5-2-21&utm_content=Aggressive%2BPolicing%2C%2BCharity%2BCare%2C%2B%2BAddiction%2B%2B%2BMore&rvgo_ee=PIsaBHiejM66z3IzHBl%2F3D%2BJLi7DAuyw1lBdDJF3D%2Bo%3D.

99. Barna M. Public Health approach to police reform gaining momentum: States, cities redirecting police funding. The Nation's Health. July 1, 2021. https://www.thenationshealth.org/content/51/5/1.2.

100. Lartey J, Griffin A. The future of policing. The Marshall Project. October 23, 2020. https://www.themarshallproject.org/2020/10/23/the-future-of-policing.

101. Grawert A, Lau T. How the first step act became law—and what happens next. Brennan Center for Justice. June 23, 2020. https://www.brennancenter.org/our-work/analysis-opinion/how-first-step-act-became-law-and-what-happens-next.

102. Wang EA, Western B, Berwick DM. Covid-19, decarceration, and the role of clinicians, Health Systems, and payers. *JAMA.* 2020;324(22):2257.

103. Acker J, Braveman P, Arkin E, Leviton L, Parsons J, Hobor G. Mass Incarceration Threatens Health Equity in America. Executive Summary. Princeton, NJ: Robert Wood Johnson Foundation, 2019: 21. https://www.rwjf.org/en/library/research/2019/01/mass-incarceration-threatens-health-equity-in-america.html

PART 4

Historically Marginalized Populations and Health Injustice

CHAPTER 10

Asian, Black, Indigenous, and Latinx People

Ruqaiijah Yearby[1]

LEARNING OBJECTIVES

By the end of this chapter you will be able to:

- Describe how the law structures citizenship rights and the social drivers of health in ways that lead to health inequities for racial and ethnic minority individuals
- Explain how the history and current trends of racism affect the rights of racial and ethnic minority individuals
- Explain some of the root causes of health inequities among Asian, Black, Indigenous, and Latinx people, including the role of racism

18 pages

Introduction

This chapter discusses the health inequities experienced by Asian, Black, Indigenous, and Latinx people. As of the 2020 Census, 24% of the U.S. population identified as a racial minority, while almost 19% identified as a Latinx.[2] Although the latest Census recognized five official racial categories (Asian American, American Indian/Alaska Native, Black or African American, Native Hawaiian/Pacific Islander, and White), there is no agreed-upon definition of what constitutes race or how it differs from ethnicity (a group's cultural identity). For example, Black heritage has often been defined by many contradictory measures, including the "one-drop" rule.[3] This rule originated from a 1662 Virginia law, which stated that if a person had one drop of Black blood, they were not considered White. More recently, this rule was used by a court in Louisiana to prevent a woman who had a Black great-great-great-great-grandmother from identifying as White on her passport.[4] Yet it is unclear how an individual proves/disproves the "one-drop" rule, since many Americans cannot trace their heritage. This is also a problem for Indigenous individuals. The federal government does not recognize all Indigenous groups as Indigenous tribes, and for those that are recognized, it is unclear what percentage of pure Indigenous blood will suffice.[5] But seemingly, any mixture of Black blood prohibits an individual from being Indigenous.[6] Furthermore, the only ethnicity currently recognized in the

United States is "Latinx," which is sometimes only used to differentiate between the Black and White racial groups. This lack of clarity is, in part, due to the fact that race and ethnicity are social constructions that have been used to separate people into "superior" and "inferior" groups.[7]

Indeed, throughout most of U.S. history, White individuals have been labeled "superior," while racial and ethnic minority groups have been labeled "inferior."[8] This racial hierarchy is used to perpetuate racism. In this chapter, we discuss how, in large part due to racism, Asian, Black, Indigenous (American Indian/Alaska Native), and Latinx individuals living in America have been denied equal access to citizenship rights, opportunities, and health-improving resources compared to White individuals, resulting in persistent racial and ethnic health inequities. Because data that are disaggregated by race and ethnicity are often missing from research studies, some of the examples provided only focus on one group. However, this does not obviate the fact that all of the groups covered in this chapter have experienced racism, which is associated with health inequities.

Treatment of Racial and Ethnic Minority Individuals Under the Law

The law has long been used to limit racial and ethnic minority individuals' citizenship rights to life, liberty, and property.[9] The main time periods of de jure discrimination (i.e., discrimination that occurs according to law) are slavery (1619–1865), Jim Crow (1875–1968), and the "race neutral"/"colorblind" era (1973–present). In each of these time periods, racism has been perpetuated by individuals and institutions as well as supported and fostered by the government.

Time Periods of Racism
Slavery (1619–1865)

When the United States was founded in 1787, a large majority of Black and Indigenous Americans were enslaved. Not only were those who were enslaved brutalized and exploited, but they were also denied the rights provided under the Constitution, including the right to life, liberty, and property. In the 1856 case of *Dred Scott v. Sanford*, the Supreme Court ruled that no Black individual, whether enslaved or free, could become an American citizen.[10] Thus, whether enslaved or free, a Black individual did not have the right to sue.[11] Free Indigenous, Asian, and Latinx individuals were also often denied full American citizenship, which provided the right to vote, own property, sue someone, or testify in court.[12]

The first Congress passed the 1790 Naturalization Act, which provided citizenship for free White individuals of good character but denied full citizenship rights for Indigenous, Black, Asian, and Latinx individuals.[13] Indigenous individuals were able to become citizens through federal treaties or marriage. However, the federal government passed several laws that allowed White individuals to forcibly remove Indigenous people from their land.[14] The laws included the 1830 Indian Removal Act[15] and the 1862 Homestead Act.[16] With the authority granted by these laws, White settlers forcibly moved the Cherokee nation to the west during the "Trail of Tears," resulting in the deaths of approximately 4,000 Cherokee individuals.[17]

The law also denied racial and ethnic minority individuals' equal governmental representation. Under Article 1 of the Constitution, slaves, who included Black and some Indigenous individuals, were only counted as three-fifths of a person, while free persons, indentured servants, and taxed Indigenous persons were counted as full persons (see **Box 10.1**).

> **Box 10.1** U.S. Constitution, Article 1, Section 2 The "Three-Fifths Clause," Ratified 1788
>
> **Preamble**
>
> Representatives and direct Taxes shall be apportioned among the several States which may be included within this Union, according to their respective Numbers, which shall be determined by adding to the whole Number of free Persons, including those bound to Service for a Term of Years, and excluding Indians not taxed, three fifths of all other Persons.[18]

Although the Civil War and the enactment of the 13th Amendment ended slavery, laws were required to provide equal citizenship rights for formerly enslaved individuals. Black individuals were promised the same citizenship rights as White individuals with the enactment of the 14th Amendment in 1868, which prohibited any state from making or enforcing "any law which shall abridge the privileges or immunities of citizens of the United States; nor shall any state deprive any person of life, liberty, or property, without due process of law; nor deny to any person within its jurisdiction the equal protection of the laws." Notwithstanding this promise, during the Jim Crow era, the federal government allowed Northern and Southern states to deny racial and ethnic minority individuals the full rights of citizenship guaranteed by the 14th Amendment.

Jim Crow (1875–1968)

During the Jim Crow era, the government (federal and state) supported both explicit and race-neutral policies that limited racial and ethnic minority people's full citizenship rights. For example, approximately 15,000 Chinese individuals worked on the transcontinental railroad, yet they were paid less than White workers and were not allowed to become American citizens.[19] When these Chinese individuals were no longer needed to work on the railroads or in other industries, the federal government enacted the Chinese Exclusion Act in 1882, barring Chinese individuals from entering the United States unless they were a diplomat or businessperson.[20] This immigration ban was extended several times and then made permanent in 1902, when Congress required "each Chinese resident to register and obtain a certificate of residence. Without a certificate, she or he faced deportation."[21] These requirements were finally repealed by Congress in 1943,[22] but Asian individuals not born in America were not allowed to become American citizens until the enactment of the Immigration and Nationality Act of 1952.[23] (See Chapter 11 for further discussion of the development of U.S. immigration law over time.)

Despite these limitations, Asian individuals born in the United States were allowed to stay in the country and were recognized as American citizens;[24] however, they were not considered White Americans and thus did not acquire the full rights of citizenship.[25] The lack of citizenship rights was used by Franklin D. Roosevelt when he issued Executive Order 9066, authorizing the placement of all individuals of Japanese descent, including American citizens, in internment camps from 1942 to 1945.[26] The Roosevelt administration tried to justify internment during World War II by asserting that Japanese Americans were a threat and their patriotism toward the United States was questionable. In addition to limiting the rights of Asian individuals, the federal and state governments denied Black Americans full citizenship rights during the Jim Crow era. In particular, the government failed to enforce the 14th Amendment and instead enacted laws that allowed for separate and unequal treatment, a concept that was upheld by the Supreme Court.[27] As a result, Black Americans lacked equal access to employment, housing, and health care during this era, as the following examples demonstrate.

Employment

The National Labor Relations Act of 1935 expanded union rights for workers, which resulted in higher wages and benefits, such as health insurance, for workers represented by unions. However, the act did not apply to the service, domestic, and agricultural industries, which were predominately filled by racial and ethnic minority individuals.[28] It also allowed unions to discriminate against racial and ethnic minority workers employed in other industries, such as manufacturing.[29] This separate and unequal protection was compounded by the federal government's failure to include racial and ethnic minority individuals in minimum wage laws and workers' retirement benefits. The Fair Labor Standards Act of 1938 (FLSA)[30] limited the workweek to 40 hours and established federal minimum wage and overtime requirements.[31] Although the FLSA did not explicitly bar racial and ethnic minority individuals from receiving these protections and benefits, it explicitly exempted from these protections domestic, agricultural, and service occupations, which, as noted previously, were predominately filled by racial and ethnic minority individuals.[32] When the FLSA was first enacted, approximately 65% of all Black workers were employed as domestic or farm workers.[33] The FLSA was eventually expanded to cover these workers, but some domestic, agricultural, and service workers, which are still predominately filled by racial and ethnic minority individuals, are still not covered.[34]

Housing

In 1926, the Supreme Court upheld the use of racial covenants that prohibited the selling of land and houses to racial and ethnic minority individuals, including Asian, Black, and Latinx individuals.[35] Even though the court later struck down these racially restrictive housing covenants in 1948 in *Shelly v. Kramer*,[36] the covenants were already being used by the

Federal Housing Administration (FHA) to limit racial and ethnic minority individuals' purchase of houses. Created in 1933, the FHA subsidized housing builders as long as none of the homes were sold to Black Americans, a practice called redlining.[37] The subsidies, received exclusively by White Americans, were used to create the suburbs. The FHA also published an underwriting manual that stated that housing loans to Black, Latinx, and Asian Americans would not be insured by the federal government. Private lenders followed suit, providing conventional mortgages to White Americans while drastically limiting the number of conventional mortgages to Black, Latinx, and Asian Americans. Due to the FHA and its policies, only 2.3% of FHA-insured mortgages outstanding in 1950 were for racial and ethnic minority Americans, while 5.0% of conventional mortgages were for racial and ethnic minority Americans.[38] President John F. Kennedy ended the FHA redlining policies with an Executive Order in 1962, but conventional mortgages remained discriminatory until the passage of the Fair Housing Act in 1968.

Health Care

The federal Hospital Survey and Construction Act of 1946, better known as the Hill-Burton Act,[39] allotted funding for the construction of public hospitals and granted states the authority to regulate this construction. Hospitals used this funding to construct, among other things, nursing home wards and freestanding geriatric hospitals to care for the elderly, the precursors to current-day nursing homes.[40] The act also provided that adequate health care facilities be made available to all state residents without discrimination based on color.[41] However, section 622(f) of the Hill-Burton Act stated

> [S]uch hospital or addition to a hospital will be made available to all persons. . . but *an exception shall be made in cases where separate hospital facilities are provided for separate population*

groups, if the plan makes equitable provision on the basis of need for facilities and services of like quality for each such group. . . (emphasis added)[42]

Under section 622(f) of the Hill-Burton Act, states could opt to participate in the federal program based on a "separate but equal" plan providing for segregated facilities.[43] Alabama, Florida, Georgia, Kentucky, Louisiana, Maryland, Mississippi, Missouri, North Carolina, Oklahoma, South Carolina, Tennessee, Virginia, and West Virginia submitted "separate but equal" applications to the Surgeon General,[44] yet the funding of the health care facilities that provided care to Black Americans was never equitable.[45] The funding to train physicians was also inequitable. In the South, "a separate system of hospitals existed to serve black communities and as a place where [Black American] physicians could be trained and practice."[46] In the North, training opportunities and staff privileges for White hospitals were limited to White physicians, resulting in "an almost equivalent degree of [racially] separate and unequal health care."[47] In response to the Civil Rights Movement, the federal government enacted the Civil Rights Acts of 1957, 1960, 1964, and 1968; the Voting Rights Act of 1965; and the Fair Housing Act of 1968, which collectively promised Black people and other racial and ethnic minority individuals equal access to education, employment, housing, health care, and voting; yet, inequities and inequalities persist.

The "Race-Neutral"/"Colorblind" Era (1973–Present)

After the end of the Jim Crow era in 1968, racial and ethnic minority individuals did make significant gains in education, employment, housing, and health care. For example, the government used Title VI of the Civil Rights Act of 1964 to force hospitals to racially integrate, increasing racial and ethnic minority individuals' access to hospitals.

However, governmental actions to affirmatively end government-sponsored racism were thwarted by state governments and the adoption of "race-neutral" policies that often disadvantaged racial and ethnic minority individuals and advantaged White individuals. For example, President Richard Nixon adopted "race-neutral" language in his War on Drugs, yet the policy measures implemented to carry out this "war" were disproportionately applied to Black Americans. According to John Ehrlichman, Nixon's assistant for Domestic Affairs, this was the purpose of the entire program (see **Box 10.2**).[48] The War on Drugs was amplified during the 1980s under the Reagan administration and led to the mass incarceration of mostly Black and Latinx people, as described in Chapter 9.

The continued use of "race-neutral" laws to limit racial and ethnic minority individuals' citizenship rights during this era is similar to the methods used during the Jim Crow era.[50] However, unlike the previous era, racial and ethnic minority individuals now enjoy the right to sue to challenge racism. However, as discussed in Chapter 6, courts

---

Box 10.2 War on Drugs

"You want to know what this [war on drugs] was really all about? The Nixon campaign in 1968, and the Nixon White House after that, had two enemies: the antiwar left and black people. You understand what I'm saying?

We knew we couldn't make it illegal to be either against the war or black, but by getting the public to associate the hippies with marijuana and blacks with heroin, and then criminalizing both heavily, we could disrupt those communities. We could arrest their leaders, raid their homes, break up their meetings, and vilify them night after night on the evening news. Did we know we were lying about the drugs? Of course we did."

John Ehrlichman, Assistant to the President for Domestic Affairs under President Richard Nixon[49]

have limited the legal definition of racism to instances where intent can be proven or racial and ethnic minority individuals can obtain data showing that the defendant's policy or behavior disproportionately impacts racial or ethnic minority individuals.[51] This prevents racial and ethnic minority individuals from addressing structural racism, which, as described in various places throughout this book, is integrated into the ways "our institutions of customs, practice and law [operate] so there need not be an identifiable perpetrator."[52] Furthermore, courts have adopted a colorblind analysis that seeks to ensure that race is not a factor in any law, even if it is to rectify past and continuing instances of racism.[53] Thus, racial and ethnic minority individuals continue to lack equal access to education, employment, housing, and health care, as the following examples demonstrate.

Employment

As described elsewhere in this book, Title VII of the Civil Rights Act of 1964 prohibits discrimination in employment based on race or sex,[54] while the Equal Pay Act of 1963 (EPA) prohibits sex-based differential pay between women and men who perform jobs that require substantially the same skill, effort, and responsibility.[55] Under Title VII, a Black woman can file a claim for discrimination based on being Black or a woman, but not for being a Black woman.[56] Even though the federal government has recognized in its guidance materials and initiatives that Women of Color experience both sex *and* race discrimination—which it notes is a violation of Title VII[57]—many courts refuse to recognize the intersection of sex and race discrimination that women of color face in Title VII claims, limiting the claims to sex *or* race discrimination.[58] For instance, in *Lee v. Walters*, an Asian American woman working as a physician at a Veterans Administration Medical Center claimed that she was denied a promotion to a higher salary level because of sex *and* race

discrimination, but the court dismissed her claim, finding that she did not experience sex *or* race discrimination because White women and an Asian man had been promoted.[59] This is also a problem under the EPA, which prohibits *only* sex discrimination.[60]

Housing

The 1975 Home Mortgage Disclosure Act required banks to report racial data in order to track racial discrimination in lending. From 2004 to 2007, Countrywide charged 10,000 Black and Latinx American borrowers more than similarly qualified White American borrowers for their loans. From 2004 to 2009, Wells Fargo charged 30,000 Black American borrowers more than similarly qualified White American borrowers for their loans. Both companies steered Black Americans into subprime loans when they qualified for conventional loans. Subprime loans generally carried higher-cost terms, such as prepayment penalties and adjustable interest rates that started with low initial rates, which significantly increased after two to three years, making the loan payments unaffordable and leaving borrowers at high risk for default or foreclosure. Both lenders were fined by the U.S. Department of Justice, but the lenders were not required to fix the inequities. In large part due these practices, Black Americans were more likely than White Americans to lose their homes during the Great Recession.

A 2018 report by the Center for Investigative Reporting analyzing Home Mortgage Disclosure Act records shows that "redlining persists in 61 metro areas—from Detroit and Philadelphia to Little Rock and Tacoma, Washington—even when controlling for applicants' income, loan amount and neighborhood."[61] Notwithstanding this report, Congress passed legislation in 2018 that cancels the requirement of credit unions and midsize and small banks to report racial data related to home mortgages. These data were not only used by the government to determine whether credit unions and banks were discriminating against racial and ethnic minority individuals, they were also used by these individuals to bring disparate impact lawsuits against banks.

Health Care and Education

Title VI of the Civil Rights Act of 1964 prohibits, among other things, racially separate and unequal health care and public education. However, some health care facilities and many public school districts remain racially segregated. Early in the enforcement of Title VI, for example, President Lyndon B. Johnson noted that unlike hospitals, nursing homes were viewed as private residences. Hence, the president and the U.S. Department of Health and Human Services were unwilling to enforce Title VI to integrate these "homes," and thus, nursing homes remain racially separate and unequal, which has led to significant racial health inequities. From 1964 through the present, studies show that most Black Americans reside in racially separate nursing homes that provide substandard care compared to the nursing homes in which Whites reside, resulting in higher incidences of pressure sores, falls, use of physical restraints, rehospitalization, and use of antipsychotic medications in Black Americans.[62] Also early in the life of Title VI, the federal government interpreted the law to only apply to health care institutions, not providers; thus, it does not prohibit racism exhibited by health care providers, such as physicians, nurses, and other health care staff.[63] This is because the government interpreted Title VI to only apply to Medicare Part B, which governs health care institutions, but not Part A, which governs health care providers.

In terms of public education, the Supreme Court ruled in the first *Brown v. Board of Education* case (1954) that racially segregated education was unconstitutional. In the second *Brown v. Board of Education* case

(1955), which was focused on implementing school desegregation, the Court determined that school integration would not be required immediately but rather "with all deliberate speed." In response, many states chose not to integrate and simply closed schools or failed to integrate them.[64] Some public schools have continued to limit integration through the "race-neutral" decision of drawing educational district lines and issuing school choice vouchers, which has resulted in hyper-segregated schools along racial and class lines.[65] Finally, as discussed in Chapter 6, the Supreme Court further limited the use of Title VI in *Alexander v. Sandoval* when it ruled that private individuals could only sue for intentional—but not disparate impact—discrimination under Title VI.[66] The failure to treat racial and ethnic minority individuals equally under the law has resulted in unequal access to the social drivers of health (education, employment, housing, and health care), perpetuating health inequities.

Treatment of Racial and Ethnic Minorities by the Health Care System

Historically, racial and ethnic minority individuals have been exploited in medical research studies and mistreated in health care. The legacy of this exploitation and mistreatment continues to affect the relationships between racial and ethnic minority people and the medical community today.

Medical Research

The most notable example of exploitation of racial and ethnic minority individuals in U.S.-funded medical research is the Tuskegee Syphilis Study. From 1932 until 1972, researchers enrolled economically disadvantaged Black men in a study to document the course of syphilis, even though the course of the disease was already known.[67] In exchange for free meals, medical exams, and burial insurance, the researchers promised the men that they would provide treatment for their "bad blood," which could include "anemic blood to muscle aches, general malaise, disorders such as parasitic infections, gonorrhea, syphilis, and other venereal disease."[68] The researchers never informed the men that they were participating in a medical research study and, therefore, never told them about the purpose of the study. Researchers also intentionally deprived these men of "demonstrably effective treatment in order not to interrupt the project, long after such treatment became generally available," causing the unnecessary disability and death of the men and causing great harm to their wives and children.[69] Yet these were not the only studies that exploited racial and ethnic minority individuals.

Between 1936 and 1960, psychiatrists and neurosurgeons conducted lobotomies on *healthy* Black American boys as young as 5 that obliterated their thought ability and personality.[70] From 1949 to 1960, the Medical College of Virginia conducted radiation tests on *healthy* Black American children, as young as 6 months old, deliberately causing third-degree burns to their skin.[71] In 1956, 17 *healthy* Black American infants were deprived of an essential nutrient, without which researchers knew the body could not survive.[72] Ten of the 17 suffered severe complications,[73] and when the study was repeated with 428 infants, seven infants died.[74] The U.S. Atomic Energy Commission (AEC) "irradiated 235 Black American newborns from 1953 to 1954 in various hospitals across the nation" for no therapeutic purpose since the infants were *healthy*.[75] Between 1960 and 1970, the AEC sponsored a study in which radioactive material was added to the oatmeal of 30 *healthy* orphans, some of whom were Black Americans.[76] The government obtained the bodies of the research participants who died to measure the levels of radioactivity and biological damage. In 1950, Puerto Rican women were used for medical research studying the safety and effectiveness of birth control pills, but they were not told that they were participating in medical research, and many suffered serious side effects.[77]

Clinical Care

In the 1980s, the federal government acknowledged in the Heckler Report on Black & Minority Health that racial and ethnic health inequities were a problem.[78] In 2003, the Institute of Medicine issued the landmark report "Unequal Treatment: Confronting Racial and Ethnic Disparities in Healthcare," which noted that racial discrimination, which limited equal access to mortgage lending, housing, employment, criminal justice, and more, leads to health inequities.[79] Since the issuance of these reports and the recognition of the importance to well-being of social drivers of health, research has shown that racism within medicine and health care is associated with health inequities.

Medicine continues to misuse the social categories of race to reinforce the misguided notion that other racial groups are genetically inferior to White people, a problem that is best illustrated by sickle cell disease. Sickle cell is labeled as a "Black disease" in medical guidelines, standards of care, and research.[80] However, people of all different races and ethnicities (Asian, White, and Latinx people) and people from a variety of places (Afghanistan, Bangladesh, Burma, Greece, Honduras, India, Indonesia, Italy, Spain, and Turkey) suffer from sickle cell.[81] Nevertheless, medical schools, articles, and guidelines still racialize the disease by primarily attributing it to Black people.[82] This classification is based on a determination in 1910 by physicians that sickle cell, like syphilis, was a Black disease.[83]

Although the first three recognized cases of sickle cell in the United States were in individuals of mixed race, the physicians designated it as a Black disease because at that time Black individuals were viewed as disease carriers, which corrupted the purity of Whiteness.[84] After this initial misclassification, the medical community continued to link the disease to being Black. Sickle cell was used by White supremacists as support for racial segregation laws and practices by claiming that Blacks were inferior both genetically and socially compared to Whites and, thus, there was a need to keep Blacks and Whites from marrying and interacting.[85] By the 1950s, researchers began to argue that the disease was linked to environmental factors, not biological race, yet the *Journal of the American Medical Association* disputed this claim, writing that "sickle cell anemia…is independent of either geography or customs and habits. Its occurrence depends entirely on the presence of Negro blood, even though in extremely small amounts."[86] The labeling of sickle cell as a Black disease harms Black people as well as non-Black individuals. First, even when non-Black individuals show symptoms of sickle cell disease, they are rarely tested or provided with appropriate care for the condition.[87] Second, since Black individuals are the ones primarily tested for the disease, the data reinforces the notion that it is a Black disease. This is not because of biology or even geography, since sickle cell is prevalent in many non-Black countries and areas; this is because they are the ones most tested for the disease. Third, because it is considered a Black disease, education about the proper treatment and management of the disease is often inadequate.

Indeed, although most physicians have been taught that sickle cell is a Black disease, they have not been taught how to treat it, as illustrated by a 2015 survey of family physicians.[88] The study showed that only 20% of more than 3,000 family physicians felt qualified and comfortable in treating sickle cell disease, leaving many sickle cell patients without proper routine care.[89] Consequently, many sickle cell patients seek care in the emergency room (ER) for acute episodes, which is called "vasco-occlusive crisis, in which an inadequate blood supply triggers excruciating pain and damages vital organs."[90] Because these patients are Black and seeking pain medication in the ER, they are often tagged as drug addicts and denied treatment, resulting in many unnecessary deaths.[91] In fact, research shows that in the emergency room, "sickle cell patients waited 60% longer to get pain medication than other patients who reported less severe pain and were triaged into a less serious category."[92]

Medical research and clinical practice guidelines often fail to account for how diseases affect people with dark skin. For example, most medical guidelines and standards of care showing the different stages of pressure sores feature White skin and fail to discuss how to identify pressure sores that develop in dark-skinned individuals.[93] Moreover, the symptom guidelines for COVID-19 note that it can result in "pink and white" COVID toes without any mention of how to identify these symptoms in those with dark skin.[94] The failure to provide training or a medical description that is relevant to all patients prevents dark-skinned people of all races and ethnicities from receiving appropriate treatment.[95]

In addition to these examples of structural/institutional racism in medicine, there are also instances of interpersonal racism, which are associated with health inequities.[96] Some health care providers in California, Virginia, North Carolina, and many other states sterilized Black and Latinx women without their consent, as described further in Chapter 12.[97] The sterilizations were often supported by state eugenic policies to try to limit the number of "inferior" racial and ethnic minority children while increasing the number of "superior" White children.[98]

Access to Quality Care

Interpersonal racism in the form of implicit and explicit bias exhibited by health care providers is also associated with health inequities. According to research studies, a patient's race can affect physicians' "question-asking in clinical interview, diagnostic decision-making, referral to specialty care, symptom management, and treatment recommendations."[99] Empirical evidence of health care providers' implicit racial bias was first published in 1999 in the now well-known Schulman study, which investigated primary care physicians' perceptions of patients and found that a patient's race and sex affected the physician's decision to recommend medically appropriate cardiac catheterization.[100] Specifically, Black Americans were less likely to be referred for cardiac catheterizations than White Americans, while Black American women were significantly less likely to be referred for treatment compared to White American males. That same year, researchers found that Black people were less likely than Whites to be evaluated for renal transplantation and placed on a waiting list for transplantation after controlling for patient preferences, socioeconomic status, the type of dialysis facility patients used, perceptions of care, health status, the cause of renal failure, and the presence or absence of coexisting illnesses.[101]

In 2000, Drs. van Ryn and Burke conducted a survey of physicians' perceptions of patients.[102] The survey results showed that physicians rated Black American patients as less intelligent, less educated, and more likely to fail to comply with physicians' medical advice.[103] Physicians' perceptions of Black patients were negative even when there was individual evidence that contradicted the physician's prejudicial beliefs. In 2006, Dr. van Ryn repeated this study using candidates for coronary bypass surgery.

Again, the physicians who were surveyed exhibited prejudicial beliefs about Black peoples' intelligence and ability to comply with medical advice.[104] The physicians acted upon these prejudicial beliefs by recommending medically necessary coronary bypass surgery for Black males less often than for White males.

More recently, a 2008 study found that physicians subconsciously favor White patients over Black patients.[105] In this study, physicians' racial attitudes and stereotypes were assessed, and then the physicians were presented with descriptions of hypothetical cardiology patients differing by race. Although physicians reported not being explicitly racially biased, most physicians *regardless of race or ethnicity* held implicit negative attitudes about Black people and thus were aversive racists (i.e., people who believe that everyone is equal but harbor contradicting, often unconscious prejudice that minorities—such as Black Americans—are inferior).[106] This is significant because research has shown that the stronger the implicit bias, the less likely the physician is to recommend the appropriate medical treatment for Black patients for heart attacks.[107] Another study revealed that "69% of medical students surveyed exhibited implicit preferences for White people" and "other studies have found that physicians tend to rate Black American patients more negatively than White patients on a number of registers, including intelligence, compliance, and propensity to engage in high-risk health behaviors."[108] Black Americans often sense this bias, resulting in delays in seeking care, an interruption in continuity of care, nonadherence, mistrust, reduced health status, and avoidance of the health care system.[109] As a result of racism in medicine and health care, many racial and ethnic minority individuals delay seeking care because they do not trust public health officials or health care workers.

The Social and Structural Drivers of Racial and Ethnic Health Inequities

Given its failure to ensure universal access to health care for all people, combined with its long history of racism, the United States has significant racial, ethnic, and socioeconomic health inequities. In the United States, no socially constructed race or ethnicity has superior health outcomes compared to all other groups in all measures. One of the challenges of assessing health inequities is that White people are generally used as the model to which racial and ethnic minorities are compared. Indeed, in some cases, racial or ethnic minorities have better health outcomes than White people. However, there is no question that minority individuals disproportionately experience health inequities based on social and structural drivers, including the legacy and persistence of racism.

Social and Structural Drivers of Health

Most Americans continue to obtain health care services through employer-sponsored insurance, as described previously in this book. Yet many racial and ethnic minority workers are employed in low-wage jobs that do not provide adequate health insurance. As of 2019, 58% of Americans were covered by employer-sponsored health insurance, with 66% of White workers covered by employer-sponsored health insurance compared to 47% of Black, 43% of Latinx, and 37% of Native American/Alaska Native workers.[110] Those without employer-sponsored health insurance are often uninsured, with Black and Latinx individuals 1.5 and 2.5 times, respectively, more likely to be uninsured than White individuals.[111] Even if racial and ethnic minority workers are insured, they are disproportionately covered by employer-sponsored plans that provide poorer coverage, leaving them with higher out-of-pocket costs (due to higher premiums and cost-sharing) than typical plans provided through the Affordable Care Act exchanges.[112] The lack of health insurance has been associated with poor health status, as discussed in Chapter 7. Furthermore, in a study conducted by National Public Radio, the Robert Wood Johnson Foundation, and the Harvard T.H. Chan School of Public Health, 52% of Black Americans said they have avoided seeking health care because of cost.[113] The study also found that between 2005 and 2006, "[t]he largest difference in doctor visits between insured and uninsured populations was seen among Black-Americans and individuals of two or more races."[114]

Housing—and particularly residential segregation—has been shown to limit Black Americans' opportunities to be healthy, as discussed elsewhere in this book.[115] Furthermore, decades of research have shown that racially segregated Black neighborhoods have "poorer housing stock and code violations for asbestos, mold and cockroaches," which have been linked to increased rates of respiratory illness, such as asthma.[116] Racially segregated neighborhoods that are predominantly filled with People of Color, usually experience less economic investment[117] than other communities and thus have fewer resources such as places to obtain healthy food [118] and places to exercise or play.[119] Indeed, residents in predominately Black neighborhoods "do not have access to healthy food due to a lack of supermarkets and a preponderance of convenience stores and fast food restaurants as the primary food outlets."[120] Such limited access to healthy food options has been shown to lead to obesity, cardiovascular disease,[121] and COVID-19.[122] Residential segregation has also been linked to Black people's higher rates of heart disease and stroke,[123] blood pressure,[124] and increased air pollution,[125] all of which are risk factors for COVID-19.[126]

Because the United States does not have a universal health care program, most Americans use some form of health insurance (Medicare, Medicaid, the Children's Health Insurance Program, or private insurance) to obtain access to health care. Prior to the passage of the ACA in 2010, racial and ethnic minority individuals were less likely to have health insurance compared to White individuals (see **Figure 10.1**). Since passage of the ACA, some racial and ethnic minority groups experienced improvements in health insurance coverage, health care access, and use of health care services.[127] Black and Latinx Americans saw the greatest improvement, followed by White, Asian, American Indian or Alaska Native, and Native Hawaiian or other Pacific Islander Americans.[128] Unfortunately, despite these improvements, Black and Latinx Americans still fared worse than

White individuals in health care coverage, access, and use of care.[129]

More specifically, between 2010 and 2019, American Indian or Alaska Native, Black, Latinx, and Native Hawaiian or other Pacific Islander Americans remained more likely to lack health insurance than White Americans,[130] as shown in **Figure 10.2**. As discussed in Chapter 7, Black and ethnic minority individuals are more likely to fall into the coverage gap that resulted from some states choosing not to expand Medicaid. But even in those states that have expanded Medicaid coverage as permitted under the ACA, racial and ethnic minority individuals are still less likely to be insured than White individuals.[131]

Research has shown that

[i]nadequate health insurance coverage is one of the largest barriers to health care access,[132] and the unequal distribution of coverage contributes to disparities in health.[133] Out-of-pocket

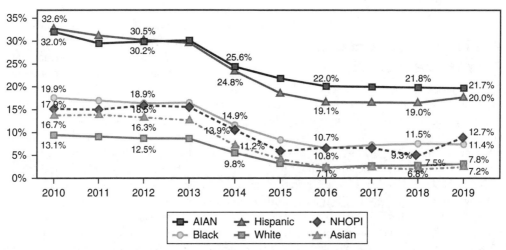

Note: Includes individuals ages 0 to 64. AIAN refers to American Indians and Alaska Natives, NHOPI refers to Native Hawaiians and Other Pacific Islanders. Persons of Hispanic origin may be of any race but are categorized as Hispanic for this analysis; other groups are non-Hispanic.

Figure 10.1 Uninsured health insurance rates among racial and ethnic minority individuals compared to White individuals

The Henry J. Kaiser Family Foundation. Key Facts on Health and Health Care by Race and Ethnicity. July 16, 2021. https://www.kff.org/racial-equity-and-health-policy/issue-brief/health-coverage-by-race-and-ethnicity/

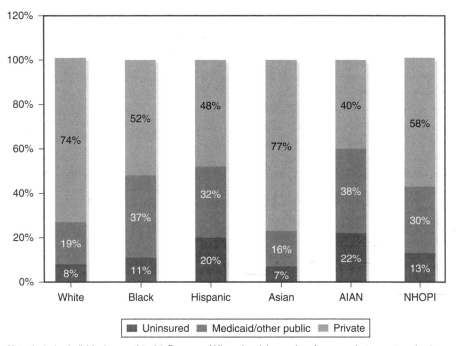

Note: Includes individuals ages 0 to 64. Persons of Hispanic origin may be of any race but are categorized as Hispanic for this analysis; other groups are non-Hispanic. AIAN refers to American Indians and Alaska Natives. NHOPI refers to Native Hawaiians and Other Pacific Islanders. Totals may not sum to 100 percent due to rounding.

Figure 10.2 Health care coverage rates among Americans, 2019

Reproduced from The Henry J. Kaiser Family Foundation. Key Facts on Health and Health Care by Race and Ethnicity. July 16, 2021. https://www.kff.org/racial-equity-and-health-policy/issue-brief/health-coverage-by-race-and-ethnicity/

medical care costs may lead individuals to delay or forgo needed care (such as doctor visits, dental care, and medications),[134] and medical debt is common among both insured and uninsured individuals.[135]

Furthermore, a recent study that considered income, race, and self-perceived health status found not only that racial identity is independently associated with lack of health insurance but also that "low-income minority [individuals] with bad health had 68% less odds of being insured than high-income White [individuals] with good health."[136] Hence, lack of health insurance has been linked to health inequities.

Racism as a Driver of Health

One explanation for health inequities is that race and ethnicity serve as proxies for socioeconomic status (SES). Because race and ethnicity are strongly correlated with SES in the United States, some argue that socioeconomic differences across racial and ethnic groups account for health inequities. "Researchers frequently find that adjusting racial disparities in health for SES substantially reduces these differences. In some cases the race [inequity] disappears altogether when adjusted for SES."[137] However, this is not always the case. In some studies, racial health inequities persist at each level of SES.[138] For example, infant mortality rates have been shown to be higher among college-educated Black women than White college-educated peers.[139] This has led researchers to investigate other factors that may influence racial and ethnic health disparities.

One theory offered by sociologist David Williams is that SES does not fully account for economic status differences. By focusing on educational attainment and income—but not wealth—measures of SES miss an important part of the picture. Because there are large racial differences in the inheritance and intergenerational transfer of wealth, Williams argues that SES does not fully capture economic disadvantage by race. He points out that net worth is significantly lower for Black and Latinx Americans than for White Americans.[140] Furthermore, as this author

and other scholars have noted, racial and ethnic differences in SES are, in part, caused by racism.[141] Racism perpetuated through law and policy has limited racial and ethnic minority individuals' equal access to education, employment, and income, which disproportionately leaves them with a lower SES than White individuals, as you will recall from Chapter 7.[142]

Thus, these and other researchers argue that the main root cause of health inequities is racism, which is illustrated by **Figure 10.3.** (In the figure, "Systems" represents the social drivers of health.)

Racism can operate at various levels, all of which may affect health: (1) interpersonal racism, or experiences of discrimination and prejudice experienced in everyday life; (2) internalized racism, in which victims

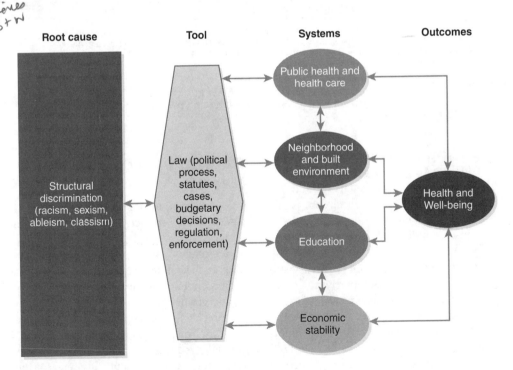

Figure 10.3 Root cause of health inequities

of racism internalize prejudicial attitudes, resulting in stress or loss of self-esteem; and (3) structural or institutionalized racism, which are "the structural elements of racism that are codified in our institutions of customs, practice and law so there need not be an identifiable perpetrator."[143] Not only is experiencing racism associated with worse health outcomes, but, as discussed in the book's Introduction, racism also influences many social drivers of health to advantage White individuals and disadvantage racial and ethnic minority individuals.[144]

Three decades of research have shown that experiencing racism is associated with health inequities for all socially constructed racial groups, but especially for racial and ethnic minority individuals.[145] For example, research has shown that experiencing racism is associated with increased rates of infant mortality, hypertension, nonadherence to medication, obesity, smoking, alcohol use, substance abuse, psychological distress, and depression[146] in Women of Color.[147] In particular, research shows that there is a positive correlation between anticipation of prejudice and increased psychological and cardiovascular stress among Latinx women.[148]

Experiencing racism has also been associated with dangerous health behaviors for all racial and ethnic groups. In a study conducted by Shariff-Malco et al., "being a current smoker" increased by 24 percent for individuals who reported experiencing racism sometimes and by 95 percent for individuals who reported experiencing racism often or all the time, compared with those who did not report experiencing racism.[149] Furthermore, the odds of binge drinking increased by 31 percent for those who reported experiencing racism often or all the time, and the odds of being overweight or obese increased by 18 percent for those who reported experiencing racism sometimes and

by 33 percent for those who reported racism often or all the time.[150] The increase in risky behaviors as a result of experiencing racism affected all racial and ethnic groups, including Blacks, Whites, Latinxs, Asians, Pacific Islanders, American Indians, and Alaska Natives.[151] Yet there were differences between groups. White individuals were more likely to be current smokers, binge drink, and be overweight and obese compared to Asians and Pacific Islanders. Additionally, Black individuals were less likely to binge drink than White individuals, and Latinx individuals were less likely than White individuals to be current smokers.[152]

Experiences of racism that serve as a significant psychosocial stressor include "everyday hassles of receiving poor service at restaurants, being followed or not helped in stores, and generally being treated with less respect and consideration than others"[153] as well as being treated differently at work, such as receiving less pay for the same work or having limited advancement opportunities.[154] As a *New York Times* article on the topic put it, "a growing body of evidence suggests that racial and sexual discrimination is toxic to the cells, organs and minds of those who experience it."[155] As described in Chapter 8, allostatic load—the daily wear and tear of chronic stress—can alter multiple body systems, leading to a wide range of poor health outcomes.[156] Internalization of racism, and its consequences for the health of Black Americans over the life course, is referred to as "weathering."[157] For instance, research has shown that experiencing racism accelerates the biological aging of Black American men, which may lead to their lower life expectancy.[158]

Racism also undergirds many social structures that drive racial and ethnic health inequities.[159] As discussed earlier in this chapter, law serves as a significant social and structural driver of health in a way that advantages White individuals and disadvantages racial and ethnic minority individuals.[160] To address racism and laws that shape the social drivers of health in ways that lead to health inequities, all levels of government should adopt a health justice lens when formulating law and policy. Next, we explore a few examples of law, policy, and structural changes that can promote health justice for racial and ethnic minority individuals and communities.

Health Inequities

Life expectancy, infant mortality, maternal mortality, and burden of disease are the measures most frequently used to determine one group's health compared to other groups, both among groups in the United States and when comparing the health of entire countries.[161] Thus, health inequities in these measures are often used to compare the health of racial and ethnic minority individuals to White individuals. The life expectancy at birth for all Americans for 2019 (the most recent year tracked) was 78.8 years,[162] compared to 82 years for Hong Kong and Switzerland.[163] Although the life expectancy rate of Black individuals was 74.7 years at birth compared to 78.8 years for White Americans, the life expectancy for Latinx Americans was 81.8 years old, better than Black and White Americans.[164] Because Latinx is considered an ethnicity, it includes the life expectancy of both Black and White Americans who select Latinx as an ethnicity. As for life expectancy premised on race and sex, Latinx women had the highest life expectancy at birth at 84.4 years, compared to 81.3 years for White women, 79 years for White men, 78.1 years for Black women, and 71.3 years old for Black men.[165] Thus, White and Black Americans have lower life expectancy compared to Latinx people. (The data do not include Asians or Indigenous people.) However, as you will read in Chapter 11, health inequities for Latinx and other ethnic minority immigrants appear to worsen the longer they live in the United States. Thus, some of the data on life expectancy should be understood through this lens.

With regard to infant mortality, which is the death of an infant before their first birthday, the highest rate was experienced by Black infants for 2018, the most recent year tracked.[166] Out of every 1,000 live births, 10.8 Black infants died, compared to 9.4 for Native Hawaiian or other Pacific Islander, 8.2 for American Indian or Alaska native, 4.9 for Latinx, 4.6 for White, and 3.6 for Asian infants.[167] Black women also had the highest maternal mortality rate at 41.7 deaths per 100,000 live births from 2014 to 2017, the most recent years for which data were available.[168] (Chapter 12 describes in detail the crisis in Black maternal mortality in the United States.) Latinx women had the lowest rate of maternal morality at 11.6 deaths per 100,000 live births, in part due to the rates of recent Latinx immigrants.[169] But the longer immigrants stay in the United States, the worse their health status becomes, including their rates of maternal mortality. This worsening health status is associated with social drivers of health, as discussed in Chapter 11.[170] The lowest rate among other racial groups was 13.4 deaths per 100,000 live births for White women, compared to 13.8 deaths for Asians or Pacific Islanders and 28.3 deaths for American Indians or Alaska Natives.[171]

Some racial and ethnic minority groups also have the highest burden of chronic disease. For example,

- From 2012 to 2014, Latinx individuals had the highest rates of new cases of diabetes compared to other groups; White individuals had the lowest rates.[172]
- From 2008 to 2010, Black individuals had the highest rates of lower extremity amputations in people with diabetes; White individuals had the lowest rates.[173]
- In 2011, Black individuals had the highest rates of new cases of colorectal cancer;

American Indian or Alaska Native individuals had the lowest rates.[174]

- In 2011, Black women had the highest rates of new cases of invasive uterine cervical cancer; Asian and Native Hawaiian or other Pacific Islander women had the lowest rates.[175]
- In 2011, Black women also had the highest rates of new cases of late-stage female breast cancer; American Indian or Alaska Native individuals had the lowest rates.[176]
- In 2010, Black individuals between the ages of 65 and 85 and older had the highest rates of heart failure hospitalizations; American Indian or Alaska Native individuals had the lowest rates.[177]
- In 2010, Black individuals 65 years and older had the highest rates of moderate to severe functional limitations; White individuals had the lowest rates.[178]

These health inequities have been tied to limited access to health care services as well as to other social (and also structural) drivers of health.

Law, Policy, and Structural Change to Achieve Health Justice

Unlike many current measures undertaken to address health inequities, health justice reform requires that communities drive change. Reforms should include not only ensuring protection from harm for Communities of Color but also affirmative actions that provide material and institutional support.[179] This approach provides a mechanism for systems-level change that goes beyond traditional notions of citizenship rights that often only prevent harm (negative rights) to a broader conception of positive rights that aim to achieve health

equity in which everyone "has the opportunity to attain . . . full health potential and no one is disadvantaged from achieving this potential because of social position or any other socially defined circumstance."[180] Following are three important steps that should be taken to promote health justice for racial and ethnic minority people.

Institute a Truth and Reconciliation Process in Health Care

First, the process of eradicating health inequities must include a *truth and reconciliation process* that acknowledges the existence of racism in medicine and health care. (A truth and reconciliation process is discussed in more detail in Chapter 16). This would offer racial and ethnic minority individuals a mechanism to recover from the trauma of experiencing racism in the health care system by, for example, providing an opportunity for communities to build trusting and respectful relationships with health care professionals and entities, which is necessary for meaningful community engagement. As the W.K. Kellogg Foundation notes, transformational and sustainable change must include "ways for all of us to heal from the wounds of the past, to build mutually respectful relationships across racial and ethnic lines that honor and value each person's humanity, and to build trusting intergenerational and diverse community relationships that better reflect our common humanity."[181] To achieve health justice, health care professionals and entities need to truthfully confront the past and current instances of exploitation and mistreatment. Currently, some stakeholders in the health care system are focused on addressing implicit bias and instilling cultural competency by training health care providers to be more reflective about how they interact with racial and ethnic minority patients.

Yet, despite these efforts, mistreatment in health care persists. Race is still treated as a biological concept in much of medical training and practice, supporting a false narrative of genetic racial differences.[182] To bring about structural change, health care professionals and entities need to listen to patients who have been harmed by the system and allow them to suggest changes to the system that would improve their care.

Engage and Empower Racial and Ethnic Minority Individuals to Transform Laws and Social Drivers of Health

Community engagement is a key priority of public health. For example, a 2011 U.S. Department of Health and Human Services toolkit and 2012 report addressing inequities during pandemics noted that "effective preparedness and response requires the ongoing and active engagement of diverse communities" before, during, and after an emergency through "sustainable partnerships between community representatives and the public health preparedness systems" that are "tailored to a community's distinct social, economic, cultural, and health-related circumstances."[183] Hence, the government should engage Communities of Color and give them the power to lead the process of revising, implementing, and evaluating laws and plans that affect their health, including those that structure the social drivers of health.

Policymakers Should Employ Racial Equity Tools to Guide Structural Change

Some cities and counties are already beginning to make structural changes to address the social drivers of health with the use of racial equity tools (e.g., racial equity impact statements/assessments, racial equity frameworks, racial equity indicators)[184] as well as through declaring racism a public health crisis.[185] For example, after using a racial equity tool in the succession planning for management hires, the first Woman of Color in over 20 years was promoted to a management position for the Madison, Wisconsin, Metro Transit.[186] Thus, by using racial equity tools, the transit system was able to change the system to address racial and gender inequities in employment. In Michigan, Washtenaw County's declaration of racism as a public health crisis outlines several ways the county plans to "address health inequities through structural change, including increasing the budget for the county's health department and racial equity office as well as enacting universal paid leave for employees (including but not limited to paid parental leave)"; the paid leave will cover many racial and ethnic minority workers who were not previously covered.[187] By providing universal paid leave, the county is trying to rectify past racial and ethnic inequities in benefits and ensure that the provision of benefits is no longer discriminatory.

Conclusion

This chapter explored health inequities among Asian, Black, Indigenous, and Latinx people in the United States. This entailed first considering how people were classified for citizenship rights and examining some of the historical and social contexts in which these classifications were derived. These rights and inequities in the social drivers of health serve as key factors in the continuation of health inequities. Racism in public health and medicine also contributes to these inequities, as the notion of biological differences among individuals persists and racism remains a part of the structures of society, public health, and medicine.

References

1. Professor of Law and Member of the Center for Health Law Studies, Saint Louis University, School of Law; Co-Founder and Executive Director, Institute for Healing Justice, Saint Louis University; B.S. (Honors Biology), University of Michigan; J.D., Georgetown University Law Center; M.P.H. in Health Policy and Management, Johns Hopkins School of Public Health.

2. United States Census Bureau. Quick Facts. https://www.census.gov/quickfacts/fact/table/US/POP010220.

3. Bradt S. "One-drop rule" persists. *The Harvard Gazette.* December 9, 2010. https://news.harvard.edu/gazette/story/2010/12/one-drop-rule-persists/.

4. Bradt S. "One-drop rule" persists. *The Harvard Gazette.* December 9, 2010. https://news.harvard.edu/gazette/story/2010/12/one-drop-rule-persists/.

5. *United States v Rogers*, 45 U.S. 4 (1846); Chow K. So what exactly is "blood quantum"? NPR. February 9, 2018. https://www.npr.org/sections/codeswitch/2018/02/09/583987261/so-what-exactly-is-blood-quantum.

6. *United States v Rogers*, 45 U.S. 4 (1846); Chow K. So what exactly is "blood quantum"? NPR. February 9, 2018. https://www.npr.org/sections/codeswitch/2018/02/09/583987261/so-what-exactly-is-blood-quantum.

7. Bonilla-Silva E. The essential social fact of race. *American Sociological Review.* 1999;64(6):899–906.

8. Bonilla-Silva E. Rethinking racism: Toward a structural interpretation. *American Sociological Review.* 1997;62(3):465–480.

9. Yearby R. Structural racism and health disparities: Reconfiguring the social determinants of health framework to include the root cause. *Journal of Law, Medicine & Ethics.* 2020;48:518–526; Perea J. Doctrines of delusion: How the history of the G.I. Bill and other inconvenient truths undermine the Supreme Court's affirmative action jurisprudence. *University of Pittsburgh Law Review.* 2014;75:583–651.

10. *Dred Scott v. Sanford*, 60 US 339 (1856).

11. *Dred Scott v. Sanford*, 60 US 339 (1856).

12. PBS. Race: The power of an illusion. 2003. https://www.pbs.org/race/000_About/002_03_d-godeeper.htm.

13. PBS. Race: The power of an illusion. 2003. https://www.pbs.org/race/000_About/002_03_d-godeeper.htm; U.S. Capitol Visitor Center. H.R. 40 Naturalization Bill (March 4, 1790). https://www.visitthecapitol.gov/exhibitions/artifact/h-r-40-naturalization-bill-march-4-1790.

14. PBS. Race: The power of an illusion. 2003. https://www.pbs.org/race/000_About/002_03_d-godeeper.htm.

15. Library of Congress. Indian Removal Act: Primary documents in American history. 2019. https://guides.loc.gov/indian-removal-act.

16. National Park Service. Native Americans and the Homestead Act. 2021. https://www.nps.gov/home/learn/historyculture/native-americans-and-the-homestead-act.htm#:~:text=The%20Homestead%20Act%20of%201862%20granted%20land%20claims%20in%20thirty,of%20many%20Native%20American%20tribes.&text=Native%20Americans%20believed%20land%20belonged,ways%20homesteaders%20conceived%20of%20ownership..

17. Library of Congress. Indian Removal Act: Primary documents in American history. 2019. https://guides.loc.gov/indian-removal-act.

18. The U.S. Constitution. Slavery and the Making of America—Thirteen/WNET New York. 2004. https://www.thirteen.org/wnet/slavery/experience/legal/docs2.html.

19. Sayej N. "Forgotten by society"—how Chinese migrants built the transcontinental railroad. *The Guardian.* July 18, 2019. https://www.theguardian.com/artanddesign/2019/jul/18/forgotten-by-society-how-chinese-migrants-built-the-transcontinental-railroad.

20. Chinese Exclusion Act of 1882. 1989. https://www.ourdocuments.gov/doc.php?flash=false&doc=47.

21. Chinese Exclusion Act of 1882. 1989. https://www.ourdocuments.gov/doc.php?flash=false&doc=47.

22. Chinese Exclusion Act of 1882. 1989. https://www.ourdocuments.gov/doc.php?flash=false&doc=47.

23. McCarran-Walter Act goes into effect, revising immigration laws. History. 2020. https://www.history.com/this-day-in-history/mccarren-walter-act-goes-into-effect.

24. *U.S. v. Wong Kim Ark*, 169 US 649 (1898).

25. PBS. Race: The power of an illusion. 2003. https://www.pbs.org/race/000_About/002_03_d-godeeper.htm.

26. Japanese Internment Camps. History. 2021. https://www.history.com/topics/world-war-ii/japanese-american-relocation.

27. *Plessy v. Ferguson*, 16 U.S .537 (1896).

28. Solomon D, Maxwell C, Castro A. Systematic inequality and economic opportunity. Center for American Progress. August 2019. https://www.americanprogress.org/article/systematic-inequality-economic-opportunity/.

29. Solomon D, Maxwell C, Castro A. Systematic inequality and economic opportunity. Center

for American Progress. August 2019. https://www.americanprogress.org/article/systematic-inequality-economic-opportunity/.

30. Fair Labor Standards Act of 1938, 29 U.S.C. § 201-19 (1938).

31. Solomon D, Maxwell C, Castro A. Systematic inequality and economic opportunity. Center for American Progress. August 2019. https://www.americanprogress.org/article/systematic-inequality-economic-opportunity/.

32. Perea J. Doctrines of delusion: How the history of the G.I. Bill and other inconvenient truths undermine the Supreme Court's affirmative action jurisprudence. *University of Pittsburgh Law Review.* 2014;75:583–651.

33. Kijakazi K, Smith K, Runes, C. African American economic security and the role of social security. Urban Institute. July 2019. https://www.urban.org/sites/default/files/publication/100697/african_american_economic_security_and_the_role_of_social_security.pdf.

34. Yearby R. Structural racism and health disparities: Reconfiguring the social determinants of health framework to include the root cause. *Journal of Law, Medicine & Ethics.* 2020;48:518–526.

35. *Corrigan v. Buckley*, 271 U.S. 3223 (1926); Perea J. Doctrines of delusion: How the history of the G.I. Bill and other inconvenient truths undermine the Supreme Court's affirmative action jurisprudence. *University of Pittsburgh Law Review.* 2014;75:583–651.

36. *Shelly v. Kraemer*, 334 US 1 (1948).

37. Rothstein R. *The Color of Law*. New York, NY: Liveright Publishing Corporation; 2017.

38. Gordon A. The creation of homeownership: How New Deal changes in banking regulation simultaneously made homeownership accessible to Whites and out of reach for Blacks. *The Yale Law Journal.* 2005;115:187–225.

39. Hospital Survey and Construction Act, 42 U.S.C. § 291e(f) (2006).

40. Smith DB. *Health Care Divided: Race and Healing a Nation*. Ann Arbor, MI: The University of Michigan Press; 1999.

41. Hospital Survey and Construction Act, 42 U.S.C. § 291e(f) (2006).

42. Hospital Survey and Construction Act, 42 U.S.C. § 291e(f) (2006).

43. U.S. Commission on Civil Rights, 1963 Report of the U.S. Commission on Civil Rights.

44. U.S. Commission on Civil Rights, 1963 Report of the U.S. Commission on Civil Rights.

45. U.S. Commission on Civil Rights, 1963 Report of the U.S. Commission on Civil Rights.

46. Gamble VN. *Making a Place for Ourselves: The Black Hospital Movement, 1920–1945*. New York, NY: Oxford University Press; 1995.

47. Smith DB. The politics of racial disparities: Desegregating the hospitals in Jackson, *Mississippi. Milbank Quarterly.* 2005;83:247–269.

48. Fulwood III S. Poisonous rhetoric, then and now. Center for American Progress. https://www.americanprogress.org/issues/race/news/2016/04/01/134450/poisonous-rhetoric-then-and-now/.

49. Drug War Confessional. Vera Institute of Justice. 2022. https://www.vera.org/reimagining-prison-webumentary/the-past-is-never-dead/drug-war-confessional; LoBianco T. Report: Aide says Nixon's war on drugs targeted blacks, hippies. CNN Politics. March 24, 2016. https://www.cnn.com/2016/03/23/politics/john-ehrlichman-richard-nixon-drug-war-blacks-hippie/index.html.

50. Perea J. Doctrines of delusion: How the history of the G.I. Bill and other inconvenient truths undermine the Supreme Court's affirmative action jurisprudence. *University of Pittsburgh Law Review.* 2014;75:583–651.

51. Lawrence III CR. The Id, the ego, and equal protection: Reckoning with unconscious racism. *Stanford Law Review.* 1989;39:317,388; Perea J. Doctrines of delusion: How the history of the G.I. Bill and other inconvenient truths undermine the Supreme Court's affirmative action jurisprudence. *University of Pittsburgh Law Review.* 2014;75:583–651.

52. Grumbach K, Braveman P, Adler N, Bindman AB. Vulnerable populations and health disparities: An overview. In King TE, Wheeler MB, Bindman AB, et al., eds. *Medical Management of Vulnerable and Underserved Populations: Principles, Practice and Populations*. New York, NY: McGraw Hill; 2007.

53. Perea J. Doctrines of delusion: How the history of the G.I. Bill and other inconvenient truths undermine the Supreme Court's affirmative action jurisprudence. *University of Pittsburgh Law Review.* 2014;75:583–651.

54. It also prohibits employment discrimination based on "color, religion, . . . and national origin." Title VII of the Civil Rights Act of 1964, 42 U.S.C. § 2000e-2(a)(1).

55. The Equal Pay Act of 1963, 29 U.S.C. § 206 (1963).

56. Pappoe YNA. The shortcomings of Title VII for the Black female plaintiff. *University of Pennsylvania Journal of Law and Social Change.* 2019;22(1):1–23; Powell ME. The claims of Women of Color under Title VII: The interaction of race and gender. *Golden Gate University Law Review.* 1996;26(2):413–436; Scarborough C. Conceptualizing Black women's employment experiences. *Yale Law Journal.* 1989;98(7):1457–1478.

57. U.S. Equal Employment Opportunity Commission, Compliance Manual: Section 15: Race and Color Discrimination 3, 8–9 (2006). https://www.eeoc.gov/policy/docs/race-color.pdf; Why Do We Need E-RACE?, U.S. Equal Employment Opportunity Commission. Accessed April 21, 2019. https://

www1.eeoc.gov/eeoc/initiatives/e-race/why _e-race.cfm.

58. *DeGraffenreid v. Gen. Motors Assembly Div.*, 413 F. Supp. 142, 143 (E.D. Mo. 1976), aff'd in part, rev'd in part on other grounds, 558 F.2d 480 (8th Cir. 1977).

59. *Lee v. Walters*, No. 85-5383, 1988 U.S. Dist. LEXIS 11336, at *7 (E.D. Pa. Oct. 11, 1988).

60. 29 U.S.C. § 206 (2018); Cal. Lab. Code § 432.3 (Deering 2019); Haw. Rev. Stat. § 378-2.4 (2019); Or. Rev. Stat. § 659A.357 (2019).

61. Jan T. *The Senate rolls back rules meant to root out discrimination by mortgage lenders.* Washington Post. March 14, 2018.

62. Rivera-Hernandez M, et al. Quality of post-acute care in skilled nursing facilities that disproportionately serve Black and Hispanic patients. *Journal of Gerontology: Series A, Biological Science and Medical Sciences.* 2019;74(5):689–697; Li Y, et al. Association of race and sites of care with pressure ulcers in high-risk nursing home residents. *Journal of the American Medical Association.* 2011;306(15):179–186; Lowenstein JK. Disparate nursing home care. *The Chicago Reporter.* 2009;38:10–14; Akamigbo A, Wolinsky F. New evidence of racial differences in access and their effects on the use of nursing homes among older adults. *The Journal of Medical Care.* 2007;45(7):672–679; Mor V, et al. Driven to tiers: Socioeconomic and racial disparities in the quality of nursing home care. *The Milbank Quarterly.* 2004;82(2):227–256; Fennell M, Miller SC, Mor V. Facility effects on racial differences in nursing home quality of care. *American Journal of Medical Quality.* 2000;15(4):174–181; Wallace SP. The consequences of color-blind health policy for older racial and ethnic minorities. *Stanford Law and Policy Review.* 1998;9(2):329–340; Smith DB. *Health Care Divided: Race and Healing a Nation.* Ann Arbor, MI: The University of Michigan Press; 1999.

63. Smith DB. *Health Care Divided: Race and Healing a Nation.* Ann Arbor, MI: The University of Michigan Press; 1999.

64. Smith-Richardson S, Burke L. In the 1950s, rather than integrate its public schools, Virginia closed them. *The Guardian.* November 27, 2021. https:// www.theguardian.com/world/2021/nov/27/integration -public-schools-massive-resistance-virginia-1950s.

65. Chatterji R. Fighting systemic racism in K–12 Education: Helping allies move from the keyboard to the school board. Center for American Progress, July 8, 2020. https://americanprogress.org/article /fighting-systemic-racism-k-12-education-helping -allies-move-keyboard-school-board/.

66. *Alexander v. Sandoval*, 532 U.S. 275 (2001).

67. Jones JH. *Bad Blood: The Tuskegee Syphilis Experiment.* New York, NY: Free Press, 1981.

68. Washington H. *Medical Apartheid.* New York, NY: Anchor Books, 2007.

69. Washington H. *Medical Apartheid.* New York, NY: Anchor Books, 2007; Alford D. Examining the "stick" of accreditation for medical schools through reproductive justice lens: A transformative remedy for teaching the Tuskegee Syphilis Study. *St. John's Journal of Civil Rights & Economic Development.* 2012; 26:153–195.

70. Washington H. *Medical Apartheid.* New York, NY: Anchor Books, 2007.

71. Washington H. *Medical Apartheid.* New York, NY: Anchor Books, 2007.

72. Washington H. *Medical Apartheid.* New York, NY: Anchor Books, 2007.

73. *Lewiston Evening Journal*, March 29 (1973).

74. Washington H. *Medical Apartheid.* New York, NY: Anchor Books, 2007.

75. Washington H. *Medical Apartheid.* New York, NY: Anchor Books, 2007.

76. Washington H. *Medical Apartheid.* New York, NY: Anchor Books, 2007.

77. The First Birth Control Pill Used Puerto Rican Women as Guinea Pigs. History. 2019. https:// www.history.com/news/birth-control-pill-history -puerto-rico-enovid.

78. Heckler MM. Report of the Secretary's Task Force on Black & Minority Health. U.S. Department of Health and Human Services. Accessed February 9, 2020. https://minorityhealth.hhs.gov/assets/pdf /checked/1/ANDERSON.pdf.

79. Institute of Medicine. *Unequal Treatment: Confronting Racial and Ethnic Inequities in Health Care.* Washington, DC: The National Academies Press; 2003.

80. Okwerekwu JA. My medical school lesson was tinged with racism. Did that affect how I treated a sickle cell patient years later? *STATNews.* September 21, 2017. https://www.statnews.com/2017/09/21 /sickle-cell-racism-doctors/; Solovieff N, Hartley SW, Baldwin CT, Klings ES, et al. Ancestry of American Americans with sickle cell disease. *Blood Cells, Molecules, and Disease.* 2011;47(1):41–45; Tanabe P. CE: Understanding the complications of sickle cell disease. *American Journal of Nursing.* 2019;119(6):26–35; National Institutes of Health, National Heart, Lung, and Blood Institute Division of Blood Disease and Resources. *The Management of Sickle Cell Disease.* 2002. NIH Publication No. 02-2117. https://www.nhlbi.nih.gov/files/docs/guidelines /sc_mngt.pdf.

81. Wilkinson D. For whose benefit? Politics and sickle cell. *The Black Scholar.* 1974;5(8):26–23. Bloom M. *Understanding Sickle Cell Disease* (Understanding Health and Sickness Series). Jackson, Mississippi: University Press of Mississippi; 1995.

82. Swetlitz I. Teaching medical students to challenge "unscientific" racial categories. *STATNews.* March 10, 2016. https://www.statnews.com/2016/03/10/medical

-schools-teaching-race/; Nelson SC, Hackman HW. Race matters: Perceptions of race and racism in a sickle cell center. *Pediatric Blood Cancer*. 2013;60(3):451 –454; Shriner D, Rotini C. Whole-genome-sequence -based haplotypes reveal single origin of the sickle allele during the Holocene Wet Phase. *American Journal of Human Genetics*. 2011;102(4):547–556; Wakefield E, Pantaleao A, Pop JM, Dale LP, et al. Describing perceived racial bias among youth with sickle cell disease. *Journal of Pediatric Psychology*. 2018;43(7):779–788.

83. Herrick JB. Peculiar elongated and sickle-shaped red blood corpuscles in a case of severe anemia. *The Yale Journal of Biology and Medicine*. 2001;74(3):179–184 (republished 1910 article); Kwateng M. Repacking racism: The role of sickle cell anemia in the construction of race as biological. Senior Capstone Projects—Paper 331. 2014. http://digitalwindow.vassar .edu/senior_capstone.

84. Wailoo K. Dying in the city of the blues: Sickle cell anemia and the politics of race and health. Chapel Hill, NC: University of North Carolina Press; 2001; Kwateng M. Repacking racism: The role of sickle cell anemia in the construction of race as biological. Senior Capstone Projects—Paper 331. 2014. http:// digitalwindow.vassar.edu/senior_capstone.

85. Nelson SC, Hackman HW. Race matters: Perceptions of race and racism in a sickle cell center. *Pediatric Blood Cancer*. 2013;60(3):451–454; Kwateng M. Repacking racism: The role of sickle cell anemia in the construction of race as biological. Senior Capstone Projects—Paper 331. 2014. http://digitalwindow .vassar.edu/senior_capstone.

86. Allison AC. Protection afforded by sickle-cell trait against subtertian malarial infection. *British Medical Journal*. 1954;1:290–294; Kwateng M. Repacking racism: The role of sickle cell anemia in the construction of race as biological. Senior Capstone Projects—Paper 331. 2014. http://digitalwindow .vassar.edu/senior_capstone; JAMA. Sickle cell anemia, a race specific disease. *Journal of the American Medical Association*. 1947;133(1):33–34.

87. Swetlitz I. Teaching medical students to challenge "unscientific" racial categories. *STATNews*. March 10, 2016. https://www.statnews.com/2016/03/10 /medical-schools-teaching-race/.

88. Bengley S. "Every time it's a battle": In excruciating pain, sickle cell patients are shunted aside. *STATNews*. September 18, 2017. https://www.statnews.com/2017 /09/18/sickle-cell-pain-treatment/; Mainous AG, Tanner RJ, Harle CA, Baker RB, et al. Attitudes toward management of sickle cell disease and its complications: A national survey of academic family physicians. *Anemia*. 2015. http://dx.doi.org/10.1155/2015/853835.

89. Bengley S. "Every time it's a battle": In excruciating pain, sickle cell patients are shunted aside. *STATNews*. September 18, 2017. https://www.statnews .com/2017/09/18/sickle-cell-pain-treatment/; Mainous AG, Tanner RJ, Harle CA, Baker RB, et al. Attitudes toward management of sickle cell disease and its complications: A national survey of academic family physicians. *Anemia*. 2015. http://dx.doi.org /10.1155/2015/853835.

90. Bengley S. "Every time it's a battle": In excruciating pain, sickle cell patients are shunted aside. *STATNews*. September 18, 2017. https://www.statnews.com/2017 /09/18/sickle-cell-pain-treatment/.

91. Bengley S. "Every time it's a battle": In excruciating pain, sickle cell patients are shunted aside. *STATNews*. September 18, 2017. https://www.statnews.com/2017 /09/18/sickle-cell-pain-treatment/.

92. Bengley S. "Every time it's a battle": In excruciating pain, sickle cell patients are shunted aside. *STATNews*. September 18, 2017. https://www.statnews.com /2017/09/18/sickle-cell-pain-treatment/; Haywood C, Naik R, Beach MC, Lanzkron S. Do sickle cell patients wait longer to see physicians in the emergency department. *Blood*. 2011;118(21):2070 (901 poster); Haywood C, Tanabe P, Naik R, Beach MC, et al. The impact of race and disease on sickle cell patient wait times in the emergency department. *American Journal of Emergency Medicine*. 2013;31(4):651–656.

93. Boyko T, Longaker M, Yang GP. Review of the current management of pressure ulcers. *Advances in Wound Care*. 2018;7(2):57–67.

94. Evans MK, Rosenbaum L, Malina D, Morrissey S, et al. Diagnosing and treating systemic racism. *The New England Journal of Medicine*. 2020;383:274–276.

95. Benfer EA, Mohapatra S, Wiley LF, Yearby R. Health justice strategies to combat the pandemic: Eliminating discrimination, poverty, and health disparities during and after COVID-19. *Yale Journal of Health Policy, Law, and Ethics*. 2020;19(3):122–171.

96. Schulman KA, et al. The effect of race and sex on physicians' recommendations for cardiac catherization. *New England Journal of Medicine*. 1999;340:618–626; van Ryn M, et al. Physicians' perceptions of patients' social and behavioral characteristics and race disparities in treatment recommendations for men with coronary artery disease. *American Journal of Public Health*. 2006;96:351–357; Green AR, et al., Implicit bias among physicians and its prediction of thrombolysis decisions for Black and White patients. *Journal of General Internal Medicine*. 2007;22(9):1231–1238.

97. Jimenez J, Telemundo N. California compensates victims of forced sterilizations, many of them Latinas. *NBCNews*. July 23, 2021. https://www

.nbcnews.com/news/Latinx/california-compensates
-victims-forced-sterilizations-many-latinas-rcna1471.

98. Jimenez J, Telemundo N. California compensates victims of forced sterilizations, many of them Latinas. *NBCNews*, July 23, 2021. https://www .nbcnews.com/news/Latinx/california-compensates -victims-forced-sterilizations-many-latinas-rcna1471.

99. van Ryn M, Burke J. The effect of patient race and socio-economic status on physicians' perception of patients. *Social Science & Medicine*. 2000; 50(6):813–828.

100. Schulman KA, et al. The effect of race and sex on physicians' recommendations for cardiac catherization. *New England Journal of Medicine*. 1999; 340:618–626.

101. Ayanian J. The effect of patients' preferences on racial differences in access to renal transplantation. *New England Journal of Medicine*. 1999;341:1661–1669.

102. van Ryn M, Burke J. The effect of patient race and socio-economic status on physicians' perception of patients. *Social Science & Medicine*. 2000; 50(6):813–828.

103. van Ryn M, Burke J. The effect of patient race and socio-economic status on physicians' perception of patients. *Social Science & Medicine*. 2000; 50(6):813–828.

104. van Ryn M, et al. Physicians' perceptions of patients' social and behavioral characteristics and race disparities in treatment recommendations for men with coronary artery disease. *American Journal of Public Health*. 2006;96:351–357.

105. Green AR, et al. Implicit bias among physicians and its prediction of thrombolysis decisions for Black and White patients. *Journal of General Internal Medicine*. 2007;22(9):1231–1238.

106. Green AR, et al. Implicit bias among physicians and its prediction of thrombolysis decisions for Black and White patients. *Journal of General Internal Medicine*. 2007;22(9):1231–1238.

107. Green AR, et al. Implicit bias among physicians and its prediction of thrombolysis decisions for Black and White patients. *Journal of General Internal Medicine*. 2007;22(9):1231–1238.

108. Paul-Emile K. Patients' racial preferences and the medical culture of accommodation. *UCLA Law Review*. 2012;60:462–504.

109. Sabin J, et al. Physicians' implicit and explicit attitudes about race by md race, ethnicity, and gender. *Journal of Healthcare Poor & Underserved*. 2009;20:896–913.

110. Employer-sponsored coverage rates for the nonelderly by race/ethnicity. Kaiser Family Foundation. October 23, 2020. https://www.kff.org /other/state-indicator/nonelderly-employer -coverage-rate-by-raceethnicity/.

111. Artiga S, Hill L, Orgera K, Damico A. Health coverage by race and ethnicity, 2010–2019. Kaiser Family Foundation. July 16, 2021. https://www .kff.org/racial-equity-and-health-policy/issue-brief /health-coverage-by-race-and-ethnicity; Rubin-Miller L, Alban C, Artiga S, Sullivan S. COVID-19 racial disparities in testing, infection, hospitalization, and death: Analysis of Epic patient data. Kaiser Family Foundation. September 16, 2020. https:// www.kff.org/report-section/covid-19-racial -disparities-in-testing-infection-hospitalization -and-death-analysis-of-epic-patient-data-issue -brief/; McMinn S, et al. Across the South COVID-19 vaccine sites missing from Black and Hispanic neighborhoods. NPR. February 5, 2021. https:// www.npr.org/2021/02/05/962946721/across -the-south-covid-19-vaccine-sites-missing-from -black-and-hispanic-neighbor.

112. Straw T. Trapped by the firewall: Policy changes are needed to improve health coverage for low-income workers. Center on Budget and Policy Priorities. December 3, 2019. https://www.cbpp .org/research/health/trapped-by-the-firewall-policy -changes-are-needed-to-improve-health-coverage-for.

113. Robert Wood Johnson Foundation et al. Discrimination in America: Experiences and views of African Americans. NPR. October 2017. https://media.npr.org/assets/img/2017/10/23 /discriminationpoll-african-americans.pdf.

114. Robert Wood Johnson Foundation et al. Discrimination in America: Experiences and views of African Americans. NPR. October 2017. https://media.npr.org/assets/img/2017/10/23/dis criminationpoll-african-americans.pdf.

115. Gilbert K, et al., Racial composition over the life course: Examining separate and unequal environments and the risk for heart disease for African American men. *Ethnicity & Disease*. 2015;25(3):295–304; Thorpe R, et al. Social context as an explanation for race disparities in hypertension: Findings from the Exploring Health Disparities in Integrated Communities (EHDIC) Study. *Social Science & Medicine*. 2008;67(10):1604–1611; Jones A. Segregation and cardiovascular illness: The role of individual and metropolitan socioeconomic status. *Health & Place*. 2013;22:56–67.

116. Scott E. 4 reasons coronavirus is hitting Black communities so hard. *Washington Post*. April 10, 2020. https://www.washingtonpost .com/politics/2020/044/10/4-reasons-coronavirus -is-hitting-black-communities-so-hard/; Benfer E. Health justice: A framework (and call to action) for the elimination of health inequity and social injustice. *American University Law*

Review. 2015:65:275–351; National Center for Healthy Housing. Timeline. 2022. https://nchh.org/sample-shortcodes/sample-timeline/.

117. Walker RE, Keane CR, Burke JG. Disparities and access to healthy food in the United States: A review of food deserts literature. *Health & Place*. 2010;16(5):876–884.

118. Walker RE, Keane CR, Burke JG. Disparities and access to healthy food in the United States: A review of food deserts literature. *Health & Place*. 2010;16(5):876–884; Goodman M, et al. How segregation makes us fat: Food behaviors and food environment as mediators of the relationship between residential segregation and individual body index. *Frontiers Public Health*. 2018;6:92.

119. Gordon-Larsen P, et al. Inequality in the built environment underlies key health disparities in physical activity and obesity. *Pediatrics*. 2006;117(2):417–424.

120. Lang ME, Bird CE. Understanding and addressing the common roots of racial disparities: The case of cardiovascular disease & HIV/AIDS in African Americans. *Health Matrix*. 2014;25:109–138.

121. Walker RE, Keane CR, Burke JG. Disparities and access to healthy food in the United States: A review of food deserts literature. *Health & Place*. 2010;16(5):876–884.

122. Centers for Disease Control and Prevention. *Obesity, race/ethnicity, and COVID-19*. 2021. https://www.cdc.gov/obesity/data/obesity-and-covid-19.html.

123. Greer S, et al. Racial residential segregation and cardiovascular mortality: Exploring pathways. *Journal of Urban Health*. 2014;91:499–509.

124. Kershaw K, et al. Association of changes in neighborhood-level racial residential segregation with changes in blood pressure among Black adults: The CARRDIA Study. *JAMA Internal Medicine*. 2017;177(7):996–1002.

125. Woo B, et al, Residential Segregation and Racial/Ethnic Disparities in Ambient Air Pollution, *Race and Social Problems*. 2019;11(1):60–67.

126. People with Certain Medical Conditions. Centers for Disease Control and Prevention. https://www.cdc.gov/coronavirus/2019-ncov/need-extra-precautions/people-with-medical-conditions.html (last updated Dec. 29, 2020).

127. Hill L, Artiga S, Haldar S. Key facts on health and health care by race and ethnicity. Kaiser Family Foundation. January 26, 2022. https://www.kff.org/racial-equity-and-health-policy/report/key-facts-on-health-and-health-care-by-race-and-ethnicity/.

128. Hill L, Artiga S, Haldar S. Key facts on health and health care by race and ethnicity. Kaiser Family Foundation. January 26, 2022. https://www.kff.org/racial-equity-and-health-policy/report/key-facts-on-health-and-health-care-by-race-and-ethnicity/.

129. Hill L, Artiga S, Haldar S. Key facts on health and health care by race and ethnicity. Kaiser Family Foundation. January 26, 2022. https://www.kff.org/racial-equity-and-health-policy/report/key-facts-on-health-and-health-care-by-race-and-ethnicity/.

130. Artiga S, Hill L, Orgera K, Damico A. Health care coverage by race and ethnicity, 2010–2019. Kaiser Family Foundation. July 16, 2021. https://www.kff.org/racial-equity-and-health-policy/issue-brief/health-coverage-by-race-and-ethnicity/.

131. Artiga S, Hill L, Orgera K, Damico A. Health care coverage by race and ethnicity, 2010–2019. Kaiser Family Foundation. July 16, 2021. https://www.kff.org/racial-equity-and-health-policy/issue-brief/health-coverage-by-race-and-ethnicity/.

132. Call K, McAlpine D, Garcia C, Shippee N, Beeba T, Adeniyi T, et al. Barriers to care in an ethnically diverse publicly insured population: Is health care reform enough? *Medical Care*. 2014;52:720–727.

133. Institute of Medicine. *Unequal Treatment: Confronting Racial and Ethnic Inequities in Health Care*. Washington, DC: The National Academies Press; 2003.; Call K, McAlpine D, Garcia C, Shippee N, Beeba T, Adeniyi T, et al. Barriers to care in an ethnically diverse publicly insured population: Is health care reform enough? *Medical Care*. 2014;52:720–727.

134. Pryor C, Gurewich D. *Getting Care but Paying the Price: How Medical Debt Leaves Many in Massachusetts Facing Tough Choices*. Boston, MA: Access Project; 2004.

135. Pryor C, Gurewich D. *Getting Care but Paying the Price: How Medical Debt Leaves Many in Massachusetts Facing Tough Choices*. Boston, MA: Access Project; 2004; Herman PM, Rissi JJ, Walsh ME. Health insurance status, medical debt, and their impact on access to care in Arizona. *American Journal of Public Health*. 2011;101(8):1437–1443; Hadley J. Sicker and poorer—the consequences of being uninsured: A review of the research on the relationship between health insurance, medical care use, health, work, and income. *Medical Care Research and Review*. 2003;60(2 Suppl):3S–75S.

136. Lee DC, Liang H, Shi L. The convergence of racial and income disparities in health insurance coverage in the United States. *International Journal of Equity Health*. 2021;20(1):96.

137. Williams DR, Collins C. U.S. socioeconomic and racial differences in health. In LaVeist TA, Isaac LA, eds. *Race, Ethnicity, and Health: A Public Health Reader*, 2nd ed. San Francisco, CA: Jossey-Bass; 2013:36.

138. Hamilton D, Cohen, J. Race still trumps class for black Americans. *The Guardian*. 2018. https://www.researchgate.net/profile/Jen-Cohen /publication/331097995_Race_still_trumps_class _for_black_Americans_-_Opinion_-_The_Guardian /links/5c6598e1299bf1d14cc74fb6/Race-still -trumps-class-for-black-Americans-Opinion-The -Guardian.pdf; Fuller-Thomson E, Nuru-Jeter A, Minkler M, Guralnik JM. Black-white disparities in disability among older Americans: Further untangling the role of race and socioeconomic status. *Journal of Aging and Health*. 2009;21(5):677–698.

139. Williams DR, Collins C. U.S. socioeconomic and racial differences in health. In LaVeist TA, Isaac LA, eds. *Race, Ethnicity, and Health: A Public Health Reader*. 2nd ed. San Francisco, CA: Jossey-Bass; 2013: 36.

140. Williams DR, Collins C. U.S. socioeconomic and racial differences in health. In LaVeist TA, Isaac LA, eds. *Race, Ethnicity, and Health: A Public Health Reader*. 2nd ed. San Francisco, CA: Jossey-Bass; 2013: 36.

141. Yearby R. Racial disparities in health status and access to health care: The continuation of inequality in the United States due to structural racism. *American Journal of Economics and Sociology*. 2018;77(3–4):1113–1152. https://doi.org/10.1111/ajes.12230; Brown T. The intersection and accumulation of racial and gender inequality: Black women's wealth trajectories. *The Review of Black Political Economy*. 2012;39:239–258; Brown D. *The Whiteness of Wealth*. New York, NY: Crown Publishing, 2021.

142. Yearby R. Racial disparities in health status and access to health care: The continuation of inequality in the United States due to structural racism. *American Journal of Economics and Sociology*. 2018;77(3–4):1113–1152. https://doi .org/10.1111/ajes.12230; Brown T. The intersection and accumulation of racial and gender inequality: Black women's wealth trajectories. *The Review of Black Political Economy*. 2012;39:239–258; Brown D. *The Whiteness of Wealth*. New York, NY: Crown Publishing, 2021.

143. Grumbach K, Braveman P, Adler N, Bindman AB. Vulnerable populations and health disparities: An overview. In King TE, Wheeler MB, Bindman AB, et al., eds. *Medical Management of Vulnerable and Underserved Populations: Principles, Practice and Populations*. New York, NY: McGraw Hill; 2007.

144. Yearby R. Structural racism and health disparities: Reconfiguring the social determinants of health framework to include the root cause. *Journal of Law, Medicine & Ethics*. 2020;48:518–526.

145. Williams R, Neighbors HW, Jackson JS. Racial/ ethnic discrimination and health: Findings from community studies. *American Journal of Public Health*. 2003;93(2):200–208; Williams, DR, Lawrence JA, Davis BA. Racism and health: Evidence and needed research. *Annual Review of Public Health*. 2019; 40:105–125.

146. Brown DR, et al. (Dis)respected and (dis)regarded: Experiences of racism and psychological distress. In Brown DR, Keith, VM, eds., *In and Out of Our Right Minds: The Mental Health of African American Women*; Columbia University Press (New York, NY). 2003; Collins Jr. JW, et al. Very low birthweight in African American Infants: The role of maternal exposure to interpersonal racial discrimination. *American Journal of Public Health*. 2004;94(12):2132–2138; Cozier Y, et al. Racial discrimination and the incidence of hypertension in US Black women. *American Journal of Epidemiology*. 2006;16(9):681–687; Cozier Y, et al. Racism, segregation, and risk of obesity in the Black women's health study. *American Journal of Epidemiology*. 2014;179(7):875–883; Krieger N. Racial and gender discrimination: Risk factors for high blood pressure? *Social Science & Medicine*. 1990;30(12):1273–1281; Owens TC, Jackson FM. Examining life-course socioeconomic position, contextualized stress, and depression among well-educated African-American pregnant women. *Women's Health Issue*. 2015;25(4):382–389; Platt J, et al. Unequal depression for equal work? How the wage gap explains gendered disparities in mood disorders. *Social Science & Medicine*. 2016;149:1–8; Sawyer PJ., et al. Discrimination and the stress response: Psychological and physiological consequences of anticipating prejudice in interethnic interactions. *American Journal of Public Health*. 2012;102(5):1020–1026; Velez BL, et al. Discrimination, work outcomes, and mental health among Women of Color: The protective role of womanist attitudes. *Journal of Counseling Psychology*. 2018;65(2):178–193.

147. Bridges KM. The dangerous law of biological race. *Fordham Law Review*. 2013;82:21–80.

148. Sawyer PJ, et al. Discrimination and the stress response: Psychological and physiological consequences of anticipating prejudice in interethnic interactions. *American Journal of Public Health*. 2012;102(5):1020–1026.

149. Shariff-Marco S, Klassen AC, Bowie JV. Racial/ethnic differences in self-reported racism and its association with cancer-related health behaviors. *American Journal of Public Health*. 2010;100(2):364–374.

150. Shariff-Marco S, Klassen AC, Bowie JV. Racial/ethnic differences in self-reported racism and its association with cancer-related health behaviors. *American Journal of Public Health*. 2010;100(2):364–374.

151. Shariff-Marco S, Klassen AC, Bowie JV. Racial/ethnic differences in self-reported racism and its association with cancer-related health behaviors. *American Journal of Public Health*. 2010;100(2):364–374.

152. Shariff-Marco S, Klassen AC, Bowie JV. Racial/ethnic differences in self-reported racism and its association with cancer-related health behaviors. *American Journal of Public Health*. 2010;100(2):364–374.

153. Bailey ZD, Krieger N, Agénor M, Graves J, Linos N, Bassett MT. Structural racism and health inequities in the USA: Evidence and interventions. *Lancet*. 2017;389:1453–1463.

154. Owens TC, Jackson FM. Examining life-course socioeconomic position, contextualized stress, and depression among well-educated African-American pregnant women. *Women's Health Issue*. 2015;25(4):382–389; Platt J, et al. Unequal depression for equal work? How the wage gap explains gendered disparities in mood disorders. *Social Science & Medicine*. 2016;149:1–8; Sawyer PJ, et al. Discrimination and the stress response: Psychological and physiological consequences of anticipating prejudice in interethnic interactions. *American Journal of Public Health*. 2012;102(5):1020–1026; Velez BL, et al. Discrimination, work outcomes, and mental health among Women of Color: The protective role of womanist attitudes. *Journal of Counseling Psychology*. 2018;65(2):178–193.

155. Khullar D. How prejudice can harm your health. *The New York Times*. June 8, 2017. https://www.nytimes.com/2017/06/08/upshot/how-prejudice-can-harm-your-health.html?mcubz=1.

156. Chae DH, Nuru-Jeter A, Adler NE, Brody GH, Lin J, Epel ES. Racial discrimination, implicit racial bias and telomeric age among African American midlife men. *American Journal of Preventive Medicine*. 2014;46(2):103–111.

157. Geronimus AT, Hicken M, Keene D, Bound J. Weathering and age patterns of allostatic load scores among Blacks and Whites in the United States. *American Journal of Public Health*. 2006;96(5):826–833.

158. Chae DH, Nuru-Jeter A, Adler NE, Brody GH, Lin J, Epel ES. Racial discrimination, implicit racial bias and telomeric age among African American midlife men. *American Journal of Preventive Medicine*. 2014;46(2):103–111.

159. Yearby R. Structural racism and health disparities: Reconfiguring the social determinants of health framework to include the root cause. *Journal of Law, Medicine & Ethics*. 2020;48:518–526.

160. Yearby R. Structural racism and health disparities: Reconfiguring the social determinants of health framework to include the root cause. *Journal of Law, Medicine & Ethics*. 2020;48:518–526; Dawes D. *The Political Determinants of Health*, Chapter 2. Baltimore, MD: Johns Hopkins University Press; 2020.

161. Ortiz-Ospina E, Roser M. Global health. Our World Data. Updated daily. https://ourworldindata.org/health-meta.

162. National Vital Statistics Report. Deaths: Final data for 2019. Centers for Disease Control and Prevention. July 2021. https://www.cdc.gov/nchs/data/nvsr/nvsr70/nvsr70-08-508.pdf.

163. The World Bank. Life expectancy at birth. 2022. https://data.worldbank.org/indicator/SP.DYN.LE00.MA.IN?most_recent_value_desc=true&view=chart.

164. National Vital Statistics Report. Deaths: Final data for 2019. Centers for Disease Control and Prevention. July 2021. https://www.cdc.gov/nchs/data/nvsr/nvsr70/nvsr70-08-508.pdf.

165. National Vital Statistics Report. Deaths: Final data for 2019. Centers for Disease Control and Prevention. July 2021. https://www.cdc.gov/nchs/data/nvsr/nvsr70/nvsr70-08-508.pdf.

166. Centers for Disease Control and Prevention. Infant mortality. September 8, 2021. https://www.cdc.gov/reproductivehealth/maternalinfanthealth/infantmortality.htm

167. Centers for Disease Control and Prevention. Infant mortality. September 8, 2021. https://www.cdc.gov/reproductivehealth/maternalinfanthealth/infantmortality.htm

168. Centers for Disease Control and Prevention. Pregnancy mortality surveillance system. November 25, 2020. https://www.cdc.gov/reproductivehealth/maternal-mortality/pregnancy-mortality-surveillance-system.htm.

169. Centers for Disease Control and Prevention. Pregnancy mortality surveillance system. November 25, 2020. https://www.cdc.gov/reproductivehealth/maternal-mortality/pregnancy-mortality-surveillance-system.htm.

170. Collins Jr. JW, et al. Very low birthweight in African American infants: The role of maternal exposure to interpersonal racial discrimination. *American Journal of Public Health*. 2004;94(12):2132–2138.

171. Centers for Disease Control and Prevention. Pregnancy mortality surveillance system. November 25, 2020. https://www.cdc.gov/reproductivehealth/maternal-mortality/pregnancy-mortality-surveillance-system.htm.

172. Centers for Disease Control and Prevention. Diabetes: Healthy People 2020 midcourse review. 2017. https://www.cdc.gov/nchs/data/hpdata2020/HP2020MCR-C08-Diabetes.pdf.

173. Centers for Disease Control and Prevention. Diabetes: Healthy People 2020 midcourse review. 2017. https://www.cdc.gov/nchs/data/hpdata2020/HP2020MCR-C08-Diabetes.pdf.

174. Centers for Disease Control and Prevention. Cancer: Healthy People 2020 midcourse review. 2017. https://www.cdc.gov/nchs/data/hpdata2020/CH05_Cancer_1.pdf.

175. Centers for Disease Control and Prevention. Cancer: Healthy People 2020 midcourse review. 2017. https://www.cdc.gov/nchs/data/hpdata2020/CH05_Cancer_1.pdf.

176. Centers for Disease Control and Prevention. Heart disease and stroke: Healthy People 2020 midcourse review. 2017. https://www.cdc.gov/nchs/data/hpdata2020/HP2020MCR-C21-HDS.pdf.

177. Centers for Disease Control and Prevention. Heart disease and stroke: Healthy People 2020 midcourse review. 2017. https://www.cdc.gov/nchs/data/hpdata2020/HP2020MCR-C21-HDS.pdf.

178. Centers for Disease Control and Prevention. Older adults: Healthy People 2020 midcourse review. 2017. https://www.cdc.gov/nchs/data/hpdata2020|/HP2020MCR-C31-OA.pdf.

179. Benfer EA, Wiley LF. Health justice strategies to combat COVID-19: Protecting vulnerable communities during a pandemic. Health Affairs Blog. 2020. https://www.healthaffairs.org/do/10.1377/hblog20200319.757883/full/; Benfer EA, Mohapatra S, Wiley LF, Yearby R. Health justice strategies to combat the pandemic: Eliminating discrimination, poverty, and health disparities during and after COVID-19. *Yale Journal of Health Policy, Law, and Ethics*. 2020;19(3):122–171.

180. CDC National Center for Chronic Disease Prevention and Health Promotion, Health Equity. 2020. https://www.cdc.gov/chronicdisease/healthequity/index.htm.

181. W.K. Kellogg Foundation, Truth, Racial Healing and Transformation. https://healourcommunities.org/.

182. Matthew DB. *Just Health: Treating Structural Racism to Heal America*. New York, NY: New York University Press, 2022; Matthew DB. *Just Medicine: A Cure for Racial Inequality in American Health Care*. New York, NY: New York University Press, 2015; Dawes D.

The Political Determinants of Health. Baltimore, MD: Johns Hopkins University Press; 2019.

183. Andrulis D, et al., H1N1 influenza pandemic and racially and ethnically diverse communities in the United States: Assessing the evidence of and charting opportunities for advancing health equity. US Department of Health and Human Services, Office of Minority Health. September 2012. https://www.researchgate.net/publication/340390150_H1N1_Influenza_Pandemic_and_Racially_and_Ethnically_Diverse_Communities_in_the_United_States_Assessing_the_Evidence_and_Charting_Opportunities_for_Advancing_Health_Equity.

184. Yearby R, et al. Governmental use of racial equity tools to address systemic racism and the social determinants of health, final report for *Are Cities and Counties Ready to Use Racial Equity Tools to Influence Policy?* Robert Wood Johnson Foundation Policies for Action grant. December 2021. https://ihje.org/wp-content/uploads/2021/12/Governmental-Use-of-Racial-Equity-Tools-to-Address-Systemic-Racism-and-the-Social-Determinants-of-Health.pdf.

185. Yearby R, Lewis C, Gilbert K, Banks K. Racism is a public health crisis. Here's how to respond. September 3, 2020. https://ihje.org/racism-is-a-public-health-crisis-report/.

186. Nelson J, Brooks L. GARE Racial Equity Toolkit: An opportunity to operationalize equity. December 2016. https://www.racialequityalliance.org/wp-content/uploads/2015/10/GARE-Racial_Equity_Toolkit.pdf.

187. DrePaul-Bruder J. Washtenaw County has declared racism a public health crisis. What are the county's next steps? Concentrate. July 15, 2020. https://www.secondwavemedia.com/concentrate/innovationnews/countypublichealthcrisis0555.aspx.

CHAPTER 11

Immigrants

16 pages

LEARNING OBJECTIVES

By the end of this chapter you will be able to:

- Describe briefly the history of U.S. immigration laws and how they have evolved based on policymakers' concerns about different immigration trends
- Explain how laws and policies governing immigrants' access to health insurance and other public benefits affect immigrants' health care access and health status
- Discuss immigrants' health status in the United States and some of the social and structural drivers that lead to existing inequities
- Consider possible options for amending laws and policies that will facilitate health justice for immigrants

Introduction

The United States has the largest number of immigrants of any country in the world. More than 40 million immigrants—people who are foreign-born—live in the United States, nearly 14% of the overall population.[1] Although some in the media and many lawmakers focus specifically on undocumented immigrants, more than three-quarters of foreign-born people in the United States have legal status, including U.S. citizenship (see **Figure 11.1**).

In recent years, there has been a rise in anti-immigrant rhetoric from U.S. lawmakers, combined with more aggressive enforcement policies designed to rid the country of undocumented immigrants and halt immigration by those presenting at the southern border—most of whom are fleeing extreme violence and poverty in their home countries. However, hostility from some policymakers and segments of the public has not only been directed at undocumented immigrants; it has often taken a racist tenor expressing hatred for foreign-born people as a whole.

Immigrant populations in the United States are not a monolithic group. Their experiences, health, and overall well-being vary significantly based on their socioeconomic status, how they were treated in their countries of origin, their reasons for migrating, and the resources and support networks available to them in the United States. Nonetheless,

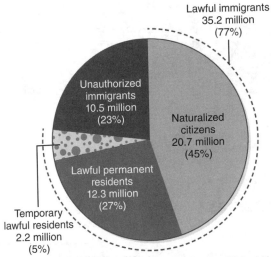

Note: Figure for the total and subgroups differ from published U.S. Census Bureau totals because census data have been augmented and adjusted to account for undercount of the population. All numbers are rounded. Unauthorized immigrants include some with temporary protection from deportation under Deferred Action for Childhood Arrivals (DACA) and Temporary Protected Status (TPS), as well as pending asylum cases.

Figure 11.1 Unauthorized immigrants are almost a quarter of U.S. foreign-born population

Budiman A. Key findings about U.S. immigrants. Pew Research Center. August 20, 2020. https://www.pewresearch.org/fact-tank/2020/08/20/key-findings-about-u-s-immigrants/

once they are in the United States, immigration status is fundamental to their ability to access a wide range of services and supports that implicate health, with direct health care services being only the most obvious. Thus, the ways in which federal, state, and local law and policy are applied to immigrant populations have serious implications for these populations' health and well-being.

This chapter explores the history and development of the law's treatment of immigration and the rights of immigrants residing within U.S. borders. It then describes how laws and policies that limit immigrants' rights compared to those of U.S.-born people serve as significant social and structural drivers of health, with consequential effects for health justice. It ends with suggestions for law and policy reforms targeted at promoting health justice for immigrants.

Treatment of Immigrants Under the Law

U.S. immigration law reaches back to the country's founding. It is one of the most complex areas of law. Thus, it is beyond the scope of this chapter to provide a comprehensive history or summary of immigration law. Instead, we present a brief overview of how immigration laws have developed and changed over time and then focus on how the law restricts immigrants' access to health care and other health-promoting supports and resources, depending on their immigration status. Indeed, as legal scholar Wendy Parmet notes, immigration laws serve as critical social and structural drivers of health.[2] Furthermore, as policymakers battle over whether and how to achieve universal health insurance coverage for U.S. citizens, immigrants continue to loom large in debates about who is deserving of government support and who is not. Before reading about the law's treatment of immigrants, first familiarize yourself with the definitions of the different types of immigration status in the United States in **Table 11.1**.

Table 11.1 Types of Immigration Status

Types of Immigration Status

U.S. citizen	A person who was born in the United States and is afforded all of the rights and privileges of U.S. citizenship.
Naturalized citizen	A person who is at least 18 years old, has been a lawful permanent resident (see below) for at least 3 years, and who has had continuous residence in the United States may apply to become a citizen. In addition, the person must demonstrate the ability to read, write, and speak English; good moral character; knowledge of U.S. history and government; loyalty to the U.S. Constitution; and willingness to take the Oath of Allegiance.[3]
Lawful permanent resident (LPR)	A person who has been granted authorization to live and work in the United States on a permanent basis. The card demonstrating proof of lawful residency is referred to as a "green card." Legal permanent residency is generally granted through sponsorship by a family member or an employer or through other status, such as being a refugee or asylee.
Refugee	A person living outside the United States who has a well-founded fear of persecution in their home country due to race, religion, nationality, membership in a particular social group, and/or political opinion.
Asylee	A person who presents at a U.S. port of entry or who is living in the United States who meets the preceding definition of *refugee*. An asylum seeker living in the United States must apply for this status within one year of entry.
Temporary protected status	A person living in the United States who cannot return home due to a natural disaster, extraordinary conditions, or ongoing armed conflict. TPS is granted for 6, 12, or 18 months and may be extended if conditions persist in the person's home country.
Other humanitarian programs that grant status	T visa Victim of Trafficking: A person who can demonstrate that they have been subject to sex trafficking (commercial sex acts through force, fraud or coercion or in which the person is under age 18) or labor trafficking (labor through force, fraud or coercion) may obtain a T Visa, which provides the benefits of lawful permanent residency. U visa Victims of crime who have suffered substantial physical or mental abuse. Violence Against Women Act protection Victims of domestic violence whose abuser is a U.S. citizen or lawful permanent resident. This protection allows the victim to self-petition for independent legal status.

VISA

A Brief History of U.S. Immigration Law

Since 1875, when the federal government began regulating immigration (prior to that it was essentially left to the states), the law has primarily been based on excluding those considered undesirable (often based on racism or other forms of discrimination) and on economics (mostly related to labor needs).[4] The Chinese Exclusion Act of 1882, for example, was a response to both the racist hostility and economic frustrations of White Californians.[5] The Immigration Act of 1882, the first federal law broadly regulating immigration, among other things, instituted screening for arriving immigrants; any person deemed a "convict, lunatic, idiot or person unable to take care of himself or herself without becoming a public charge"[6] was not allowed to enter the United States. (As discussed later, the "public charge" provision has remained part of immigration law since that time, and recent changes to the law under the Trump administration have been detrimental to immigrants' health and well-being.)

By 1921, due to concerns about the growing number of immigrants coming to the United States post–World War I, Congress passed the Emergency Quota Act, its first foray into setting quotas based on nationality.[7] Then, in 1942, during World War II labor shortages (many men were abroad fighting in the war), the United States entered into the Bracero Agreement with Mexico, allowing Mexicans to work in U.S. agricultural jobs. The act required that these workers be paid wages equal to American farmworkers and that transportation and living expenses be covered by employers. The agreement remained in place until 1964.[8] The quota system was then extended in the McCarren-Walter Act of 1952, this time including quotas for Asian countries, which had prior to this time been excluded. But by 1965, Congress changed course: Through the Hart-Cellar Act, it replaced the quota system with one that authorized admission based on employment or family unification. Apparently, some policymakers believed that using family unification as the basis of admission would lead mostly to European immigration, but the number of immigrants from Asia actually increased significantly during this time.[9] The law also set a cap on immigration from the Western Hemisphere, largely to reduce immigration of Latinx populations.[10]

It was not until 1980 that Congress created a system for admitting refugees and processing asylum seekers. (Refer back to Table 11.1 for definitions of refugees and asylees.) Although European refugees were admitted after World War II, the Refugee Act of 1980 laid out a statutory framework that defined who would be considered refugees and asylum seekers and that institutionalized the process by which these groups would be admitted and treated.[11] The number of refugee admissions is set by the president in consultation with Congress. Since 1980, the number has fluctuated, but it dropped precipitously in 2016 after the election of Donald Trump, who was hostile to any immigration, even for refugees and asylum seekers. Although the Biden administration raised the annual ceiling in 2020, the number of refugees is still well below the numbers admitted in past years.

By 1986, concerns about an influx of undocumented immigrants from Mexico prompted new federal legislation. The Immigration Reform and Control Act (IRCA) was a compromise between those seeking amnesty for undocumented immigrants living in the United States and those who wanted to crack down on illegal border crossings. The law provided a path to legal status for certain agricultural workers and for those immigrants living in the United States since 1982. At the same time, the law represented the first time that lawmakers made it a crime for employers to knowingly hire undocumented immigrant workers, and it significantly increased funding for border security. In the 1990s, as part of the "tough on crime" laws described in Chapter 9, Congress targeted immigrants, passing legislation that expanded grounds for deportation to "aggravated felonies" and again increasing border patrol funding. The linking of undocumented immigrants and crime culminated in the Illegal Immigration Reform and Immigrant Responsibility Act of 1996. This law, among other things, created new grounds for inadmissibility and deportation; increased the types of crimes defined as "aggravated felonies"; reduced judicial review of immigration decisions; and expanded detention for those immigrants previously convicted of a crime. The law also tightened procedural requirements for asylum seekers and developed a pilot program allowing states and local governments to enforce immigration laws.[12]

After the 9/11 terrorist attacks, Congress acted quickly in 2002 to increase terrorism-based exclusions for foreigners (especially people from the Middle East and from Islamic nations) entering the United States and create the Department of Homeland Security to oversee all aspects of immigration enforcement. Since the mid-2000s, Congress has been unable to achieve compromise on major immigration reform despite it being a priority on both sides of the aisle. Unable to reach agreement with Congress on a legislative solution, President Barack Obama signed an executive order in 2012 announcing the Deferred Action for Childhood Arrivals (DACA) program. The new policy allowed undocumented immigrants who entered the country before the age of 16 and who had lived in the United States since 2007 to be protected from deportation and to apply for work permits. Permits were renewable so long as the applicant continued to meet program requirements. Litigation challenging President Obama's authority to create the DACA program has been ongoing since its initiation; in July 2021, a U.S. District Court in Texas held that DACA is unlawful, but it maintained protection and benefits for DACA

recipients who applied before the date of its decision, pending further appeal.[13]

Like Obama, Trump used his executive authority to determine the fates of immigrants, though Trump's actions were focused on placing limits on admissions of immigrants and restricting the rights of immigrants living in the United States. The Migration Policy Institute issued a report in 2020 cataloguing the more than 400 policy changes made through executive action between 2016 and 2020. These changes were wide-reaching, affecting, among other policies, immigration enforcement at the border and inside the United States; judicial discretion in immigration cases; rules governing treatment of refugees, asylum seekers, child immigrants, and victims of trafficking; and the response to the COVID-19 pandemic as it related to immigrants.[14] While it is possible for the Biden administration to reverse many of these policy changes because they were instituted through executive action, policy change will take time and requires prioritization by the administration.

Laws Governing Immigrants' Access to Health Care and Other Government Supports

One of the most controversial issues related to immigration policy is the law's role in defining immigrants' access to publicly funded education, health care, and government assistance programs—as the Temporary Assistance for Needy Family program, the Supplemental Nutrition Assistance Program, and housing subsidies. (See Chapter 7 for detailed discussion of these programs). As described later, an individual's immigration status plays a large role in determining that person's access to government programs and benefits.

In general, undocumented immigrants are excluded from access to publicly funded programs. But when faced with whether undocumented immigrant children have a right to a public education, the Supreme Court was persuaded that they do. In *Plyler v. Doe* (1982), the court considered whether the Equal Protection Clause of the U.S. Constitution was violated by a Texas law that withheld state funds from school districts for the education of undocumented children and authorized districts to deny enrollment to these kids. The level of scrutiny the Court applies in equal protection cases depends on whether the group experiencing differential treatment is considered a suspect class, as noted in Chapter 4. In this case, the class was undocumented immigrant children, not a specific ethnic or racial group. (Race and ethnicity are both treated as suspect classes.) Thus, the Court applied a rational basis standard of review—meaning that the state only needed to demonstrate that the differential treatment was rationally related to a legitimate government interest. In finding that Texas did not have a rational basis for the law, the Court rejected the state's argument that it had an interest in the "preservation of the state's limited resources for the education of its lawful residents."[15] The Court acknowledged that laws treating undocumented immigrants may be permissible when aligned with federal immigration policy. But it found that the denial of a public education would render a "lifetime hardship on a discrete class of children not accountable for their disabling status."[16]

While *Plyler* was a landmark case in prohibiting states and local school districts from discriminating against children based on their immigration status, the Court's decision was narrow; it did not expand antidiscrimination law to all undocumented immigrants in every context. State laws that discriminate against immigrants with legal status, however, are subject to strict scrutiny under the Equal Protection Clause because, as applied to lawful immigrants, the state would be treating people differently based on their alienage, not whether they are in the country without legal documentation.[17] At the same time, federal laws treating immigrants—even those with legal status—differently from U.S.

citizens are only subject to rational basis review. This is because the Court views the federal government's plenary constitutional authority to regulate immigration as providing wide leeway for how it treats immigrants of all kinds.[18]

The complexity of the law's treatment of immigrants reflects some of the country's ambivalence about—and often hostility toward—the role of immigrants in American society and policymakers' uncertainty about how to structure immigration policies, particularly as they pertain to immigrants who have lived in the United States for a long period of time. The idea of granting amnesty to immigrants who have come to the United States without going through the legal process strikes some as rewarding bad behavior, while others focus on the contribution that immigrants—documented or undocumented—make to the U.S. economy and cultural diversity. Hence, taxpayer-funded government assistance programs become a flashpoint both for polarized views about how to control the flow of immigrants and for moral arguments about how to treat those who do—and do not—follow the rules.

Access to Health Care and Other Government Assistance Programs

Immigrants' access to health care under the law is complicated by the maze of government policies, public and private insurance providers, and the diversity of clinical institutions and programs that make up the U.S. health care system. As there is no universal right to health care services or insurance in the United States, immigrants' health care rights are carved out of various programs and policies. First, as discussed in Chapter 4, the one universal right to access health care in federal law is through the Examination and Treatment for Emergency Medical Conditions and Women in Labor Act (commonly referred to as "EMTALA," after its original title), which prohibits hospitals that participate in the Medicare program from turning away without an examination any person—including documented and undocumented immigrants—who presents at a hospital emergency department. To help cover hospital costs associated with treating low-income undocumented immigrants in emergencies or during labor, Congress appropriates "Emergency Medicaid" funding to states. To qualify for Emergency Medicaid, the immigrant must meet all of the eligibility requirements for the traditional Medicaid program (e.g., income eligibility). With EMTALA, the American public and Congress have demonstrated an unwillingness to let undocumented immigrants go without lifesaving care in an emergency. But this largesse does not extend to any legal rights that grant immigrants the ability to access regular primary or specialty care.

Another area of law pertaining to health care access for immigrants is the availability of language services for patients with limited English proficiency (LEP). Title VI of the Civil Rights Act (discussed in Chapter 6) says that "[n]o person in the United States shall, on the ground of race, color, or national origin, be excluded from participation in, be denied the benefits of, or be subjected to discrimination."[19] In 2000, President Bill Clinton signed Executive Order 13166: Improving Access to Persons with LEP, which provided guidance to federally funded entities, including health care institutions, to ensure that "their programs and activities normally provided in English are accessible to LEP persons and thus do not discriminate on the basis of national origin."[20] Despite the interpretation of Title VI as including access to language services, many health care institutions fail to provide adequate access, resulting in poor quality care and sometimes adverse events that harm health.[21]

Concerns about spending taxpayer dollars on health care for immigrants and wariness about immigrants coming into the United States to take advantage of its health care system, have also led to differential treatment in public and private insurance coverage. Undocumented immigrants are ineligible for Medicaid and Medicare; they are also ineligible for subsidies or to buy private insurance through the health insurance exchanges created by the Affordable Care Act (ACA). There are also restrictions placed on lawful permanent residents' access to publicly funded health insurance. When Congress passed the Personal Responsibility and Work Opportunity Reconciliation Act (PRWORA) in 1996—the so-called "welfare reform" law (see Chapter 7)—it created a new category of immigrants called "qualified aliens," deemed to be eligible for federal public benefits.[22] Qualified immigrants include legal permanent residents, refugees and asylees, and others with specific types of legal status. Along with undocumented immigrants, people on short-term visas (e.g., student visas, some work visas) are unqualified.

But being deemed a qualified immigrant does not provide automatic access to Medicaid and Medicare eligibility. With PRWORA, Congress established that some qualified immigrants are only eligible for Medicaid after 5 years from the time they entered the United States. Legal permanent residents are subject to the 5-year waiting period. However, some qualified immigrants, such as refugees, victims of trafficking, and those granted asylum, are eligible for Medicaid upon entry to the country. Notably, DACA recipients are not considered lawfully present and are therefore ineligible for all types of publicly supported health insurance coverage available through Medicaid and the ACA, including the subsidies and tax credits available to purchase coverage through the insurance exchanges.[23] See **Table 11.2** for a list of immigrants who are eligible and ineligible for Medicaid.

While some qualified immigrants are subject to a waiting period before they can access Medicaid and unqualified immigrants

Table 11.2 Non-Exhaustive Description of Noncitizen Eligibility for Medicaid Under Federal Law

Eligible Without Five-Year Ban (upon entry)	Eligible but Subject to Five-Year Ban	Ineligible
■ Refugees, asylees, victims of trafficking, veterans, Supplemental Security Income recipients	■ Lawful permanent residents (i.e., noncitizens holding green cards); parolees (if parole is one year or more); self-petitioners under the Violence Against Women Act	■ Unauthorized immigrants, DACA beneficiaries, asylum seekers, Certain employment-based visa and student visa holders

Data from Lacarte V, Greenburg M, Capps R. Medicaid Access and Participation: A Data Profile of Eligible and Ineligible Immigrant Adults. Migration Policy Institute. October 2021.

may not access it under federal law, states do have the option to use their own funds to provide coverage to any immigrants they choose. About half of the states provide Medicaid coverage to eligible qualified immigrants (i.e., if they are deemed qualified and they meet the other eligibility criteria for Medicaid, such as income limits) who otherwise would be subject to the 5-year waiting period.[24] Five states and the District of Columbia fund Medicaid-like coverage for many immigrants who are excluded under federal program rules. California covers undocumented immigrants ages 19 to 26 and will extend that coverage to adults over age 50 in 2022.[25]

The "complex maze of waiting periods, exceptions, and exceptions to those exceptions"[26] created by PRWORA does not just apply to government-funded health care coverage. As with Medicaid, some qualified immigrants are subject to the 5-year waiting period before they can access the Temporary Assistance for Needy Family (TANF) program and the Supplemental Nutrition Assistance Program (SNAP). Again, states may use their own funds to extend eligibility to those subject to the waiting period or to unqualified immigrants. Legal permanent residents are eligible for federal subsidized housing programs; undocumented immigrants and those with temporary status are not.[27]

The Public Charge Rule

As it stands, even immigrants who are eligible for a range of government benefits may be reluctant to apply for them. As mentioned earlier, even before federal immigration laws were enacted, some states barred entry to immigrants who were deemed likely to be a "public charge," meaning that the immigrants were poor and considered likely to burden state budgets. The Immigration Act of 1882 excluded any immigrant deemed unable to care for themselves without becoming a public charge. Since then, federal regulations have governed the criteria for determining when an immigrant entering the country or one seeking permanent residency would be considered likely to become a public charge. While controversial among some immigration advocates, the public charge rule did not receive a great deal of attention until the Trump administration dramatically revised the long-standing criteria for public charge determination.

In August 2019, U.S. Citizenship and Immigration Services (USCIS) announced the new rule, which would classify an immigrant seeking admission to the country or for lawful permanent resident status as likely to become a public charge if that person had participated in any of the following public benefit programs for more than 12 months in any 36-month period: TANF, SNAP, Medicaid, and public housing assistance programs.

Prior guidance had only considered public benefit programs that focused on cash assistance (e.g., TANF), income maintenance (Social Security Disability Income), or long-term care funded by Medicaid. The Trump rule only applied to those immigrants seeking permanent residency, not to those who were already lawful permanent residents. It did not apply to humanitarian immigrants, such as refugees, asylees, or survivors of domestic violence or trafficking. Nonetheless, the rule's inclusion of a broad array of public benefits that many people—citizens and noncitizens alike—rely on, coupled with the Trump administration's harsh rhetoric against immigrants in other contexts, invoked tremendous fear in immigrant communities regardless of status. Many immigrants feared that their participation in public benefit programs would lead to deportation.

President Biden has refused to support the Trump-era amended rule; as a result, several states have sued the administration for refusing to defend the rule after a federal court stopped it from going into effect. At the time of this writing, the case is still pending in the Supreme Court.[28] Nonetheless, as discussed previously, fear of the rule has had a devastating effect on legal immigrants' access to public benefits that are key social drivers of health—health insurance, food assistance, and housing. (See Chapter 7 for discussion of how these programs are linked to health.)

The public charge rule was not the only Trump administration policy with serious ramifications for the health of immigrants. Researchers have documented how anti-immigration rhetoric and policy have harmful effects on immigrants' mental health, physical health, and health care utilization.[29] For example, one study found that preterm births increased for Latina mothers after the 2016 election, in which anti-immigrant rhetoric and policy proposals were highly publicized.[30] Immigrants at the U.S. border

experienced numerous health harms associated with changes in immigration policy. Most visible was the policy of separating immigrant children from their parents. Parent–child separation is associated with significant toxic stress, leading to a range of negative health outcomes. A 2018 study found that children who were separated from their families at the border had a significantly higher risk of emotional and behavioral problems.[31]

Treatment of Immigrants by the Health Care System

Medical Examination of Immigrants Entering the United States

Medical historians Howard Markel and Alexandra Minna Stern note that in American history, immigrants have long been associated with disease: "Anti-immigrant rhetoric and policy have often been framed by an explicitly medical language, one in which the line between perceived and actual threat is slippery and prone to hysteria and hyperbole."[32] Throughout history, policymakers have drawn on the notion that immigrants export diseases—infectious, chronic, disabling, and mental—from their home countries to the United States and that to protect the public's health, immigrants must be excluded or at least meticulously screened. As the federal government began to take control of processing new immigrants at U.S. borders at the turn of the twentieth century, immigrants were subjected to rigorous government-sponsored medical and psychological testing. While most immigrants passed medical exams and were admitted into the country, some were sent back to their home countries or detained in border hospitals until they were deemed free from disease.[33]

The medical screening process was often tainted by racist and anti-Semitic assumptions about the physical inferiority of foreigners: "Asians were portrayed as feeble and infested with hookworm, Mexicans as lousy, and eastern European Jews as vulnerable to trachoma, tuberculosis, and—a favorite 'wastebasket diagnosis of nativists in the early 1900s—'poor physique.'"[34] At Ellis Island, where thousands of immigrants were processed in the late nineteenth and early twentieth centuries, medical screening was viewed as preventing entry of "undesirable people," and the physicians conducting the screenings often regarded immigrants as deviously attempting to conceal their ailments or disabilities by evading examination.[35]

Association of immigrants with "germs and contagion" helped fuel American fears about how immigrants would alter the nation's health and also its social fabric. For example, the U.S. ban on HIV-positive immigrants entering the country—which lasted from 1988 to 2010—was presented to the public as necessary to protect Americans from a communicable disease. However, HIV is not spread through casual contact, and, in fact, at the time the ban was implemented, there were more cases of HIV in the United States than in other countries. The HIV ban helped further cement the false notion that immigrants were bringing HIV into the United States and were coming to the United States to avail themselves of the health care system.[36] As Patricia Illingsworth and Wendy Parmet demonstrate in their book *The Health of Newcomers: Immigration, Health Policy, and the Case for Global Solidarity,* many misconceptions about immigrants' health fuel public perceptions and public policy. The authors point out that immigrants are often believed to be sicker than natives and perceived to live unhealthy lifestyles, neither of which are borne out by the evidence.[37] Indeed, as discussed later in the chapter, immigrants actually have better health than native residents of the United States, at least initially.

There is no question that, as all aspects of life have become more global and as new and emerging infectious disease outbreaks—avian flu, SARS, Ebola, and now COVID-19—continue to threaten public health, the role of medical screening in the immigration context remains highly relevant. Yet the racist political rhetoric and hate crimes against Asian Americans during the COVID-19 pandemic demonstrate the power of deeply imbedded misperceptions about immigrants and the origins of disease. Linking the pandemic to a specific group of immigrants (or people perceived to be immigrants) perpetuates a long-standing faulty (and, in this case, dangerous) narrative.

Access to Quality Health Care

Immigrants face a number of access barriers to health care. These barriers often depend upon an immigrant's legal, socioeconomic, insurance, and health status as well as literacy level, English proficiency, and cultural expectations and prior experiences of health care. We begin by describing the many challenges immigrants face in accessing health insurance and then consider different types of barriers to health care based on legal status.

Immigrants, both those who are lawfully present and those who are undocumented, are significantly less likely to have health insurance than U.S. citizens. While roughly one in 10 citizens is uninsured, a quarter of legal permanent residents and nearly half of undocumented immigrants are uninsured (see **Figure 11.2**). While 5% of citizen children with citizen parents are uninsured, 21% of lawfully present children and 35% of undocumented children are uninsured.[38]

Some immigrants with legal status may forgo enrolling in publicly funded programs out of fear that doing so will be used by the government to deport them or deny a later application to adjust their status. Confusion over how immigration policies apply to different categories of immigrants, especially

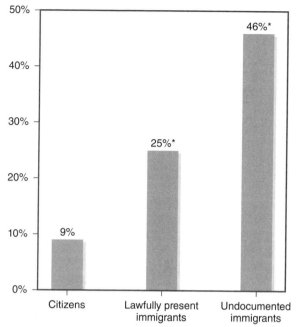

Note: *Indicates a statistically significant difference from citizens at the *p* < 0.05 level.v

Figure 11.2 Uninsured rates among nonelderly population by immigration status, 2019

Henry J. Kaiser Family Foundation. Health Coverage of Immigrants. July 15, 2021. https://www.kff.org/racial-equity-and-health-policy/fact-sheet/health-coverage-of-immigrants/

with regard to the proposed public charge rule changes and other punitive enforcement policies by the Trump administration, has led to some immigrants not applying for or disenrolling in publicly funded and supported health insurance programs, even when they were eligible and were not subject to the public charge rule changes.[39] Additionally, even when immigrants are able to maintain health insurance coverage, perceptions about anti-immigrant hostility from policymakers, state and local authorities, and even health care providers may stifle health care utilization. For example, a study of local enforcement of federal immigration laws, as authorized by the Section 287(g) of the Immigration and Nationality Act and Secure Communities program, found that pregnant Latina women, fearful of local authorities, delayed prenatal care and received lower-quality care than non-Latina pregnant women. The study authors note that fears were generalized across populations (undocumented and documented) and that increasing immigrants' knowledge of the legal rights and eligibility for health care services is important.[40]

Cultural and language barriers can also make accessing quality health care extremely challenging for some immigrants. Depending on their country of origin, immigrants may have little experience of formal health care and especially of complex systems like the ones in the United States. Navigating U.S. health care is challenging enough for people who are accustomed to it and who speak, read, and write English fluently. For many immigrants, especially those from low-income countries and those who do not speak English, the U.S. health care maze can be overwhelming.

Roughly 25 million people in the United States have limited English proficiency.

While, as discussed previously, Title VI of the 1964 Civil Rights Act requires health care institutions accepting federal funding to provide appropriate language services to patients, many do not employ a sufficient number of trained interpreters or have functional technology for interpretation (such as telephone or videoconferencing with a trained interpreter). Indeed, studies show that only 13% of hospitals meet all four of the U.S. Department of Health and Human Services' National Standards for Culturally and Linguistically Appropriate Services (CLAS) for health care.[41] It is not uncommon for health care providers to rely on patients' family members or bilingual medical staff who are not trained interpreters. This is despite the fact that the federal guidelines from the HHS Office for Civil Rights explicitly require health care providers to "inform LEP patients that they have the right to an interpreter without charge."[42] Even when professional interpreters are available, some clinicians may not employ their services in order to save time.[43] Yet "[u]se of professional medical interpreters is associated with decreased health disparities for patients with LEP, improved patient comprehension, fewer medical errors, and greater patient and clinician satisfaction compared to use of ad hoc interpreters, such as family members or bilingual staff."[44] Language barriers can have profound consequences not only for quality of care but also for health. For example, one study showed that Latinx children living in households with non-English primary language "have a significantly higher odds of perforation of the appendix than non-Latino children in English primary language households."[45]

Given their ineligibility for public health insurance programs, combined with the challenges discussed previously, undocumented immigrants face the greatest barriers to health care. Undocumented immigrants are more likely to be of lower socioeconomic status, exacerbating health inequities and poor access

to care.[46] Fear of deportation and poor bargaining power with employers when seeking time off from work also contribute to delayed or avoided health care. Federally qualified health centers (FQHCs) and "free clinics" supported by philanthropy and volunteer clinicians are open to immigrants without regard to status. But structural barriers, such as lack of transportation and/or child care, the inability to take off time from work, and fears about encountering immigration enforcement authorities, create obstacles to regular, preventive care. Tellingly, clinicians at FQHCs reported an increase in "no shows" among immigrant patients during the Trump administration's heightened immigration enforcement efforts.[47]

The COVID-19 pandemic has illuminated many of the access barriers experienced by immigrants—particularly undocumented immigrants—and these barriers' grave consequences for health. First, because immigrants disproportionately work in service industry jobs (e.g., restaurants, food services) that were lost during shutdowns, they were at heightened risk for becoming uninsured.[48] Second, immigrants may have been more reluctant to seek health care due to lack of insurance or fears about deportation. Third, COVID-19 was a "compounder of disadvantage (fear of unemployment and eviction, lack of safeguards for undocumented immigrants, inability to protect self from COVID-19, and high-density housing)"[49] that demonstrated inequities for immigrants. Fourth, the typical barriers to care experienced by immigrants described earlier (lack of language services, poor provider communication, challenges in system navigation) are even more acute during the public health crisis. Although there is an absence of national data comparing COVID-19 outcomes between foreign-born and U.S.-born people, a study in Minnesota found that COVID-19 deaths of foreign-born people were two times higher in the state than those of U.S.-born people. Foreign-born people were also more likely to die earlier in the pandemic and outside residential settings.[50]

Policies governing access to health insurance pose significant barriers to immigrants' access to care, especially for undocumented immigrants. U.S. policymakers and the public continue to debate whether undocumented immigrants should have access to taxpayer-funded services. Opponents argue that providing access to these programs will both stimulate more immigration by offering immigrants better health care than that available in their home countries and encourage people to immigrate outside the legal process. Proponents of providing access to health insurance and health care to undocumented immigrants suggest that not only is it unethical and unjust to deny access to care based on immigration status, but it is also costly. Immigrants who delay or forgo preventive health care become sicker, making them more likely to require more expensive emergency and inpatient services.

Addressing language access in health care requires both short-term and long-term structural changes in the health care system. As noted earlier, language services are profoundly inadequate in many health care institutions and practices. Health care system investment in these services not only improves quality of care for LEP patients and improves efficiency for providers, but it also improves health outcomes and reduces inequities. Working with interpreters and language interpretation technology should be part of routine training for health care providers. But research also demonstrates that quality of care is better and patient and provider satisfaction are higher when there is language concordance between the provider and the patient.[51] Clearly, in a country as diverse as the United States, matching the health care workforce to the patient population will take time. However, policymakers and health care institutions can commit to

building language proficiency among and increasing the diversity of the health care workforce. Because immigrants often have greater unmet social needs than the general population and experience intersectional issues—discrimination based on race, ethnicity, socioeconomic status, language, gender—health institutions and practices that serve large immigrant patient populations should also invest in comprehensive services and team-based care models that are responsive to these needs.[52]

Clinicians also play a critical role in supporting refugees through the resettlement process. While, as discussed earlier, the number of refugees coming to the United States has declined dramatically in recent years, the number will likely fluctuate over time with each new presidential administration. Refugees often have complex physical and mental health care needs having fled from violence, war, and oppressive regimes. There are not enough clinical practices that are devoted to caring for refugees. Specialized refugee clinics provide a welcoming environment and employ well-trained clinicians who are familiar with the common health conditions, risks, and barriers to care prevalent in the refugee populations they serve and who are multilingual and/or skilled at working with interpreters. Since many refugees have experienced trauma, comprehensive trauma-informed care is also vital.[53]

Social and Structural Drivers of Immigrant Health Inequities

Social and Structural Drivers of Health

As noted at the beginning of the chapter, immigration law is a potent social and structural driver of health. The chapter thus far has highlighted how immigration policies that restrict access to health care based on an immigrant's legal status have a powerful impact on health. But by structuring immigrants' access to a diverse array of social and economic supports—public benefits like SNAP, TANF, and housing subsidies—restrictive laws and policies also implicate health by relegating many immigrants to perpetually low socioeconomic status.[54] As discussed earlier, anti-immigrant political rhetoric and policies discourage immigrants who are eligible for these supports from seeking them out of fear. Indeed, trauma generated by fear of deportation and family separation has been shown to have a profound effect on children's physical and mental health. During the Trump presidency, pediatricians treating children of immigrant parents noted an increase in trauma-induced health concerns—psychosomatic issues like headaches and stomachaches, behavioral changes such as problems with sleeping and eating and acting out in school, and mental health problems including depression and anxiety. They also expressed concerns about the long-term consequences of this trauma on future health, given the research on toxic stress.[55]

Furthermore, immigrants' experiences of discrimination in the United States are a significant social driver of health. Daily experiences of discrimination are important contributors to chronic stress affecting both physical and mental health. (See Chapters 7 and 10 for further discussion of research on discrimination and health.) Immigrants' experiences of discrimination vary, at least initially, from those of U.S.-born People of Color. Immigrants "acquire minority status within U.S. society after arrival."[56] Minority status and the discrimination that is often associated with it can be jarring to immigrants who have lived in more ethnically homogenous countries. Experiences of discrimination reportedly increase for immigrants over time, and the degree and

prevalence of these experiences may be related to darkness of skin tone and English language proficiency.[57] Depending on status, immigrants are more susceptible to exploitation by employers and may experience discrimination in housing and in health care. For undocumented immigrants, the insecurity and fear associated with the threat of deportation and family separation, combined with discrimination, exploitation, and the inability to exercise many legal rights afforded to U.S. citizens and immigrants with legal status, produce very stressful lives. Indeed, if "stress is a physiological response of the body in the presence of stressors, 'conditions of threat, challenge, demands, or structural constraints,'"[58] then it would appear that immigrants—and, most especially, undocumented immigrants—and their families encounter health-harming chronic stress. Social support—strong family and friend relationships and ties to one's community—can provide an important buffer against discrimination and stress.[59]

Many immigrants, particularly refugees and those seeking asylum, come to the United States to escape poverty, violence, torture, persecution, and oppression in their home countries, and some, especially undocumented immigrants, suffer extreme hardship in their migration journeys, affecting both their physical and mental health. This history, coupled with significant social disadvantage in the United States—as a group, immigrants are more likely than natives to be poor, live in substandard housing, work in low-wage jobs without benefits, have language barriers affecting access to health care and education, and experience stigma and discrimination—sets many immigrants up for poor health.[60]

Health Inequities

Given that immigrants are generally of lower socioeconomic status than U.S. citizens, the fact that immigrants tend to have better health than U.S.-born people has been called the "immigrant health paradox."[61] Some have explained this paradox by suggesting that immigrants may return to their home countries when they become sick or disabled (and thus those who stay are relatively healthy); others suggest that there is selection bias in those who immigrate to the United States (i.e., those who manage to leave their homes and journey to a new country are likely to be healthy and resourceful).[62] However, a large body of evidence demonstrates that the immigrant health advantage disappears over time.[63] In particular, studies show that the prevalence of obesity—an important predictor of chronic diseases like diabetes, coronary heart disease, and high blood pressure—increases over time in immigrants across multiple ethnic groups. Researchers speculate that the decline in health over time is a function of acculturation—the adoption of an American lifestyle, including relatively high-calorie diets and sedentary way of living—leading to worsening health over time and over generations for immigrants and their families.[64]

Socioeconomic and other social drivers of health appear to catch up with immigrants, particularly for second and third generations. For example, Latina immigrants "enjoy surprisingly favorable birth outcomes despite their social disadvantages."[65] Researchers posit that this may be due to "protective factors" associated with "strong cultural support for maternity."[66] Foreign-born Latinas are also less likely than U.S.-born women to smoke, drink alcohol, or use drugs during pregnancy. But with acculturation, these protective factors erode with each successive generation, and birth outcomes of later-generation Latinas worsen. As some researchers point out, low birth weight, typically used to measure birth outcomes, fails to account for high pregnancy risks associated with being overweight (e.g., gestational

diabetes, preeclampsia), which are more prevalent in Latinas.[67]

Because immigrants are a heterogeneous population, coming from many different countries of origin, rates of chronic and infectious disease vary significantly across groups. While foreign-born immigrants generally are less likely to have chronic diseases than U.S.-born residents, this not true for all immigrant groups. For example, South Asian immigrants have a higher cardiovascular risk profile upon entry to the country than other immigrant groups, and this risk remains high for this group as they reside in the United States.[68] Latinx children are 1.8 times more likely to be obese than White children, setting them on a course for a number of chronic diseases in adulthood.[69] The incidences of cancers associated with diet, exercise, and other health behaviors are generally lower among immigrants than native-born people, but as with other chronic diseases, these risks increase with a longer duration spent in the United States. Some cancers associated with infectious disease are more prevalent in immigrant groups, depending on country of origin.[70]

Mental health disorders also vary greatly depending on the circumstances by which an immigrant migrates to the United States. Overall, rates of depression and mood disorders tend to be lower among new immigrants than for U.S.-born residents; however, rates among children of immigrants are more comparable with their peers. Refugees are at high risk for mental health problems related to trauma associated with violence, torture, war, and forced migration. They have substantially higher rates of posttraumatic stress disorder, somatic complaints, and depression.[71] As detailed earlier, immigrants also confront stigma, discrimination, and fear driven by anti-immigrant policies, all of which take a significant toll on their mental health.

Law, Policy, and Structural Change to Achieve Health Justice

Immigration policy is one of the most polarizing issues confronting the American public and U.S. lawmakers. Agreement over key concerns seem distant on the horizon. Nonetheless, we focus below on a few law, policy, and structural reforms targeted toward achieving health justice for immigrants.

Create a Path to Legal Status for Undocumented Immigrants

Of 10.5 million undocumented immigrants, 66% have lived in the United States for more than 10 years.[72] More than 7 million immigrant workers—about 4.6% of the U.S. workforce—are undocumented. It is estimated that immigrants pay as much as $23 billion in taxes each year.[73] These people have built their lives in the United States. Many have children who were born in the United States and contribute meaningfully to their communities. Rather than creating narrow programs to provide temporary status to immigrants who have lived most of their lives in the United States (e.g., DACA recipients), immigration policy should provide reasonable opportunities for undocumented immigrants to achieve permanent status. Punitive U.S. policies that relegate undocumented immigrants to the shadows of American society and that instill constant fear of detention, deportation, and/or family separation, harm the health of immigrant families and tear apart local communities. The consequences of the aggressive enforcement policies of the Trump administration to root out and deport undocumented immigrants produced fear in many immigrant communities, even for those who are documented. Demonizing certain immigrant groups has caused long-term damage for immigrants' health, particularly for children.

Provide Access to Health Care to People Living within U.S. borders, Regardless of Status

The U.S. patchwork system of eligibility for health insurance coverage and access to health care, with the exception of emergency care, takes a heavy toll on immigrants' health. Although the United States fails to provide access to health care for all U.S. citizens (see Chapter 7), immigrants—both those with status and those without—are most likely to be uninsured. The 5-year waiting period for lawful permanent residents to qualify for Medicaid leaves them vulnerable to health threats that harm their long-term health and that of the U.S. economy. The inability to access preventive care only leads to costlier long-term health care needs. Excluding undocumented immigrants from access to insurance, except in life-threatening circumstances, is shortsighted and inhumane.

Only slightly more than a third of Americans polled say that they favor providing health insurance to undocumented immigrants.[74] Few policymakers are willing to publicly support such a policy. But studies show that forgoing preventive care is extremely costly to the U.S. health care system as undocumented immigrants seek acute care in emergency rooms for serious conditions that could have been averted.[75] As has been evident from the COVID-19 pandemic, immigrants' access to health care, without fear of repercussions, is vital to stopping the spread of infectious disease; it is also ethical and just.

[handwritten margin note: cost benefit Studies ?]

Other high-income countries have made health care available to all immigrants regardless of documentation. Countries like Italy, Belgium, and the Netherlands extend the same access to their health care systems to undocumented immigrants as they do to their citizens.[76] Indeed, international law supports health care equity for immigrants, including those who are undocumented. The UN's Global Compact for Safe, Orderly and Regular Migration calls for equal access to health care for all migrants regardless of status. Among all 193 United Nations members, the United States is the only country unwilling to endorse the compact.[77]

[handwritten margin note: W/ above & not legally binding compact]

Address the Social and Structural Drivers That Harm Immigrants' Health

The Trump administration's proposed changes to the public charge rule raised awareness among some policymakers and segments of the public about the importance of equitable access to safety net programs for immigrants. Although there is still heated debate about extending access to these programs to undocumented immigrants, many viewed the proposed public charge rule as intending to encourage many immigrants, even those with legal status, to forgo applying for these supports. The growing attention to the social and structural drivers of health—being able to access health care, sufficient income, food, and housing as well as being free from stigma, discrimination, and violence—has made clear that immigrants' health is strongly correlated to social disadvantage and legal exclusion. This disadvantage may stem from experiences in their home countries, but the evidence that immigrants' health worsens the longer they live in the United States strongly suggests that social factors in this country play a large role in immigrant health inequities.

Concerns that extending access to health care and other health-promoting supports to immigrants will lead to a deluge of new undocumented immigrants are not borne out by the evidence.[78] Rather than perpetuating shortsighted policies that U.S. services and jobs are a zero-sum game—citizens win if immigrants lose, and vice versa—a more nuanced policy approach accounts for the contributions immigrants make to the U.S. economy and social fabric and recognizes that extending preventive health and other services to all residents is a win-win for the country. Not only does doing so reduce long-term costs associated with inequality, poverty, and preventable disease, it also invests in the second and third generations—fostering a productive workforce that will contribute to the United States for years to come.

Conclusion

This chapter outlined the history of immigration laws in the United States and some of the attitudes and misconceptions about immigrants upon which they have been built. The perpetual tension between those who view immigrants as important contributors to the country's economy and diverse culture and those who fear immigrants as a threat to the American way of life makes thoughtful and practical legal and policy change extremely unlikely anytime soon. Meanwhile, laws and policies directed at making immigrants' lives more dangerous and difficult—and how aggressively they are enforced—have enormous consequences for immigrants' health and well-being. Although policies may fluctuate with changing presidential administrations, the insecurity felt by immigrants; their limited access to health care; and their experiences of stigma, discriminatory treatment, and hostility make health justice difficult to achieve. Rethinking the country's approach to immigration requires an even-handed, evidence-based assessment of what is equitable, just, and beneficial to immigrants and the country.

References

1. Budiman A. Key findings about U.S. immigrants. Pew Research Center. August 20, 2020. https://www.pewresearch.org/fact-tank/2020/08/20/key-findings-about-u-s-immigrants/.

2. Parmet W. Immigration law as a social determinant of health. *Temple Law Review*. 2020;92:931.

3. U.S. Citizenship and Immigration Services. Become a U.S. citizen through naturalization. https://www.uscis.gov/forms/explore-my-options/become-a-us-citizen-through-naturalization.

4. Reimers D. The impact of immigration legislation: 1875 to the present. In *Bayor RH. The Oxford Handbook of American Immigration and Ethnicity*. Oxford: Oxford University Press; 2016.

5. Reimers D. The impact of immigration legislation: 1875 to the present. In *Bayor RH. The Oxford Handbook of American Immigration and Ethnicity*. Oxford: Oxford University Press; 2016.

6. Migration Policy Institute. Timeline of major US immigration laws, 1790–present. March 2018. https://www.migrationpolicy.org/research/timeline-1790.

7. Reimers D. The impact of immigration legislation: 1875 to the present. In *Bayor RH. The Oxford Handbook of American Immigration and Ethnicity*. Oxford: Oxford University Press; 2016.

8. Migration Policy Institute. Timeline of major US immigration laws, 1790–present. March 2018. https://www.migrationpolicy.org/research/timeline-1790.

9. Reimers D. The impact of immigration legislation: 1875 to the present. In *Bayor RH. The Oxford Handbook of American Immigration and Ethnicity*. Oxford: Oxford University Press; 2016.

10. Reimers D. The impact of immigration legislation: 1875 to the present. In *Bayor RH. The Oxford Handbook of American Immigration and Ethnicity*. Oxford: Oxford University Press; 2016.

11. Migration Policy Institute. Timeline of major US immigration laws, 1790–present. March 2018. https://www.migrationpolicy.org/research/timeline-1790.

12. Migration Policy Institute. Timeline of major US immigration laws, 1790–present. March 2018. https://www.migrationpolicy.org/research/timeline-1790.

13. U.S. Department of Homeland Security. Deferred Action for Childhood Arrivals (DACA). Important information about DACA requests. October 2021. https://www.dhs.gov/deferred-action-childhood-arrivals-daca.

14. Pierce S, Bolter J. Dismantling and reconstructing the U.S. immigration system: A catalog of changes under the Trump presidency. The Migration Policy Institute. July 2020. https://www.migrationpolicy.org/sites/default/files/publications/MPI_US-Immigration-Trump-Presidency-Final.pdf.

15. *Plyler v. Doe*, 457 U.S. 202 (1982).

16. *Plyler v. Doe*, 457 U.S. 202 (1982).

17. *Graham v. Richardson*, 403 U.S. 365, 371–372 (1971).

18. Parmet W. Who's in?: Immigrants and healthcare. In Cohen IG, Hoffman AK, Sage WM. *The Oxford Handbook of U.S. Health Law*. Oxford: Oxford University Press; 2017: 1043.

19. Title VI of the Civil Rights Act of 1964, 42 U.S.C. 2000d et seq.

20. United States Department of Justice. Overview of Executive Order 13166. August 2021. https://www.justice.gov/crt/executive-order-13166.

21. Flores G. Language barriers and hospitalized children: Are we overlooking the most important risk factor for adverse events. *JAMA Pediatrics*.2020;174(12):e203238.

22. The Personal Responsibility and Work Opportunity Reconciliation Act, 110 Stat. 2105 (1996).

23. Parmet W. Who's in?: Immigrants and healthcare. In Cohen IG, Hoffman AK, Sage WM. *The Oxford Handbook of U.S. Health Law*. Oxford: Oxford University Press; 2017: 1041.

24. Broder T, Lessard G, Moussavian A. Overview of immigrant eligibility for federal programs. National Immigration Law Center. October 2021. https://www.nilc.org/issues/economic-support/overview-immeligfedprograms/.

25. Lacarte V, Greenburg M, Capps R. Medicaid access and participation: A data profile of eligible and ineligible immigrant adults. Migration Policy Institute. October 2021. https://www.migrationpolicy.org/sites/default/files/publications/mpi-hsi_medicaid-brief_final.pdf.

26. Parmet W. Who's in?. Immigrants and healthcare. In Cohen IG, Hoffman AK, Sage WM. *The Oxford Handbook of U.S. Health Law*. Oxford: Oxford University Press;2017:1041.

27. Congressional Research Service. Noncitizen eligibility for federal housing programs. July 23, 2020. https://sgp.fas.org/crs/misc/R46462.pdf.

28. Fritze J. Supreme Court to hear case seeking to revive Trump "public charge" rule nixed by Biden. *USA Today*. October 29, 2021. https://www.usatoday.com/story/news/politics/2021/10/29/supreme-court-takes-case-seeking-revive-trump-public-charge-rule/6044802001/

29. Saadi A, Taleghani S, Hampton K, Heisler M. Clinicians' perspectives on the impacts of post-2016 immigration enforcement on immigrant health and

health care use. *Journal of Health Care for the Poor and Underserved*. 2021;32(4):1778–1797.

30. Gemmill A, Catalano R, Casey JA, et al. Association of preterm births among US Latina women with the 2016 presidential election. *JAMA Network Open*. 2019 Jul 3;2(7):e197084.

31. Lu T, He Q, Brooks-Gunn J. Diverse experience of immigrant children: Do separation and reunification shape development? *Child Development*. 2020;91(1):e146–e163.

32. Markel H, Stern AM. The foreignness of germs: The persistent association of immigrants and disease in American society. *The Milbank Quarterly*. 2002;80(4):757–788.

33. Markel H, Stern AM. The foreignness of germs: The persistent association of immigrants and disease in American society. *The Milbank Quarterly*. 2002; 80(4):757–788.

34. Markel H, Stern AM. The foreignness of germs: The persistent association of immigrants and disease in American society. *The Milbank Quarterly*. 2002; 80(4):757–788.

35. Bateman-House A, Fairchild A. History of medicine: Medical examination of immigrants at Ellis Island. Virtual Mentor. American Medical Association *Journal of Ethics*. 2008;10(4):235–241.

36. Winston SE, Beckwith CG. The impact of removing the immigration ban on HIV-infected persons. *AIDS Patient Care and STDs*. 2011;25(12):709–711.

37. Illingsworth P, Parmet W. *The Health of Newcomers: Immigration, Health Policy, and the Case for Global Solidarity*. New York, NY: New York University Press; 2017.

38. Henry J. Kaiser Family Foundation. Health Coverage of Immigrants. July 15, 2021. https://www.kff.org/racial-equity-and-health-policy/fact-sheet/health-coverage-of-immigrants/.

39. Artiga S, Ubri P. Living in an immigrant family in America: How fear and toxic stress are affecting daily life, well-being, & health. Henry J. Kaiser Family Foundation. December 13, 2017. https://www.kff.org/racial-equity-and-health-policy/issue-brief/living-in-an-immigrant-family-in-america-how-fear-and-toxic-stress-are-affecting-daily-life-well-being-health/.

40. Rhodes SD, Mann L, Simán FM, et al. The impact of local immigration enforcement policies on the health of immigrant Hispanics/Latinos in the United States. *American Journal of Public Health*. 2015;105(2):329–337.

41. Diamond LC, Wilson-Stronks A, Jacobs EA. Do hospitals measure up to the national culturally and linguistically appropriate services standards? *Medical Care*. 2010;48(12):1080–1087.

42. U.S. Department of Health and Human Services. Office for Civil Rights. Guidance to federal financial assistance recipients regarding Title VI and the prohibition against national origin discrimination affecting limited English proficient persons. July 2013. https://www.hhs.gov/civil-rights/for-providers/laws-regulations-guidance/guidance-federal-financial-assistance-title-vi/index.html.

43. Hsieh E. Not just "getting by": Factors influencing providers' choice of interpreters. *Journal of General Internal Medicine*. 2015;30(1):75–82.

44. Espinoza J, Derrington S. How should clinicians respond to language barriers that exacerbate health inequity? *AMA Journal of Ethics*. 2021;23(2):E109–E116.

45. Flores G. Families facing language barriers in healthcare: When will policy catch up with the demographics and evidence? *Journal of Pediatrics*. 2014;164(60):1261–1264.

46. Beck T, Le TK, Henry-Okafor Q, Shah MK. Medical care for undocumented immigrants: National and international issues. *Primary Care: Clinics in Office Practice*. 2017;44(1).

47. Gale R. Legal counsel: A health care partner for immigrant communities. *Health Affairs*. 2021; 40(8):1184–1189.

48. Henry J. Kaiser Family Foundation. Health coverage of immigrants. July 15, 2021. https://www.kff.org/racial-equity-and-health-policy/fact-sheet/health-coverage-of-immigrants/.

49. Cervantes L, Martin M, Frank MG, et al. Experiences of Latinx individuals hospitalized for COVID-19. *JAMA Network Open*. 2021;4:e210684.

50. Horner KM, Wrigley-Field E, Leider JP. A first look: Disparities in COVID-19 mortality among US-Born and foreign-born Minnesota residents. *Population Research and Policy Review*. August 2, 2021.

51. Espinoza J, Derrington S. How should clinicians respond to language barriers that exacerbate health inequity?. *AMA Journal of Ethics*. 2021;23(2):E109–E116.

52. Espinoza J, Derrington S. How should clinicians respond to language barriers that exacerbate health inequity?. *AMA Journal of Ethics*. 2021;23(2):E109–E116.

53. Walden J, Valdman O, Mishori R, et al., Building capacity to care for refugees. *Family Practice Management*. 2017;24(4):21–27.

54. Parmet W. Immigration law as a social determinant of health. *Temple Law Review*. 2020;92:931.

55. Artiga S, Ubri P. Living in an immigrant family in America: How fear and toxic stress are affecting daily life, well-being, & health. Henry J. Kaiser Family Foundation. December 13, 2021. https://www.kff.org/racial-equity-and-health-policy/issue-brief/living-in-an-immigrant-family-in-america-how-fear-and-toxic-stress-are-affecting-daily-life-well-being-health/.

56. Szaflarski M, Bauldry S. The effects of perceived discrimination on immigrant and refugee physical and mental health. *Advances in Medical Sociology*. 2019;19:173–204.

57. Szaflarski M, Bauldry S. The effects of perceived discrimination on immigrant and refugee physical and mental health. *Advances in Medical Sociology.* 2019;19:173–204.

58. Szaflarski M, Bauldry S. The effects of perceived discrimination on immigrant and refugee physical and mental health. *Advances in Medical Sociology.* 2019;19:173–204.

59. Szaflarski M, Bauldry S. The effects of perceived discrimination on immigrant and refugee physical and mental health. *Advances in Medical Sociology.* 2019;19:173–204.

60. Chang CD. Social determinants of health and health disparities among immigrants and their children. *Current Problems in Pediatric and Adolescent Health Care.* 2019;49:3–30.

61. Dubowitz T, Bates LM, Acevedo-Garcia D. The Latino health paradox: Looking at the intersection of sociology and health. In Bird CE, Condrad P, Fremont AM, Timmermans S. *Handbook of Medical Sociology.* 6th ed. Nashville, TN: Vanderbilt University Press; 2010:106–123.

62. Hall E, Cuellar NG. Immigrant health in the United States: A trajectory toward change. *Journal of Transcultural Nursing.* 2016;27(6):611–626.

63. Hall E, Cuellar NG. Immigrant health in the United States: A trajectory toward change. *Journal of Transcultural Nursing.* 2016;27(6): 611–626.

64. Singh G, Siahpush M, Hiatt R, Timsina L. Dramatic increases in obesity and overweight prevalence and body mass index among ethnic-immigrant and social class groups in the United States, 1976–2008. *Journal of Community Health.* 2011;36:94–110.

65. Barr DA. Health disparities in the United States: Social class, race, ethnicity and the social determinants of health. 3rd edition. Baltimore: Johns Hopkins University Press;2019:151.

66. Barr DA. Health disparities in the United States: Social class, race, ethnicity and the social determinants of health. 3rd edition. Baltimore: Johns Hopkins University Press;2019:151.

67. Richardson DM, Andrea SB, Ziring A, et al. Pregnancy outcomes and documentation status among Latina women: A systematic review. *Health Equity.* 2020;4:158–182.

68. Payton C, Kimball S, Ahrenholz NC, Wieland ML. Preventive care and management of chronic diseases in immigrant adults. *Primary Care.* 2021 Mar;48(1):83–97.

69. U.S. Department of Health and Human Services, Office of Minority Health. Obesity and Hispanic Americans. March 2020. https://minorityhealth.hhs.gov/omh/browse.aspx?lvl=4&lvlid=70.

70. Payton C, Kimball S, Ahrenholz NC, Wieland ML. Preventive care and management of chronic diseases in immigrant adults. *Primary Care.* 2021 Mar;48(1):83–97.

71. Kirmayer LJ, Narasiah L, Munoz M, et al. Common mental health problems in immigrants and refugees: General approach in primary care. *Canadian Medical Association Journal.* 2011;183(12):E959–E967.

72. Budiman A. Key findings about U.S. immigrants. Pew Research Center. August 20, 2020. https://www.pewresearch.org/fact-tank/2020/08/20/key-findings-about-u-s-immigrants/.

73. Campbell AF. Trump says undocumented immigrants are an economic burden. They pay billions in taxes. *Vox News.* October 25, 2018. https://www.vox.com/2018/4/13/17229018/undocumented-immigrants-pay-taxes

74. Krogstad JM, Passel JS, Cohn D. 5 facts about illegal immigration in the U.S. Pew Research Center. June 12, 2019. https://www.pewresearch.org/fact-tank/2019/06/12/5-facts-about-illegal-immigration-in-the-u-s/.

75. Gostin L. Is affording undocumented immigrants health coverage a radical proposal? *JAMA Forum.* September 25, 2019. https://jamanetwork.com/channels/health-forum/fullarticle/2759639.

76. Friedman E. The right to health for all: Ending discrimination against undocumented migrants. O'Neill Institute for Global and National Health Law. Georgetown Law School. June 9, 2016. https://oneill.law.georgetown.edu/the-right-to-health-for-all-ending-discrimination-against-undocumented-migrants/.

77. Gostin L. Is affording undocumented immigrants health coverage a radical proposal? JAMA Forum. September 25, 2019. https://jamanetwork.com/channels/health-forum/fullarticle/2759639.

78. Gostin L. Is affording undocumented immigrants health coverage a radical proposal? JAMA Forum. September 25, 2019. https://jamanetwork.com/channels/health-forum/fullarticle/2759639.

CHAPTER 12

Women

LEARNING OBJECTIVES

By the end of this chapter you will be able to:

- Describe the development of antidiscrimination laws and laws affecting reproductive rights and their influence on women's health and well-being
- Discuss historical and current treatment of women as participants in the health care system and how gender bias affects women's access to quality medical care
- Detail health inequities between women and men and among women and consider how these inequities are driven by laws, policies, and other social and structural factors
- Highlight how the intersections of gender with other marginalized statuses (e.g., race, ethnicity, socioeconomic status, disability) exacerbate health inequities

Introduction

This chapter and the next explore the role of gender in health inequities. Specifically, they discuss how these inequities are rooted in laws, policies, and systemic practices. This chapter focuses on gender-based inequities that apply to women in relation to men. Chapter 13 details gender-based inequities deriving from sexual orientation and gender identity. Clearly, women are not a monolithic group for which experience can be generalized. At the same time, discrimination based on gender can affect all women regardless of social status. Furthermore, gender-neutral policies that have been formed and implemented

with men in mind disproportionately affect all women. Nonetheless, intersectionality is also key to understanding how laws, policies, and social structures differentially affect the health of women based on their race, ethnicity, socioeconomic status (SES), gender identity, sexual orientation, and/or disability. This chapter provides an overview of the treatment of women under the law and as participants in the health care system and how social norms based on men's experiences have shaped this treatment with significant consequences for women's health. Throughout the chapter, we consider how intersectionality affects women's health outcomes. In addition to this chapter, specific inequities experienced by Women of

Color, LGBTQ+ women, immigrant women, and women with disabilities are described in other chapters.

Treatment of Women Under the Law

Women have long been affected by the law in ways that are distinct from men. Historically, the law treated women differently from men in many areas of life: property ownership, educational opportunity, employment, child custody, criminal law, and more. Although the Equal Protection Clause of the federal Constitution and various civil rights statutes are intended to protect women from many types of discrimination, there remain significant challenges in enforcing gender-based antidiscrimination laws, as we explore in this chapter; this ongoing discrimination has important implications for women's health. Because of women's reproductive capacity and traditional role as caretakers of children and other family members, legal rights pertaining to reproductive health care, parenting, and caretaking disproportionately impact women in ways that have serious repercussions for their health as well as their equal status in society. Women who face intersectional discrimination and marginalization based on their race, ethnicity, sexual orientation, gender identity, and/or disability experience additional burdens.

Antidiscrimination Laws

It is beyond the scope of this chapter to comprehensively present the history of gender-based antidiscrimination laws in the United States. Here, we highlight briefly the trajectory from legalized discrimination against women to current legal protections. Historically, differential treatment between men and women under the law was typically premised on the notion that women were more vulnerable than men and required protection from society to protect their health and well-being.

A classic example of this thinking is the 1908 case *Muller v. Oregon*. In *Muller*, the Supreme Court was tasked with deciding the constitutionality of an Oregon state law that limited the number of hours a woman could work in factories and laundries. The court had recently held that a limit on the number of hours a person could work violated the 14th Amendment's Due Process Clause by restraining a worker's right to contract. In *Muller*, however, the court viewed women workers as different from men. They require special protection from the state, the court reasoned, based on their physical frailty and reproductive capacity.

Citing voluminous medical testimony, the court viewed long work hours as detrimental to women's health because they are likely to become mothers and therefore long work hours will harm "the strength and vigor of the race."[1] Ultimately, the court rationalized restricting women's work hours based on their natural dependence on men: "Still again, history discloses the fact that woman has always been dependent upon man. He established his control at the outset by superior physical strength, and this control in various forms, with diminishing intensity, has continued to the present."[2] It's important to note that workplace protections such as the ones in *Muller* were not applied to Women of Color, who worked long hours in low-wage, often dangerous jobs. Notions about protecting women from harm were solely focused on White women. Nonetheless, the *Muller* decision highlights two important themes in American law related to women's rights and their health. First, because women's bodies are different from men's, they are considered more physically vulnerable and, therefore, in need of men's protection. Second, the state has an interest in promoting human reproduction and thus may legitimately place restrictions on women in order to protect that interest. As discussed later, even today these themes continue to play a significant role in law and legal discourse.

The notion that women should be treated differently based on their biological differences from men has influenced hundreds of laws over the course of American history. Assumptions about women's physical strength, lesser intelligence, psychological and emotional precarity, and submissive nature have supported differential legal treatment. Beginning the 1970s, lawyers such as the late Supreme Court Justice Ruth Bader Ginsburg began to challenge the foundational basis for legal discrimination against women by challenging sex-based state laws under the 14th Amendment to the U.S. Constitution. In these cases, the Supreme Court had to confront what circumstances justified differential treatment.

When deciding what type of scrutiny courts should apply to laws that treat men and women differently, the Supreme Court settled on "intermediate scrutiny," meaning that sex-based laws would be considered "quasi-suspect," but not as suspect as laws treating people differently based on race, citizenship, and national origin, as noted in Chapter 4. Instead of having to meet the burden of showing that a law has a *compelling* interest, the state must only show that its sex-based law serves *important* governmental objectives.[3] In reaching the doctrine of intermediate scrutiny, the Supreme Court noted that state laws could not be based on stereotyped assumptions about the differences between men and women (e.g., that women are better suited to housework than men).

Consider why the Supreme Court chose intermediate, rather than strict, scrutiny in assessing whether sex-based laws violate the 14th Amendment. The justification for applying intermediate scrutiny to sex-based laws is that, in some instances, women are not "similarly situated" with men. What situations might justify treating women differently from men under the law? Do biological differences between men and women, including a woman's capacity to become pregnant, warrant unequal treatment? Think about these questions as you read further about contemporary legal treatment of women.

In addition to the Supreme Court's interpretation of the 14th Amendment as protecting women from discrimination is some contexts, Congress began taking action to protect women from specific types of sex-based discrimination through passage of several key civil rights laws. The Equal Pay Act of 1963 requires that employers provide equal pay for equal work without regard to sex; Title VII of the Civil Rights Act of 1964 affords women the ability to challenge sex-based employment discrimination; Title IX of 1972 bars any education program receiving federal funding from excluding from participation, denying benefits, or discriminating on the basis of sex; and the Pregnancy Discrimination Act of 1978 makes it illegal for employers to discriminate on the basis of pregnancy, childbirth, or a related medical condition (see Chapter 6). All of these laws were major steps forward in addressing centuries-old discrimination against women in education and employment based on assumptions about innate differences between men and women and stereotypes about women's proper roles in society.

However, as was also discussed in Chapter 6, individuals who believe they have experienced disparate treatment must demonstrate that the discrimination was intentional, which can be challenging in today's work environment in which gender-biased decision-making is rarely explicit. Despite enormous progress in gender equality in education and employment, progress appears to have stalled. For example, even though women are now more likely to receive undergraduate and doctoral degrees than are men, they are still more likely to be segregated into lower-paying jobs and less likely to reach positions of leadership. They are also likely to be paid less than men.[4] (Chapter 7 highlighted the stubborn pay gap that perpetuates gender inequity.) In a 2019 survey of women, 41% said they had been discriminated against in equal pay and promotions, and 20% indicated they had experienced discrimination in higher education; Native, Black, and Latina women had the highest odds of reporting discrimination; and LGBTQ+ women were more likely to report sexual harassment.[5] Despite legal protections afforded by the Pregnancy Discrimination Act, women also continue to report employment discrimination based on pregnancy, most commonly that they were discharged when they became pregnant. Nearly a third of all charges of pregnancy discrimination are made by Black women.[6]

While not technically antidiscrimination laws, workplace protections such as family and medical leave laws disproportionately impact women. Women are more likely than men to serve as primary caretakers of children and for ill, disabled, or elderly family members.[7] The United States is the only nation among wealthy (and many middle- and low-income) nations that does not guarantee paid leave when an employee gives birth, adopts a child, or needs to care for a sick family member.[8] As described in Chapter 7, U.S. law only guarantees unpaid leave for certain employees working for large employers and for those who work a minimum number of hours. Later in this chapter we explore further how these legal gaps affect women's health and well-being.

Reproductive Rights

In 1992, in the case of *Planned Parenthood of Southeastern Pa. v. Casey*, Justice Sandra Day O'Connor asserted this about reproductive rights: "The ability of women to participate equally in the economic and social life of the Nation has been facilitated by their ability to control their reproductive lives."[9] The law's role in regulating women's reproduction—how much autonomy they have in making the decision whether and when to have children—has a long and complex past. It is also among the most, if not *the* most, controversial and polarized topics in U.S. law today. Next, we consider the law's role in impeding some women's

fertility while at the same time restricting access to contraception and abortion.

The history and development of reproductive rights in the United States are closely tied to racial-, ethnic- and class-based inequities that shape a woman's ability to decide when to have a child and when not to have a child. Chapter 10 described legally sanctioned sexual and reproductive exploitation of enslaved women and the history of nonconsensual gynecological experimentation on Black women. As late as the 1980s, Black women were forcibly sterilized by doctors who determined that their offspring were undesirable. Black, ethnic minority, disabled, and poor women have been subject to eugenic sterilization over the course of U.S. history. Eugenic sterilization was legally sanctioned by the U.S. Supreme Court in the infamous case of *Buck v. Bell* in 1927. At issue in the case was whether a state law that permitted compulsory sterilization of women considered to be unfit due to intellectual disability violated the 14th Amendment's Due Process and Equal Protection Clauses.

In the case, 18-year-old Carrie Buck, who was institutionalized at the "Virginia State Colony for Epileptics and Feebleminded," was alleged by the superintendent of the facility to be genetically deficient and "incorrigible." She had been committed to the institution after having become pregnant at age 17. Basing the court's decision on the protection of the public's welfare, Justice Oliver Wendell Holmes asserted that compulsory sterilization would "prevent our being swamped with incompetence. It is better for all the world, if instead of waiting to execute degenerate offspring for crime, or to let them starve for their imbecility, society can prevent those who are manifestly unfit from continuing their kind."[10] Historians have pointed out that Carrie Buck was neither intellectually disabled nor incorrigible. Her mother had been abandoned by her husband and had been committed to the Virginia State Colony based on "immorality" and prostitution. Carrie was placed in foster care at birth.

Her pregnancy at age 17 was the result of rape by the nephew of her foster mother. The family committed Carrie to the institution in order to preserve its reputation.[11] Carrie Buck was not alone: Sterilization of mentally ill, disabled, and poor women occurred in states across the country during the eugenics movement from the 1900s into the 1940s. Forced sterilizations were carried out in 32 states during that time. Recently, North Carolina and Virginia passed laws approving reparations to the families of women who were sterilized during the movement.[12]

But nonconsensual sterilization of women deemed "unfit" and whose children are regarded to be a burden to society did not stop with the end of the eugenics movement in the 1940s. As late as the 1980s, Black mothers were threatened with termination of welfare benefits and loss of medical care if they refused sterilization or contraception methods that were often dangerous.[13] As recently as 2010, pregnant inmates in a California prison were coerced into undergoing tubal ligation.[14] In 2020, immigrant women detainees at a U.S. Immigration and Customs Enforcement facility revealed that they were subjected to nonconsensual hysterectomies.[15]

Legal sanctioning of nonconsensual sterilization and use of state power to coerce women into not having children can be juxtaposed with the law's restrictions on whether and when women may decide to prevent or terminate a pregnancy. In 1965 the Supreme Court held in *Griswold v. Connecticut* that a state law making it a crime to provide contraception or to aid and abet the prevention of conception was unconstitutional. The law applied to both married and unmarried people. The Court found that the law was a violation of a constitutionally protected "zone of privacy"[16] that could be deciphered from various constitutional amendments and principles. In a subsequent case, *Eisenstadt v. Baird*, in 1972, the Supreme Court struck down a Massachusetts law that prohibited distribution of contraception to non-married couples.[17] While these

Court decisions prevented states from excluding access to contraception for married and unmarried couples, they did not address the question of equitable access to contraception for low-income people and those with poor access to reproductive health care. Congress sought to address access barriers to contraception through passage of Title X of the Public Health Service Act of 1970. Title X prioritizes funding of reproductive health care for low-income and uninsured patients, with funding distributed to community-based hospitals, health centers, university health centers, and faith-based organizations. Services provided by Title X grantees include family planning, contraception, education and counseling, breast and pelvic cancer screening and exams, and screening and treatment of sexually transmitted diseases and HIV. Under the law, Title X funds may not be used for abortion services.

Beginning with the Reagan administration in the 1980s, funding for and restrictions on the use of Title X funds have been a political football. Through rule making, Republican administrations have imposed restrictions on Title X funding, such as withholding funds to any family planning organization that provides abortion services. The Trump administration imposed a "gag rule" that forbade any organization receiving Title X funds from counseling patients about abortion. Democratic administrations have been less restrictive. In 2021, the Biden administration announced that it would replace the Trump administration rules, essentially restoring the less restrictive rules governing Title X funding that were present under the Obama administration. According to the Biden administration, the new rules will ensure "access to equitable, affordable, client-centered, quality family planning services."[18]

In addition to the reproductive health services provided through Title X funding, regulations passed by the U.S. Department of Health and Human Services (DHHS) under the Affordable Care Act include prescription contraception as part of a list of preventive services that must be covered—without any copayments—through health insurance plans. This contraceptive mandate has been controversial among religious conservatives who view the mandate as an attack on the religious beliefs and liberty of employers. In response to concerns from religious organizations, the Obama administration implemented an opt-out provision allowing insurance companies to provide contraceptive coverage without direct involvement from a religious employer. This compromise was rejected by some religious organizations, including the Conference of Catholic Bishops, which sued the federal government. In *Burwell v. Hobby Lobby* (2014), the Supreme Court ruled that the mandate violated closely held corporations' religious liberty rights under the federal Religious Freedom Restoration Act.[19] (A closely held corporation is a company that has only a small number of shareholders, such as a family-owned company.) Then, in *Little Sisters of the Poor v. Pennsylvania* (2020), the Supreme Court upheld broad exemptions for employers who do not wish to offer contraception under their health plans, further undermining access to contraception for women employees.[20]

While the government's and private employers' obligation to provide access to contraception and reproductive health care continues to be contested, the law's role in access to abortion remains one of the most bitterly divided issues of our time. Given space considerations, a comprehensive history of abortion law is not possible. Instead, we offer a brief overview of the law's development and the current legal controversies surrounding abortion. To date, two key Supreme Court cases have governed when and how states may restrict access to abortion. The first is the seminal case of *Roe v. Wade*, decided with a seven-justice majority in 1973, which found unconstitutional a Texas law that made all abortions illegal except "for purposes of saving the life of the mother." In its decision, the Court held that in balancing the privacy rights of women seeking abortions and the state's interest in the "potentiality of human life," restrictions on abortion should be structured by the stages of pregnancy. In the first trimester of pregnancy, the decision must be "left to the medical judgment of the pregnant woman's attending physician"; in the second trimester, the state may regulate "the abortion in ways that are reasonably related to maternal health"; and "subsequent to viability" of the fetus (i.e., the ability of the born child to live on its own), the state "may regulate, and even proscribe, abortion," except as necessary to protect the health of the mother.[21]

Just four years later, the Supreme Court made clear that, even though states could not prohibit abortion, they had no obligation to facilitate access to abortion for low-income women who could not afford one. Upholding a Connecticut law that only provided state funding for abortions deemed medically necessary, the Court did not see this as a "disadvantage" for poor women: "The indigency that may make it difficult and in some cases, perhaps, impossible for some women to have abortions is neither created nor in any way affected by the Connecticut regulation."[22] The Court subsequently upheld the Hyde Amendment, which prohibited the use of federal funds to pay for abortions; again, the Court found that this restriction did not represent an unreasonable obstacle to the right to abortion.[23]

A second landmark Supreme Court decision shaping abortion rights was *Planned Parenthood of Southeastern Pennsylvania v. Casey*, decided in 1992. Between 1973 (when *Roe v. Wade* was decided) and 1992, states had continued to test in the courts different restrictions on access to abortion. In *Planned Parenthood*, the court was confronted with several restrictions imposed by Pennsylvania on the abortion right. These were requirements that women seeking abortions must wait 24 hours after providing written informed consent before obtaining an abortion (informed consent requirements included that the woman be given information about fetal development), parental consent for minors seeking abortions, notification of a woman's spouse prior to an abortion, and reporting of the number of abortions performed by each facility. In a landmark five-to-four decision penned by Justice Sandra Day O'Connor, the court upheld all of the state restrictions, with the exception of the spousal notification requirement. The court set a new standard for determining the constitutionality of state abortion restrictions: A state restriction is constitutionally permissible if it does not create an "undue burden" on a woman's access to abortion. "Undue burden" was defined as placing a "substantial obstacle in the path of a woman seeking an abortion before the fetus attains viability."[24] Commentators have viewed O'Connor's decision as an attempt to find a middle ground in the abortion debate. But the case did little to bring closure to the debate about legal restrictions on abortion.

The next major Supreme Court decision interpreting the undue burden standard was not until 2016. At issue in *Whole Women's Health v. Hellerstedt* was a Texas law requiring abortion providers to have admitting privileges at a local hospital and mandating that facilities providing abortions meet the standard for ambulatory surgical centers. Whole Women's Health, an abortion provider, challenged the law, claiming that it represented an undue on women's access to abortion. In a five-to-four decision, the court found that these provisions did create an undue burden because the law would lead most abortion clinics in Texas to close, leaving women with few options other than going out of state to obtain an abortion. *Whole Women's Health* brought to the foreground one of the key disputes in abortion law. In defending the law, Texas officials argued that the law was designed to protect women's health and safety, not to reduce access. But abortion advocates and the Supreme Court majority questioned the true intent of the law, which they saw as using women's health and safety as pretext for restricting access. The American Medical Association and many other medical societies filed "friend of the court" briefs in the case, arguing that provisions of the Texas law were medically unnecessary and did little to protect women's health.[25]

Indeed, restrictions on abortion have often been based on the idea of "protecting" women from later regrets about their choices. (Recall the earlier discussion of *Muller v. Oregon*, in which restrictions on women's work hours were based on protecting their health and well-being as mothers.) In *Carhart v. Gonzalez* (2007), a decision that upheld a restriction on an abortion procedure, Justice Anthony Kennedy based his decision, in part, on the idea that women need to be protected from bad decisions that could lead to "depression and a loss of self-esteem."[26] He noted that "[w]hile we find no reliable data to measure the phenomenon, it seems unexceptionable to conclude some women come to regret their choice."[27] Research on women's post-abortion mental health does not support Kennedy's assertion.[28]

In 2021, states enacted more than 100 abortion restrictions. In December 2021, the Supreme Court heard the case *Dobbs v. Jackson Women's Health*, challenging a Mississippi law banning abortions after 15 weeks. The law clearly conflicts with the Court's holdings in *Roe v. Wade* and *Planned Parenthood v. Casey,* which treat abortion as a Constitutional right, albeit with many restrictions placed on that right.[29] Legal commentators suggest that the Court will likely either uphold the Mississippi law, allowing other states to follow suit and restrict access to abortion to the first 15 weeks of pregnancy, or it will strike down *Roe v. Wade* altogether, allowing states to make all or virtually all abortions illegal.[30] Meanwhile, Texas enacted Senate Bill 8 ("SB8") in May 2021, which prohibits abortion after 6 weeks of pregnancy. The law was constructed to avoid a challenge under *Roe v. Wade* by providing that the law may only be enforced through private civil lawsuits brought by "any person" against "any person" who performs any abortion or who "knowingly engages in conduct that aids or abets the performance or inducement of an abortion."[31] This unprecedented enforcement provision is an attempt to prevent lawsuits against the state that aim to strike down the law, since enforcement is carried out by private citizens. Abortion providers were unsuccessful in persuading the Supreme Court to freeze the law while it could be fully challenged as a constitutional violation. The law went into effect in September 2021, and as of the time of this writing, the Supreme Court had still refused to stop enforcement of the law pending further litigation.[32]

In addition to contested state restrictions on abortion, there have been other important developments in health law that relate to the abortion debate. For example, "conscientious objection" laws have been passed to protect clinicians from having to provide medical services to certain patients based on religious or other conscientious objections. These laws have been enacted in some states, and during the Trump administration, conscientious objection protections were advanced through federal regulation. Specifically, the administration created an exemption for health care providers to the requirements of Section 1557 of the Affordable Care Act. (Recall from Chapter 6 that this section of the ACA protects patients, including women, from discrimination in health care.) Specifically, the Trump administration regulation provided an exemption for clinicians based on their objection to abortion. In other words, clinicians were not bound by the sex-based nondiscrimination provisions of the Affordable Care Act if they chose not to provide care to a patient who had previously had an abortion if the clinician found abortion objectionable. In 2021, the Biden administration announced that it would rewrite the rule; however, the issue of whether clinicians have the right to refuse care to certain patients (including women who have had abortions) based on religious objections is still being litigated.[33] The law's role in determining when women may make autonomous decisions about their health and well-being and in governing when

clinicians may deny them care has a major bearing on women's health and well-being. Next, we turn to the treatment of women in medical research and clinical care and to how gender bias plays a role in access to quality medical care.

Treatment of Women by the Health Care System

Medical Research

Feminist theorists have challenged the ways in which medical science has been shaped by defining male physiology and psychology as the norm, as Chapter 1 described. For example, feminists have pointed out that women have often been excluded from medical research because their hormones and menstrual cycle were thought to alter the results of clinical trials. Furthermore, failing to take into account how women's bodies may respond differently to pharmaceuticals, medical researchers have traditionally tested new therapies on men, assuming that findings of effectiveness and side effects could be extrapolated to women.[34]

In response to concerns about exclusion of women from medical research, the National Institutes of Health (NIH) enacted the Revitalization Act in 1993 recommending that women be included in phase 3 clinical trials. (These are trials that test whether a new treatment is better than existing treatments.) In 2010, the Institute of Medicine published the report "Women's Health Research, Progress, Pitfalls and Promise," which found that:

> There…has been inadequate enforcement of requirements that representative numbers of women be included in clinical trials and that women's results be reported. A lack of taking account of sex and gender

differences in the design and analysis of studies, and a lack of reporting on sex and gender differences, has hindered identification of potentially important sex differences and slowed progress in women's health research and its translation to clinical practice.[35]

That same year, the newly passed Affordable Care Act required that Offices of Women's Health be established in the different federal agencies within the U.S. Department of Health and Human Services. The FDA Office of Women is responsible for ensuring that women are appropriately represented in pharmaceutical trials. But a 2020 study of clinical trials found that, despite the current regulatory framework and guidelines for inclusion of women, "notable gaps exist in the integration of sex and gender in pharmaceutical research" and "stronger governance and oversight from regulatory agencies" is needed.[36] In addition to failing to include women in clinical trials, gender biases are often built into health services research studies. For example, men are often not asked in surveys about child health and care, while women are.[37]

Clinical Care

Gender bias also affects clinical care. Most often gender bias results from implicit biases that clinicians have about women and men based on gender stereotypes. For example, despite the fact that women are more likely than men to experience chronic pain, they are often dismissed as complainers, too sensitive, or overly emotional.[38] On the other hand, some doctors may prescribe less pain medication to women under the assumption that they are used to pain from menstruation and childbirth.[39] Research also demonstrates that heart attacks in women are underdiagnosed because their symptoms manifest differently from men's.[40] This is particularly

concerning since heart disease is the leading cause of death for women in the United States.[41] Lack of understanding of or attention to menstruation has also been shown to influence underdiagnosis of bleeding disorders in women.[42]

There is a long history of gender bias in the diagnosis and treatment of mental health concerns in women, as described in Chapter 1. Hippocrates, the Greek physician, first used the term *hysteria* to describe a disease of the uterus caused by lack of sexual activity that manifested in women as anxiety, tremors, and convulsions. This notion of hysteria, or "uterine fury," lasted well into the nineteenth and early twentieth centuries.[43] Historians note that psychiatry has often played a "prominent role in maintaining the status quo and controlling individuals who rebelled against the social norm."[44] In the early twentieth century, for example, husbands and fathers often sent their wives and daughters to the asylum when they were perceived as defying social rules.[45] The notion that women are more prone to emotional problems than men persists in psychiatry today.

The World Health Organization (WHO) reports that women and girls are much more likely to experience depression and anxiety than men and boys. "The feeling of a lack of autonomy and control over one's life is known to be associated with depression. Socially determined gender norms, roles and responsibilities place women, far more frequently than men, in situations where they have little control over important decisions concerning their lives."[46] Women are more likely than men to seek help for mood disorders, such as depression and anxiety, and are more likely to be prescribed psychotropic medications.[47] This has led to concerns about the medicalization of women's mental health concerns rather than focusing on social and structural factors.[48] Indeed, medicalizing women's mental health dismisses social causes related to gender inequity, particularly trauma resulting from sexual violence, discrimination, and restrictive gender roles.[49]

Access to Quality Health Care

Women experience unique barriers to health care. Barriers are both individual—related to patient-provider interactions—and structural—driven by extant laws, policies, and systems. Individual-level barriers involve clinician traits and skills, such as expressing implicit or explicit gender bias, failing to listen or answer questions effectively, and/or treating a female patient disrespectfully or dismissively. Studies of women's preferences with regard to patient-centered care show that they value exchange of information with a provider, being able to ask questions, and involvement in decision-making.[50] Research findings on whether gender concordance in the provider–patient relationship improves female patients' satisfaction with care are mixed. However, some studies suggest that women physicians "tend to exhibit more encouragement, empathy, and more patient-centric behaviors in their conversations with patients," things that seem to be highly valued by women patients.[51] Having a woman doctor is associated with some better patient outcomes: Female patients are less likely to die from a heart attack and all patients (male and female) are less likely to die within 30 days of admission to the hospital when treated by a woman doctor.[52] Yet women physicians remain in lower tiers of the medical hierarchy (e.g., only 15% of medical school deans are women) and make up a disproportionate share of low-status and low-paid health care workers, such as nurses and community health workers.[53] A study by the Steering Committee of the Lancet Series on Gender Equality, Norms, and Health suggests that failing to address gender inequity in health care systems is problematic for providers and patients: "Health systems reflect and reinforce the gender biases and restrictive gender norms in society, and these biases and norms undermine the functioning of health systems and compromise the safety and wellbeing of providers and the health of communities."[54]

Gender inequities are present in access to health insurance as well. As of 2020, roughly 11% of women ages 19 to 64 were uninsured and more likely to be covered as a dependent than to carry their own health insurance.[55] Lack of health insurance significantly affects the amount and quality of care that women receive. Uninsured women are less likely to access preventive services such as mammograms and Pap tests and to have a regular source of care, including prenatal care. Women of Color, immigrant women, low-income women, and single mothers have higher rates of uninsurance.[56] However, as of 2010 with passage of the Affordable Care Act (ACA), gender-rating insurance (in which health insurance plans charge women more than men for the same benefits) is now prohibited. Furthermore, ACA plans must cover certain preventive services without a copayment, including well-women visits, Pap tests, mammograms, bone density tests, the human papilloma virus (HPV) vaccine, breastfeeding supplies, and prescription contraceptives. Clearly an effort to expand and improve women's access to care—especially preventive services that are particularly important to women's health—the ACA made great strides in reducing inequity in women's health care.

Nonetheless, as discussed earlier in this chapter, Supreme Court decisions have undermined the ACA's contraception mandate, and the COVID-19 pandemic has exacerbated existing access barriers for women in obtaining regular preventive health care services. A study by Becker et al. showed that "the overall odds of a woman receiving a given preventive service [breast cancer screening, cervical cancer screening, sexually transmitted infection (STI) screening, long-acting reversible contraception (LARC) insertions, and pharmacy-obtained contraception] in 2020 was 20% to 30% lower than 2019."[57]

Women's reproductive health continues to be subject to social, economic, and political forces, creating significant barriers to quality care. These forces affect women's daily lives: "Because so much of women's lives is devoted to reproductive issues—trying to avoid pregnancy, trying to get pregnant, raising children, and being familial caretakers—women are directly affected by the politicization of reproductive health care."[58] Sixty-one million women in the United States are of reproductive age. Roughly 70% of those are sexually active and are not wishing to become pregnant; 45% of all pregnancies are unintended.[59] Cost barriers most significantly affect low-income women, making them more susceptible to unintended pregnancy. Research shows that the ACA's elimination of cost-sharing for contraception was associated with higher contraception use and with lower birth rates for women, especially for low-income women.[60] At the same time, women who are charged a copayment of greater than $30 for contraception are less likely to consistently use it.[61] Persistent racial and ethnic inequities in access to care also put Women of Color at higher risk of unintended pregnancies and sexually transmitted diseases:

> Data suggest that the disproportionate risk for [W]omen of [C]olor for reproductive health access and outcomes expand beyond individual-level risks and include social and structural factors, such as fewer neighborhood health services, less insurance coverage, decreased access to educational and economic attainment, and even practitioner-level factors such as racial bias and stereotyping.[62]

Nearly one in four women in the United States will have an abortion during her lifetime. The growing number and type of state restrictions on abortion have taken a toll on access. Thirty-five states enacted 227 laws restricting access to abortion between January 2017 and November 2020.[63] Laws imposing more requirements on abortion providers have affected access by reducing the number of available providers in some geographic areas, particularly rural areas. One study found that increasing travel time to abortion services is significantly associated with the median abortion rate in that geographic area.[64] Restrictions on access to abortion are also associated with adverse birth outcomes (preterm birth and low birth weight) for Black and low-SES women.[65] Black women are disproportionately harmed by the lack of access to abortion, as they are more likely to live in states with abortion restrictions.[66] As described later in this chapter, the Black maternal health crisis has also been linked to poor access to abortion for Black women. Next, we detail further health inequities among women.

Social and Structural Drivers of Women's Health Inequities

Social and Structural Drivers of Health

The health status of women is affected by multiple structural and societal issues: power differentials between men and women, restrictive gender roles, economic inequity, lack of access to resources, restrictions on self-determination, and concerns for physical safety. Thus, women's health is deeply connected to their position in society. Here, we explore how structural and social drivers impact health inequities between men and women and among women. We start with economic inequality.

Women are more likely to live in poverty than are men across all racial and ethnic groups, but Women of Color have the highest rates of poverty of any group in the United States. Nearly a quarter of Black and Native women live in poverty.[67] Women with disabilities are more likely to live in poverty than men with disabilities and people without disabilities. One explanation for the higher rates of poverty among women is that they are both paid less than men and more likely to work in low-wage jobs. Women earn between 56% and 78% of what White men earn, with Women of Color on the low end of that scale, as noted in Chapter 7. Another reason for the higher rates of poverty among women is that they are more likely than men to be single parents. Eighty percent of single parents in the United States are women.[68] Nearly a quarter of unmarried women with children live in poverty.[69] Child care expenses, combined with the multiple and compounding costs associated with raising children (e.g., food, clothing, health insurance, housing), leave many mothers, particularly those working low-wage jobs, susceptible to falling into poverty.

Poverty and the stress of financial hardship are closely correlated with poor health. For low-income mothers, economic instability makes them vulnerable to eviction and food insecurity, two critical social drivers of health. (See Chapters 7 and 8 for a detailed discussion of the links between food insecurity, housing instability, and health.) But there are also economic and health repercussions associated with being a mother even when not living in poverty. Overall, mothers are paid about 75% of what fathers earn.[70] Women pay a price in lower wages when they have children. One study found that mothers who change jobs after giving birth experience a 7.1% wage gap by being segregated into lower-paying jobs.[71] Women also receive fewer employment-based benefits—82% of health insurance, 76% of paid leave, and 67% of pension benefits—relative to men.[72] Black women and Latinas have significantly less access to paid parental leave than White and Asian women.[73] The United States is the only country among wealthy nations that does not mandate paid maternity leave (see **Figure 12.1**). Indeed, the United States is one of seven countries without national paid parental leave.[74]

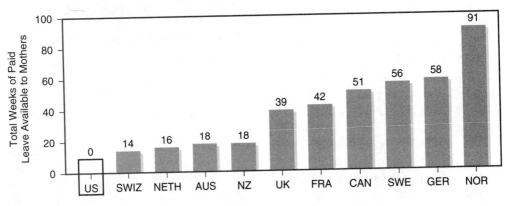

Figure 12.1 Weeks of paid maternity leave, 2018

Reproduced from Roosa Tikkanen et al., Maternal Mortality and Maternity Care in the United States Compared to 10 Other Developed Countries (Commonwealth Fund, Nov. 2020). https://doi.org/10.26099/411v-9255

Research shows that women, particularly mothers, continue to be responsible for a disproportionate share of caretaking and housework compared with men.[75] The COVID-19 pandemic highlighted the unequal roles played by women and men in the home. Studies of employment during the pandemic show that women were more likely than men to reduce their employment when child care facilities closed.[76] Women also had substantially more job losses than men did during the pandemic. Between February 2020 and September 2020, women accounted for 68.5% of U.S. job losses.[77] Although all workers may experience work–home conflicts from time to time, women, especially mothers, are more prone to the stress of balancing child care, home responsibilities, and work demands. Studies show that there are health consequences for women associated with caretaking.

As discussed at various points in this text, research demonstrates the important role that stress plays in health outcomes. A 2017 American Psychological Association study showed that women report substantially higher levels of stress than men.[78] Stress is associated with a range of poor health outcomes (as detailed in Chapter 7). In particular, recent studies have investigated the potential role of stress in cardiovascular disease and differences in prevalence between men and women. Rates of heart attack and fatal coronary heart disease are higher for older women than older men. While men have higher incidence of coronary heart disease overall, women actually have higher incidence as they age.[79] While researchers are still assessing the links between stress and coronary heart disease, women's stress burden may help explain health inequalities over the life course.[80] Another study found that mothers who care for a child with a serious health issue had shorter telomeres than peers without a seriously ill child. Telomeres "cap the end of chromosomes and generally shorten with age"; shorter telomeres are predictive of cardiovascular disease and death. The study suggested that the shorter telomere length of mothers caring for ill children was associated with 9 years of aging.[81] Thus, cumulative stress related to heavier responsibilities for caretaking and the challenges related to work–family balance may take a toll on women's long-term health.

For low-income and other marginalized women, the combination of structural and social drivers—including the greater burdens associated with caretaking, poverty, food insecurity, housing instability, and experiences of discrimination based on gender, race, ethnicity, and/or SES—can make healthy behaviors extremely difficult if not impossible:

> Can women eat well when their income is used to pay for housing, when poor quality food is most readily available, when due to work and home responsibilities they have little time or energy to devote to cooking? Can women exercise when they have no time due to multiple roles, when the neighbourhoods where they live are not safe for walking, when there is little accessible, affordable recreation, when they have no child care? Can they effectively manage stress when they work in jobs that offer them little control, when they have little hope for change, when they have no personal time for adult relationships? Will women give up smoking, alcohol, or drugs when these seem to be the only sources of relief from stress?[82]

"Weathering" (the hypothesis that "the health of African American women may begin to deteriorate in early adulthood as a physical consequence of cumulative socioeconomic disadvantage")[83] likely plays an important role in Black women's health inequities. Likewise, the experiences of being an immigrant, LGBTQ+, and/or disabled woman each bring unique stressors that implicate health.

Social drivers and structural factors (i.e., gender inequality and law and policy failures) and their contribution to allostatic load (chronic and cumulative stress) also influence women's reproductive health. These factors influence many reproductive health outcomes, including unintended pregnancy, cervical and breast cancer, infertility, preterm birth, and maternal mortality.[84] Lack of access to quality, affirming reproductive health care is associated with worse breast and cervical cancer outcomes for Women of Color and LGBTQ+ women. For example, mortality from breast cancer is 40% higher for Black women than for White women. Black women are not only more likely have delayed diagnosis, but they are also more likely to have breast cancer at a younger age (40 to 45).[85] Poor access to care for low-SES women and higher incidence of chronic disease (e.g., diabetes, cardiovascular disease) may explain these disparities.[86]

Weathering may also play a role in Black women experiencing more aggressive forms of breast cancer.[87]

Perhaps the greatest reproductive health problem in the United States is the nation's shockingly poor maternal health outcomes as compared to the rest of the world. The United States has the highest maternal mortality rate among high-income countries—twice the rate of Canada and 10 times the rate of New Zealand (see **Figure 12.2**).

Explanations for the maternal mortality crisis in the United States are multifactorial. First, the data show that there are gross racial inequities at play. Black mothers die at three times the rate of White mothers,[88] and their babies are more than twice as likely to die in the first year of life as White babies.[89] Black mothers also experience more severe maternal morbidities than White women. Black women, for example, have a 60% higher rate than White women of preeclampsia (high blood pressure during pregnancy that, if not treated, can lead to serious complications and even death).[90]

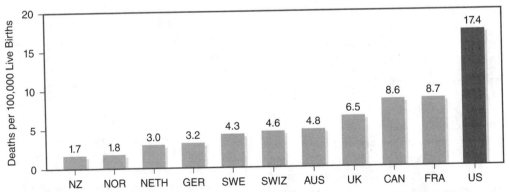

Notes: The maternal mortality ratio is defined by the World Health Organization as the death of a woman while pregnant or within 42 days of termination of pregnancy, irrespective of the duration and site of the pregnancy, from any cause related to or aggravated by the pregnancy or its management but not from accidental or incidental causes.

Figure 12.2 Maternal mortality ratios in selected countries, 2018 or latest year

Reproduced from Roosa Tikkanen et al., Maternal Mortality and Maternity Care in the United States Compared to 10 Other Developed Countries (Commonwealth Fund, Nov. 2020). https://doi.org/10.26099/411v-9255

Preterm birth is also disproportionately higher among Black women. Because racial disparities persist in maternal morbidity and mortality even when controlling for SES, many researchers have concluded that experiences of racism affect reproductive health for Black women. For example, with regard to racial disparities in preterm births, public health researcher Paula Braveman and colleagues note that "…Black women's potentially subtle but repeated experiences of feeling judged or treated unfairly or anticipating unfair treatment because of their race could contribute to increased PTB [preterm birth] risk through physiologic pathways involved in stress."[91] High rates of Black maternal morbidity and mortality reflect a constellation of factors: higher rates of chronic disease (often associated with social drivers and allostatic load as described above), the experience of racism and discrimination over a lifetime, and lack of access to quality, unbiased, reproductive health care.[92]

A second factor in the maternal mortality crisis is the type of reproductive health care available in the United States and the inadequacy of the care and support mothers receive during the postpartum period. Many countries cover through insurance or government-funded programs access to midwives, doulas (individuals who provide guidance and support to a woman during pregnancy, childbirth, and postpartum), and other supportive care providers for women throughout their pregnancies. The United States has a long history of resistance to non-physician care providers. The Sheppard-Towner Act of 1921 enacted onerous regulatory barriers, including education and licensure requirements, that shifted power over births from mothers and communities to the medical establishment (mainly, male physicians). This was particularly harmful to Black women, as they have historically relied on a community of women supporting one another during pregnancy, birth, and the postpartum period.[93] Despite evidence that

midwives and doulas improve maternal health outcomes, the United States has not developed this aspect of the health care workforce in the way that other countries have. Furthermore, private and public insurance plans have traditionally not covered these services. In particular, Medicaid, which covers nearly half of all births in the United States and 66% of births to Black women, has not traditionally supported these services. However, some states are beginning to change these policy dynamics.[94]

Half of all maternal deaths in the United States occur postpartum. Indeed, a third of all deaths occur between 1 week and 1 year after delivery.[95] But the United States lags in providing supportive in-home follow-up care to mothers postpartum (see **Figure 12.3**). Because of the patchwork health insurance system in the United States, access to postpartum care is highly dependent on insurance policies. Specifically, Medicaid, which, as noted previously, covers a large portion of pregnant women—especially Black women—varies dramatically by state regarding postpartum coverage. Under federal rules, Medicaid programs must cover maternal care for at least 60 days postpartum. Therefore, women living in states that have not expanded Medicaid coverage under the ACA to all adults living below 138% of the federal poverty level often lose their health insurance after 60 days. A study in 2018 showed that 47% of new mothers lost Medicaid or health insurance coverage after pregnancy.[96] With more attention to maternal mortality, some states have begun extending Medicaid coverage to up to 12 months postpartum. Additionally, through the American Rescue Plan Act in 2020, the Biden administration began authorizing states to extend Medicaid eligibility for up to 12 months postpartum beginning on April 1, 2022. However, this provision of the act only lasts for 5 years and will have to be renewed by Congress.[97]

A third factor in the high rate of maternal mortality is the prevalence of violence

Postpartum Home Visits

	Covered by national insurance?	Timing and number of covered visits	Provider
Australia	Yes	Within week 1, typically one to three visits	Midwife
Canada	Yes	Contacted or visited within 24 to 48 hours after going home	Public health nurse
France	Yes	Starting within 24 hours after discharge, one to three visits	Midwife
Germany	Yes	Daily if needed until day 10, plus 16 visits as needed until eight weeks postpartum	Midwife
Netherlands	Yes	Daily, starting immediately after birth and up to 10 days postpartum, staying at a minimum 4 hours per day	Maternity nurse
New Zealand	Yes	At least five visits over six weeks, starting within 48 hours postpartum	Midwife
Norway	Yes	Midwife: Starting at 24 to 48 hours, or three days (for low-risk multiparous women) after going home Nurse: First visit on days 7 to 10 postpartum; second visit on days 14 to 21	Midwife, nurse
Sweden	Yes	First visit during week 1; visits thereafter every one to two weeks until week 8	Midwife, nurse
Switzerland	Yes	Daily, up to 10 days postpartum	Midwife
United Kingdom	Yes	At least until 10 days postpartum	Midwife, nurse
United States	Covered by some state Medicaid programs and certain health plans	Varies by state Medicaid program and by individual insurer	Nurse, physician, community health worker, doula, home health worker

Figure 12.3 Postpartum home visits

Reproduced from Roosa Tikkanen et al., Maternal Mortality and Maternity Care in the United States Compared to 10 Other Developed Countries (Commonwealth Fund, Nov. 2020). https://doi.org/10.26099/411v-9255

and substance use disorders in the United States (see Chapter 7). According the Centers for Disease Control and Prevention, the leading causes of pregnancy-associated death are homicide, suicide, and drug overdose.[98] Women are more likely to die from homicide during pregnancy than when not pregnant. Black women are seven times more at risk for homicide during pregnancy than White women.[99] Homicide is highly correlated with intimate partner violence, which tends to escalate during pregnancy, and rates of pregnancy-associated homicide are higher in the United States than other countries.[100] The higher prevalence of both suicide and homicide during pregnancy in the United States is likely connected to its propensity for gun violence.[101]

Another social driver of the high rates of maternal mortality is the drug overdose crisis that has devastated communities across the United States. Between May 2020 and April 2021, more than 100,000 people died from drug overdose.[102] A review of state Maternal Mortality Review Committee reports by 26 states found that pregnancy-associated overdose deaths doubled between 2007 and 2016.[103] White women are most at risk of overdose death.[104] Furthermore, in 2021, the CDC reported that in a review of six states, 73% of pregnancy-associated overdose deaths occurred in the late postpartum period (43 to 365 days after delivery), and 89% were potentially preventable.[105]

Women may be reluctant to seek help for a substance use disorder (SUD) or even to engage in prenatal care during pregnancy and postpartum because they fear being reported to child protective services and losing custody of their newborn and/or other children. The Guttmacher Institute, a reproductive rights organization, reports that 23 states and the District of Columbia (D.C.) define substance use during pregnancy as child abuse; 25 states and D.C. require health care providers to report prenatal drug use to child protective services, and eight states require testing when drug use is suspected. But only 19 states fund drug treatment programs that specifically focus on pregnant women, and only 10 states prohibit discrimination against pregnant women in publicly funded treatment programs.[106] In some states, such as Alabama, pregnant women have been arrested under "chemical endangerment laws."[107] Punitive laws and policies that prosecute pregnant women or remove children from their custody when they use illicit substances have been found to actually reduce the likelihood that pregnant women receive treatment. These laws also fail to reduce neonatal abstinence syndrome (the withdrawal a baby experiences when born to a mother with SUD).[108]

Health Inequities

Overall, women are generally viewed as having better health than men. After all, they enjoy a longer life expectancy at birth than men—5 years longer. But women's unique experiences, including their social, economic, and political position in society and their greater role in reproduction, make them susceptible to health inequities. In fact, life expectancy for lower-educated women, particularly White women, actually has declined in recent years.[109] While women are less likely to die at each age than men, they are more likely to rate their health as poor and to visit the hospital more than men. This paradox may be explained, at least in part, by differences in the prevalence of chronic conditions women face. Women experience higher rates of pain (migraine headaches, arthritis) and some respiratory conditions, including bronchitis, asthma, and lung problems not related to cancer. They are also much more likely than men to suffer from reproductive cancers, hypertension, vision problems, and depression.[110]

On the other hand, earlier mortality for men may be tied to riskier unhealthy behaviors.

"Their higher rates of cigarette smoking, heavy drinking, gun use, employment in hazardous occupations, and risk taking in recreation and driving are responsible for males' higher death rate due to lung cancer, accidents, suicide, and homicide."[111] Data on women's health also illustrate significant racial and ethnic health inequities among women. As described earlier, these include higher rates of diabetes and higher mortality rates from heart disease, stroke, and cancer among Black women and Latinas than White women. These inequities are influenced by social disadvantages specific to Women of Color, as outlined previously.[112] LGBTQ+ women and women with disabilities also suffer from health inequities, topics that are explored in greater detail in Chapters 13 and 14, respectively.

No discussion of inequities in women's health would be complete without discussion of violence. One in four women in the United States will experience intimate partner violence in her lifetime, while one in six will experience an attempted or completed rape.[113] Far more will experience sexual harassment and other types of sexual assault. The health consequences of violence against women and girls are far-reaching. Physical health consequences commonly experienced by women who are victims of violence are heart disease, asthma, arthritis, chronic pain, migraine headaches, ulcers and other gastrointestinal disorders, and gynecological problems. They are also at higher risk for HIV or sexually transmitted diseases.[114] Furthermore, as discussed in Chapter 7, the trauma associated with being the survivor of violence may also have lifelong effects on mental health. Survivors are more likely than those who have not experienced violence to be diagnosed with posttraumatic stress disorder, depression, eating disorders, and substance use disorders.[115] Given the prevalence of violence against women, experts define this crisis as both a public health problem and a human rights issue.[116]

Law, Policy, and Structural Change to Achieve Health Justice

Imbedded in U.S. laws and policies are deeply ingrained notions about appropriate gender roles for men and women. Women continue to experience gender-based discrimination and to have less economic, social, and political power than men. Coupled with their reproductive capacity and higher burden of unpaid caretaking work, women disproportionately live in poverty or experience precarity in managing their daily expenses. Women's reproductive rights continue to be highly politicized, while low-income women and Women of Color, in particular, continue to lose access to reproductive health care. All of these inequities in the distribution of power and resources affect women's health.

Laws, as written, implemented, and enforced, and policy decisions (often made predominantly by men) play an enormous role in women's health. While addressing all of the legal and policy changes necessary to eliminating gender-based health inequities is beyond the scope of this chapter, we highlight some of the law and policy changes important to realizing health justice for women.

Protect and Promote Reproductive Rights and Justice

Court decisions prioritizing the religious rights of the few over women's reproductive rights, coupled with state and federal policies that chip away at public funding for contraception and abortion, harm all women, but especially low-income women and Women of Color. Women's reproductive rights implicate multiple aspects of their lives—their physical health, mental health, and overall well-being; their economic independence; and their self-determination. But as the

reproductive justice movement suggests, reproductive justice is not only about the legal right to abortion and public investment in contraception; rather, it should focus on "the complete physical, mental, spiritual, political, social, and economic well-being of women and girls."[117] Ultimately, as Elizabeth Sepper points out:

> It demands the equal importance of rights to have a child, rights to avoid procreation, and the right to parent one's children with the recognition that these rights are intimately linked to the conditions in one's community from environment to education to crime....[and] demands radical change to eradicate the legal, social, and cultural oppression of women and women of color in particular."[118]

Access to safe, affordable, and supportive reproductive health care that empowers women to make their own decisions about whether and when to have children is a function of policy choices. At this time, the United States is moving further and further away from reproductive justice.

Invest in and Prioritize Women's Health

The U.S. health care system was not formed with women's particular health interests and needs in mind. Centering women's health involves confronting not only how gender bias manifests in women's encounters with individual providers and health care institutions but also how laws and policies shape those encounters. The maternal health crisis, particularly the shameful maternal mortality rate for Black mothers, reflects the convergence of long-standing racism and gender bias in American society. But it also exhibits a very flawed health care system that does not prioritize women's health, especially Black women's health, and that undervalues and underpays a health care workforce that is predominantly made up by Women of Color.

While some states are beginning to cover the services of midwives, doulas, and other community health workers, reimbursements are grossly inadequate, and bureaucratic hurdles make development of this mostly female workforce overly burdensome.[119] States and the federal government can impose accountability requirements for health care systems based on their maternal health outcomes and can, through Medicaid and insurance rules, require adequate coverage for evidence-based care practices and different types of providers that support maternal health. While proposals to extend Medicaid coverage to women postpartum is a step forward, it also implies that women's health is *only* important as it relates to childbirth. Expanding Medicaid to low-income women, whether they are mothers or not, supports women's health across the life span.

Implement Policies That Support Women's Economic Security

The COVID-19 pandemic has laid bare the multiple ways that women are economically vulnerable. Disproportionately working in low-wage "essential" jobs, Women of Color continue to endure financial precarity as well as significant health risks associated with poverty—housing instability, food insecurity, and the stress of discrimination and racism. Women as a group bear a greater burden of caretaking that can threaten their financial stability, mobility, and independence. The Biden administration has proposed significant investments in government subsidization of child care and in the paid caregiver workforce (e.g., elder and child care workers). As of this writing, the administration's proposals for government-funded paid sick and family leave have been abandoned. Gender-neutral paid leave policies would most benefit women, especially low-income women, who face untenable work–family conflicts. These policies also have the potential to encourage men to invest more time in caretaking responsibilities and relieve some of the burden from women. For low-income women who struggle to care for their children, stay housed, put food on the table, and keep their jobs—and endure ruthless stress associated with these struggles—government policy has a huge stake in their health. Investments in child care, family and medical leave, and other workplace supports for parents and caregivers are crucial to improving health justice for women.

Reframe Women's Rights as Human Rights

It is often said that "women's rights are human rights." But as this chapter has demonstrated, the history of discrimination against women and the structuring of systems around male norms without regard for women's needs and interests undermine women's self-determination and equal access to power. The United States has failed in its leadership of and even commitment to international human rights norms, as described in Chapter 5. For example, it remains one of only six countries in the world that has not ratified the Convention on the Elimination of All Forms of Discrimination Against Women, even though the convention simply states that countries agree "to take all appropriate measures, including legislation, to modify or abolish existing laws, regulations, customs and practices which constitute discrimination against women." Elimination of discrimination against women in the United States first requires recognition of the problem; it then demands that women's health, well-being and equitable treatment are prioritized in law and policy. In the workplace, the persistent pay gap and the gender disparities in leadership are still often dismissed as inherent to women's "choices" to have and care for children or family members. Similarly, sexual harassment and violence continue to diminish women's opportunities and devastate their health and well-being. The feminization of poverty harms the health and well-being of a large proportion of U.S. women and their children. U.S. policymakers and much of the public view the country as leading when it comes to women's rights. Yet its failure to enact laws and policies that prioritize women's health, well-being, and self-determination tells another story. The United States has a long way to go to treat women's rights as human rights.

Conclusion

This chapter highlighted both the history and persistence of gender-based discrimination in American society and its effects on women's health and well-being. U.S. policymakers and the public continue to debate foundational issues related to women's equality: reproductive rights, legal and policy remedies for women's lack of economic and political power, and how to begin to acknowledge and address the gross inequities among women that continue to relegate a disproportionate number of Women of Color to poverty and low social status. As outlined here, there are multiple opportunities for policymakers to enact laws and policies that ensure equitable treatment of women and that promote women's rights as human rights. In the next chapter, we turn to gender-based health injustice through the lens of gender identity and sexual orientation.

References

1. *Muller v. Oregon*, 208 U.S. 412 (1908).
2. *Muller v. Oregon*, 208 U.S. 412 (1908).
3. *Craig v. Boren*, 429 U.S. 190 (1976).
4. England P, Levinea A, Mishela E. Progress toward gender equality in the United States has slowed or stalled. *PNAS*. March 31, 2020;117(13):6990–6997.
5. Steelfisher GK, Findling MG, Bleich SN, et al. Gender discrimination in the United States: Experiences of women. *Health Services Research*. 2019;54:1442–1453.
6. National Partnership for Women and Families. By the numbers: Women continue to face pregnancy discrimination in the workplace: An analysis of U.S. Equal Employment Opportunity Commission charges (fiscal years 2011–2015). October 2016. https://www.nationalpartnership.org/our-work/resources/economic-justice/pregnancy-discrimination/by-the-numbers-women-continue-to-face-pregnancy-discrimination-in-the-workplace.pdf.
7. Family Caregiver Alliance. Women and caregiving: Facts and figures. Who are the caregivers? 2003. https://www.caregiver.org/resource/women-and-caregiving-facts-and-figures/.
8. Robert Wood Johnson Foundation. Improving access to paid family leave to achieve health equity: How the United States can advance health equity by guaranteeing all people have access to paid family leave. May 27, 2021. https://www.rwjf.org/en/library/research/2021/05/improving-access-to-paid-family-leave-to-achieve-health-equity.html?rid=0034400001rm8RkAAI&et_cid=2495830.
9. *Planned Parenthood of Southeastern Pa. v. Casey*, 505 U.S. 833, 856 (1992).
10. *Buck v. Bell*, 274 U.S. 200 (1927).
11. Lombardo P. *Three Generations, No Imbeciles: Eugenics, the Supreme Court and Buck v. Bell*. Baltimore, MD: Johns Hopkins Press; 2008.
12. Hawkins D. California once forcibly sterilized people by the thousands. Now the victims may get reparations. *Washington Post*, July 9, 2021. https://www.washingtonpost.com/nation/2021/07/09/california-once-forcibly-sterilized-people-by-thousands-now-victims-may-get-reparations/.
13. Fuller TR, Prather C, et al. Racism, African American women, and their sexual and reproductive health: A review of historical and contemporary evidence and implications for health equity. *Health Equity*. 2018;2:249.
14. Hawkins D. California once forcibly sterilized people by the thousands. Now the victims may get reparations. *Washington Post*, July 9, 2021. https://www.washingtonpost.com/nation/2021/07/09/california-once-forcibly-sterilized-people-by-thousands-now-victims-may-get-reparations/.
15. Bekiempis V. More immigrant women say they were abused by ICE gynecologist. *The Guardian*. December 22, 2020. https://www.theguardian.com/us-news/2020/dec/22/ice-gynecologist-hysterectomies-georgia.
16. *Griswold v. Connecticut*, 381 U.S. 479 (1965).
17. *Eisenstadt v. Baird*, 405 U.S. 438 (1972).
18. Frederiksen B, Salganicoff A, Sobel L, et al. Key Elements of the Biden Administration's Proposed Title X Regulation. Kaiser Family Foundation. May 5, 2021. https://www.kff.org/womens-health-policy/issue-brief/key-elements-of-the-biden-administrations-proposed-title-x-regulation/.

19. *Burwell v. Hobby Lobby*, 573 U.S. 682 (2014).

20. Keith K. Supreme Court upholds broad exemptions to contraceptive mandate—for now. Health Affairs Blog. July 9, 2020. https://www.healthaffairs.org/do/10.1377/hblog20200708.110645/full/.

21. *Roe v. Wade*, 410 U.S. 113 (1973).

22. *Maher v. Roe*, 432 U.S. 464 (1977).

23. *Harris v. McRae*, 448 U.S. 297, 316 (1980).

24. *Planned Parenthood of Southeastern Pennsylvania v. Casey*, 505 U.S. 833 (1992).

25. Brief for American College of Obstetricians & Gynecologists American Medical Association, American Academy of Family Physicians, American Osteopathic Association, & American Academy of Pediatrics, as Amici Curiae Supporting Petitioners, *Whole Woman's Health v. Hellerstedt,* No. 15–274 (June 27, 2016).

26. *Carhart v. Gonzalez*, 550 U.S. 124 (2007).

27. *Carhart v. Gonzalez*, 550 U.S. 124 (2007).

28. Guttmacher Institute. Emotional and mental health after abortion. 2022. https://www.guttmacher.org/perspectives50/emotional-and-mental-health-after-abortion.

29. *Dobbs v. Jackson Women's Health Organization* (citation pending).

30. How a majority of court appears poised to roll back abortion rights. SCOTUSblog. December 1, 2021. https://www.scotusblog.com/.

31. Tex. Health & Safety Code Ann. §§171.208(a), (b)(3) (West 2021).

32. *United States v. Texas*, 595 U. S. _____ (2021).

33. Rosenthal A, George P, Tobin-Tyler E, et al. The past and future of gender nondiscrimination policy under the Affordable Care Act. *American Journal of Preventive Medicine.* 2021. doi:10.1016/j.amepre.2021.06.019.

34. Chilet-Rosell E. Gender bias in clinical research, pharmaceutical marketing, and the prescription of drugs. *Global Health Action.* 2014;7:25484.

35. Institute of Medicine. Summary. Women's health research: progress, pitfalls, and promise. Washington, DC: The National Academies Press; 2010. https://www.nap.edu/read/12908/chapter/2.

36. Ravindran T., Teerawattananon Y, Tannenbaum C, Vijayasingham L. Making pharmaceutical research and regulation work for women. *BMJ.* 2020; m3808. doi:10.1136/bmj.m3808.

37. Gupta GR, Oomman N, Grown C, Conn K, et al. Gender equality and gender norms: Framing the opportunities for health. *The Lancet.* 2019;393:2550–2562.

38. Samulowitz A, Gremyr I, Eriksson E, Hensing G. "Brave men" and "emotional women": A theory-guided literature review on gender bias in health care and gendered norms towards patients with chronic pain. *Pain Research and Management.* 2018;1–14.

39. Leonard J. Gender bias in medicine. Medical News Today. June 16, 2021. https://www.medicalnewstoday.com/articles/gender-bias-in-medical-diagnosis.

40. Dennis B. Heart attacks in women can be different—and more deadly—than in men. *The Washington Post.* January 25, 2016. https://www.washingtonpost.com/news/to-your-health/wp/2016/01/25/why-heart-attacks-in-women-are-often-different-than-in-men/.

41. Centers for Disease Control and Prevention. Women and heart disease. https://www.cdc.gov/heartdisease/women.htm.

42. Weyand AC, James PD. Sexism in the management of bleeding disorders. *Research and Practice in Thrombosis and Haemostasis.* 2021;5:51–54.

43. Tasca C, Rapetti M, Carta MG, Fadda B. Women and hysteria in the history of mental health. *Clinical Practice & Epidemiology in Mental Health.* 2012;8:110–119.

44. Hunter N. The scarlet diagnosis: Trauma, psychosis, and pathologizing the feminine. In *Women and the Psychosocial Construction of Madness.* Lanham, MD: Lexington Books; 2019: 149.

45. Hunter N. The scarlet diagnosis: Trauma, psychosis, and pathologizing the feminine. In *Women and the Psychosocial Construction of Madness.* Lanham, MD: Lexington Books; 2019: 149.

46. World Health Organization. Gender and mental health. 2002. https://apps.who.int/iris/bitstream/handle/10665/68884/a85573.pdf.

47. World Health Organization. Gender and mental health. 2002. https://apps.who.int/iris/bitstream/handle/10665/68884/a85573.pdf.

48. Bacigalupe A, Martín U. Gender inequalities in depression/anxiety and the consumption of psychotropic drugs: Are we medicalising women's mental health? *Scandinavian Journal of Public Health.* 2021;49(3):317–324.

49. World Health Organization. Gender and mental health. 2002. https://apps.who.int/iris/bitstream/handle/10665/68884/a85573.pdf.

50. Ramlakhan JU, Foster AM, Grace SL, et al. What constitutes patient-centred care for women: A theoretical rapid review. *International Journal for Equity in Health.* 2019;18:182.

51. Prasad T, Buta E, Cleary PD. Is patient–physician gender concordance related to the quality of patient care experiences? *Journal of General Internal Medicine.* 2021;36:3058–3063.

52. Greenwood BN, Carnahan S, Huang L. Patient-physician gender concordance and increased mortality among female heart attack patients. *Proceedings of the National Academy of Sciences of the United States of America.* 2018;115(34):8569; Tsugawa Y, Jena AB, Figueroa JF. Comparison of hospital mortality and readmission rates for Medicare patients treated by male vs female physicians. *JAMA Internal Medicine.* 2017;177:206.

53. Hay K, Mcdougal L, Percival V, et al. Disrupting gender norms in health systems: Making the case for change. *The Lancet.* 2019;393:2535–2549.

54. Hay K, Mcdougal L, Percival V, et al. Disrupting gender norms in health systems: Making the case for change. *The Lancet.* 2019;393:2535–2549.

55. Kaiser Family Foundation. Women's health insurance. November 8, 2021. https://www.kff.org/other/fact-sheet/womens-health-insurance-coverage/.

56. Kaiser Family Foundation. Women's health insurance. November 8, 2021. https://www.kff.org/other/fact-sheet/womens-health-insurance-coverage/.

57. Becker NV, Moniz MH, Tipirneni R, et al. Utilization of women's preventive health services during the COVID-19 pandemic. *JAMA Health Forum.* 2021; 2:e211408.

58. Harleman E, Steinauer J. Women's health: Reproduction and beyond in poor women. In King TE, Wheeler MB, Bindman AB, et al. Medical management of vulnerable and underserved populations: Principles, practice and populations. New York, NY: McGraw Hill; 2007: 297.

59. Marshall C, Schmittdiel J, Chandra M, et al. The relationship between prescription copayments and contraceptive adherence in a new-user cohort. *Medical Care.* 2018;56:577–582.

60. Dalton VK, Moniz MH, Bailey MJ. Trends in birth rates after elimination of cost sharing for contraception by the Patient Protection and Affordable Care Act. *JAMA Network Open.* 2020;3(11):e2024398.

61. Marshall C, Schmittdiel J, Chandra M, et al. The relationship between prescription copayments and contraceptive adherence in a new-user cohort. *Medical Care.* 2018;56:577–582.

62. Sutton M, Anachebe NF, Lee R, Skanes H. Racial and ethnic disparities in reproductive health services and outcomes. *Obstetrics & Gynecology.* 2021;137(2):225–233.

63. Gaj EB, Sanders JN, Singer PM. State legislation related to abortion services, January 2017 to November 2020. *JAMA Internal Medicine.* May 2021;181(5):712.

64. Thompson KMJ, Sturrock HJW, Foster DG, Upadhyay UD. Association of travel distance to nearest abortion facility with rates of abortion. *JAMA Network Open.* 2021;4(7):e2115530.

65. Redd SK, Rice WS, Aswani MS, et al. Racial/ethnic and educational inequities in restrictive abortion policy variation and adverse birth outcomes in the United States. *BMC Health Services Research.* 2021;21:1139.

66. National Partnership for Women and Families. Maternal health and abortion restrictions: How lack of access to quality care is harming Black women. October 2019. https://www.nationalpartnership.org/our-work/resources/repro/maternal-health-and-abortion.pdf.

67. Bleiweis R, Boesch D, Gaines AC. The basic facts about women in poverty. Center for American Progress.

August 3, 2020. https://www.americanprogress.org/article/basic-facts-women-poverty/.

68. Livingston G. The changing profile of unmarried parents. Pew Research Center. April 25, 2018. https://www.pewresearch.org/social-trends/2018/04/25/the-changing-profile-of-unmarried-parents/.

69. Bleiweis R, Boesch D, Gaines AC. The basic facts about women in poverty. Center for American Progress. August 3, 2020. https://www.americanprogress.org/article/basic-facts-women-poverty/.

70. National Women's Law Center. The wage gap: The who, how, why, and what to do. Fact sheet. September 2021. https://nwlc.org/wp-content/uploads/2020/10/2021-who-what-why-wage-gap.pdf.

71. Fuller S. Segregation across workplaces and the motherhood wage gap: Why do mothers work in low-wage establishments? *Oxford Academic Journal.*2017;96:1443–1476.

72. Belsey-Priebe M, Lyons D, Buonocore JJ. COVID-19's impact on American women's food insecurity foreshadows vulnerabilities to climate change. *International Journal of Environmental Research and Public Health.* 2021;18(13):6867.

73. Goodman JM, Williams C, Dow WH. Racial/Ethnic Inequities in Paid Parental Leave Access. *Health Equity.* 2021;5.1:738–749.

74. Miller C. The World 'Has Found a Way to Do This': The U.S. Lags on Paid Leave. *The New York Times.* November 3, 2021. https://www.nytimes.com/2021/10/25/upshot/paid-leave-democrats.html

75. Hess C., Ahmed T., Hayes J. Providing unpaid household and care work in the United States: Uncovering inequality. *Institute for Women's Policy Research.* 2020;26:4.

76. Feyman Y, Fener NE, Griffith KN. Association of childcare facility closures with employment status of US women vs men during the COVID-19 pandemic. *JAMA Health Forum.* 2021;2(6):e211297.

77. Wolfe R, Harknett K, Schneider D. Inequalities at work and the toll of Covid-19. *Policy Brief. Health Affairs.* June 2021. https://www.healthaffairs.org/do/10.1377/hpb20210428.863621/full/

78. American Psychological Association. *Stress in America: The State of Our Nation.* Washington, DC: American Psychological Association; 2017.

79. Taylor JL, Makarem N, Shimbo D, Aggarwal, B. Gender differences in associations between stress and cardiovascular risk factors and outcomes. *Gender and the Genome.* 2018;2(4):111–122.

80. Taylor JL, Makarem N, Shimbo D, Aggarwal, B. Gender differences in associations between stress and cardiovascular risk factors and outcomes. *Gender and the Genome.* 2018;2(4):111–122.

81. Epel ES, Blackburn EH, Lin J, et al. Accelerated telomere shortening in response to life stress.

Proceedings of the National Academy of Sciences of the United States of America. 2004;101(49):17312–17315.

82. Wuest J, Merritt-Gray M, Berman H, Ford-Gilboe M. Illuminating social determinants of women's health using grounded theory. *Health Care for Women International.* 2002;23:794–808,797.

83. Geronimus AT. The weathering hypothesis and the health of African-American women and infants: Evidence and speculations. *Ethnicity & Disease.* 1992 Summer;2(3):207–221.

84. American College of Obstetrics and Gynecologists. Importance of social determinants of health and cultural awareness in the delivery of reproductive health care. Committee Opinion Number 729. January 2018. https://www.acog.org/clinical/clinical -guidance/committee-opinion/articles/2018/01 /importance-of-social-determinants-of-health-and -cultural-awareness-in-the-delivery-of-reproductive -health-care?utm_source=redirect&utm _medium=web&utm_campaign=otn.

85. Breast Cancer Research Foundation. Black women and breast cancer: Why disparities persist and how to end them. January 14, 2021. https://www.bcrf .org/blog/black-women-and-breast-cancer-why -disparities-persist-and-how-end-them/.

86. Breast Cancer Research Foundation. Black women and breast cancer: Why disparities persist and how to end them. January 14, 2021. https://www.bcrf .org/blog/black-women-and-breast-cancer-why -disparities-persist-and-how-end-them/.

87. Linnenbringer E, Gehlert S, Geronimus AT. Black-White disparities in breast cancer subtype: The intersection of socially patterned stress and genetic expression. *AIMS Public Health.* 2017;4(5):526–556.

88. Petersen EE, Davis NL, et al. Racial/ethnic disparities in pregnancy-related deaths—United States, 2007–2016. *Morbidity and Mortality Weekly Report.* 2019; 68:762.

89. Collins JW, David RJ. Racial disparity in low birth weight and infant mortality. *Clinical Perinatology.* 2009;36:63.

90. Fingar KR, Mabry-Hernandez I, Ngo-Metzger Q, et al. Delivery hospitalizations involving preeclampsia and eclampsia, 2005–2014 (Statistical Brief #222). April 2017. https://www.hcup-us.ahrq.gov/reports /statbriefs/sb222-Preeclampsia-Eclampsia-Delivery -Trends.pdf.

91. Braveman PA, Heck K, Egerter S, et al. The role of socioeconomic factors in Black–White disparities in preterm birth. *American Journal of Public Health.* 2015;105(4):694–702.

92. Tobin-Tyler E. Black mothers matter: The social, political and legal determinants of Black maternal health across the lifespan. *Journal of Health Care Law and Policy.* 2022;25(1):49–89.

93. Williams JM. The midwife problem: The effect of the 1921 Sheppard-Towner Act on Black midwives in Leon County. Southern Conference on African-American Women Studies. Southern University and A & M College, Baton Rouge, LA, February 2014.

94. Tobin-Tyler E. Black mothers matter: the social, political and legal determinants of black maternal health across the lifespan. *Journal of Health Care Law and Policy.* 2022;25(1):49–89.

95. Tikkanen R, Gunja MZ, Fitzgerald M, et al. Maternal mortality and maternity care in the United States compared to 10 other developed countries. *Commonwealth Fund.* November 2020. https://doi .org/10.26099/411v-9255.

96. McMorrow S, Dubay L, et al. Uninsured new mothers' health and health care challenges highlight the benefits of increasing postpartum Medicaid coverage. The Urban Institute. May 2020. https://www .urban.org/sites/default/files/publication/102296 /uninsured-new-mothers-health-and-health-care -challenges-highlight-the-benefits-of-increasing -postpartum-medicaid-coverage_0.pdf.

97. Chappel A, DeLew N, Grigorescu V, Smith SR. Addressing the maternal health crisis through improved data infrastructure: Guiding principles for progress. Health Affairs Blog. August 11, 2021. https://www .healthaffairs.org/do/10.1377/hblog20210729.265068 /full/?utm_medium=email&utm_source=hasu&utm _campaign=blog&utm_content=chappel&utm _source=Newsletter&utm_medium=email&utm_cont ent=ACA+Updates%2C+Innovation+At+CMS+%26+M ore&utm_campaign=HASU%3A+8-15-21&vgo_ee=P IsaBHiejM66z3IzHBl%2F3D%2BJLi7DAuyw1lBdDJF3 D%2Bo%3D.

98. Campbell J, Matoff-Stepp S, Velez ML, Cox HH, Laughon K. Pregnancy-associated deaths from homicide, suicide, and drug overdose: Review of research and the intersection with intimate partner violence. *Journal of Women's Health.* 2021;30(2):236–244.

99. Campbell J, Matoff-Stepp S, Velez ML, Cox HH, Laughon K. Pregnancy-associated deaths from homicide, suicide, and drug overdose: Review of research and the intersection with intimate partner violence. *Journal of Women's Health.* 2021;30(2):236–244.

100. Campbell J, Matoff-Stepp S, Velez ML, Cox HH, Laughon K. Pregnancy-associated deaths from homicide, suicide, and drug overdose: Review of research and the intersection with intimate partner violence. *Journal of Women's Health.* 2021;30(2):236–244.

101. Campbell J, Matoff-Stepp S, Velez ML, Cox HH, Laughon K. Pregnancy-associated deaths from

homicide, suicide, and drug overdose: Review of research and the intersection with intimate partner violence. *Journal of Women's Health.* 2021;30(2):236–244.

102. Keating D, Bernstein L. 100,000 Americans died of drug overdoses in 12 months during the pandemic. *The Washington Post.* November 17, 2021. https://www.washingtonpost.com/health/2021/11/17/overdose-deaths-pandemic-fentanyl/.

103. Gemmill A, Kiang MV, Alexander MJ. Trends in pregnancy-associated mortality involving opioids in the United States, 2007–2016. *American Journal of Obstetrics & Gynecology.* 2019;220:115–116.

104. Schiff DM, Nielsen T, Terplan M, et al. Fatal and nonfatal overdose among pregnant and postpartum women in Massachusetts. *Obstetrics & Gynecology.* 2018;132:466–474.

105. Smoots AN, Zaharatos J, Beauregard JL, Trost SL, Goodman DA. Pregnancy-Associated Overdose Deaths: Data from 6 states in the Rapid Maternal Overdose Review Initiative, 2015-2019. Atlanta, GA: Centers for Disease Control and Prevention, U.S. Department of Health and Human Services; 2021.

106. Guttmacher Institute. State laws and policies. Substance use during pregnancy. November 1, 2021. https://www.guttmacher.org/state-policy/explore/substance-use-during-pregnancy.

107. Martin N. Take a Valium, lose your kid, go to jail. ProPublica. September 23, 2015. https://www.propublica.org/article/when-the-womb-is-a-crime-scene.

108. Atkins DN, Durrance CP. State policies that treat prenatal substance use as child abuse or neglect fail to achieve their intended goals. *Health Affairs.* 2020;39(5):756–763.

109. Montez JK, Zajacova A. Why is life expectancy declining among low-educated women in the United States? *American Journal of Public Health.* 2014;104(10):e5–e7.

110. Population Reference Bureau. Gender disparities in health and mortality. Accessed October 9, 2017. http://www.prb.org/Publications/Articles/2007/genderdisparities.aspx.

111. Population Reference Bureau. Gender disparities in health and mortality. Accessed October 9, 2017. http://www.prb.org/Publications/Articles/2007/genderdisparities.aspx.

112. Harleman E, Payne C, Steinauer J. Women's health: Reproduction and beyond in poor women. In King TE, Wheeler MB, Bindman AB, et al. *Medical Management of Vulnerable and Underserved Populations: Principles, Practice and Populations.* New York, NY: McGraw Hill; 2016.

113. Harleman E, Payne C, Steinauer J. Women's health: Reproduction and beyond in poor women. In King TE, Wheeler MB, Bindman AB, et al. *Medical Management of Vulnerable and Underserved Populations: Principles, Practice and Populations.* New York, NY: McGraw Hill; 2016.

114. Institute of Medicine. *Women's Health Research: Progress, Pitfalls, and Promise.* Washington, DC: The National Academies Press; 2010:57. https://www.nap.edu/read/12908/chapter/4#57.

115. Institute of Medicine. *Women's Health Research: Progress, Pitfalls, and Promise.* Washington, DC: The National Academies Press; 2010:57. https://www.nap.edu/read/12908/chapter/4#57.

116. Harleman E, Payne C, Steinauer J. Women's health: Reproduction and beyond in poor women. In King TE, Wheeler MB, Bindman AB, et al. *Medical Management of Vulnerable and Underserved Populations: Principles, Practice and Populations.* New York, NY: McGraw Hill; 2016.

117. Ross L, Solinger R. *Reproductive Justice: An Introduction.* Oakland, CA: University of California Press; 2017.

118. Sepper E. The right to avoid procreation and the regulation of pregnancy: A US perspective. In Orentlicher D, Hervey TK. *The Oxford Handbook of Comparative Health Law.* Oxford: Oxford University Press; 2021.

119. Tobin-Tyler E. Black mothers matter: The social, political and legal determinants of Black maternal health across the lifespan. *Journal of Health Care Law and Policy.* 2022;25(1):49–89.

CHAPTER 13

LGBTQ+ People

Co-authored by Heather Walter-McCabe

20 pages

LEARNING OBJECTIVES

By the end of this chapter you will be able to:

- Describe the status of anti-discrimination and other laws affecting LGBTQ+ people
- Discuss historical and current treatment of LGBTQ+ people in health care, including the ways in which bias and stigma affect LGBTQ+ people's access to quality care
- Describe the social and structural drivers of LGBTQ+ health inequities
- Highlight how the intersections of LGBTQ+ status with other marginalized statuses (e.g., race, ethnicity, socioeconomic status, disability) exacerbate health inequities

Introduction

Chapter 12 described how gender has traditionally been defined in medicine, public health, and law as solely about the binary difference between men and women. Because women as a group continue to experience sex discrimination and marginalization based on a long legacy of policies and practices favoring men, discussing their particular experiences with the medical and legal systems—and the effects of social and structural drivers on their health—is critical to an understanding of gender and health justice. At the same time, the outmoded definition of gender as binary—male versus female—excludes and dismisses people who do not identify in the traditional regime of cisgender, heterosexual, and binary.

This chapter explores how LGBTQ+ communities continue to battle against discrimination and marginalization in health care, public health, and especially law, with grave consequences for their health and well-being. Because, as discussed in Chapter 1, language and self-identification are fundamental to how people are perceived and treated, we begin with a discussion about why language is so critical to LGBTQ+ people's dignity and rights. The chapter then explores the legal treatment of LGBTQ+ people over time and current controversies in the law. Next, it turns to LGBTQ+ people's experiences with medicine and health care, the many social and structural drivers of LGBTQ+ health, and the health inequities that continue to plague LGBTQ+ communities. The chapter ends with a discussion of some of the legal, policy, and structural changes that would facilitate health justice for LGBTQ+ people.

The Importance of Language and Self-Identification

While often described as a monolithic group, sexual and gender minorities encompass a wide variety of identities.[1] Even the acronym "LGBTQ+" has multiple forms, with some using simply LGBT and others expanding it to include additional identities, most commonly "IA" for *intersex* and *asexual*. We use "LGBTQ+" to indicate inclusion of all sexual and gender minorities, however they identify. When working with LGBTQ+ populations in health care, public health, and the policy arena, it is important to understand the meaning behind the language people use to identify themselves in order to provide culturally appropriate care and to promote meaningful structural reforms. The U.S. Department of Health and Human Services (HHS) recognizes the importance of language as a mediator of health inequities, reporting that "one of the most modifiable factors [for health inequities] is the lack of culturally and linguistically appropriate services, broadly defined as care and services that are respectful of and responsive to the cultural and linguistic needs of all individuals."[2]

Language is powerful, as noted in Chapter 1. It has been used "to discriminate, abuse, marginalize, disrupt, and destabilize individuals and communities,"[3] including LGBTQ+ communities. As described later, while sexual and gender minorities have existed throughout history, until recently, health and behavioral health professionals and systems categorized variance in sexuality and gender identity and expression as deviant and even sociopathic.

LGBTQ+ rights advocates have been active in changing social norms to increase acceptance, including defining and identifying themselves through labels that have evolved over time. (See **Table 13.1** demonstrating how language has changed.) Claiming their own experiences through language empowers these communities to challenge societal expectations that are based on heteronormative and cisnormative assumptions—respectively, that everyone is heterosexual or that only heterosexuality is "normal" and that everyone is cisgender, that their sex and gender align, or that anything other than cisgender is not "normal." For example, whereas *gay* (G) was traditionally used as a blanket term for any person who had an emotional or physical attraction to others of the same sex, lesbians (L)—women who are emotionally and/or physically attracted to women—asserted their need to be named and recognized on their own terms.[4] Similarly, *bisexual* (B) used to describe those who are emotionally and/or physically attracted to men and women. Over time, however, the term has been conceptualized to include being attracted to more than one gender, with some using it as inclusive of trans men, trans women, and non-binary people, adopting the term to explicitly challenge the notion of a binary gender structure. Others use the term *pansexual* to indicate that they are attracted to all gender identities.[5] Those identifying as *asexual* are people who experience little to no sexual attraction.[6] Queer (Q), used historically as a slur, has been reclaimed by some in the LGBTQ+ community whose sexuality falls outside traditionally socially accepted labels and norms. This term, which gained popularity during the AIDS pandemic, is sometimes used as a political statement in defiance of negative and imposed social norms. While some have reclaimed this term, others in LGBTQ+ communities continue to view this term as offensive.[7] The Q can also be used to describe those who are questioning their sexuality or gender identity.

Transgender (T) communities have similarly asserted their right to identify on their own terms. *Transsexual* was an early term used by the medical community for those who now refer to themselves as *transgender*. *Transsexual* is no longer used widely and is generally considered an

Table 13.1 LGBTQ+ Outdated and Recommended Terms

Outdated term	Recommended term
Berdache	Two spirit
Biological female/male	Assigned female/male at birth
Cross sex hormone therapy; hormone	Gender affirming hormone therapy
Disorders/differences of sex development	Intersex
Female to male (FTM) and Male to female (MTF)	Transgender man and transgender women
Gender nonconforming	Gender non binary
Hermaphrodite/Ambiguous genitalia	Intersex
Homosexual	Gay or lesbian
Legal name	Administrative name or Name on legal documents
Preferred name	Choose name or Name used
Preferred pronouns	Pronouns
Sex change/Sex reassignment surgery/Gender reconstruction surgery	Gender affirming surgery
Sexual preference/lifestyle	Sexual orientation
Transgendered	Transgender

Reproduced from Fenway Institute National LGBTQIA+ Health and Education Center. LGBTQIA+ Glossary of Terms for Health Care Teams. Published online February 2, 2020. https://www.lgbtqiahealtheducation.org/publication/lgbtqia-glossary-of-terms-for-health-care-teams/

outdated and offensive term. Though a small number of people in the transgender community still use this term to emphasize their belief that medical transition is important, the term is viewed by many as an offensive medicalization of their lived experience. People should never be referred to as transsexual unless they specifically request it.[8] *Transgender* is an inclusive term, including those who identify as trans men or women (those whose assigned sex at birth does not match their gender identity, regardless of medical transition), nonbinary or genderqueer (those who do not identify with the gender binary), genderfluid (those whose gender identity varies, including at times identifying as both or neither binary genders), and agender (those who do not view themselves as having a gender), among many more. Additionally, some include intersex people (those who develop secondary sex characteristics in a way that does not conform to traditional expectations of male or female) in transgender communities, but it is important to understand that, though some who are intersex also identify as transgender, this is a distinct community with its own identity.[9] Another inclusive term for these diverse groups is *gender diverse people (GDP)*. Similar to queer (Q) as a defiant sexuality, genderqueer is a gender identity popularized in the 1990s that is rooted in a rejection of societal norms about binary genders.[10]

Honoring and using the terms with which a person identifies is a critical component of competent health care and health justice more generally.[11] Given that the language people use changes over time, it is important for health care providers, public health practitioners, and policymakers dedicated to health justice to ensure they understand and employ the terms used by LGBTQ+ communities. Additionally, using incorrect pronouns to identify individuals—termed *misgendering*—can further marginalize and stigmatize people. Particularly in the health care context, insensitivity to people's sexual or gender identity can negatively impact their mental health and discourage engagement in treatment.[12] A good resource, which is regularly updated, is the *LGBTQIA+ Glossary of Terms for Health Care Teams* created by the Fenway Institute.[13]

As discussed in Chapter 1, LGBTQ+ people's identities and experiences may vary dramatically based on their race, ethnicity, socioeconomic status, and disability status. The intersectionality of sexual and gender identity with these other types of social statuses may influence how an individual is treated by law enforcement and the legal system, health care providers, and many other systems. Defining people just by their sexual or gender identity ignores the complexity of their experiences and may force them to choose a particular community or group when they feel part of many. Respecting how people identify themselves—including all of their social and cultural identities—affirms them as individuals. As discussed in Chapter 6, LGBTQ+ status has yet to achieve the same legal protections as race, ethnicity, gender (as it applies to notions about differences between men and women as traditionally defined), and disability. As explored later, while there have been enormous strides made in LGBTQ+ rights, there are still many challenges ahead in achieving equality and health justice for these communities. We explore these challenges through the lenses of constitutional law, civil rights laws,

religious rights, and the particular legal issues affecting transgender rights.

Treatment of LGBTQ+ People under the Law

Progress Toward Equal Treatment under the U.S. Constitution

LGBTQ+ people have for centuries been subject to discrimination and criminal prosecution based on who they are. Homosexuality was criminalized largely through state sodomy laws. It was not until 2003 that the U.S. Supreme Court, in the case of *Lawrence v. Texas*,[14] declared these laws an unconstitutional violation of equal protection, privacy, and liberty interests under the 14th Amendment. While sodomy laws are unenforceable, 14 states still had such statutes in their state legal codes as of 2020.[15]

While the *Lawrence* decision was momentous in improving the treatment of LGBTQ+ populations under the law, significant legal barriers persist in accomplishing full recognition of LGBTQ+ rights. LGBTQ+ people have no explicit protections in federal civil rights laws. As described later in the chapter, recent court decisions have interpreted protections against sex discrimination to include sexual orientation and gender identity, but lawsuits seeking to restrict these protections are still pending in federal courts. State-level legal protections vary by type of discrimination and whether the protection applies to sexual orientation, gender identity, or both.

In 2015, LGBTQ+ people experienced a major legal advancement when the U.S. Supreme Court recognized the constitutionality of marriage equality. Prior to 2004, across all states and at the federal level, marriage was legally defined as only between a man and a woman. In the late 1980s, LGBTQ+ advocates began to push states to legalize marriages between two people of the same sex. In 1993, the Hawaii Supreme Court ruled in *Baehr v. Lewin* that the state's refusal to grant a marriage license to two individuals of the same sex should be reviewed by the court using the strict scrutiny standard (which, as you will recall from Chapter 4, requires the state to show that its action was based on a compelling state interest and was narrowly tailored to meet that interest).[16] Although the Hawaii court ultimately did not find in favor of a right to same-sex marriage, the case attracted national attention and initiated a backlash by Congress against LGBTQ+ rights. In 1996, Congress passed the Defense of Marriage Act (DOMA). DOMA defined marriage as between one man and one woman, applied this definition to all federal programs, and clarified that no state was required to recognize a same-sex marriage that was legal in another state.[17] As a result of DOMA, LGBTQ+ people in same-sex marriages were unable to access federal benefits available to other legally married people.

Nonetheless, in 2004, states began passing laws allowing same-sex couples to legally marry. As discussed previously, recognition of these marriages was limited to the states that had chosen to legalize such marriages and did not include recognition by the federal government or other states per DOMA. However, in 2013, in *United States v. Windsor*, the Supreme Court found that application of DOMA as it pertained to the federal government under Section 3 was unconstitutional under the Fifth Amendment of the U.S. Constitution. The decision made more than 1,000 federal statutes applicable to all marriages regardless of the sex of the individuals. The Court was not, however, asked to consider the constitutionality of Section 2, which allowed states to decline recognition of same-sex marriages from other states.[18] In 2015, after decades of LGBTQ+ legal advocacy in conjunction with efforts to change public perception of same-sex marriage, the Supreme Court held, in *Obergefell v. Hodges*, that marriage was a fundamental right

that must not be denied to same-sex couples.[19] The Court's ruling was a vital moment for recognition and inclusion of LGBTQ+ people in American society, but as with the *Lawrence* case, it did not eliminate disparate treatment under the law. Even in the area of marriage, two states still have laws allowing state and local officials to refuse to perform marriages with which they disapprove.[20]

The Rise of Religious Rights and Its Effect on LGBTQ+ Equality

Legal rights for LGBTQ+ people are inextricably linked to assertions of rights by people who oppose homosexuality and gender diversity based on their religious beliefs. Opposition to marriage equality, access to public accommodations, workplace equality, and provision of gender-affirming health care have all been premised on protecting religious rights. In 1993, just as new LGBTQ+ rights were starting to take hold, Congress passed the Religious Freedom Restoration Act (RFRA). The law applies strict scrutiny to any governmental action that implicates a person's religious freedom—even when the law is one of general applicability, meaning that it is applied to all people equally without targeting a particular group for differential treatment.[21] RFRA sought to change the way courts analyze laws that implicate religious rights after the 1990 Supreme Court case of *Employment Division v. Smith*. In *Smith*, the Court found that when a law implicates religious rights only "incidentally" and is applied to religious and nonreligious individuals equally, then an individual may be required to comply with the law, even if doing so violates that person's religious beliefs. Legislators concerned with protecting religious rights perceived the *Smith* analysis as a major departure from previous Court analyses of religious rights.[22]

By ensuring that courts apply strict scrutiny to any law seeking to compel action in conflict with a person's religious beliefs, RFRA has been employed as a vehicle to undermine LGBTQ+ rights. Although in *City of Boerne v. Flores* (1997) the Supreme Court limited the applicability of RFRA to federal laws—holding that Congress exceeded its authority when applying the law to states—the law remains important in supporting religious rights claims.[23] Additionally, 21 states enacted their own versions of RFRA, making it more difficult to overcome challenges to discrimination against LGBTQ+ people when the alleged offender asserts a religious rationale for their behavior.[24] For example, Indiana passed a state version of RFRA that broadly interprets protection of religious rights to include both businesses and individuals. While Indiana's law resulted in state and national corporations exerting fiscal pressure on the state to modify the law because of its implications for LGBTQ+ people, the law succeeded in further stigmatizing and marginalizing LGBTQ+ communities.[25]

In addition to the implications of RFRA-type laws in states, the Supreme Court has recently begun shifting its interpretation of religious rights under the federal Constitution. In *Fulton v. City of Philadelphia* (2021), the Court held that the city of Philadelphia could not enforce its nondiscrimination policy by refusing to contract with Catholic Social Services (CSS) for provision of foster care services because CSS refused to license same-sex couples as foster parents. The Court found that the city's nondiscrimination policy was not "generally applicable" to all people because it provided some discretion to the commissioner of the Department of Health to determine whether to contract with specific agencies. The Court's decision allows lower courts to strike down any law as not "generally applicable" if it includes *any* secular exemptions as violating religious rights when religious groups are not also given an exemption.[26] It remains to be seen how and in what circumstances the Court will apply this logic, but as seen in *Fulton*

v. City of Philadelphia, it could have major implications for LGBTQ+ communities' freedom from discrimination.

Protection Under Civil Rights Laws

As mentioned previously, LGBTQ+ populations have been omitted from federal civil rights statutes. While the universe of issues in the legal treatment of LGBTQ+ people is beyond the scope of this chapter, we focus below on several areas of law that are specifically relevant to LGBTQ+ health justice. Additionally, we describe recently enacted and proposed state legislation that is explicitly targeted at undermining the rights of transgender and gender diverse people.

Public Accommodations

Like all people, LGBTQ+ people use public accommodations regularly and should reasonably have an expectation to do so without experiencing discrimination. Public accommodations are those places generally open to the public (e.g., restaurants, stores, hotels). Private clubs and religious organizations, as organizations that do not hold themselves out to be open to the general public, are generally not considered public accommodations. For example, bathrooms, which are of particular importance to the health and safety of gender diverse people, are considered part of the facilities put forth to the public for use as a part of public accommodations.[27]

Federal civil rights laws that protect people from discrimination in places of public accommodation do not include sexual orientation and gender identity. Twenty-one states and the District of Columbia explicitly bar discrimination based on sexual orientation and gender identity in public accommodations; an additional six states have interpreted their prohibitions against discrimination on the basis of sex to include sexual orientation and/or gender identity (see **Figure 13.1**).[28]

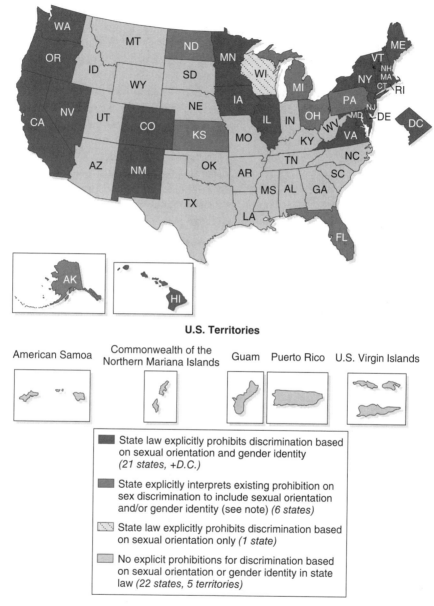

Figure 13.1 Map of public accommodations laws

There have been multiple court cases examining the extent to which those whose religious beliefs do not condone homosexuality or gender diversity[29] must provide public accommodations and services to LGBTQ+ people. These cases have often centered around the provision of wedding services. In some of the recent cases examining LGBTQ+ rights, the Supreme Court has avoided explicit declarations regarding how they will balance these rights with religious objections by focusing on technical and process-related issues.[30] How the Supreme Court will treat cases in which a person claims that providing accommodation to LGBTQ+ people is a violation of the Free Exercise Clause of the U.S Constitution (which prevents the government from interfering with a person's right to practice their religion) remains unsettled. But advocates for LGBTQ+ rights are concerned about how the current Supreme Court may rule in this area.[31]

Interpretation of "Discrimination on the Basis of Sex"

Until 2020, LGBTQ+ people were not protected under Title VII of the 1964 Civil Rights Act (which, as discussed in Chapter 6, is a federal civil rights law that protects certain classes of people against workplace discrimination). The law prohibits employment discrimination "on the basis of sex"—meaning that a worker may not be discriminated against solely because she is a woman or he is a man, but the law is silent with regard to protections based on sexual orientation or gender identity. In other words, until recently, it was perfectly legal for employers to make hiring and firing decisions based on an applicant's or worker's sexual orientation or gender identity.[32] In June 2020, in *Bostock v. Clayton County*, the Supreme Court ruled that despite the fact that sexual orientation and gender identity are not explicitly included as protected classes in Title VII, they are subsumed under the definition of "on the basis of sex," the antidiscrimination language in the statute.[33] The ruling that sex discrimination protections included sexual orientation and gender identity has had broad impact. On his first day in office in 2021, President Joe Biden signed an executive order that extended the Court's interpretation of sex discrimination to multiple laws—including Title IX of the 1972 Education Amendments (which prohibits sex discrimination in education), the Fair Housing Act, and the Immigration and Nationality Act—to "prohibit discrimination on the basis of gender identity or sexual orientation, so long as the laws do not contain sufficient indications to

the contrary."[34] He further ordered all administrative agencies to review current regulations for changes needed to implement the order. President Biden's decision to ensure implementation of the *Bostock* holding will protect the health of LGBTQ+ people by reducing the negative effects of multiple social and structural drivers of health.

Although these newly recognized antidiscrimination provisions have broad impact, religious opponents to LGBTQ+ rights stand poised to try to mitigate some of the progress. For example, the 2021 case of *Bear Creek Bible Church and Braidwood Management v. Equal Employment Opportunity Commission* posed this question to a federal trial court in Texas: Is a private, for-profit business that is considered a Christian business governed by the post-*Bostock* interpretation of Title VII as protecting LGBTQ+ people from discrimination in employment? The Texas court's decision in the case broadly interpreted the rights of religious businesses to sidestep Title VII's prohibition against discrimination based on sexual orientation and gender identity. It held that the antidiscrimination requirements of Title VII, as applied to LGBTQ+ people, violated the rights of religious businesses under RFRA and the Constitution's Free Exercise Clause.[35] Furthermore, the plaintiffs had asked the Texas court to consider the extent to which a secular employer "opposed to homosexual and transgender behavior" is governed by Title VII's newly interpreted nondiscrimination protections under the Constitution's Free Association Clause. The Texas court decided that gender-neutral provisions, such as those addressing dress codes and bathroom usage, may be applied to employees as governed by their assigned sex at birth. The case will almost certainly be appealed, but the broad exemption inherent in the court's holding is concerning. Despite the positive progress made in the *Bostock* decision, the court's holding in *Bear Creek Bible Church* makes it clear that for LGBTQ+ communities, the fight continues for expansive and all-inclusive rights in employment.[36] As employment rights are fundamental to people's ability to meet their basic needs, they clearly have significant implications for health and well-being.

Housing Discrimination

The Fair Housing Act "protects people from discrimination when they are renting or buying a home, getting a mortgage, seeking housing assistance, or engaging in other housing-related activities. Additional protections apply to federally-assisted housing" (see Chapter 6).[37] As of February 2021, per President Biden's executive order discussed previously, the U.S. Department of Housing and Urban Development (HUD) began enforcing a prohibition on discrimination in housing on the basis of sexual orientation and gender identity.[38] This is an important policy change for those needing stable housing, which, as discussed in Chapter 8 and elsewhere in this book, is a vital social driver of health. Though the federal government is now enforcing protections against discrimination for LGBTQ+ people in federal housing programs, some states have not yet implemented laws providing the same protections in state-funded housing programs or in private housing. Twenty-two states and the District of Columbia have housing laws prohibiting discrimination on the basis of sexual orientation and gender identity. Nine states interpret their existing laws prohibiting discrimination on the basis of sex as inclusive of sexual orientation and gender identity. One state prohibits discrimination on the basis of sexual orientation only. The remaining 18 states do not explicitly prohibit discrimination on the basis of sexual orientation or gender identity.[39] Failure to include LGBTQ+ people in housing discrimination laws in some states means that they do not have the same legal protections as virtually all other people in those states.

Health Care Access and Financing

In May 2021, the U.S. Department of Health and Human Services (HHS) published a notification of interpretation and enforcement of Section 1557, the section of the Affordable Care Act (ACA) that prohibits discrimination in health care. As you may recall from Chapter 6, Section 1557 is the most expansive antidiscrimination law ever passed regulating health care programs and activities. The HHS publication explicitly reaffirmed the protections against discrimination on the basis of sexual orientation and gender identity that were included in Section 1557 regulations promulgated by the Obama administration in 2016.[40]

An important aspect of the Obama administration rule was that it prohibited public and private health insurance plans from writing blanket provisions prohibiting gender-confirming care for transgender populations. The rule essentially required that hormone therapy and gender-confirming surgery be deemed medically necessary treatment for those with gender dysphoria. Thus, it was critical to increasing access to needed services for those previously unable to pay out of pocket for costly treatments. Within months, a group of Catholic and Christian medical providers challenged the rule in the case of *Franciscan Alliance, Inc. v. Burwell*. A federal trial court in Texas issued a nationwide preliminary injunction (meaning that the rule would not go into effect until challenges could be fully vetted by the courts) but stated that the Obama administration, in interpreting Section 1557's antidiscrimination provisions as including gender identity, may have overstepped its authority under the Administrative Procedures Act. The rule, the court warned, was also likely to violate the RFRA.[41]

Shortly after the court's decision in *Franciscan Alliance*, Donald Trump was elected president. The Trump administration declined to challenge the injunction and agreed to write a new rule that would comply with the court's findings.[42] Finally, in 2019, HHS proposed a new rule, reversing the Obama administration's interpretation of Section 1557, excluding gender identity from protection, and explicitly including broad exemptions for entities controlled by religious institutions from enforcement of the rules governing nondiscrimination on the basis of sex.[43] But the Trump administration rule was short-lived. In *Whitman-Walker Clinic, Inc. v. U.S. Dep't of Health & Hum. Servs*, the new rule was challenged as inconsistent with the Supreme Court's decision in *Bostock*, which incorporated gender identity in the definition of sex discrimination.[44]

Under the Biden administration, the federal government is interpreting Section 1557 to prohibit health care programs and activities from discriminating based on sexual orientation and gender identity, with some narrow exemptions for religious entities in compliance with RFRA. HHS plans to release a new notice of proposed rulemaking interpreting Section 1557 early in 2022 and has already begun conducting research for that proposed rule. While this is positive progress, court challenges continue, primarily with regard to how the law relates to health care rights for transgender people. The scope of antidiscrimination protections in health care for LGBTQ+ people remain unsettled.[45]

Legal Issues of Importance to Transgender Communities

Discussion of the legal treatment of LGBTQ+ populations would not be complete without inclusion of specific legal issues facing transgender communities. Next, we highlight some of the types of laws that impact these communities. It is particularly important to understand these issues at a time of unprecedented legal and physical attacks on members of transgender communities. In 2021 alone, states enacted 15 laws that are harmful to transgender communities; more than 250 bills restricting the rights of transgender people were introduced in state legislatures.[46]

Transgender communities have sought legal recognition for decades. For example, they have advocated for laws allowing access to appropriate gender marker on legal documents (e.g., birth certificates and passports), which indicate their gender identity rather than assigned sex at birth. Having appropriate documents reduces harassment when, for example, seeking health care services or submitting job applications. Appropriate documentation enables transgender people to express their identities without continually providing explanations for who they are. In June 2021, the U.S. Department of State began issuing passports that align with gender identity without requiring medical documentation. This change not only increases ease for the applicant but also provides the choice of "X," allowing those who identify outside the gender binary the ability to have documents that reflect their identity in ways that were previously unavailable.

In recent years, the fight for transgender rights has also been waged in school athletics. Opponents to transgender rights in athletics object to transgender students participating in team sports—often by citing concerns about physical advantages—that match the their gender identity rather than the sex assigned a birth (e.g., a transgender girl playing on a girls' basketball team). Yet transgender students participating in sports activities that match their gender identity is not new. It often occurs in higher education, and transgender people are currently eligible to participate in the Olympics, provided that certain medical criteria are met.

The number of youth identifying as transgender is increasing as representation in the media and online help support people to recognize and name their experiences. But even as the number of self-identified transgender people has increased, a recent study reports that only 1.8% of youth self-identify as transgender.[47] Given this small percentage, the legislative attention to restricting transgender youth from participating in school activities seems vastly disproportionate to the day-to-day realities experienced in most schools. Nevertheless, 10 states currently have laws or executive orders banning participation by transgender youth in school athletics. In two states (West Virginia and Idaho), a court has ordered a preliminary injunction temporarily preventing the law from taking effect.[48]

Another area of activity for state legislatures is the movement to bar provision of age-appropriate gender-affirming medical services. Transgender youth under 18 are rarely candidates for gender-affirming surgeries, but puberty blockers—medications that pause puberty until children are old enough to decide for themselves if they would like to pursue hormone therapy—and hormone therapy for older adolescents are the standard of care for youth experiencing gender dysphoria.[45] As discussed later in the chapter, failing to provide appropriate medical care for gender dysphoria can have devastating consequences for transgender people's health and well-being. While only Arkansas has passed legislation forbidding such care, 15 such bills were introduced in 2020–2021. The Arkansas bill is currently being litigated.[49]

In addition to laws targeting transgender youth, some state Medicaid laws ban gender-affirming medical care across all ages. Despite federal laws prohibiting discrimination in health care, 10 state Medicaid programs explicitly forbid coverage of transgender-related health care, while 17 states have no legislative language on the issue. There are court challenges in some states. In 2021, an Iowa district court found the exclusion of gender-affirming care from the state's Medicaid program unconstitutional under the Iowa constitution.[50]

The past two decades have ushered in many positive changes in legal protections for LGBTQ+ communities, yet recent state legislative actions creating greater restrictions on transgender rights present new challenges. The failure to afford LGBTQ+ people full equality under the law has serious implications for health justice.

Treatment of LGBTQ+ People by the Health Care System

There is a long history of pathologizing and stigmatizing LGBTQ+ people by the medical community. Scientific research and the medical community have reinforced notions of gender nonconformance and homosexuality as pathological. In 1952, the American Psychiatric Association's (APA) first edition of the *Diagnostic and Statistical Manual of Mental Disorders* (DSM) listed homosexuality as "psychopathological and as a sociopathic personality disturbance."[51] Classifying homosexuality as a disease had profound consequences for the lives of LGBTQ+ people, who were demonized as deviant and dangerous; the DSM included them in the same category as pedophiles. On this basis, laws excluding them from employment were common, and some psychiatrists advocated for confining LGBTQ+ people in order to prevent sex crimes. "Cures" for homosexuality, such as electroshock, castration, lobotomy, hormone treatment, and psychotherapy, were offered by psychiatrists and psychologists.[52]

In 1968, after activists—such as the Mattachine Society, discussed in Chapter 2—challenged the criminalization and pathologizing of homosexuality, the sociopathic disturbance category was removed from the DSM-II (2nd edition), but it continued to list homosexuality as psychopathologic and a "sexual deviation."[53] In 1980, after much lobbying by activists, including some in the medical profession, the DSM-III did not include homosexuality but instead added new diagnostic categories called "Gender Identity Disorder in Childhood" (GIDC) and "transsexualism." GIDC focused on the development of atypical behavior, particularly in boys, who displayed "effeminate behavior" and who were thought likely to become gay in adulthood. GIDC was maintained as a category of mental illness in the APA's DSM-III-R in 1987, when a third diagnosis was also added: gender identity disorder in adulthood and adolescence.[54] The DSM-IV (1994) included a single diagnosis: gender identity disorder, which incorporated GIDC and "transsexualism."[55] Finally, in DSM-V (2013), GIDC was replaced with "gender dysphoria," which the APA describes as "psychological distress that results from an incongruence between one's sex assigned at birth and one's gender identity."[56]

The category of gender dysphoria is intended to address the mental health consequences and stress created by gender nonconformity in children and adults. Nonetheless, as queer theorists point out: "What the diagnostic history of homosexuality, GIDC, and gender dysphoria in children point to is to the ways in which biomedical knowledge is structured around the polarity of the normal and the pathological to the extent that all have served to maintain heteronormative gender norms."[57] Furthermore, despite the lack of evidence supporting it and the extreme harm caused by it,[58] "conversion therapy"—which attempts to convert LGBTQ+ people to heterosexuality and/or cisgender identity—continues to be practiced, though 25 states have made it illegal for mental health providers to employ it.[59]

Access to Quality Health Care

The legacy of stigmatizing sexual minorities as mentally ill or deviant from the norm has fundamentally shaped LGBTQ+ people's connection to the health care system, creating significant barriers to trusting provider–patient relationships. Gender-affirming health care that supports the physical, mental, and emotional health of LGBTQ+ people is still relatively rare. In its report *The Health of Lesbian, Gay, Bisexual and Transgender People: Building a Foundation for Understanding*, the Institute of Medicine outlined the personal barriers to care faced by LGBTQ+ individuals. Personal barriers include (1) "enacted stigma," in which LGBT[Q+] patients face discrimination that results in denial of care or hostility from health care providers; (2) "felt stigma," in which people change their behavior or hide their sexuality to prevent experiencing stigma, leading to delayed care or receiving inadequate care; and (3) "internalized stigma," in which LGBT[Q+] individuals do not believe they are entitled to appropriate, respectful health care.[60] LGBTQ+ people who also face discrimination based on their race, ethnicity, SES, immigration status, disability, or geographic location may experience intersectional stigma and discrimination. Another way to describe different levels of stigma affecting the LGBTQ+ population is individual, interpersonal, and structural.

Since health care is generally provided through large institutions, LGBTQ+ patients often confront structural or institutional stigma, even if individual providers do not exhibit bias toward them. For example, a hospital policy that does not recognize a same-sex partner as a health care proxy, even when that person has been designated by the patient, would indicate structural stigma.[61]

Understanding the role of stigma in producing obstacles to high-quality health care for LGBTQ+ individuals is crucial because, as discussed later in the chapter, as a group, they experience significant health inequities. As **Figure 13.2** displays, in 2020, LGBTQ+ people were more likely to report negative experiences with health care providers than were non-LGBTQ+ people. But as noted earlier, lumping people together in the LGBTQ+ category often obscures their different experiences.

Fear of stigmatization and discrimination often means that LGBTQ+ people do not disclose their sexual orientation or gender identity to health care providers. Failing to disclose can have serious ramifications for access to appropriate, quality care and for one's overall health and well-being. One study summarizes some of the barriers to disclosure as lack of opportunity (e.g., the provider does not ask or indicate any interest in the patient), fear of homophobia and discrimination, dismissive and/or hostile behavior or heteronormative attitudes

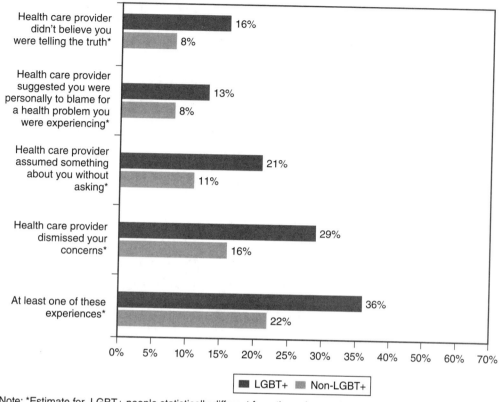

Note: *Estimate for LGBT+ people statistically different from those for non-LGBT people (*p* < 0.05).

Figure 13.2 Larger shares of LGBT+ adults report negative experiences with their providers compared with non-LGBT+ adults

Dawson L, Frederiksen B, Long M, et al. LGBT[Q]+ People's Health and Experiences Accessing Care. Kaiser Family Foundation. July 22, 2021. https://www.kff.org/report-section/lgbt-peoples-health-and-experiences-accessing-care-report/

of the provider, projected discomfort with the topics of sexuality and gender identity by the provider, and lack of supportive services in the provider's practice (e.g., failing to offer a welcoming atmosphere that indicates acceptance and respect for all people).[62] Young people are especially reluctant to disclose their sexuality or gender identity to a clinician unless appropriately encouraged.[63] A study of LGBTQ+ people living in rural areas found that stigma plays an important role in the likelihood that sexual and gender identity minorities will access primary care and preventive screenings.[64] For example, LGBTQ+ women are less likely to obtain a mammogram and to have a gynecological exam than non-LGBTQ+ women.[65]

Studies show that poor access to behavioral health care for LGBTQ+ youth is a chronic, national problem. This is particularly problematic because, as discussed later, this population has some of the highest rates of mental health and substance use disorders in the country.

A 2020 study conducted by the Trevor Project found that only 54% of LGBTQ+ youth who indicated that they desired mental health care actually received it. LGBTQ+ youth living in the South were less likely to access mental health care than those living in the North.[66] Concerns about cost, parental permission, and provider bias were some of the reasons attributed by the survey respondents for inability to access care.[67] Access to reproductive health care that is tailored to the LGBTQ+ population is also lacking; in particular, there is a dearth of family planning counseling and services available.[68] Indeed, transgender people who wish to parent frequently do not access information about reproductive health options from their health care providers.[69]

Access to high-quality health care for LGBTQ+ people begins with gender affirmation—respectful, nonjudgmental, and supportive care for all patients regardless of their sexual orientation or gender identity. Gender affirmation is particularly critical for gender diverse people (GDP). Not all GDP experience gender dysphoria—distress experienced when gender identity does not match their assigned sex at birth. The medical standard of care for gender dysphoria is to provide appropriate, evidence-based medical treatment including, for example, puberty blockers, hormone therapy, or gender-affirming surgeries that align patients' bodies with their gender identity.[70] But gender-affirming care is still relatively inaccessible because of blanket exclusions in health insurance plans for gender-affirming treatments and the prohibitively high out-of-pocket costs of care. Inability to access gender-affirming care often results in behavioral health crises and even suicide.[71]

Scholars and advocates have identified several structural changes required to improve health care for LGBTQ+ populations, especially the provision of gender-affirming care. First, they point to needed reforms to medical and other health professional education. As a start, proponents of reform argue that health education programs should require a basic curriculum on diversity in sexuality and gender identity and competency with LGBTQ+ terminology.[72] A second structural change is expansion of gender-affirming health care services for LGBTQ+ patients. This may be accomplished through health care system investment in specialized clinics that specifically target the needs of LGBTQ+ patients and training *all* health care providers how to deliver gender-affirming care to their patients. Expansion is vital because access to gender-affirming care is uneven geographically.[73]

Social and Structural Drivers of LGBTQ+ Health Inequities

Social and Structural Drivers of Health

Even before LGBTQ+ people reach a clinician's office, they experience social and structural barriers that impede access to health care and that impact their health status. A 2021 study by the Kaiser Family Foundation found that although roughly the same percentage of LGBTQ+ people have health insurance as their non-LGBTQ+ peers, they are more likely to report difficulties with health care costs (30%) than non-LGBTQ+ people (19%). One in four LGBTQ+ people reported that their preferred health care provider is not covered by their insurance.[74] The study also showed that LGBTQ+ people are more likely than non-LGBTQ+ people to live below 200% of the federal poverty level.[75]

As discussed earlier, LGBTQ+ people are not a monolithic group, and therefore their social experiences vary. The experience of being a transgender woman, for example, is different from that of being a lesbian. Furthermore, intersectionality (the interconnected nature of social categorizations such as race, ethnicity, SES, and disability status) plays a role in how sexual minorities and gender-nonconforming people are treated and the degree to which they experience stigma and discrimination. Moreover, family and community also may affect how and when people express their sexual orientation and gender identity, and this can ultimately affect their health:

> The racial and ethnic communities to which one belongs affect self-identification, the process of coming

out, available support, the extent to which one identifies with the LGBT community, affirmation of gender-variant expression, and other factors that ultimately influence health outcomes.[76]

Recall the social-ecological model of health presented in Chapter 1. Individual health may be influenced by families, relationships, community, and the larger society. For many LGBTQ+ people, rejection by family, unhealthy relationships, lack of access to social supports in the community, and societal stigma and discrimination are a recipe for poor mental and physical health. Family affirmation, support, and connectedness are all important social drivers of health. A safe and stable family home environment is closely correlated with healthy child development and with adult health outcomes, as discussed in Chapter 8. Studies show that LGBTQ+ adolescents are less likely than heterosexual and cisgender peers to report strong connection to family.[77] There is also a higher prevalence of sexual and physical child abuse among LGBTQ+ adolescents than straight youth.[78] Consequently, they are overrepresented in the child welfare system, where they often encounter further marginalization and rejection. They are also less likely to be placed in home settings and more likely to live in group homes.[79] Young LGBTQ+ people who are rejected by family are also more likely to experience homelessness: Between 20% and 40% of homeless youth identify as LGBTQ+.[80] Hence, family rejection and violence have a spiraling effect on the health of LGBTQ+ youth, as these experiences lead to other significant social drivers of health: child welfare involvement and homelessness.

LGBTQ+ youth and adults experience higher rates of bullying, harassment, victimization, and violence than heterosexual and cisgender people.[81] Studies show that school bullying and violence against LGBTQ+ youth are common. Among high school students, they are the most likely to experience threats and violence from peers.[82] A review of 102 studies on violence and victimization experienced by LGBTQ+ individuals found that victimization is common across the life span, with the greatest prevalence during childhood and adolescence and later in adulthood. Transgender people in particular experience disproportionate victimization from violence: They are four times more likely than cisgender people to experience violence.[83] The Human Rights Campaign reported that in 2020 there were a record number of violent deaths of transgender and gender-nonconforming people. **Figure 13.3** demonstrates the convergence of factors—including harmful laws, policies, and practices—that lead to a higher risk of violent death among transgender and gender-nonconforming People of Color.

Health Inequities

As a result of the distinct challenges that they face—stigmatization and discrimination in health care and in society as a whole, lack of access to quality gender-affirming care, higher rates of family rejection and social isolation, and disproportionate exposure to violence—LGBTQ+ people are subject to a number of health inequities. Increasingly, there is recognition by researchers, clinicians, and policymakers that routine and standardized data collection on sexual orientation and gender identity is critical to understanding health inequities and trends in this population.[84] Research focused on studying the health and well-being of LGBTQ+ community is growing. Overall, these studies show that LGBTQ+ adults report worse health, more disabilities, and lower quality of life related to health than do non-LGBTQ+ peers (see **Table 13.2**). The groups most vulnerable to health inequities appear to be bisexual, transgender, and nonbinary people.[85] Next, we highlight some of these research findings.

Figure 13.3 The higher risk of violence for transgender and gender-nonconforming people

Chronic Disease

Being overweight or obese is more prevalent among LGBTQ+ women. In particular, lesbians and bisexual women are more likely to be overweight and obese than heterosexual women, putting them at higher risk for other health problems, such as cardiovascular disease and diabetes.[86] Recent research demonstrates that LGBTQ+ people have higher rates of cardiovascular disease than non-LGBTQ+ peers and that among the LGBTQ+ population, most affected are Black lesbians and transgender and bisexual

Table 13.2 Many LGBT+ People Are Living with Ongoing Health Conditions or Disabilities

Share of people ages 18–64 who report having at least one of the following		
	Ongoing health condition requiring regular monitoring, medical care, or medication	Disability or chronic disease preventing full participation in work, school, housework, or other activities
Sexual Orientation		
LGBT.	47%*	21%*
Non-LGBT+	40%	14%
LGBT+		
Gender		
Women	44%	22%
Men	52%	19%
Age		
18–44	39%	19%
45–64	77%*	25%
Insurance Type		
Medicaid	51%	34%*
Private	48%	14%

Note: *Estimates are statistically different within column and group (p < 0.05).
KFF Women's Health Survey 2020 (Nov. 19–Dec. 17, 2020).
Dawson L, Frederiksen B, Long M. LGBT+ People's Health and Experiences Accessing Care. Kaiser Family Foundation. July 22, 2021. https://www.kff.org/report-section/lgbt-peoples-health-and-experiences-accessing-care-report/

individuals.[87] Long-term use of hormonal therapy may also play a role in cardiovascular disease among transgender people.[88] However, as discussed later, inequalities in obesity and cardiovascular disease among the LGBTQ+ population are thought to be primarily related to their experiences of stigma and stress.

There is also evidence that rates of cancer are higher among some subgroups in the LGBTQ+ population. For example, gay and bisexual men are at higher risk for contracting HIV and hepatitis C, which, in turn, increase their risk of cancer.[89] But poor access to care also seems to play an important role. Feeling stigmatized by the medical care system, for example, may contribute to fewer LGBTQ+ women (35%) than non-LGBTQ+ women (64%) receiving routine mammograms.[90]

Mental Health Disorders, Substance Use Disorders, and Suicide Risk

Of major concern for the LGBTQ+ population are mental health disorders, particularly depression and anxiety. These disorders are "not inherent to being a sexual minority person but can manifest as a result of leading marginalized lives, enduring the stress of hiding one's sexuality, or facing verbal, emotional, or physical abuse from intolerant family members and communities."[91] The Centers for Disease Control and Prevention reports a shocking statistic: 47% of LGB youth reported in a national survey in 2019 that they had seriously considered suicide.[92] Studies consistently show that LGBTQ+ youth are at higher risk than their peers for anxiety, depression, posttraumatic stress disorder, eating disorders, substance use disorders, and suicide. Furthermore, mental health and substance use disorders often persist into adulthood. Indeed, rates of anxiety, depression, and eating and substance use disorders are higher in the adult LGBTQ+ population than the general population.[93] Persistence of mental health and substance use problems is often associated with lack of social and family support.[94]

Recently, researchers have begun to specifically investigate the mental health status of transgender individuals. In one study, transgender identity was associated with higher risk for reported discrimination, depression, and attempted suicide. However, self-acceptance of transgender identity was correlated with lower rates of reported depression.[95] The U.S. Transgender Survey in 2015 found that 40% of transgender people had attempted suicide in their lifetimes—nearly nine times the rate of the rest of the U.S. population. Of those, racial and ethnic minorities and Indigenous transgender people were more likely to report suicide attempts than White LGBTQ+ peers.[96] While the research base is growing with regard to mental health in the LGBTQ+ population, there is still very little research on the mental health status of intersex individuals.[97] Data collection that does not delineate among different gender identities and sexual orientations leaves many questions and makes intervention more difficult. The failure to ask research subjects about their gender identity and sexual orientation, for example, was illuminated during the COVID-19 pandemic. Only a handful of states

collect this data, making it difficult to assess the impact of the pandemic on the LGBTQ+ population.[98] Nonetheless, smaller surveys of LGBTQ+ people during COVID indicate that they experienced worse mental health and problems with alcohol during the pandemic.[99]

Minority Stress Theory

The growing body of evidence about the mechanisms through which stress manifests in negative physical and mental health outcomes is helping researchers better understand root causes of population health inequities. Experiences of marginalization, stigma, and discrimination are believed to be correlated with poor physical and mental health outcomes. (Recall the discussion in Chapter 10 of weathering, which described how discrimination and structural racism contribute to racial health inequities.) Minority stress theory asserts that LGBTQ+ individuals "are exposed to a variety of 'distal' stressors unique to their status as a stigmatized minority (e.g., exposure to prejudicial attitudes, experiences of discrimination) and that these activate 'proximal' stress processes within individuals (e.g., expectations of rejection, a desire to conceal sexual orientation), and together these accumulate to affect health."[100] Hence, all of the negative experiences associated with being a sexual and gender minority—societal, community, and family marginalization and stigma; discrimination in health care, employment, and housing; and a lack of social support and affirmation—compound to negatively affect health.

In a 2021 study, researchers were interested in determining if a group of LGBTQ+ research subjects would be more likely to manifest biomarkers of a stress response when told that they were completing interview questions on their "likeability, competence and intelligence" designed by an interviewer with homophobic attitudes, as compared with a LGBTQ+ peer group who were told nothing about the attitudes of the person designing the questions. The study showed that the group who anticipated bias by the interviewer were more likely to exhibit physiological markers of stress when completing the questions than those who knew nothing about their interviewer's bias. The study provides important insight into the ways in which perceptions about and experiences of discrimination and stigma alter physiological functioning.[101] Thus, higher rates of cardiovascular disease, metabolic disease (which influences weight gain), and some types of cancer—all of which are associated with allostatic load (chronic stress)—are likely correlated with minority stress for LGBTQ+ people. Minority stress theory also helps explain LGBTQ+ mental and behavioral health inequalities. For example, the higher prevalence of mental health disorders, substance use, and suicide risk among LGBTQ+ youth is thought to be correlated with family rejection and peer harassment and bullying.[102] Researchers point to the ways in which social support is vital to buffering minority stress.

Law, Policy, and Structural Change to Achieve Health Justice

U.S. laws and policies are slowly recognizing the rights of LGBTQ+ people. However, health care systems and providers often continue to reflect stigmatizing societal attitudes and discriminatory practices that harm the health of LGBTQ+ people. Despite some recent advances in the law, years of legalized discrimination and systemic bias continue to perpetuate disparate health outcomes for LGBTQ+ communities. Next, we highlight three areas in law, health care, and public health that will promote health justice for LGBTQ+ communities.

Civil Rights

Recent Supreme Court cases and legal interpretations of civil rights laws have helped move the United States toward full recognition of the rights of LGBTQ+ people to live free from discrimination in the places where they are born, live, learn, work, play, worship, and age.[103] Recognition of equal rights for LGBTQ+ people must be accompanied by changes in social norms and in systems to meaningfully implement these rights. While federal antidiscrimination laws are becoming more inclusive of LGBTQ+ people, actions at the state and local level are undermining equal treatment, particularly for transgender people. In addition, there remain numerous court challenges brought by businesses seeking exemptions from federal civil rights laws. These developments point to a landscape in need of continued vigilance.

Legal, health, and community advocates should work collectively to ensure that state laws targeting the rights of transgender people and efforts in the courts challenging newly recognized rights do not reverse progress on civil rights for LGBTQ+ communities. Research suggests that merely introducing anti-LGBTQ+ policies, even when they are not ultimately adopted, can have a negative impact on the social well-being and health of LGBTQ+ people. A 2021 research study found that "[t]he number of texts to Crisis Text Line in a state where anti-LGBTQ legislation was proposed increased in the four weeks after such legislation was proposed; this difference was small but statistically significant."[104] Whereas between 2015 and 2019 there were over 200 pieces of anti-LGBTQ+ legislation introduced, in 2021 alone, 200 anti-LGBTQ+ bills were introduced in 35 states.[105]

In addition to anti-LGBTQ+ legislation, anti-LGBTQ+ activity appears to be growing in local communities as well. For example, local school boards across the country are being asked to remove books and curriculum that acknowledge and accept all sexual orientations and gender identities. The requested changes create less-accepting school environments for LGBTQ+ youth. Some parents, local advocacy groups, and elected officials are attending school board meetings where they express anti-transgender rhetoric.[106] This type of community engagement has a negative impact on the social environment that reaches beyond schools. As discussed previously, supportive homes, schools, and communities can help mitigate experiences of bias, discrimination, and stigma that harm the health of LGBTQ+ youth. The federal government should use its enforcement powers under Title IX to ensure that school environments are safe for LGBTQ+ youth. Advocates should also push for state policies that protect LGBTQ+ youth from discrimination in schools, though the political climate in some states may make policy change difficult.

Furthermore, courts' granting of religious exemptions from civil rights protections that enable discrimination against LGBTQ+ people continues to threaten equality. Protections against workplace discrimination that have recently been applied to LGBTQ+ communities hold the possibility of not only improving their economic security but also reducing the health and mental health consequences of discriminatory behavior. Economic security can support multiple dimensions of health, including food security, health care coverage, and housing. But the U.S. Supreme Court has signaled a willingness to privilege religious rights over LGBTQ+ rights. Legal, health care, and public health practitioners concerned with health justice for LGBTQ+ people must remain vigilant in documenting the negative health effects of discrimination in all of the social spheres with which LGBTQ+ people interact—the workplace, schools, housing, health care, the legal system, and others.

Culturally Appropriate Health Care

Health care providers and systems must begin to view the care of people of varying sexual orientations and gender identities as an intrinsic part of their services. States and the federal government can provide incentives and accountability for the provision of culturally appropriate care by health care providers. One policy mechanism for ensuring the availability of appropriately trained health care providers is for the federal Health Resources and Services Administration (HRSA) to use the administrative rulemaking process to designate LGBTQ+ populations as Medically Underserved Populations (MUP) and as a Health Professional Shortage Area (HPSA). These shifts would increase financial and other resources to expand access to care that is supportive, knowledgeable, and inclusive of all sexual and gender identities.[107] In order to increase access to health care coverage, the federal government should incentivize states that have not expanded Medicaid to do so, as many LGBTQ+ people depend on Medicaid coverage to access health care. Furthermore, HHS should ensure that health care plans governed by the ACA comply with the nondiscrimination requirements of Section 1557, including coverage of gender-affirming care. Lastly, HHS should aggressively exercise its enforcement powers under Section 1557 to pursue cases of discrimination by health care institutions, providers, and insurance plans based on sexual orientation and gender identity.[108]

Data Collection

In order to ensure that efforts targeted at reducing health inequities in LGBTQ+ populations are effective, interventions must be rigorously evaluated. As discussed previously, many data collection mechanisms do not collect data on sexual orientation and gender identity. Even when the information is collected, it is not always collected in a way that represents research subjects' full experiences. *Healthy People 2030*—a report issued every 10 years by the U.S. Department of Health and Human Services—includes objectives specifically related to increasing data collection on LGBTQ+ populations in national health surveys. *Healthy People 2020* was the first time that goals related to LGBTQ+ communities were included in this important national plan "[t]o promote, strengthen, and evaluate the nation's efforts to improve the health and well-being of all people."[109] Public health and health services researchers should seek input from LGBTQ+ people from various sexual orientations and gender identities in devising data collection metrics and methods. As discussed at the beginning of the chapter, language and terms related to gender are changing; thus, it is important that research studies employ language that is identifiable to research subjects.[110]

There are currently no federal mandates requiring collection of LGBTQ+ data.[111] In 2015, the Office of Management and Budget (OMB) convened the Federal Interagency Working Group on Measuring Sexual Orientation and Gender Identity to examine and improve federal data collection on LGBTQ+ communities. The working group produced reports analyzing federal surveys for inclusion of relevant data collection mechanisms and made recommendations for culturally appropriate, coordinated national data collection efforts. The federal government should reconvene the working group and task it with developing guidelines to be implemented by the Office of Management and Budget (OMB) for federal data collection. At a minimum, federal guidelines for data collection should ensure that all federal surveys and forms include questions that capture information on sexual orientation and gender identity.

Conclusion

Laws and policies affecting the rights of LGBTQ+ people are evolving rapidly, even as this book goes to publication. While there has been major progress in legal recognition of the rights of LGBTQ+ communities, the uncertainty about how the Supreme Court will balance religious rights with civil rights for these communities, along with the onslaught of enacted and proposed anti-LGBTQ+ legislation in states, continues to threaten the health and well-being of these populations. LGBTQ+ communities have shown enormous resilience as they fight for social and legal recognition of their identities and human rights. Health justice advocates should work alongside LGBTQ+ communities to ensure that laws, policies, and practices are structured with their needs and interests in mind.

References

1. McCabe HA, Kinney MK. LGBTQ+ individuals, health inequities, and policy implications. *Creighton Law Review.* 2019;52:24.
2. U.S. Department of Health and Human Services, Office of Minority Health. National standards for culturally and linguistically appropriate services in health and health care. 2013.
3. Bouman WP, Schwend AS, Motmans J, et al. Language and trans health. *International Journal of Transgenderism.* 2017;18(1):1–6. doi:10.1080/15532739.2016.1262127.
4. Auchmuty R, Jeffreys S, Miller E. Lesbian history and gay studies: Keeping a feminist perspective. *Women's History Review.* 1992;1(1):89–108. doi:10.1080/09612029200200006.
5. Flanders CE, LeBreton ME, Robinson M, Bian J, Caravaca-Morera JA. Defining bisexuality: Young bisexual and pansexual people's voices. *Journal of Bisexuality.* 2017;17(1):39–57. doi:10.1080/15299716.2016.1227016.
6. Fenway Institute National LGBTQIA+ Health and Education Center. LGBTQIA+ glossary of terms for health care teams. February 2, 2020. https://www.lgbtqiahealtheducation.org/publication/lgbtqia-glossary-of-terms-for-health-care-teams/.
7. Levy DL, Johnson CW. What does the Q mean? Including queer voices in qualitative research. *Qualitative Social Work.* 2012;11(2):130–140. doi:10.1177/1473325011400485.
8. What's the difference between being transgender and transsexual? Healthline. November 21, 2019. https://www.healthline.com/health/transgender/difference-between-transgender-and-transsexual; Zambon V. Transgender vs. transsexual: Definitions

and differences. February 25, 2021. https://www.medicalnewstoday.com/articles/transgender-vs-transexual.

9. Fenway Institute National LGBTQIA+ Health and Education Center. LGBTQIA+ glossary of terms for health care teams. February 2, 2020.

10. Stryker S. *Transgender History: The Roots of Today's Revolution*. 2nd ed. New York, NY: Seal Press; 2017.

11. Patterson CJ, Sepúlveda MJ, White J, eds. *Understanding the Well-Being of LGBTQI+ Populations*. National Academies of Sciences, Engineering, and Medicine. The National Academies Press; 2020. doi:10.17226/25877.

12. Dolan IJ, Strauss P, Winter S, Lin A. Misgendering and experiences of stigma in health care settings for transgender people. *Medical Journal of Australia*. 2020;212(4):150. doi:10.5694/mja2.50497.

13. Fenway Institute National LGBTQIA+ Health and Education Center. *LGBTQIA+ Glossary of Terms for Health Care Teams*. February 2, 2020.

14. *Lawrence v. Texas*, 539 U.S. 558, 123 S. Ct. 2472, 156 L. Ed. 2d 508 (2003).

15. Dawsom J. Idaho sodomy suit revives specters of the law's dark history. Boise State Public Radio. January 21, 2021. https://www.boisestatepublicradio.org/law-justice/2021-01-21/idaho-sodomy-suit-revives-specters-of-the-laws-dark-history.

16. *Baehr v. Lewin*, 74 Haw. 530, 852 P.2d 44 (1999).

17. DEFENSE OF MARRIAGE ACT, PL 104–199, September 21, 1996, 110 Stat 2419.

18. *United States v. Windsor*, 570 U.S. 744, 133 S. Ct. 2675, 186 L. Ed. 2d 808 (2013).

19. *Obergefell v. Hodges*, 576 U.S. 644, 135 S. Ct. 2584, 192 L. Ed. 2d 609 (2015).

20. Movement Advancement Project. *Marriage solemnization*. https://www.lgbtmap.org/equality-maps/religious_exemption_laws.

21. Religious Freedom Restoration Act of 1993, PL 103–141, November 16, 1993, 107 Stat 1488.

22. *Employment Div., Dept. of Human Resources of Oregon v. Smith*, 494 U.S. 872 (1990); *Sherbert v. Verner*, 374 U.S. 398 (1963).

23. *City of Boerne v. Flores*, 521 U.S. 507, 117 S. Ct. 2157, 2158, 138 L. Ed. 2d 624 (1997).

24. Griffin J. *Religious freedom restoration acts—legal brief*. May 2015. https://www.ncsl.org/research/civil-and-criminal-justice/religious-freedom-restoration-acts-lb.aspx.

25. Adams D. RFRA: Why the "religious freedom law" signed by Mike Pence was so controversial. *The Indianapolis Star*. May 18, 2018. https://www.indystar.com/story/news/2018/04/25/rfra-indiana-why-law-signed-mike-pence-so-controversial/546411002/.

26. *Fulton v. City of Philadelphia, Pennsylvania*, 141 S. Ct. 1868, 210 L. Ed. 2d 137 (2021).

27. 42 U.S.C. § 2000a.

28. Movement Advancement Project. Public Accommodations. January 27, 2022. https://www.lgbtmap.org/equality-maps/non_discrimination_laws/public-accommodations.

29. *State v. Arlene's Flowers, Inc.*, 193 Wash. 2d 469, 480, 441 P.3d 1203, 1209 (2019), *cert. denied*, 141 S. Ct. 2884 (2021); *Masterpiece Cakeshop, Ltd. v. Colorado C.R. Comm'n*, 138 S. Ct. 1719, 201 L. Ed. 2d 35 (2018).

30. *Masterpiece Cakeshop, Ltd. v. Colorado C.R. Comm'n*, 138 S. Ct. 1719, 201 L. Ed. 2d 35 (2018); *Fulton v. City of Philadelphia, Pennsylvania*, 141 S. Ct. 1868, 210 L. Ed. 2d 137 (2021).

31. Shanor A. LGBTQ+ need not apply. *The Regulatory Review*. June 21, 2021. https://www.theregreview.org/2021/06/21/shanor-lgbtq-need-not-apply/.

32. Civil Rights Act of 1964 § 7, 42 U.S.C. § 2000e et seq (1964).

33. *Bostock v. Clayton County* 140 S. Ct. 1731, 1737, 207 L. Ed. 2d 218 (2020).

34. Executive Order on Preventing and Combating Discrimination on the Basis of Gender Identity or Sexual Orientation, 2021 WL 197405:*1.

35. Executive Order on Preventing and Combating Discrimination on the Basis of Gender Identity or Sexual Orientation, 2021 WL 197405:*1.

36. *Bear Creek Bible Church v. Equal Employment Opportunity Commission*. No. 4:18-CV-00824-O, 2021 WL 5052661, at *2 (N.D. Tex. Oct. 31, 2021).

37. US Department of Housing and Urban Development. Housing Discrimination Under the Fair Housing Act. https://www.hud.gov/program_offices/fair_housing/_equal_opp/fair_housing_act_overview.

38. U.S. Department of Housing and Urban Development. HUD to enforce Fair Housing Act to prohibit discrimination on the basis of sexual orientation and gender identity. February 11, 2021. https://www.hud.gov/press/press_releases_media_advisories/hud_no_21_021

39. Movement Advancement Project. Equality maps: State nondiscrimination laws—housing. https://www.lgbtmap.org/equality-maps/non_discrimination_laws/housing.

40. Nondiscrimination in Health Programs and Activities, 81 Fed. Reg. 31,375 (May 18, 2016).

41. *Franciscan Alliance, Inc. v. Burwell*, 227 F. Supp. 3d 660 (N.D. Tex. 2016).

42. *Franciscan Alliance, Inc. v. Azar*, 414 F. Supp. 3d 928, 947 (N.D. Tex. 2019).

43. Nondiscrimination in Health and Health Education Programs or Activities, Delegation of Authority, 85 Fed. Reg. 37,160 (June 19, 2020); Title IX of the Education Amendments of 1972 (20 U.S.C. §1681(a)(3)).

44. *Whitman-Walker Clinic, Inc. v. U.S. Dep't of Health & Hum. Servs.*, 485 F. Supp. 3d 1, 10 (D.D.C. 2020).

45. Keith K. Judge blocks enforcement against Franciscan Alliance plaintiffs of prohibition on discrimination based on gender identity, pregnancy termination. August 11, 2021. https://www.healthaffairs.org/do/10.1377/hblog20210811.110777/full/; Musumeci M, Dawson L, Sobel L, Kates J. *Recent and anticipated actions to reverse Trump administration Section 1557 non-discrimination rules*. Kaiser Family Foundation. June 6, 2021. https://www.kff.org/racial-equity-and-health-policy/issue-brief/recent-and-anticipated-actions-to-reverse-trump-administration-section-1557-non-discrimination-rules/; See, e.g., *Franciscan All., Inc. v. Becerra*, No. 7:16-CV-00108-O, 2021 WL 3492338 (N.D. Tex. Aug. 9, 2021); *Bos. All. of Gay, Lesbian, Bisexual & Transgender Youth v. United States Dep't of Health & Hum. Servs.*, No. CV 20-11297-PBS, 2021 WL 3667760 (D. Mass. Aug. 18, 2021).

46. Ronan W. *2021 Officially becomes worst year in recent history for LGBTQ state legislative attacks as unprecedented number of states enact record-shattering number of anti-LGBTQ measures into law*. HRC. May 7, 2021. https://www.hrc.org/press-releases/2021-officially-becomes-worst-year-in-recent-history-for-lgbtq-state-legislative-attacks-as-unprecedented-number-of-states-enact-record-shattering-number-of-anti-lgbtq-measures-into-law.

47. The Trevor Project. *Data on transgender youth*. 2019. https://www.thetrevorproject.org/research-briefs/data-on-transgender-youth/.

48. *B. P. J. v. W. Virginia State Bd. of Educ.*, No. 2:21-CV-00316, 2021 WL 3081883 (S.D.W. Va. July 21, 2021); *Hecox v. Little*, 479 F. Supp. 3d 930 (D. Idaho 2020).

49. *Brandt v. Rutledge*, No. 4:21CV00450 JM, 2021 WL 3292057, at *1 (E.D. Ark. Aug. 2, 2021).

50. *Vasquez v. Iowa Department of Human Services*, No.CVCV061729 (D. Iowa, Nov. 22, 2021).

51. Spurlin WJ. Queer theory and biomedical practice: The biomedicalization of sexuality/the cultural politics of biomedicine. *Journal of Medical Humanities*. 2019;40:7–20,9.

52. Institute of Medicine (IOM). *The Health of Lesbian, Gay, Bisexual, and Transgender People: Building a Foundation for Better Understanding*. Washington, DC: The National Academies Press; 2011: 36.

53. Spurlin WJ. Queer theory and biomedical practice: The biomedicalization of sexuality/the cultural politics of biomedicine. *Journal of Medical Humanities*. 2019;40:7–20,10.

54. Institute of Medicine (IOM). *The Health of Lesbian, Gay, Bisexual, and Transgender People: Building a Foundation for Better Understanding*. Washington, DC: The National Academies Press; 2011: 50.

55. Institute of Medicine (IOM). *The Health of Lesbian, Gay, Bisexual, and Transgender People: Building a*

Foundation for Better Understanding. Washington, DC: The National Academies Press; 2011: 50.

56. American Psychiatric Association. *What is gender dysphoria?* November 2020. https://www.psychiatry.org/patients-families/gender-dysphoria/what-is-gender-dysphoria.

57. Spurlin WJ. Queer Theory and Biomedical Practice: The Biomedicalization of Sexuality/The Cultural Politics of Biomedicine. *Journal of Medical Humanities*. 2019;40:7-20,11.

58. King M. Stigma in psychiatry seen through the lens of sexuality and gender. *BJPsych International*. 2019;16:77–80.

59. Movement Advancement Project. *Conversion therapy laws*. January 27, 2022. https://www.lgbtmap.org/equality-maps/conversion_therapy.

60. Institute of Medicine (IOM). *The Health of Lesbian, Gay, Bisexual, and Transgender People: Building a Foundation for Better Understanding*. Washington, DC: The National Academies Press; 2011:63–64.

61. Institute of Medicine (IOM). *The Health of Lesbian, Gay, Bisexual, and Transgender People: Building a Foundation for Better Understanding*. Washington, DC: The National Academies Press; 2011:65.

62. Banerjee SC, Staley JM, Alexander K, et al. Encouraging patients to disclose their lesbian, gay, bisexual, or transgender (LGBT) status: Oncology health care providers' perspectives. *Translational Behavioral Medicine*. 2020;10(4):918–927.

63. Institute of Medicine (IOM). *The Health of Lesbian, Gay, Bisexual, and Transgender People: Building a Foundation for Better Understanding*. Washington, DC: The National Academies Press; 2011:167.

64. Whitehead J, Shaver J, Stephenson R. Outness, stigma, and primary health care utilization among rural LGBT populations. *PLOS One*. 2016;11:e0146139.

65. Dawson L, Frederiksen B, Long M. *LGBT+ people's health and experiences accessing care. Kaiser Family Foundation*. July 22, 2021. https://www.kff.org/report-section/lgbt-peoples-health-and-experiences-accessing-care-report/.

66. The Trevor Project. Breaking barriers to quality mental health care for LGBTQ youth. August 18, 2020. https://www.thetrevorproject.org/research-briefs/breaking-barriers-to-quality-mental-health-care-for-lgbtq-youth/.

67. The Trevor Project. Breaking barriers to quality mental health care for LGBTQ youth. August 18, 2020. https://www.thetrevorproject.org/research-briefs/breaking-barriers-to-quality-mental-health-care-for-lgbtq-youth/.

68. Klein DA, Berry-Bibee EN, Keglovitz Baker K, Malcolm NM, Rollison JM, Frederiksen BN. Providing quality family planning services to LGBTQIA individuals: A systematic review. *Contraception*. 2018 May;97(5):378–391.

69. Tornello SL, Bos H. Parenting intentions among transgender individuals. *LGBTHealth.* 2017;4(2):115–120.

70. World Professional Association for Transgender Health. *Standards of Care for the Health of Transsexual, Transgender, and Gender Nonconforming People* (7th version). 2011. https://www.wpath.org/publications/soc.

71. Almazan AN, Keuroghlian AS. Association between gender-affirming surgeries and mental health outcomes. *JAMA Surgery.* 2021;156(7):611. doi:10.1001/jamasurg.2021.0952.

72. Keuroghlian AS, Ard KL, Makadon HJ. Advancing health equity for lesbian, gay, bisexual and transgender (LGBT) people through sexual health education and LGBT-affirming health care environments. *Sexual Health.* 2017;14:119.

73. Tuller D. For LGBTQ patients, high-quality care in a welcoming environment. *Health Affairs.* 2020;39(5):736–739.

74. Dawson L, Frederiksen B, Long M. LGBT+ people's health and experiences accessing care. Kaiser Family Foundation. July 22, 2021. https://www.kff.org/report-section/lgbt-peoples-health-and-experiences-accessing-care-report/.

75. Dawson L, Frederiksen B, Long M. LGBT+ people's health and experiences accessing care. Kaiser Family Foundation. July 22, 2021. https://www.kff.org/report-section/lgbt-peoples-health-and-experiences-accessing-care-report/.

76. Institute of Medicine (IOM). *The Health of Lesbian, Gay, Bisexual, and Transgender People: Building a Foundation for Better Understanding.* Washington, DC: The National Academies Press; 2011: 33.

77. Institute of Medicine (IOM). *The Health of Lesbian, Gay, Bisexual, and Transgender People: Building a Foundation for Better Understanding.* Washington, DC: The National Academies Press; 2011: 164.

78. Institute of Medicine (IOM). *The Health of Lesbian, Gay, Bisexual, and Transgender People: Building a Foundation for Better Understanding.* Washington, DC: The National Academies Press; 2011: 163.

79. McCormick A, Schmidt K, Terrazas S. LGBTQ youth in the child welfare system: An overview of research, practice, and policy. *Journal of Public Child Welfare.* 2017;11(1):27–39.

80. Cunningham M, Pergamit M, Astone N. *Homeless LGBTQ youth. The Urban Institute.* August 2014. https://www.urban.org/sites/default/files/publication/22876/413209-Homeless-LGBTQ-Youth.PDF.

81. Institute of Medicine (IOM). *The Health of Lesbian, Gay, Bisexual, and Transgender People: Building a Foundation for Better Understanding.* Washington, DC: The National Academies Press; 2011: 158.

82. Johns MM, Lowry R, Haderxhanaj LT, et al. Trends in violence victimization and suicide risk by sexual identity among high school students—Youth Risk Behavior Survey, United States, 2015–2019. *Morbidity and Mortality Weekly Report.* 2020;69(1):19–27.

83. UCLA Williams Institute. *Transgender people over four times more likely than cisgender people to be victims of violent crime.* March 23, 2021. https://williamsinstitute.law.ucla.edu/press/ncvs-trans-press-release/.

84. National Academies of Sciences, Engineering, and Medicine. *Understanding the Well-Being of LGBTQI+ Populations.* Washington, DC: The National Academies Press; 2020. https://doi.org/10.17226/25877.

85. National Academies of Sciences, Engineering, and Medicine. *Understanding the Well-Being of LGBTQI+ Populations.* Washington, DC: The National Academies Press; 2020. https://doi.org/10.17226/25877.

86. Azagba S, Shan L, Latham K. Overweight and obesity among sexual minority adults in the United States. *International Journal of Environmental Research and Public Health.* 2019;16:1828.

87. National Academies of Sciences, Engineering, and Medicine. *Understanding the Well-Being of LGBTQI+ Populations.* Washington, DC: The National Academies Press; 2020: 293–294. https://doi.org/10.17226/25877.

88. National Academies of Sciences, Engineering, and Medicine. Understanding the Well-Being of LGBTQI+ Populations. Washington, DC: The National Academies Press; 2020: 294. https://doi.org/10.17226/25877.

89. National Academies of Sciences, Engineering, and Medicine. *Understanding the Well-Being of LGBTQI+ Populations.* Washington, DC: The National Academies Press; 2020: 296. https://doi.org/10.17226/25877.

90. Dawson L, Frederiksen B, Long M. LGBT+ people's health and experiences accessing care. Kaiser Family Foundation. July 22, 2021. https://www.kff.org/report-section/lgbt-peoples-health-and-experiences-accessing-care-report/.

91. Mayer KH, Bradford JB, Makadon HJ, Stall R, Goldhammer H, Landers S. Sexual and gender minority health: What we know and what needs to be done. *American Journal of Public Health.* June 2008;98(6):989–995.

92. Centers for Disease Control and Prevention. *Health Disparities Among Youth: Understanding Unequal Health Risks and Experiences of LGBTQ+ Youth.* November 2020. https://www.cdc.gov/healthyyouth/disparities/index.htm.

93. National Academies of Sciences, Engineering, and Medicine. *Understanding the Well-Being of LGBTQI+ Populations.* Washington, DC: The National Academies Press; 2020: 308. https://doi.org/10.17226/25877.

94. Lothwell LE, Libby N, Adelson SL. Mental health care for LGBT youths. *FOCUS.* 2020;18:268–276.

95. Su D, Irwin JA, Fisher C, Ramos A. Mental health disparities within the LGBT population: A comparison between transgender and

nontransgender individuals. *Transgender Health.* 2016;1(1):12–20.

96. James SE, Herman JL, Rankin S, et al. *The Report of the 2015 U.S. Transgender Survey.* Washington, DC: National Center for Transgender Equality; 2016. https://transequality.org/sites/default/files/docs/usts/USTS-Full-Report-Dec17.pdf.

97. National Academies of Sciences, Engineering, and Medicine. *Understanding the Well-Being of LGBTQI+ Populations.* Washington, DC: The National Academies Press; 2020: 308. https://doi.org/10.17226/25877.

98. Perret M, Jillson K, Danielson AC, et al. COVID-19 Data on trans and gender-expansive people, stat! Health Affairs Blog. May 12, 2021. https://www.healthaffairs.org/do/10.1377/hblog20210510.756668/full/?utm_medium=email&_hsmi=129907151&utm_content=129907151&utm_source=hs_email&_hsenc=p2ANqtz--OJQOP5K9iAL7xV7Z2oxTtP-AVjzjVebpCc8kbeGmO_IJEWsSziaI-yNUilWyvlCTwPAyCiYG_KKH4Dr_v5YZfX6aybLBsijOT-UR9s61ww6mqZM4; Cahill SR. Still in the dark regarding the public health impact of COVID-19 on sexual and gender minorities. *American Journal of Public Health.* 2021;111:1606–1609.

99. Akré ER, Anderson A, Stojanovski K, et al. Depression, anxiety, and alcohol use among LGBTQ+ people during the COVID-19 pandemic. *American Journal of Public Health.* 2021;111:1610–1619.

100. Huebner DM, McGarrity LA, Perry NS, et al. Cardiovascular and cortisol responses to experimentally-induced minority stress. *Health Psychology.* 2021;40(5):316–325,317.

101. Huebner DM, McGarrity LA, Perry NS, et al. Cardio-vascular and cortisol responses to experimentally-induced minority stress. *Health Psychology.* 2021; 40(5):316–325.

102. Adelson SW, Stroeh OM, Ng YKW. Development and mental health of lesbian, gay, bisexual, or transgender youth in pediatric practice. *Pediatric Clinics of North America.* 2016;63(6):971–983.

103. World Health Organization. Social determinants of health. 2021. Accessed February 3, 2021. https://www.who.int/westernpacific/health-topics/social-determinants-of-health.

104. Parris D, Fulks E, Kelley C. Anti-LGBTQ policy proposals can harm youth mental health. *Child Trends*; 2021. https://www.childtrends.org/publications/anti-lgbtq-policy-proposals-can-harm-youth-mental-health.

105. Parris D, Fulks E, Kelley C. Anti-LGBTQ policy proposals can harm youth mental health. *Child Trends*; 2021. https://www.childtrends.org/publications/anti-lgbtq-policy-proposals-can-harm-youth-mental-health.

106. Alas H. Activists continue campaign against transgender policy, vaccine mandates at school board meeting. *The Loudoun Times.* September 29, 2021. https://www.loudountimes.com/news/activists-continue-campaign-against-transgender-policy-vaccine-mandates-at-school-board-meeting/article_86ef41aa-214d-11ec-853c-67a333e31f8a.html; Pitman MD. What happened with Josh Mandel at the Lakota school board meeting? Video and interviews detail events. *Springfield News-Sun.* October 13, 2021. https://www.springfieldnewssun.com/local/what-happened-with-josh-mandel-at-the-lakota-school-board-meeting-video-and-interviews-detail-events/2RYJ37UTEVHMHBFQGG6DZKKMIU/.

107. The Fenway Institute. The case for designating LGBT people as a medically underserved population and as a health professional shortage area population group. August 2014. https://fenwayhealth.org/documents/the-fenway-institute/policy-briefs/MUP_HPSA-Brief_v11-FINAL-081914.pdf.

108. Center for American Progress. *Improving the Lives and Rights of LGBTQ People in America.* January 12, 2021. https://americanprogress.org/articleimproving-lives-rights-lgbtq-people-america/.

109. Office of Disease Prevention and Health Promotion. *LGBT—Healthy People 2030.* 2021. https://health.gov/healthypeople/objectives-and-data/browse-objectives/lgbt.

110. Persad X. *LGBTQ-Inclusive Data Collection: A Lifesaving Imperative.* Washington, DC: Human Rights Campaign Foundation; 2019.

111. State Health Access Data Assistance Center. *A New Brief Examines the Collection of Sexual Orientation and Gender Identity (SOGI) Data at the Federal Level and in Medicaid*; 2021. https://www.shadac.org/news/new-brief-examines-collection-sexual-orientation-and-gender-identity-sogi-data-federal-level.

CHAPTER 14

People with Disabilities

Elizabeth Pendo

12 page

LEARNING OBJECTIVES

By the end of this chapter you will be able to:

- Describe the antidiscrimination and health care laws that influence access to health care and other social drivers of health for people with disabilities
- Explain historical and current treatment of people with disabilities by the health care system and how assumptions, biases, and lack of knowledge impact health care for people with disabilities
- Identify health inequities experienced by and among people with disabilities and explain some of the root causes of these inequities, including laws, policies, and other social and structural factors
- Describe legal, policy, and structural changes necessary to eliminate health inequities experienced by and among people with disabilities

Introduction

According to the World Health Organization, disability is a "a continuum, relevant to the lives of all people to different degrees and at different times in their lives," and a "natural feature of the human condition."[1] We are all at risk of acquiring a disability at any time. Some people are born with a disability, while others acquire disabilities during the course of their lives as a result of illness, injury, age, or other causes. A report on the future of disability in the United States noted that considering the sizable number of people with disabilities and also people who will develop disabilities in the future, disability will affect the lives of most Americans.[2]

With that reality in mind, this chapter explores the health and well-being of people with disabilities through the lens of health justice. Specifically, it discusses how the significant health inequities experienced by people with disabilities are rooted in policies, practices, and beliefs that reflect long-standing stigma, unequal treatment, and discrimination. The chapter begins with an overview of the large and diverse group of people with disabilities in the United States. Here and throughout the chapter, the intersection of disability with race, ethnicity, gender,

LGBTQ+ status, socioeconomic status, and other characteristics is considered. Next, it introduces the key federal laws that govern access to health care and other structural drivers of health for people with disabilities. It then addresses the past and present treatment of people with disabilities by the health care system, followed by discussion of the social and structural drivers of health inequities for people with disabilities, including negative attitudes, stereotypes, misconceptions, and discrimination. The chapter concludes by highlighting some legal, policy, and structural changes that are necessary to realize health justice for people with disabilities.

Overview of Disability in the United States

Until recently, numerous federal surveys collected information about disability using different definitions. As a result, estimates of disability prevalence varied widely.[3] The Patient Protection and Affordable Care Act (ACA)[4] addressed this problem by directing the federal government to create a standard minimum set of questions for identifying disability that would be used across federal surveys. The six questions developed are shown in **Box 14.1**.[5] These questions were already in use by the American Community Survey (ACS) and are now used in multiple federal surveys.[6]

Based on the six ACS disability questions, one in four American adults who live outside of care or criminal justice institutions—a diverse group of 67 million people—experiences some form of disability.[7] This figure reflects a 1% increase from 2016 due in part to the aging of the population.[8] Mobility was the most prevalent disability type (13.3%), followed by cognitive or mental (12.1%), independent living (7.2%), hearing (6.1%), vision (5.2%), and self-care (3.9%). Over 3 million children experienced disability in 2019.[9] An estimated 2.1 million more people with disabilities live in institutions such as nursing

> **Box 14.1** Six ACS Disability Questions
>
> 1. Are you deaf or do you have serious difficulty hearing?
> 2. Are you blind or do you have serious difficulty seeing, even when wearing glasses?
> 3. Because of a physical, mental, or emotional condition, do you have serious difficulty concentrating, remembering, or making decisions? (5 years old or older)
> 4. Do you have serious difficulty walking or climbing stairs? (5 years old or older)
> 5. Do you have difficulty dressing or bathing? (5 years old or older)
> 6. Because of a physical, mental, or emotional condition, do you have difficulty doing errands alone such as visiting a doctor's office or shopping? (15 years old or older)
>
> Question responses: ☐ Yes ☐ No

"How Disability Data are Collected from The American Community Survey," United States Census Bureau

homes, prisons, jails, mental hospitals, and juvenile correctional facilities.[10] **Figure 14.1** displays by age and sex the distribution of different types of disability.

Disability affects every demographic group but affects some groups much more than others. Overall, adults with disability are more likely to be older, female, and Latinx; have less than a high school education and a lower income; and be unemployed.[11] Although women reported higher prevalence across most disability types,[12] Black women had higher prevalence of disability than women of other races and ethnicities.[13] Adults with disability were also more likely than those without a disability to be bisexual, transgender, or gender-nonconforming.[14] There are also differences in the prevalence of disability types between groups. For example, hearing, mobility, and independent living disabilities are higher among older adults, while cognitive disability is highest among middle-aged and young adults.[15]

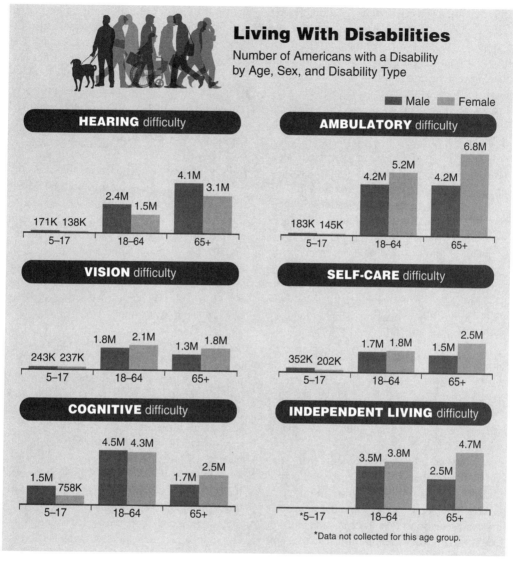

Figure 14.1 Living with disabilities

Treatment of People with Disabilities under the Law

This section highlights key antidiscrimination and health care laws that affect the health and well-being of people with disabilities. As with some marginalized groups discussed in other chapters, the protections of the Equal Protection Clause of the 14th Amendment to the U.S. Constitution apply to people with disabilities. However, in *Cleburne v. Cleburne Living Center*, the Supreme Court held that unlike laws classifying persons based on race or sex, laws classifying people based on disability are subject only to rational basis review.[16] Rational basis review, as you will recall from Chapter 4, only requires that the law be rationally related to any legitimate government purpose. Although the Supreme Court applied a relatively low level of judicial scrutiny to laws classifying people based on disability, Congress has passed robust protections for people with disabilities.

In addition to the laws discussed later, other federal laws address disability discrimination in areas such as education, housing, air travel, voting, and telecommunications.[17] Notably, the Individuals with Disabilities Education Act (IDEA)[18] transformed the educational landscape for children with disabilities by ensuring that they be provided a free, appropriate public education in the least restrictive environment. The law requires that public schools provide special education services to eligible students as described in an Individualized Education Program (IEP) designed to meet the student's individual needs. The IDEA also provides federal funding to assist states with the costs of educating children with disabilities. By 2019–2020, 14% of children aged 3 through 21 in public schools received special education services under the IDEA.[19]

States and local governments may also have additional laws that protect people with disabilities from discrimination in different settings. In some cases, these laws provide greater protections than federal laws do. For example, the ADA's definition of "service animal" excludes animals that provide emotional support or comfort.[20] However, some states provide protections for individuals who use dogs and other animals for emotional support and comfort.[21] Another example is the Georgia Accessibility Code, which, unlike the ADA, requires religious or other private institutions to comply with the law's physical access requirements.[22]

Antidiscrimination Laws

The Americans with Disabilities Act (ADA)[23] was enacted over 30 years ago to eliminate widespread discrimination against people with disabilities and to ensure equal opportunity across many areas of American life. The ADA expands the protections of an earlier law, Section 504 of the Rehabilitation Act,[24] which bans disability discrimination in programs and activities that receive federal financial assistance. The requirements of the ADA are summarized in **Table 14.1**.

The ADA and the Rehabilitation Act protect individuals who meet the statutory definition of "disability." An individual with a disability is one who has a physical or mental impairment that substantially limits one or more major life activities, has a record of such impairment, or is regarded as having such an impairment.[25] The ADA was amended in 2008 to clarify that this definition should be construed broadly. Disabilities can be physical, sensory, cognitive, intellectual, or developmental. Mental health conditions, substance use disorders (SUD), and chronic illnesses can qualify as disabilities. For example, SUD is a disability when the condition substantially limits a major life activity, which includes major bodily functions such as neurological and brain function. Individuals with a history of SUD or who are incorrectly assumed to have a SUD are also protected.

Significantly, the ADA imposes an affirmative obligation to ensure that people with disabilities have equal opportunities within certain limits. For example, Title I requires employers to provide reasonable accommodations, which are changes to the way a job is done or to the work environment that allow an employee to do their job. Examples of employment accommodations in the ADA regulations include removing physical barriers, job restructuring, part-time or modified work schedules, reassignment to a vacant position, purchasing accessible equipment or devices, providing readers or interpreters, and modifications to workplace policies, practices, and procedures.[26] Accommodation decisions are made on an individualized basis through an informal, interactive process between the employer and employee. Employers do not

Table 14.1 Summary of ADA Requirements by Title

Title	Covered Entities and Requirements
Title I (Employment)	Requires equal access to employment opportunities and that employers provide reasonable accommodations for applicants and employees with disabilities (i.e., changes to the way a job is done or to the work environment that allow an employee to do their job).
Title II (Public Entities)	Bars disability discrimination in state and local services, programs, and activities such as public education, transportation, recreation, health care, social services, courts, and voting and requires reasonable modifications to ensure that people with disabilities can participate in and enjoy these services, programs, and activities.
Title III (Public Accommodations)	Bars disability discrimination by private places of public accommodation, such as restaurants, retail establishments, private clinical practices, and other businesses open to the public and requires reasonable modifications to afford access to people with disabilities.
Title IV (Telecommunications)	Requires telephone and television access for people with hearing and speech disabilities.
Title V (Miscellaneous Provisions)	Includes provisions that apply to the ADA as a whole including direction to specific federal agencies to provide information and guidance about the requirements of the law.

have to provide the specific accommodation requested, as long as any accommodation offered addresses the employee's needs. Nor do employers have to provide accommodations that would pose an undue hardship (involving significant difficulty or expense) to the employer or a direct threat to others. For example, an employer can require an employee who has tested positive for COVID-19 infection or who has COVID-19 symptoms to stay home.[27] However, if the employee is still well enough to perform the job, the employer must consider whether the threat can be eliminated or reduced through a reasonable accommodation, such as working remotely.[28]

Health Care Laws

Laws that govern health care services and programs also impact the health and health care of people with disabilities. Title XIX of the Social Security Act established the joint federal and state Medicaid program (discussed in Chapter 7), which is a key source of health insurance coverage for nonelderly adults with disabilities. As discussed elsewhere, the ACA has many different provisions addressing the health care system, including policies intended to expand access to public and private insurance coverage, enhance health care quality, improve health care delivery systems, control health care costs, and identify and eliminate health inequities. Many of the ACA's general provisions have the potential to benefit individuals with disabilities.[29] Coverage of preexisting conditions, for example, is especially important for individuals with disabilities. Prior to the ACA, many health insurers were allowed to exclude or restrict coverage for individuals with preexisting conditions such as cancer, asthma, or other chronic conditions or disabilities.[30] The ACA also has disability-specific provisions, including the antidiscrimination provision (Section 1557) and data collection requirements, both of which are discussed later in this chapter.

Treatment of People with Disabilities by the Health Care System

People with disabilities have experienced a history of discrimination and unequal treatment by the health care system, including denial of needed services, inadequate or inappropriate treatment, unjustified institutionalization, compulsory sterilization, exploitation in research, and other harms. The Supreme Court's decision in *Buck v. Bell* (discussed in Chapter 12), for example, upheld the compulsory sterilization of Carrie Buck, a young woman who experienced harms based on stereotypes and stigma related to her (perceived) disability, gender, and poverty.

The ADA and the Rehabilitation Act were intended to address many of these harms, and together they apply to nearly all health care settings and programs. These laws require equitable access for individuals with disabilities to health care services offered by public hospitals, to state and local policies and programs, and to private offices and hospitals, subject to some limitations. Section 1557 of the ACA amends the Rehabilitation Act to provide additional protections against discrimination in health care and adopts many of the ADA's requirements.[31]

Under these laws, providers and institutions may not refuse to see a patient on the basis of disability. Physical access to clinical and other health care settings must be provided. Under Title III of the ADA, a private practice that serves the public is required to ensure physical access and remove barriers where it is "readily achievable" (i.e., not too difficult or expensive). Title II of the ADA requires state and local governments to ensure general access to service and programs. If barrier removal is not feasible (e.g., too expensive given the entity's resources), then an alternate way to deliver the health care services must be provided. Effective communication is required, including provision of auxiliary aids and services (e.g., the provision of sign language interpreters or materials in alternative formats) unless it would be an undue burden. Finally, there is an overall requirement of reasonable modification of policies, practices, and procedures when necessary to accommodate individual needs unless the modifications would fundamentally alter the nature of the services. In health care settings, decisions about reasonable modifications should include discussions between the physician and the patient and emphasize the preferences of the patient.[32] ADA regulations also clarify that patients cannot be required to provide their own accommodations (e.g., a companion to transfer the patient to an exam table or a family member who can act as a translator) or be required to pay for the accommodations.[33]

Health Care Services

Despite these legal protections, people with disabilities continue to face significant barriers to health care. Some health care providers continue to refuse to treat individuals on the basis of disabilities such as HIV/AIDS and SUD.[34] Others may refuse to treat individuals with disabilities because they are unable or unwilling to provide needed accommodations. One "secret shopper"–style investigation found that 22% of physician practices refused to make an appointment for a fictional patient described as unable to transfer independently onto an exam table.[35]

These types of refusals to treat were highlighted by the COVID-19 pandemic when concerns arose regarding medical resource allocation policies and practices that disadvantaged people with disabilities. The death of Michael Hickson exemplified these concerns. Mr. Hickson was a 46-year-old Black man with disability who sought care for COVID-19. According to his family, the hospital refused to provide Mr. Hickson with lifesaving care for COVID-19 disease based on assumptions that he had a low quality of life due to preexisting quadriplegia and head injury.[36] In response to this and similar reports, the U.S. Department of Health and Human Services Office for Civil Rights (OCR) issued a statement affirming that people with disabilities should not be denied medical care on the basis of "stereotypes, assessments of quality of life," or "judgments about a person's relative 'worth' based on the presence or absence of disabilities or age."[37] Instead, decisions concerning whether an individual is a candidate for treatment should be "based on an individualized assessment of the patient based on the best available objective medical evidence."[38] The OCR statement also emphasizes other requirements of Section 1557 and the Rehabilitation Act, including the obligation to ensure effective communication with individuals who are deaf, hard of hearing, or blind; have low vision; or have speech disabilities and to make reasonable modifications to address the needs of individuals with disabilities. Reasonable modifications for a patient who is deaf or hard of hearing, for example, could include providing a qualified notetaker, a qualified sign language interpreter, real-time captioning of video or virtual communications, or written materials.[39] Decisions about modifications should take into account the specific circumstances and the communications needs and preferences of the individual. For example, ADA guidance suggests that a qualified interpreter generally will be needed for taking the medical history of a patient who uses sign language for discussing a serious diagnosis and its treatment options.[40] OCR's emphasis on these requirements is important, as lack of effective communication continues to be a problem for many deaf or hard-of-hearing patients.[41]

People with disabilities also face physical barriers in health care settings. Despite legal accessibility requirements required by law, studies document a lack of accessible medical diagnostic equipment, such as examination tables and chairs, weight scales, and imaging equipment as a significant barrier to the receipt of quality health care services.[42] A national survey found that only about one-fifth of physicians reported using accessible scales to weigh patients with mobility disabilities, and only two-fifths of physicians reported using accessible exam tables and chairs or using lifts to transfer those patients.[43] Quality of care many be compromised in the absence

of reasonable modifications such as accessible equipment and lifts. Patients who use wheelchairs, for example, report being examined in their wheelchairs rather than being transferred onto exam tables.[44]

With the increase of telemedicine, particularly during the COVID-19 pandemic, access to technology—smartphones and computers—is becoming even more important. Yet people with disabilities are less likely than people without disabilities to have access to these devices (see **Figure 14.2**). Furthermore, websites, apps, and other digital health tools may not be accessible to people with disabilities.[45]

Health-Related Services and Programs

People with disabilities face barriers to participation in health-related services and programs. Historically, some states chose to provide Medicaid services to individuals in institutional settings but not to individuals living in the community. The Supreme Court held in *Olmstead v. L.C.* that the ADA requires state Medicaid programs to provide community-based services to persons with disabilities in the most integrated setting appropriate to their needs.[46] This means that individuals with disabilities, including persons with cognitive and intellectual disabilities and individuals with mental illness, cannot be required to live in institutions or group settings to obtain the health care and other services they need. However, resource constraints might delay a community-based placement—a transfer from an institutional setting to a community-based setting is required if it can be reasonably accommodated, taking into account the resources available to the state and the needs of other individuals with disabilities.[47] Activities and services designed to promote health and wellness more broadly should also be accessible to people with disabilities, such as opportunities for physical fitness[48] and health promotion and disease prevention activities.[49]

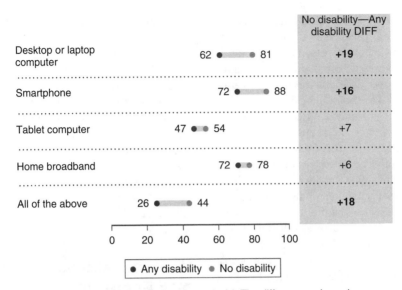

Note: Statistically significant differences in **bold**. The difference values shown are based on subtracting the rounded values in the chart. Respondents who did not give an answer are not shown.

Figure 14.2 Access to computers and smartphones by people with disabilities

ANDREW PERRIN AND SARA ATSKE, "Americans with disabilities less likely than those without to own some digital devices," Pew Research Center

Assumptions, Biases, and Lack of Knowledge

Assumptions, biases, and lack of knowledge about what it is like to live with disability contribute to the types of barriers described. Implicit biases about people with disabilities and other marginalized groups can greatly impact health and health care (see Chapter 1). Research consistently shows that physicians hold negative views of people with disabilities and fail to fully appreciate the value and quality of life with a disability.[50] One recent study found that more than 82% of physicians in the United States believe that people with significant disabilities have a worse quality of life than nondisabled people.[51] More than 20 years ago, *Healthy People 2010*, a U.S. Department of Health and Human Services (HHS) initiative that sets 10-year goals and objectives for improving population health, suggested that common misconceptions about individuals with disabilities contribute to disparities in their receipt of health care services, especially lower rates of screening tests, and an underemphasis on health promotion and disease prevention activities.[52] More recently, a series of reports from the National Council on Disability explored how persistent devaluation of the lives of people with disabilities by the medical community, legislators, researchers, and others have perpetuated inequities in health and access to health care.[53]

Lack of training of health care providers about the health care needs of people with disabilities also hinders access to quality care for these populations.[54] A report by the National Council on Disability identified lack of training on disability competence issues and on legal requirements for health care practitioners among the most significant barriers to health and health care experienced by people with disabilities.[55] One example is "diagnostic overshadowing," a process by which symptoms are misattributed to the underlying disability, leaving the presenting injury or disease undiagnosed and untreated. This process appears especially common for people with mental health issues or intellectual or developmental disabilities.[56]

Social and Structural Drivers of Disability Health Inequities

Attention to people with disabilities as a population experiencing significant health inequities is relatively recent. Recognition has been hindered by misconceptions of disability and assumptions that disability equals poor health. Historically, the "medical model" "treats disability as a problem of the person, directly caused by disease, trauma or another health condition, which required medical care," as described in Chapter 1.[57] This model assumes that health differences for people with disabilities are individual and a consequence of disability itself.

In contrast, the "social model" recognizes that "disability is not an attribute of the individual, but rather a complex collection of conditions which are created by the social environment."[58] *Healthy People 2020* reflects the social model of disability, recognizing "that what defines individuals with disabilities, their abilities, and their health outcomes more often depends on their community, including social and environmental circumstances."[59] This view is consistent with the International Classification of Functioning Disability and Health (ICF), published by the World Health Organization in 2001, which views disability less as a biomedical label and more as an experience that should be understood in social and environmental contexts.[60] The social model of disability also is reflected in laws—such as the ADA—that require removal of socially created barriers. Embrace of the social model of disability and robust antidiscrimination

protections are important, as people with disabilities continue to experience structural and social disadvantages as well as inequities in health and health care access.

Social and Structural Drivers of Health

People with disabilities are a diverse group, in terms of both types and severity of disabilities and characteristics such as race, ethnicity, and gender, among others. However, on average, individuals with disabilities are much more likely than nondisabled individuals to experience social and environmental circumstances that threaten their health and well-being. According to a recent review of the evidence, people with disabilities experience

- Higher rates of poverty
- Higher rates of food insecurity
- Lower levels of education
- Lower rates of employment among those seeking jobs
- Significant problems finding safe, affordable, accessible housing
- Substantial difficulties finding safe, reliable, affordable, and accessible transportation
- Higher probabilities of being victims of crime or domestic violence[61]

Intersections with race, ethnicity, gender, or other characteristics may compound these disparities.[62] Women with disabilities, for example, experience even greater inequities in income, education, and employment.[63] **Figure 14.3** shows the substantially higher rate of poverty among people with disabilities, as compared to the general population.

The overlap of disability with poverty and race/ethnicity contributes to inequities in education, a key social driver of health.[64] Although the IDEA was intended to guarantee a free and appropriate public education for all children with disabilities, research points to gaps and inequities in receipt of special education services that disproportionately

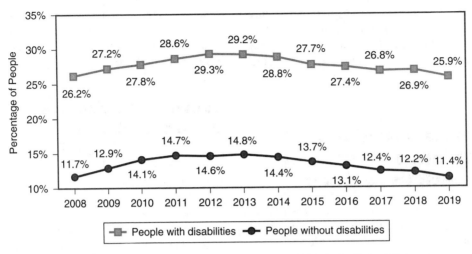

Figure 14.3 Poverty rate among people with and without disabilities in the United States from 2008 to 2019

impact poor children and Black and Latinx children.[65] Challenges related to inadequate funding, federal monitoring and enforcement, and continued segregation and discipline of students with disabilities have also been documented.[66]

Health and Health Care Inequities

As discussed earlier, recognition of disability-based health inequities has been hampered by misconceptions of disability as an individual medical issue that inevitably leads to worse outcomes. In fact, *Healthy People 2010*, released in 2000, was the first in the *Healthy People* series to identify people with disabilities "as a potentially underserved group … [that] would be expected to experience disadvantages in health and well-being compared with the general population."[67] The report took note of inequities in the receipt of health care services by people with disabilities—especially lower rates of screening tests—and an under-emphasis on health promotion and disease prevention activities.

The 2005 report *The Surgeon General's Call to Action to Improve the Health and Wellness*

of Persons with Disabilities highlighted inequities such as poorer reported health status and specific risk of secondary conditions as well as barriers to health and health care including lack of transportation, provider attitudes and misconceptions, and inaccessible facilities and services.[68] A few years later, in 2009, the National Council on Disability published *The Current State of Health Care for People with Disabilities,* an evaluation of decades of research on health inequities and barriers experienced by people with disabilities.[69] The report found that people with disabilities report poorer health status than people without disabilities, use fewer preventive services despite using health care services at a significantly higher rate overall, and face more problems accessing health care than other groups. The report also identified lack of training on disability competence issues and on legal requirements for health care practitioners among the most significant barriers.

Reports from governmental agencies, advocacy organizations, academic researchers, and others continue to document health inequities experienced by people with disabilities. Major findings show that people with disabilities

- Have higher rates of common chronic conditions, such as diabetes, hypertension, and chronic pulmonary disease
- Are more likely to be current or past tobacco smokers
- Are more likely to be overweight or obese
- Report lower rates of leisure time physical activity
- Are more likely to report experiencing symptoms of depression, stress, anxiety, and fears[70]

People with disabilities also experience inequalities in health care services, including lower rates of the following:

- High-value cancer screening tests, such as screening mammography and Pap tests
- Preventive dental care
- Services relating to contraception, sexuality, and reproductive health
- Quality prenatal care, such as routine weight measurement[71]

It is important to appreciate that people with certain disabilities may experience greater stigma and unequal treatment across different health care settings and types of health care. For example, people with SUD face distinct forms of stigma and unequal treatment in health care. But there are gaps in the data across disability subpopulations, such as comparisons between different types of disability or different levels of severity of disability in terms of health status, health care access, and health care outcomes.[72]

It is also the case that members of underserved racial and ethnic groups with disabilities experience relatively greater disparities in health status and access to health care than their counterparts.[73] Additionally, women with mobility limitations are also more likely to experience late-stage breast cancer detection.[74] However, a 2019 report published by the National Academies, called *Compounded Disparities: Health Equity at the Intersection of Disability, Race, and Ethnicity*, noted that "research on health and health disparities at the intersection of disability and race/ethnicity

is very limited."[75] More research is needed to understand and address overlapping disparities experienced at the intersection of disability, race, ethnicity, gender, LGBTQ+ status, and other characteristics.

Law, Policy, and Structural Change to Achieve Health Justice

More than 30 years after passage of the ADA, people with disabilities continue to experience health inequities and social disadvantages and fare worse in terms of the negative effects of many social drivers of health. Addressing these inequities will require a multipronged approach that recognizes the social, environmental, economic, and health system factors that contribute to the health and well-being of people with disabilities. While addressing the range of changes necessary to eliminate disability-based health inequities is beyond the scope of this chapter, following are some of the legal and policy changes that are necessary to realizing health justice for people with disabilities.

Strengthen and Enforce Existing Laws

Existing laws are strong tools to promote the health and wellness of individuals with disabilities, but they require enforcement to be effective. The ADA, the Rehabilitation Act, and Section 1557 of the ACA are designed to be enforced by specific federal agencies and through actions brought by private individuals and groups. Public and private enforcement actions and settlement agreements have addressed a wide range of barriers to health care services for individuals with disabilities. However, many experts claim that these laws are underenforced.[76] Strong and consistent public enforcement efforts are needed.

There are also opportunities to strengthen existing laws in ways that could advance health justice for people with disabilities. For example, the ACA directed the U.S. Access Board—an independent federal agency responsible for developing accessibility guidelines and standards under disability antidiscrimination laws—to develop technical standards for the accessibility of examination tables, examination chairs, weight scales, mammography equipment, and other diagnostic imaging equipment.[77] Adopting the accessibility standards as enforceable under the ADA and Rehabilitation Act would clarify requirements for health care offices and institutions and help reduce a significant barrier to care.[78]

Educational Initiatives

While there are many reasons for health inequities and barriers to quality care for people with disabilities, well-documented negative attitudes, assumptions, and lack of information about disability play a role. Research shows a lack of knowledge of and noncompliance with disability antidiscrimination laws in health care settings.[79] Health care providers, institutions, and systems need to ensure that all medical professionals and staff receive training about barriers to care for people with disabilities, along with the existing antidiscrimination protections that protect and promote accessible health care for individuals with disabilities.[80] There also are opportunities to incorporate disability competence curricula more broadly in graduate and professional schools and in health care settings.[81]

Data to Support Research and Policy

Better disability data are needed to inform policies and programs designed to address issues of health equity for people with disabilities. This means that people with disabilities must be included in a wide range of health data collection initiatives. The ACA already requires all federally conducted or supported health care and public health programs to collect data on disability status using, at a minimum, the six ACS disability questions. These data are critical to identifying and addressing inequities experienced by people with disabilities as well inequities at the intersections of disability, race, ethnicity, gender, and other characteristics.

There are also opportunities to collect disability-specific data. The ACA directs HHS to identify locations where individuals with disabilities access different types of care and to determine the number of providers with accessible facilities and accessible medical and diagnostic equipment, along with the number of employees trained in disability awareness and in caring for patients with disabilities. However, this data has not been collected.

People with disabilities must also be included in clinical trials and other health research. As researchers have noted, people with disabilities remain "largely absent from mainstream health research," and we must "[increase] the amount and coordination of disability research and routinely include[e] people with disabilities in general health research" in order to "close the knowledge gap in effective interventions."[82]

Conclusion

This chapter examined how the significant health inequities experienced by people with disabilities are rooted in policies, practices, and beliefs that reflect and reinforce long-standing stigma, unequal treatment, and discrimination. It provided an overview of key federal disability and health care laws that can be leveraged to address inequities in access to health care and other structural drivers of health for a large and diverse group of Americans. Although there is much work to be done, this chapter highlighted opportunities for legal, policy, and structural changes that are necessary to promote the health and well-being of people with disabilities within the health justice framework.

References

1. World Health Organization, ed. *International Classification of Functioning, Disability and Health: ICF.* World Health Organization (Geneva); 2001.

2. Institute of Medicine (US) Committee on Disability in America. *The Future of Disability in America.* (Field MJ, Jette AM, eds.). National Academies Press (US); 2007. http://www.ncbi.nlm.nih.gov/books/NBK11434/.

3. Walsh ES, Peterson JJ, Judkins DZ. Searching for disability in electronic databases of published literature. *Disability and Health Journal.* 2014;7(1):114–118. doi:10.1016/j.dhjo.2013.10.005.

4. Patient Protection and Affordable Care Act, Pub. L. No. 111-148, § 4203, 124 Stat. 119, 570 (2010) (Codified as Amended at 29 U.S.C. § 794f (2010)).

5. Data collection standards for race, ethnicity, sex, primary language, and disability status. Office of Minority Health, U.S. Dept. of Health and Human Services. https://www.minorityhealth.hhs.gov/omh/browse.aspx?lvl=2&lvlid=23. Dorsey R, Graham G, Glied S, Meyers D, Clancy C, Koh H. Implementing health reform: Improved data collection and the monitoring of health disparities. *Annu Rev Public Health.* 2014;35(1):123–138. doi:10.1146/annurev-publhealth-032013-182423.

6. Pendo E, Iezzoni LI. The role of law and policy in achieving healthy people's disability and health goals around access to health care, activities promoting health and wellness, independent living and participation, and collecting data in the United States. Department of Health and Human Services, Office of Disease Prevention and Health Promotion. 2020. https://www.healthypeople.gov/sites/default/files/LHP_Disability-Health-Policy_2020.03.12_508_0.pdf.

7. Varadaraj V, Deal JA, Campanile J, Reed NS, Swenor BK. National prevalence of disability and disability types among adults in the US, 2019. *JAMA Network Open.* 2021;4(10):e2130358. doi:10.1001/jamanetworkopen.2021.30358.

8. Varadaraj V, Deal JA, Campanile J, Reed NS, Swenor BK. National prevalence of disability and disability types among adults in the US, 2019. *JAMA Network Open.* 2021;4(10):e2130358. doi:10.1001/jamanetworkopen.2021.30358. Okoro CA. Prevalence of disabilities and health care access by disability status and type among adults—United States, 2016. *Morbidity and Mortality Weekly Report.* 2018;67. doi:10.15585/mmwr.mm6732a3.

9. Young NAE. Childhood disability in the United States: 2019. U.S. Census Bureau. 2021. https://www.census.gov/library/stories/2021/03/united-states-childhood-disability-rate-up-in-2019-from-2008.html.

10. Understanding disability statistics. ADA National Network. 2017. https://adata.org/factsheet/understanding-disability-statistics.

11. Varadaraj V, Deal JA, Campanile J, Reed NS, Swenor BK. National prevalence of disability and disability types among adults in the US, 2019. *JAMA Network Open.* 2021;4(10):e2130358. doi:10.1001/jamanetworkopen.2021.30358.

12. Okoro CA. Prevalence of disabilities and health care access by disability status and type among adults—United States, 2016. *Morbidity and Mortality Weekly Report.* 2018;67. doi:10.15585/mmwr.mm6732a3.

13. Varadaraj V, Deal JA, Campanile J, Reed NS, Swenor BK. National prevalence of disability and disability types among adults in the US, 2019. *JAMA Network Open.* 2021;4(10):e2130358. doi:10.1001/jamanetworkopen.2021.30358.

14. Varadaraj V, Deal JA, Campanile J, Reed NS, Swenor BK. National prevalence of disability and disability types among adults in the US, 2019. *JAMA Network Open.* 2021;4(10):e2130358. doi:10.1001/jamanetworkopen.2021.30358.

15. Okoro CA. Prevalence of disabilities and health care access by disability status and type among adults—United States, 2016. *Morbidity and Mortality Weekly Report.* 2018;67. doi:10.15585/mmwr.mm6732a3.

16. *Cleburne v. Cleburne Living Ctr.* 473, 432 (U.S. 1985).

17. U.S. Department of Justice Civil Rights Division Disability Rights Section. A guide to disability rights laws. 2009. https://www.ada.gov/cguide.htm.

18. Individuals with Disabilities Education Act. Vol 20 U.S.C. § 1400 et seq. (2004).

19. Irwin V, Zhang J, Wang X, et al. *Report on the condition of education 2021.* U.S. Department of Education, National Center for Education Statistics; 2021:43.

20. U.S. Department of Justice Civil Rights Division, Disability Rights Section. Frequently asked questions about service animals and the ADA. 2015. https://www.ada.gov/regs2010/service_animal_qa.pdf.

21. U.S. Department of Justice Civil Rights Division, Disability Rights Section. Frequently asked questions about service animals and the ADA. 2015. https://www.ada.gov/regs2010/service_animal_qa.pdf. Wisch RF. Table of state service animal laws. Michigan State University College of Law, Animal Legal & Historical Center. 2021. https://www.animallaw.info/topic/table-state-assistance-animal-laws.

22. Georgia State Financing and Investment Commission, State ADA Coordinator's Office. Accessibility in state-owned buildings and facilities. 2009: 1–60. https://ada.georgia.gov/.

23. Americans with Disabilities Act. Vol 42 U.S.C. § 12101 et seq. (2008).

24. Rehabilitation Act. Vol 29 U.S.C. § 701 et seq. (1973).

25. Definition of Disability. Vol 42 U.S.C. §12120. (2008).

26. U.S. Equal Employment Opportunity Commission. Enforcement guidance on reasonable accommodation and undue hardship under the ADA. 2002. https://www.eeoc.gov/laws/guidance/enforcement-guidance-reasonable-accommodation-and-undue-hardship-under-ada#N_7_.

27. U.S. Equal Employment Opportunity Commission. What you should know about COVID-19 and the ADA, the Rehabilitation Act, and other EEO laws. 2022. https://www.eeoc.gov/wysk/what-you-should-know-about-covid-19-and-ada-rehabilitation-act-and-other-eeo-laws.

28. U.S. Equal Employment Opportunity Commission. What you should know about COVID-19 and the ADA, the Rehabilitation Act, and other EEO laws. 2020. https://www.eeoc.gov/wysk/what-you-should-know-about-covid-19-and-ada-rehabilitation-act-and-other-eeo-laws.

29. National Council on Disability. Implementing the Affordable Care Act: A roadmap for people with disabilities. 2016. https://www.ncd.gov.

30. Claxton G, Cox C, Damico A, Levitt L, Pollitz K. Pre-existing conditions and medical underwriting in the individual insurance market prior to the ACA. Kaiser Family Foundation. 2016. https://www.kff.org/health-reform/issue-brief/pre-existing-conditions-and-medical-underwriting-in-the-individual-insurance-market-prior-to-the-aca/.

31. Patient Protection and Affordable Care Act, Pub. L. No. 111-148, § 4203, 124 Stat. 119, 570 (2010) (Codified as Amended at 29 U.S.C. § 794f (2010)).

32. *General.* Vol 28 C.F.R. §35.160(b)(2) (2011). *Auxiliary Aids and Services.* Vol 28 C.F.R. 36.303 (2011).

33. *General Prohibitions against Discrimination.* Vol 28 C.F.R. § 35.130 (2011). *Eligibility Criteria.* Vol 28 C.F.R. § 36.301 (1991).

34. Dineen KK, Pendo E. Substance use disorder discrimination and the CARES Act: Using disability law to inform part 2 rulemaking. *Arizona State Law Journal.* 2021;52:1143.

35. Lagu T, Hannon NS, Rothberg MB, et al. Access to subspecialty care for patients with mobility impairment: A survey. *Ann Intern Med.* 2013;158(6):441. doi:10.7326/0003-4819-158-6-201303190-00003

36. Cha AE. Disability rights activists rally around wife of quadriplegic man with COVID-19 who sought continued treatment. *The Washington Post.* July 5, 2020. https://www.washingtonpost.com/health/2020/07/05/coronavirus-disability-death/.

37. BULLETIN: Civil Rights, HIPAA, and the Coronavirus Disease 2019 (COVID-19).

38. BULLETIN: Civil Rights, HIPAA, and the Coronavirus Disease 2019 (COVID-19).

39. *ADA Requirements: Effective Communication. U.S. Dept. of Justice, Civil Rights Division.* 2014. Accessed June 28, 2021. https://www.ada.gov/effective-comm.htm.

40. *ADA Requirements: Effective Communication. U.S. Dept. of Justice, Civil Rights Division.* 2014. Accessed June 28, 2021. https://www.ada.gov/effective-comm.htm.

41. See, e.g., Baystate Medical Center agrees to settle allegations of Americans with Disabilities Act violations. November 16, 2021. https://www.justice.gov/usao-ma/pr/baystate-medical-center-agrees-settle-allegations-americans-disabilities-act-violations.

42. Pendo E, Iezzoni LI. The role of law and policy in achieving healthy people's disability and health goals around access to health care, activities promoting health and wellness, independent living and participation, and collecting data in the United States. Department of Health and Human Services, Office of Disease Prevention and Health Promotion. 2020. https://www.healthypeople.gov/sites/default/files/LHP_Disability-Health-Policy_2020.03.12_508_0.pdf.

43. Iezzoni LI, Rao SR, Ressalam J, et al. Use of accessible weight scales and examination tables/chairs for patients with significant mobility limitations by physicians nationwide. *The Joint Commission Journal on Quality and Patient Safety.* June 2021:S1553725021001598. doi:10.1016/j.jcjq.2021.06.005.

44. Iezzoni LI, Kilbridge K, Park ER. Physical access barriers to care for diagnosis and treatment of breast cancer among women with mobility impairments. *Oncology Nursing Forum.* 2010;37(6):711–717. doi:10.1188/10.ONF.711-717. de Vries McClintock HF, Barg FK, Katz SP, et al. Health care experiences and perceptions among people with and without disabilities. *Disability and Health Journal.* 2016;9(1):74–82. doi:10.1016/j.dhjo.2015.08.007.

45. Perrin R, Atske S. Americans with disabilities less likely than those without to own some digital devices. Pew Research Center. Accessed December 18, 2021. https://www.pewresearch.org/fact-tank/2021/09/10/americans-with-disabilities-less-likely-than-those-without-to-own-some-digital-devices/.

46. *Olmstead v. L.C. Ex Rel. Zimring.* U.S. 527, 581 (1992).

47. *Olmstead v. L.C. Ex Rel. Zimring.* U.S. 527, 581 (1992).

48. Pendo E, Iezzoni LI. The role of law and policy in achieving healthy people's disability and health goals around access to health care, activities promoting health and wellness, independent living and participation, and collecting data in the United States. Department of Health and Human Services, Office of Disease Prevention and Health Promotion. 2020. https://www.healthypeople.gov/sites/default/files/LHP_Disability-Health-Policy_2020.03.12_508_0.pdf.

49. Health and Human Services Department, Satcher D. *Healthy People 2010, Vols. 1–2: With understanding and improving health and objectives for improving health*. 1st ed. 2001.

50. Pendo E, Iezzoni LI. The role of law and policy in achieving healthy people's disability and health goals around access to health care, activities promoting health and wellness, independent living and participation, and collecting data in the United States. Department of Health and Human Services, Office of Disease Prevention and Health Promotion. 2020. https://www.healthypeople.gov/sites/default/files/LHP_Disability-Health-Policy_2020.03.12_508_0.pdf.

51. Iezzoni LI, Rao SR, Ressalam J, et al. Physicians' perceptions of people with disability and their health care: Study reports the results of a survey of physicians' perceptions of people with disability. *Health Affairs*. 2021;40(2):297–306. doi:10.1377/hlthaff.2020.01452.

52. Health and Human Services Department, Satcher D. *Healthy People 2010, Vols. 1–2: With understanding and improving health and objectives for improving health*. 1st ed. 2001.

53. National Council on Disability. *Bioethics and disability report series*. 2019. https://ncd.gov/.

54. Agaronnik ND, Pendo E, Campbell EG, Ressalam J, Iezzoni LI. Knowledge of practicing physicians about their legal obligations when caring for patients with disability. *Health Affairs*. 2019;38(4):545–553. doi:10.1377/hlthaff.2018.05060.

55. National Council on Disability. The current state of health care for people with disabilities. 2009.

56. Molloy R, Munro I, Pope N. Understanding the experience of diagnostic overshadowing associated with severe mental illness from the consumer and health professional perspective: A qualitative systematic review protocol. *JBI Evidence Synthesis*. 2020. doi:10.11124/JBIES-20-00244.

57. World Health Organization, ed. *International Classification of Functioning, Disability and Health: ICF*. World Health Organization (Geneva); 2001.

58. World Health Organization, ed. *International Classification of Functioning, Disability and Health: ICF*. World Health Organization (Geneva); 2001.

59. Disability and Health | Healthy People 2020. 2016. https://www.healthypeople.gov/2020/topics-objectives/topic/disability-and-health.

60. Krahn GL, Walker DK, Correa-De-Araujo R. Persons with disabilities as an unrecognized health disparity population. *American Journal of Public Health*. 2015;105(S2):S198–S206. doi:10.2105/AJPH.2014.302182.

61. Pendo E, Iezzoni LI. The role of law and policy in achieving healthy people's disability and health goals around access to health care, activities promoting health and wellness, independent living and participation, and collecting data in the United States. Department of Health and Human Services, Office of Disease Prevention and Health Promotion. 2020. https://www.healthypeople.gov/sites/default/files/LHP_Disability-Health-Policy_2020.03.12_508_0.pdf.

62. Yee, S, Breslin ML, Goode TD, et al. *Compounded disparities: Health equity at the intersection of disability, race, and ethnicity*. National Academies of Sciences, Engineering, and Medicine. 2018: 1–177. https://dredf.org/wp-content/uploads/2018/01/Compounded-Disparities-Intersection-of-Disabilities-Race-and-Ethnicity.pdf.

63. Nosek MA. Health disparities and equity: The intersection of disability, health, and sociodemographic characteristics among women. In Miles-Cohen SE, Signore C, eds. *Eliminating Inequities for Women with Disabilities: An Agenda for Health and Wellness*. American Psychological Association. 2016: 13–38. doi:10.1037/14943-002.

64. Bonuck K, Hill LA. Special education disparities are social determinants of health: A role for medical–legal partnerships. *Progress in Community Health Partnerships*. 2020;14(2):251–257. doi:10.1353/cpr.2020.0028.

65. Bonuck K, Hill LA. Special education disparities are social determinants of health: A role for medical–legal partnerships. *Progress in Community Health Partnerships*. 2020;14(2):251–257. doi:10.1353/cpr.2020.0028.

66. National Council on Disability. Individuals with Disabilities Education Act report series. 2018. https://ncd.gov/.

67. Health and Human Services Department, Satcher D. *Healthy People 2010, Vols. 1–2: With understanding and improving health and objectives for improving health*. 1st ed. 2001.

68. Office of the Surgeon General (US), Office on Disability (US). The Surgeon General's call to action to improve the health and wellness of persons with disabilities. 2005. http://www.ncbi.nlm.nih.gov/books/NBK44667/.

69. National Council on Disability. The current state of health care for people with disabilities. 2009.

70. Pendo E, Iezzoni LI. The role of law and policy in achieving healthy people's disability and health goals around access to health care, activities promoting health and wellness, independent living and participation, and collecting data in the United States. Department of Health and Human Services, Office of Disease Prevention and Health Promotion. 2020. https://www.healthypeople.gov/sites/default/files/LHP_Disability-Health-Policy_2020.03.12_508_0.pdf.

71. Pendo E, Iezzoni LI. *The role of law and policy in achieving healthy people's disability and health goals around access to health care, activities promoting health and wellness, independent living and participation, and collecting data in the United States.* Department of Health and Human Services, Office of Disease Prevention and Health Promotion. 2020. https://www.healthypeople.gov/sites/default/files/LHP_Disability-Health-Policy_2020.03.12_508_0.pdf.

72. Peterson-Besse JJ, Walsh ES, Horner-Johnson W, Goode TD, Wheeler B. Barriers to health care among people with disabilities who are members of underserved racial/ethnic groups: A scoping review of the literature. *Medical Care.* 2014;52:S51–S63. doi:10.1097/MLR.0000000000000195.

73. Yee, S, Breslin ML, Goode TD, et al. *Compounded disparities: Health equity at the intersection of disability, race, and ethnicity.* National Academies of Sciences, Engineering, and Medicine. 2018: 1–177. https://dredf.org/wp-content/uploads/2018/01/Compounded-Disparities-Intersection-of-Disabilities-Race-and-Ethnicity.pdf.

74. Andresen EM, Peterson-Besse JJ, Krahn GL, Walsh ES, Horner-Johnson W, Iezzoni LI. Pap, mammography, and clinical breast examination screening among women with disabilities: A systematic review. *Women's Health Issues.* 2013;23(4):e205–e214. doi:10.1016/j.whi.2013.04.002.

75. Yee, S, Breslin ML, Goode TD, et al. *Compounded disparities: Health equity at the intersection of disability, race, and ethnicity.* National Academies of Sciences, Engineering, and Medicine. 2018: 1–177. https://dredf.org/wp-content/uploads/2018/01/Compounded-Disparities-Intersection-of-Disabilities-Race-and-Ethnicity.pdf.

76. National Council on Disability. Monitoring and enforcing the Affordable Care Act. 2016. https://ncd.gov/. National Council on Disability. The current state of health care for people with disabilities. 2009.

77. Architectural and transportation barriers compliance board, standards for accessible medical diagnostic equipment. Vol 82 Fed. Reg. 2810 (codified at 36 C.F.R. Part 1195). 2017.

78. Iezzoni LI, Pendo E. Accessibility of medical diagnostic equipment—implications for people with disability. *New England Journal of Medicine.* 2018;378(15):1371–1373. doi:10.1056/NEJMp1800606.

79. Agaronnik ND, Pendo E, Campbell EG, Ressalam J, Iezzoni LI. Knowledge of practicing physicians about their legal obligations when caring for patients with disability. *Health Affairs.* 2019;38(4):545–553. doi:10.1377/hlthaff.2018.05060.

80. Agaronnik ND, Pendo E, Campbell EG, Ressalam J, Iezzoni LI. Knowledge of practicing physicians about their legal obligations when caring for patients with disability. *Health Affairs.* 2019;38(4):545–553. doi:10.1377/hlthaff.2018.05060.

81. Garland-Thomson R, Iezzoni LI. Disability cultural competence for all as a model. *The American Journal of Bioethics.* 2021;21(9):26–28. doi:10.1080/15265161.2021.1958652.

82. Rios D, Magasi S, Novak C, Harniss M. Conducting accessible research: Including people with disabilities in public health, epidemiological, and outcomes studies. *American Journal of Public Health.* 2016;106(12):2137–2144. doi:10.2105/AJPH.2016.303448.

© Johnny Miller/Unequal Scenes

PART 5

Striving for Health Justice: Structural and Policy Change

CHAPTER 15

Existing Efforts to Achieve Health Justice

LEARNING OBJECTIVES

18pts

By the end of this chapter you will be able to:

- Explain some existing health care system reforms aimed at identifying patients' social risks and addressing their social needs
- Describe initiatives focused on better aligning goals in health care, public health, and social services
- Discuss cross-sector state and local efforts that promote health justice through enforcement of legal rights and policy change

Introduction

The previous chapters in this book have detailed the many, complex pathways between and among social and structural drivers of health, laws, policies, and the long-standing and persistent health inequities in the United States. Fortunately, there has been much greater attention given to health inequities in recent years. This attention has led to new ways of thinking about the roles of medicine, public health, and law in confronting and addressing social and structural drivers of health. Recognition of the disconnect between the health care system and the community-based services and resources people need to stay healthy has initiated the development of new intersectoral partnerships. Many of these efforts have been guided and supported by the Affordable Care Act (ACA),

which, in addition to expanding access to health insurance, promotes payment reforms and population health–focused projects that encourage a more holistic approach to health. In public health, greater focus on upstream, structural drivers of health has promoted intersectoral and community-initiated changes to public health practice and policy. Furthermore, discussion of the role of law in constructing the conditions in which people live, combined with the crisis in access to justice for marginalized and low-income people, has precipitated approaches that partner lawyers, public health practitioners, health care providers, and community health advocates. In this chapter, we explore some of these reforms and initiatives with an eye toward how effective they have been in addressing health inequities and promoting health justice. As you read this chapter, think back to the many structural challenges, gaps and complexities in health and other social service systems, and health injustices described in earlier chapters; how well do the existing strategies presented in this chapter mitigate and remediate those problems?

Health Care System Reform

A New Focus on Population Health Management

In 2008, Donald M. Berwick, Thomas W. Nolan, and John Whittington published an article in *Health Affairs* in which they coined the term "the triple aim" of health care reform. In the article, they set out three simultaneous goals for reform: improving the experience of care, improving the health of populations, and reducing per capita costs of healthcare."[1] To be successful, they argued, a health care organization must accept responsibility for all three goals for the population that it serves. In 2014, Thomas Bodenheimer and Christine Sinsky, recognizing the systemwide problem of clinician burnout, argued that health care reform should include a fourth aim—improving the work satisfaction of health care providers— hence, creating the quadruple aim.[2] Recently, reformers have extended this even further, incorporating equity as a key goal of health care reform (see **Figure 15.1**).

The idea that health care organizations and providers are responsible not just for individual patients but for population health outcomes has become widely accepted, particularly in the delivery of primary care. This population health focus has led to a whole host of health care system delivery innovations. These include greater consideration of the root causes of illness; more attention to preventing illness and promoting wellness rather than waiting for people get sick; deeper focus on coordination of care across a siloed and fragmented health care system to not only improve the experience of care but also reduce unnecessary health care costs; strategic use of data to track patient and population health outcomes; incentives for payment reform that shifts from traditional fee for service (i.e., paying by the visit or procedure) toward value-based payment (centered on effective management of a population of patients); and efforts to identify and address social needs that drive poor health outcomes, health inequities, and high health care costs.[3]

One of the driving forces behind health care reformers' greater attention to social drivers of health was data demonstrating escalating costs associated with chronic disease management. The United States has a higher burden of chronic disease than 16 peer nations for conditions including diabetes, obesity, chronic lung disease, heart disease, and disability, as alluded to in this text's Introduction.[4] Indeed, the Centers for Disease Control and Prevention report that 90% of the

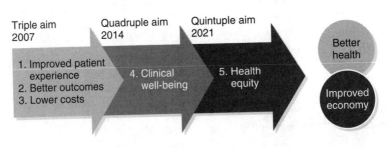

Figure 15.1 Evolution of the Quintuple Aim

Reproduced from Itchhaporia D. The Evolution of the Quintuple Aim: Health Equity, Health Outcomes, and the Economy. *Journal of the American College of Cardiology.* 2021;78(22):2262–2264.

$3.8 trillion the United States spends annually on health care services is for people with chronic and mental health conditions.[5] People with lower socioeconomic status, racial and ethnic minorities, and people in other disadvantaged and marginalized communities have a higher burden of chronic disease, as we have highlighted in other chapters. Therefore, the costs of chronic disease management and the inequities associated with it have helped to fuel innovations in the health care system aimed at improving the health of (and reducing the cost of care for) underserved populations.

Payment Reform: Opportunities to Address Health Inequities

The paradox in the United States—that it spends enormously on health care while having comparatively poor population health outcomes—has shined a light on how the nation pays for health care services as well as how costs are distributed across patient populations. The U.S. approach to health care spending has largely been driven by a "fee-for-service" model: Health care providers are either paid directly by patients at the time of treatment or reimbursed by a patient's health insurance company for each individual service rendered. Imagine a hospital bill for a patient who has just received a hip replacement, for example. Under a fee-for-service model, each interaction with a health care provider (e.g., the surgeon, anesthesiologist, nurse), each medication, and each bandage used for the dressing would be itemized separately on the bill, often at significant administrative cost. While a patient may not be responsible for these costs because of insurance, these are costs to the system nonetheless. Health care reformers have pointed out that fee-for-service payment incentivizes providers and hospitals to provide as many services as possible rather than focus on the necessity and effectiveness of these services for achieving patient health.

Value-Based Payment

The quintuple aims of health care reform—improved patient experience, lower costs, better population health outcomes, clinician well-being, and equity—have supported shifting to a value-based payment model. Value is essentially defined as "the quality of care (the sum of outcomes, safety, and service) divided by the cost of care over time."[6] Value-based payment is generally achieved through some sort of "bundled" or "global" payment mechanism rather than through the traditional fee-for-service model. A bundled payment is episode-based. For example, a provider is paid a lump sum (bundled payment) to cover the costs of a patient's hip replacement surgery (rather than, as described previously, for each individual service associated with the procedure and follow-up care). A global payment is made to a provider or group of providers to cover all of the costs of caring for a particular patient or patient population. The idea is to incentivize providers to use health care resources wisely and efficiently. The "value" in value-based payment models is measured by patient outcomes, patient satisfaction and other quality metrics, and demonstration of meeting cost containment goals. In value-based purchasing contracts with payers (e.g., Medicare, Medicaid, or commercial insurance plans that have adopted value-based purchasing), providers may be fully responsible for meeting cost goals—potentially taking a loss if they are over budget (downside risk)—or they may negotiate the opportunity to share any savings achieved by more efficient and high-quality delivery of care (upside risk).

The primary organizational model for value-based payment is the accountable care organization (ACO). ACOs are organizations that coordinate care among a group of health care providers (e.g., primary care practices, hospitals), which together manage the care for a defined population of patients and are held accountable for the quality of care, costs, and outcomes of that population. Most ACOs utilize a value-based purchasing model, sometimes employing a "capitated" model in which the ACO receives a per-patient, per-month payment to care for its designated population. Generally, ACOs share the financial risk of providing care with the government (Medicare and Medicaid) or a private insurance carrier by contracting up front to meet specific quality measures and cost targets. If those targets are met, the ACO providers are rewarded with a bonus payment; if not, they may be financially penalized.

You may be wondering at this point: How do these payment reforms and ACOs relate to health equity and justice? While not explicitly focused on health equity, value-based payment models and the adoption of ACOs have forced health care organizations and insurance providers to pay attention to health inequities in a number of ways. First, while capitated payment models, such as the per-patient, per-month model, may suggest that all patients are roughly equal in health care needs and costs, clearly they are not. Healthier patients require less care, while sicker patients—particularly those with chronic disease(s)—may require a far more significant amount of care. Consider this:

> The sickest patients are in the smallest percentage (5 percent) of the population and are often described as [high-need, high-cost patients]. They often are elderly, frail, disadvantaged socioeconomically, have psychosocial barriers to care, and have multiple health issues and/or many emergency department visits and hospitalizations. They account for 45 to 50 percent of the healthcare costs in a population.[7]

To be effective in meeting quality, cost, and outcome measures, an ACO must pay close attention not only to the health care needs of its population but also to how it can better coordinate care across systems and address nonmedical and social needs that may be leading to health care overutilization. It also must show better outcomes for its entire patient population, something that was not measured under the old fee-for-service payment model.

Second, many health care providers, particularly in primary care, have long sought options to fund services—such as behavioral and mental health care and assistance with accessing social services—that support a more holistic vision of health, but these types of services were not allowable charges under most health insurance plans. By negotiating value-based contracts with insurers, providers have more flexibility in defining what services may be covered. With the development of value-based care models, nonmedical services are more widely viewed as beneficial to patient health outcomes and important to reducing unnecessary and costly health care utilization.[8] Increasingly, value-based payment models tie payment to interventions that address social needs and connect performance on quality metrics to social needs interventions. This is true in Medicare (both traditional models and Medicare Advantage), state Medicaid programs, and commercial plans.[9]

State Medicaid programs have experimented in a number of ways with connecting value-based payment to social needs interventions through Medicaid Act Section 1115 waivers (under federal law, states may apply for a waiver from federal Medicaid program requirements to test and evaluate program innovations); Medicaid Managed Care organization contracts with providers; and Medicaid Accountable Care Organizations. Rhode Island, Massachusetts, and Oregon all require providers participating in Medicaid ACOs either to demonstrate that they are spending some of their funding to address social needs and/or to partner with community-based organizations to do so.[10] (We discuss partnerships between clinical and social services providers in more detail later in the chapter.) There is some evidence that marrying value-based payment with social needs interventions is effective in improving care and reducing health care costs:

> [S]everal [social] interventions have shown reductions in unnecessary utilization and spending for higher risk, high-cost patients, especially people with multiple chronic medical conditions and social needs (e.g., those with severe mental illness, chronic homelessness) who frequently use emergency department care. Cost reduction, and corresponding return on investment, evidence is strong (based on randomized trials) when healthcare and community-based organizations work together on housing or nutrition interventions.[11]

Finally, value-based payment models have supported a shift in focus from the individual patient in the exam room to the needs of the population living in the community. Rather than focus solely on the personal attributes of an individual patient, many health care providers are now being asked to account for, track, and address social factors that influence their patients' health. Later in the chapter, we describe some of the challenges and critiques of the health care sector's role in addressing social drivers of health.

Data-Driven Strategies to Address Social Drivers of Health

One thing that the health care and public health systems have in abundance is data. The electronic medical record, in which patients' health histories and medical care are recorded and updated each time they interact with the health care system, has become a valuable source of information—not just for the patient and provider but also for tracking individual and population-level health outcomes. Another source of data that is helpful to understanding population health, including health inequities, are insurance claims databases, which can help identify high-need, high-risk patients whose complex social needs may drive overutilization of medical care. And, finally, long an important resource for public health surveillance of disease trends, public health data are increasingly being employed to better track health inequities. Here, we highlight three examples of ways that health care institutions have employed data to guide equity-focused delivery system reforms and to target social needs interventions.

Hotspotting

One approach to using data to identify patients with multiple and complex social and medical needs is "hotspotting." This approach, conceived in 2002 by Dr. Jeffrey Brenner at a not-for-profit organization called the Camden Coalition, strategically uses data "to identify and engage patients with medical and social complexity and poor healthcare outcomes."[12] The coalition builds collaborations among community-based primary care providers, frontline hospital staff and social workers, and other community partners from across Camden to provide a team-based approach to managing patients with complex medical and social needs. The teams receive daily information about hospitalizations, which helps them track these patients and identify when interventions are needed. The model is based on building trust and long-term relationships with patients and their families.[13] Brenner's hotspotting model has been replicated in many locations across the country. In 2017, the National Center for Complex Health and Social Needs was launched to inform and support data-driven and patient-centered approaches to patients with complex needs through collaborations among clinicians, social service partners, policymakers, researchers, and consumers.[14]

2. Geomarkers

While Dr. Brenner used data to target interventions toward patients with complex needs, others are linking clinical data with community-level data to identify particular health risks. Dr. Andrew Beck and colleagues coined the term *geomarkers* (like biomarkers used to predict disease) to demonstrate place-based (e.g., neighborhood-level) risk factors for poor health outcomes. Beck and colleagues define geomarkers as "'any objective, contextual, or geographic measure' that influences or predicts the incidence of outcome or disease. By complementing biology with geography, we are able to tap into health-relevant data that generally exist in isolation from clinical care."[15] Geomarkers can include a range of neighborhood factors known to affect health—for example, the poverty rate, housing code violations, and accessibility of health care.

Linking community-based data with health data provides the opportunity to better understand individual susceptibility to disease based on community factors and to guide interventions and community-based partnerships. But databases are not the only way to gather and use data to address community health needs. Involving patients and community members in health care system change and reallocation of resources is vital to developing effective and responsive social needs interventions.

3. Community Health Needs Assessments

Hospitals have little, if any, financial incentive to invest in primary prevention, since their revenue derives from people needing acute medical care and from keeping their hospital beds full. Drafters of the ACA, however, sought to involve hospitals in population health improvement and hold them accountable for health care systems costs. The law requires that, in order to maintain their tax-exempt status, not-for-profit hospitals must conduct a community health needs assessment (CHNA) at least every 3 years. These needs assessments must include input from the community, including the local public health department as well as from medically underserved, low-income, and minority communities. Hospitals must also devise an implementation strategy to address the community health needs identified in the CHNA.

Under what is known as the "community benefit" standard, the federal Internal Revenue Service (IRS) has long required that a not-for-profit hospital demonstrate that it is contributing to the community in exchange for a tax exemption. Prior to the ACA, most community benefit spending took the form of reimbursing the hospital for charity care—providing care to the uninsured or making up for the gap between the cost of treating Medicaid patients and the amount reimbursed by the government—but not for community-based activities focused on health improvement.[16] The ACA's CHNA mandate was an attempt to refocus not-for-profit hospitals on upstream population health efforts through engagement with their local communities. The IRS regulations supporting the ACA mandate are explicit that CHNAs must address social needs.[17] However, a 2021 study found that

since the passage of the ACA's CHNA and implementation strategy regulations, most hospitals reported that they are conducting CHNAs and adopting related implementation strategies. However, only 60.0% of the hospitals in our sample had both a CHNA report and an implementation strategy on their website, and many of the documents were missing the required documentation elements.

It appears that a significant number of not-for-profit hospitals treat the ACA requirements for CHNAs as a "check-the-box" exercise rather than a genuine opportunity to connect clinical care to public health strategies and community needs.

Medical and Social Care Integration

As discussed previously, there has been significant movement in U.S. health care toward adopting strategies to address social needs as part of health care delivery. As these strategies have evolved, so too has the language used to describe them. Before reading this next section, it is helpful to delineate terminology. The term *social determinants of health* became commonly used in the mid-1990s.

It is often used in clinical settings to refer to interventions related to mitigating social factors that affect health. However, individual clinicians are typically not in a position to alter social conditions; they can assist patients and sometimes a population of patients to address social factors affecting their health. Consider the definitions in **Box 15.1** as you read the rest of the chapter. Think about who is in a position to respond to each of these: social drivers of health, social risk factors, and social needs.

With these definitions in mind, we turn to medical and social care integration. The overview of health care reform strategies—such as value-based payment and data-driven approaches to social drivers of health—provided some context for governmental and health care system investments in integrated care models, but how does this actually work in practice? Next, we explore

---

Box 15.1 Definitions

Social drivers of health (SDOH) are generally described as the "the conditions in the environments where people are born, live, learn, work, play, worship, and age that affect a wide range of health, functioning, and quality-of-life outcomes and risks."[18] These conditions are "shaped by the distribution of money, power and resources"[19]; put differently, if structural drivers of health are the methods and tools utilized by those in power to shape society and distribute resources and opportunities, then social drivers of health are the actual conditions and material circumstances that result from the use of those methods and tools. Social drivers may either positively or negatively affect health. Many medical and public health scholars and practitioners use the term *social determinants of health*, as discussed in Chapter 1; in this text, we use *social drivers* to acknowledge that, because of the many complex pathways between and among social factors that influence health, it is difficult to "determine" specific links between one factor and a resulting health outcome.

Social risk factors are "specific adverse social conditions that are associated with poor health, like social isolation or housing instability,"[20] that affect people at the individual or family level. These may be identified in clinical care through screening. Also, data collected about social risk factors may be employed to target individual or community-level interventions.[21]

Social needs are "[a] patient-centered concept that incorporates a person's perception of his or her own health-related needs."[22] Therefore, these are the needs that the patient identifies and prioritizes to address.

Social care integration refers to how "services that address health-related social risk factors and social needs [are integrated] into clinical practice and what kinds of infrastructure will be required to facilitate such activities."[23]

Social services are services that are provided by the government and private for-profit and not-for-profit organizations that promote health and social well-being.[24]

three common approaches employed by clinical programs to integrate social care: screening for social risks, interprofessional health care teams, and partnerships between clinical and social services.

Screening for Social Risks

With growing attention to the importance of social drivers of health, many primary care practices (and some specialty care providers) routinely screen for social risks.[25] Several professional medical associations have embraced social risk screening as a best practice, and there has been a proliferation of screening tools.[26] See **Box 15.2** for an example of a social risk screening tool used in a clinical setting. Some health care systems are integrating social risk screening questions into their electronic medical records.[27]

Screening for social risks as a part of clinical practice begs a few questions. Who

---

Box 15.2 Example of a Social Risk Screening Tool Used in a Clinical Setting

Box 1 | Accountable Health Communities Core Health-Related Social Needs Screening Questions

Underlined answer options indicate positive responses for the associated health-related social need. A value greater than 10 when the numerical values for answers to questions 7–10 are summed indicates a positive screen for interpersonal safety.

Housing Instability

1. What is your housing situation today?
   - I do not have housing (I am staying with others, in a hotel, in a shelter, living outside on the street, on a beach, in a car, abandoned building, bus or train station, or in a park)
   - I have housing today, but I am worried about losing housing in the future.
   - I have housing

2. Think about the place you live. Do you have problems with any of the following? (check all that apply)
   - Bug infestation
   - Mold
   - Lead paint or pipes
   - Inadequate heat
   - Oven or stove not working
   - No or not working smoke detectors
   - Water leaks
   - None of the above

Food Insecurity

3. Within the past 12 months, you worried that your food would run out before you got money to buy more.
   - Often true
   - Sometimes true
   - Never true

4. Within the past 12 months, the food you bought just didn't last and you didn't have money to get more.
   - Often true
   - Sometimes true
   - Never true

Transportation Needs

5. In the past 12 months, has lack of transportation kept you from medical appointments, meetings, work or from getting things needed for daily living? (Check all that apply)
   - Yes, it has kept me from medical appointments or getting medications
   - Yes, it has kept me from non-medical meetings, appointments, work, or getting things that I need
   - No

Utility Needs

6. In the past 12 months has the electric, gas, oil, or water company threatened to shut off services in your home?

- Yes
- No
- Already shut off

Interpersonal Safety

7. How often does anyone, including family, physically hurt you?
   - Never (1)
   - Rarely (2)
   - Sometimes (3)
   - Fairly often (4)
   - Frequently (5)

8. How often does anyone, including family, insult or talk down to you?
   - Never (1)
   - Rarely (2)
   - Sometimes (3)

- Fairly often (4)
- Frequently (5)

9. How often does anyone, including family, threaten you with harm?
   - Never (1)
   - Rarely (2)
   - Sometimes (3)
   - Fairly often (4)
   - Frequently (5)

10. How often does anyone, including family, scream or curse at you?
    - Never (1)
    - Rarely (2)
    - Sometimes (3)
    - Fairly often (4)
    - Frequently (5)

should be responsible for administering the screening? Physicians have limited time with patients (often as little as 15 minutes), and some stakeholders suggest that it is not reasonable to add a social risks screening to an already harried and full agenda for the primary care visit. The advent of the health care team (which will be discussed in more detail later) has helped alleviate this problem since screening may be completed by other health care professionals, including physician assistants, care managers, community health workers, or others. This way, information from the screening can be shared with the physician or nurse, who can incorporate it into a treatment plan and with a social worker or case worker who in turn can help connect patients and families with needed resources.

The second question that often arises when social risk screening is integrated into health care is: What if the health care team is unable to respond to the need identified? This is a common problem for primary care providers, as many do not work with onsite social workers or other professionals whose job it is to follow up on social risks and needs. Providers may feel overwhelmed by the level of need of their patients as well as ill-equipped to direct patients to appropriate resources or to follow up to see if patients have actually accessed those resources. A 2020 report by the National Academies of Science, Engineering, and Medicine on integration of social care into medicine found that there is not substantial evidence as to the effectiveness of social risk screening. The report also raised vital questions about the potential harms of screening if there is no follow-up intervention to address the risks and needs identified.[28] This can cause deep frustration for providers as well as for patients who have been asked sensitive personal questions for seemingly no reason.[29] Before discussing some of the ways that clinical programs are attempting to mitigate these problems, we first turn to new models of care that incorporate interprofessional health care teams.

Interprofessional Health Care Teams

To address the enormous problem of fragmentation in the health care system—in other words, the problem of focusing on various parts of an individual in search of a "cure" or remedy without adequately appreciating the totality of the person and the person's life circumstances—several models of care integration have taken shape in the past two decades. Here we focus on models that are primarily focused on better coordination and integration of a range of health and social services through the use of a health care team.

Patient-Centered Medical Homes

First developed by the American Academy of Pediatrics in 1967, the patient-centered medical home (PCMH) model has gained significant traction in primary care in the past decade. The goal of this model is to provide "comprehensive, continuous, patient-centered, team-based, and accessible primary care in the context of a patient's family and community."[30] The ACA promotes the implementation of the PCMH model in primary care, and with the growing adoption of value-based payment, many PCMH practices have become part of ACOs. Because PCMH is based on a recognition that health care should be provided with the whole person (and often whole family) in mind, the model has led the way in expanding who is considered vital to the health care team. In addition to a primary care physician, the PCMH team may include a registered nurse,

a care coordinator, a social worker, a pharmacist, a behavioral health specialist, and, as discussed in greater detail later, a community health worker.

By including multiple types of professionals under one roof, the PCMH improves access to and coordination of care and increases attention to the multiple factors that play a role in patient and population health. PCMHs are generally accessibly placed in the community and offer flexible hours to facilitate access to care. Many PCMH programs colocate with behavioral health and social service organizations (such as food banks), further supporting patients' access to basic needs.

Community Health Workers and Community Health Teams

In addition to being members of interprofessional clinical teams, community health workers are employed to serve as a link between the clinic and community. The American Public Health Association describes the role of the CHW this way: "A frontline public health worker who is a trusted member of and/or has an unusually close understanding of the community. This trusting relationship enables the worker to serve as a liaison/link/intermediary between health/social services and the community to facilitate access to services and improve the quality and cultural competence of service delivery."[31] CHWs not only help patients navigate the health care system but also often make home visits to support patients with medication, chronic disease management, home safety, and a wide range of social needs (e.g., access to food and other basic needs). A 2020 randomized, controlled trial testing a health-system based community health worker intervention in several clinical settings and across multiple diseases found that the intervention did not improve self-rated health but did lead to substantial and sustained improvements in perceived quality of primary care and reductions in hospital use."[32] Other studies have shown that CHWs improve health outcomes and reduce disparities in cardiovascular disease.[33]

Partnerships Between Health Care and Community-Based Organizations

Since passage of the ACA in 2010, the federal government, state governments, health care systems, and philanthropic organizations have invested in partnerships between health care and community-based organizations (CBOs) that provide social services. The federal Center for Medicare and Medicaid Innovation (CMMI) created the Accountable Health Communities (AHC) grant program "based on emerging evidence that addressing health-related social needs through enhanced clinical-community linkages can improve health outcomes and reduce costs."[34] Grantees are testing the effectiveness of health care–CBO collaboration through a community bridge organization that links patients and community members to the services they need. **Figure 15.2** demonstrates how this model is intended to work.

At the state level, policymakers are also experimenting with state investments in social service integration through Medicaid Section 1115 waivers. Some states have applied for waivers to expand services not typically offered through the Medicaid program. For example, through its 1115 waiver, Oregon created regional coordinated care organizations that have the authority to fund a range of services addressing health-related social needs, including cell phones for telehealth visits; home goods, such as air filters and slow cookers; nonmedical transportation to, for example, access social service agencies; and temporary housing or rental supports.[35]

Health care systems are also making direct investments in social services and community-based supports for their patient communities.

A 2020 study found that from January 1, 2017, to November 30, 2019, 57 health care systems (which included 917 hospitals) invested at least $2.5 billion in social needs–related programs; $1.6 billion of those dollars were committed to housing interventions. Other programs focused on employment, transportation, food security, and education.[36] In 2018, Kaiser Permanente, the largest health care system in the United States, announced that it was committing $200 million in affordable housing because its leadership saw the investment as important to improving health outcomes.[37] Increasingly, philanthropy is funding multisector partnerships to address health inequities.[38] Public and private funding have helped clinical programs experiment with ways to develop and implement partnerships with CBOs aimed at providing more coordinated, comprehensive, and integrated care, especially for communities with many unmet social needs.

As these new clinic–CBO partnerships are formed, however, they are shining a light on the lack (and fragmentation) of community-based resources. One approach to improving coordination, collaboration, and tracking of referrals is the development of a number of web-based searchable database platforms. These platforms help clinicians and health care staff identify appropriate community resources for patients, make referrals, and track outcomes (e.g., whether the patient was able to access the referred CBO and receive needed services or resources).[39]

Nonetheless, even with the assistance of technology to help facilitate information sharing and communication, these partnerships are attempting to link two very different systems and cultures, and that often comes with significant challenges: "Many partnerships end up being costly, hard to manage, and struggle to navigate the various cultural, organizational, and accountability issues they face."[40] Studies on the perceptions of CBO leadership that partner with health care institutions demonstrate some of the barriers to effective

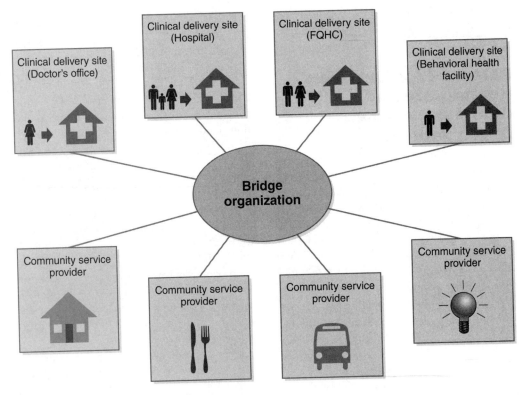

Figure 15.2 Accountable health community
Courtesy of Centers for Medicare and Medicaid Services (CMS) – visit www.cms.gov.

collaboration. Because the financial incentives to develop partnerships typically come from federal Center for Medicare and Medicaid Services (CMS) and/or state Medicaid agencies, they tend to apply health care language, goals, and metrics to the partnerships. Cash-strapped CBOs often view these partnerships as potential ["new sources of critically needed revenue" and therefore adapt their services to fit the health care–driven model. It is not clear that this is beneficial for service provision.[41] While CBOs may value health care partnerships that can support more comprehensive service provision, they are often not treated as equal partners in planning and implementation of the partnerships. Furthermore, since the partnerships are often part of pilot projects,

they may invest resources and time when these efforts are not sustainable.[42]

These partnerships also illuminate larger systemic and policy issues. As we have highlighted elsewhere, the United States is exceptional among peer nations in its mismatch between funding for health care and social services. Because government-funded safety net programs—such as subsidized housing, income supports, and health insurance—are limited and do not meet the need, connecting people to adequate supports is often not possible. Like the health care system, social service systems are often fragmented, difficult to navigate, and usually extremely overburdened and under-resourced. But even if a patient is successfully referred to a CBO for help in finding housing, there simply is not enough safe, affordable housing available. Indeed, there is not a state without an affordable housing gap.[43] And recall from Chapter 8 that waiting lists for public housing and housing subsidies can be years long. Thus, these partnerships sometimes simply illustrate that a clinical referral is a "bridge to nowhere" since resources are not available.[44]

Critics of the movement toward integration of social care into medicine point out that it is problematic because it "medicalizes" social needs:

> Medicalization provides medical professionals the primary authority to "diagnose" and "treat" what are ostensibly social problems within the boundaries of biomedical expertise and clinical practice. And, importantly, medicalization leads to a conflation of "health" and "health care," giving credence to the fallacy that societal problems having to do with health primarily need health care solutions.[45]

These critics note the many integration efforts focus primarily on positive returns to the health care system (e.g., improving scores on quality metrics, reducing costs) and not on addressing structural (i.e., root) causes of health inequity. Thus, they argue that by using the language *social drivers (or determinants) of health*, the health care sector is helping alleviate policymakers' responsibility for investing in upstream public health and social services that would reduce unmet social needs to begin with. In other words, to effect real change and eliminate health inequities, the focus should be on policy failures and structural inequity.[46] Indeed, while these partnerships may be highly valuable to individual patients and families, they are not a fix to the serious social and structural drivers of population health inequities.

Moving Further Upstream: Equity-Focused Public Health Interventions and Policy

Public Health Agencies: Federal and State Focus on Equity

Well before the COVID-19 pandemic laid bare the vast inequities in health in the United States, the Centers for Disease Control and Prevention (CDC) and many state and local public health agencies were prioritizing health equity in their goals and funding priorities. Primarily through its Office of Minority Health and its National Center on Chronic Disease Prevention and Health Promotion, the CDC has multiple equity-focused initiatives.[47] In 2021, the Public Health Accreditation Board—which accredits state and local public health departments—announced that it was strengthening its emphasis on health equity by "infusing" it in all 10 domains of its standards and measures.[48] The events of 2020—the media attention to racial, ethnic, and socioeconomic disparities in COVID-19 cases and deaths alongside the country's reckoning with the legacy of racism, especially in police violence—also emboldened some public health leaders and policymakers to call out the role of racism in public health.[49] This has led to more focused discussion about what types of interventions are necessary to reduce racial and ethnic health inequities, including the need for legal, policy, and other structural reforms.

There has also been a shift in language used by many public health leaders, scholars, and professionals from "health equity" to "health justice." There is greater recognition that a vast number of laws, policies, and funding decisions—many that are not public health related per se—actually play an important role in public health:

Laws transform the underpinnings of the health system and also act at various points in and on the complex environments that generate the conditions for health. Those environments include the widely varied policy context of multiple government agencies, such as education, energy, and transportation agencies, as well as many statutes, regulations, and court cases intended to reshape the factors that improve or impede health.[50]

Hence, many public health interventions require law and policy change. **Figure 15.3** highlights how laws and policies can support public health actions across the spectrum from individual encounters between patients and providers to large-scale societal change. (You may recognize Figure 15.3 from Chapter 1. Here the public health impact pyramid is expanded to include legal interventions.)

Health Impact Assessments

To carefully assess the potential health consequences of different laws and policies, the health impact assessment (HIA) is "a tool that can help communities, decision makers, and practitioners make choices that improve public health through community design."[51] Specifically, "HIA brings potential positive and negative public health impacts and considerations to the decision-making process for plans, projects, and policies that fall outside traditional public health arenas, such as transportation and land use."[52]

At the local level, there are efforts to bring together the community development and public health sectors to address issues such as access to health care and healthy food, early childhood education, and opportunities for physical activity and health promotion in schools, workplaces, and neighborhoods. Increasingly, banks and other financial institutions support these community development efforts.[53] In addition, state and local redevelopment agencies charged with planning and financing community improvement and economic development projects are considering population health in their designs. Specifically, these agencies are often tasked with addressing blight—which may be defined under state or local law as including "public health risks like unsafe or unhealthy buildings

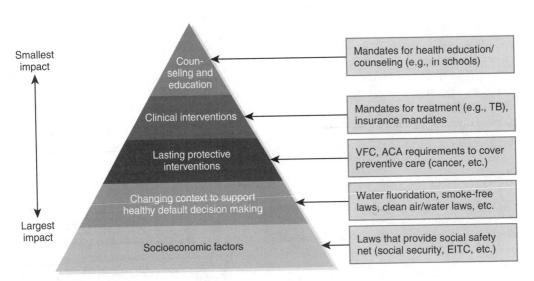

Figure 15.3 Health impact pyramid with legal intervention

Smallest impact → Largest impact

- Counseling and education — Mandates for health education/counseling (e.g., in schools)
- Clinical interventions — Mandates for treatment (e.g., TB), insurance mandates
- Lasting protective interventions — VFC, ACA requirements to cover preventive care (cancer, etc.)
- Changing context to support healthy default decision making — Water fluoridation, smoke-free laws, clean air/water laws, etc.
- Socioeconomic factors — Laws that provide social safety net (social security, EITC, etc.)

Data from Frieden, TR. A framework for public health action: the health impact pyramid. *American Journal of Public Health*. April 2010;100(4):590–595.

and the presence of hazardous waste"—as well as the "lack of access to services such as grocery stores and pharmacies."[54] Focusing community development and redevelopment efforts on population health is critical to addressing social drivers of health and for leveling the playing field for people living in low-income neighborhoods.

Health in All Policies

The fact that law and policy are accepted as key drivers in shaping the conditions that either support or harm health has led to calls for a "Health in All Policies" (HIAP) approach to policymaking. HIAP is "a collaborative approach to improving the health of all people by incorporating health considerations into decision-making across sectors and policy areas."[55] This approach has been adopted by some state governments, most notably in California. HIAP recognizes the multifactorial nature of health determinants:

> Health in All Policies is a response to a variety of complex and often inextricably linked problems such as the chronic illness epidemic, growing inequality and health inequities, rising healthcare costs, an aging population, climate change and related threats to our natural resources, and the lack of efficient strategies for achieving governmental goals with shrinking resources.[56]

Community-Driven Efforts

While policy and planning are fundamental to improving the social conditions of people living in disadvantaged communities, top-down efforts that do not engage people living in those communities are not equitable and are less likely to be successful. Chapter 16 describes in more detail the role of community organizing and engagement in social change and community health. Here we highlight two examples of efforts designed to engage community members in prioritizing actions focused on improving health. First is

THRIVE (the Tool for Health and Resilience In Vulnerable Environments), which was created by a California not-for-profit organization called the Prevention Institute to help communities assess and act on the "community determinants of health." THRIVE is a "a framework for understanding how structural drivers, such as racism, play out at the community level in terms of the social-cultural, physical/built, and economic/educational environments."[57] **Figure 15.4** demonstrates the factors considered by communities in striving toward health equity and justice.

The tool has been used by some public health institutes (nonprofit organizations focused on advancing public health systems and practice) to develop multisector strategies and action plans and participate in local and state policy reforms.[58]

A second example is Rhode Island's Health Equity Zone (HEZ) Initiative. Supported by the Rhode Island Department of Health, the HEZ initiative uses a braided funding model—pooling of multiple sources of funding including federal, state, and local dollars combined with investor and foundation funding—to direct more than $10 million to community-led HEZs in 10 areas across the state.

> "Health Equity Zones are geographic areas where existing opportunities emerge and investments are made to address differences in health outcomes. Through a collaborative, community-led process, each Health Equity Zone conducts a needs assessment and implements a data-driven plan of action to address the unique social, economic, and environmental factors that are preventing people from being as healthy as possible."[59]

HEZs have achieved a number of public health improvements: initiating Rhode Island's first "Complete and Green Streets" ordinance in a predominantly low-income Latinx community, embedding behavioral health specialists with police to divert people with substance use

People

Social networks and trust

Participation and willingness to act for the common good

Norms and culture

Equitable opportunity

Education

Living wages and local wealth/assets

Place

What's sold and how it's promoted

Look, feel, and safety

Housing

Parks and open space

Air, water and soil

Getting around

Arts and cultural expression

Figure 15.4 Tool for health and resilience in vulnerable environments factors

Reproduced from Prevention Institute. Tool for Health and Resilience in Vulnerable Environments. https://www.preventioninstitute.org/tools/thrive-tool-health-resilience-vulnerable-environments

disorders to treatment instead of the criminal justice system, bringing together community members and developers to remediate blighted housing, and many other efforts.[60] Community-driven initiatives not only improve the conditions in which people live, they target policy, funding, and other resources based on what communities value and prioritize.

Linking Health, Law, and Justice

Throughout this text, we have described the multiple and complex pathways between structural and legal factors and health inequities. We have also outlined how the health of low-income and marginalized populations suffers from severely inadequate access to justice and from laws and policies that fail to support the conditions necessary for health and well-being. There is no right to a lawyer in most civil legal matters, as you will recall from Chapter 4. These matters include those affecting people's basic needs and well-being—housing instability (e.g., evictions,

habitability, wrongful utility shutoffs), public benefit needs (e.g., access to public health insurance programs and Social Security income), food insecurity, special education plans, immigration status determinations, family matters (e.g., custody/visitation rights, domestic violence), and more. The gap between the availability of legal assistance that enables low- and moderate-income people to exercise their legal rights that protect their health and well-being and the need is enormous. In closing out this chapter, we explore how the justice gap harms individual and population health and how partnerships among lawyers, clinicians, public health practitioners, and community health advocates is playing a role in promoting health justice.

During his administration, President Obama created the Office on Access to Justice to focus on initiatives designed to increase the availability of legal assistance for people unable to pay. This office was shuttered during the Trump administration. In May 2021, President Biden issued a "Memorandum on Restoring the Department of Justice's Access-to-Justice Function and Reinvigorating the White House Legal Aid Interagency

Roundtable." In restoring this effort, President Biden stated:

> This Nation was founded on the ideal of equal justice under the law. Everyone in this country should be able to vindicate their rights and avail themselves of the protections that our laws afford on equal footing. Whether we realize this ideal hinges on the extent to which everyone in the United States has meaningful access to our legal system. Legal services are crucial to the fair and effective administration of our laws and public programs, and the stability of our society.[61]

The memorandum acknowledges data showing that "low-income Americans receive inadequate or no professional legal assistance with regard to over 80 percent of the civil legal problems they face in a given year."[62] Legal aid lawyers and legal scholars have drawn attention to this justice gap for years without much response from federal policymakers.

Medical–Legal Partnerships

Partnerships between social justice–focused lawyers and medical and public health professionals targeting the social drivers of health began in the 1960s when a physician named Jack Geiger hired a lawyer at the nation's first federally funded rural health center in Mound Bayou, Mississippi. Recognizing the gross inequities affecting the health of patients in one of the poorest areas in the country, Geiger saw health inequities as a matter of injustice, requiring the subject matter expertise and skills of a lawyer.[63] Partnerships were also developed between the medical community and lawyers in the 1980s during the AIDS crisis to protect the rights and end-of-life needs of people with the disease.[64] In 1993, Boston Medical Center began hiring lawyers as members of the pediatric health care team to address health-harming legal issues for patients and their families. This approach is referred to as

medical–legal partnership (MLP). Since 1993, the MLP approach has been adopted in 450 health care institutions across 49 states and the District of Columbia, serving a wide range of marginalized and underserved populations—older adults, children, veterans, people with disabilities, justice system–involved individuals, refugees, those experiencing homelessness, and more.[65]

MLPs are premised on the understanding that health justice—people's opportunity to reach their full health potential—is strongly influenced not just by their ability to meet their basic needs but also by their capacity to exercise their legal rights. Indeed, these two things are connected. As mentioned previously, being able to live in safe housing, exercising one's rights to government programs like Medicaid and food assistance, and protection from intimate partner violence all have profound effects on health, and all have roots in law. See **Figure 15.5** for examples of how civil legal aid work addresses the negative effects of social drivers of health. Thus, lawyers play a key role in addressing social drivers of health:

> Attorneys in general—and poverty lawyers in particular—have an in-depth understanding of relevant policies, laws, and systems, and seek out solutions at the individual and policy levels to a range of health-related social and legal needs. When embedded as specialists in a healthcare setting, lawyers can directly resolve specific problems for individual patients, while also helping clinical and non-clinical staff navigate system and policy barriers and transform institutional practices.[66]

Like other clinic-to-community partnerships, MLPs screen for patients' social risk factors but do so with a focus on unmet legal needs and identifying what legal or systemic advocacy will help achieve health justice for a patient and/or their family. Since many people are unaware of their legal rights, screening enables the MLP team to identify and address problems before

I-HELP issue	Common social determinant of health	Civil legal aid interventions that help	Impact of civil legal aid intervention on health/health care
Income	Availability of resources to meet daily basis needs	**Benefits unit:** Appeal denials of food stamps, health insurance, cash benefits, and disability benefits	1. Increasing someone's income means s/he makes fewer trade-offs between affording food and health care, including medications. 2. Being able to afford enough healthy food helps people manage chronic diseases and helps children grow and develop.
Housing and utilities	Healthy physical environments	**Housing unit:** Secure housing subsidies; improve substandard conditions; Prevent eviction; Protect against utility shut-off	1. A stable, decent, affordable home helps a person avoid costly emergency room visits related to homelessness. 2. Consistent housing, heat and electricity helps people follow their medical treatment plans.
Education and employment	Access to the opportunity to learn and work	**Education and employment units:** Secure specialized education services; Prevent and remedy employment discrimination and enforce workplace rights	1. A quality education is the single greatest predictor of a person's adult health. 2. Consistent employment helps provide money for food and safe housing, which also helps avoid costly emergency health care services. 3. Access to health insurance is often linked to employment.
Legal status	Access to the opportunity to learn and work	**Veterans and immigration units:** Resolve veteran discharge status; Clear criminal/credit histories; Assist with asylum applications	1. Clearing a person's criminal history or helping a veteran change their discharge status helps make consistent employment and access to public benefits possible. 2. Consistent employment provides money for food and safe housing, which helps people avoid costly emergency health care sevices.
Personal and family stability	Exposure to violence	**Family law unit:** Secure restraining orders for domestic violence; Secure adoption, custody and guardianship for children	1. Less violence at home means less need for costly emergency health care sevices. 2. Stable family relationships significantly reduce stress and allow for better decision-making, including decisions related to health care.

Figure 15.5 How civil legal aid helps health care address the social determinants of health

Reproduced from "Framing Legal Care as Health Care," National Center for Medical-Legal Partnership.

they become crises (e.g., preventing eviction by identifying landlord–tenant problems early; protecting a victim from escalating violence). But MLP practice is more than the resolution of specific health-harming social and legal needs—it also promotes institutional change at both health and legal organizations by aligning their goals and strategies around health justice. Furthermore, MLP facilitates upstream law and policy change using experiences from practice and by connecting practitioners from health care, public health, community-based organizations, and law around a common advocacy goal: health justice (see **Figure 15.6**).

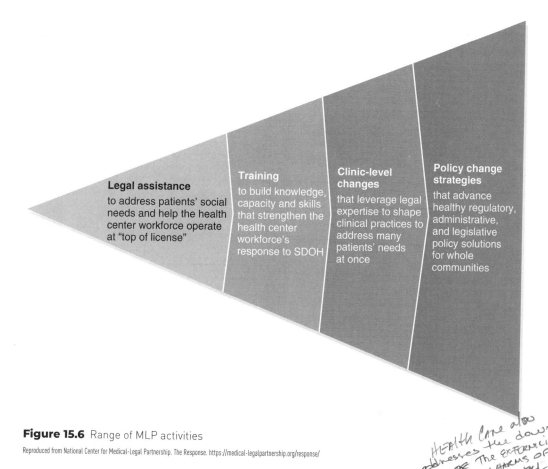

Figure 15.6 Range of MLP activities

Reproduced from National Center for Medical-Legal Partnership. The Response. https://medical-legalpartnership.org/response/

Conclusion

This chapter highlighted some of the efforts being undertaken in the health care, public health, and legal fields to account for and attempt to address health inequities. You might have noticed that much of this chapter was devoted to describing reforms in the health care system. This is not surprising. Because health care absorbs upward of 18% of the U.S. gross domestic product, it is where the money is and, therefore, is where most of the action has been. While efforts to link clinical care with community-based services and supports are critically important to protecting and improving individual and community health and establishing better coordination and collaboration across sectors, they do not supplant the

large-scale structural changes that are necessary to achieve health justice. Health care addresses the downstream effects of social policy failures. To effect upstream structural change, federal and state laws, policies, and funding priorities should align with the evidence: that treating all people with dignity and supporting them to meet their basic needs is vital to improving population health and promoting health justice. Community-level efforts, even those that effectively pursue local and state policy changes, cannot create or expand resources that do not exist, such as affordable housing or health insurance for the millions of Americans who lack them. In the final chapter, we explore the types of large-scale structural, legal, and policy-focused initiatives that are necessary to truly achieve health justice.

References

1. Berwick DM, Nolan TW, Whittington J. The triple aim: Care, health, and cost. *Health Affairs.* 2008; 27(3):759–769.

2. Bodenheimer T, Sinsky C. From triple to quadruple aim: Care of the patient requires care of the provider. *The Annals of Family Medicine.* 2014;12:573–576.

3. Wilson N, George P, Huber JM.Population health. In Skochelak SE, Hawkins RE, Lawson LE, et al., eds. *Health Systems Science.* Philadelphia, PA: Elsevier; 2017:121–122.

4. Roosa Tikkanen, Melinda K. Abrams. U.S. healthcare from a global perspective, 2019: Higher spending, worse outcomes? *The Commonwealth Fund. January 20.* 2020. https://www.commonwealthfund .org/publications/issue-briefs/2020/jan/us-health-care -global-perspective-2019.

5. Centers for Disease Control and Prevention. Health and economic costs of chronic diseases. https://www.cdc .gov/chronicdisease/about/costs/index.htm.

6. Starr SR, Nesse RE. The healthcare delivery system. In Skochelak SE, Hawkins RE, Lawson LE, et al., eds. *Health Systems Science.* Philadelphia, PA: Elsevier; 2017:26.

7. Starr SR, Nesse RE. The healthcare delivery system. In Skochelak SE, Hawkins RE, Lawson LE, et al., eds. *Health Systems Science.* Philadelphia, PA: Elsevier; 2017:32–33.

8. Crook HL, Zheng J, Bleser WK, et al. How are payment reforms addressing social determinants of health? Policy implications and next steps. Milbank Memorial Fund and Duke Margolis Center for Health Policy. February 2021. https://www.milbank.org /publications/how-are-payment-reforms-addressing -social-determinants-of-health-policy-implications -and-next-steps/.

9. Crook HL, Zheng J, Bleser WK, et al. How are payment reforms addressing social determinants of health? Policy implications and next steps. Milbank Memorial Fund and Duke Margolis Center for Health Policy. February 2021. https://www.milbank.org /publications/how-are-payment-reforms-addressing -social-determinants-of-health-policy-implications -and-next-steps/.

10. Tobin-Tyler E, Ahmad B. Marrying value-based payment and the social determinants of health through Medicaid ACOs: Implications for policy and practice. Milbank Memorial Fund; 2020: 1–24. https://www.milbank.org/wp-content/uploads/2020 /05/Medicaid-ACOs-and-SDOH.ver5_.pdf.

11. Crook HL, Zheng J, Bleser WK, et al. How are payment reforms addressing social determinants of health? Policy implications and next steps. Milbank Memorial Fund and Duke Margolis Center for Health Policy. February 2021. https://www

.milbank.org/publications/how-are-payment-reforms -addressing-social-determinants-of-health-policy -implications-and-next-steps/.

12. The Camden Coalition of Healthcare Providers. Using data to identify and engage patients with complex health and social needs is the foundation of our work. 2022. https://camdenhealth.org /connecting-data/.

13. MacArthur Foundation. Jeffrey Brenner. September 25, 2013. https://www.macfound.org/fellows/886/.

14. Camden Coalition of Healthcare Providers. Our National Center. 2022. https://www.camdenhealth.org /national-center/.

15. Beck AF, Sandel MT, Ryan PH, Kahn RS. Mapping neighborhood health geomarkers to clinical care decisions to promote equity in child health. *Health Affairs.* June 2017;36(6):1000.

16. Young GJ, Chou C, Alexander JA, Lee SD, Raver E. Provision of community benefits by tax-exempt U.S. hospitals. *New England Journal of Medicine.* April 18, 2013;368(16):1519–1527; Crossley M, Tobin Tyler E, Herbst, J. Tax-exempt hospitals and community health under the Affordable Care Act: Identifying and addressing unmet legal needs as social determinants of health. *Public Health Reports.* January–February 2016;131(1):195–199.

17. U.S. Department of the Treasury. Additional requirements for charitable hospitals; community health needs assessments for charitable hospitals; requirement of a Section 4959 excise tax return and time for filing the return. *Federal Register.* 2014;79:78954.

18. Healthy People 2030. *Social Determinants of Health.* 2022. https://health.gov/healthypeople /objectives-and-data/social-determinants-health.

19. World Health Organization, Commission on Social Determinants of Health. Closing the gap in a generation: Health equity through action on the social determinants of health. Commission on Social Determinants of Health. Final Report. 2008. https:// www.who.int/social_determinants/final_report/csdh _finalreport_2008.pdf.

20. Alderwick H, Gottlieb LM. Meanings and misunderstandings: A social determinants of health lexicon for healthcare systems. *The Milbank Quarterly.* 2019 Jun;97(2):407–419.

21. Alderwick H, Gottlieb LM. Meanings and misunderstandings: A social determinants of health lexicon for healthcare systems. *The Milbank Quarterly.* 2019 Jun;97(2):407–419.

22. Alderwick H, Gottlieb LM. Meanings and misunderstandings: A social determinants of health lexicon for healthcare systems. *The Milbank Quarterly.* 2019 Jun;97(2):407–419.

23. National Academies of Sciences, Engineering, and Medicine. *Integrating Social Care into the Delivery of Healthcare: Moving Upstream to Improve the Nation's Health.* Washington, DC: The National Academies Press; 2019. https://doi .org/10.17226/25467.

24. National Academies of Sciences, Engineering, and Medicine. *Integrating Social Care into the Delivery of Healthcare: Moving Upstream to Improve the Nation's Health.* Washington, DC: The National Academies Press; 2019. https://doi .org/10.17226/25467.

25. Andermann A. Screening for social determinants of health in clinical care: Moving from the margins to the mainstream. *Public Health Reviews.* 2018;39(1). doi:10.1186/s40985-018-0094-7.

26. Characteristics of Social Prescribing Statements by Professional Medical Associations. SIREN. 2019. https://sirenetwork.ucsf.edu/PMAstatements.

27. Olsen D, Oldfield, B, et al. Standardizing social determinants of health assessments. Health Affairs Blog. March 2019. doi:10.1377 /hblog20190311.823116.

28. National Academies of Sciences, Engineering, and Medicine. *Integrating Social Care into the Delivery of Healthcare: Moving Upstream to Improve the Nation's Health.* Washington, DC: The National Academies Press; 2019.

29. Browne J, Mccurley J, Fung V, et al. Addressing social determinants of health identified by systematic screening in a Medicaid accountable care organization: A qualitative study. *Journal of Primary Care & Community Health.* 2021;12:1–8.

30. Berenson RA, Hammons T, Gans DN, et al. A house is not home: Keeping patients at the center of practice redesign. *Health Affairs.* 2008;27(5):1219–1230.

31. American Public Health Association. Community health workers. 2021. https://www.apha.org/apha -communities/member-sections/community -health-workers.

32. Kangovi S, Mitra N, Norton L, et al. Effect of community health worker support on clinical outcomes of low-income patients across primary care facilities. *JAMA Internal Medicine.* 2018;178:1635–1643.

33. Centers for Disease Control and Prevention. Division of Heart Disease and Stroke Prevention. Integrating community health workers on clinical care teams and in the community. 2020. https://www .cdc.gov/dhdsp/pubs/guides/best-practices/chw .htm.

34. Centers for Medicare and Medicaid Services. Accountable Health Communities Model. 2021. https://innovation.cms.gov/innovation-models/ahcm.

35. Center for Healthcare Strategies. Oregon leverages Medicaid to address social determinants of health and health equity. Issue brief. June 2021.

https://www.ohsu.edu/sites/default/files/2021-06 /Oregon%20Medicaid%20addresses%20SDOH%20 and%20health%20equity1.pdf.

36. Horwitz LI, Chang C, Harmony N, Arcilla HN, Knickman JR. Quantifying health systems' investment in social determinants of health, by sector, 2017–19. *Health Affairs.* 2020;39:192–198.

37. U.S. Department of Housing and Urban Development. Office of Policy Development and Research. Kaiser Permanente's Housing for Health Fund Provides Agile Investing. 2022. https://www.huduser.gov/portal /casestudies/study-012420.html.

38. Brunton C, Duong TC, Jacobs F, et al. Multisector partnerships such as ACHs: How can they improve population health and reduce health inequities? Health Affairs Blog. April 6, 2021. https://www .healthaffairs.org/do/10.1377/hblog20210406 .792026/full/?utm_medium=email&utm _source=hasu&utm_campaign=blog&utm _content=bruntin&utm_source=Newsletter&utm _medium=email&utm_content=Health+Affairs ++April+Issue%3A+Access%2C+ACA%2C+Spending +++More&utm_campaign=HASU%3A+4-11-21 &vgo_ee=PIsaBHiejM66z3IzHBl%2F3D%2BJLi7 DAuyw1lBdDJF3D%2Bo%3D.

39. Heath S. Building social services referral platforms to meet SDOH needs. Patient Engagement HIT. September 21, 2020. https://patientengagementhit .com/news/building-social-services-referral-platforms -to-meet-sdoh-needs.

40. Alderwick H, Hutchings A, Briggs A, Mays N. The impacts of collaboration between local healthcare and non-healthcare organizations and factors shaping how they work: A systematic review of reviews. *BMC Public Health.* 2021 Apr 19;21(1):753.

41. Taylor LA, Byhoff E. Money moves the mare: The response of community-based organizations to healthcare's embrace of social determinants. *The Milbank Quarterly.* 2021;99(1):171–208.

42. Agonafer EP, Carson SL, Nunez V, et al. Community-based organizations' perspectives on improving health and social service integration. *BMC Public Health.* 2021;21:452.

43. National Low-Income Housing Coalition. The gap: A shortage of affordable rental homes. No state has an adequate supply of affordable rental housing for the lowest income renters. 2022. https://reports.nlihc .org/gap.

44. Tobin-Tyler E, Ahmad B. Marrying value-based payment and the social determinants of health through Medicaid ACOs. Milbank Memorial Fund. May 2020. https://www.milbank.org/publications /marrying-value-based-payment-and-the-social -determinants-of-health-through-medicaid-acos -implications-for-policy-and-practice/.

45. Lantz PM. The medicalization of population health: Who will stay upstream? *The Milbank Quarterly.* 2019;97(March). https://www.milbank.org/quarterly/articles/the-medicalization-of-population-health-who-will-stay-upstream/.

46. Castrucci B, Auerbach J. Meeting individual social needs falls short of addressing social determinants of health. Health Affairs Blog. January 16, 2019. https://www.healthaffairs.org/do/10.1377/hblog20190115.234942/full/.

47. See Centers for Disease Control and Prevention (CDC). Health equity. 2020. https://www.cdc.gov/healthequity/index.html; National Center for Chronic Disease Prevention and Health Promotion. Health equity. https://www.cdc.gov/chronicdisease/healthequity/index.htm.

48. Public Health Accreditation Board (PHAB). Focus on equity. September 2021. https://phaboard.org/wp-content/uploads/Focus-on-Equity-One-Pager-6.pdf.

49. American Public Health Association. Racism is a public health crisis. Racism declarations: Opportunities for action. 2021. https://www.apha.org/Topics-and-Issues/Health-Equity/Racism-and-health/Racism-Declarations.

50. Institute of Medicine. For the public's health: Revitalizing law and policy to meet new challenges; 2011: 12. https://www.nap.edu/read/13093/chapter/1.

51. Centers for Disease Control and Prevention. Health impact assessments. 2016. https://www.cdc.gov/healthyplaces/hia.htm.

52. Centers for Disease Control and Prevention. Health impact assessments. 2016. https://www.cdc.gov/healthyplaces/hia.htm.

53. Mattessich PW, Rausch EJ. Cross-sector collaboration to improve community health: A view of the current landscape. *Health Affairs.* 2014;33(11):1968–1974.

54. Nguyen J, Glass P. Focusing on equity in the planning process. Change Lab Solutions. May 24, 2021. https://www.changelabsolutions.org/blog/focusing-equity-planning-process.

55. Public Health Institute and the American Public Health Association. Health in all policies: A guide for state and local governments; 2013:6. http://www.phi.org/resources/?resource=hiapguide.

56. Public Health Institute and the American Public Health Association. Health in all policies: A guide for state and local governments; 2013:7. http://www.phi.org/resources/?resource=hiapguide.

57. Prevention Institute. THRIVE: Tool for Health & Resilience In Vulnerable Environments. 2022. https://www.preventioninstitute.org/tools/thrive-tool-health-resilience-vulnerable-environments.

58. Prevention Institute. THRIVE: Tool for Health & Resilience In Vulnerable Environments. 2022. https://www.preventioninstitute.org/tools/thrive-tool-health-resilience-vulnerable-environments.

59. Rhode Island Department of Health. Health equity zones. September 2021. https://health.ri.gov/publications/brochures/HealthEquityZones.pdf.

60. Rhode Island Department of Health. Health equity zones. September 2021. https://health.ri.gov/publications/brochures/HealthEquityZones.pdf.

61. The White House. Memorandum on restoring the Department of Justice's access-to-justice function and reinvigorating the White House Legal Aid Interagency Roundtable. May 18, 2021. https://www.whitehouse.gov/briefing-room/presidential-actions/2021/05/18/memorandum-on-restoring-the-department-of-justices-access-to-justice-function-and-reinvigorating-the-white-house-legal-aid-interagency-roundtable/.

62. The White House. Memorandum on restoring the Department of Justice's access-to-justice function and reinvigorating the White House Legal Aid Interagency Roundtable. May 18, 2021. https://www.whitehouse.gov/briefing-room/presidential-actions/2021/05/18/memorandum-on-restoring-the-department-of-justices-access-to-justice-function-and-reinvigorating-the-white-house-legal-aid-interagency-roundtable/.

63. Lawton E. The history of the medical-legal partnership movement. Community Health Forum. National Center for Community Health Centers. Fall/Winter 2014. https://medical-legalpartnership.org/wp-content/uploads/2015/01/NACHC-Magazine-A-History-of-the-Medical-Legal-Partnership-Movement.pdf.

64. Lawton E. The history of the medical-legal partnership movement. Community Health Forum. National Center for Community Health Centers. Fall/Winter 2014. https://medical-legalpartnership.org/wp-content/uploads/2015/01/NACHC-Magazine-A-History-of-the-Medical-Legal-Partnership-Movement.pdf.

65. National Center for Medical-Legal Partnership. 2022. https://medical-legalpartnership.org/.

66. National Center for Medical-Legal Partnership. The need. Lawyers as specialists on the healthcare team. 2022. https://medical-legalpartnership.org/need/.

CHAPTER 16

Law, Policy, and Structural Change: New Directions for Health Justice

15 pages

LEARNING OBJECTIVES

By the end of this chapter you will be able to:

- Describe how the United States can confront past and present injustices and remediate past harms in order to ensure justice and equity for all people in the future
- Discuss the roles of democratic engagement and collective action in health justice
- Explain current proposals for investments that would curtail social and economic inequality and promote health justice
- Describe some of the ways that advocates can hold health care leaders and government officials accountable through a movement for health justice

Introduction

In many ways the United States is at a crossroads; will the country reap the benefits of its diversity or further suppress the rights and opportunities of those whose voices have long been excluded? Will it invest in policies, practices, and resources that promote and protect health and well-being for all people or perpetuate laws, systems, and policies that advantage a small number at the expense of the many? Will it embrace power-sharing and engagement in American democracy among all stakeholders or reinforce a power structure that preserves privilege, prosperity, and opportunity for the few? Answers to all of these questions will determine health justice in the United States; after all, there can be no health justice without broader social justice.

Law professors Emily Benfer, Seema Mohapatra, Lindsay Wiley, and Ruqaiijah

Yearby propose a three-part framework for health justice:

First, legal and policy responses must address the structural determinants of health. Second, interventions mandating healthy behaviors must be accompanied by material support and legal protections to enable compliance while minimizing harms. Third, historically marginalized communities must be engaged and empowered as leaders in the development and implementation of interventions and the attainment of health justice.[1]

In this chapter, we expand upon this framework to explore the necessary precursors and strategies for achieving health justice. We begin with discussion about the need for the United States to confront its long-standing denial about racial injustice and how a process of truth and reconciliation is vital to moving toward a more just and equitable society. The chapter then explores the roles of democratic engagement and collective action in health equity, the types of investments necessary to eliminating structural inequity, and ways to hold policymakers accountable for health justice. It ends by describing how you can join a multisector movement for health justice and advocate for structural change.

Health Justice Starts with Confronting America's Past

Author and activist James Baldwin famously wrote that "[n]ot everything that is faced can be changed, but nothing can be changed until it is faced."[2] American denial of racial injustice and social and economic inequities has enabled policymakers to perpetuate laws, policies, and practices that advantage particular groups while marginalizing and subjugating others. The "racial reckoning" that was accelerated in 2020 by the Black Lives Matter movement and, in particular, by the murder of George Floyd has facilitated new conversations about the role of racism in U.S. systems and government practices. However, Americans' and policymakers' views of how racism, like many other issues, shapes opportunity are extremely polarized. Indeed, even how people should represent American history is now hotly debated, with some papering over the evils of the past in order to maintain a patriotic sense of America's righteous place in the world. While there is no question that progress toward racial justice has been made through legal reform, in many ways, policies, practices, and court decisions have subtly embedded racism in systems, making it harder to challenge.

Some other countries with histories of racism, oppression, violence, and genocide have found ways to confront their pasts, moving beyond denial to accept the truth and discuss a path forward. The United States has never done this. Some countries have employed a truth and reconciliation commission (TRC) to create a forum that recognizes systemic injustices from the past and their effect on the lives of people today. TRCs hear the testimony of people who themselves or whose family members have been harmed by oppressive government policies, violence, and human rights violations. In the past 50 years, 46 countries—including South Africa, El Salvador, Rwanda, and Canada—have used TRCs to confront their histories and seek healing for those harmed.[3] The role of the TRC is to promote *truth-seeking*—to acknowledge and overcome government denial of past atrocities through testimony by those with lived experience; *reconciliation*—to engage in restorative justice, repairing harm and restoring the well-being of those involved through a process of reconciliation; and *justice and accountability*—to ensure that just government laws, policies, and practices are adopted based on learning from the TRC process.

At a time when American citizens and policymakers often do not even agree on facts, the importance of truth-telling could not be more urgent. Learning from those who have experienced injustice at the hands of the government is a powerful means of promoting dialogue about where the country has been and where it should go in the future. Consider this statement from the Report of the Canadian Royal Commission on Aboriginal Peoples, which called for a TRC on residential schools that were designed to "reshape the identity and consciousness of First Nations, Inuit, and Métis children":

> …[T]he incredible damage—loss of life, denigration of culture, destruction of self-respect and self-esteem, rupture of families, impact of these traumas on succeeding generations, and the enormity of the cultural triumphalism that lay behind the enterprise—will deeply disturb anyone who allows this story to seep into their consciousness and recognizes that these policies and deeds were perpetrated by Canadians no better or worse intentioned, no better or worse educated than we are today. This episode reveals what has been demonstrated repeatedly in the subsequent events of this century: the capacity of powerful but grievously false premises to take over public institutions and render them powerless to mount effective resistance. It is also evidence of the capacity of democratic populations to tolerate moral enormities in their midst.[4]

The legacy of America's past atrocities—including the oppression of Indigenous peoples, slavery, and Jim Crow laws—have perpetuated racial and ethnic injustice and have taken their toll on generations of Indigenous, Black, and ethnic minority Americans. These crimes against humanity are equally egregious to—if not more egregious than—what the Canadian government sought to acknowledge and remedy. These injustices continue to perpetrate an enormous toll on the health, well-being, and life potential of affected populations, as discussed throughout this book. Hence, before health justice can be achieved, a process that promotes truth-telling must come first. As human and civil rights lawyer Bryan Stevenson says, "… if you're genuinely engaged and recovering from human rights abuses, you have to commit to truth-telling first. You can't jump to reconciliation. You can't jump to reparation or restoration until you tell the truth."[5] Of course, initiating a truth and reconciliation process in the United States to address historic harms and their legacy would take courageous and committed leadership. As we discuss at the end of this chapter, structural change—including a reckoning with the past to bring about a more just future—will only happen with sustained efforts from advocates.

Health Justice, Self-Determination, and Democratic Engagement

The evidence from medicine and public health demonstrating the complex ways in which racism, discrimination, stigma and minority stress manifest in health disparities has important implications for health justice. Different groups—racial and ethnic minorities, immigrants, women, LGBTQ+ people, people with disabilities—have challenged norms defined by dominant social and political discourse and have instead sought to name and claim their own experiences through language and the right to self-determination, as noted in Chapters 1 and 2. The health harms to individuals and groups of exclusion and stigmatization, as documented throughout this book, demand structural changes that facilitate the expansion of un-inclusive norms and language that acknowledges diverse experiences. For example, the growing acceptance among some—particularly younger—people of gender-inclusive language and pronouns represents important progress in this area. Recognition of ableist assumptions and policies in educational institutions also demonstrates movement toward more inclusive practices. These practices not only acknowledge human differences, but they also help to protect and promote health and well-being.

But as encouraging as these developments are, structural change requires that historically marginalized groups have a voice in decision-making that affects their lives. Self-determination, empowerment, and community engagement in and of themselves have been shown to improve people's health. One of the primary drivers of allostatic load (chronic stress) is a person's sense of a lack of control over his/her/their destiny. (see Chapter 8).[6] Furthermore, community empowerment—to the extent that it enables people to challenge exclusionary power structures and have a voice in structuring the conditions in which they live—has positive benefits for health: "There is growing evidence that increased collective control at the population level is associated with improved social determinants of health and population health outcomes."[7]

Increasingly, public health scholars are studying the role of democratic engagement in population health and health equity. This inquiry is especially apt at a time when democratic principles and voting rights are being undermined by courts, government officials, and social media platforms. Democratic engagement involves not just voting but also expressing a political view—support for or opposition to a proposed law or policy, awareness of government actions and their effects on a particular community, and taking an interest in promoting the common good.[8] Voting and democratic engagement are pertinent to health justice in three important ways. First, most

simply, when a large number of people from a community vote, "it translates into greater influence over determining who holds political power. Those in power in turn put forward and support policies that respond to the needs and demands of their constituents that shape the social determinants of their health."[9]

Second, research shows that voting is associated with self-rated health: Several studies have found that those who report that they vote also report better health. On the other hand, those with chronic diseases and disabilities are less likely to vote, often due to structural barriers. These data support the third point about voting and health: Those experiencing the greatest health inequities are least likely to vote. One study suggests that this partly stems from general voting patterns that affect people with low socioeconomic status differently. Young people tend not to vote, and low-SES people are more likely to die earlier than high-SES people; thus, "through the early disappearance (i.e., death) of the poor, continuing socio-political participation of high-SES survivors helps to perpetuate inequality in the status quo."[10] Another study of the 2004 election found that excess deaths among Black people due to health inequities were responsible for the loss of 1 million potential votes and also concluded that some state elections may have come out differently without these excess deaths.[11]

The ability to participate in the political process, therefore, is shaped by the social and structural drivers of health that perpetuate health inequities, and those social drivers are largely determined by elected officials who endorse policies that ignore or fail to address those inequities. Policies that suppress the vote for certain segments of the population—which have only proliferated in recent years—have enormous implications for addressing health inequities. In most states, people with felony records are disenfranchised, as noted in Chapter 9. Given the disproportionate effect of these laws on People of Color, particularly

Black men, these policies play an important role in restricting political participation in these communities. Redistricting policies also serve to suppress the vote and limit the democratic voice of Communities of Color. Finally, the inability of legally present immigrants to vote reduces their political participation and capacity to advocate for better policies that affect their lives and self-determination. Under federal law, even lawful permanent residents cannot access government benefits like Medicaid and SNAP until they have resided in the country for 5 years, as discussed in Chapter 11. Since they are also disenfranchised, they have little lobbying power to change this law. In December 2021, however, the New York City Council passed a bill allowing immigrants with legal status to vote, becoming one of the few cities, and by far the largest, to do so.[12]

Another positive development in expanding the power of minority communities' democratic engagement is the large turnout of LGBTQ+ people in the 2020 elections. People identifying as LGBTQ+ made up between 7 and 8% of the voting population in 2020, compared to 3 to 5% in 2018.[13] Finally, the representation of U.S. senators and representatives who identify as Black, Latinx, Asian/Pacific Islander, or Native American increased from 82 in 2011 to 124 in 2021, or fully 23% of Congress. The percentage of congresswomen is also higher than ever before, at 23%.[14] Though elected officials are still far from representative of the U.S. population at large, the growing diversity of Congress is encouraging.

Investments That Target the Root Causes of Health Injustice

As described throughout this text, laws and policies structure the distribution of power and resources in U.S. society, and this distribution is fundamental to health justice. These laws and policies include the federal Constitution and its interpretation by federal courts—most importantly by the Supreme Court; state constitutions; federal and state statutes and regulations that govern working conditions, wages, paid leave, health insurance, housing safety, and more; and budgetary decisions that direct resources to social safety net programs, schools, community development and safety, and more. Here, we focus on the types of investments that are needed to improve overall U.S. population health, reduce health inequities and promote health justice.

Addressing the Black–White Wealth Gap

The income and wealth gaps for Black Americans—which civil rights laws have failed to close—have led to calls for the U.S. government to make reparations to the descendants of people who were enslaved. Proposals for reparations span from individual direct payments to college tuition to business and housing grants and loans for descendants of enslaved Black Americans.[15] As discussed in Chapters 6 and 10, Supreme Court decisions have severely restricted policymakers' ability to direct resources to individuals and communities based on their race. While this does not proscribe the possibility of reparations for Black Americans whose ancestors were enslaved, it makes structuring them challenging.

The question of prioritizing the distribution of resources based on race and ethnicity came up during the height of the COVID-19 pandemic. Some public health officials, concerned about higher death rates among Black and ethnic minority populations, argued that it was ethical and equitable to prioritize distribution of (at that time) a scarce supply of vaccines to these communities. Indeed, the CDC guidance asserted that states identify "critical populations" including "people from racial and ethnic minority groups" for prioritization of vaccine distribution.[16] Legal scholars warned that while targeting vaccines to people based on certain characteristics might survive court scrutiny, a race-based approach would not: "A vaccine distribution formula…could lawfully prioritize populations based on factors like geography, socioeconomic status, and housing density that would favor racial minorities de facto, but not explicitly include race."[17]

Thus, legal restrictions on the use of race as a basis for distributing resources undercut reparations as a means to remedy past racial injustice and facilitate more economic equity. These restrictions do not prevent the private sector from making race-based investments. In 2021, for example, Target Corporation announced that it was investing $100 million in organizations led by Black people.[18] Nonetheless, government investments to repair Black communities harmed by the country's long racist history and to eliminate the wealth gap will need to be constructed based on criteria other than race. Racial and economic injustice will not change without targeted policies and investments: "Blacks cannot close the racial wealth gap by changing their individual behavior—i.e. by assuming more 'personal responsibility' or acquiring the portfolio management insights associated with 'financially literacy'—if the structural sources of racial inequality remain unchanged."[19] To eliminate racial health inequities, structural economic injustices must be remedied.

Reversing Economic Inequality

Growing economic inequality in the United States results from decades of policy decisions that shape economic opportunity, as discussed in Chapter 7. As economist Joseph Stiglitz argues, rising inequality in the United States is "a matter of choice: a consequence of our policies, laws, and regulations….A vicious spiral

has formed: economic inequality translates into political inequality, which leads to rules that favor the wealthy, which in turn reinforces economic inequality."[20] As noted previously, those with less economic opportunity are more likely to experience worse health, and having poor health and limited resources often translates into less political participation. While it is beyond the scope of this chapter to outline all of the possible options for reversing economic inequality in the United States—and thus improving health justice—we highlight some that are being discussed among economists, social scientists, and policymakers.

There has been significant attention in recent years to the ways in which U.S. tax policy is structured to advantage the wealthy and undercut economic opportunities for low-income Americans. The Tax Cuts and Jobs Act of 2017 added to the advantage of the wealthy by providing new deductions for businesses, with 50% of the accrued savings going to the top 1% (in terms of income) of taxpayers and 72% going to the top 5%.[21] Corporate tax cuts provided under the law mostly benefited corporate shareholders, with between 37% and 47% going to the top 1% of taxpayers.[22] Some policy experts and lawmakers propose progressive tax policies that would impose higher taxes on wealthy individuals to pay for services and supports that would expand economic stability and opportunity for middle- and low-income Americans. Ideas for improving economic stability for non-wealthy individuals and families include using greater tax revenue to subsidize child care, paid leave, college tuition, educational loan forgiveness, public schools, and more.[23]

Another proposal that gained some traction during the 2020 presidential election was universal basic income (UBI), which features recurrent, unconditional cash payments made to all members of a community. The goal of UBI is to ensure that all people can meet their basic needs and not live in poverty. Another form of cash assistance that is being touted is guaranteed income programs that are targeted to specific populations based on where they live or their income level. Guaranteed income programs have been employed in several countries around the world as a way to alleviate poverty and stimulate the economy. But recently, the idea has been adopted in the United States: As of December 2021, 27 U.S. states and cities had initiated these programs.[24]

One of the main arguments against UBI and direct cash transfers is that they will disincentivize work. However, a synthesis of the research on UBI from Stanford University found the following:

> The evidence from diverse interventions in low-, middle-, and high-income contexts indicates minimal impact on aggregate measures of labor market participation, with some studies reporting an increase in work participation. When reductions do occur, time is channeled into other valued activities such as caregiving.[25]

With regard to health, the authors report that "there is consistent evidence across contexts for improvements to health status and to the myriad behavioral and social factors that are linked to leading causes of premature ill health, disability, and death."[26]

Proponents of cash transfers argue that they not only help people meet their basic needs and improve their health and productivity, but they also reduce the administrative burden of social safety net programs. The eligibility requirements for federal and state safety net programs (e.g., TANF, SNAP, WIC, Medicaid) require recipients and government agencies to spend countless hours determining whether an individual or family is entitled to benefits, as described in Chapter 7. One of the premises of UBI is that it simplifies the process, reducing government resources needed for program administration. The identification of social risks in health care settings is a downstream approach to meeting social needs,

as discussed in Chapter 15. And as mentioned, governments, health care institutions, and philanthropic organizations are spending substantial resources to initiate systems and protocols for screening, referral, and development of partnerships between clinical and social services organizations. These new initiatives, while potentially beneficial to individual patients, also tax already-burdened health care staff. Would guaranteed income programs alleviate the need for these expenditures as well (i.e., if people could afford to meet their basic needs for food, housing, etc.)? If so, would these programs be a better use of resources?

The COVID-19 pandemic illuminated both the challenges with and potential for U.S. safety net programs. During the pandemic, Congress passed several economic relief bills designed to provide financial security and stability to workers who lost their jobs and to prevent downstream negative effects, such as eviction of families from their homes. These relief bills were the largest infusion of federal money toward economic relief in U.S. history. Government accountability experts are still assessing what lessons can be learned from this effort. However, there are two points worth mentioning here. First, bureaucratic hurdles made distribution of funds to individuals, communities, and businesses extremely difficult; in some cases, people lost their homes while waiting for relief. Second, despite its faults, the federal government demonstrated its vital role in responding to economic insecurity and deprivation.

At the time of this writing, the Biden administration is proposing to vastly expand the federal government's role in addressing economic inequality and supporting financially vulnerable individuals and families. The Build Back Better plan, for example, includes funding for child care, an expanded child tax credit, affordable housing, premium support for health insurance under the ACA, environmental justice, and climate change initiatives.[27] After months of debate and compromise, the plan is substantially smaller than initially proposed but would still take a major step toward addressing some of the social drivers of health described in this text. However, passage of the bill is far from certain, given political polarization and disagreement about funding priorities in the Democratic party.

Access to Health Care

Debate about of the federal government's role in establishing and funding programs to help people meet their basic needs is as old as federalism itself. No topic incites this debate more than health care. People's access to health care in the United States is dependent on a litany of threshold questions: Are they U.S. citizens? If not, have they met the 5-year waiting period for lawful permanent residents? Do they have employer-sponsored insurance? If not, can they afford insurance through an ACA insurance exchange? If not, do they qualify for Medicaid? If so, do they live in a state that expanded Medicaid to people with their status? Like other systems in the United States (e.g., safety net programs), the rules for obtaining health insurance are exceedingly complicated. Thus, even those who may qualify for coverage may not obtain it.

The ACA helped expand health insurance coverage to millions of Americans, but its implementation still falls far short of reaching universal coverage, as discussed elsewhere in this book. Currently, there are three main policy proposals for further expansion of coverage: (1) increasing government subsidies for people to purchase commercial insurance through ACA health insurance exchanges while continuing to urge and incentivize state governments to expand Medicaid, (2) adding a "public option" to the exchanges that would allow people to select a government-sponsored insurance plan (such as Medicaid), and (3) a single-payer system like Medicare for All.

Some Democrats propose sweetening the deal for states that have not expanded Medicaid to do so by having the federal government pick up nearly all of the cost.

But some argue that depending on intransigent state governments to expand coverage to their low-income populations could take years and that increasing financial incentives only penalizes the states that expanded Medicaid early on. They argue that the federal government should create its own public health insurance option so that people in all states have the opportunity to access it. Still, others view these solutions—increased subsidies to purchase private insurance, incentives to states to expand Medicaid, and a federal public option—as only perpetuating a system that leaves too many Americans with options that are too costly or with no insurance at all. Consider this: The average employer-sponsored health insurance plan for a family now costs more than $28,000 per year, with the employee paying roughly $12,000 of that. Advocates for a single-payer system argue that health care is a right that should not depend on a person's ability to afford insurance. Further, they contend, the fact that the United States spends more on health care while ranking near the bottom on multiple health indicators among its peers demonstrates the need for structural change, not incremental change within the existing system.[28] Simply adding additional options to a dysfunctional, market-based system that is overly complex, inefficient, and costly to administer is not structural reform.

Seventeen countries, including the United Kingdom, Norway, Italy, Spain, and Canada, have single-payer health care systems.[29] Single-payer systems provide universal access by publicly financing (through tax revenues) and administering health care.[30] In other words, a single-payer system essentially pays the costs associated with basic health care for a country's residents. In the United States, the Veteran's Health Administration and

Medicare are single-payer systems that serve particular populations—veterans and older adults, respectively. Although there have been proposals for single payer health care in the United States over the years, the best known is Medicare for All, which has been, in one form or another, proposed by various Democratic senators and representatives in recent years. Opponents of implementing a single-payer system in the United States argue that government-run health care is too costly, will reduce patient choice, will harm quality by reducing competition, and will create waiting lists for some procedures and types of care.[31] Given the health inequities you have read about in this text, do you believe the United States should take an incremental approach to expanding health care coverage or a more radical one? Clearly, a single-payer system would bring about more structural change. What are the pros and cons for health justice of doing so?

OR AT LEAST A public option

Accountability for Health Injustice

Major structural changes—such as changing tax policy to fund basic needs and reconfiguring the health care system from market-based to rights-based—are vital to achieving health justice. But structural change also involves holding current systems accountable for inequities and injustice. Systems develop cultures, and humans adapt to those cultures. Rarely do humans change their behavior without a stick—consequence for not changing—or a carrot—incentive to change. Furthermore, well-intentioned people working in health care, public health, government agencies, law enforcement, and courts may want to provide services in equitable ways but may find it difficult to overcome entrenched bureaucracy and a toxic culture. You have read examples throughout the book of ways that systems might be held accountable to support equity. Here, we explore some broader themes related to accountability necessary to promote health justice.

Data and Evidence-Based Policy

You can't change what you don't know. The data that health care systems, public health departments, law enforcement agencies, courts, and a whole array of other government actors collect are vital to decision-making and targeting of resources. At the start of the COVID-19 pandemic, public health advocates and scientists decried the gaps in data on race and ethnicity for COVID-19 deaths. They again raised the alarm when vaccination data was missing specific information about the pickup rate for racial and ethnic minorities. Without this data, the CDC and state health departments could not accurately report racial and ethnic disparities, nor could they appropriately target resources to support vaccination. Fortunately, attention to poor reporting of race and ethnicity data sharpened the focus of state policymakers on the need to ensure that agencies are both collecting and reporting accurate data. A 2021 report by the National Governors Association and others, *Achieving Progress Toward Health Equity Using Race and Ethnicity Data: State Strategies and Lessons Learned*, reported that "vaccine data by race and ethnicity increased from 17 states in January 2021 to 47 states in September 2021."[32]

Lack of data means lack of accountability. For systems—and the people who work in those systems—to be held accountable, they need to have good information, but there must also be the expectation that people use that information. Health care systems can track patient outcomes by race, ethnicity, gender, sexual orientation, and disability in order to monitor health inequalities. Data from patient surveys should inform institutions about perceptions of bias and provider–patient relationships. One way to hold health care providers and institutions accountable for discriminatory treatment toward patients is to tie patient surveys to quality metrics reported to the Agency for Healthcare Research and Quality and the Centers for Medicare and Medicaid Services, both of which are federal agencies housed in the Department of Health and Human Services. Requiring health care institutions to report this data to the public would also support greater accountability.

COVID-19 exposed the ill-equipped public health infrastructure in the United States. Investment in public health is not just important for responding to public health crises like the pandemic, it is also vital to health justice. Chronic underfunding of state health departments means that they do not have the capacity to monitor health inequities and to adopt appropriate interventions.[33] For advocates to lobby health departments and hold them accountable, these departments must have the capacity to collect and analyze the data needed for sound public health policy. They also need to be able to demonstrate to the public that their policies are based on evidence and responsive to the needs of the community.

Similarly, policymakers should be held accountable for the laws they enact. How does the public know if a law is having its intended effect or an unintended consequence? How can government agencies monitor whether a given policy is harming or benefiting health? Legal epidemiology is "the study of law as a factor in the cause, distribution, and prevention of disease and injury,"[34] and it is emerging as an important mechanism for better understanding how laws as implemented and enforced affect people's health. Legal epidemiology is not only the study of what are typically regarded as public health laws; it can also help assess the potential public health effects of a range of laws, regulations, and policies—including eviction, aggressive policing, sick leave policies, and many more. Linking the effects of laws to public health supports health justice by making transparent the effects of certain policies and practices on marginalized communities. For example, recall the compelling research presented in Chapter 9 about the public health effects of police use of force in Communities of Color. Hence, underenforcement of protective public health laws and overenforcement of laws criminalizing minor infractions in Communities of Color also have significant implications

for public health. Government actors may only be held accountable for inequitable enforcement policies and practices when advocates have access to data about disparate treatment.[35]

Equal Access to the Legal System

Access to justice in the U.S. legal system is highly inequitable, as discussed in Chapters 4 and 15. In civil legal matters, those who have the means hire lawyers; those who don't must fend for themselves, usually with little knowledge about their legal rights and responsibilities. The American Bar Association and some states are promoting the idea of a civil right to counsel or "Civil Gideon" (a reference to the famous Supreme Court decision giving individuals charged with a serious crime the right to counsel). Civil Gideon would require that those who cannot afford a lawyer be provided one at no charge in cases involving fundamental needs and rights—such as health, safety, housing, food, and child custody.[36] Civil Gideon would promote accountability by government officials (e.g., those administering government benefits like SNAP and Medicaid and judges deciding cases involving eviction, domestic violence, or removal of children from a parent).

Ensuring that people have access to legal counsel also supports individual and community empowerment by educating people about their legal rights. Inequity thrives on keeping some people in the dark about their rights while others with more power use the letter of the law to their advantage. Knowing when a government official has erroneously denied an application for Medicaid, a landlord has violated a housing safety code, or an employer has illegally discriminated based on disability not only empowers people to exercise their rights, it also helps them protect and promote their health. The concept of "legal empowerment" is taking hold around the world as a human rights practice geared toward listening to the stories of people who have been marginalized by the legal system and supporting their capacity to use the law to address their needs and problems.[37] As described earlier, democratic engagement and collective action are key social drivers of population health.

3 Health Justice as Human Rights

A human rights approach to health justice demands more than holding government officials accountable for actions and inactions that implicate population health. It also helps define health justice through positive, rather than just negative, rights (see Chapter 5). The United States has failed to realize equality through its civil rights laws. This failure is in part due to narrowing of antidiscrimination principles by the Supreme Court. But inequality and marginalization are also driven by the country's failure to reckon with economic injustice that not only subordinates a large swath of the American public but also places the United States at the end of the line among its peers in terms of population health. Redistributing public resources (e.g., to nutritious food, safe housing, and health care) is indeed the only way that the United States will begin to level the playing field.[38]

The United States is an outlier in its failure to ratify many of the international human rights treaties that hold countries accountable for progressive realization of human rights (see Chapter 5). This includes the International Covenant on Economic, Social and Cultural Rights (ICESCR), which speaks to a country's willingness to sign on to "progressive realization" of positive rights (e.g., making basic public resources available to all). The notion of human rights is that they are "birth rights—that is, rights all people have at birth by virtue of being human—and generally require the state to treat all humans equally and consistent with human dignity."[39] The right to the "highest attainable standard of health" included in the Constitution of the World Health Organization is dependent upon confronting and eliminating all of the many health-harming factors (e.g., vast economic inequality; racial, ethnic, gender, and disability discrimination; the mass incarceration

system) detailed in this text. The United States has a long way to go in realizing the right to health; as of now, it does not even purport to aspire to the goal. How can those concerned with health justice hold elected officials accountable for failing to even embrace this goal? Before reading about advocacy strategies, consider **Figure 16.1** which outlines the values and goals of health justice that have been discussed in this chapter.

A Multisector Movement for Health Justice: What You Can Do

With the seeming intransigence of health injustice, you may be asking yourself, "What can I do to make a difference?" In many ways, despite the challenges of the past several years, advocates for health justice are more poised for action than ever. The upheaval caused by the COVID-19 pandemic, while painful, disruptive, and devastating to those who have lost loved ones, has helped shine a light on the enormous inequities in the United States. Discourse about the role of racism in U.S. institutions is driving change, albeit slowly. The understanding among scientists and public health professionals that structural factors and policy decisions are the primary drivers of health inequities provides advocates with new opportunities to center justice as fundamental to health.

Chapter 2 explored the social movements that have driven social and structural change in the United States. Advocates are coming together from across sectors—medicine, public health, law, social work, community organizing, environmental justice, and more—to call for a health justice movement. In arguing for a new "civil rights of health," Angela Harris and Aysha Pamukcu suggest that "the health justice framework treats public health, law, and social movement advocacy as collaborative and also potentially adversarial, creating a system of check and balance against abuse of power."[40]

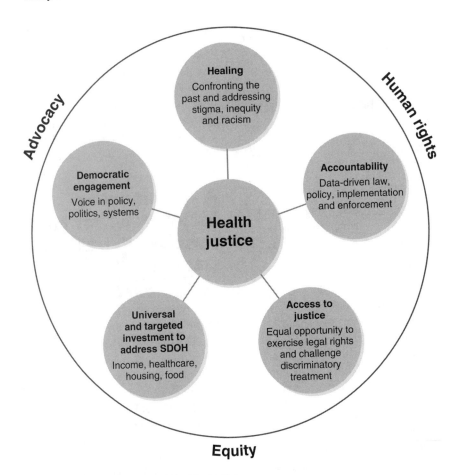

Figure 16.1 The Values and Goals of Health Justice

This approach, they suggest, "allows for many possible alliances between legal power, scientific power, and people power."[41] The power of a multisector health justice movement depends on advocates collaboratively setting goals driven by community voices. It also depends on skilled and effective advocacy. Next, we highlight some of the goals and strategies for effective health justice advocacy.

Goals and Strategies of Health Justice Advocacy

"Advocacy should ultimately be aiming to remedy injustices, not simply to make those injustices more bearable."[42] Thus, advocating for structural change requires patience, persistence

and holding those in power accountable for injustice. Advocacy can take several forms—individual (e.g., assisting a person navigate health care, social service, or government systems), institutional (e.g., lobbying to change policies in a hospital, public health department, or court), and policy (working with partners to effect legislative and regulatory change as well as holding government officials accountable for their actions or inactions). Here, we focus on the third type of advocacy: policy change. Chapter 3 provided an overview of the roles and responsibilities of the different branches of government and the principle players in drafting laws, the government agencies that promulgate regulations to carry out those laws, and the structure of courts in interpreting and ruling on those laws and regulations. There are a variety of ways in which advocates may engage in the legislative and rulemaking process to ensure that laws and policies are drafted with health justice in mind and/or to prevent unjust laws and policies from being enacted. These include the following:

- Formulating policy positions on specific bills
- Preparing and presenting testimony before legislative committees
- Providing public comment on agency rules and regulations
- Initiating telephone calls and writing e-mails or letters to legislators to urge a particular action on specific or categorical legislation
- Sponsoring or holding meetings, furnishing speakers, or preparing and distributing pamphlets and other literature to stimulate reaction to legislation
- Submit an op-ed to a newspaper, engage in a social media campaign, and/or solicit press interest to call attention to your policy change agenda

But equally important, health justice advocates should hold government officials accountable for implementing and enforcing existing laws and policies equitably. Consider the inequitable health impact of insufficient enforcement of housing safety codes on low-income People of Color (see Chapter 7). Often, injustice stems not from a law or policy as written but from the failure to enforce it on behalf of marginalized communities. Identifying through the experiences of affected communities health-harming enforcement failures—and holding government actors accountable for these failures—is vital to health justice.

Federal Policy Advocacy

With the ongoing dysfunction and gridlock in Congress, it may be tempting to write off the benefit of federal policy advocacy. But obviously, ceding advocacy efforts to the powerful interests that tend to control the policy levers in Washington would do a huge disservice to disenfranchised populations. For example, advocates were critical

to beating back attempts to repeal the Affordable Care Act in 2017. The Black Lives Matter movement has helped spur several bills in Congress that address racism and police violence.

As described earlier, there are many entry points for influencing proposed legislation and regulations. While traveling to Washington may not always be possible, you should not discount the opportunity to lobby your member of Congress or to submit comments on proposed federal regulations. Additionally, members of Congress spend time in their home districts, and most have legislative aides who focus on various matters pertaining to health and other social policies. Most members of Congress value input from health advocates, particularly when the advocate can offer new information, data, or a different perspective on the topic or bill. Similarly, as described previously, administrative agencies seek out comments from individuals and organizations that bring expertise to a particular issue during the rulemaking process. Comments can be submitted electronically. Advocates can also ensure that federal policymakers hear from affected communities by elevating the voices of patients, clients, and community members.

State Policy Advocacy

Advocacy for health justice at the state level can be a powerful means of effecting policy changes that impact a large number of people. Because state legislators' constituencies are smaller than those of members of the U.S. Congress, state policymakers are much more accessible and often more willing to meet individually with advocates to hear their concerns. Unlike in Congress, where advocates must be invited to offer testimony in support of or opposition to a bill, in state legislatures, citizens can generally sign up to testify on a bill of interest. Health care providers and public health advocates, in particular, may be in a unique position to offer information about the disparate impact of particular policies on population health through data and patient anecdotes. Advocates have successfully lobbied for state laws that are critical to health justice—such as access to Medicaid for immigrants, extending the right to vote to justice-involved people, expanded antidiscrimination protections for people with disabilities, and many more.

Local Policy Advocacy

While policy at the state or federal level is more likely to effect change for a greater number of people, there is much to be said for engaging in policy advocacy at the local level. First, policy change at the local level is often easier to achieve in a short amount of time. Advocates are more likely to have access to decision makers and to be able to make their voices heard by testifying at city council or mayoral meetings. They are also in a better position to hold government officials accountable for policy failures or inadequate enforcement of laws by sharing stories from affected communities. Second, as we discussed earlier, advocacy is most effective when it engages multiple constituencies by creating effective coalitions. Although there are certainly effective state and federal level coalitions working toward health and social policy change, local coalitions can effectively empower members of the community affected by laws and policies to shape sustainable change. In promoting health justice, it is particularly important that health advocates not usurp power from marginalized populations. Instead, they can provide information in support of the agenda driven by the community and help facilitate multisector coalition building. A final note about the importance of state and local policy advocacy: Although policy changes at these levels affect fewer people, they often influence federal policy. Thus, many of the laws and policies that states and municipalities enact capture the attention of federal policymakers. Examples are the $15 minimum wage, universal basic income, paid leave, and payment for doulas and midwives to reduce maternal mortality.

All of these policy ideas have come from state and local governments and are now receiving consideration at the federal level.

Skills for Effective Health Justice Advocacy

Developing advocacy skills takes time and experience. For people new to advocacy, identifying and cultivating relationships with mentors who are effective advocates in your community can be helpful in avoiding common mistakes. Learning from patients, clients, and community members about the daily injustices they experience and tracking patterns that point to system and policy failures are critical to developing advocacy strategies. Working with allies to build consensus about goals and tactics can avoid some inconsistent or ill-timed messaging. Grassroots advocacy requires that diverse voices are heard, but to be effective, those voices must be aligned around a common and consistent message.

Framing the Need for Change

One of the greatest challenges of health justice advocacy is framing the need for structural and policy change within a political context that is often deaf to the voices and needs of marginalized communities. As we discussed earlier in the text, the United States has a uniquely individualistic and market-driven approach to social policy, including health policy. Because health care is generally viewed as a market commodity rather than a service that the government is obliged to provide its citizens, persuading policymakers that the government has a responsibility for improving the conditions in which people live can be difficult. Similarly, as we described in Chapter 7, notions about the "deserving and undeserving poor" continue to heavily influence social policies, and Americans are deeply divided by political party with regard to their views on the government's responsibility to provide basic services to all Americans.

Given these challenges, what evidence and arguments are most effective in persuading policymakers and the public that a particular policy change is warranted? Since many health professionals are scientists, they often rely on scientific evidence and data to demonstrate the problem and need for change. But political will is often shaped by intuition, not necessarily rational arguments supported with data. The COVID-19 pandemic has illuminated just how difficult it is to persuade people of the need for a policy or practice, even when there is good scientific evidence to support it. This is not to argue that advocates should avoid using sound evidence to construct and support their policy arguments. It is, however, important to consider how data can be combined with stories and anecdotes that help the public and policymakers understand the human impact of a particular policy or policy failure. Individual stories can be helpful in "tearing at the heartstrings." For example, individual stories of cancer patients unable to acquire health insurance were used by advocates to persuade policymakers that there was a need for expanded access to health insurance through the ACA.

On the other hand, it is also important to recognize how individual stories and anecdotes can be used to paint a negative picture of particular groups of people, even when the evidence suggests that these anecdotes do not represent the majority of people in that group. During the 1980s, President Ronald Reagan used the stereotype of the Black "welfare queen" to persuade the public and other policymakers that the Aid to Families with Dependent Children (welfare) program was being abused by recipients (particularly Black mothers) and that taxpayer dollars were being wasted. The "welfare queen" was depicted this way by Reagan:

> She has eighty names, thirty addresses, twelve Social Security cards and is collecting veteran's benefits on four non-existing deceased husbands. And she is collecting Social Security on her cards. She's got Medicaid, getting food stamps, and she is collecting welfare under each of her names. Her tax-free cash income is over $150,000.[27]

Despite the lack of evidence that mothers receiving welfare benefits were abusing the program in this way, this anecdote was extremely powerful in moving the public and policymakers to believe that the welfare program was creating laziness and dependency among the poor and that taxpayers were footing the bill. The title of the welfare reform law passed in 1996 indicates the power this welfare queen depiction had; it was titled "The Personal Responsibility and Work Opportunity Act."

Framing persuasive arguments about the policy failures that lead to health inequity can be complex. Ultimately, advocates rely on a range of narratives. While some advocates choose to focus on a values-based argument that health is a human right and the government has responsibility to support its citizens' basic needs, others rely on the more pragmatic economic argument that prevention (through health care and social services) will reduce downstream costs in health care spending (thereby saving taxpayers money). Both approaches, and others, may be needed for short- and long-term policy change. Advocates must decide what strategies they believe will be most effective in bringing about the change they seek, but framing of arguments should always follow the lead of people who are most affected by the policy change sought.

Conclusion

Persistent advocacy in support of health justice is critical to changing the laws, policies, and systems that can either positively support or negatively impact the health of marginalized populations. Achieving health justice is a full agenda for advocates, but persistent focus on remedying policy failures and promoting innovative solutions can bring about incremental change:

> While large-scale reform leading to just institutions is not a near-term probability, striving for fairer treatment of mothers and their children,

greater gender equity, less social exclusion and racism, more inclusive and supportive communities, better environmental stewardship, more accountable government and corporations, fairer employment practices, and physical and social environments more conducive to human activity is possible. Doing so is our surest path—in fact, our only path—to improving population health.[43]

In the 1960s, civil rights movement leaders coined the phrase "keep your eyes on the prize" in recognition that change is slow and that it will only come with persistence and clear focus. A multisector health justice movement requires joining forces among empowered communities, health care, public health, legal advocates, and others who share a common purpose and who are committed to structural change and more just laws and policies.

References

1. Benfer EA, Mohapatra S, Wiley LF, Yearby R. Health justice strategies to combat the pandemic: Eliminating discrimination, poverty, and health disparities during and after COVID-19. *Yale Journal of Health Policy Law and Ethics.* 2020;19:122–123.

2. Baldwin J. As much truth as one can bear. *The New York Times Book Review.* January 14, 1962. https://www.nytimes.com/1962/01/14/archives/as-much-truth-as-one-can-bear-to-speak-out-about-the-world-as-it-is.html.

3. Souli S. Does America need a truth and reconciliation commission? *Politico.* August 16, 2020. https://www.politico.com/news/magazine/2020/08/16/does-america-need-a-truth-and-reconciliation-commission-395332.

4. Castellano MB, Archibald L, De Gagné M. From truth to reconciliation transforming the legacy of residential schools. *Aboriginal Healing Foundation.* 2008. https://www.ahf.ca/downloads/from-truth-to-reconciliation-transforming-the-legacy-of-residential-schools.pdf.

5. Klein E. Bryan Stevenson on how America can heal. *Vox.* July 20, 2020. https://www.vox.com/21327742/bryan-stevenson-the-ezra-klein-show-america-slavery-healing-racism-george-floyd-protests.

6. McEwen BS, Gianaros PJ. Central role of the brain in stress and adaptation: Links to socioeconomic status, health, and disease. *Annals of the New York Academy of Sciences.* 2010;1186:190.

7. Popay J. Community empowerment and health equity. *Oxford Research Encyclopedias: Global Health.* 2021.

8. Brown CL, Raza D, Pinto AD. Voting, health and interventions in healthcare settings: A scoping review. *Public Health Reviews.* 2020;41:16.

9. Brown CL, Raza D, Pinto AD. Voting, health and interventions in healthcare settings: A scoping review. *Public Health Reviews.* 2020;41:16.

10. Rodriguez JM. Health disparities, politics, and the maintenance of the status quo: A new theory of inequality. *Social Science and Medicine.* 2018;200:36–43.

11. Rodriguez JM, Geronimus AT, Bound J, Dorling D. Black lives matter: Differential mortality and the racial composition of the U.S. electorate, 1970–2004. *Social Science and Medicine.* 2015;136–137:193–199.

12. Mays JC, Correal A. New York City gives 800,000 noncitizens right to vote in local elections. *The New York Times.* December 9, 2021. https://www.nytimes.com/2021/12/09/nyregion/noncitizens-voting-rights-nyc.html?campaign_id=60&emc=edit_na_20211209&instance_id=0&nl=breaking-news&ref=cta&regi_id=79692342&segment_id=76580&user_id=5b4723d558eceb1f1f7cfa11e126c359.

13. Flores A, Magni G, Reynolds A. Had LGBT voters stayed home, Trump might have won the 2020 presidential election. *The Washington Post.* December 1, 2020. https://www.washingtonpost.com/politics/2020/12/01/had-lgbt-voters-stayed-home-trump-might-have-won-2020-presidential-election/.

14. Schaeffer K. The changing face of Congress in 7 charts. Pew Research Center. March 10, 2021. https://www.pewresearch.org/fact-tank/2021/03/10/the-changing-face-of-congress/.

15. Ray R, Perry A. Why we need reparations for Black Americans. Brooking Policy 2020. April 15, 2020. https://www.brookings.edu/policy2020/bigideas/why-we-need-reparations-for-black-americans/.

16. Covid-19 vaccination program interim playbook for jurisdiction operations. Centers for Disease Control and Prevention. September 16, 2020. https://www.cdc.gov/vaccines/imz-managers/downloads/COVID-19-Vaccination-Program-Interim_Playbook.pdf.

17. Schmidt H, Gostin LO, Williams MA. Is it lawful and ethical to prioritize racial minorities for COVID-19 vaccines? *JAMA.* 2020;324(20):2023–2024.

18. Norfleet N. Target to invest $100 million in Black-led organizations. *StarTribune.* October 12, 2021. https://www.startribune.com/target-to-invest-100-million-in-black-led-organizations/600105958/.

19. Darity W, Hamilton D, Paul M, et al. What we get wrong about closing the racial wealth gap. Samuel DuBois Cook Center on Social Equity, Insight Center for Community Economic Development. April 2018. https://socialequity.duke.edu/wp-content/uploads/2019/10/what-we-get-wrong.pdf.

20. Stiglitz JE. The American economy is rigged and what we can do about it. *Scientific American.* November 1, 2018. https://www.scientificamerican.com/article/the-american-economy-is-rigged/.

21. Looney A. Funding our nation's priorities: Reforming the tax code's advantageous treatment of the wealthy. Brookings. May 12, 2021. https://www.warren.senate.gov/newsroom/press-releases/warren-jayapal-boyle-introdsuce-ultra-millionaire-tax-on-fortunes-over-50-million.

22. Looney A. Funding our nation's priorities: Reforming the tax code's advantageous treatment of the wealthy. Brookings. May 12, 2021. https://www.warren.senate.gov/newsroom/press-releases/warren-jayapal-boyle-introduce-ultra-millionaire-tax-on-fortunes-over-50-million.

23. See Stiglitz JE. The American economy is rigged and what we can do about it. *Scientific American.* November 1, 2018. https://www.scientificamerican.com/article/the-american-economy-is-rigged/; Elizabeth Warren Press Release. Warren, Jayapal, Boyle introduce ultra-millionaire tax on fortunes over $50 million. March 1, 2021. https://www.warren.senate.gov/newsroom/press-releases/warren-jayapal-boyle-introduce-ultra-millionaire-tax-on-fortunes-over-50-million.

24. Lalljee J. 27 basic and guaranteed income programs where cities and states give direct payments to residents, no strings attached. *Business Insider.* December 11, 2021. https://www.businessinsider.com/how-many-ubi-guaranteed-basic-income-programs-us-cities-states-2021-12.

25. Hasdell R. What we know about universal basic income: A cross-synthesis of reviews. Stanford Basic Income Lab. July 2020:16. https://basicincome.stanford.edu/uploads/Umbrella%20Review%20BI_final.pdf.

26. Hasdell R. What we know about universal basic income: A cross-synthesis of reviews. Stanford Basic Income Lab. July 2020:17. https://basicincome.stanford.edu/uploads/Umbrella%20Review%20BI_final.pdf.

27. The White House. President Biden announces the Build Back Better Framework. October 28, 2021. https://www.whitehouse.gov/briefing-room/statements-releases/2021/10/28/president-biden-announces-the-build-back-better-framework/.

28. Arno P, Caper P. Medicare for all: The social transformation of US health care. Health Affairs Blog. March 25, 2020. https://www.healthaffairs.org/do/10.1377/hblog20200319.920962/full/.

29. World Population Review. Countries with single payer 2022. 2022. https://worldpopulationreview.com/country-rankings/countries-with-single-payer.

30. World Population Review. Countries with single payer 2022. 2022. https://worldpopulationreview.com/country-rankings/countries-with-single-payer.

31. Blumberg LJ, Holahan J. The pros and cons of single-payer health plans. Urban Institute. March 2019. https://www.urban.org/sites/default/files/publication/99918/pros_and_cons_of_a_single-payer_plan.pdf.

32. National Governors Association. Achieving progress toward health equity using race and ethnicity data. November 8, 2021. https://www.nga.org/center/publications/achieving-progress-toward-health-equity-using-race-and-ethnicity-data/.

33. Maani N, Galea S. COVID-19 and underinvestment in the public health infrastructure of the United States. *The Milbank Quarterly.* June 2020;98. https://www.milbank.org/quarterly/articles/covid-19-and-underinvestment-in-the-public-health-infrastructure-of-the-united-states/.

34. Centers for Disease Control and Prevention. Division for Heart Disease and Stroke Prevention. Legal Epidemiology. What is legal epidemiology. May 12, 2021. https://www.cdc.gov/dhdsp/policy_resources/legal_epi.htm#:~:text=Legal%20epidemiology%20is%20the%20study,how%20laws%20affect%20population%20health.

35. ChangeLab Solutions. Equitable enforcement to achieve health equity: An introductory guide for policymakers and practitioners. June 2020. https://www.changelabsolutions.org/product/equitable-enforcement-achieve-health-equity.

36. American Bar Association. Civil right to counsel. At a glance. 2022. https://www.americanbar.org/groups/legal_aid/indigent_defense/civil_right_to_counsel1/?q=&json.facet=%7B%22null%22%3A%7B%22type%22%3A%22terms%22%2C%20%22field%22%3A%22ABA_Board_of_Governors%22%7D%7D&fq=(id%3A%5C%2Fcontent%2Faba-cms-dotorg%2Fen%2Fgroups%2Flegal_aid:indigent_defense%2F*)&wt=json&start=0.

37. Dhital S. Reimagining justice: Human rights through legal empowerment. Open Global Rights. April 23, 2018. https://www.openglobalrights.org/Reimagining-justice-human-rights-through-legal-empowerment/.

38. Harris A, Pamukcu A. The civil rights of health: A new approach to challenging structural inequality. *University of California Law Review.* 2020; 67:758–832.

39. Mariner WK, Annas GJ. A culture of health and human rights. *Health Affairs.* 2016;35(11):1999–2004.

40. Harris A, Pamukcu A. The civil rights of health: A new approach to challenging structural inequality. *University of California Law Review.* 2020;67:765.

41. Harris A, Pamukcu A. The civil rights of health: A new approach to challenging structural inequality. *University of California Law Review.* 2020;67:765.

42. Parsons I. *Oliver Twist Has Asked for More: The Politics and Practice of Getting Justice for People with Disabilities.* Victoria, Australia: Villamanta Publishing Service; 1994:40.

43. Davidson A. *Social Determinants of Health: A Comparative Approach.* Vancouver, Ontario: Oxford University Press; 2014:265–266.

Conclusion

This text may not have been a comforting read. In fact, it may have left you feeling distressed or dejected. If so, we hope these feelings trigger a desire to bring about change. Bryan Stevenson, an internationally acclaimed public interest lawyer and the executive director of the Equal Justice Initiative in Montgomery, Alabama, often talks about the need to do uncomfortable things as a precursor to change. Because people are biologically programmed to do what's comfortable, it's easy for us all to place ourselves in environments and situations that are, subjectively speaking, well known and comfortable. Inertia and the status quo can, unsurprisingly, result. According to Stevenson, it is thus incumbent upon people who seek change to fight against norms and their own proclivities—in other words, to do uncomfortable things. Perhaps reading some part of this text was uncomfortable to you because it challenged certain beliefs or exposed you to unsavory societal practices or structural infirmities of which you were unaware. If so, what will you do in response? How will you help create environments—whether a classroom, a conference room, a boardroom, a health clinic, a neighborhood, a state, or someplace else—that promote health justice?

There is little doubt that the United States, compared even to other high-income, industrialized nations, has unique political, social, and cultural attributes. Some of these attributes include limited governmental power, a belief in self-governance, capitalism, unprecedented wealth, a strong sense of individualism, and racial and ethnic diversity. These characteristics have much to offer. At their worst, however, they contribute to an environment that

allows health injustice to flourish. Consider the following:

- Susan Fiske and Shelley Taylor, two pre-eminent social psychologists working in the subfield of social cognition, have spent their professional careers trying to better understand how people initially process and store information about other people and how individuals then apply that information in social situations. As part of their work, Fiske and Taylor scanned the brains of high-achieving people in the United States to ascertain how these high achievers processed information about poor people. They found that the scanned brains processed images of poor people as if they were things rather than human beings.[1]

- In a 2017 study, researchers analyzed population surveys from 32 high- and middle-income countries to determine how Americans' acceptance of health and health care disparities stacked up against the views of people in other similarly situated political and/or economic contexts. They found that the United States is an outlier in the very large share of people who don't find it unfair that many people lack access to needed health care. As the authors put it: "Relatively low levels of moral discomfort over income-based health care disparities despite broad awareness of unmet need indicate more public tolerance for health care inequalities in the United States than elsewhere."[2]

- Thirty-two percent of Black people surveyed in 2017 said they had personally experienced racial discrimination at a physician's office or a health clinic. Twenty-two percent indicated that they have gone so far as to avoid seeking medical care out of concern about discrimination.[3]

- Thirty of the 85 richest people in the world are from the United States, and their combined net worth is nearly $2 trillion.[4] Two trillion dollars represents almost one-tenth of the entire U.S. economy, which itself represents almost one-quarter of the entire global economy. The eight wealthiest people in the world—seven of whom are from the United States—hold as much wealth as half of all humanity.[5] This constitutes phenomenal, and phenomenally destructive, wealth concentration.

- Of all age groups, children are the most likely to live in poverty, a failure that exists purely for political reasons: Children can't vote, and too frequently low-income parents don't vote (see Chapter 16 for a discussion about the relationship between voting and health justice); as a result, child poverty does not live near the top of the nation's political agenda. Even *existing* funding that would keep the already terrible problem of childhood poverty from getting worse is not sacrosanct. For instance, in 2017, federal funding for the Children's Health Insurance Program (CHIP) dried up. CHIP provides health insurance coverage to nearly 10 million children in families that earn too much to qualify for Medicaid but who cannot afford private coverage. The program costs the federal government approximately $17 billion annually, or about 0.36% of the federal budget. Yet while Congress debated tax cuts for large corporations in the fall of 2017, the deadline to renew CHIP funding passed. After allowing funding for the program to lapse for an unprecedented 114 days, funding was eventually extended through September 2023.

- The nation's social contract—the implicit agreement among the members of U.S. society to cooperate in the name of widespread social benefit—appears to be tattered. One needs to look no further than the national response to the COVID-19 pandemic for evidence of this. One key provision of all functioning social contracts is that people will sacrifice some individual freedom in the name of safeguarding—or, at the very least, not harming—others, and the use of face coverings to control the spread of COVID-19 is a safe, effective, and noninvasive example of the type of individual sacrifice that could have been routinized in response to the pandemic. Yet this has been anything but the case, as the wearing of face coverings in the United States appears to have been far more influenced by politics, culture, and personal identity[6] than by any generalized support for the social contract. While the potential impact of pandemic responses (both the use of face coverings and otherwise) on interpersonal and institutional trust has not yet been thoroughly investigated,[7] there is plenty of anecdotal evidence to suggest that the U.S. response to the pandemic will erode trust between citizens and between citizens and government leaders.[8] As Shinobu Kitayama, president of the Association for Psychological Science, put it: "It appears as though many Americans have maximized their psychological welfare by not covering their mouths. This behavior, however, has come at a grave cost for the collective….Unfortunately, again and again, many Americans prioritized their personal convenience or preference while ignoring the collective consequences of doing so."[9]

Large-scale health justice—the opportunity for all people to reach their full health potential through structural equity and recognition of their human rights, civil rights, value, and dignity—simply cannot be achieved in this environment. While the nation has the power to correct its own health inequities and inequalities, major systemic change is required. Education has an important role to play. To be sure, health professions education should be expanded and deepened to better train clinicians of all types in the social complexities that dominate the lives of low-income and other marginalized patient populations. But again, as you have learned, health justice encompasses far more than access to high-quality, nondiscriminatory health care services, and many jobs pertinent to health justice reside outside the confines of the health professions. As a result, higher education generally should become more adept at training students in the multiple dimensions of inequity and poor health. Among other things, this requires educational programming across academic disciplines. Because of the many different and intersectional pathways to health inequities, the various stakeholders who together can lead the nation down a new path toward health justice should be educated together as early as possible to understand one another's professional language, interventions, and goals. It has to be said that law schools—our own training ground—have historically been particularly siloed in their approach to education. Though lawyers are unsurpassed in their understanding of complex administrative, constitutional, and poverty law, they typically have been trained as downstream interventionists for already-existing legal crises (e.g., attempting to ward off an already-initiated eviction). Training lawyers from the outset as "upstreamists" and as part of a broader team focused on holistic well-being would help immensely.

Change for the better would also require the shifting of resources. We've discussed this at multiple points, but it bears repeating: The nation's social needs are outstripping available resources, while nearly *$4 trillion* is spent annually on medical care to address some of the very problems created by the nation's historical underfunding of social services. A shift in resources from medical to social care would be especially compelling where it was channeled into early childhood programming and toward people who have been caught in the cycle of intergenerational poverty.

Finally, a movement toward health justice requires policymaking that at all levels addresses the devastating health effects of the nation's structural illnesses—economic, social, and environmental.[10] As one author notes:

> Meaningful progress in addressing health inequities requires complementary policies to reduce inequities in education, employment, housing, transportation, and public safety. The decision makers with the greatest power to shape health outcomes are not health workers: Instead, they work on school boards or in municipal government, legislative bodies, housing authorities, transit agencies, and the business sector. They are employers, developers, investors, banks, economists, voters, and journalists.

But the policy change has to involve more than just the shifting of physical resources and more than just an acknowledgment that health justice requires a quiver of many different types of arrows. It must embrace an empathic and tolerant approach to governing that seeks to reverse the accumulated social disadvantage suffered by a wide range of marginalized populations—including racial, ethnic, and Indigenous minorities; immigrants; women; LGBTQ+ people; people with disabilities; and populations who live in poverty or struggle for opportunity and resources in geographically limited areas[12]—and affirms that respect for all people is an essential condition of a just and healthy society.

References

1. Fiske ST, Taylor SE. *Social Cognition: From Brains to Culture*. London, UK: Sage Publications Ltd.; 2017.

2. Hero JO, Zaslavsky AM, Blendon RJ. The United States leads other nations in differences by income in perceptions of health and health care. *Health Affairs*. June 2017;36(6):1032–1040.

3. Williams DR. Why discrimination is a health issue. Robert Wood Johnson Foundation. 2021. https://www.rwjf.org/en/blog/2017/10/discrimination-is-a-health-issue.html.

4. Dolan KA, Wang J, Peterson-Withorn C., Eds. World's billionaires list: The richest in 2021. *Forbes*. 2022. https://www.forbes.com/billionaires/.

5. Hirschler B. World's eight richest as wealthy as half humanity, Oxfam tells Davos. Reuters. 2017. https://www.reuters.com/article/us-davos-meeting-inequality/worlds-eight-richest-as-wealthy-as-half-humanity-oxfam-tells-davos-idUSKBN150009.

6. See, e.g., Struck K. Study confirms political influence on preventing COVID spread. VOA. (September 2021). https://www.voanews.com/a/study-confirms-political-influence-on-preventing-covid-spread/6239657.html; Powdthavee N, Riyanto YE, Wong ECL, Yeo JXW, Chan QY. When face masks signal social identity: Explaining the deep face-mask divide during the COVID-19 pandemic. *PLOS One*. June 2021. https://journals.plos.org/plosone/article?id=10.1371/journal.pone.0253195; Lua JG, Jina P, English AS. Collectivism predicts mask use during COVID-19. *Proceedings of the National Academy of Sciences of the United States of America (PNAS)*. 2021. https://www.pnas.org/content/pnas/118/23/e2021793118.full.pdf.

7. Thoresen S, Blix I, Wentzel-Larsen T, Skogbrott Birkeland M. Trusting others during a pandemic: Investigating potential changes in generalized trust and its relationship with pandemic-related experiences and worry. *Frontiers in Psychology*. August 2021. https://www.frontiersin.org/articles/10.3389/fpsyg.2021.698519/full; but see van der Cruijsen C, de Haan J, Jonker N. Has the COVID-19 pandemic affected public trust? Evidence for the US and the Netherlands. DNB Working Paper. August 2021. https://www.dnb.nl/media/ic2fknyz/working_paper_no-_723.pdf.

8. See, e.g., John M. Public trust crumbles under COVID-19, fake news—survey. Reuters. January 2021. https://www.reuters.com/business/media-telecom/reuters-next-public-trust-crumbles-under-covid-19-fake-news-survey-2021-01-13/.

9. Kitayama S. Psychological science in the era of infectious disease. APS Observer. September 2020. https://www.psychologicalscience.org/observer/era-of-infectious-disease.

10. Benfer EA. Health justice: A framework (and call to action) for the elimination of health inequity and social justice. *American University Law Review*. 2015;65(2):275,283.

11. Woolf SH. Progress in achieving health equity requires attention to root causes. *Health Affairs*. June 2017;36(6):984–991.

12. Weil AR. Pursuing health equity. *Health Affairs*. June 2017;36(6):975.

Index

Note: Page numbers followed by b, f, or t indicate material in boxes, figures, or tables, respectively.

A

ableism, 23
#AbolishICE, 42
abuse
  emotional, 148
  physical, 148
  sexual, 148
ACA. *See* Patient Protection and
  Affordable Care Act of 2010
access to health care, 344–345
access to quality health care, 208,
  236–239, 237f
  LGBTQ+ people, 282–284, 283f
  women, 256–257
accountable care organizations
  (ACO), 317–318, 324
Accountable Health Communities
  (AHC), 325
ACEs. *See* adverse childhood
  experiences
ACF. *See* Administration for
  Children and Families
ACL. *See* Administration for
  Community Living
ACO. *See* accountable care
  organizations
ACOG. *See* American College of
  Obstetrics and Gynecology
ACS. *See* American Community
  Survey
ACT UP (AIDS Coalition to Unleash
  Power), 37–38
ADA. *See* Americans with
  Disabilities Act of 1990
Administration for Children and
  Families (ACF), 61t
Administration for Community
  Living (ACL), 61t
administrative law, 60
Administrative Procedure Act of
  1946, 60, 279

Adoption and Safe Families Act of
  1997, 148
adverse childhood experiences
  (ACEs), 146–147, 151, 152,
  185
AFDC. *See* Aid to Families with
  Dependent Children
  program
Affordable Care Act of 2010 (ACA).
  See Patient Protection and
  Affordable Care Act of 2010
  (ACA)
African Charter on Human and
  Peoples' Rights, 84
Agency for Healthcare Research and
  Quality (AHRQ), 61t, 345
Agency for Toxic Substances and
  Disease Registry (ATSDR),
  61t
"aggravated felonies," 231
AHC. *See* Accountable Health
  Communities
AHRQ. *See* Agency for Healthcare
  Research and Quality
Aid to Families with Dependent
  Children (AFDC) program,
  72, 125, 351
*Alabama Association of Realtors, et al.
  v. Department of Health and
  Human Services, et al.* (2021),
  153
Alexander v. Sandoval (2001),
  103–104, 205
allostasis, 147
allostatic load, 147
American Bar Association, 181,
  183, 346
American College of Obstetrics and
  Gynecology (ACOG), 187
American Community Survey
  (ACS), 301, 308
  disability questions, 298, 298b
American exceptionalism, 91

American Health Dilemma, An (Byrd
  and Clayton), 98
American Medical Association, 92
  *Declaration of Professional
  Responsibility Medicine's Social
  Contract with Humanity,* 5
American Poison (Porter), 98
American Psychiatric Association
  (APA)
  *Diagnostic and Statistical Manual
  of Mental Disorders* (DSM),
  281–282
American Psychological Association,
  259
American Public Health
  Association
  2019 Code of Ethics, 10
American Rescue Plan Act of 2020,
  261
Americans with Disabilities Act
  (ADA), 40, 300, 303, 305,
  307, 308
  requirements by Title, 300, 301t
  Title II, 302
  Title III, 302
Americans with Disabilities Act of
  1990 (ADA), 56–57, 102
antidiscrimination laws, 248–250
  people with disabilities, 300–301
anti-essentialism, 19
APA. *See* American Psychiatric
  Association
"appropriate screening
  examination," 69
Aristotle, 18
Armey, Dick, 69
asthma triggers, housing-related,
  157–158
ATSDR. *See* Agency for Toxic
  Substances and Disease
  Registry
autonomy, 6, 7
Avila, Cecile Joan, 127